MEDIA
NOW

MEDIA NOW

Understanding Media, Culture, and Technology

TENTH EDITION

JOSEPH STRAUBHAAR
University of Texas, Austin

ROBERT LaROSE
Michigan State University

LUCINDA DAVENPORT
Michigan State University

CENGAGE
Learning·

Australia • Brazil • Mexico • Singapore • United Kingdom • United States

CENGAGE
Learning·

Media Now: Understanding Media, Culture, and Technology, Tenth Edition
Joseph Straubhaar, Robert LaRose, and Lucinda Davenport

Product Director: Monica Eckman

Product Manager: Kelli Strieby

Content Development Manager: Janine Tangney

Senior Content Developer: Jessica Badiner

Marketing Manager: Jillian Borden

Senior Content Project Manager: Andrea Wagner

Senior Art Director: Marissa Falco

Manufacturing Planner: Doug Bertke

IP Analyst: Ann Hoffman

IP Project Manager: Kathryn Kucharek

Production Service: Lumina Datamatics, Inc.

Compositor: Lumina Datamatics, Inc.

Cover Designer: Red Hangar Design

For product information and technology assistance, contact us at
Cengage Learning Customer & Sales Support, 1-800-354-9706

For permission to use material from this text or product, submit all requests online at **www.cengage.com/permissions**.
Further permissions questions can be emailed to
permissionrequest@cengage.com.

Library of Congress Control Number: 2016945590

ISBN-13: 978-1-305-95084-9

Cengage Learning
20 Channel Center Street
Boston, MA 02210
USA

Cengage Learning is a leading provider of customized learning solutions with office locations around the globe, including Singapore, the United Kingdom, Australia, Mexico, Brazil, and Japan. Locate your local office at **www.cengage.com/global**.

Cengage Learning products are represented in Canada by Nelson Education, Ltd.

To learn more about Cengage Learning Solutions, visit **www.cengage.com**.

Purchase any of our products at your local college store or at our preferred online store **www.cengagebrain.com**.

Printed at CLDPC, USA, 01-17

BRIEF CONTENTS

CONTENTS

PART TWO   The Media

CHAPTER 11 The Third Screen: Smartphones and Tablets 287

PREFACE

Smartphones are the latest manifestation of media convergence, the continuing evolution of conventional media forms into digital communication platforms. In today's world, interpersonal communication and the creative efforts of billions of individual users have been absorbed into the media environment that was once the exclusive domain of the print, broadcasting, advertising, and film industries. Media consumption has become a personalized as well as a mass phenomenon as messages are targeted to ever narrower segments of the audience and distributed through smartphones and tablets that are with us at all times, wherever we go.

Our theme is that the evolution of traditional media industries and newer technologies has created a new communications environment that impacts society and culture. Our goal throughout this book is to prepare students to cope with that environment as both critical consumers of media and aspiring media professionals.

We reach for that goal by providing an approach to mass media that integrates traditional media (magazines, books, newspapers, music, radio, film, and television) and newer media (the Internet, tablets, smartphones, and video games), and emphasizes the intersection of technology, media, and culture. Change continues apace as the new electronic media of the twentieth century are challenged by the Internet, which in turn is giving way to a new wave of disruptive technology embodied in smartphones and tablets. It remains important to consider the historical trends that got us here and to observe long-term trends that extend beyond the latest Internet memes and infatuations with tech gadgets. We have already witnessed astounding changes in the structure of the radio and telecommunications industries and the rapid evolution of the newspaper, film, and television industries as they meet the challenges of new technologies and new ways of doing business on a global scale. These are changes that affect our society as well as those across the globe, and our students need to learn about them in their introductory courses to prepare them to be productive citizens.

NEW TO THIS EDITION

The tenth edition of *Media Now* provides the most current coverage possible of media industries old and new and reflects the field's latest research as well as the challenges that confront industries in transition. Social media and the rapid spread of smartphones represent an overarching trend toward audience-originated content and mobile media consumption that force media executives, advertisers, public relations executives, and governments around the world to rethink their strategies. We believe that these changes afford "teachable moments" in which students can reflect on the future of the media and their own life plans while recognizing the impact that external events can have on providers of entertainment, information, and communication. To place these changes in their proper historical context, we have revised the historical narratives to emphasize events that have a direct impact on the media today and to point out that many seemingly "new" developments are really nothing new but rather paths not taken and choices not made at different points in time. We have also separated magazines and books (previously Chapter 3) into two chapters (now Chapter 5 and Chapter 3) because they have distinct industries composed of different economies, audiences, and technologies.

Chapter by chapter, here are examples of the updates you will find in this edition:

- **The Changing Media** examines how smartphone and tablet apps expand conventional typologies of communication and charts the end game in the conversion of conventional media to digital forms.

- **Media and Society** considers the new business models that are emerging in social media and tracks recent trends in the adoption of media forms old and new.

- **Books** traces the evolution of technology, content, audiences, and multiple delivery methods (print, audio, and digital) for books, and the effects of those changes on the industry and consumers.

- **Print and Digital Newspapers** looks at the positive impact of journalism on the growth of democracy and analyzes the industry as it evolves with the digital landscape toward immersive journalism, and experiments with changes in its business model.

- **Magazines** is now its own chapter and examines the good influence of (muckraking) content on society, the expansion of genres, and the shifts that technology, audiences, and owners have caused in the industry.

- **Recorded Music** tracks how the music industry copes with declining sales by exploring new outlets for music on the Internet, such as streaming music services.

- **Radio** examines the Internet "cloud music" trend, evolving Internet radio, and their impact on conventional broadcasting.

- **Film and Video** analyzes how the industry prospers through premium ticket sales in 3-D and IMAX venues, while changing global distribution to fight piracy and maximize growing international revenues.

- **Television** explores how the basic nature of television and its conventional business models is evolving in response to the challenge of streaming media with new business models even as a new golden age of television drama fills the home screen.

- **The Internet** scrutinizes trends that are leading to a decline in Internet use in American homes as social media apps challenge the conventional PC-oriented model.

- **Public Relations** shows how social media present new opportunities, tools, and ways to communicate to various publics across the country and to other cultures throughout the world.

- **Advertising** examines mobile advertising trends and the growing threats to consumer privacy the growing.

- **The Third Screen** monitors the latest trends in mobile apps and the evolution of smartphones into an entertainment and advertising medium.

- **Video Games** profiles a rapidly changing industry and anticipates the impact of virtual reality and augmented reality.

- **Media Uses and Impacts** expands coverage of the impacts of new media with a closer look at the relationship between media consumption and well-being.

- **Media Policy and Law** considers the implications of new FCC rulings on network neutrality and universal access.

- **Media Ethics** expounds on professional responsibility to society, the processes of ethical decision-making, and the importance of ethical behavior that has magnified with the new challenges brought about by social media.

- **Global Communications Media** investigates the impact of social media on democratic revolutions in the Middle East and accelerating global film, television, and music flows.

UPDATED PROVEN FEATURES

This book comes with a rich set of features to aid in learning, all of which have been updated to help students better understand the ongoing changes in media, culture, and technology:

- **Figures:** These visuals, some of which were labeled "infographics" in previous editions, capture key trends and statistics in an accessible and graphically appealing style common to the new media, updated with the latest data.

- **Media Literacy:** Included within each media chapter, these sections focus on key issues regarding the impact of media on culture and society, encouraging students to think critically and analyze issues related to their consumption of media. This edition focuses on privacy issues and changes in media ownership patterns that affect consumers.

- **Glossary:** Key terms are defined in the margins of each chapter and are listed at the end of each chapter, and a complete glossary is included in the back of the book.

- **Media Then... Media Now:** Major events in each medium's industry are highlighted. Important dates are also called out in the margins of the text in each chapter.

- **Featured Boxes:** Four types of boxes appear in the text, each designed to target specific issues and further pique students' interest:
  - **MEDIA AND CULTURE** boxes highlight cultural issues in the media.
  - **TECHNOLOGY DEMYSTIFIED** boxes explain technological information in a clear and accessible way.
  - **YOUR MEDIA CAREER** guides readers to the "hot spots" in media industries updated with the latest projections from the Bureau of Labor Statistics. New to this edition, these include:
    - ○ **CAREER PROFILES** are thumbnail biographies of successful media professionals who started out with degrees in media studies.
  - **WORLD VIEW** expands thinking from beyond the front door to a more global perspective.

- **Stop & Review:** Appearing periodically throughout each chapter, these questions help students incrementally assess their understanding of key material.

- **Summary & Review:** Each chapter concludes with summary and review sections, which are presented as questions with brief narrative answers.

TEACHING AND LEARNING RESOURCES

MindTap Communication for *Media Now* is a personalized, online digital learning platform that provides students with an immersive learning experience that builds critical thinking skills. Through a carefully designed chapter-based learning path, MindTap allows students to easily identify the chapter's learning objectives, read the chapter, test their content knowledge, and reflect on what they've learned. The course is as flexible as you want it to be: you can add your own activities, PowerPoint slides, videos, and Google docs or simply select from the available content, and you can rearrange the parts to suit the needs of the course. Analytics and reports provide a snapshot of class progress, time in course, engagement, and completion rates.

The **Instructor Companion Website** is an all-in-one resource for class preparation, presentation, and testing for instructors. It is accessible by logging on to login.cengage.com with your faculty account. You will find an Instructor's Resource Manual, Cognero® test bank files, and PowerPoint presentations specifically designed to accompany this edition.

- The Instructor's Resource Manual provides you with extensive assistance in teaching with the book, including sample syllabi, suggested assignments, chapter outlines, individual and group activities, and more.

- Cengage Learning Testing Powered by Cognero® is a flexible, online system that allows you to import, edit, and manipulate content from the text's test bank or elsewhere, including your own favorite test questions; create multiple test versions in an instant; and deliver tests from your LMS, your classroom, or wherever you may be, with no special installs or downloads required.

- PowerPoint® Lecture Tools are ready-to-use outlines of each chapter. They are easily customized for your lectures.

ACKNOWLEDGMENTS

We wish to thank our spouses, Sandy Straubhaar, Betty Degesie-LaRose, and Frederic W. Greene, for their patience and valuable ideas. We also want to thank a number of our students and graduate assistants, Camille Douglas, Stuart Davis, Josh Gleich, Julie Goldsmith, Nicholas Robinson, and Tim Penning, for their reviews and comments on the chapters. Also, thanks to Rolf and Chris Straubhaar, Julia Mitschke, and Rachael and Jason Davenport Greene for insights into their culture and concerns. Special thanks to Tammy Lin for reviewing drafts of the video games chapter.

We would also like to acknowledge the tremendous efforts of everyone at Cengage Learning who worked with us to create an outstanding book and accompanying learning materials. There are many who have worked tirelessly behind the scenes. Great appreciation also goes to Andrea Wagner, content project manager; Sarah Seymour, marketing manager; and our product manager, Kelli Strieby. The team at Lumina Datamatics did an outstanding job managing this project, in particular Valarmathy Munuswamy, Manoj Kiran, and Magesh Rajagopalan. We also gratefully acknowledge the assistance of Dr. Teresa Mastin, for her previous work on the advertising chapter; Julia Crouse Waddell, for her excellent work on this book's MindTap content; and Stuart Davis and Kevin Tankersley, for their help with the supplementary resources. Finally, we wish to thank the following reviewers for their thoughtful suggestions and guidance in the development of the tenth edition:

Arnold Mackowiak, Eastern Michigan University

Tim Moreland, Catawba College

Kevin Tankersley, Baylor University

Dr. David Nelson, University of Central Oklahoma

We also thank the following individuals for their reviews of the previous editions: Arnold Mackowiak, Eastern Michigan University; Tim Moreland, Catawba College; Kevin Tankersley, Baylor University; Dr. David Nelson, University of Central Oklahoma; Robert Abeman, Cleveland State University; Jon Arakaki, State University of New York, College at Oneonta; Thomas Berner, Pennsylvania State University; Elena Bertozzi, Indiana University; Larry Bohlender, Glendale Community College; Sandra Braman, University of Wisconsin, Milwaukee; Dr. Jim Brancato, Cedar Crest College; Michael Brown, University of Wyoming; Erik Bucy, Indiana University; Karyn S. Campbell, North Greenville University; Larry Campbell, University of Alaska, Anchorage; Richard Caplan, University of Akron; Meta Carstarphen-Delgado, University of Oklahoma; Jerry G. Chandler, Jackson State University; Tsan-Kuo Chang, University of Minnesota, Twin Cities; John Chapin, Rutgers University; Joseph Chuk, Kutztown University of Pennsylvania; Dan Close, Wichita State University; Gene Costain, University of Central Florida; Dave D'Alessio, University of Connecticut, Stamford; Robert Darden, Baylor University; Krishna DasGupta, Worcester State College; Staci Dinerstein, County College of Morris; David Donnelly, University of Houston; Mike Dorsher, University of Wisconsin, Eau Claire; Michael Doyle, Arkansas State University; Dr. Jim Eggensperger, Iona College; Lyombe Eko, University of Maine; Emily

Erickson, Louisiana State University; Nickieann Fleener, University of Utah, Linda Fuller, Worcester State College; Ivy Glennon, University of Illinois at Urbana-Champaign; Donald Godfrey, Arizona State University; Mark Goodman, Mississippi State University; Tom Grimes, Kansas State University; Larry Haapanen, Lewis and Clark State College; Ken Hadwiger, Eastern Illinois University; Linwood A. Hagin, North Greenville University; Junhao Hong, State University of New York, Buffalo; Kevin Howley, Northeastern University; Jack Hodgson, Oklahoma State University; Rick Houlberg, San Francisco State University; James Hoyt, University of Wisconsin, Green Bay; Susan Hunt-Bradford, St. Louis Community College; Matthew Jackson, Penn State University; Harvey Jassem, University of Hartford; Howard Keim, Tabor College; Randall King, Point Loma Nazarene University; Seong H. Lee, Appalachian State University; Bradley Lemonds, Santa Monica College; Charles Lewis, Minnesota State University, Mankato; William Lingle, Linfield College; Linda Lumsden, Western Kentucky University; Robert Main, California State University, Chico; Reed Markham, Salt Lake Community College; Judith Marlane, California State University, Northridge; Stephen McDowell, Florida State University; Timothy P. Meyer, University of Wisconsin, Green Bay; Jonathan Milien, Rider College; Suman Mishra, Temple University; Joel Moody, University of Toronto, Mississauga; Jennifer Nelson, Ohio University; John S. Nelson, Dakota State University; Kyle Nicholas, Old Dominion University; Daniel Panici, University of Southern Maine; Karen Pappin, Huntington University, Laurentian; Norma Pecora, Ohio University; Ben Peruso, Lehigh Carbon Community College; Cristina Pieraccini, State University of New York, Oswego; Michael Porter, University of Missouri; Peter Pringle, University of Tennessee, Chattanooga; Hoyt Purvis, University of Arkansas; Arthur Raney, Indiana University; Divyesh K. Raythatha, Delaware State University; Mike Reed, Saddleback College; Humphrey Regis, University of South Florida; Mark D. Ricci, State University of New York College at Brockport; Ronald Rice, Rutgers University; Karen E. Riggs, Ohio University; Shelly Rodgers, University of Minnesota, Twin Cities; Marshall Rossow, Mankato State University; Gay Russell, Grossmont College; Joseph Russomanno, Arizona State University; Marc Ryan, Marist College; Christian Sandvig, University of Illinois at Urbana, Champaign; Tom Shaker, Northeastern University; Laura Sherwood, University of Nerasak, Kearney; Roger Soenksen, James Madison University; Jeffrey C. South, Virginia Commonwealth University; Don Stacks, University of Miami; Michelle J. Stanton, California State University, Northridge; Patrick J. Sutherland, Bethany College; Jill D. Swenson, Ithaca College; Michael Ray Taylor, Henderson State University; Don Tomlinson, Texas A&M University; Max Utsler, University of Kansas; Hazel Warlaumont, California State University, Fullerton; Alden L. Weight, Arizona State University, Polytechnic Campus; Susan Weill, Texas State University, San Marcos; Debora Wenger, Virginia Commonwealth University; Clifford Wexler, Columbia-Greene Community College; Glynn R. Wilson, Loyola University, New Orleans; Alan Winegarden, Concordia University; J. Emett Winn, Auburn University; and Phyllis Zagano, Boston University.

ABOUT THE AUTHORS

DR. JOSEPH D. STRAUBHAAR is the Amon G. Carter Centennial Professor of Communications in the Radio-TV-Film Department and Latino Media Studies Director in the Moody College of Communication of the University of Texas at Austin. He was the Director of the Center for Brazilian Studies within the Lozano Long Institute for Latin American Studies. His most recent book is *Latin American Television Industries* (2013), with John Sinclair. He has published books, articles, and essays on international communications, global media, digital inclusion, international telecommunications, Brazilian television, Latin American media, comparative analyses of new television technologies, media flow and culture, and other topics appearing in a number of journals, edited books, and elsewhere. His primary teaching, research, and writing interests are in global media, international communication and cultural theory, the digital divide in the United States and other countries, and global television studies. He does research in Latin America, Asia, and Africa, and has taken student groups to Latin America and Asia. He has presented seminars abroad on media research, television programming strategies, and telecommunications privatization. He is on the editorial board for *Communication Theory, Media Industries, Chinese Journal of Communication, Journal of Latin American Communication Research, Studies in Latin American Popular Culture, Comunicación e Cultura,* and *Revista Intercom.*

Visit Joe Straubhaar on the Web at
http://rtf.utexas.edu/faculty/joe-straubhaar

DR. ROBERT LaROSE is an emeritus full professor in the Department of Media and Information at Michigan State University. Dr. LaRose was recently recognized as a distinguished faculty member with the MSU William J. Beal Outstanding Faculty Award. Other awards include the Outstanding Article Award of the year in the field of communication from the International Communication Association, and the McQuail Award for the Best Article Advancing Communication Theory from Amsterdam School of Communication Research for his 2010 paper, "The Problem of Media Habits." He conducts research on the uses and effects of the Internet. He has published and presented numerous articles, essays, and book chapters on computer-mediated communication, social cognitive explanations of the Internet and its effects on behavior, understanding Internet usage, privacy, and more. In addition to his teaching and research, he is an avid watercolor painter and traveler.

Visit Robert LaRose on the Web at
http://www.msu.edu/~larose

DR. LUCINDA D. DAVENPORT is the Director of the School of Journalism at Michigan State University, a nationally accredited program since 1949. She was Associate Dean for Graduate Studies in the College of Communication Arts and Sciences, among other administrative positions. She has been recognized with the Michigan State University Excellence in Teaching Award and the College of Communication Arts and Sciences Faculty Impact Award. She has earned national awards for her research, which focuses mainly on news media and innovative technology, media history, and journalistic ethics. She has professional experience in newspaper, radio, television, public relations, and digital news. And, she is known to be an innovator with digital news and journalism education. Her credentials include a Ph.D. in mass communication from Ohio University, an MA in journalism from the University of Iowa, and a BA double major in journalism and Radio/TV/Film from Baylor University. Her master's thesis and doctoral dissertation were firsts in the country on computerized information services and online news.

Visit Lucinda D. Davenport on the Web at
http://jrn.msu.edu

THE CHANGING MEDIA

LEARNING OBJECTIVES

After studying the topics in this chapter, you will be able to:

1 Give at least two examples of the convergence of traditional and new media.
2 Summarize the technological changes that have occurred over the three basic stages of economic development to create today's information society.
3 Apply the Source Message Channel Receiver (SMCR) model to intrapersonal, interpersonal, small-group, large-group, and mass media communication exchanges.
4 Give at least one example of a mediated communication exchange that does not fit within the SMCR model.
5 Classify a communication exchange as asynchronous or synchronous, and digital or analog.
6 Regarding the technological affordances of social media and interactive new media, reflect on their growing impact on media industries, government regulations, individual lifestyles, careers, and social issues.

THE MEDIA IN OUR LIVES

If you were the typical American media consumer, you would consume over 3,400 hours of media content per year. That is the equivalent of a full-time job, with a long commute and no vacation days. The only way to cram that much media into your schedule is to surf the Internet, text, read, or play a game at the same time you are watching TV (see Figure 1.1). Since this is the information age, we can break that figure down into the bits and bytes of computer data. The world's capacity to communicate information through broadcast (e.g., television) and two-way communication technologies (e.g., the Internet) combined is estimated at 2 sextillion (i.e., 2 followed by 21 zeros) bytes (Hilbert & Lopez, 2011), or about 300 billion bytes per person. What do you do with your share?

We consume information, but we also create it when we update Facebook profiles, upload "selfies" to Instagram, or control avatars in

© charnsitr/Shutterstock.com

DIGITAL MEDIA reach us anytime, anywhere on a growing array of devices such as Apple's iWatch that exemplify the media convergence we will examine in this chapter.

1

MEDIA THEN··· MEDIA NOW

3100 BCE
> Writing is first developed

1455 CE
> The Gutenberg Bible is published

1690
> The first American newspaper appears

1910
> The United States becomes an industrial society

1949
> The Shannon–Weaver communication theory is published

1960
> The United States transitions to become the first information society

1962
> Digital communication is deployed.

> Video games are created

1975
> Personal computers are invented

1982
> CDs are introduced to consumers

1989
> Carey's Communication as Culture is published

1991
> World Wide Web begins

1995
> Computer-generated films are introduced

> DVDs are first sold to consumers

1996
> Telecommunications Act passes Congress

1998
> Digital cable first reaches U.S. homes

> The Copyright Term Extension Act is enacted by Congress

2009
> HDTV takes over the airwaves

MindTap®

Start with a quick warm-up activity.

multiplayer online games like "Guild Wars." Most of us will enter careers in which we gather, organize, produce, or distribute information. This includes media professionals employed as journalists, movie actors, musicians, television producers, writers, advertising account executives, researchers, Web page designers, announcers, and public relations specialists. Information workers make up over half the employment in a wide range of industries including

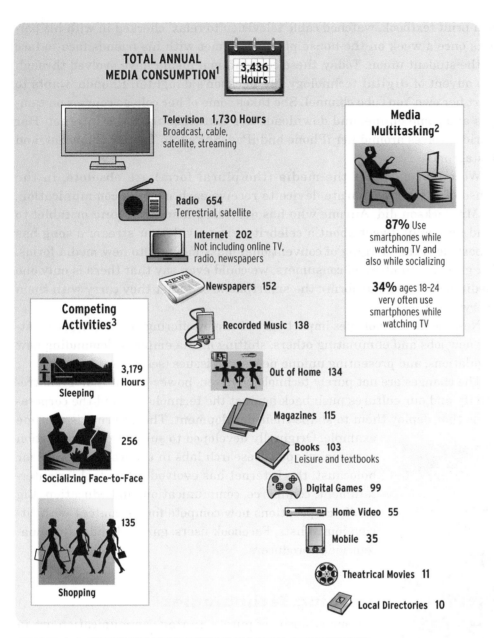

TOTAL ANNUAL MEDIA CONSUMPTION¹ 3,436 Hours

Television 1,730 Hours
Broadcast, cable, satellite, streaming

Radio 654
Terrestrial, satellite

Internet 202
Not including online TV, radio, newspapers

Newspapers 152

Recorded Music 138

Out of Home 134

Magazines 115

Books 103
Leisure and textbooks

Digital Games 99

Home Video 55

Mobile 35

Theatrical Movies 11

Local Directories 10

Media Multitasking²

87% Use smartphones while watching TV and also while socializing

34% ages 18-24 very often use smartphones while watching TV

Competing Activities³

3,179 Hours Sleeping

256 Socializing Face-to-Face

135 Shopping

FIGURE 1.1 **SPENDING TIME WITH THE MEDIA REFERENCES**

¹Veronis Suhler Stevenson, Communications Industry Forecast 25th Ed., 2011; ²Based on adult smartphone owners. Deloitte. 2015 Global Mobile Consumer Survey: US Edition http://www2.deloitte.com/content/dam/deloitte/us/documents/technology-media-telecommunications/us-tmt-global-mobile-executive-summary-2015.pdf; ³Averages for age 18 and over. Bureau of Labor Statistics (2014). American Time Use Survey. http://www.bls.gov/tus/

education, wholesaling, retailing, insurance, and real estate (Apte, Karmarkar, & Nath, 2012) and many organizations large and small, across all industries, have in-house public relations specialists, video producers, and web designers. So, we now work and play in an **information society.**

MEDIA IN A CHANGING WORLD

Media technology changes with every generation: for example, Mr. Jackson, who is 45 years old, is a television producer. When he was in a college **mass communication** survey course, our fictional Mr. Jackson studied books, newspapers, magazines, radio, television, and film. He read about them

Information society In an information society, the exchange of information is the predominant economic activity.

Mass communication is one-to-many, with limited audience feedback.

MindTap®

Read, highlight, and take notes on the complete chapter text in a rich interactive online platform.

in a print textbook, watched cable television to relax, checked in with his parents once a week on the house phone, and met with his friends face-to-face in the student union. Today, these conventional media have evolved through the advent of **digital** technology. Mr. Jackson's daughter, Rhonda, wants to start her own YouTube channel. She takes some of her college courses on campus and some online, and downloads her textbooks from the Internet. Her world revolves around her iPhone and iPad. She's into Twitter, Snapchat, and Instagram.

We might say that the media (the plural form) are obsolete, in the sense of having a separate device to receive each mode of communication, as Mr. Jackson did. Anyone who has ever used a **smartphone** or tablet to read an e-mail, tweet about a celebrity, view a video, or stream a song has experienced the merging of conventional mass media into new media forms. For growing numbers of consumers, we could even say that there is only one medium (the singular form): the smartphone or tablet they carry with them everywhere.

New media technologies impact our culture by offering new lifestyles, creating new jobs and eliminating others, shifting media empires, demanding new regulations, and presenting unique new social issues (see Figure 1.2).

The changes are not purely technology driven, however. Our individual creativity and our cultures push back against the technologies and the corporations that deploy them to shape their development. The Internet is a prime example. Originally developed to support communication between weapons research labs in the wake of a nuclear holocaust, the Internet has evolved into a tool for entertainment, commerce, communication, and education. Big media corporations now compete for its content with citizen journalists, Facebook users, garage bands, and amateur video producers.

Merging Technologies

Not many forms of purely **analog** communication are in common use today. We continue to experience purely analog communication when we are in a room with another person listening to what he or she says and observing his or her facial expressions or when we pass him or her a handwritten note. Interpersonal communication has been made over by digital forms including texting, e-mail, online chatting, and social networking.

The digital domain now encompasses all media industries, including broadcasting (radio and television), cable, film, music, and publishing (newspapers, magazines, and books). With few exceptions, all media can be consumed online and many conventional media outlets also provide **apps** for consumption on smartphones, e-readers, and tablets.

Digital technology converts sound, pictures, and text into computer-readable formats by changing the information into strings of *binary digits (bits)* made up

> **Digital** means computer-readable information formatted in 1s and 0s.

> **Smartphones** are mobile phones that can access the Internet.

> **Analog** communication uses continuously varying signals corresponding to the light or sounds originated by the source.

> **Apps** (short for *applications*) are software applications for use on smartphones.

DIGITAL MEDIUM The special effects of blockbuster films like *Avengers: Age of Ultron* (2015) are computer generated. Copies are distributed on digital discs and shown to the public on digital projectors. The last analog theaters in the United States closed in 2014.

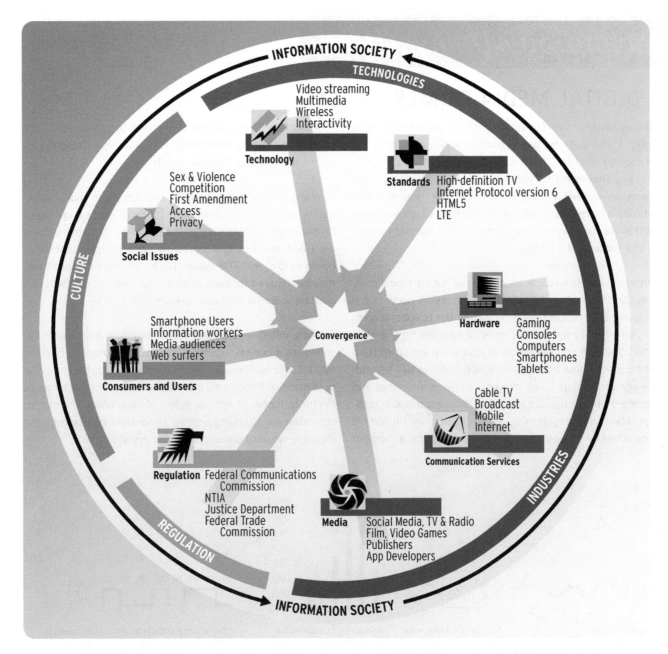

FIGURE 1.2 **MEDIA CONVERGENCE** Media and information technologies, industries, and regulations are converging to impact our culture in the information society.

of electronically encoded 1s and 0s (see Technology Demystified: A Digital Media Primer). A particularly useful quality of digital information is that many different sources can be combined in a single transmission medium. That is the key to combining formerly distinct **channels** of communication, such as telephone and television for delivery to a single digital device, such as a smartphone or tablet.

> **Channel** A channel is an electronic or mechanical system that links the source to the receiver.

Changing Industries

The **convergence** of media technologies is propelling changes in media industries as newer media firms like Google, Apple, and Facebook compete with old media companies for dominance (see Figure 1.2). Apple became the

> **Convergence** is the integration of mass media, computers, and telecommunications.

Technology Demystified

A DIGITAL MEDIA PRIMER

All digital transmissions are composed of only two digits: 1 and 0. These are actually a series of on (for 1)–off (for 0) events. These can be encoded in a variety of ways, including turning electrical currents or light beams on and off in Internet connections, changing the polarity of tiny magnets on the surface of a computer hard drive, or varying the patterns of microscopic pits on the surface of a DVD.

Consider a simple landline telephone call, where digital communication was born. The digital conversion occurs on a computer card that connects the line to the telephone company's switch. First, brief excerpts, or samples, of the electrical waveform corresponding to your voice are taken from the telephone line at a rate of 8,000 samples per second. The size, or voltage level, of each sample is measured and "rounded off" to the closest of 256 different possible readings. Then, a corresponding eight-digit binary number is transmitted by turning an electrical current on for a moment

to indicate a 1 and turning it off for a 0. This process produces a faithful representation of the analog sound waves we create ourselves (see Figure 1.3).

To make computer graphics, a computer stores digital information about the brightness and color of every single point on the computer screen. On many computer screens, there are 1,024 points of light (or picture elements, pixels for short) going across and 768 down. Up to 24 bits of information may be required for each point so that millions of colors can each be assigned their own unique digital code.

Similarly, when we type text into a computer, each key corresponds to a unique sequence of eight computer bits (such as 1000001 for A). These sequences are stored inside the computer or transmitted through the Internet, in the form of tiny surges of electricity, flashes of light, or pulses of magnetism. The human senses are purely analog systems, so for humans to receive the message, we must convert back from digital to analog.

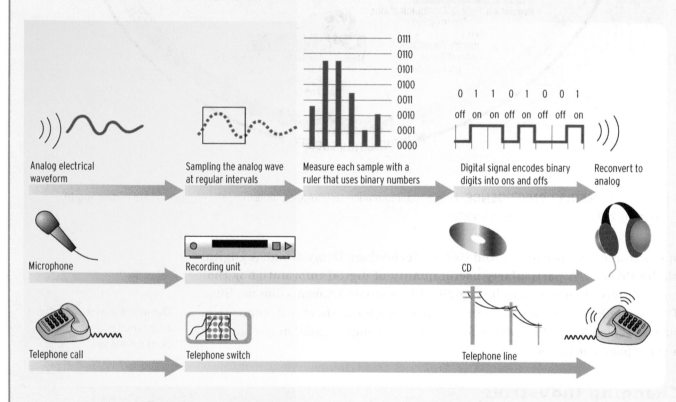

| Analog electrical waveform | Sampling the analog wave at regular intervals | Measure each sample with a ruler that uses binary numbers | Digital signal encodes binary digits into ons and offs | Reconvert to analog |

0111 0110 0101 0100 0011 0010 0001 0000

0 1 1 0 1 0 0 1
off on on off on off off on

Microphone → Recording unit → CD → (headphones)

Telephone call → Telephone switch → Telephone line → (telephone)

FIGURE 1.3 **CONVERTING ANALOG TO DIGITAL** The analog-to-digital conversion process occurs in a variety of media. Here, we illustrate the examples of a music CD recording and a telephone call.

most powerful player in the recorded music industry with iTunes, rocked the telephone industry with the iPhone, and is shaking up print and video with the iPad and AppleTV. Google has emerged as the largest advertising medium of all as advertisers learn how to target ads based on the online behaviors of consumers. Meanwhile, Facebook is prospering as an advertising and content distribution platform for its billions of users worldwide. Apple and Google hope to lead a transition to Internet television that could replace conventional broadcast and cable television, while Amazon, Netflix, and Google's YouTube are investing in professionally produced original video content.

Conventional media firms are changing their ways and reorganizing to meet the new media challenge. In 2011, the cable television giant Comcast bought NBCUniversal after revenues from the NBC Television network declined. NBC's old broadcast network rivals, CBS, ABC, and Fox, are staying afloat with new revenue streams by selling the rights to their programs to **streaming video** companies like Netflix and Hulu. Although most news organizations continue to operate profitably, they have ramped up their online publishing and many have changed owners. Magazine publishers are developing smartphone apps that they hope will revitalize their appeal among young readers.

Old media are also finding it profitable to hire recent college graduates who can advise them how to take advantage of social media. So, changing industries also mean challenging careers for those entering media professions (see Your Media Career: Room at the Bottom, Room at the Top, page 8).

Changing Lifestyles

When new media enter our lives, media consumption patterns evolve. Each month, for example, more than 194 million U.S. Internet users now watch video on their computers, averaging about 20 hours of viewing monthly (comScore, 2015). During the 2014 mid-term elections, 28 percent of eligible voters used their cell phones to keep up with the campaigns, including over 40 percent of young adults aged 18–29 (Smith, 2015). Top video games like "Call of Duty" make as much money in the first week of their release as top movies like *Iron Man 3* make in their entire run.

A lifestyle change among the college-age population makes media executives and advertisers take notice: young adults are no longer easily reached by conventional mass media. They spend so much time juggling their iPods, iPads, iPhones, and video games (often simultaneously) that there is little time or interest

INTERNET TELEVISION The latest TVs are Internet appliances that illustrate the convergence of Web, video, audio, print, games, and interpersonal communication media in a single device.

1962

Digital communication is deployed

Streaming video converts video to continuous streams of data for transmission over the Internet.

left for traditional newspapers or television. They consume media on demand, where and when they please, freeing them from the schedules of television networks, radio DJs, and newspaper deliveries. That's why the old media run websites to sustain interest in long-running TV shows like *Survivor,* create "buzz" for new movies, or add live discussion forums to printed stories. It's also why media and advertisers look for new ways to recapture the young adult audience, such as making TV shows available online and inserting ads

Your Media Career

ROOM AT THE BOTTOM. ROOM AT THE TOP.

The rewards of top-echelon media careers are well publicized: multimillion-dollar salaries, hobnobbing with the rich and famous, globe-hopping lifestyles. From among the tens of thousands who enter the media industry each year from courses like the one you are taking now, only a few make it to the level of Lester Holt, Steven Spielberg, Bob Woodward, or Howard Stern. Still, fulfilling professional success can be attained in less visible media occupations, either behind the scenes of global productions or in local markets, where the rewards may come from creative self-expression or from the satisfying feeling of "making a difference." Media industries feed on the creative energies of young professionals who give them insights into young consumers and the social media they use. This means positions are continually opening up at all levels. And today's media stars have to be replaced someday, so why not you?

The challenges of media careers are many. Some young college graduates never move beyond internships or entry-level "go-for" positions. Making the jump to steady professional employment sometimes depends on things we do not learn in college, such as having family connections or being born with basic creative talent or entrepreneurial drive. Convergence makes media-related careers highly volatile. Whenever you read about a media merger or a new form of digital media production or distribution, it means that some media jobs may disappear, but newly created ones like "social media guru" might appear. So, it is a good idea to consider a media degree as a springboard to other opportunities. Most people entering the workforce today will have four or five different careers regardless of the field they enter, and this is also true of media careers. When we say "different careers," we don't mean working your way up through a progression of related jobs inside an industry, say, from the mailroom at NBC Television to vice president for network programming at CBS.

So, you may find yourself on a very different course later in life (see Career Profile: Sallie Krawcheck). For many of our readers it will mean starting out in a media industry but retraining to enter health care, education, or computer careers where employment is expected to grow the fastest over the next decade. How to get there? Multimedia computer skills not only are in demand in media industries but also will help you leap into other careers if necessary. The abilities to write a coherent paragraph and to produce professional photos, videos, audio, and Web pages are in demand across the information economy and are not limited to media industries.

To assess your options, you can visit the *Occupational Outlook Handbook* (http://www.bls.gov/OCO/), an authoritative source of information about the training and education needed, earnings, expected job prospects, workers' responsibilities on the job, and working conditions for a wide variety of media occupations. Or, keep reading. In each chapter, you will find features about media careers in related fields.

Career Profile: Sallie Krawcheck

Sallie graduated from the University of North Carolina with a degree in journalism. After attaining a master of business administration degree from Columbia University, she put her journalism and business skills to work as a Wall Street analyst, winning recognition for her objectivity and honesty. After holding senior positions at Citibank and Bank of America, she became the chairperson of Ellevate Network, an investment fund-targeting company that has women in important leadership positions. Sallie contributes to business journalism today through columns for business publications, appearances on CNBC, and as a thought leader on the LinkedIn social media network. Her issue is financial reform.

http://www.washingtonspeakers.com/speakers/biography.cfm?SpeakerID=6718

into video games. New media introduce us to alternative ways to live. About two-thirds of U.S. adults use social networking to keep up with their friends and families (Perrin, 2015). However, the new media may also displace close human relationships with superficial ones online (Turkle, 2012), lower the quality of public discourse by substituting Internet rumors for professional journalism, or drag popular culture to new lows.

Shifting Regulations

With the **Telecommunications Act of 1996,** Congress stripped away regulations that protected publishing, broadcasting, cable and satellite television, telephone, and other media companies from competing with one another. Lawmakers had hoped to spark competition, improve service, and lower prices in all communications media. Unfortunately, the flurry of corporate mergers, buyouts, and bankruptcies has outpaced consumer benefits.

Changes in copyright laws shifted the balance of power between media companies and their audiences. The Copyright Term Extension Act of 1998 broadened the **copyright** protection enjoyed by writers, performers, songwriters, and the giant media corporations that own the rights to such valued properties as Bugs Bunny. The Digital Millennium Copyright Act weakened the fair use rights of students and professors to reproduce copyrighted printed works for noncommercial, educational use. It also cracked down on "sharing" music and videos online and made it a crime to tamper with copy protections on music and videos.

Vital consumer interests are also at stake in the battle over **net neutrality.** This is the principle that Internet providers should remain neutral in handling information on the Internet to avoid favoring content provided by their affiliates and business partners and charging their competitors—and ultimately the public—excessive fees. In 2015, the Federal Communications Commission decided to treat Internet providers, like Comcast, as public utilities to strengthen net neutrality protections for consumers.

Rising Social Issues

Social issues are intrinsic to the media. Television is often singled out for the sheer amount of time that impressionable youngsters spend watching it. Children aged 2 to 11 years average nearly 22 hours a week in front of the television screen (Nielsen, 2015). Over the years, television has been criticized for its impacts on sexual promiscuity, racial and ethnic stereotypes, sexism, economic exploitation, mindless consumption, childhood obesity, smoking, drinking, and political apathy. The impact of television on violence is an enduring concern of parents and policy makers alike.

New media are fast replacing television as the number one concern about media effects. Cyberbullying is just as harmful and nearly as prevalent as offline bullying among school children

1996

Telecommunications Act passes Congress

> **Telecommunications Act of 1996** The Telecommunications Act of 1996 is federal legislation that deregulated the communications media.

1998

The Copyright Term Extension Act is enacted by Congress

> **Copyright** is the legal right to control intellectual property. With it comes the legal privilege to use, sell, or license creative works.

> **Net neutrality** means users are not discriminated against based on the amount or nature of the data they transfer on the Internet.

MEDIA EFFECT The Egyptian government was concerned about the effects the Internet was having on society after it was used to organize a rebellion, so they shut it down. Here, Egyptian reporters protest the shutdown. The rebellion overthrew a dictatorship but ultimately resulted in a new regime that cracked down on press freedom.

Digital divide The digital divide is the gap in Internet usage between rich and poor, Anglos and minorities.

STOP & REVIEW

1. List four examples of the convergence phenomenon.
2. What is meant by the term *information society*?
3. What are the three conventional types of mass media?
4. What is the difference between analog and digital?
5. Name three areas in which communication regulations are shifting.

(Kowalski & Limber, 2013), amid highly publicized incidents of teenage suicides associated with online harassment. Does the spread of the Internet create a **digital divide** that spawns a new underclass of citizens who do not enjoy equal access to the latest technology or to the growing array of public services available online? (See Media & Culture: A New Balance of Power?)

On a global scale, a wave of pro-democracy rebellions that swept through the Middle East in the last decade seemed to feed on Facebook, Twitter, text messages, and cell phone videos. However, most of those revolts ultimately led to new dictatorial regimes or to chaos that fostered terrorists who use the Internet as a recruitment tool.

CHANGING MEDIA THROUGHOUT HISTORY

Although changes in the media and the accompanying changes in society sometimes appear to be radically new and different, the media and society have always adapted to each other. In this section, we examine how the role of the media has evolved as society developed—and vice versa—from the dawn of human civilization (see Figure 1.4) through agricultural, industrial, and information societies (Bell, 1973; Dizard, 1997; Sloan, 2005).

Media & Culture

A NEW BALANCE OF POWER?

Just how powerful are the media? Do they affect the very underpinnings of the social order, by determining who holds power in society and how they keep it?

The new media can put us all at the mercy of "digital robber barons." The late Steve Jobs was widely praised and much admired upon his death, but he was a prime example of someone who sets out to dominate new media, to create interesting new things, but also to enrich himself at our expense. The dominance of this type of person reduces the diversity of content and raises the cost of information. For example, Apple maintains control over the apps that are allowed on its iPhone. Innovative apps developed by entrepreneurs that might save consumers money on music, but that would diminish the profits from Apple's iTunes, are not allowed. Or, do the new media consign the poor to continuing poverty? The digital divide describes the gap in Internet access that persists between whites and minorities, rich and poor (NTIA, 2015). As the Internet grows into an important source of employment, education, and political participation, that digital divide could translate into widening class division

and social upheaval. Equal opportunity in the information economy already lags for both minorities and women, who are underrepresented in both the most visible (i.e., on-camera) and most powerful (i.e., senior executive) positions in the media. And although the gap in Internet access for women has largely closed (except for those who are poor or who are recent immigrants), women are poorly represented in computer-related professions and the proportion of women enrolled in undergraduate computer science majors is now in the teens (National Science Foundation, 2015), about a third of the peak level in the 1980s. The issue is global. The nations of the world are divided between those with access to advanced communication technology and those without it.

Or could the new media be a catalyst for a shift away from traditional ruling classes? Blogs raise issues that are ignored by the mainstream press. The diverse and lively communities of the Internet may contribute to the fragmentation of culture and power—for many, identity is defined as much by the Internet communities in which we participate as by the countries we live in or the color of our skin.

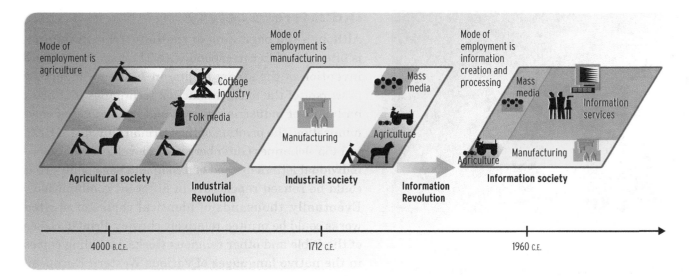

FIGURE 1.4 **STAGES OF ECONOMIC DEVELOPMENT** The three basic stages of economic development, from agricultural to industrial to informational.

Pre-Agricultural Society

Before agricultural societies developed, most people lived in small groups as hunters of animals and gatherers of plants. These cultures depended on the spoken words and songs to transmit ideas among themselves and between generations. Shamans and storytellers spread the news. The oral tradition is an extremely rich one, bringing to us Homer's *Iliad* and *Odyssey* and the epic stories, folktales, ritual chants, and songs of many other cultures. These works that originated in oral forms live on today in the fairy tales and campfire stories that we tell our children.

Agricultural Society

Once agricultural society developed, most work was found on farms or in resource extraction, such as mining, fishing, and logging. Agricultural societies were more settled and more complex than pre-agricultural societies. It was the ancient Sumerian culture, located in what is now modern-day Iraq, that is often credited with developing writing in 3100 BCE. The Greco-Roman method of writing developed into our present-day alphabet.

In early civilizations, literacy was common only among priests and the upper classes. In some cultures, literacy was intentionally limited because the ruling class wanted to keep the masses ignorant of new ideas. Reproduction of printed works was painstaking. Christian monks copied books by hand. The Chinese developed printing with a press that used carved wooden blocks, paper, and ink. With much of the populace still illiterate, couriers skilled at memorizing long oral messages were valuable communication specialists.

3100 BCE

Writing is first developed

AGRICULTURAL SOCIETY This illustration of life on the farm from the nineteenth century provides an idealized picture of pre-industrial America. The critical reader will note the obvious prominence of the white male farmer in the picture and also the African-American laborer chopping wood at the far right.

START THE PRESSES! The advent of the printing press in the late fifteenth century was a precursor of mass literacy and the Industrial Revolution. The Bibles printed by Johannes Gutenberg and others launched a revolution in religious beliefs and culture in the Western world.

1455

The Gutenberg Bible is published

1690

The first American newspaper appears

1910

The United States becomes an industrial society

1960

The United States transitions to become the first information society

1975

Personal computers are invented

1991

World Wide Web begins

Industrial Society

Although the beginning of the Industrial Revolution is often dated to correspond with Thomas Newcomen's invention of the steam engine in 1712, an important precursor of the mass production techniques that are a hallmark of industrialism is found in the field of communication: the printing of the German Gutenberg Bible in 1455. Johannes Gutenberg used movable metal type—individual letters instead of a complete page plate—that could be reused repeatedly in different combinations. Eventually, thousands of identical copies of printed works could be printed relatively cheaply. Printed copies of the Bible and other religious works, including copies in the native languages of various Western European cultures, were instrumental in spreading the Protestant Reformation of the sixteenth century, which in turn spurred the further diffusion of literacy.

The mass production of printed works and the spread of literacy to new classes of society helped create a demand for sporadic printed news sheets that eventually evolved into newspapers.

In a sense, the Industrial Revolution extended Gutenberg's methods to the manufacture of not just print media, but virtually all types of goods. Industrial production (and higher wages) was centered in large cities, triggering a mass migration from rural areas to cities and from agricultural jobs to manufacturing. Growing urban populations with money to spend on manufactured goods provided ready audiences as newspapers expanded to become the first advertising-supported medium of mass communication.

By 1910, the United States had become an industrial society: manufacturing had outstripped agricultural employment for the first time. Industrialization further encouraged the spread of literacy to cope with more complex job requirements and the demands of urban life. Soon, industrial methods of mass production were applied to speed up the printing process of newspapers and magazines and to invent newer communication technologies for the urban populations. Film, radio, and television, as well as newspapers and magazines, are the characteristic media of industrial societies.

Information Society

Today, we live in an information society—our economy depends primarily on the production and consumption of information. When the United States was still an agricultural society, only about 10 percent of the population was employed as **information workers.** The point at which information work starts to dominate the workforce marks the transition to an information society. This transition happened in the United States in 1960, but relatively few other nations have made the transition so far. The proportion of information workers has reached about three-fifths of the U.S. workforce (Wolff, 2006). Since the media reflect the societies that spawn them, it comes as no surprise that the dominant tool in an information society is one that helps to create, store, and process information: the computer.

The evolution of media in the information society can be marked by points at which various media first adopted digital technology and the point at which they became complete, end-to-end digital production and distribution channels.

Telephone. The first consumer communications medium to be digitized was the telephone, beginning in 1962 with digital equipment buried deep within AT&T's network. Today, telephone conversations are converted to digital form in your smartphone handset and travel as computer data along with music and video through advanced telephone networks (see Figure 1.2, page 5).

Print Media. Digitization first hit the production rooms of print media in the late 1960s. Today, thousands of newspapers and magazines are also available electronically on the Internet and as e-books and smartphone apps.

Film. In Hollywood, the computer movement started with the special effects for *Star Wars* in 1974 and continued with the release of all-digital *Toy Story* in 1995. The conversion to digital movie projectors in U.S. movie theaters was completed in 2014.

Video Games. First developed for computers in 1962, they moved to arcades and home consoles in 1971–1972, and later onto personal computers and handhelds.

Recordings. The first digital compact disc (CD) recordings reached consumers in 1982. Despite a recent resurgence in sales of (analog) vinyl LPs, 95 percent of all recorded music sales are digital, including CDs and digital music downloads and streams.

Cable and Satellite Television. In 1998, cable companies began to convert to digital and completed the shift when TV broadcasting in the United States went digital in 2009. Now many cable subscribers enjoy high-speed Internet access and telephone service as well.

Broadcasting. High-definition television (HDTV) replaced conventional television completely in the United States in 2009. Digital audio broadcasting (known as high-definition radio) went on the air in 2004.

Home Video. Beginning in 1995, analog video cassette recorders were supplanted by digital video disc (DVD) players and, four years later, by digital video recorders (DVRs). Video streaming also dates back to the 1990s, and now smartphones, tablets, and smart TVs are gradually replacing the preceding generations of stand-alone home video players.

Thus, digital media are becoming an integral part of our information society. Indeed, employees of newspapers, radio and television stations, and film and recording studios now are grouped together with telecommunications workers and computer programmers as part of the information sector of the economy. College students also create, transform, and store information, although for no pay. So, now and in the future, we are all information workers.

THE WORLD IN YOUR HAND Smartphones are the endpoint of a digital revolution in telephony that began in the 1960s and has resulted in competition for conventional video, audio, and print channels.

Information workers create, process, transform, or store information.

1995

Computer-generated films are introduced

NOW AT YOUR LOCAL THEATER Digital movie projectors using CD-like digital storage media instead of film represent the digital revolution at your local movie theater.

1962

Video games are created

1982

CDs are introduced to consumers

1998

Digital cable first reaches U.S. homes

2009

HDTV takes over the airwaves

1995

DVDs are first sold to consumers

Reuters/Mario Anzuoni

WOW FACTOR Filmmakers hope 3-D movies will encourage the masses to lay down their game consoles and return to movie theaters. However, 3-D movies are still examples of conventional mass communication in that they address a mass audience with limited feedback.

CHANGING CONCEPTIONS OF THE MEDIA

Reading highly encapsulated accounts of the evolution of the media, such as the above, you might get the mistaken impression that society has always followed a logical, linear progression driven by changes in communication technology. However, economics, culture, and politics must come together for technologies like movable type or smartphones to develop. This reality raises the fundamental question that we will consider at length in Chapter 2: do the media determine culture and society, or do culture and society determine the media? Here, we will review a conventional model of human communication and then examine how new media challenge that model.

The SMCR Model

The classic **Source-Message-Channel-Receiver (SMCR)** model was first developed by Shannon and Weaver (1949) and later refined by David Berlo (1960) and Wilbur Schramm (1954).

- The *source* is the originator of the communication.
- The *message* is the content of the communication, the information that is to be exchanged.
- An *encoder* translates the message into a form that can be communicated—often a form that is not directly interpretable by human senses.
- A *channel* is the medium or transmission system used to convey the message from one place to another.
- A *decoder* reverses the encoding process.
- The *receiver* is the destination of the communication.

STOP & REVIEW

1. What were the media forms in pre-agricultural society?
2. Which media evolved in industrial societies?
3. What changes led to the development of the information society?
4. Which media have not become purely digital, end to end?

Source-Message-Channel-Receiver (SMCR) The Source-Message-Channel-Receiver (SMCR) model of mass communication describes the exchange of information as the message passes from the source to the channel to the receiver, with feedback to the source.

- A *feedback mechanism* between the source and the receiver regulates the flow of communication.

- *Noise* is any distortion or errors that may be introduced during the information exchange.

This model can be applied to all forms of human communication, but here we will just illustrate it with a conventional mass communication example, that of television viewing (see Figure 1.5). According to the model, when you are at home watching a television program, the television network (a corporate source) originates the message, which is encoded by the microphones and television cameras in the television studio. The channel is not literally the number on the television dial to which you are tuned, but rather the entire chain of transmitters, satellite links, and cable television equipment required to convey the message to your home. Although we sometimes call a TV set a "receiver," it is really the decoder, and the viewer is the receiver. Feedback from viewers is via television rating services. Electronic interference with the broadcast and the distractions of the neighbor's barking dogs are possible noise components in this situation.

In this classic view, mass communication is a one-to-many communication, and the mass media are the various channels through which mass communication is delivered; for example, through newspapers, radio, TV, or film. The message is communicated from a single source to many receivers at about the same time, with limited opportunities for the audience to communicate back to the source.

Conventional mass media were produced by large media corporations. There an elite corps of media commentators and professional producers acted as **gatekeepers,** deciding what the audience should receive. These editors and producers, recognizing their own power, were aware of themselves as shapers of public opinion and popular tastes (Schramm, 1982).

Mass media messages were addressed to the widest possible audience. The underlying motive was to homogenize tastes and opinions to further the goals of a mass-market industrial economy. Feedback was largely limited to reports from audience research bureaus, which took days or weeks to compile in those days. Beyond the basic demographic distinctions of gender and age found in research reports, the audience was an undifferentiated mass, anonymous

1949

The Shannon–Weaver communication theory is published

Gatekeepers decide what will appear in the media.

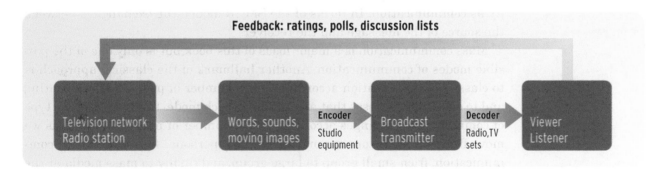

FIGURE 1.5 SMCR MODEL The SMCR model is one way of describing the communication process as applied to broadcast media. In this example, we apply the model to television and radio broadcasting.

1989

Carey's *Communication as Culture* is published

Social media are media whose content is created and distributed through social interaction.

to the source and a passive receptacle for the message. Social critics like Horkheimer and Adorno (1972) called this approach the industrialization of culture.

Carey (1989) criticized the SMCR model for being too linear, seeing media only as a one-way flow from creators to audiences. He and others began to see communication as a more circular, interactive, or even ritual process—one in which audiences not only choose from but also interact with media content, changing its meaning.

Facebook, Twitter, and YouTube are **social media** that challenge the SMCR model, and they embody and even extend the critiques of Carey and others. Social media users continually interact with one another and provide instant feedback not only to their own communication partners but also to the creators of conventional mass media productions that are frequent topics of online commentary. Now we create our own media content, share it with hundreds or thousands of our online "friends," and contest the power of authoritative mass media sources in ways and on a scale that neither Schramm nor Carey could anticipate. Media professionals keep track of the buzz created by their productions and news organizations incorporate clips from smartphones and report about trending topics in social media. YouTube videos conform in some ways to the conventional mass communication model in that they are one-to-many, but feedback in the form of audience downloads and comments is nearly instantaneous and the sources are often amateur video producers rather than media professionals. So, social media perhaps constitute a fundamentally new type of communication. Instead of a linear process, we might reconceptualize the SMCR model as a circle in which the receivers in the audience are positioned closer to the source to provide instant feedback and, in many cases, become the source of communication themselves.

Types of Communication

Communication is an exchange of meaning.

Communication is simply the exchange of meaning. This definition covers a lot of ground. It obviously includes texting your friends, reading a newspaper, watching television, and surfing the Internet. Less obvious examples of communication might include the graphic design on a T-shirt, a fit of laughter, or the wink of an eye. And the meaning exchanged does not have to be profound: a sonnet by Shakespeare and a verse scratched on a bathroom wall both qualify as communication. In terms of the SMCR model, the exchange is between the source of the message and the receiver.

Mass communication is a major focus of this book but is only one of the possible modes of communication. Another hallmark of the classical approach is to classify communication according to the number of people communicating and to examine processes that are unique to each mode. In Figure 1.6, the type of communication changes according to the number of people involved: as we move from top to bottom, we move from intrapersonal to interpersonal communication, from small group to large group, and finally to mass media at the bottom of the pyramid. We can also distinguish between analog (on the left) and digital forms of communication (on the right) in each category. An example of each type is found in the corresponding layer of the pyramid.

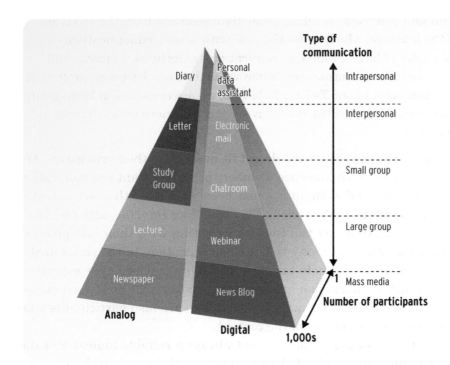

FIGURE 1.6 TYPES OF COMMUNICATION Types of communication may be distinguished according to the number of participants and the nature of the communication process.

- *Intrapersonal communication* is an exchange of information we have with ourselves, such as when we think over our next move in a video game or sing to ourselves in the shower. Typing a to-do list into a smartphone is electronically mediated intrapersonal communication.

- *Interpersonal communication* includes exchanges in which two or more people take part, but the term is usually reserved for situations in which just two people are communicating. Sometimes we call that one-to-one communication. Having a face-to-face conversation over lunch and writing a postcard to a friend are everyday examples. When interpersonal communication is electronically **mediated,** as in a cell phone conversation, the term *point-to-point communication* is sometimes used.

> **Mediated** refers to communication transmitted through an electronic or mechanical channel.

- *Small-group communication* usually involves fewer than a dozen people, extending interpersonal communication into situations where group dynamics become important. For example, when students get together to "scope out" an exam, their interaction is likely to follow one of several well-known patterns of small-group interaction as they define a study plan. For example, one person in the group may dominate. Or, they may take turns speaking and let everyone have their say; we could call that many-to-many communication. Online, small-group communication happens in chat rooms and in multiuser video conferences.

- *Large-group communication* involves anywhere from a dozen to several thousand participants, and the communication situation restricts active involvement to only a few of the parties. However, large-group communication still involves immediate feedback from the receivers of the message, which is not the case with mass communication. Examples of large-group communication are lectures, concerts, and live theatrical performances. When we update our Facebook profiles or post messages to our Twitter followers, we are engaging in large-group communication—provided we have a dozen or more online friends or followers.

Many communication situations do not fit neatly into these categories. Are talk-radio shows, in which audience members provide instant communication back to the source—and even, in a sense, become sources themselves—still true mass media forms? What about TV shows like *Dancing with the Stars* that invite viewers to direct the content by voting with their cell phones? We could perhaps call that many-to-one communication. In the social media sphere, wall postings and photo tags are further examples. Other aspects of social media, such as discussion groups in Facebook, might be termed many-to-many communication since audience members are also participants who are themselves also the sources of the content.

Also, the number of participants is not always a reliable indicator of the type of communication involved. A college lecture delivered on the last day before spring break to only six students or a Facebook posting made by someone with only a few online friends would still be a large-group communication (because of the style of presentation), even though the audience is a small group in terms of the number of people involved. Thus, both the nature of the communication setting and the size of the gathering must be considered.

Other classifications of communication reflect the setting for the communication or the nature of the communication process. *Organizational communication* takes place in formally structured organizations, spans the entire spectrum of communication types as classified by size, and is affected by a person's position and function within the organization. For example, in certain highly structured organizations, most communication travels in one direction—from the bosses to the workers—with little flowing either back up the chain of command or laterally to workers in other departments. Other organizations use social media to promote horizontal communication between employees and "bottom up" feedback from employees to management. Communication can also be distinguished between one-way communication, in which the flow of information goes from the source exclusively to the receiver, and two-way communication, in which both participants take an active role. Finally, *intercultural communication* takes place across international or cultural boundaries.

So, are social media a fundamentally new type of communication? That is debatable. Social networking sites like Facebook are unique in that their various functions provide examples of virtually every type of communication we have mentioned here. Social media also bring relatively rare types of communication, such as many-to-one and many-to-many, within the reach of millions and make it routine for their users to originate their own large-group communications. Empowering the audience or user to produce media content as well as consume it, sometimes known as **Web 2.0,** also occurs in social media venues on a very large scale, but is not entirely unprecedented. Letters to the

Web 2.0 are Internet applications in which users provide content as well as consume it.

editor and radio call-in programs are time-honored old media examples of audience-produced content as well.

What Are the Media Now?

At one time, *media* simply meant the mass media of radio, television, newspapers, magazines, and film. We now talk about **new media**—a term usually associated with interactive media technology, such as the Internet and video games. The defining aspects of the new media are that they are digital, interactive, social, **asynchronous,** multimedia, and narrowcasted. These particular characteristics are important in distinguishing a new, audience-focused conception of the media from the older SMCR model, which emphasized one-way transmission of messages.

Digital. What differences do digital media make? Digitization improves the quality of transmission because digital signals are less susceptible to interference and distortion. Digital messages also can be compressed by allowing multiple channels to be carried where only one was possible before. Many users can also share the same transmission channel simultaneously by taking turns. The Internet uses this approach: if we cut up the stream of digits for your e-mail into chunks (called "packets"), and cut up the YouTube video file your neighbor is receiving, then both of you can share the same channel. Furthermore, digitization is the key to multimedia—combining text, image, and sound in two-way communication channels—representing an important departure from the old media where each modality was confined to separate channels and was one-way only.

Interactive. Just what is "interactivity"? Sometimes the word is used as a synonym for two-way communication, but few interactive media are truly two-way in the same sense as interpersonal communication. In a conversation, two people not only take turns responding to each other but also modify their interaction on the basis of preceding exchanges (Rafaeli, 1988). Social media like Facebook and Twitter are interactive in that sense, but it is the responsiveness of the people involved as much as the **affordances** of the technology, such as the Like button found in Facebook, that make it so.

Interactivity may also be defined in terms of the variety of functional controls that users can manipulate (Sundar et al., 2015). By this definition, the options afforded by a user interface, such as clicking, scrolling, and commenting at a website or jumping, dodging, and shooting in a video game embody interactivity. But by this definition, TV remote controls, textbook indexes, and light switches are interactive, too, although at a low level.

Social Media. A particularly transformative aspect of interactivity is the ability of audiences to contribute content of their own. Since this involves sharing words and images with other users in the course of social interactions, social media have emerged as an umbrella term for this phenomenon. Affordable TV cameras, audio recorders, digital editing software, and cell phone cameras put

DIGITAL INTERPERSONAL Smartphones are an example of digital interpersonal communication when used alone, and an example of digital small-group communication if you text messages to your closest friends. Uploading pictures to Snapchat from your smartphone is large-group communication while viewing movies on a mobile is mass communication.

New media are digital, interactive, social, asynchronous, multimedia, and narrowcasted.

Asynchronous media are not consumed simultaneously by all members of the audience.

Affordances are the technical features of communication channels that allow their users to perform useful functions.

Interactive communication allows the user to modify and control a message as it is presented.

Photos 12 / Alamy Stock Photo

ASYNCHRONOUS HIT *THE WALKING DEAD* is one of the most watched TV show on DVRs. Its audience grows substantially among those aged 18–49 years when delayed viewing is counted over a week's time.

Blogs A blog, short for *Web log*, is commentary addressed to the Web audience. A blog is similar to an online opinion journal.

Narrowcasting targets media to specific segments of the audience.

people from all walks of life in the producer's chair. Facebook, Twitter, YouTube, Pinterest, and Wikipedia are well-known examples. **Blogs** that are filled with personal and professional commentary and the many online support groups devoted to cancer and other serious diseases are further examples.

The interactive features of social media grant the audience new power, not merely to select content but also to contest the messages supplied by the media, and even contribute to the media content. The ability of social media to define culture may be eroding the power of the conventional media. Ever-growing amounts of the news and entertainment are generated by those who do not work for established "big media" organizations. This trend liberates the creative energies of millions of people and makes it possible for viewpoints that are not acceptable in mainstream media to find an audience. However, that also undermines the role of the conventional media in separating fact from fiction and weeding out truly awful and harmful content.

Asynchronous Communication. Simultaneity, the notion that everyone in the audience receives the message at about the same time (or *synchronously*), was once another defining characteristic of the mass media. That view made sense before consumer recording technology became commonplace in the 1960s and 1970s. Before then, you had to catch a program the first time it aired or wait for the reruns. However, the notion never applied very well to film, not without stretching "the same time" to cover a period of several weeks.

Situations that lack simultaneity are examples of asynchronous communication. Consumers' ability to "time shift" programs using DVRs and Internet video renders the notion of simultaneity obsolete, as they can choose when to watch a program regardless of the time and day it originally airs. On-demand options such as cable pay-per-view programs and streaming video services like Netflix are further examples. Postal mail and e-mail are two common examples of asynchronous interpersonal communication.

Narrowcasting. Another sign of the growing power of the audience in the new media is the practice of targeting content to smaller audiences, sometimes called **narrowcasting** (as opposed to broadcasting). Advanced audience research methods help the media cater to smaller audiences by enhancing the richness and speed of audience feedback. The result is that narrowcasting—dedicating communication channels to specific audience subgroups, or market segments—is now practical. Demographic characteristics, such as sex and age, once the sole means of defining audiences, are being replaced by a focus on lifestyles and user needs, and even individual preferences including purchasing and online surfing behavior. Rather than homogenize audiences, the new communications media cater to specialized groups and define new niches and even customize content for individuals by sifting through vast databases of information that consumers leave behind as they navigate the Internet. Narrowcasting is variously referred to as audience segmentation, target marketing, or audience fragmentation.

Multimedia. Converging technologies break down conventional distinctions between channels of communication. Consider online newspapers that show

webpics / Alamy Stock Photo

ASYNCHRONOUS FUN Streaming media services like Netflix and Hulu are the latest technology that puts control of the viewing schedule in the hands of the audience so that there is no longer any need to watch our favorite shows at the time designated by network programing executives.

us the text of the latest story about scandal in high places, but also include links to additional resources such as animated graphics that "follow the money trail" and live video of the Congressional hearings on the matter, as well as to instant polls and a discussion group where we can express our outrage. This multitude of news components means we can choose to experience the same story in five different ways, including as a conversation with other audience members. So what are the media now? Older media forms such as newspapers, television, and film and conventional media institutions like the *New York Times,* CBS Television, and MGM Studios are still with us and will continue to be for a long time. But throughout the media environment, numerous changes in the media, both big and small, are being driven by the continuing evolution of technology, regulation, media ownership, our economy, our culture, our world, and ourselves. As this evolution continues, the old media of generations past are gradually taking on new media forms.

STOP & REVIEW

1. What does SMCR stand for?
2. Use the SMCR model to describe Facebook.
3. Is an automated teller machine interactive? Explain.
4. Name three examples of social media.
5. How do the "new media" differ from the "old media"?

SUMMARY&REVIEW

WHAT IS THE INFORMATION SOCIETY?

The information society is one in which the production, processing, distribution, and consumption of information are the primary economic and social activities. In an information society, an ever-increasing amount of time is spent with digital communications media. Most people are employed as information workers: people who produce, process, or distribute information as their primary work activity. The information society is a further step in the evolution of society from its former bases in agriculture and manufacturing.

HOW ARE MASS MEDIA AND INFORMATION TECHNOLOGIES CONVERGING?

Increasingly, communication is created and distributed in a computer-readable digital form. This change means that the same basic technologies can be used to transmit all forms of communication—text, audio, or video—in an integrated communication system such as the Internet. Thus, separate channels of communication are no longer needed for each medium. The mass media, telecommunications, Internet, and computer software industries are all part of the same information sector of the economy—they are, in other words, converging. Laws and public policies governing the media, career opportunities in communications industries, social and personal issues arising from media consumption, and even theories of the media and their role in society are all changing.

WHAT ARE THE COMPONENTS OF THE COMMUNICATION PROCESS?

All communication processes can be described in terms of a simple model in which a corporate or individual source encodes a message and transmits it through a physical channel to the person for whom the message is intended—the receiver. We call this the SMCR model. In most communication situations, feedback is also provided between the receiver and the source. Contemporary views of the process stress that it takes place in the context of a culture shared by the source and the receiver and that both source and receiver contribute to the creation of meaning.

WHAT IS MASS COMMUNICATION?

The conventional view is that mass communication involves large professional organizations, audiences of hundreds or thousands or millions of people, and no immediate feedback between source and receiver. Newspapers, magazines, radio, television, and film are all examples of mass media.

WHAT OTHER TYPES OF COMMUNICATION EXIST?

When the communication channel is an electronic or mechanical device—such as a radio station or a movie projector—we call it mediated communication. Mediated communication may be point-to-point, one-to-many, or multipoint-to-multipoint.

Communication can be characterized according to the number of people involved. Intrapersonal communication involves one person, interpersonal communication usually includes only two people, and small-group communication usually encompasses more than two but fewer than a dozen participants. Large-group communication involves dozens or hundreds of people, but feedback is still immediate. Communication can also be characterized according to the setting in which it takes place. For example, organizational communication happens inside a formally structured organization. Social media combine multiple types of communication and empower audiences to contribute content on an unprecedented scale.

WHERE DID THE MASS MEDIA COME FROM?

Although mass media had forerunners in agricultural and pre-agricultural societies, they are generally regarded as creations of the Industrial Age. Mass production methods coupled with the rise of large urban audiences for media during the Industrial Age led to the rise of print and later mass media.

WHAT IS INTERACTIVITY?

A variety of meanings have been attached to the term *interactive*, ranging from the simple ability to select content from a large number of options to media that mimic interpersonal interactions. The degree of interactivity can be defined in terms of the number of features that the user has available in an interface to control media content.

WHAT ARE THE NEW MEDIA?

The long-term trend is to integrate the many specialized channels of communication into all-purpose digital networks that will provide access at the convenience of the audience. Familiar mass media forms such as newspapers, radio, and television are evolving into, or learning to coexist with, new forms that are all-digital, such as the World Wide Web. Interactive capabilities give users a new measure of control over the media channels they consume, where and when they consume the media, and even the content of those channels. Messages are customized for smaller specialized audience segments, sometimes even tailored to individuals, and are narrowcast to these segments rather than broadcast to a homogeneous audience.

THINKING CRITICALLY
ABOUT THE MEDIA

1. How would you tell the story of the development of the information society to your parents?

2. Describe what convergence has meant in your life and how it affects you.

3. What will your future life in the information society be like?

4. Does the SMCR model adequately explain social media?

5. If you send a text message to your entire "friends circle," is that mass communication? Explain.

6. Are social media a fundamentally new type of communication or not? Justify.

KEY TERMS

affordances (p. 19)

analog (p. 5)

apps (p. 5)

asynchronous (p. 19)

blog (p. 20)

channel (p. 5)

communication (p. 16)

convergence (p. 5)

copyright (p. 9)

digital (p. 4)

digital divide (p. 10)

gatekeepers (p. 15)

information society (p. 3)

information workers (p. 13)

interactive (p. 19)

mass communication (p. 3)

mediated (p. 17)

narrowcasting (p. 20)

net neutrality (p. 9)

new media (p. 19)

smartphone (p. 4)

social media (p. 16)

Source-Message-Channel-Receiver (SMCR) (p. 14)

Streaming video (p. 7)

Telecommunications Act of 1996 (p. 9)

Web 2.0 (p. 18)

MindTap

Test your knowledge with online printable flashcards and online quizzing.

MindTap Log on to the MindTap for *Media Now to* access a variety of additional materials, including this chapter's e-book, learning objectives, comprehension quizzes, videos, and more!

MEDIA AND SOCIETY

LEARNING OBJECTIVES

After studying the topics in this chapter, you will be able to:

1 Explain how your media choices are affected by economies of scale in today's converging media industry.
2 Distinguish the profit motives and subsequent consumer costs behind advertising-supported media, the movie industry, the book publishing industry, and social media.
3 List the nine sources of media revenue.
4 Identify examples of the four functions of the media.
5 According to Everett Rogers' diffusion of innovations process, classify media users based on when they adopted a piece of new technology.
6 Evaluate the influence of media gatekeepers on swaying public opinion of a news event.
7 Explain Marshall McLuhan's statement that "the medium is the message."
8 Assess new media technology's social function as either a determinant or product of modern culture.

UNDERSTANDING THE MEDIA

This chapter is organized around one of the most fundamental debates about media and society: do media change society or reflect society? For example, is the adoption of Internet-connected smart TVs determined by their cost, or does the way audiences use the Internet change the economics of television distribution? Or do both take place?

We begin this chapter with the arguments that society drives the changes in media content and technology. We end the chapter by presenting opposing positions about how media content and media technologies impact society and culture. In between, we will consider

EAGER MEDIA CONSUMERS like these movie patrons help us understand why the media exist. We will examine many other explanations for the media here in this chapter.

Philip Game/Alamy Stock Photo

MEDIA THEN··· MEDIA NOW

1867
> *First volume of* Das Kapital *is published*

1869
> *Matthew Arnold's* Culture and Anarchy *is published*

1900
> *First edition of Freud's* The Interpretation of Dreams *comes out*

1949
> *David White publishes* The Gatekeeper

1960
> *Charles Wright first publishes his* Functional Analysis of Mass Communication

1962
> *First edition of Rogers'* Diffusion of Innovations *is published*

1964
> *McLuhan's* Understanding the Media *is published*

1972
> *MacCombs and Shaw define agenda setting*

viewpoints that occupy the middle ground, emphasizing the mutual relationships among media, economics, and culture.

We'll examine the issue through **theories** of media and society. Theories reflect our assumptions about patterns of behavior of individuals, media institutions, and society at large. Media theories can help us predict future actions in similar circumstances, take a more critical look at what media do, and interpret the broader meaning of the media and their content. In this chapter, we will focus on theories about how media institutions function in society. In Chapter 15, we will examine theories of media impacts on society and individuals. Theories are the work of scholars typically employed as university professors, so we would also like to introduce you to that profession (see Your Media Career: Media Scholar, page 29).

> **Theories** are general principles that explain and predict behavior.

MindTap
Start with a quick warm-up activity.

MEDIA ECONOMICS

If you were to ask people who work in the media why their companies exist, many might say something like, "to make money." Notwithstanding some important nonprofit exceptions such as Public Broadcasting and noncommercial community radio stations, America is a capitalist society and its media institutions reflect that fact, so we will start there.

MindTap
Read, highlight, and take notes on the complete chapter text in a rich interactive online platform.

Economics studies the forces that allocate resources to satisfy competing needs (Picard, 2011). Classical economists believe that media institutions, as well as the cultures and societies in which they exist and the media consumption behavior of individuals, reflect economic forces. For these economists, our purchase of Microsoft's Xbox One results from a cold and calculated economic comparison of its price and features to Sony's PS4 and the costs of other competing entertainment alternatives, "rational choice," rather than from our passion to play games.

Mass Production, Mass Distribution

Throughout the history of the mass media, mass production and mass distribution have been the keys to economic success. Recalling our discussion of the historical development of the media in Chapter 1, we can say that the transition from the folk media that characterized agricultural society to the mass media associated with industrial society came about as standardized media products were distributed to ever-expanding mass markets (see Figure 2.1).

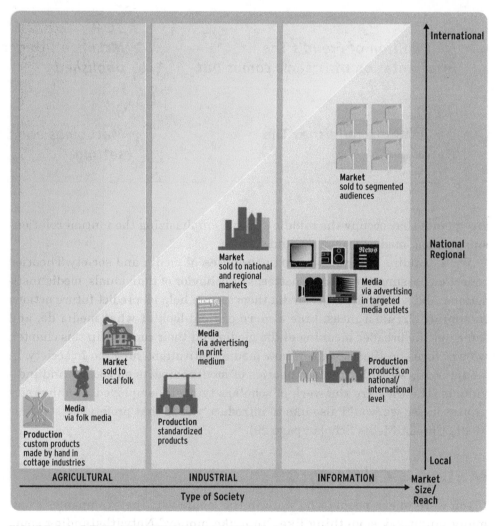

FIGURE 2.1 DEVELOPMENT OF MASS MEDIA Mass media developed during the Industrial Age by building on economies of scale to reap increasing profits from larger mass markets. They replaced folk media and in turn are being transformed into highly targeted and personalized forms.

In this respect, the media follow an industrial economic model in which profits are reaped by producing many copies of a product at the lowest possible cost to the producer. However, for media more than other industries, most of the cost is in the first copy. As media companies get larger, expand their scope, and find larger audiences, they can spread the first-copy costs over more consumers. They can reap immense profits if their production costs go down while audiences expand.

Thus, all media companies constantly strive to produce media products more efficiently to reduce their costs, but large firms enjoy some natural advantages in doing so. For example, CBS Television can better afford investments in labor-saving technologies like robotic cameras for the big-market television stations it owns than can family-owned, small-town television stations. This is because the large stations produce more programs and sell ads in the programs at higher rates so that they can more quickly recover the cost of the equipment from what they save on labor.

Sometimes media organizations combine their companies and slash staff. In the newspaper industry, many formerly independent local papers have been reorganized under common management so that a single advertising sales staff serves two papers instead of one. We call these efficiency measures **economies of scale.** Production efficiencies are hard to come by in the electronic media because each movie, television program, or home page is an original product. Yet the incremental, or marginal, cost of each additional copy is very low after that first copy is made, even moreso with digital copies than with physical ones, giving digital media an advantage over conventional ones.

> **Economies of scale** result when unit costs go down as production quantities increase.

Economies of scale also give big media companies an advantage when dealing with the firms that supply their operations with products and services. When a CBS-owned television station places an order for editing equipment, its corporate parent may further fatten the order by buying equipment for several other CBS-owned stations at the same time. To achieve their own economies of scale, equipment suppliers will negotiate a volume discount for CBS, whereas the "mom-and-pop" station pays the full price because it makes fewer purchases. However, when the costs of production technologies drop rapidly, this barrier to entry declines and smaller producers can take advantage of lower production equipment costs to jump in to parts of the market. For example, small record labels and video producers now compete with "Big Media" companies on the Internet.

The Benefits of Competition

In the presence of competition, cost savings resulting from economies of scale may be passed along to consumers. When this happens, the **law of supply and demand** dictates that more people will consume the product, leading to further economies of scale, further improvements in production and products, and so on in a spiral effect.

> **Law of supply and demand** The law of supply and demand describes the relationship among the supply of products, prices, and consumer demand.

It is perhaps easiest to grasp the benefits of competition using mass-produced consumer products such as color television sets. Improvements in electronics and manufacturing techniques yielded economies of scale that cut the price of a 15-inch color TV set from $8,700 (in today's dollars) in 1954 to less than $50 by the time that the last TV sets with conventional picture tubes were being sold in the United States in 2014. As the price decreased, more people bought color sets, and the most efficient manufacturers earned profits to invest in larger plants and newer, faster production techniques that further lowered the costs relative to their competition and created more and improved products. To stay in business, TV manufacturers continually come up with new premium products such as ultra high-definition TVs (see Chapter 9). Lower prices and improved products meant still more sales, and so on. Today, for the equivalent cost of the 1954 color TV, you can buy a 78-inch ultra high-definition TV. Other media, such as newspapers and magazines, with substantial **marginal costs** associated with producing each additional copy, follow a similar formula: the more units they produce, the less each unit costs and also the more incentive they have to innovate with new production processes and consumer products.

> **Marginal costs** are the incremental costs of each additional copy or unit of a product.

Competition still benefits the consumer even when marginal costs are low, such as television programming distribution. For example, cable television operators have to be mindful of Internet options such as Netflix and Hulu. The law of supply and demand dictates that if they set cable prices too high, their customers will consider "cutting the cord" that connects them to the cable TV provider and go "over the top" (see Chapter 9) to Internet providers that offer access to online video at less cost.

Media Monopolies

What happens when there is little or no competition? The producer of a media product can pocket the cost savings realized from economies of scale in the form of higher profits—especially if there is no competition to undercut the price or introduce attractive new products. In fact, why bother to become more efficient? Sometimes producers can make more money by simply raising prices, provided they are not so steep that consumers forgo making the purchase. For example, when there are two newspapers in town, they compete for subscribers by undercutting each other's prices and adding features to win new readers. But if one drives the other out of business, or if they merge, the newsstand price may rise higher than ever.

Thus, the economics of media industries can lead to ownership patterns that are not in the best interest of consumers. These patterns include **monopoly,** in which one company dominates an industry and can set its prices, and **oligopoly,** in which a few companies dominate (see Figure 2.2). For example, having only one newspaper in town creates a newspaper monopoly. New York City has three daily newspapers—that is an oligopoly. And when there are two independent outlets, it is called a **duopoly.**

> **Monopoly** is the domination of a market by a single company.

> **Oligopoly** is the domination of a market by a few firms.

> **Duopoly** A duopoly exists when two companies dominate a market.

Big is not invariably bad. The greatest economies of scale should result when there is only a single provider, because the initial costs are spread among the greatest possible number of consumers (Noam, 1983). Unfortunately, big companies can behave badly when they dominate a market. They might not want to invest in product research and development or new equipment to better serve the public. They may abuse their market power with underhanded tactics, such as giving speedier access to Internet networks they own to websites they control than to websites owned by other companies. Or they'll take

MEDIA SCHOLAR

On the surface, the job of a media scholar looks like a cushy one: between press interviews about her latest research and travel junkets, the scholar may spend only 6 or 7 hours a week to teach her classes, attend the occasional faculty meeting, and manage her teaching assistants. Once she gets tenure, she has the guarantee of lifetime employment and gets a sabbatical year off every few years. Meanwhile, she is free to enjoy those long summer, winter, and spring vacations!

In reality, she may never have a real vacation (or a free weekend) from the time she embarks on her career as a scholar until the day she gets tenure. Most of those breaks and all of those sabbaticals are devoted to scholarly work. For every hour she spends in class, several more are devoted to preparation, grading, and advising students. Additional hours go into serving on university committees, reviewing scholarship produced by others, and doing outreach in the community. The pursuit and administration of external grants from government agencies like the National Science Foundation, the National Endowment for the Humanities, and the National Institutes of Health may be part of her job as well. It's really four jobs in one (teaching, research, service, grant seeking) that add up to far more than 40 hours a week. What sustains her is a passion for creating knowledge and a desire to make the world a better place through the students she mentors and the new knowledge she creates. Those are the prime qualifications for a career as a media scholar. A total of 4 to 7 years of formal education beyond a bachelor's degree are also required, during which time the aspiring scholar will serve as a low-paid apprentice while obtaining her "terminal degree." One route (followed by Susan Robinson, see below) is to obtain a Master of Arts (MA) degree followed by a Doctor of Philosophy (PhD) in communication, mass media, or journalism or in a related field such as sociology or psychology. Following that route, she will write articles for scholarly journals such as the *Journal of Communication, Journalism Quarterly, Journal of Advertising Research, or Journal of Computer-Mediated Communication.* Alternatively, she could obtain a Master of Fine Arts (MFA) degree and become a creative scholar by having her films, videos, photos, or graphics presented at peer-juried creative competitions. Either way, "publish or perish" is her credo, since if she hasn't produced enough scholarship to obtain tenure, usually after 7 years of teaching and 7 years of graduate studies, she may have to find another line of work.

According to the *Occupational Outlook,* employment for postsecondary (i.e., post-high school) teachers is expected to grow faster than for other occupations over the next several years. Increasing enrollments assure continued growth, although uncertainties about government funding for higher education and a trend toward hiring part-time instructors are cautionary notes. About 30,000 postsecondary teachers work in the field of communication. Their average annual salary was about $69,000 in 2014. Full professors at prestigious institutions located on the East or West Coasts or the upper Midwest earn salaries well into the six figures—and that's for 9 or 10 months of work—and they can supplement their incomes with consulting fees, publication royalties, and extra money for summer teaching and research.

Source: BLS (2016). *Occupational Outlook Handbook.* Available: http://www.bls.gov/ooh/

BLS (2016). Occupational Employment and Wages, May 2014: 25–1122 Communications Teachers, Postsecondary. Available: http://www.bls.gov/oes/current/oes251122.htm

Career Profile: Susan Robinson

Susan is an associate professor in the School of Journalism and Mass Communication at the University of Wisconsin. Her work on the impact of new media technologies on the reporting of public affairs is published in the *Journal of Communication* and *New Media and Society,* among others. She holds a BA in Journalism from the University of New Hampshire, an MA in Journalism from Northeastern, and a PhD in Mass Media and Communication from Temple University. In 2012, she was honored by the Association for Education in Journalism and Mass Communication for outstanding achievement and effort in teaching, research, and public service for scholars under 40 years of age.

Source: https://journalism.wisc.edu/sjmc_profile/susan-robinson/

profits from a business in which they enjoy monopoly dominance, such as personal computer operating system software, and use those profits to dominate other competitive businesses, such as the market for Internet browser software. (Microsoft was found guilty of this.) Another abuse is to slash prices

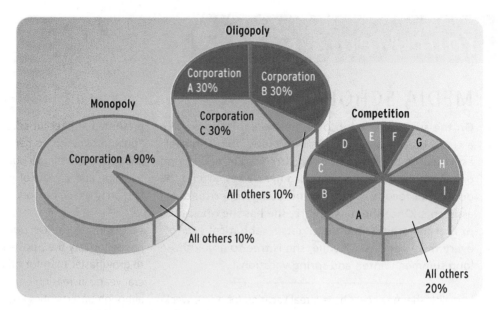

FIGURE 2.2 **MEDIA OWNERSHIP PATTERNS** Media ownership patterns reflect the number of competing media and how they divide the market. In a monopoly one firm dominates, while in an oligopoly a small number of firms split the market among themselves.

below costs to ruin smaller competitors. For instance, Amazon.com initially offered electronic books at low prices, which undercut local bookstores. After the giant has bankrupted its smaller competitors, it can raise prices again to boost profits.

Similarly, monopolies and oligopolies can afford high entry costs that pose **barriers to entry** to new competitors. If a mom-and-pop radio station wanted to compete against the big media groups by buying dozens of stations of its own, chances are it could not raise the money necessary. Large media companies can find the financing, even if they are already deeply in debt, because they have a track record with bankers and valuable assets that banks could seize. Newer, smaller entrants have few assets and inspire less confidence in investors. So, the big get bigger and the small are forced out of business, resulting in greater concentration of ownership.

When companies dominate a market, they can raise their prices—and their profits—with impunity. Some communications media are regarded as such necessities that many consumers grudgingly pay far more than the companies' actual costs. Cable television rates have consistently risen well above inflation, for example. And sometimes oligopolies forge "gentlemen's agreements" to fix prices among themselves, with nearly the same effects on the consumer as a monopoly. Major book publishers colluded with Apple to force Amazon to raise the prices for electronic books to match the retail prices of printed books in support of their traditional business model, for example, even though the e-books cost far less to produce and distribute than printed books.

Monopolies in communications media are especially troubling because they can also reduce the diversity of content. What could happen if the same company owned the local newspaper, the leading local TV and radio stations, and the local cable TV franchise and commanded all of its outlets to back the same candidate for mayor? It would be very difficult for other candidates to present their

Barriers to entry are obstacles companies must overcome to enter a market.

position to the public. Such issues raise questions of regulation. The media industries continually push the Federal Communications Commission to relax prohibitions on such cross-ownership, while some consumer advocates would like to see them strengthened (see Chapter 16).

The Profit Motive

Let's change our unit of analysis and examine more closely how economic forces that operate at the industry level affect individual media organizations. For privately owned media companies, everything is ultimately subordinate to the flow of **profits,** including the content of the media and the audiences they seek. The owners of the media must turn a profit after paying all their operating costs and their taxes. Continuing costs are also involved, such as the paper and ink the news is printed with and the personnel for reporting, designing, advertising, selling, and distributing the newspaper. Media companies also have to pay back their entry costs, the money they borrowed from banks or their investors to put their production and distribution apparatus in place, and also loans they take to upgrade their operations, with interest. The rate of profit has to match or exceed that which investors could realize if they invested in other types of businesses or just left their money in the bank (Picard, 2011) or they will desert the company's stock for more profitable investments.

All media firms have to recoup their costs somehow, but why is there such a wide disparity in their cost to the consumer? Some media, such as broadcast radio and television, are seemingly free, whereas newspapers charge for subscriptions by the month, and movies charge hefty admissions for a single viewing. The answer lies in the different methods the media use to recoup their first-copy costs.

First consider moviemaking, where costs are largely recovered from direct payments from the consumer in the form of movie theater admissions. The first-copy costs include the salaries for the actors and the production staff, rental of the studios and cameras, location fees where the film is shot, the sets, the special effects, and all of the management overhead associated with getting the film made and shown to the public. Thus, first-copy costs include everything that goes into making the master print of the film.

The production costs of the recent Star Wars installment, *The Force Awakens,* were reportedly over $250 million; another $250 million was spent on promotion and advertising before the film opened and the studio charged about $30 million for managing the project (Barnes, 2016). The film grossed $517 million worldwide in its first weekend, but that did not make it instantly profitable. Those box office proceeds have to be split with the theater owners, who typically get half, but the theater owners' shares were smaller than usual since Disney could command a better cut of the proceeds for a sure fire hit. Still, the film was a quarter billion dollars in the red after the opening week

BUSINESSMAN OR MONOPOLIST? The dominance of social networking by Facebook's Mark Zuckerberg raises antitrust issues about monopolistic practices. Has Facebook become so powerful that it limits innovation and discourages competition?

Profits are what is left after operating costs, taxes, and paybacks to investors.

FIRST-COPY COSTS The salaries paid to the stars of the *Star Wars* films are examples of the costs of making the first copy of a film that must be spread over millions of moviegoers.

and did not make a profit for Disney studios until about half way through its first run. *The Force Awakens* eventually grossed $2 billion in ticket sales, and thus returned huge profits by the end of its first run. Further revenues are generated by selling rights to home video, broadcast, cable, pay-per-view, and streaming video distributors, adding another half billion or so, although revenue sharing fees and royalties paid to participants in the film (e.g., the director and the stars) will subtract about a quarter billion dollars from Disney's profits over time. And, beginning with the first *Star Wars* release in 1977, the franchise has been a merchandising bonanza, and the current installment may well gross more revenue from the toys it promotes than from the theater tickets it sells, so Disney hopes that the sales force will be with you. All told, the film will generate well over a billion dollars in profits.

In advertising-supported electronic media such as television, radio, and social media, the cost of each additional copy is virtually zero. That is, whether one person or 20 million people view *The Big Bang Theory,* the cost to the network is the same. But the value to the advertiser increases with the increased number of households. The cost of broadcasting a program to 1,000 homes is the same as broadcasting it to 2,000 homes, but the fee to the advertiser may double. And so, the broadcaster can recoup the first-copy costs exclusively from advertising sales and offer the program "free" to the viewer.

In publishing, the first-copy costs include the salaries of all the writers and editors who prepare the stories and the designers and preproduction workers who get them ready for the printing press and online publication. In addition, newspapers and magazines incur substantial per-unit marginal costs when they print and distribute each copy to their readers—the amount of paper and the ink consumed and the payments to delivery people rise with each copy. To offset these marginal costs, most newspapers and magazines have three revenue streams: advertising sales, subscriptions (including online subscriptions), and newsstand purchases. Advertising is usually the most important of the three, typically contributing three-fourths of newspaper revenues. When revenues from advertisers and consumers exceed production costs, profits result. The media reinvest some of their profits to make improved products that even more consumers will want. For example, television networks invest their profits in new programs that they hope will be hits; newspaper publishers invest in faster printing presses.

But profits are not always paramount. The Public Broadcasting Service (PBS) is the prime example of a not-for-profit media organization in the United States. Government funds and voluntary charitable contributions cover its operating costs so it can be independent of advertisers, although the on-air acknowledgments of corporate contributions may appear to be ads to the viewer. No profits are expected. Still, these not-for-profit media are also money-minded;

they must continually raise money from grants and corporate donors—and "from viewers like you"—to cover their capital costs and operating budgets.

How Media Make Money

The formula for staying profitable is seemingly simple. The payments received from media consumers (see Figure 2.3) must exceed the total spent on content, distribution, daily operations, taxes, and investment. A number of different business models for making money exist in the media:

- *Direct sales* occur when consumers pay lump sums to purchase products that they own, such as iTunes downloads.

- *Rentals* also involve direct payment for a product, except that the consumer only borrows the product, such as video game rentals. A retail outlet buys the product from a manufacturer and recoups the purchase price by renting it multiple times.

- *Subscriptions* are payments for a continuing service rather than a single product. Newspapers, magazines, pay TV companies, and streaming media make money this way.

- *Usage fees* include admission fees to theaters and pay-per-view movies on TV.

- *Advertising* is the main economic base for most newspapers and magazines and all commercial television and radio stations. Advertisers buy commercial time or page space from the media, and the rates are set in relation to the number of people who are likely to be exposed to the ad.

FIRST-RUN SYNDICATION *Judge Judy* is syndicated to local TV stations throughout the country by CBS Television Distribution. The episodes have not previously appeared on network television and so are first-run syndication.

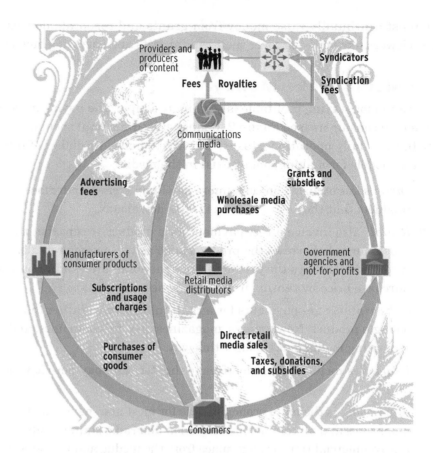

FIGURE 2.3 **MEDIA REVENUE SOURCES** There are four main ways of paying for media: advertising, direct sales, subscriptions, and public subsidies. Media organizations in turn pay the producers of the content, either directly or through syndication agreements and royalty fees.

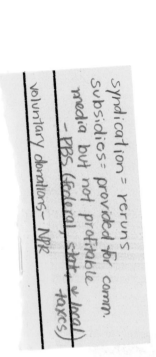

Syndication = reruns
Subsidies = provided for comm. media but not profitable.
– PBS (federal, state, + local taxes)

voluntary donations– NPR

- *Syndication* is the rental of content to media outlets, rather than to the consumer. Newspaper comic strips and reruns of old television series are syndicated to the media outlets that distribute them locally.

- *License fees* compensate the creators of media content for the use of their original ideas. For example, songwriters receive a **copyright royalty fee** collected from Internet radio stations that play their songs.

- *Subsidies* are provided for communications media that society considers desirable but that commercial interests do not find profitable. PBS is subsidized by federal, state, and local taxes.

- *Voluntary donations* are made by corporations, private foundations, and individuals to media that provide a public service, like National Public Radio. Also, some creators let you download their software and games, and then pay if you like them.

> **A copyright royalty fee** is a payment for use of a creative work.

From Mass Markets to Market Segments

From our discussion so far, it might seem natural to you that communications media should strive for products that have the broadest possible appeal. Indeed, until recently this was the case. Now, however, technological changes and receptivity by audiences and advertisers encourage media to engage in *narrow casting,* to target smaller, more specific audience segments with more specialized content. Revisiting Figure 2.1 (see page 26), this development marks the transition from the mass media of industrial society to the targeted media of the information society.

In television, the 1970s were a time when CBS, NBC, and ABC ruled the screen. Together, they accounted for over 90 percent of the prime-time audience, and top shows like *All in the Family* reached up to half the people watching television. Their sponsors sold mass-market products like Lay's potato chips that appealed to a broad spectrum of viewers. For the sponsors, this was a good deal—a relatively inexpensive way to present a mass-market item to a mass audience.

Now, with competition from specialized cable and satellite channels and Internet videos, top-rated network television shows reach less than a fifth of the audience they once did, or under 10 percent of possible viewers, and advertisers offer a dizzying array of variations on their products. Several factors contribute to such finely grained audience segmentation. First, information technologies, such as desktop publishing and computerized video editing, have lowered media production costs. That makes it possible to profit from smaller audiences. Second, advertisers value small audiences if they contain high proportions of their target market. A computer software ad that appears in *Personal Computing* magazine might reach more potential computer software buyers than one that appears in *People* magazine. Thus, *Personal Computing* is more worthwhile to the software advertiser, even though the cost of reaching each individual *People* reader (many of whom are not in the market for software) is lower. Third, sophisticated research techniques and databases of consumer information make it practical to aggregate a large audience of potential customers across multiple, narrowcast media more efficiently than by making a single mass-media buy (see Chapter 14). Finally, conventional media forms like the broadcast TV networks, which have lost audiences to narrowcasters, have had to respond with more narrowly targeted programs of their own.

New Media Economics

Popular sites on the World Wide Web and social media have pushed segmentation to a new extreme: personalization. The logic behind personalized content, customized for individuals, is similar to that of narrowcasting, except that the market segments shrink to specific individuals. Personalization works to the advertisers' benefit, giving them the ability to target ads very precisely to specific people who are actually in the market for their products. For example, if someone enters *smartphone* as a search term into Google, he or she is greeted with several sponsored links featuring special deals, but a conventional television station has no way of "knowing" if a viewer is interested in that particular product.

SELLING THE AUDIENCE Advertising is the major revenue source for mass media. The media sell advertising space on the basis of the size of the audience but users of TV remote controls and DVRs undermine that business model.

© Kekyalyaynen/Shutterstock.com

New media challenge other basic assumptions of media economics, since reproduction and distribution costs are greatly reduced (Kahin & Varian, 2000). Conventional mass media had to make expensive investments in printing presses, broadcast transmitters, and movie theaters to distribute their products whereas for new media much of these costs are absorbed by end users who pay for the Internet infrastructure with their monthly service fees and, in the case of college students, with their institution's technology fees. Websites that sell media products like books and CDs can also afford to offer a wider selection of specialized products that brick-and-mortar bookstores and record stores cannot afford to stock on their shelves.

The initial public stock offerings for new media companies like Facebook in 2012 were covered as "get rich quick" stories or popularity contests, but they actually reflect a the basic mechanisms of a capitalist economy. Facebook founder Mark Zuckerberg became an "instant" billionaire only after years of struggle to develop, promote, and finance his social media empire. Facebook uses the proceeds from its initial stock offering and subsequent rises in its stock price to buy hardware, develop software, and acquire other companies, such as Instagram, that help it expand into new markets.

However, the economics of social media differs somewhat from conventional media. Social media benefit from the *critical mass* or network effect (see below), by which their adoption, and hence their value, increases in relation to the number of users who have already adopted it. After a certain point, their popularity accelerates and the new service "takes off." Once established, social media pose a significant barrier to entry to later entrants: the *switching costs* involved in recreating one's profile and network of contacts on a new platform, for example. Thus, investors are eager to get in on the ground floor of a new company that they believe can be the prime mover of a new social media craze. That is why, some start-up companies that have never turned a profit, and in some cases have never even had a product to sell, can attract billions from investors.

Many websites and mobile apps make money in the proven traditional media way—through advertising—but with some interesting twists. For example, Google advertisers bid for prime space at the top and right-hand margins of their search pages, whereas conventional media charge fixed rates for ads. Google charges "by the click" so that advertisers pay only when someone clicks on their ad. Those ad rates can run from a few pennies to as much as $100 per click. Online advertisers bid for potential customers in real time, based on detailed information about the Web surfing habits of individual consumers. By comparison, broadcast TV advertisers reach Super Bowl viewers for only about 4 cents each. The difference is that the Google ads reach consumers as they actively seek the product through a keyword search (Google calls them "adwords"), and the click-through assures the advertiser that the consumer is interested in their particular brand. In contrast, the Super Bowl

SHARING YouTube shares its advertising revenues with social media stars who upload popular videos, such as the men of Smosh, shown here.

viewer may not notice the ad, may not be in the market for the product, may be the loyal customer of some other company's products, may forget the ad because he or she is not going to shop until the next day, or may not even be in the room when the ad runs.

Websites run by traditional media companies such as the *New York Times* have an edge over those run by Internet companies such as Salon.com. The older media companies have deeper pockets to subsidize unprofitable websites, and they can recycle content that is supported by conventional media cash flows. The incremental advertising dollars from Web ads help cover the cost of running the website. However, now that the Internet is becoming the dominant news medium, less and less content is free. Now only about 1 day's worth of the *Times* each month (10 articles) is free. After that, you have to pay a monthly subscription to offset the decline in print subscriptions.

Social media websites, eBay and Facebook included, have a further economic advantage over older media: their content is provided free to the website proprietor. Think about it: when you update your Facebook profile, you are providing free content to those who profit from the advertising sales. Where is your cut of the profits from Facebook stock? If you contribute popular original content, YouTube will give you a 50 percent cut of the ad revenue, with top partners like PewDiePie earning millions of dollars a year (Berg, 2015).

STOP & REVIEW

1. What are *economies of scale?*

2. Why is the first copy of a mass-media production the most expensive?

3. What are the basic types of media ownership patterns?

4. How do the mass media make profits? Why are profits necessary?

5. What is the role of stock offerings in media economics?

6. What are some of the ways new media economics differ from conventional media?

CRITICAL STUDIES

Critical scholars have alternative theories for the relationship of media industries, content, and society. They examine the connection between media and society from political-economic, feminist, ethnic, and media criticism perspectives. These perspectives focus on the need for **media literacy** and a critical understanding of media structure and its power, as well as the meaning of its content. That means that we should not just accept the media at face value, as though it were a natural phenomenon like the weather. We should try instead to understand the causes underlying media change and to be skeptical about the motives of the media industry. In contrast to the SMCR model introduced in Chapter 1, the **critical studies** approach emphasizes the feedback link and an active process in which the human receiver "decodes" the messages that the human source encodes.

Media literacy means learning to think critically about the role of media in society.

Critical studies examine the overall impact of media.

1867

First volume of *Das Kapital* is published

Political Economy

Political economy draws inspiration from the work of nineteenth-century political economist Karl Marx. In *Das Kapital*, Marx wrote that society is based on the relations between those who own the means of production (e.g., consumer electronics factories and printing presses) and those who work for them. In this view, it is the owners' interests that are reflected by media and culture, because the dominant groups in a society—usually those who own the major corporations—want to create an underlying consensus, or **hegemony,** of ideology favoring their continued domination (Gramsci, 1994). For example, billionaires buy television ads for political candidates who advocate tax cuts for the wealthy. Hegemony consists of creating a consensus around certain self-serving ideas, like "the poor will always be with us," or "globalization will

Political economy analyzes patterns of class domination and economic power.

Hegemony is the use of media to create a consensus around certain ideas so that they come to be accepted as common sense.

benefit everyone," through a variety of means, including the media. Although consumer needs and the law of supply and demand still affect the media, they operate in an economic system devoted to preserving the interests of the ruling classes.

This analysis suggests that media reflect the interests of media owners, advertisers, and, through the advertisers' corporations, the general nature of what the people in power want said (McChesney, 2015). The same groups of people who sit on the boards of directors of major media companies also sit on the boards of other major corporations and the banks that support them. Now the same economic class that dominates the older media is asserting control over the new media as well (Fuchs, 2009) and the ruling class includes new media entrepreneurs like Mark Zuckerberg of Facebook as well as old media barons like Rupert Murdoch of News Corp. Even public service media like PBS are supported, in part, by businesses through direct donations and through large charitable foundations, such as the Ford Foundation, that are controlled by the same class of people who own the large corporations. Thus, the media cover protests demanding an increase in the minimum wage as a labor dispute or a political battle without calling into question the legitimacy of the economic system that perpetuates low wages but that also supports the media industry.

Communication media support the political and economic status quo in other ways. Citizens who can afford the price of an iPhone or iPad and have the skills to get information from the Internet can participate more fully in politics by accessing coverage of political issues and contributing their "tweets" to the ongoing public conversation. Unequal access becomes even more important in the Information Age, as political communication shifts online (Varnelis, 2012). African-American, Hispanic, and low-income households and those headed by someone aged 65 or over or with less than a college education are much less likely than others to have high-speed Internet access (NTIA, 2015). Low-income, less educated, and older consumers are also much less likely to have smartphones than others (Anderson, 2015), making access to technology a new dimension of social stratification between the "haves/have nots" and the "information rich/information poor" segments of society. However, the tensions arising from such inequalities do not usually undermine the underlying social order, according to Gramsci (1971), who argued that the media (and educational institutions) convince the poor and the middle class to accept the hegemony of ideas that keeps the ruling class on top. For example, support-ers of the underlying social order

AP Images/Jim Cooper

WHAT'S YOUR POINT? Do cable talk shows like *Bill O'Reilly* offer fresh perspectives or do they merely reinforce a hegemony of ideas? When Bill rails against class warfare, does he act in the interests of "the 1 percent?"

might offer the excuse that the poor don't want Internet access, rather than being unable to afford it or being excluded from opportunities to learn how to use it effectively (Strover, 2003).

Political economy has cultural implications as well. As commercial media reach into more societies, people in different parts of the world become aware of Coca-Cola and Nike shoes. That may undermine ties to their traditional **cultures** and spur the growth of consumer culture (Ewen, 2008). The danger is that commercial messages may impact our innermost desires and perceptions of ourselves, making us feel dependent upon consumer products for our happiness. While we become more indebted, pursuing materialistic dreams, manufacturers become fat with profits (McChesney, 2015).

> **Culture** is a group's pattern of thought and activity.

The *cultural industries* approach (Hesmondhalgh, 2013) offers a more hopeful outlook. While recognizing the tendencies of media conglomerates to control cultural products through copyright restrictions and marketing campaigns, this school of thought also considers the implications of the preeminence of creative labor in the information economy. Public policies that subsidize artists and seek to cluster them in creative communities can improve the cultural resources of society as well as fuel the creative economy (Flew, 2012).

The *commodification* of what was once public information, such as census data, into a product that can be bought and sold by private companies, such as market research databases, furthers the dominance of the owners of information industries (Schiller, 1996). The modification of copyright and patent laws to favor their owners is another example (Lessig, 2004). Now, the personal information that we provide to websites (Campbell & Carlson, 2002) or social networks (Koponen, 2010) has also become a commodity, as when Facebook sells your posts and personal data to advertisers. Political economists believe that such actions further reinforce hegemony of power, which acts against the interests of common citizens.

Feminist Studies

Feminist critics of the media have concerns that parallel those of political economists to some degree, but focus on the oppression of women by a male-dominated society rather than the oppression of the working or middle classes by the ruling class. Thus, communication media serve the purposes of the patriarchy that runs society. The oppression also has economic dimensions. Women typically earn only about two-thirds of what men make in comparable jobs, so the perpetuation of sexism in the images we see in the media benefits the owners of media organizations and their associates who run corporate America (Kim, 2009).

Over the years, feminist media scholars (Hust and Brown, 2008) have focused on the fact that too few women appear in the media and are limited to a few stereotypical roles (e.g., housewife, mother, nurse, secretary, helper). We will examine those patterns of content and their impact in greater depth in Chapter 14 when we examine media representations and impacts. Here we are concerned more with the reasons why such portrayals exist. These include the underrepresentation of women as media producers and in the corporate decision structure, which led to protests about the Hollywood gender power structure in 2015, as well as social norms that prescribe only certain roles for women. For instance,

FEMINISM ON THE LINE Women reinvented the telephone, converting it to an instrument of social interaction. In doing so, they contested the dominance of a patriarchal society.

women are bombarded by advertising messages that stress their role as consumers of mass-produced goods and push unrealistic ideals of feminine beauty that in turn drive sales of products targeted to women. These critiques link feminism with political economy in looking at underlying reasons for the structure and content of the media.

Feminists also take issue with the way media are targeted by gender. They argue that media for women, such as romance novels or soap operas, have been denigrated as less serious than male-oriented spy novels. They see the pleasure women take in such media as a form of resistance to male dictates about what is enjoyable (Spence, 2005). Other studies examine women's particular subjectivity, or sense of interpretation of what media mean (Livingstone, 1998). Meanwhile, video games (Cassell & Jenkins, 1998; Jenson & De Castell, 2010) seem designed to stereotype, alienate, and exclude women and direct them to "girl games," and in so doing, exclude them from the inner world of computer knowledge reserved for men. The "gamergate" controversy of 2015 produced vulgar criticism of and even threats to feminist commentators who dared to challenge video game sexism (Chess & Shaw, 2015).

Women influence the development of technology. The telephone was intended as an instrument of communication for the (male-dominated) business world, and telephone companies discouraged "trivial" social use of the telephone (mostly by women) to keep the lines clear for important (i.e., male-originated) business calls. However, women staged a quiet rebellion against these restrictions, forcing the redesign of the telephone system, by expanding its capacity to handle the social and other uses women made (Fischer, 1992).

We see the "communications specialist" emerge again in new media as women became the dominant bloggers on the Internet (Lin, 2007; Synovate, 2007). But they still communicate from within their homes, limiting personal social contact and continuing the perception that they are not "businessmen." And the impact of women on new media is limited by their low level of representation in the ranks of undergraduate computer science majors, which has in the past 20 years decreased to less than 20 percent (NSF, 2015).

Ethnic Media Studies

Many of the same issues apply to minority racial and ethnic groups, including African Americans, Latinos, and Asians. Many scholars and social groups have criticized media for disproportionately showing African Americans, Latinos, and Arabs in such stereotypical roles as maids, criminals, or even terrorists (Shaheen, 2012). Minority representation among computer science majors has increased since the early 1990s but, still at less than 20 percent, lags minority representation in the general U.S. population (NSF, 2015).

Scholars such as Herman Gray (1995) critique a deeper level of structural problems with race and media. They argue that racial depictions are a form of ideology, designed to keep whiteness associated with dominance and power, whereas black and brown minorities are pointed toward inferior social roles. The media have been described as a system of racialization that defines race and ethnicity; for example, by portraying African-American women as nameless sex objects in music videos (Littlefield, 2008). Those images perpetuate a "new racism" in a society that believes that the problem of racism has been solved even as the sexualized images allow viewers to blame the victims of teen pregnancy and unwed mothers who are enduring consequences of the "old racism." And, does media coverage of the "Black Lives Matter" movement that emphasizes protests and social disorder revert to the level of media coverage of the civil rights movement of the 1960s that treated it as a law and order "problem"?

Racial disparities are also reflected in the economics of the media. Advertisers undervalue minority audiences, for example, even after correcting for income levels (Napoli, 2002); that benefits advertisers of products targeted to minorities by reducing their advertising costs. Minorities have a difficult time obtaining financing, which is a barrier to minority ownership in broadcasting (Braunstein, 2000); that reduces competition for white-owned media outlets serving minority communities.

Media Criticism

Another critical studies approach looks at the media as a kind of literature and applies traditions of literary criticism (Lotz, 2015). Here, long-standing cultural conventions dictate the content of the media rather than capitalist economics or power relationships in society. This approach focuses on **genres,** categories of creative works that have a distinctive style and format, such as horror or science fiction. Over time, genres become storytelling formulas that evolve out of the interaction between producers and audiences (Sharma, 2013). They transfer from one medium to another. For example, romance and adventure genres were transported from print novels to film, radio, and television. We can also find adventure games (although romance games are hard to find), but game critics caution against applying either conventional film genres (e.g., adventure) or typologies from the game industry (e.g., first-person shooters) to video games since game mechanics as well as aesthetic styles play a role (Arsenault, 2009). For example, many first-person shooter games require actions other than shooting to destroy or escape from opponents and 2-D and 3-D shooters might be regarded as separate genres.

Media criticism scholars also probe for verbal and visual symbolism in media (Berger, 2013). In this *semiotic analysis,* words, sounds, and images are interpreted individually as signs or symbols of something other than the literal action. The sign has two components: a concept, or the thing signified, and a sound-image, or the signifier. For example, in a *Star Trek* episode, a musical theme (signifier) functions as a sign to announce that the starship *Enterprise* is about to come to the rescue (concept).

Where do symbols come from, and what makes some symbols more powerful than others? To answer these questions, one can use a related approach—looking for *archetypes* and symbols taken from psychological theories. Analysis of media content is often seen as analogous to Freud's interpretation of dreams, since both media creators and audiences are relying on images created through psychological processes like condensation (fusing symbols together)

Genres are distinctive styles of creative works. The term is also used to represent different types or formats of media content.

1900

First edition of Freud's *The Interpretation of Dreams* comes out

POSTMODERNISM

Modern society began with the Enlightenment in the eighteenth century. Modernity is a way of viewing the world in which reason is the source of progress and science has universal explanations for all natural phenomena. Modernity is characterized by technological innovation, dynamism, and the view that change is positive. It is also reflected in social institutions, such as representative forms of government, large companies, and banks. The dawn of the modern era also coincided with the Industrial Revolution, so we can think of it in terms of industrialization, the growth of science and technology, urbanization, and the evolution of mass media and culture.

Many scholars argue that in art, culture, and society, we are now in a *postmodern* era. What took place is a break with modernity, both in modes of thinking and in economic and political institutions. We have moved from an era of economic determinism, in which economic phenomena determine all others, to a time of cultural determinism (Baudrillard, 1983). Now messages carried by communications technologies can take on new meanings, different from or even opposed to what was originally intended, decoding meanings that were not necessarily encoded by their creators (Hall, 1980). We have moved from an era of universal laws and truths based on rational science to one in which local, particularistic, subjective understandings are more important and more valid. The postmodern view is that there is no universal truth, that what you think depends on your own experience, which depends on what groups you belong to, what media

you pay attention to, and what your family taught you. And what you think is as valid as what anyone else thinks, even if he or she belongs to a privileged elite and carries a title like "president" or "college professor."

A corollary of this view is that developments in the information society encourage cultural fragmentation. According to the French philosopher Jean-François Lyotard (1984), the proliferating forms of media permit many new forms of expression, creating new forms of knowledge and new social formations, so that fewer people share the same ideas and understandings. As more groups express their own ideas through proliferating multimedia channels— and even define their identities in terms of those channels—society becomes more focused on these groups. In consequence, society becomes less concerned with widespread ideas of nation-states and other vestiges of the modern era, creating a postmodern world.

But what comes after postmodernism, and are we already there? Those who hope to promote new universal ideas, such as a radical interpretation of Islam, use the Internet to post videos and social media to recruit followers, whereas nation-states like China assert control over online discourse (see "The Great Firewall of China" in Chapter 18). In the media realm, giant media corporations still assert themselves on the Internet in ways that may further homogenize popular culture, even as millions of people and groups post their own ideas and media productions. Old ways, and media, survive as new ones assert themselves.

STOP & REVIEW

1. What is a political economist?
2. How can the evening TV news create a hegemony of ideas?
3. What is the essence of the feminist critique of the media?
4. Does media coverage of the "Black Lives Matter" movement perpetuate racism or lessen it?
5. How do genres develop?

and displacement (replacing one symbol with another) (Freud, 1949). Other scholars draw upon the work of Carl Jung (1970), who interpreted recurring cultural themes as the expression of underlying archetypes, unconscious symbols of concepts like motherhood that all cultures share.

We see that the audience has a role to play in the selection of content. Media creators have to follow certain conventions and produce media that fit the expectations of their audiences. Otherwise, they risk alienating those audiences. So, the audience wields a great deal of power in the media content creative process. Scholars also point out that audiences frequently interpret media in a way very different from what its writers or producers had in mind. So the question of the power of media to impose meanings versus the power of the audience to interpret them remains a lively debate, depending on which studies and scholars you choose to believe.

DIFFUSION OF INNOVATIONS

1962

First edition of Rogers' *Diffusion of Innovations* is published

Individuals and society also have the power to influence the success of media technology. The diffusion of innovations theory has its roots in sociology and helps us understand why people adopt new communication behaviors (Rogers, 1995). **Diffusion** is a process by which an innovation—a new way of doing things—is communicated through media and interpersonal channels over time among the members of a community.

> **Diffusion** is the spread of innovations.

For example, researcher Everett Rogers (1986) observed that VCRs diffused very quickly in the United States, from 1 percent of American households in 1980 to 20 percent in 1985 (peaking at 90% in 2006; Nielsen Media Research, 2010). Prices are important in diffusion. VCR prices declined rapidly, from $9,500 (in today's dollars) in 1975 to under $125 in 2014. Traditional forms of media consumption are continually replaced by new technologies, innovations that are themselves continually supplanted by yet newer technologies (see Figure 2.4). In the 1990s,

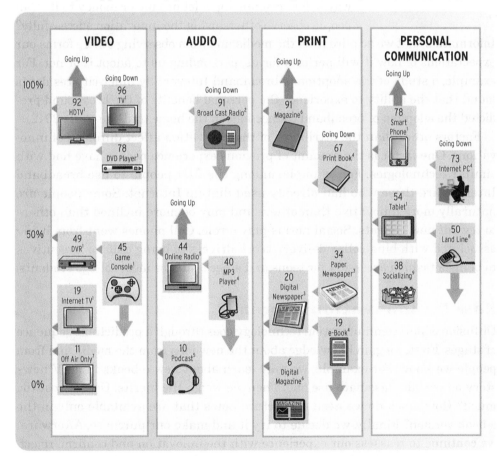

FIGURE 2.4 MEDIA INNOVATIONS AND PRACTICES: GOING UP, GOING DOWN Media technologies and practices are in a constant state of flux. The percentage of users of HDTVs, online radio, online newspapers, and e-mail continues to rise while watching TV off the air, broadcast radio, print, broadband Internet connections, and face-to-face socializing are in decline.

Source: 1. Based on U.S. TV households. Nielsen Media Research (2013). The Media Universe in 2013. Available: http://www.nielsen.com/us/en/newswire/2013/consumerelectronics- ownership-blasts-off-in-2013.html 2. Weekly readership based on all U.S. adults. Newspaper Association of America (2013).http://www.naa.org/Trends-and- Numbers/Readership.aspx 3. Based on all U.S. Households.NTIA (2013).Exploring the Digital Nation: America's Emerging Online Experience. Washington, DC.Economics and Statistics Administration, U.S. Department of Commerce.http://www.ntia.doc.gov/files/ntia/publications/exploring_the_digital_nation_-_americas_emerging_online_ experience.pdf 4. Annual, based on all U.S. residents age 16 or older Rainie, L. & Duggan, M. (2012). E-book Reading Jumps; Print Book Reading Declines. Available: http:// libraries.pewinternet.org/ 2012/12/27/e-book-reading-jumps-print-book-reading-declines/ 5. Weekly, based on all U.S. residents age 12+ Arbitron (2013). The Infinite Dial. Available: http://www.edisonresearch.com/wp-content/uploads/2013/04/Edison_Research_Arbitron_Infinite_Dial_2013.pdf 6. Based on U.S. TV households. Zero-TV Doesn't Mean Zero Video. http://www.nielsen.com/us/en/newswire/2013/zero-tv-doesnt-mean-zero-video.html 7. Based on U.S. TV Households. The Cross Platform Report. Available: http://www.nielsen.com/content/dam/corporate/us/en/reports-downloads/2013%20Reports/The-Cross-Platform-Report-A-Look-Across-Media-3Q2013.pdf" "8. Based on U.S. Households.Extended Measures of Well-Being: Living Conditions in the United States: 2011. Available:http://www.census.gov/prod/2013pubs/p70-136.pdf 9Based on U.S. civilian population 15+.American Time Use Survey, 2012. Available: http://www.bls.gov/tus/

BETTER LUCK THIS TIME The new iPad is Apple's second try at a tablet computer. The Newton was a failure due to a faulty handwriting recognition program.

DVD players replaced VCRs and they are in turn being replaced by digital video recorders and Internet video. As a general rule, all new technologies follow a similar price pattern: the first few units sold cost 10 or more times as much as the last units sold, a direct consequence of the economies of scale discussed earlier in this chapter.

Why Do Innovations Succeed?

How quickly an innovation diffuses depends on several other factors besides its cost: what do people think are the relative advantages of the new idea compared to existing ways of doing things? How compatible is it with existing ways of doing things? How complex is the new technology to operate? How easy is it to try out the new way before committing a lot of time or money to it? Can people observe others using the innovation successfully? Information that we acquire from the media and from observing others forms our expectations of how it will perform for us, persuading us to adopt it or not. For example, a study of the adoption of broadband Internet by inner-city residents found that the ability to experience the personal benefits of the broadband predicted the adoption of broadband connections in the home (LaRose et al., 2012).

Factors other than the attributes of the innovation affect diffusion of innovations. One factor is the amount of previous experience people have had with similar technologies. For example, among the first people to use broadband Internet are those who had already used dial-up Internet. Some people are naturally more innovative than others and may be more inclined than others to try out new gadgets. Social norms play a role. Cell phones went from being associated with blue-collar delivery truck drivers to being chic for executives to being a fashion accessory for teens and a necessity for most college students.

How Do Innovations Spread?

Diffusion of new communication technology goes through a predictable sequence of stages. First, we gain knowledge about the new idea from the media and from people we know. For example, we may learn about new e-books in a TV news story or see our classmate use one. Then we weigh the merits. Does it cost too much? How much do we need the lecture notes that are available only in the e-book version? Finally, we decide to try it and make our purchase. Afterward, we continue to reassess our experience with the innovation and confirm, reject, or modify our use of it. We may find that our own handwritten lecture notes are more useful than the e-books and regret our purchase. In other words, we decide which innovations to pursue according to the expected outcomes of our adoption decision, and we then continually monitor the fulfillment of those expectations.

People do not adopt new ideas at the same rates (see Figure 2.5). Those who first use an innovation are called innovators. People who follow up on innovative ideas through specialized media such as trade journals or interpersonal contacts are early adopters. Those who join the trend as it begins to go mainstream make up the early majority. Those who wait to see what most people are going to do constitute the late majority. Those who wait until the very end are called laggards.

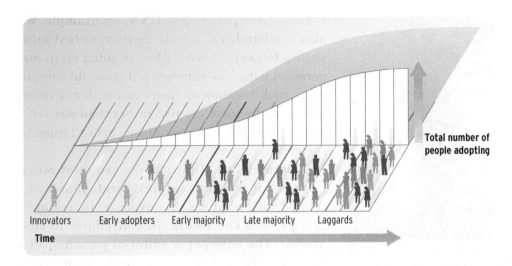

FIGURE 2.5 **DIFFUSION** Some people adopt new ideas earlier than others. The majority of people do so only after innovators and early adopters have forged the way. Growth accelerates when the early majority latch onto new innovations.

Interactive communication technologies diffuse in a characteristic way. First, a certain minimum number, or *critical mass*, of adopters is necessary for it to be useful enough for most people to go along with the trend (Lin, 2003). E-mail is a good example. What good was e-mail to the first two Internet users in 1969? They couldn't send messages to their family or friends. E-mail spread very slowly at first. Now over three-fourths of the U.S. population uses e-mail, so it is very useful.

Since information technologies are relatively flexible tools, they tend to be used in new, unanticipated ways by their adopters. Rogers (1986) called this *reinvention*. For instance, early adopters of home computers were attracted by educational software for children. Once the children had the computers, they used them to play computer games instead. Then the personal computer was reinvented again, as a tool to send e-mail and obtain information on the Internet. Now the computer is housed in a smartphone and used for instant messages and online access. Thus, in its emphasis on the attributes of innovations, the diffusion of innovations approach initially may seem technologically deterministic. Although it stresses on the ability of people and their cultures to act as influences in the spread of innovations, it falls short of the *social shaping of technology* perspective (Lievrouw, 2006) that emphasizes the ways in which social forces influence the design of new technologies as well as decisions to adopt or not adopt them.

WHAT ARE THE MEDIA'S FUNCTIONS?

Now we turn to sociological theories that emphasize the mutual dependence of media and society. These theories represent a middle ground between cultural determinism and **technological determinism.** Functionalism states that society cannot function without the media and that the media exist to serve the needs of our societies and cultures (Wright, 1974). The media help us to achieve these social needs:

Surveillance. Certain media specialize in providing information to help people with their surveillance of the environment, alerting them to important

1960

Charles Wright first publishes his *Functional Analysis of Mass Communication*

> **Technological determinism** explains that the media cause changes in society and culture.

NEWSFLASH: IT'S RAINING! The news media perform the surveillance function by alerting us to important things going on around us, such as the approach of a hurricane. Later coverage of events may serve an interpretation function by helping us understand the need for better emergency response procedures.

events—newspapers and CNN, for example. We also use Facebook, e-mail, Twitter, or text messaging to keep up with what is going on in our personal lives. The Internet is a powerful surveillance tool, because its users can seek out information on topics of interest rather than passively waiting for the older media to bring topics to them.

Interpretation. Information is not of much use until it is processed, interpreted, and correlated with what we already know. Individuals, groups, and the media all contribute to this process. The newspaper editorial page helps us interpret the headlines, *The Daily Show* interprets headlines with humor, and Internet blogs comment upon and interpret current events and social trends.

Values Transmission/Socialization. As soon as human beings had language, they used it to pass on ideas to their children. Today the media have assumed the roles of storytellers, teachers, and even parents. For example, textbooks like this one pass along concepts about the media to a new generation of students. But this function is not limited to media with an obvious educational or informational purpose, such as *Sesame Street*. Generations of movie buffs have learned about the values of loyalty and friendship from watching installments of the Star Wars saga.

Entertainment. With the exception of magazine-style information programs such as *60 Minutes,* the top 10 programs on network television have always been entertainment oriented. Newspapers complement their news and commentary with entertaining diversions on sports and lifestyle. Americans spend enormous amounts of time and money attending or renting feature films, listening to music, watching television comedies, playing video games, and checking social media just for fun.

New media are bringing about new functions. The Internet has attracted attention for its role in building and maintaining social bonds through the likes of Facebook. Social media like YouTube, Flickr, and blogs also function as outlets for creative self-expression that conventional media afforded only to an elite few.

MEDIA AND PUBLIC OPINION

In this section, we examine social theories that tie together the relationship between the events of the day and the decisions of media professionals about what becomes media content.

1949

David White publishes *The Gatekeeper*

Gatekeeping

Of all the events that happen in a community, who decides which ones will be covered and recorded for posterity and which ones will silently fade into oblivion? The *gatekeeping* theory (Shoemaker, 1991; White, 1949) emphasizes the crucial role of the so-called *gatekeepers*, the media managers and editors who can either open or close "the gate" on a story or shape how it is presented.

Gatekeepers are influential. They can squelch new ideas and suppress the news of events that others might find important. For instance, if an editor decides not to send a camera crew to a local environmental group gathering, she excludes the views of the activists from the public debate. However, media outlets compete with each other for audiences, so the gatekeeping actions of any one news editor are unlikely to have much impact. Gatekeepers get fired if they leave out too many stories that their viewers want to see and that the competition is willing to show them. So, the consensus among editors to keep certain stories in the news while excluding others may bias the public agenda and reinforce a hegemony over ideas.

Some think that the hinges are falling off the gate with the profusion of online news sources, amateur "citizen journalists," bloggers, and tweeters who challenge conventional news editors when determining what is newsworthy and what is not. However, gatekeeping theorists argue that these new sources, even if not conventional media managers, are new manifestations of the gatekeeping phenomenon (Shoemaker & Vos, 2009).

AGENDA SETTING

Who sets the public agenda—or topics of interest—in an election year: the media gatekeepers or the candidates? Some figures, like the president, can routinely command media attention (Gandy, 1982). Other public figures and interest groups try to set the agenda by harping on an issue in their public statements, social media postings, or TV ads, but they succeed only if their words are picked up in the news.

1972

MacCombs and Shaw define agenda setting

SETTING THE AGENDA Presidential news conferences receive extensive media coverage, giving the president an opportunity to set the public policy agenda.

Other times, the media set the agenda for the candidates. For instance, media coverage of big bonuses paid to failing financial firms in the midst of the financial crisis of 2009 quickly turned this into a political issue. Thus, agenda setting bestows political power on the media. However, the media are not all-powerful. The media's constant harping on the Clinton-Lewinsky sex scandal in the 1990s had no effect on the president's approval ratings, perhaps because adultery was not a highly relevant issue for the public (Yioutas & Segvic, 2003). Also, the new media environment, with its many competing (and sometimes unprofessional) voices, may be undermining the power of the older media to set the public agenda (Williams & Delli Carpini, 2004).

Agenda-setting theory also describes how media coverage affects public opinion (McCombs et al., 2014). Merely by publishing some stories and not others, the media influence perceptions of what the important issues of the day are. The impact is not so much on how to think about the issues and candidates but rather what issues to think about. Our opinions on the issues are further shaped by the communities we belong to and our personal beliefs.

Framing

Whereas the media's agenda setting tells us *what* topics to think about, the framing of issues by the media also influences *how* to think about those topics. *Framing theory* examines how writers frame or present a story (Altheide, 1974; Gitlin, 1983). Reporters decide what to include within the view, or frame, of a story and what to leave out, much as a painter chooses what to put on the canvas of a painting. They decide not only which tone, words, and facts to include, but also the conceptual framework, context, and interpretation of the facts.

Where do frames come from? French media critic Pierre Bourdieu (1998) contended that even in countries where there is supposed to be freedom of expression, there is invisible self-censorship. If they wish to remain employed, journalists realize what is permissible and pre-edit their own work to be consistent with those perceived norms. For example, news producers at ABC "just know" they should avoid stories about animated movies that are not produced by their corporate parent, Disney.

TECHNOLOGICAL DETERMINISM

Now we arrive at the end of the continuum that is opposite to cultural determinism. Some social critics maintain that communications media change everything in society. In this view, technology drives social change, so it is sometimes called *technological determinism.* Variations on this theme stress the social effects of media messages, covered in Chapter 14, and the technological culture that gives rise to them.

THE MEDIUM IS THE MESSAGE

1964

McLuhan's *Understanding the Media* is published

The most famous technological determinist, Marshall McLuhan, argued that print (*The Gutenberg Galaxy,* 1962) and electronic media (*Understanding the Media,* 1964) were truly revolutionary, an idea captured in his famous aphorism "The medium is the message." He proposed that new communication technologies determine culture and that it is the form of the media rather than their content that matters. For example, in McLuhan's view, the invention of the printing press led to the rise of the scientific method and later to our technological society by forcing thinkers to put their words in linear order and their arguments in a logical progression—just like the words on a printed page. This led to thinking about the natural world in the same linear fashion, instilling the notion that it, too, had a beginning and an end, causes and effects.

McLuhan did not live to witness the Internet, but he coined a phrase that perhaps describes it well. The "global village" draws the entire world together into an electronically mediated small town. "By electricity we everywhere resume person-to-person relations as if on the smallest village scale" (McLuhan, 1964, p. 255). When he wrote that in the 1960s, he was thinking of broadcast television and the telephone, long before Facebook was a reality.

McLuhan further theorized that in society's zeal to conquer technology, we might progress in technology, but we would regress as a culture. Whereas technology could extend human capabilities in one way, it would cut off others. For example, the telephone would extend the voice, but amputate printed correspondence. These amputations could have long-term cultural consequences with new media, too. Digital archives extend memories about prior generations, but cut off the need to save original documents. Sometimes a reversal of the original intent occurs: digital archives save memories, yet in 5 to 10 years the hardware and software used to retrieve the computerized files will be obsolete and the memories gone forever (Davenport, Randle, & Bossen, 2007).

Bernard Gotfryd/Getty Images

THE MEDIUM IS THE MESSAGE Marshall McLuhan, the late communication scholar, argued that the way we think is determined by the nature of the media we consume. For example, does reading this text in a linear progression from left to right and top to bottom subtly lead us to believe that the world is an ordered place governed by cause and effect?

Technology as Dominant Social Force

Other media theorists emphasize that social systems and worldviews promote technology and dominate culture. Neil Postman (1992) argued that computers foster *technopoly,* in which technology is deified and extends its control to all aspects of life. Technopoly compounds the excesses of technocracy, in which the scientific method is applied by experts to technology for the improvement of life, but also to the destruction of culture.

Similarly, French sociologist Jacques Ellul (1990) argued that the pursuit of technological improvement led to the social dominance of an elite tier of scientists, engineers, and managers for whom technology became an end in itself, devoid of moral foundation. But for Ellul, the technologists' efforts were ultimately ineffective. Technologists promise a great deal to ensure their status in a society conditioned to welcome technological progress. But they deliver very little: not even a truly satisfying evening's entertainment on TV, an effective magazine ad, or a true relationship on the Internet.

In *The Rise of the Network Society* (2000), Manuel Castells described the impact of information technologies on society as nothing less than a revolution comparable to the Industrial Revolution of three centuries before (see Chapter 1). In his view, not only have technological innovations changed society, but the process of innovation itself has been accelerated by the application of those technologies, creating a self-perpetuating revolution.

Media Drive Culture

Still other viewpoints emphasize media content over technology. In the early nineteenth century, Oxford professor and poet Matthew Arnold held that people moving from the countryside into the cities would become refined by coming in contact with "high culture" media such as the ballet and the opera. Implicit was the idea that media should exist to educate, not entertain, a point echoed by some present-day critics, such as Postman (1992). This was reflected in the concept of the BBC, which was founded to educate, not entertain (see Chapter 6).

Sociologist and philosopher Theodor Adorno (Horkheimer & Adorno, 1972) argued, however, that mass-produced cultural goods of low quality replaced high culture and traditional folk culture. If people were easily entertained by pop music, would they ever attend a classical opera? As mass audiences consumed **popular culture,** would everyone begin to think and act alike? For example, they might believe that the perfect 1950s family portrayed in *Leave It to Beaver* was a realistic model for their own family (Real, 1989). Another observation is that mass media overwhelm the "true" culture of the people in the interest of perpetuating class hegemony (Carey, 1972). Postman argued that literacy and reasoning skills decline as a result of overexposure to popular culture. In his words, we are "amusing ourselves to death" (Postman, 1986). Or, in the words of another critic, we are living in a "filter bubble" (Pariser, 2011) in that the personalized algorithms that Google, Amazon, Facebook, and others use to feed us online information trap us in a world where we are never subject to new ideas or people that diverge from those we "liked" or searched for in the past.

As we learn more about the relationship between media and society, scholars continue to debate which perspective is most valid. Throughout *Media Now*, we try to present both sides of the debate so that you, the reader, can decide for yourself what the best explanation is.

1869

Matthew Arnold's *Culture and Anarchy* is published

Popular culture is made up of elements mass produced in a society for the mass population.

STOP & REVIEW

1. Give examples of people who are gatekeepers.

2. What are the main social functions of the mass media?

3. Using the "diffusion of innovations" paradigm, explain how Facebook spread through society.

4. How does technological determinism differ from cultural determinism?

SUMMARY & REVIEW

HOW DO ECONOMICS INFLUENCE THE MEDIA?

First-copy costs in mass media entail virtually all the investment in the production of a work. Economies of scale occur when producers make so many copies of something that they learn how to make each of those copies more cheaply. By the law of supply and demand, cheaper copies can reach far more people, creating a broader audience. Producers want to spread production costs and also their entry costs—the initial costs of establishing a media enterprise—across a broad audience in order to increase profits and satisfy their investors. Investors back media organizations that offer an acceptable return on their investments relative to other options.

HOW IS MEDIA OWNERSHIP STRUCTURED?

Media can be structured as monopolies, where one company dominates the industry; as oligopolies, where a few companies dominate; or in competition, where a number of companies vie for dominance. The patterns of ownership have a great deal to do with the diversity and nature of the media's content, their availability and accessibility to people, and their role in society. Generally speaking, the more the ownership is concentrated in the hands of a few, the less diverse and more expensive the media are.

WHAT ARE THE SOURCES OF MEDIA REVENUE?

Most revenues come directly from the end user of media products. Direct sales of media products occur when consumers pay out a lump sum and take a media product such as a CD home with them. A rental also involves payment for a product, except that the consumer pays only to borrow it, as in a videogame rental. Subscriptions permit newspapers and magazines to be sold on a continuing basis over time for a standard fee. Usage fees are charged for temporary access to media products, such as movie theater admissions, that consumers can't literally take home. The media collect advertising revenues by selling access to their audiences to advertisers, who in turn pay for advertising by charging consumers.

WHAT IS THE ROLE OF PUBLIC SUBSIDIES?

Public subsidies, from either voluntary contributions or taxes, are provided for socially desirable content that commercial interests do not find profitable to provide. The educational and cultural programs on PBS are prime examples.

WHAT IS SEGMENTATION?

Technological changes, industry changes, and receptivity by audiences and advertisers are all encouraging media to segment their audiences, that is, to focus on smaller, more specific audiences with more specialized programs or contents. The targeting of media content to appeal to the tastes of a particular narrow audience segment is called *narrowcasting*.

WHAT ARE THE NEW MEDIA ECONOMICS?

The Internet takes segmentation to its logical conclusion by personalizing content and ads for individual users. Websites profit from having their users supply the content free of charge and by having users absorb a large share of the distribution costs. Others profit by repurposing content created for conventional media for distribution on the Internet. Unlike conventional media, Internet companies like Google can charge advertisers on the basis of those who respond to their ads (by the click) as well as according to the number who were exposed to the page carrying the ad.

HOW DO POLITICAL ECONOMISTS EXPLAIN MEDIA?

Social structure is determined by the efforts of dominant classes to maintain their wealth and power. The dominant class in society uses its ownership of the media to influence their content. This class creates a consensus, or hegemony, of ideas that reinforces its position of dominance. In this view, maintaining class dominance is furthered by the profitability of media enterprises. This tends to keep media content within the bounds of this hegemonic set of ideas.

WHAT DO FEMINIST AND ETHNIC STUDIES CONTRIBUTE?

The sex-role and ethnic stereotypes that appear in the media may be there for a reason: to perpetuate the dominance of white males in society.

WHAT IS SEMIOTICS?

Semiotics is a branch of critical studies. It is a systematic way of looking at media content to examine the symbols and signs contained in it. The signs in media communicate something of symbolic value to the audience; they include visual images, music, camera angles, words, and so on. The producer creates or encodes a meaning into the sign, but the audience may decode or interpret a different meaning.

WHAT ARE GENRES?

In media content, formulas, or genres, evolve over time. These formulas are things like soap operas, mystery novels, and action cartoons. They represent an agreement between producer and audience on what kinds of stories ought to be told and how, or on how a music video ought to look, or on how a talk show host ought to act.

WHAT ARE AGENDA SETTERS AND GATEKEEPERS?

A variety of media professionals make decisions about what goes into and what stays out of news and entertainment media. They are the gatekeepers. The media set the public agenda by defining the important issues of the day in conjunction with the personal beliefs of their audiences and the groups that audience members belong to. Leaders from government, business, and public interest groups try to influence the agenda set by the media.

WHAT SOCIAL FUNCTIONS DO MEDIA SERVE?

Among the functions sociologists have identified for communications media are surveillance (keeping track of our world or environment), interpretation (making sense of what we learn), value transmission (passing values on from one generation to the next), and entertainment.

HOW DO NEW MEDIA SPREAD?

New technologies spread like a disease, from person to person, slowly at first but gradually picking up speed. People consider an innovation's relative advantages, its compatibility with existing practices, its complexity, and any opportunities they have to observe the innovation in action before they try it out themselves. Some people are innovators, some are early adopters, followed by the majority of adopters, late adopters, and laggards. Interactive technologies seem to require a critical mass of users before large numbers will adopt it.

WHAT IS TECHNOLOGICAL DETERMINISM?

Technological determinists argue that changes in society and culture are driven by advances in media technology and by the content of the media to a large extent. They oppose the view of cultural determinists, who maintain that culture determines the nature of the media and their content.

THINKING CRITICALLY
ABOUT THE MEDIA

1. Is Mark Zuckerberg of Facebook a monopolist or not? Explain your position.

2. How has the hegemony of ideas affected you personally?

3. List all the media you used today, and define the functions associated with each one.

4. What is your favorite medium, and how do its owners make money from you?

5. Twitter was slow to catch on among college students. How can you explain that in terms of diffusion of innovations?

KEY TERMS

barriers to entry (p. 30)

copyright royalty fee (p. 34)

critical studies (p. 37)

culture (p. 39)

diffusion (p. 43)

duopoly (p. 28)

economics (p. 26)

economies of scale (p. 26)

genres (p. 41)

hegemony (p. 37)

law of supply and demand (p. 27)

marginal costs (p. 28)

media literacy (p. 37)

monopoly (p. 28)

oligopoly (p. 28)

political economy (p. 37)

popular culture (p. 50)

profits (p. 31)

technological determinism (p. 45)

theories (p. 25)

MindTap

Test your knowledge with online printable flashcards and online quizzing.

MindTap Log on to the MindTap for *Media Now* to access a variety of additional material, including this chapter's e-book, learning objectives, comprehension quizzes, videos, and more!

BOOKS

LEARNING OBJECTIVES

After studying the topics in this chapter, you will be able to:
1 Summarize the major technological changes in print media that contributed to increasing literacy rates throughout Europe and the United States, from the development of the printing press through the early twentieth century.
2 Describe how digital evolutions have dramatically impacted the tradition of book publishing in the last 20 years.
3 Explain how the Internet has caused libraries to strike a new balance between censorship and access.

HISTORY: FROM INK TO DIGITAL, FROM PRESS TO COMPUTER

Founding father and colonial-era publisher Benjamin Franklin would have appreciated the historical path from printed pamphlets and books to the Kindle. If a modern-day Franklin developed book apps and used social media to interact with his audiences, he would have understood that where we are today is the result of a continual cycle of technological innovations and social acceptances, competition between forms and uses of media, consumer demand, growing literacy, and changes in society wrought by media.

Early Print Media

Technology influences what formats are possible in media, but it does not define their contents. For example, **novels** flourished with printing because mechanical reproduction allowed quantities of books to be produced less expensively. However, the concepts and forms that characterize the novel originated much earlier: Greek oral poets produced epic works such as the *Iliad* and the *Odyssey* by Homer, who lived between 700 and 800 BCE. And the Japanese *Tale of Genji*, recognizable as a novel by current standards, was written by Lady Murasaki

FROM MANUSCRIPTS hand-copied by medieval monks to e-books distributed through the Internet, publishing the written word is an ever-changing media form.

© Radu Bercan/Shutterstock.com

54

MEDIATHEN··· MEDIANOW

105

> Chinese develop ink, brushes, and paper

1234

> Movable metal type invented in Korea

1455

> Gutenberg Bible published

1640

> First book published in the American colonies

2004

> Google starts scanning books' content online

2012

> Apple's iPad, Barnes & Noble's Nook, and Amazon's Kindle compete for consumers

---

Shikibu in the eleventh century. Thus, the antecedents of novels about daily life, romances, mysteries, and horror existed well before the advent of printing.

The earliest experiments with an alphabet are thought to be from the Middle East in 1900–1800 BCE, and it continued to be developed by the Phoenicians, Greeks, and Romans. However, the oldest script still in existence today is from China, a country that also developed brushes, ink, and paper in 105 CE. Brushes used a type of ink made from soot or black soil, and Tsai-Lun, the superintendent of a weapons-manufacturing factory, created a form of paper by mashing together different plants, rags, and water and drying them on screens of bamboo (Sloan, 2005). The Chinese built upon their knowledge by developing printing blocks—they carved symbols in pieces of wood and inked them—and pressing them on paper, which they used to produce books. These inventions were passed along to the Japanese and Koreans and then to the Arabs, who brought them to the West. By 1051, the Chinese put together a metal, clay, and wooden press. The Koreans further refined the printing process by developing movable metal type in 1234. Printing did not evolve further (it was difficult to deal with 40,000 Asian characters) until 1455, when Johannes Gutenberg of Germany (re)discovered movable type and printed the first (German) Bible. Innovations continued from there.

Until Gutenberg's press, books were a limited medium throughout the world because they had to be hand-copied. For thousands of years, handwritten and printed materials were available only to the few best-educated people,

MindTap

Start with a quick warm-up activity.

105

Chinese develop ink, brushes, and paper

> **Novels** are extended fictional works, usually of book length.

1234

Movable metal type invented in Korea

such as the Mandarin bureaucratic elite of China. In many cultures, rulers did not want their subjects gaining new ideas and questioning government policies. Thus, few people in the early civilizations of Greece, Egypt, China, the Middle East, and Rome were literate or had access to libraries. As the more sophisticated cultures were destroyed by barbarians, reading and writing were carried on by monks, who passed along all sorts of information about farming and irrigation to peasants. Many monks also devoted their lives to copying text and creating beautiful illustrations by hand. Some surviving examples, among them the Irish *Book of Kells* (800 CE), are considered major works of art today. Books tended to build on earlier oral traditions, for instance, early Greek epics such as the *Iliad* and the *Odyssey* (800 BCE), medieval European literature such as Icelandic sagas, and the folk stories and fairy tales collected by the brothers Grimm.

The growth of **literacy** in Europe and the writing of books in the everyday language spoken by most people in a particular region, such as Italian or Swedish, were key for the development of print media. Before 1100, written communication was nearly always in Latin, the language of the Roman Catholic Church. Thus, to be literate, people had to learn a second language. By the 1200s, written versions of daily languages were more frequent, and as a result, literacy became more commonplace in the 1300s and 1400s among the political elite, the commercial and trading class, and such professionals as the sea captain Christopher Columbus. Outside this group, though, most people remained illiterate.

Throughout the Middle Ages in Europe, few books other than the Bible and religious or philosophical commentaries were available for people to read. This began to change by the 1300s and 1400s. Universities were established to train more people as clergy and clerks. Also, the most important books printed and circulated in Europe came from the Hebrew Middle East (the Bible, the Torah) or the Arab Middle East (focusing on science, math, astronomy, and navigation). Many also came from ancient Greece: classic works of science, literature, and philosophy, such as Plato's *Republic*, that influenced European ideas of government. Whereas books had survived only in hand-copied form for centuries, the printing of these classic works gave a greater number of people access to ideas about life and work. For instance, in the late 1400s, Columbus learned from an Arab book on geography that he might be able to reach India and Southeast Asia by sailing west across the Atlantic Ocean. It is highly likely that if Columbus had been born 100 years earlier, he would not have had access to such books. Clearly, the European explosion of print technology and printed contents built a much larger world context.

> **Literacy** is the ability to read and understand a variety of information.

Scala/Art Resource, NY

HANDMADE Among the earliest books were illustrated manuscripts that were carefully created by hand, like this page from Statute of a council from the fourteenth century.

1455

Gutenberg Bible published

The Gutenberg Revolution

The Gutenberg Bible was published in 1455, the result of Johannes Gutenberg's development of movable type and mechanical printing five years earlier. This German press was a technology breakthrough that made new forms of mass production possible—people could print many more books, handbills, and newsletters at a much lower cost. For example, within 15 years of Gutenberg, a French-printed Bible cost one-fifth of what a hand-copied manuscript had cost. As the new technology gained momentum, printing and reading became a cyclical process that reinforced itself. As more people had sufficient money and interest to buy books, book production increased and benefited from economies of scale, which made individual books cheaper (see Chapter 2). This permitted even more people to buy books (see Media & Culture: Goodbye, Gutenberg).

The Bible, prayer books, and hymnals were among the earliest publications. Beyond the Bible and religious pamphlets, new products were often more entertainment oriented and aimed at broader groups of people with less education. *Broadside ballads* were single sheets of words for popular songs, whereas chapbooks were cheaply bound books or pamphlets of poetry, ballads, or prose that were aimed at a broader audience. Libraries provided one

Media & Culture

GOODBYE, GUTENBERG

Did reading change the way our brains work? As we saw in Chapter 2, Canadian media scholar Marshall McLuhan (1962) argued in *The Gutenberg Galaxy: The Making of Typographic Man* that printing fostered linear modes of thinking about ordered sequences of events that in turn led to thinking about cause and effect, then science, then the modern industrial world.

At a social level, readers were more likely to identify with people and issues beyond their immediate communities. In another book *The Imagined Communities*, Benedict Anderson (2006) argued that reading was largely responsible for the development of nationalism: the intense individual identification that countries have with their nations that enables them to command such loyalty that people are willing, even excited, to go to war. Anderson traced such individual passion for the nation to the experience of reading the same novels and newspapers across the breadth of the national territory, so that people began to imagine themselves as part of a larger community defined by all the people reading the same things. As our media today become more fragmented, critics wonder if audiences will, too.

In his later book *Understanding Media,* McLuhan (1964) observed that electronic media had further changed most people to a new sort of orientation, not based on the typographical logic, but focused instead on decoding and understanding television. Some studies of earning among young people in the United States and Germany seem to show new patterns in which many children who are not good at

Bettmann/AS400 DB/Corbis

GUTENBERG'S PRESS The invention of the printing press allowed reading as a leisure activity to flourish, helping people identify with communities beyond their immediate locale.

reading are sophisticated at learning from computer games and television screens with complex arrays of numbers and images (Bachmair, 2006). However, *Typographic Man* still has many advantages in our society. People who are good at deep involvement and comprehension in reading still tend to do better in school, particularly college, which is still the main avenue to the best-paying jobs in our society.

means of popularizing books and making them more accessible to the public. Sir Thomas Bodley started the first modern lending library of printed books in 1602 in Oxford, England. Years later, as printing and binding costs continued to decline and thus made books more affordable, publishers began to distribute books directly to the public by selling them through bookstalls in railway stations. Then, book publishing accelerated rapidly: 2 million titles were issued worldwide in the 1700s and 8 million in the 1800s.

1640

First book published in the American colonies

> **Almanacs** are book-length collections of useful facts, calendars, and advice.

AP Images/Jim Cole

CONVENIENT AND USEFUL *The Old Farmer's Almanac* has provided weather forecasts, gardening tips, and other useful information since 1792. Farmers wanted it handy throughout the year, so they ran nails and string through the top left corner to hang it on the wall in the kitchen, barn, or outhouse. Today, publishers use machinery to punch holes in the press run of 400 million books for the same reason.

The First American Print Media

In the United States, also, print media began with copies of religious books; after all, the colonists came to the United States to pursue religious freedom. *The Bay Psalm Book* was the first book published in the United States, printed in 1640 by Elizabeth Glover, who set up the first printing press in the new Massachusetts college called Harvard. As most families encouraged their children to read the Bible, the literacy rate in the colonies was high. As more people could read, other publications followed religious ones. Soon thereafter came newspapers, magazines, and **almanacs,** published in Boston, New York, and Philadelphia (see Chapter 4).

One of the more influential publishing figures in the American colonies was Benjamin Franklin, a major innovator in printing, science, politics, and practical inventions. As a printer, Franklin constantly experimented to see what kinds of publications would attract an audience. (If he had had social media, he might have asked them directly!) In 1732, he published one of America's first successful nonreligious books, *Poor Richard's Almanack,* which contained moral advice, farming tips, amusements, and maxims for American colonists. Almanacs, along with educational primers, religious books, and law books, were among the most popular books in the colonies. The oldest regularly published periodical in North America is *The Old Farmer's Almanac,* started by Robert B. Thomas in 1792 with a new issue appearing each September. Franklin and other book printers also produced political pamphlets. Thomas Paine's *Common Sense,* which urged readers to support independence from Great Britain, sold 100,000 copies in 10 weeks.

Franklin also started the first **subscription library** in the United States, beginning a tradition that greatly helped popularize book reading. Still, the high cost of books and the difficulty of gaining access to them aided the rise of less expensive newspapers and magazines.

In the mid-1800s, improving social conditions fostered a mass audience for books and magazines. An expanding public education system taught more people to read. As wages increased, young people moved to the cities to work in the burgeoning industrial economy, and an urban middle class grew. Prices fell with economies of scale, improved printing technology, and more demand for print media. Access to books increased as the number of public libraries tripled in the first half of the nineteenth century.

Perhaps most important, however, was the popularization of book content. Many American novelists earned loyal fans by addressing the uniquely American national experience and interests. James Fenimore Cooper wrote compelling stories about the struggles of both white settlers and indigenous people on the frontier. In novels such as *The Last of the Mohicans* (1826), Cooper dramatized the attraction of the West. Immigrants sometimes cited his work as part of what they knew about the United States, a contributing factor of what drew them to the West.

Novels had political effects. A prime example is Harriet Beecher Stowe's *Uncle Tom's Cabin* (1852), which sold 300,000 copies in its first year and did much to inspire popular opposition to slavery (Davis, 1985).

In the second half of the nineteenth century, a new cheap format popularized reading even more. **Dime novels** (called "Penny Dreadfuls" in Great Britain) were often colorful humor that involved a broader audience, including working-class people. For instance, Horatio Alger wrote 100 books that collectively sold about 250 million copies. His popular hero was usually a poor boy who managed to rise out of poverty through hard work, honesty, thrift, planning, and other virtues. The phrase "Horatio Alger hero" eventually became a popular term for anyone who gained social mobility and success through hard work and honest living. Mark Twain (Samuel Clemens) also wrote for the average person. *The Adventures of Tom Sawyer, The Adventures of Huckleberry Finn,* and *The Prince and the Pauper* are only a few of his literary works.

Many great American novelists also lived during the twentieth century. Ernest Hemingway wrote *The Sun Also Rises, A Farewell to Arms, For Whom the Bell Tolls, A Moveable Feast,* and *The Old Man and the Sea,* which won a Pulitzer. He also won the Nobel Prize in Literature. F. Scott Fitzgerald found a publisher for Hemingway's first novel and Gertrude Stein was considered a mentor. Other successful, literary friends at this time included James Joyce and T. S. Eliot.

Today, of course, we have J. K. Rowling, Veronica Roth, John Green, Stephen King, John Grisham, and James Patterson. Nora Roberts and Danielle Steele appear to have a monopoly on romance novels.

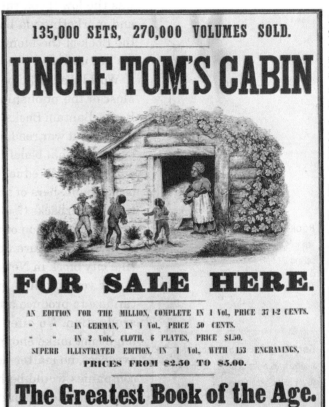

Poster advertising 'Uncle Tom's Cabin', 1852 (colour litho), American School, (19th century) / © Collection of the New-York Historical Society, USA / The Bridgeman Art Library

AGAINST SLAVERY Harriet Beecher Stowe's *Uncle Tom's Cabin* was a best seller in its day and also helped set the agenda for opposition to slavery.

Book Publishing Giants Evolve

Many publishing houses have been around since the early 1800s, although they may have changed hands and been renamed. Harpers Publishing is an example. The Harper brothers (J. and J. Harper) started their publishing business in 1817. Two more brothers joined the business and the name was changed in

STOP &
REVIEW

1. What key elements of print media developed first outside Europe?
2. What was the impact of printing in Europe?

Book publishers offer an array of services, from editing to promoting to selling a book.

Book was defined traditionally and narrowly as a set of pages bound together between covers.

E-books are book content that appear in digital text format. They can be read on mobile devices, computer tablets, and e-readers.

Audiobooks can be heard on a CD, the radio, or downloaded onto a mobile device.

2004

Google starts scanning books' content online

the 1830s to Harper & Brothers. About 130 years later, the company merged with Row, Peterson & Company and became Harper & Row. Rupert Murdoch's News Corp., the current owner, acquired the company in 1987 and merged it with a British company; the company was renamed HarperCollins and is one of the world's largest publishing companies. Harper Paperbacks is a new line, and Harper Audio offers audio books.

Other active American publishers, such as McGraw-Hill, Prentice Hall, and Random House, the world's largest general interest trade book publisher, set up shop in the early twentieth century. As printing costs declined, more Americans could afford books, and the publishing industry grew.

For both books and pulp magazines that specialized in short stories, the first half of the twentieth century was a boom era for detective stories, science fiction, and westerns (Folkerts & Teeter, 1994). Behind this publishing boom was the low "book rate" for mailing books, which made both mail-order sales and marketing via book clubs much cheaper. Mail-order book clubs, such as the Book-of-the-Month Club and the Literary Guild, initially worried publishers but ultimately benefited them by popularizing book reading and buying.

World War II helped popularize reading by ushering in the paperback era. Most of the publishing houses established during this time, such as Pocket Books, Bantam Books, and Penguin Books, profited from paperbacks. Young people away at war read more. As they returned home and entered college (assisted by educational benefits for veterans), they read textbooks and mass-marketed paperbacks. As educational institutions and the public demanded more textbooks, publishers of serious literature and nonfiction introduced larger-format trade paperbacks ("soft cover") to complement "pocket-size" paperbacks.

The connotation of a **book publisher** is changing. To your grandfather, the term would conjure up a huge publishing building—such as Random House—on a city block in New York, the main publishing center of the United States.

For your mother, "publishing" might mean the companies online that she can use to produce a book that holds memories and photos as a gift for your graduation. No offense to your mother, but the large publishing company might not make enough sales with your mother's memory book to cover their expenses, no matter how cute you looked in second grade. However, the online companies would be happy to take her book manuscript, charging different fees for the design, number of books, and optional marketing support. Another alternative for your mother is to take her book directly to a printing company. Many writers don't care if there is a large enough market to make it profitable; they just want to publish their book.

For you, the definition of **book** has changed to be more inclusive. Although an **e-book** is electronic, it is still a book. While **audiobooks** are not read, they are still stories or information that people consume—just in a different form (audio). The number of books overall—no matter the form or platform—continues to rise.

Today's book publishing industry are stretching and growing in new directions. Publishers have experimented with distributing books directly to the public themselves, while some bookstore chains have tried publishing their own books. Non-traditional publishing companies took a giant step forward, acting as reprint companies that produce on-demand public domain titles—printed books whose copyright or intellectual property rights have expired.

AUTHOR! AUTHOR!

It is a competitive market, so you need to be good and relentless in the promotion of your work. The average salary for writers and authors is $69,000, with the highest 10 percent earning about $114,000, according to the Bureau of Labor Statistics. This is a very general category that covers many types of writing (screen writers, PR, etc.).

One type of writer is a book author, most of whom are self-employed or work part-time jobs while writing their great American novel. Authors do not get a salary, but are paid a royalty—a percentage of the net revenue (after all costs are deducted out) from sales of the book—from traditional publishing houses.

You can expect book royalties between 8 and 15 percent, depending on how good you are and how well you negotiate. In the current book industry, the costs are divided among the author (10 percent), publisher (30 percent), printer (10 percent), distributor (10 percent), and retailer (40 percent). You can also negotiate an increase in royalties based on increased sales. If you are a coauthor, then the 10 percent is split among you. Sometimes the publisher will give you an advance to get you started and then deduct that amount from your royalties. Depending on the type of book (fiction novels are the most popular) and projections for success, publishers will send you on book tours.

Authors no longer have to depend solely on publishing houses to be a success. Many authors self-publish or write e-books. Some are doing well at it. They are more hand-on in the process and spend a lot of time on social media promoting and selling their books. Most self-published authors earn about $10,000 a year (Chmielewski, n.d.). Some large publishing houses pick up successful e-book writers.

A success story is of Amanda Hocking (*Kanin, Trylle, Watersong* series, etc.), a group home worker, writing novels on the side. She couldn't find a publisher interested in her books and began self-publishing them as e-books in 2010. A year later, she sold about million copies of nine of her books and made about $2.5 million. She continues to release books, with a new series in 2016 and another in 2017.

Do your research on self-publishing options and expectations, so you know how to do it right to be a success. A book is like any business product. It has to be good, but it also needs marketing and promotion for people to know about it.

In the United States and internationally, book publishers and bookstores are redefining themselves. High-tech companies, including Amazon and Google, challenge conventional print institutions ranging from publishers to bookstores to public libraries. For example, Amazon.com started its Kindle Direct Publishing only a few years ago. You can haul in a 70 percent royalty (whereas authors of textbooks split about a 10% royalty) for books that appear in Kindle stores worldwide and in print, digital, or audio. Google Library Project has scanned more than 30 million books from libraries and authors and made them available in their entirety (usually if copyright is out of date) or in varied proportions (whatever amount the author deems). If you want a copy of a book, then Google Books tells you where it is available (the publisher) and includes a nearby link for buying it from its Google Play eBook store. Try finding this textbook, for example, at books.google.com.

TECHNOLOGY TRENDS: FROM CHAPBOOK TO E-BOOK

In the 560 years since Gutenberg, most improvements in publishing technology have revolved around finding faster ways to press ink on paper, although progress was slow for about 400 years.

E-Publishing

Four evolutions to the computer age have had an impact on the traditional book publishing industry: Kindle's impact toward society's acceptance of e-books, e-commerce on the Internet, books-on-demand and self-publishing, and Google's digitization of printed books.

A challenge to those who provide digital information is that many people don't like reading a lot of text from a computer monitor (Davenport, 1987). Computer text is harder—and about 60 percent slower—to read than ink on paper (Frost, 1996), although technology is making improvements all the time. As a result, many people find themselves scanning information online that they would read more thoroughly in print.

E-reader and larger **mobile device** screens are easier to read than computer monitors, and people find they are enjoying the act of reading—and read more. The top picks for e-readers in 2016 appear to be various Amazon Kindles, Barnes & Noble Nooks, and Kobos. If all else fails in reading, then you can have your Kindle read aloud to you.

Although printed books still sell more than any other book form, the popularity of e-books continues to increase multifold—especially post-Christmas when everyone is trying out their new e-readers and buying e-books with bookstore gift cards. During this time, more e-books than printed books sell the 10 most popular book titles. Amazon's annual sales for e-books now surpass printed books.

Amazon and other companies online would not exist without **e-commerce.** Without leaving home, shoppers can browse and buy books. The Hunger Games series in hardcopy can be delivered in overnight mail or instantly downloaded to your e-reader. Virtual bookstores "remember" that you purchased *Game of Thrones* and, the next time you visit, automatically recommend *Dance with Dragons* or the latest in the series for pre-purchase—even before it is published. It's almost like having a personal librarian and shopper.

But, what should you do if you are looking to publish your own Great American Novel? Custom publishing with online independent publishers is your answer. You can bypass conventional publishers altogether to custom publish your Great American Novel for $1,000 for the standard (lowest) package deal at www.iuniverse.com, for example. The company's experts will help you design the cover, the layout and the design of the pages, and if visuals should be used. The books will be shipped to your house and you can give them away or sell them. (Many churches raise money by publishing and selling cookbooks this way.) Some authors don't care about seeing their book in print, but just want to sell the digital versions online. Self-published books make up about 3 percent of all books purchased by Americans (Bowker, 2013).

What if you want a book that is no longer being published? Small publishers, who may not have the resources for their own bookstores, will **print-on-demand** requested books, using the vast inventories and searchable databases of the Internet to give new life to **backlisted books.** Large companies, such as Google, are also making **orphaned books** available. Google recently won a case to digitize and make searchable the collections of several large research libraries. Portions of books are available to the public, and if the book is out of copyright and in the public domain, then it is viewable or

---

2012

Apple's iPad, Barnes & Noble's Nook, and Amazon's Kindle compete for consumers

---

E-readers are devices that are used to display digital content found in books, magazines, and newspapers.

Mobile devices are handheld computers or cell phones with display screens. They access and send information using cell phone or Wi-Fi connections to the Internet.

E-commerce is the ability to buy and sell online.

Print-on-demand technology prints books only when they are ordered by customers.

Backlist books are older books that are not actively promoted but are still in print.

Orphaned books are older books, perhaps still under copyright, whose authors are unknown.

downloadable to the public. Critics worry that Google will have a monopoly on all information and access. On the one hand, Google could obtain digital versions of all books in all libraries and special collections in universities and museums, many of which house classical literature and valuable historical works, and make these classics more available. On the other hand, what happens once Google becomes a monopoly of information and can choose whether or not to sell its databases to university and community libraries?

And, speaking of universities and learning, what do you do if you need a textbook for class? Technology has evolved so that you no longer have to go the school bookstore, but can order online from the textbook publisher, Amazon or an e-text company, such as Vitalsource.com. So, you have several choices: (1) new print text, (2) used print text, (3) e-text to keep, and (4) e-text to rent. Be careful if you want to borrow your roommate's e-book, because companies that sell and rent e-books are developing ways to avoid people's swapping of copyrighted works online—the problem that the music industry initially encountered with Napster.com (see Chapter 6). Cost-conscious professors try to help your budget when they ask textbook publishers to print-on-demand a limited number of chapters they feel are important for their students. The cheapest bet is a used paper book.

The Economics of Book Publishing

People like to buy books, no matter if they are print, digital, audio, or e-books. U.S. sales rose to $28 billion in 2014 (an almost 5% increase from the prior year) from the sale of 2.7 billion books, the latest annual figures from the Association of American Publishers (Bluestone, 2015). This is the net revenue for U.S. publishers from retailers or other distribution methods (bookstore, online, or directly to the consumer), but not retailer/customer sales. Categories of books are trade (fiction, nonfiction, and religion for all ages), K–12 instructional, higher education instructional, university presses, and professional books. Table 3.1 shows the number and types of books sold within the "trade" book category.

MOVING UP About 30 percent of the population read e-books and 70 percent read books in print. Many people read books in both formats.

TABLE 3.1 **Number of U.S. "Trade" Books Sold by Publishers in 2014**

Paperbacks	942 million
Hardbacks	568 million
E-books	510 million
Audiobooks	26.8 million

Source: Bluestone, M. (2015). U.S. Publishing Industry's Annual Survey Reveals $28 Billion in Revenue in 2014. *Association of American Publishers*. Available online at http://publishers.org/news/us-publishing-industry's-annual-survey-reveals-28-billion-revenue-2014

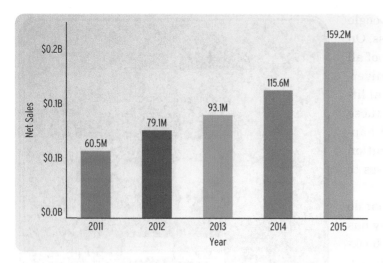

FIGURE 3.1 **PUBLISHERS' REVENUE FOR DOWNLOADED AUDIOBOOKS IN ALL CATEGORIES**

Source: Association of American Publishers (2016). http://newsroom.publishers.org/aap-statshot-publisher-net-revenue-from-book-sales-declines-20-through-third-quarter-of-2015/

Of special note is that audiobooks have become especially popular in recent years. Figure 3.1 shows publishers' revenues and sales for downloaded audiobooks have doubled in the past 3 years. (This does not include physical audiobooks.)

Business was also good for exporting books abroad: up 7.3 percent to $833.4 million. Just imagine shipping about 150 million books worldwide! Of course, a growing percentage of the market was downloaded e-books and audiobooks, so booking passage on a barge has decreased as a line item in the budget (Sporkin, 2013). Publishers can thank the movie business for helping them. On one hand, some movies are turned into best-selling books. On the other hand, some books have made great movies. A popular movie can resurge book sales (printed, e-book, and audio) and put new and old books on the best-seller list. For example, the *Diary of a Wimpy Kid* series has helped both industries. *The BFG* movie in 2016, adapted from Roald Dahl's book in 1982, has made the book popular again. Other Dahl books that did the same were *Charlie and the Chocolate Factory, James and the Giant Peach, Matilda,* and *Fantastic Mr. Fox,* for example. The movies from the Divergent series, *Deadpool, The Martian, Paper Town,* and *Ender's Game* all made their books popular again. Every time the *The Great Gatsby,* an American classic by *F. Scott Fitzgerald* published during the Roaring 20s, is remade as a movie (1926, 1949, 1974, 2013), the book reappears as a best seller.

Many books are read by millions of people. Print books are still the staple of readers' diets, even though more are also reading e-books. Almost 75 percent of American adults read one or more books in any form, and about 30 percent read an e-book and 12 percent listen to audiobooks. These numbers have stayed consistent since 2012 (Rainie & Perrin, 2015).

Every publisher gambles on successful authors and stories and hopes to find the book that becomes the next best seller. There are hundreds of small publishers—academic presses, political groups, and religious organizations—that leave publishing the best sellers to the large publishing houses, but they still strive to reach many people with their message in book form. They are more motivated by the urge to publish a certain kind of book that they feel is important to the world.

BEST-SELLING BOOKS CAN TURN INTO BLOCKBUSTER MOVIES The Game of Thrones six-book series, written by George R. R. Martin, was successful on its own. The success of the blockbuster TV series that followed was in part because of the already-loyal book fans.

The Book Publishing Process: From Publishing Houses to You

Publishing houses are the organizations that acquire manuscripts and supervise the overall production of books in print, e-book, and audio versions. They can be housed in a building or online. Their work includes acquiring and investing in new ideas, developing, producing, curating, editing, marketing, protecting copyright, and delivering books in every form and platform.

The publishing houses might be commercial, independents, universities, religious groups, trade associations, and even vanity presses that will publish anything as long as the author provides the money. Cengage, the publisher of this textbook, is a company devoted to education, whereas other publishing houses, such as Random House, may have several divisions.

Even though the computerized publishing technologies discussed earlier in this chapter make the publication of smaller, more specialized projects possible, major mass-market books continue to be expensive to produce because marketing and other costs have increased. As a result, many publishers feel that they have to concentrate on selling more copies of fewer books.

Publishing houses make room for new formats—or the presentation and distribution—of book content, depending on what consumers want. You probably have bought a variety of book formats for different purposes. As you look around your room, you might see physical books that you can hold (hardcover, **softcover,** mass-market paperback, and packaged audiobooks), display devices for nonphysical books that have no packaging around the content (e-books, downloaded audiobooks, paid mobile apps, and Internet products), or a combination of printed and digital components.

> **Softcover books** are usually printed and distributed in a manner similar to that of hardcover books. They are larger, exhibit more intricate artwork on the cover, and are more expensive than mass-market paperbacks.

A few authors have sold their works directly to the public, cutting out publishers, paralleling developments in the music business (see Chapter 6). For example, Amanda Hocking, author of popular vampire romances, self-published her early works, publicized them through social media, including Twitter and book blogs, and distributed them through Amazon before signing a multimillion dollar deal with a conventional publisher.

Retail Bookstores

Publishers stock the shelves of bookstores, which range from national chains to small, independent bookstores and from physical stores to e-stores. Barnes & Noble is the largest bookstore chain in the United States with 700 physical stores in malls and other community locations (in addition to about 635 college bookstores), followed by Books-A-Million, or BAM!, with 250 bookstores.

Barnes & Noble reinvented itself from a brick-and-mortar store to the largest e-bookstore with an inventory of about 1 million printed books and about 4 million e-book titles that can be read on its Nook, the first color e-reader. In addition to print and e-books, Barnes & Noble sells audiobooks, magazines, DVDs, music, games, toys, and other gifts that you can buy online or think about purchasing while having coffee in their bookstores' cafes.

Bookstore strategies must be working. Independent bookstore retail sales increased almost 10 percent, comparing December months in 2014 and 2015, according to the Bureau of Census (Jarrad, 2016). Keep in mind that these sales include everything in bookstores, not just books.

Amazon has never had a storefront, saving lots of capital on real-estate storefronts and personnel. When its products are not in its warehouses, it takes orders over the Internet and arranges to have books shipped to customers

DISTRACTIONS, COMPREHENSION, AND SLEEP: PRINTED TEXTBOOKS, E-TEXTS, AND THE COST OF LEARNING

Students spent about $1,200 on books and supplies in 2015, according to the College Board (Burke, 2015).

So, you want to carefully consider your options. You can buy or rent a new or used printed textbook, borrow from the library, or buy or rent an e-text. Cost-conscious instructors can request publishers to print-on-demand a text with a few chapters or a text with no binding or cover. Some growing initiatives are offering free courseware and licensing.

Similar to all e-books, the price for e-texts is climbing: about $115 to buy *Media Now* as an e-text, $113 to rent it for a year, or $83 to rent it for 180 days from Vitalsource.com. (Amazon is cheaper, but it might prorate for the days remaining in the semester.) Of course, you need to buy a device to read the e-text.

There are other considerations that go into your purchasing decision. If you buy a printed textbook, then you can keep it forever or sell it. For learning purposes, you can dog-ear a page for reference, highlight significant passages, write comments in the margins, or stick post-it notes on pages (Catalano, 2015). These are valuable techniques when identifying and reviewing pertinent information for learning and retaining information for tests.

An e-text is lighter to carry. You can search and highlight important points, but it may take a few moves. You also have to search for your electronic post-it notes (Catalano, 2015). Anything that takes your attention away from reading will disrupt your learning. That includes pop-up notifications for e-mails, program updates, social media, and other distractions on e-reader devices. And, e-books have been modified or disappeared from one's collection, depending on the retailer (um, Amazon).

In addition to distractions on devices, comprehension diminishes when reading from a screen. Readers skim, skip, jump around, and repeat text on a screen, taking more time and effort to gain comprehension than reading line-by-line on a page, according to eye-tracking and other studies (Catalano, 2015).

Thus, more students are returning to paper, after having tried both. Several projects, including one by Hewlett-Packard, found that students have a strong preference for printed textbooks (about 60% preferred paper and 20% e-text). They preferred a printed textbook because it is easy to use and to take notes. Others chose e-texts because of its lighter weight and accessibility (not learning capability). Most of these students (almost 70%) were willing to pay upward of $40 more for a printed textbook above the cost of an $80 e-text (Tan, 2014).

In addition to better learning and studying processes with print (increased comprehension, fewer distractions), students engage better, stay focused longer, and prefer to read in-depth from the printed page (Foasberg, 2014).

And one more important thing: it's bad to use electronic devices for any reason before bed. Read a paper book instead. The light emitted from a screen has an effect that increases alertness and prolongs the time it takes to fall asleep, reduces the quality of sleep (REM), retards sleep-promoting hormones (melatonin), messes up your sleep rhythm (circadian clock), and promotes lethargy in the morning (Chang et al., 2015). This is bad for your health and diminishes your ability to learn and retain information.

If you are going to put forth the time and effort (and funds) toward learning, then make good choices to study wisely and well.

from publishers or used-book sellers. Amazon has become the nation's largest online retailer with books and e-books as only one line of its merchandise. It continues to increase sales, and its Kindle has been doing well, especially as it just announced a new Kindle for $50.

Independent bookstores that survived the Amazon and e-book waves are gaining in strength: about 1,710 stores in 2,230 locations compared to 1,410 stores in 1,660 U.S. locations 5 years ago, according to the American Booksellers Association (Alter, 2015). Several well-known bookstores are expanding significantly to hold more shelves or increase their warehouses. This comes at a time when sales of e-readers have dropped to 12 million from 20 million 5 years ago. And, e-book sales, making up 20 percent of the market to consumers, have slowed while print books increased (Alter, 2015). Many readers tried the new technology and returned to print, while others combine e-books and print. Many readers prefer to buy a paperback that costs less than its digital counterpart.

Before leaving this topic about retail sales, we wish we could be high brow and tell you that print sales increased because people thirst for literary knowledge. Well, that's partially true, because *Go Set A Watchman*, the prequel of *To Kill A Mockingbird* by Lee Harper, contributed to the higher sales figures, but so did the new fad of adult coloring books and books by YouTube "stars" such as PewDiePie, Tyler Oakley, and Shane Dawson (Ingram, 2015).

Book Readers and Purchasers

People love to read. They are buying more books than ever before. Computers make publishing easier and the Internet makes it easier for people to be exposed to new books and advertising about books. As you add up the numbers for books published and sold in recent years (see Table 3.1 on p. 63), it is a far cry from the 11,000 books published in 1950 (Vinjamuri, 2014)!

So, who reads the most books? You'll find the answer next time you are waiting for an airplane and observing what men and women are reading. (Women read more books. They average 14 books a year while men average nine.) Book readers are younger, have higher incomes and more education than those who don't read books (Rainie & Perrin, 2015).

As you look around at your airport gate or in the airplane, you'll see that most of the books are fiction—espionage, mysteries, and romance (Schmidt & Park, 2013). And, you probably won't be surprised to know that within the trade book category, children and young adult fiction books experienced the biggest growth partially because of trends in graphic novels and coloring books. Nielson BookScan tracks 85 percent of book sales and its researchers identified four types of book consumers: (1) disengaged households (not highly interested in media of any kind, so they probably wouldn't be taking this course), (2) gamers (care more about games than books as media entertainment), (3) social omnivores (they like all media), and (4) avid readers (you guessed it). In a 6-month study, researchers found

READ AS YOU DRIVE The audiobook market continues to grow. According to the Association of American Publishers, audio downloads grew from just over 60 million in 2011 to almost 160 million in 2015. (http://newsroom.publishers.org/aap-statshot-publisher-net-revenue-from-book-sales-declines-20-through-third-quarter-of-2015/)

that the disengaged bought five books, gamers four, social omnivores seven, and avid readers nine. Can you guess which group holds the most potential for buying more books? That's right—social omnivores could respond to the right type of marketing by purchasing more than they usually do (Button, 2016).

Most people find out about a book from a friend or relative or look at bestseller lists. They often buy books they see while out shopping or from searching the websites of a familiar author. However, e-book purchasers tend to find out about a book while online (reading an excerpt, seeing an ad, browsing on online bookstore) (Schmidt & Park, 2013).

WHAT'S TO READ? BOOK GENRES AND CONTENT

Books are diverse and hard to characterize in general terms. Some books are sacred, some are sensational, some are read for pleasure, and some are assigned reading in college courses. The Association of American Publishers identifies four publishing divisions. These divisions are listed below and can be further grouped according to subject area (e.g., fiction, nonfiction) or form (e.g., paperback, audiobook, digital) or publishing house (e.g., university press, independent) or age group (e.g., young adult, adult).

Trade. General-interest fiction and nonfiction (cookbooks, biographies, self-help books, religion, etc.) for adults and children.

Professional and scholarly. Aimed at research, new ideas and innovation in all areas.

PreK–12 Learning. Instructional materials for any level of learning, from toddlers to high schoolers.

Higher Education. Post-secondary learning materials, such as this textbook.

It's sometimes hard to put a book in only one category because it can cross into more. Publisher's Weekly lists the top selling books, and in different categories. Table 3.2 shows the top selling print books in 2014. Most are also the top e-books sold.

TABLE 3.2 Top 10 Print Bestsellers, 2014

RANK	TITLE	AUTHOR	PUBLISHER	TOTAL UNITS
1	The Fault in Our Stars (trade paper)	John Green	Penguin/Speak	1,813,574
2	The Long Haul	Jeff Kinney	Abrams/Amulet	1,560,410
3	Divergent	Veroncia Roth	HarperCollins/Tegen	1,426,292
4	Insurgent	Veronica Roth	HarperCollins/Tegen	1,310,210
5	Killing Patton	O'Reilly/Dugard	Holt	1,190,152
6	Allegiant	Veronica Roth	HarperCollins/Tegen	1,146,369
7	Gone Girl	Gillian Flynn	Broadway	962,797
8	The Fault in Our Stars (movie tie-in)	John Green	Penguin/Speak	923,182
9	The Fault in Our Stars (hardcover)	John Green	Dutton	769,065
10	Frozen	Victoria Saxon	Random/Disney	784,691

Source: Swanson, C. (2015). The Bestselling Books of 2014. *Publishers Weekly.* Available online at http://www.publishersweekly.com/pw/by-topic/industry-news/bookselling/article/65171-the-fault-in-our-stars-tops-print-and-digital.html

Many classics continued to be popular for decades and centuries. Most are fiction, history, or biography. Great stories inspire movies (and their remakes) that, in turn, make people want to read the classics again. For example, a whaling event in 1820 inspired *Moby-Dick* and, much later, the movie *In the Heart of the Sea*. It is doubtful that the movie would have been made if it had not been for the book. You'll recognize many of the top 10 books of the 1800s, which are still popular today (see Table 3.3).

Although print and digital books are in transition, it is likely that some genres will determine their book form. For example, some people prefer to carry around a hardback or paperback book for leisure reading and like to put books on their bookshelves or pass books along to friends and family. Other books, however, such as travel guides, might be predisposed to digitization because they can be searched easily while you are on a trip, but won't take up storage space once you return home (similar to maps and GPS systems). They have a one-time use; after all, the prices and restaurants may no longer be viable the next time you visit. And, the form of the book may depend on habits. Learning is acquired and remembered better and longer as one engages with tactile print (reading, highlighting, and making notes in the margins of books), while one can search digital forms quickly and easily for a general understanding of a topic.

TABLE 3.3 Top 10 Works of the Nineteenth Century

1	*Anna Karenina* by Leo Tolstoy
2	*Madame Bovary* by Gustave Flaubert
3	*War and Peace* by Leo Tolstoy
4	*The Adventures of Huckleberry Finn* by Mark Twain
5	The stories of Anton Chekhov
6	*Middlemarch* by George Eliot
7	*Moby-Dick* by Herman Melville
8	*Great Expectations* by Charles Dickens
9	*Crime and Punishment* by Fyodor Dostoevsky
10	*Emma* by Jane Austen

Source: http://www.theatlantic.com/entertainment/archive/2012/01/the-greatest-books-of-all-time-as-voted-by-125-famous-authors/252209/

MEDIA LITERACY

As we have seen in this chapter, the role that publishing and literacy play in society is continually evolving. Here we consider some of the issues that confront the publishing industry today.

NEW LITERACIES, OLD LITERACIES

Learning how to create, access, analyze, and evaluate news and information from different media is defined as *media literacy*. The Center for Media Literacy also notes that media literacy "builds an understanding of the role of media in society as well as essential skills of inquiry and self-expression necessary for citizens of a democracy" (www.medialit.org).

Instead of simply letting media bombard you with a cacophony of messages, you can learn to use different media effectively to obtain the information you need to make productive decisions. You can be an active seeker of information and an active participant, contributing to the market place of ideas and a democratic form of governance. To become this critical thinker, you have to understand how the different media work—who makes decisions and why and how are they made.

However, conventional literacy in the sense of being able to read and understand the printed word is also a concern. A national survey in the early 2000s found that 15 percent of adults in the United States had less than basic literacy skills, meaning that although they could sign their names to a document, they were not necessarily able to understand what they had signed (National Center for Educational Statistics, 2005). An additional 6 percent of college students were unable to understand documents as "complex" as a television program guide and 56 percent were unable to synthesize information, such as comparing viewpoints between newspaper editorials (Baer, Cook, & Baldi, 2006). And that study was completed just as texting and tweeting began eroding the literacy skills of youth.

Things are finally looking up. The National Endowment for the Arts (NEA) has conducted surveys about literacy since 1985. Its most recent survey, in 2008, showed that literary reading is on the upswing in almost all adult groups—across age, gender, ethnicity, and education levels—reversing a 20-year downward trend. Why? The writing was on the wall (no pun intended). When faced with this growing problem, families, communities, libraries, and educational institutions rose to the challenge to encourage reading.

BOOKS AS IDEAS, BOOKS AS COMMODITIES

Before the Internet, relatively few people had access to media to voice their opinions, except in letters-to-the-editor columns in local newspapers. Yet it has been assumed that competition would bring out diverse points of view and approximate a fairly free discussion among knowledgeable people. Now most of the readership of books is concentrated on the output of a few publishers. To make the best profit, those publishers tend to promote a handful of potential best sellers, rather than a broad catalog of fiction and nonfiction. People wonder whether the trend toward maximizing sales of a few books in the U.S. book publishing industry means a reduction in the ability of a diversity of authors to find publishers for their ideas. Given that books are very important in national intellectual and political life, some writers and publishers fear that it will be hard for manuscripts other than probable blockbuster best sellers to find a publisher if the number of publishing houses were to decline.

This concern is partially met by a steady rise of new, small publishing houses that target different audiences, by the number of people who are self-publishing their own manuscripts through the Internet, and by print-on-demand requests for older books whose ideas and discussion are still relevant today. Although it may seem as if book publishers continue to consolidate and monopolize the decisions for what makes a "good" book, many new publishing houses continue to spring up, signaling growth and diversity in the print industry. These new publishers tend to be small and to reach far fewer people than the largest book publishers, yet collectively they are a significant force.

The concern about publisher monopolies is met also by the less expensive and wider distribution of books through e-book stores and through e-books and e-readers, all of which help to promote the spread of different ideas and voices. Now that much of the U.S. population has access to the Internet, new electronic publishers, digital magazines, online bookstores, and a growing market certainly increase the potential for competition and a greater diversity of viewpoints.

Unfortunately, members of low-income households may have limited access to the Internet, either because of the cost of computers or mobile devices or because of Internet connection charges. So, although diverse points of view are available, not everyone can access them easily. This is why libraries are important to our democratic society. Anyone is welcomed to read printed material at a library, borrow books or journals, or access information online through a library computer, thus becoming exposed to different points of view.

PUBLIC LIBRARIES, FREEDOM OF SPEECH, AND THE FIRST AMENDMENT

Libraries are great places. Most people aren't concerned about the clothes you wear or your patter in a library. Instead, they'd prefer that you didn't talk. People go to libraries for news, information, and help. About 90 percent of Americans felt that a library is important to their community and almost as many said it was important to their family, according to the American Library Association (2014). They look for information in books, computers connected to the Internet, magazines, and journals to help them with decisions about their lives. In addition to borrowing material, most patrons purchase particular authors and other sources of information, as a result of being introduced to them at a library. And, if you are a power patron, then you probably visit a library about once a week and are an active voter. As society changes, so do libraries in an effort to keep relevant in people's lives. Borrowers may find a printed book to their liking, but they also are checking out audiobooks and e-books and using the library's computers for social media.

If you were in your school's library last week, then you probably contributed to one of the 31 million weekly searches on databases and your question to the librarian may have been one of 470,000 questions they answer weekly (ALA, n.d.). Librarians in the Brooklyn Public Library system (60 libraries) alone answered 3.5 million queries in 2013—an increase from the prior year (Blau, 2014).

Libraries also fight censorship issues in an effort to champion free speech. Thus, First Amendment issues are crucial to the publishing industry. Freedom of speech and of expression in print media is well established in the United States, but over the years, community and religious groups have objected to the contents of various books, magazines, and digital publications. The top reasons for objections are sexually explicit material, offensive language, material unsuitable to an age group, violence, homosexuality, religious viewpoint, and being antifamily (ALA, 2008). Since the turn of the twentieth century, most books in the United States have been exempt from overt **censorship,** although novels like *Lady Chatterley's Lover* (1928), by D. H. Lawrence, went through periods of being censored. By today's standards, many readers would consider Lawrence's sexually explicit passages fairly tame, but the book challenged the conventional limits of its time.

STOP & REVIEW

1. What are the main trends in book publishing?

2. What are the four major divisions of books?

3. As you consider your habits, when might you use different formats of books (hardback, paperback, audiobook, e-book, etc.)?

4. What could happen if the book industry becomes monopolized?

Censorship is when authorities or perhaps others in positions of power suppress types of information or news to audiences.

TABLE 3.4 Some Top Challenged/Banned Books of the Twenty-First Century

TITLE	REASONS
Captain Underpants (series), by Dav Pilkey	Offensive language, unsuited to age group, violence
The Absolutely True Diary of a Part-Time Indian, by Sherman Alexie	Drugs/alcohol/smoking, offensive language, racism, sexually explicit, unsuited to age group
The Perks of Being a Wallflower, by Stephen Chbosky	Drugs/alcohol/smoking, homosexuality, sexually explicit, unsuited to age group
And Tango Makes Three, by Peter Parnell and Justin Richardson	Homosexuality, unsuited to age group
The *Internet Girls* Series, by Lauren Myracle	Offensive language, sexually explicit, religious viewpoint
The *Alice* Series, by Phyllis Reynolds Naylor	Sexually explicit content, homosexuality, drug use, religious viewpoint, and offensive language
What My Mother Doesn't Know, by Sonya Sones	Sexually explicit content, offensive language
The Kite Runner, by Khaled Hosseini	Homosexuality, offensive language, religious viewpoint, and sexually explicit material
The *Hunger Games* series, by Suzanne Collins	Violent content, religious viewpoint
The *Harry Potter* series, by J. K. Rowling	Satanic themes

Source: Stone, A. (no date). 10 Twenty-First Century Bestsellers People Tried to Ban (and Why). Mental Floss. Online at http://mentalfloss.com /article/59059/10-twenty-first-century-bestsellers-people-tried-ban-and-why

Even today, books get pulled from library shelves for various reasons. The American Library Association lists the top 10 books annually that receive the most complaints. For example, *Captain Underpants* has headed the list several times. *The Catcher in the Rye* (1951), by J. D. Salinger, is often challenged for rough language; *The Adventures of Huckleberry Finn* (1885), by Mark Twain, for racial stereotypes and epithets; and the *Harry Potter* and *Twilight* books for witchcraft and sorcery. Table 3.4 shows some popular bestsellers of twenty-first century that are frequently challenged.

The focal point for discussions about censorship of books is usually the local library or school system, because campaigns to ban books usually focus on what is available through libraries or assigned in schools. Librarians have evolved a number of strategies for reconciling freedom of access with the desire to protect children or other vulnerable audiences from adult content. Some books are not shelved but have to be requested; access to others is restricted by age.

The Internet poses similar challenges for libraries, because local libraries now offer Internet access as one of their services to the public. Their challenge is to figure out how to keep the screen clean for all ages. This is difficult when their search engines can be used to seek out a wide variety of controversial material that may contain sex, violence, or hate speech. (See Chapter 16 for discussions of laws that require libraries to use filtering programs to screen out controversial material.)

SUMMARY & REVIEW

WHAT KEY ELEMENTS OF THE PRINT MEDIA WERE DEVELOPED FIRST OUTSIDE EUROPE?

A number of essential ideas were brought to Europe—for example, using rags to make paper was imported from China. Other printing techniques, such as movable metal type, developed in parallel form outside Europe but were probably not a direct influence on the development of European print media.

WHAT WAS THE IMPACT OF PRINTING IN EUROPE?

The advent of printing by Gutenberg greatly accelerated the growth of literacy by making books cheaper and more widely available. Education became more widespread because texts were easier to get. Printing affected religion by making the Bible widely available, politics by boosting news circulation, and economics by increasing knowledge and skills.

WHAT IS HAPPENING WITH BOOK PRINTING?

Desktop publishing is the creation of publication-quality documents using the increased power and speed of desktop computers, laser printers, and scanners that digitize photos or illustrations into computer-readable form. Desktop publishing has done much to decentralize print media. The average person can now produce local or specialized media. This advance in technology has led to the proliferation of books-on-demand, something not possible with older technology.

WHAT ARE THE MAIN TRENDS IN BOOK PUBLISHING?

Increasing numbers of books are being published and purchased by consumers, students, and businesses. Large publishing houses are consolidating even as smaller ones proliferate.

THINKING CRITICALLY

ABOUT THE MEDIA

1. Which culture should receive the most credit for the invention of printing? Please explain.

2. Debate the following proposition: books are an obsolete medium.

KEY TERMS

almanac (p. 58)

audiobook (p. 60)

backlist book (p. 62)

book (p. 60)

book publisher (p. 60)

censorship (p. 71)

dime novel (p. 59)

e-book (p. 60)

e-commerce (p. 62)

e-reader (p. 62)

literacy (p. 56)

mobile device (p. 62)

novels (p. 54)

orphaned book (p. 62)

print-on-demand (p. 62)

softcover book (p. 65)

subscription library (p. 58)

CHAPTER

4

PRINT AND DIGITAL NEWSPAPERS

LEARNING OBJECTIVES

After studying the topics in this chapter, you will be able to:

1. Discuss the impact that John Peter Zenger's libel trial had on the First Amendment.
2. Show how the history of journalism is intertwined with the history of democracy in the United States.
3. Compare the journalism strategies used to increase circulation by rivals William Randolph Hearst and Joseph Pulitzer.
4. Discuss ways in which the newspaper industry has adapted to new media to maintain profitability.
5. Debate the newspaper industry's responsibility to balance reporting news accurately and objectively with the pressures of a 24-hour news cycle and competition with popular tabloid journalism.
6. Discuss how the world would be without journalists providing news and information that audiences need to know.

Nine in 10 U.S. residents follow local news closely. Where do they get their news? A vast majority read printed or digital newspapers weekly (about 71%), according to the Newspaper Association of America (2013). Most of these newspaper readers get their news exclusively from the printed page (about 60%), and almost all young people who are online are also reading digital newspapers (93%) (Newspaper Association of America, 2015a; Pew Research Center, 2015).

And, who delivers news to audiences? Journalists gather, present, and disseminate news that is helpful to diverse audiences and they are professionals with critical thinking, news judgment, writing and visual communication skills, and ethics.

This chapter focuses on the journalism in newspapers and covers the newspaper-publishing platforms of print and digital (online and mobile).

© Settawat Udom/Shutterstock.com

THE ONLY PROFESSION PROTECTED BY THE U.S. CONSTITUTION, journalism, is about the freedom to report what is going on in the world and in communities.

MEDIA THEN··· MEDIA NOW

1690
> First American newspaper, Publick Occurrences Both Forreign and Domestick, *published*

1733
> John Peter Zenger trial establishes truth as a defense for press against libel charges

1783
> First daily newspaper in America, Pennsylvania Evening Post and Daily Advertiser, *published*

1789
> First Amendment to Constitution enshrines freedom of press

1833
> The New York Sun, *first Penny Press daily, begins publication*

1878
> Joseph Pulitzer originates the Yellow Journalism movement

1972
> Watergate scandal inspires new era of investigative reporting

1982
> USA Today *national daily launched*

1986
> Knight Ridder's and Times-Mirror's *experiments with videotex close down*

1994
> The development of the World Wide Web signals a change in the newspaper industry

1997
> The Wall Street Journal *implements a paywall and gains 200,000 subscribers in the first year*

2009
> Detroit Free Press and Detroit News begin hybrid model of 3-day home delivery while providing news online daily

2014
> News organizations develop immersive journalism stories that combine writing with visual communication and new media technologies

2015
> Gannett offers international and national news to local audiences by including a section of USA TODAY *in their community newspapers.*

HISTORY: JOURNALISM IN THE MAKING

MindTap°

Start with a quick warm-up activity.

More people are seeking more news and information in more and different ways than ever before. They might read a printed newspaper in the morning, listen to the news on the radio on the way to class or work, check the latest updates on their computers or smartphone at lunch, and watch TV news in the evening. News content appears as text, audio, or visuals, such as photos, video, design, information graphics, animation, and virtual reality.

"News" is information we didn't know before (it's "new" to us). Anyone can provide or get information. Yet, professionally trained journalists find out more about the issues and events that affect society and put them into a context that makes the information meaningful. This type of journalism helps us to form opinions about the world around us and gives us the kind of information that helps us lead better lives.

The history of our ideas about what journalism should be is reflected in the history of newspapers. Newspapers have always wrestled with commercial interests and political powers, but their history reflects the evolution of a free press from European and American Revolution models. Many publishers and editors worked hard to battle government censorship and commercialism. The struggles are the same today as they were centuries ago, but the circumstances have changed. The history of journalism is crucial to understanding the role and function of journalism today—such as combating a European stranglehold on the news during colonial times, moving from a party press to an independent press, transforming technology in a ravaged Civil War existence to an industrialized nation, and moving forward from the sensational in yellow journalism to a reformist "muckraking" mind-set in the Progressive Era and on to modern media. In the history of newspapers, we can see the evolution of social responsibility—the development of better journalistic practices and ethics.

Newspapers Emerge

MindTap°

Read, highlight, and take notes on the complete chapter text in a rich interactive online platform.

First there were town criers announcing news to an intrigued audience in city courtyards, and then there were newsletters. Starting in 59 BCE, Julius Caesar's *Acta Diurna (Journal of Daily Events)* was posted daily for 200 years in public places; it announced news concerning the Roman senate, merchant business, weather, disasters, individuals, and later, even gossip. During the 1500s, financial institutions in Europe, particularly Germany's House of Fugger, gathered and published financial and trade news for all interested businesspeople. Meanwhile, Italians were charged a gazzetta (about a penny) to hear the daily newsletter on merchant news read aloud. In 1618, patterning their newsletters after German and Belgian newsletters, the Dutch published their **corantos** (currents of news) to include local news and gossip. And England's first daily newsletter, first published in 1641, was the *Diurnal Occurrences in Parliament,* listing government business. In 1702, Mrs. Elizabeth Mallet published England's first daily newspaper—the *Daily Courant*—that continued for 33 years. She listed **datelines** and clearly separated objective news from opinion and advertising (Sloan, 2005).

> **Corantos** were news sheets that appeared around 1600.

> **Datelines** appear at the beginning of a story and note the location where a story happens.

Freedom of the press was nonexistent in the early days of newspapers in Europe. The ruling class granted licenses to printers and had their authorities censor every article before it was printed. Over time, open societies recognized the importance of freedom of speech and criticized censorship. By the early 1600s, British citizens were leaving the country in droves, many of them coming to America in hopes of freedom to practice their religion—and with it the freedom to talk and write about their beliefs. In anger over the Church's refusal to allow publication of his essay on divorce, John Milton wrote his famous *Areopagitica* in 1644 and entreated Parliament to cease licensing and censorship. He advocated that a free press would allow a diversity of voices and that in the **marketplace of ideas,** truth would emerge and rise above.

> **Marketplace of ideas** is the concept that the truth and the best ideas will win out in competition.

The Colonial and Revolutionary Freedom Struggles

Early American newspapers struggled with the question of control by colonial authorities, and that fight gave birth to freedom of the press. The first colonial newspaper, Benjamin Harris's *Publick Occurrences Both Forreign and Domestick,* published in 1690, contained stories that scandalized the British Crown and Puritan authorities; it was shut down after one issue. Boston postmaster John Campbell started the rather boring *Boston News-Letter* in 1704, published "by authority" of the royal governor, and it lasted 72 years.

> **1690**
>
> First American newspaper, *Publick Occurrences Both Forreign and Domestick,* published

James Franklin began an independent newspaper, the *New-England Courant,* without "by authority" approval. As a result of his unapproved, scandalous opinions, he was jailed and forbidden to publish. To evade further punishment, James registered his apprentice brother's name as editor. Benjamin Franklin had a flair for words and writing, and he soon moved to Philadelphia to start his successful publishing business with the *Pennsylvania Gazette.*

The question of editorial independence and criticism of authority was raised again in 1733, when John Peter Zenger published a newspaper openly critical of the British governor of New York and was jailed for criminal **libel.** Zenger's lawyer, Andrew Hamilton, argued that the truth of a published piece was itself a defense against libel. Appealing to the American jury not to rely on British law and precedent, Hamilton won the libel case, which established the important principle that true statements are not libelous.

> **1733**
>
> John Peter Zenger trial establishes truth as a defense for press against libel charges

> **Libel** is harmful and untruthful written criticism from the media that intends to damage someone.

In the Zenger case and other events that followed, the British colonial authorities still tried to control the fledgling American press, particularly as calls for revolution increased. British domination left colonists, particularly journalists and printers, convinced that freedom of speech and of press was essential. They insisted that even radical statements, such as calling for the overthrow of an unjust government, be permitted. Benjamin Franklin drew the first American editorial cartoon in 1754, showing a snake chopped into eight pieces and the caption "Join or Die," which represented the colonies in a united stand, protesting France's power in America. It was used again to urge the colonies to unite against the British. The political press that emerged was very important in building support for the American

UNITED WE STAND, DIVIDED WE FALL

The first editorial cartoon to appear in a newspaper was drawn by Benjamin Franklin, who urged the colonists to join together in their fight against other countries that sought to dominate them.

Partisan press are newspapers sponsored by a person or groups that support particular ideas, causes, politics, or individuals.

Seditious speech is aimed at overthrowing the government.

1789

First Amendment to Constitution enshrines freedom of press

Diversity includes all points of view from people of different races, cultures, political leanings, gender, age, and life experiences, for example.

1783

First daily newspaper in America, *Pennsylvania Evening Post and Daily Advertiser,* published

Revolution (1776–1783) and in defining the role of the American free press. **Partisan** newspapers proliferated. Newspapers published key documents including the Declaration of Independence (1776) and the debates over the Constitution in 1787.

The First Amendment

Freedom of the press was formally established in the United States at the Constitutional Convention. The desire to protect freedom of speech and freedom of the press resulted in the First Amendment to the Constitution. It says:

Congress shall make no law respecting an establishment of religion, or prohibiting the free exercise thereof, or abridging the freedom of speech, or of the press; or the right of the people peaceably to assemble, and to petition the Government for a redress of grievances.

Despite this strong stand for freedom of the press, there was soon an attempt to limit **seditious speech** under the Alien and Sedition acts, signed into law by John Adams in 1798, and several newspaper writers and editors were charged with sedition at the turn of the eighteenth century. The new president Thomas Jefferson allowed the acts to expire in 1800 because a consensus had grown for freedom of the press.

Diversity in the Press

Diverse viewpoints are essential to the functioning of the press in a free society. After the American Revolution, the politicization of newspapers continued, representing a wide **diversity** of political views, similar to what we see today with online newspapers. These publications took on more partisan leanings and were often openly involved in political campaigns, such as the abolition of slavery.

Advertising and commercial interests began to be important as well. Benjamin Franklin was successful in part because he was a clever writer and designer of advertising copy. In 1783, the first daily newspaper in the United States, the *Pennsylvania Evening Post and Daily Advertiser,* was begun. By 1800, most large cities had at least one daily, but circulations were limited because printing presses were slow, and readers had to be literate and relatively wealthy: one copy cost as much as a pint of whiskey, around 5 cents. Newspapers were one of the forces that drew people into thinking about themselves as Americans, forming a community of people who had access to the same information and identified with each other (Anderson, 1983). However, real differences existed among Americans, and not everyone was welcomed into the larger community. Thus, in addition to the "mainstream" press, other newspapers were published to address the needs of diverse audiences.

Native American Press. The first Native American newspaper, the *Cherokee Phoenix,* was established by the Cherokee Nation in 1828. A year later, the Georgia legislature took away all the legal rights of Native Americans,

Bettmann/CORBIS

LEADING STAR Frederick Douglass used the African-American paper the *North Star* to promote and push for the abolition of slavery.

Abolitionists wanted to abolish slavery.

Penny Press included daily newspapers that sold for 1 cent and had content that interested the average person.

including freedom of speech. In 1832, the editor of the *Cherokee Phoenix* resigned in protest, and its publication became erratic and eventually ended. It was not until 10 years later—after the Cherokee were removed from their lands—that a new Cherokee Nation newspaper was firmly established. Several other Native American groups published newspapers, and some of them suffered similar discrimination, such as suppression by state authorities to limit sympathy for Native American claims to retain their lands.

African-American Press. About 40 African-American newspapers were published before the Civil War. The first, *Freedom's Journal,* was published in 1827 in New York City. This newspaper had strong ties to the **abolitionist** press, and its goal was to encourage racial unity and the progress of African Americans in the North.

Another important African-American paper, the *North Star,* was founded in 1847 and edited by Frederick Douglass, an escaped slave and probably the best-known African American at the time. It had the following prospectus:

Frederick Douglass proposes to publish in Rochester, New York, a weekly antislavery paper with the above title. The objective of the *North Star* will be to attack slavery in all its forms and aspects; advocate universal emancipation; exact the standard of public morality; promote the moral and intellectual improvement of the colored people; and . . . hasten the day of freedom to our three million enslaved fellow-countrymen.

He called it the *North Star* because slaves escaping at night used the North Star as their guide. Along with others, Douglass helped push what abolitionists called "the War to Free the Slaves"—the U.S. Civil War.

The Penny Press

For democracy to function, ideas must be widely circulated as well as diverse. The early 1800s saw technological innovations in the field of printing (see Chapter 3), which in turn permitted lower-cost papers aimed at a broader audience. At the same time, social conditions favorable for the creation of the mass audience and mass newspapers were building. More people were learning to read via the expanding public education system, wages were increasing, more people were moving to the cities, and an urban middle class was growing. Whereas most newspapers had been aimed at an elite class and were expensive, innovative publishers responded to this new market by covering local news and selling cheaper newspapers. Thus, in both the United States and Britain, the mid-1800s brought forth the **Penny Press.** However, many people still could not read or afford newspapers, particularly among the waves of immigrants who arrived in the United States from the 1840s on.

In 1833, Benjamin Day launched the first low-cost daily mass newspaper in New York. Called *The Sun*, the paper sold for a penny—hence the nickname Penny Press. To offer his paper at that price, Day relied on advertising and sales, and reached out farther to the urban audience, using newsboys to sell papers in greater volume. Five years later, James Gordon Bennett, Sr., publisher of the successful *New York Herald*, was the first to publish news promptly and give daily coverage to business, sports, and women's news. He also added a personals (classified) section and required advertisers to change their ads every day. The Penny Press was one of the first media to create a truly mass audience, big enough to attract advertisers and justify their investment. And with the advent of faster rotary presses in the early nineteenth centurycosts decreased even further (see Chapter 3 for early printing press development). As newspapers began to address larger, more diverse, and less clearly partisan audiences, modern journalism also began to evolve. Although most newspapers had covered business and politics, the Penny Press reached across party lines and used common language to tell stories about the average person. This combination of factors spawned the modern daily newspaper.

ONLY A PENNY *The Sun* was the first low-cost daily mass newspaper, first published in 1833.

Another boon to the mass newspaper was Samuel Morse's telegraph in 1844, which led to a marked improvement in speed and reach in news gathering. By the time of the Mexican-American War (1846–1848), telegraph technology enabled newspapers to get news of the war as soon as their reporters returned by ship from the front in Mexico City. (Ten years later, the first transatlantic cable was laid for the telegraph.)

Additionally in 1848, several New York newspapers started the New York Associated Press (AP) news service to share the cost of covering stories. AP member newspapers sold their reporters' stories to all the papers, so each newspaper could provide more news to its readers, especially if the newspaper couldn't send someone to cover an event. The service expanded with the ability to send stories over the telegraph, thus becoming the first **wire service.** This and other regional wire services joined in 1892 to become what is now called the Associated Press. Wire services helped newspapers lower their costs, add more general-interest material, and appeal to a wider audience, with the side effect of news becoming more objective and less partisan in coverage.

1833

The New York Sun, the first Penny Press daily, begins publication

Wire services supply news to multiple paying news organizations; they were named originally for their use of telegraph wires. Modern wire services are digital and are called "news services."

Following the Frontier

Newspapers expanded westward with the American population in the years before the Civil War. Mark Twain began his career as a frontier newspaper journalist and later became famous for his books and short stories. As presses were made lighter in weight with hollow legs and became transportable to the West, newspapers proliferated and diversified. For example, the second half of the 1800s saw more than 130 Spanish-language newspapers started in the Southwest (Huntzicker, 1993). Frontier newspapers were often blunt and antagonistic, and their editors were opinionated. Many chastised eastern liberals for sympathizing with the "Indians." Jane Grey Swisshelm, founder of the *St. Cloud Visiter,* criticized the politicians of St. Cloud, Minnesota. They retaliated by destroying her press, but they made her reputation, as she rebuilt her press and exposed the members of the mob who destroyed it (Huntzicker, 1993).

Civil War Coverage

Newspapers helped Americans build a nation, but they also played a catalytic role in the conflict that tore it apart. A prime example is Harriet Beecher Stowe's *Uncle Tom's Cabin* (1852), which exposed the evils of slavery and was published in serial form in the *National Era,* the most popular abolitionist newspaper of the time. The story was then published in a book form and sold more than a million copies in 2 years.

The debate over slavery and the events leading up to the Civil War were well covered by the Penny Press. The Civil War (1861–1865) expanded newspaper readership because everyone wanted immediate news from the battlefield and politicians' viewpoints. That interest, fueled by reports telegraphed directly from the front, reinforced newspapers' focus on up-to-date events and headlines. Not surprisingly, northern and southern papers often saw things very differently.

The New Journalism

Newspapers plunged into the post-Civil War industrial expansion, flourishing in the cities where industries grew and people flocked to get jobs. Along with other industries, newspapers saw a chance to grow, and they more aggressively pursued advertising and newspaper sales.

Headlines were large, gossip was news, and pictures showed emotion. **New journalism** was lively, brash, self-conscious, impetuous, and sensational. It concentrated more on news, increasingly defined as the latest events of the day, and less on editorials and essay columns.

Scoops that beat rival newspapers to press became more important, as did crusades against corruption. For example, William "Boss" Tweed in New York City stole hundreds of millions of taxpayers' dollars while paying unscrupulous newspaper editors to look the other way (*New York Times,* 1901). Although most newspapers were on the Tweed Ring's payroll in 1870, the *New York Times* rose to prominence partly as the result of its successful campaign against the corrupt legislator and his cronies. *Harper's Weekly* magazine editorial cartoonist Thomas Nast supported the *Times* with strong visual statements against the Tweed Ring. The campaign eventually brought down the Ring, and subsequent investigations showed that, among other things, the politicians bought off many newspapers through $500,000 of advertising. Most of those 89 newspapers folded afterward (Parton, 1874).

Furthering their appeal, newspapers of this era added a new visual element, the news photograph. During the Civil War, photographer Mathew Brady had popularized photographic images, but they could not be reproduced

New journalism was the investigative reporting of the nineteenth century.

To **scoop** a rival newspaper is to be the first one to get the story and publish it.

in newspapers or magazines (see Chapter 5 for Civil War illustrations). However, in 1880 a process for integrating photos and text on the same page was developed, and the first bona fide newspaper photos appeared.

Toward the end of the 1800s, newspapers reached broader audiences. In the largest cities of the day, large-circulation papers, such as the *National Police Gazette* tabloid, pursued a mass audience with sensational stories on sex, murder, scandal, popularized science and medicine, and other human-interest events accompanied by large headlines and lurid illustrations. As European immigration increased, many immigrants published foreign language newspapers.

Yellow Journalism

Yellow journalism was a product of new journalism. It grew from the rivalry of two late nineteenth-century media moguls, Joseph Pulitzer and William Randolph Hearst, and from changing newspaper economics. The term itself was an outgrowth of the first newspaper cartoon strip, called the *Yellow Kid,* which depicted a clueless youth from the New York tenements who wore a yellow nightshirt. One of Hearst's stunts was to hire away Pulitzer's staff, including the artist of the *Yellow Kid.* Another artist filled his place and for a while, New York had two versions of the *Yellow Kid,* whose ridiculous adventures reminded people of the publishers' rivalry.

NAST'S FAMOUS CARTOON, "LET US PREY"

EFFECTIVE WIT *Harper's Weekly* magazine editorial cartoonist Thomas Nast was famous for cartoons denouncing corrupt politicians.

North Wind/North Wind Picture Archives

Hungarian immigrant Joseph Pulitzer came to the United States, joined the army, and turned to journalism after the war. In 1878, he pulled together enough money to merge two struggling St. Louis newspapers into one, the *St. Louis Post-Dispatch,* and he established himself as a nonpartisan social critic by conducting popular crusades against corruption and complacency. Pulitzer also bought the *New York World,* intending to publish a newspaper for the underdogs in New York City. For example, he hired Elizabeth Cochrane, known as Nellie Bly, who became famous by feigning insanity to investigate the notorious Blackwell Island insane asylum. Her stories on the poor conditions and abuse of patients prompted official investigations and improvements (Everett, 1993). In another instance, the *World* championed her as she competed with Phileas Fogg by going around the world in less than 80 days. Because of its successful escapades and escalating circulation, the *World* became the paper that others imitated.

1878

Joseph Pulitzer originates the Yellow Journalism movement.

Yellow journalism was the sensationalistic reporting of the nineteenth century.

ELIZABETH COCHRANE ("NELLIE BLY") was one of the first investigative reporters and one of the first women recognized for serious reporting. She also was a champion for women's rights and social reform.

STOP & REVIEW

1. What case established the precedent for freedom of the press in colonial America?

2. What was the Penny Press? What led to it?

3. What are the differences between new journalism and yellow journalism?

4. What effect did the telegraph have on newspapers?

5. How did wire services influence a change in the newspaper business?

One of the imitators was William Randolph Hearst. Hearst inherited his family's fortune and came to New York City to buy the ailing *New York Morning Journal*. There followed a dramatic war between Hearst's *Journal* and Pulitzer's *World*. A legendary example of Hearst's yellow journalism was when he sent his best reporter and best artist to cover the Cuban unrest. After a week or so they cabled Hearst that there was no revolt and they were coming home. His purported response was, "Please remain. You furnish the pictures and I'll furnish the war."

Another myth reflecting the zeal of yellow journalism was Hearst's and Pulitzer's spectacular coverage of the 1898 explosion of the U.S. battleship *Maine* in the Havana harbor, which the *Journal* blamed on the Spanish, although the cause of the explosion was found in later years to be a spontaneous combustion in the battleship's ammunition magazine. Many historians credit the *Journal's* frenzied coverage with helping to push the United States into war with Spain over Cuba and the Philippines (Sloan, Stovall, & Startt, 1993). So, in a sense, Hearst did furnish the war.

Yellow journalism was more than just a result of the competition between two men. During the 1880s and 1890s, papers were no longer read only by the elite but also by the general population. With this shift in the marketplace came a shift in the sources of income from circulation to advertising and in the story content. The newspapers sold their ads and subscriptions at the greatest profit, and these sales depended on the size of the paper's audience. The journalistic style that was used to amass a bigger audience emphasized sensational photos and story selections, large headlines, an abundance of personality and human-interest stories, and sometimes even hoaxes and fake interviews. The sensationalism and over-the-top stories were also a product of how journalists were paid. The longer the story, the better the quotes, and the more exclusive the interview, the bigger the pay rate. This caused journalists to forget ethics as they used flowery language, made up quotes, and hid sources from other newspapers. In other words, the lowering of journalistic quality was a combined result of change in the marketplace; Hearst and Pulitzer were simply responding to the change. But in the process, commercialism grew as a threat to the ideal of the press in a free society.

Responsible Journalism

Although yellow journalism may have gotten out of hand, both Hearst and Pulitzer contributed substantially to the development of the profession. Pulitzer created a journalism that defined social responsibility for newspaper coverage. Hearst encouraged higher salaries, bylines, and other recognition for journalists. These innovations were important milestones in the evolution of journalism as a valued and respectable profession. Both Pulitzer and Hearst helped mentor and create a number of good journalists.

Publishers shifted formats to keep pace with changing social conditions. They focused on things that preoccupied city dwellers trying to make sense of their rapidly changing world, such as divorce, murder, and other crime. Newspapers adjusted direction to keep up with the changing times. For example, African-American papers shifted to a more urban focus as their audiences migrated north. Furthermore, immigrant ethnic press overall declined as readers assimilated into American society and as their children learned to read English.

Responsible journalism advanced when Adolph Ochs bought the *New York Times* in 1896. Ochs turned the nearly dead paper into an exceptional twentieth-century newspaper of record. He resisted sensationalism in photos, extravagant typefaces, fake stories, and stunts, of which many readers had tired. He stressed impartiality and independence—which today we call **objectivity.** He made sure that advertising was clearly distinguishable from stories, unlike other papers that made money by allowing ads to masquerade as legitimate stories.

The *Chicago Tribune* was also making headway as a serious newspaper. Whereas most newspapers pushed sensationalism to attract readers, the *Tribune* invested in color technologies that would print art on the front page for the public. It published comic strips in color in the early 1900s and was the first newspaper that printed four-color illustrations.

> **Objectivity** fosters news stories free of biases and opinions.

Muckraking

The early 1900s, called the Progressive Era, was a time in which society wanted reform legislation for politicians, big business, and social ills. President Theodore Roosevelt likened the passion of investigative reporters to that of someone who exposed filth and raked the muck away. Most of the **muckraking** exposés were published in the national magazines (discussed in Chapter 5), but many of the journalists who exposed corruption and helped achieve reform also wrote for newspapers.

> **Muckraking** is investigative journalism that "rakes off the muck"—dirt and filth—to expose corruption and scandal.

The Effect of Chain Ownership and Conglomerates

Printed papers peaked as a mass medium between 1890 and 1920. Newspaper circulation increased 20-fold, while the U.S. population tripled between 1850 and 1900 (McKearns, 1993). In 1900, there were 1,967 English-language dailies, and 562 American cities had competing dailies. New York City alone had 29 dailies. Many small towns had more than one newspaper, each shedding a different light on reported issues and events. People would buy the various newspapers to read the different views and opinions about an issue, and feel informed.

By 1910, the newspaper industry had grown larger than its resources of advertising and circulation could support. Inevitably, mergers and consolidations began to trim the numbers back. Usually, stronger papers acquired smaller, profitable ones to get their circulation and advertising base. The new group owners were business people who bought and then closed down the competition or consolidated papers to maximize profits. The largest owners were the Hearst and the Scripps-Howard chains that closed more than 30 papers between them. The chain phenomenon continued into the 1930s, as Harry Chandler (the Times-Mirror group), Frank Gannett (the Gannett group), John Knight (Knight Ridder Publications), and others joined the chain ownership trend. By the end of the 1930s, six chains controlled about a quarter of newspaper circulation (Folkerts & Teeter, 1994).

Thus, the diversity in newspapers that marked the late nineteenth-century press began to erode with group ownership. In addition, antitrust regulators became concerned about diversity in content as *monopolies* or *oligopolies* emerged, particularly among the news services that supplied the newspapers with much of their material: the AP, United Press, and the International News Service. This concern has increased as chains also own weekly newspapers, television stations, and other media holdings in the United States and elsewhere.

Critics are also worried that **conglomerates** have the same effect of narrowing diversity in content. Conglomerates might own several different types of companies, including news organizations. Thus, owners could discourage the publication of critical news on their other holdings. The opposite also could occur, with only good news about company holdings being published. (See Chapter 17 for more discussion on conglomerates and media ethics.)

> **Conglomerates** are big businesses or corporations that own seemingly unrelated holdings. They are made up of diverse parts from across several media industries and are involved in multiple areas of business activity.

Professional Journalism

New journalism and muckraking were to be admired. However, the excesses of yellow journalism and the rising tide of commercialism in newspaper operations sparked the further evolution of the journalistic profession from a free press to a **social responsibility model.** One of the key points was the evolution of journalists from anyone who could write and had a nose for news in the nineteenth century to the college-educated professionals of the twentieth century. That depended on professional education and the rise of accredited journalism schools. Another key development was the rise of professional associations with well-structured codes of ethics (see Chapter 17 for ethics codes).

> **Social responsibility model** calls on journalists to monitor the ethics of their own newsgathering and reporting.

Daily newspapers helped shape the events of the late nineteenth and early twentieth centuries, so much so that attempts were made to make the press behave more responsibly in times of national crises. During the first half of the 1900s, newspapers crusaded both for and against government policies, such as entering World War I (1914–1918). For example, sensational newspaper coverage of the 1915 German sinking of the British ocean liner *Lusitania,* which killed more than 100 U.S. citizens, aroused public sentiment in favor of entering World War I against Germany.

The government created the Office of War Information to ensure that official government decisions would be covered and publicized. It also closed German-language newspapers and censored news during World War I to make sure that no military secrets leaked out through the newspapers. U.S. government propaganda was more restrained during World War II, but was still

Scott Peterson/Getty Images

MOBILE JOURNALISTS Many journalists are skilled in writing, shooting photos and video, and uploading stories to a website without ever going into the newsroom.

presented to the public through newspapers, magazines, movie reels, and cartoons. Controls were still placed on newspaper coverage to avoid divulging military secrets. Censorship was abolished with the end of hostilities in 1945, but the give-and-take between the government and the press over the preceding decades of crises helped to entrench the social responsibility model, and the press assumed a rather uncritical stance toward national policy.

The Watchdogs

Many countries look to the United States as a role model of what it means to citizens to have a free press in a democratic society. Through the First Amendment and other laws, journalists can request information to enlighted residents about what their government representatives are doing—and whether government activities are in the best interests of its citizens.

Since World War I, most media supported the government out of a sense of patriotic duty. But with the Cuban Missile Crisis, the Vietnam War (1959–1975), and the Watergate scandal, journalists began to distrust the government's official announcements and to see themselves as "watchdogs"—outside critics with a primary responsibility to keep an eye on government mistakes and public deception. Through their coverage of civil rights and the emergence of advocacy movements championing the rights of ethnic minorities, women, and alternative lifestyles, many papers were critical of the status quo.

Throughout history, journalists had generally protected the reputation and decisions of presidents and, in turn, government officials usually trusted the press with information to be publicized later. But the Cuban Missile Crisis was a turning point as John F. Kennedy gave the press and the public inaccurate or incomplete information while recovering from the Bay of Pigs disaster (an aborted invasion of communist Cuba).

In another crucial test of press freedom, the *New York Times* published secret government documents, known as the Pentagon Papers, proving that the United States had been illegally bombing neutral Cambodia during the Vietnam War. Such coverage set the news media in conflict with government authorities (Braestrup, 1977).

Also during the Vietnam conflict, Carl Bernstein and Bob Woodward, two junior investigative reporters working for the *Washington Post,* broke the story of the Watergate scandal. In 1972, Republican Party operatives burglarized Democratic Party headquarters in the Washington, D.C., Watergate complex, looking for documents that might damage Democratic Party candidates. With the help of a confidential informant in the Nixon administration, Bernstein and Woodward exposed the foul play and the cover-up that followed. These revelations ultimately led to Richard Nixon's resignation from the presidency.

1972

Watergate scandal inspires new era of investigative reporting

Many observers wonder who will watch the government if a free press diminishes. More recently, *Detroit Free Press* reporters Jim Schaefer and M. L. Elrick used the Freedom of Information Act (FOIA) to obtain text (and sexting) messages that led to the downfall of former Detroit mayor Kwame Kilpatrick, who continuously lied to the public and spent taxpayers' money for personal use.

TECHNOLOGY TRENDS

Advances in publishing technology were reviewed in Chapter 3. Here we will consider innovations that have shaped the newspaper industry, where speed is of the essence in all phases of gathering, presenting, publishing, and disseminating the news.

Newsgathering

Before the telegraph, the speed of news was the speed of transportation systems from the clipper ship to the pony express to trains and even to carrier pigeons. A generation later, the telephone also improved the speed of news gathering, even though some late nineteenth-century reporters disdained it as a "lazy" way to avoid honest footwork (Sloan, Stovall, & Startt, 1993).

In times past, journalists did almost all of their news gathering (interviewing, examination of documents, etc.) away from the office and hurried back to type up their stories. Today, they can do much of their newsgathering from the newsroom. They monitor other news organizations, police communication frequencies, and use Facebook, Twitter, and other social media (blogs, chat rooms, listservs) to get tips, track down rumors, and confirm stories.

Now, because much of this technology is small and mobile, journalists are again doing much of their reporting in the field. They can easily carry their equipment for newsgathering and producing (writing, recording audio, shooting visuals) in the field and then send it to an editor to review and place in the news lineup. **Backpack journalism** is a term for reporters in the field who combine different forms of the story into multiple versions for different media.

Technology has also made it possible to analyze large amounts of information or mine "big data," a skill that has been known as computer-assisted reporting (CAR). By examining government databases, reporters write stories about trends in crime and poverty, and objectively compare areas or groups of people without relying on self-serving handouts from politicians or lobbying

> **Backpack journalism** is the term for reporters who carry a digital video camera (a mini DV; see Chapter 8), tape recorder, notebook, telephone, and computer, often in a backpack.

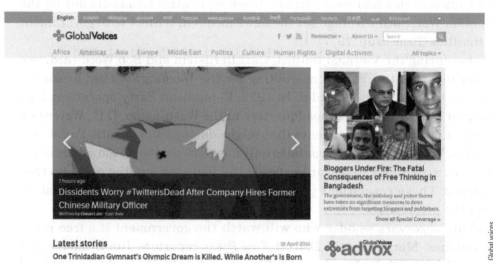

BREAKING BARRIERS Global Voices publishes news stories that happen in 167 countries and translates them into 30 languages. The news site is a nonprofit organization with more than 800 writers, analysts, media experts, and translators.

groups. They use campaign finance databases to find financial connections between the way politicians vote and the businesses that support them. Some reporters use social science methods (see Chapter 15) by analyzing trends in voter behavior, finding correlations between crime and poverty rates and their possible causes, and producing detailed maps of poverty or crime in a region (Davenport, Fico, & DeFleur, 2002).

The technology **convergence** or combination of different forms of media has allowed many news organizations to combine multiple media into a single story or to use various pieces of the same story for different media platforms or to share their resources with other media.

> **Convergence** is the integration of mass media, computers, and telecommunications. It occurs when news organizations share different formats of information for multimedia news.

Print Publishing

As innovations in printing presses continued to evolve, developments such as the rotary press, linotype, and phototypesetting greatly increased the number of pages printed in an hour's time. These innovations changed the industry as newspaper pages went from a few to many, prices decreased, and circulation grew into the hundreds of thousands as a result. (For discussion on early printing press development, see Chapter 3.)

Teletypesetting was a significant improvement in the 1950s. Stories were set in type by a highly skilled typesetter employed by a wire service, then punched out onto paper tape by the local newspaper, and then automatically fed into the newspaper's own typesetting machines to produce a near-perfect copy. By the late 1960s and the early 1970s, data contained on paper tapes were stored in computer memory, paving the way for the computerization of print production. Today, reporters compose and edit their stories and designers lay out the pages of newspapers on computers. The latest computer-to-plate processes generate the printing plates directly from computer images, using sophisticated cousins of the ink-jet and laser printers found in the home. This eliminates the expensive step of photographing the layouts and chemically processing them for the press run.

2015

Gannett offers international and national news to local audiences by including a section of *USA TODAY* in their community newspapers.

Satellite delivery of copy to remote printing plants also speeds the news to your door or device. *USA Today* print edition, for example, is put together in McLean, Virginia. It is then sent by satellite to 36 printing plants across the United States and to five printing plants in Europe and Asia. It travels about 45,000 miles at the speed of light to make local same-day print delivery possible for its 3 million readers.

More geographically diverse news organizations are working with each other to produce local news. For example, most of Gannett's local newspapers now include a section of *USA Today* (also owned by Gannett) to give national and global news to local readers.

Online and Digital Publishing

Digital news makes sense also for publishers because it cuts the costs of expensive ink, paper, and delivery methods (trucks and personnel). The idea of distributing news electronically is not new. Nineteenth-century financial barons had stock tickers in their homes. In the 1930s, newspapers experimented with "faxing" newspapers to special home radio receivers (Shefrin, 1993). In the 1980s, several newspapers invested millions in experiments to transmit news and information digitally over phone lines and by cable.

1986

Knight Ridder's and Times-Mirror's experiments with videotex close down

Videotex was an early way to transmit digital news by phone lines for display on TVs or early desktop computers. A modem and special software were needed to transmit the analog signals to digital ones and vice versa.

Teletext was an early way to transmit digital news by cable or broadcast signals for display on TVs.

1994

The development of the World Wide Web signals a change in the newspaper industry

2009

Detroit Free Press and *Detroit News* begin hybrid model of 3-day home delivery while providing news online daily

2014

News organizations develop immersive journalism stories that combine writing with visual communication and new media technologies

Knight Ridder developed a **videotex** service called Viewtron, which sent digitized news to the home over phone lines for display on television sets. *Times Mirror* did a similar experiment called Gateway, but used cable as the transmission line. These trials failed because of the high cost to consumers and the idea of putting dense textual information on a television set, which people used for entertainment. More successful consumer online services, such as CompuServe and America Online, followed suit using early desktop computers. Meanwhile, other countries used **teletext** piggy-backed on broadcast signals to transmit news to the television set (Davenport, 1988). Online news has substituted for broadcast teletext in several countries, and over time, these teletext operations have shut down. However, digital and other types of teletext are still viable in various countries, such as Ireland and the Netherlands, for the transmission of news.

Online newspapers have many features that their print versions lack: up-to-the-minute breaking news, sports scores, and stock prices; computer-searchable classified ads; interactive forums where readers exchange views; audio and video clips for major stories; and automatic news alerts to your tablet or phone.

Some offer personalized news. You select the type of coverage, topics, and formats that fit your personal lifestyle. Then a software program develops a profile of what you like to read, listen to, or watch and gathers those stories for you. Critics of this system worry that we would become a fragmented audience, narrowing our fields of interest, and have nothing in common with others. With printed and mobile app newspapers, readers are attracted to headlines and read information they would not seek otherwise, and become more informed about what is happening in their communities or around the world. Many believe that the serendipitous nature of reading a newspaper with a printed or digital page layout is beneficial.

Online news and digital developments in news production also helped newspapers cut costs and keep afloat during the Great Recession, which began in 2007. Many print-only news outlets, such as the *Detroit Free Press* and the *Detroit News* experimented with a hybrid system of delivering newspapers to doorsteps for fewer days of the week while providing more news online every day. As other news organizations moved in the direction of online news, executives realized the importance of providing news and information content for the developing media technologies that audiences use, such as computers, tablets, and apps.

Immersive Journalism—Virtual Reality

As technology becomes more innovative, newspapers can put you in the middle of a story as you see events unfold around you in every direction. Some newspapers use Oculus Rift for animated 3-D experiences and others use Google Cardboard and a smartphone. (See Technology Demystified box in this chapter for more news about immersive journalism.)

A few newspapers have also experimented with augmented content. Audiences can scan the printed page with their phone to retrieve more information on the subject, such as a recorded interview with a source in the story.

Readers like news on the Internet or their phone or tablet because they can check the news quickly. For some news consumers who are accustomed to the printed newspaper, however, the layout and design of news on a website looks too different; they are not comfortable with it. For others, the ergonomics are all wrong for relaxing with casual reading from a desktop or even laptop computer that is often used for work.

However, many of these same readers enjoy the look of the traditional newspaper on their iPad or tablet and they like the feel of being able to "turn" the page. With mobile apps, people are spending more time with the news and they have more choices as to how they want to get their news. Some enjoy using their tablets or e-readers so much that they are reading more news, reading it for longer periods of time, and going to several mainstream media places to get that news (Pew Research Center, 2010).

Consumers also use social media to find out about news. Reporters and friends use Twitter, to alert "followers" to breaking news or to news stories online. And **blogs** are used mostly for opinion and insight about news events and issues. Blogs have morphed from electronic bulletin boards systems (BBSs) to newsgroups to weblogs. There are about 160 million blogs on the Web, written by anyone, from teenagers about their high school soccer team to political candidates on issues of the election. Some blogs are predominantly text, whereas others incorporate digital photos, links to other sites, audio download links, or podcasts.

Consumers Habits

More people than ever before are accessing more news, and they are doing it in more and different ways than ever before.

About eight in 10 newspaper readers get news from a printed newspaper—by itself or in addition to digital (NAA, 2015b). A little more than half get their news from printed newspapers only. The other half is using digital only or a combination of digital and print. (See Figure 4.1 in this section for a breakdown of news devices that people use.)

THE NEWS COMES TO YOU Email newsletters like theSkimm provide readers with a fast, snappy overview of the day's news.

> A **blog,** short for *Web log,* is commentary addressed to the Web audience. A blog is similar to an online opinion journal.

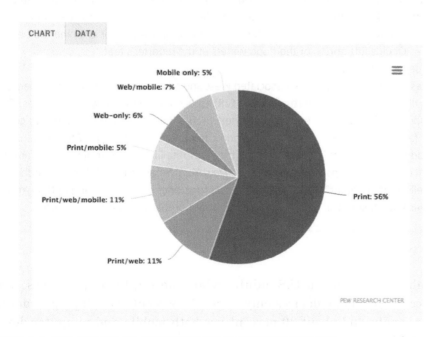

FIGURE 4.1 PIE CHART OF AUDIENCE BY PLATFORM/DEVICE

http://www.journalism.org/media-indicators/newspaper-audience-by-platform/
Source: Nielsen Scarborough USA+ 1999–2014, Release 1.

Technology Demystified

IMMERSIVE JOURNALISM AND VIRTUAL REALITY

Time traveling to distant lands doesn't take a teleporter—it just takes media. But, how you are transported depends on technology and innovation.

Readers have always traveled to imagined worlds . . . just by reading the words of great journalism storytellers.

Listeners are drawn into a story . . . by hearing sounds happening around reporters describing a scene.

And viewers have front-row seats to unfolding events . . . by watching photojournalists focus on environments and key players.

From print to digital to multimedia newspapers, journalists have used words, sound, pictures, and motion to take their audiences to news as it happens. And, now newspapers are using 3-D (three-dimensional) technology to place their audiences inside their stories.

Using virtual reality, journalists immerse you into stories where you can look behind and above, walk distances, and hear and see people interact with each other.

Remember what newspapers told you about the trapped Chilean miners? Did you wonder what was it like for the miners to be trapped for 69 days? Now you can have a better idea, using immersive technologies, such as Oculus Rift and 3-D animation, that you control. Newspapers can transport you into an underground network of caves in Chile, seeing only what the headlamp on your helmet illuminates in the darkness. You can see your cold breath bounce off a damp rock wall only 3 inches away which, the farther you walk, opens into a large cavern. You hear a steady plink . . . plink . . . plink . . . in the claustrophobic silence as water drips from the slick ceiling into the shallow, yellow pool behind you. An abrupt swoosh! makes you cover your head and

duck instinctively as a million tiny bats swarm into a small tunnel above, cutting off all shadows of light for moment or two. Then, suddenly, the ground shakes and you run toward the distant shouts of other miners, not caring that your "waterproof" boots are getting heavier with dirty water as they slip and splash through uneven, wet ground. The closer you get, the more you can see of the wall of rocks that sealed the only way out to fresh air. As you continue your immersive experience, you listen to the miners deliberate with each other and the outside world on chances of survival, and talk about loved ones. And you watch them become tired, but still hopeful. And . . . now you know what it's like to be buried 2,000 feet underground for 69 days with 33 Chilean miners . . . waiting for the successful rescue.

Newspapers can give you another type of immersive experience live-streamed, using Google Cardboard and your smartphone (or by using your computer and cursor). This experience might be a 360 camera strapped to the helmet of a reporter covering the evacuation of residents of the Gulf of Mexico during a hurricane. As the reporter strains to see ahead through the pounding rain, yelling to be heard above flapping clothes, 95 mile-per-hour winds and crashing Gulf waves, you can physically move your head or turn around while looking through Google Cardboard and your smartphone, to see people stranded on their roofs behind you, or look into the angry clouds above you, or examine the height of the flood waters at the reporter's feet.

The Associated Press and newspapers are bringing audiences' virtual reality (VR) to accompany their written stories. For example, Gannett used a 360 camera and recorder to cover the Alpine World Championships. The *Des Moines Register* used Oculus Rift to illustrate life on a four-generation farm in Iowan. And the *New York Times* delivered Google Cardboard to a million readers for stories called "Walking in New York" and "Displaced," about orphans in war-torn countries.

Of about 180 million U.S. adults who read digital newspapers, about 40 percent use mobile devices only, about 30 percent use a laptop or desktop computer only, and about 30 percent use both mobile and computer devices (NAA, 2015c).

Newspapers have found that they have more visits from people using mobile devices, but people stay longer when using their desktop computers.

Young people (18–24) get much of their news and information from social media and online-only sites—everyone knows that. Yet, most said they feel more informed about current issues when using printed newspapers (67%) and traditional newspaper websites (56%)—as opposed to using online-only news sites (NAA, 2015d).

INDUSTRY: THE NEWS LANDSCAPE

Competition for Audiences and Advertisers

As the first mass medium to carry news, the newspaper has long encountered competition from every new mass medium that has come along. And the newspaper has survived as each new medium squared off, stretched, and grew into its niche. Along the way, its content changed in the dance with other media.

Magazines contained some content similar to newspapers, such as literary stories and long narratives about news events. They also had woodcut illustrations. But magazines were expensive and published quarterly or monthly. Newspapers were cheaper and got the news out quicker.

Radio burst on the scene in the late 1920s and could offer immediate news updates. To set themselves apart, newspapers pursued deeper news analysis and interpretation. Newspapers could deal with complex government programs and economic crises, reporting various points of view in and out of government with in-depth investigative reporting, a technique not well suited to radio. They were also able to display pictures of products on sale—something that radio couldn't do.

But television could. In the early 1950s, television ate into the national advertising base that newspapers had once dominated.

New journalistic voices have appeared as community weekly newspapers followed the middle class away from city centers into the suburbs. Many people subscribe to both a community weekly and a daily. Weeklies have loyal, local advertisers and are not as affected by a volatile economy as are metropolitan newspapers. However, they compete with weekly "shoppers," alternative press publications, and city and regional magazines for advertising.

As news organizations compete for audiences and advertisers, they have added online and mobile platforms to readers and advertisers, and this has had an effect on circulation and advertising revenue:

- Total circulation (print, online, and mobile) increased 22 percent from 2013 to 2014, followed by a decline of 3 percent in the past year (Pew Research Center, 2015). A lot of information can be obtained free on the Internet.

- However, total circulation revenue has increased, mostly because newspaper companies raised their 7-day home rates about 57 percent in the past 5 years and many subscribers don't mind paying for reliable news (NAA, 2015a).

- Total advertising revenue continues to decrease because of a loss in print ads. Although spending for both online and mobile advertising rose to $50 billion in 2014 (at the same rate of 18% annually for the past several years), the increases do not yet compensate for print advertising's revenue loss (Pew Research Center, 2015).

STOP & REVIEW

1. What was the impact of Watergate on American journalism?

2. What are the main recent trends in newspaper delivery technologies?

3. What are potential problems with citizen journalism news sites run by nonprofessional journalists?

4. Compare how news on the Web and e-readers, tablets, and other mobile devices influence the news business.

REPORTING THE NEWS THAT OTHERS USE

This is an exciting career, where something new happens every day. Journalists begin the day by hitting the ground running and learning about new issues and events. Their minds and bodies are continually at work, helping local and global communities.

People always want news and information. It is important to know about issues and events that affect our decisions on how to lead productive lives. And we must be able to trust the journalists who do the reporting and writing.

Journalists come in all packages: as reporters, news analysts, correspondents, writers, editors, designers, information graphics experts, photographers, videographers, and even 3-D animators, to name a few. With digital technologies come new job descriptions such as social media manager, aggregator, technologist, and director of technology. They use honed news judgment to discern what their audience needs to know and how to tell it best—to report the news. These journalists are experts in gathering, organizing, and presenting information in various formats (text, visual, auditory, multimedia) for distribution on different platforms (newspaper, magazine, radio, television, online, and mobile devices).

Critical thinking, great news judgment, clear writing, and good visual communication skills are ingredients of successful journalists.

Journalists also have insatiable curiosity about the world around them and a desire to find answers. They might go to a scene to observe the situation, take pictures of it, record it on video, do background research on the people or topics involved, interview bystanders or relatives, and then put the different pieces of information together in such a way that best tells the story of what happened or why it happened. Reporters use qualitative research skills (observing, interviewing, studying documents) and quantitative social science research skills (analyzing databases or putting numbers into a spreadsheet) to give events and issues context and meaning to their audiences.

Most journalists learn reporting and writing skills by pursuing a major in journalism at a college or university. Students take journalism courses to gain critical thinking, writing, and reporting (or story telling). Students also take courses outside of journalism to learn about the world, because journalists report on life. In addition, journalism students should have several internships or part-time jobs in journalism to experience the work before they graduate and to make themselves more marketable to employers.

Journalists can be general reporters, covering all aspects of a community; or specialists in a particular area, such as science and health, sports, environment, medicine, government, fashion, or education; or foreign correspondents, traveling to report on events and issues in other countries.

Nationwide, there are more than 69,000 news analysts, reporters, and correspondents, about half of whom are employed in print media. Many more are employed writing news for new and different forms of digital news available to audiences through technologies, such as the Web, tablets, e-readers, and mobile devices. The best opportunities are expected to be in new media fields and in smaller print and electronic media markets, according to the Bureau of Labor Statistics.

Journalism students should train in all aspects of multimedia in order to be prepared to work in any news environment. The more knowledgeable the applicant, the better the chance at being hired. Furthermore, many journalists move around in the news industry; feature writers might switch from TV to print, editors become columnists or opinion writers, newspaper reporters become TV reporters, and radio journalists become podcast interviewers.

Source: Bureau of Labor Statistics (2014). News analysts, reporters, and correspondents.

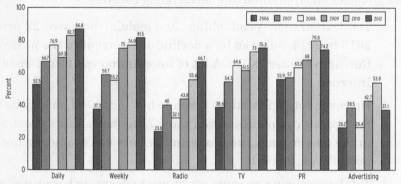

Employed Bachelor's Degree Recipients in Communications Doing this Work

Source: Vlad, T., Becker, L.B., Simpson, H., & Kalpen, K. (2013). 2012 Annual Survey of Journalism & Mass Communication Enrollments. Retrieved from http://www.grady.uga.edu/annualsurveys/

The World View

Much of this chapter is about U.S. newspapers. But let's step back a moment to look at the situation globally so that we can see the United States compared to the rest of the world. Newspapers worldwide generated about $180 billion in revenue—more than the book, music, or film industries. Circulation revenue outpaced the advertising revenue—$92 billion compared to $87 billion for the first time. This changes the basic assumption that advertising revenue is needed to support the newspaper industry. It is moving away from a business-to-business model (publishers to advertisers) to a business-to-consumers model (publishers to audiences), according to the World Association of Newspapers (Edmonds, 2015).

Although the circulation and advertising revenue percentages differ according to each country, Europe and Asia have a general 50-50 split. They charge higher prices and depend on newsstand sales. Revenue in the United States had been generally 30-70 with a low cost to the reader and a higher reliance on advertising.

Print (news and advertising) still attracts 93 percent of all revenue even though digital is increasing. About 2.7 billion people read printed newspapers compared to 770 million who access it on their desktop. More people are reading the news in other ways as digital devices become accessible.

> The **news industry business model** was totally dependent on advertising revenues. Thus, revenues fluctuate with the advertising whims and budgets of other businesses.

A New Business Model for the United States

Throughout the years, U.S. newspapers continue to remain profitable, although revenues fell during the 2009 Great Recession, with profits ratcheted down from what shareholders demanded 20 years ago. That revenue comes from newspaper circulation and advertising. Circulation revenue has grown since the end of the recession, but advertising, a much larger piece of the revenue pie, has continued to take a hit and is a worry for news executives. Revenue overall was $38 billion for the U.S. newspaper industry in 2013 and has continued to increase.

> **Paywall model** limits the number of free articles that a reader can access.

The traditional business model and innovative technologies have caused newspapers to reexamine how they build revenue. Newspapers traditionally have a business model of being supported by advertising. But the recession made it plain that this **business model** left the industry at the mercy of others because in hard economic times, many companies don't advertise if they can't afford it.

> **Metered pay models** require readers to pay a price to read more than a few articles.

One initiative to improve revenue has been to raise the cost of news content—to increase single-copy sales and circulation rates and no longer offer credits to subscribers on vacation (because they can read daily news online). In the past 5 years, newspapers have increased their home delivery rate of print and digital by almost 60 percent (NAA, 2015b).

Another initiative is to implemented **paywall models** for digital news. A hard paywall allows no access to information without a paid subscription. A soft or **metered pay model** allows some free articles, and if readers want more, then they must become a subscriber. More than 450 American newspapers and an additional others across the globe have a paywall model. For many, including *The Wall Street Journal* and the *New York Times*, paywalls are producing significant revenue. News organizations are hoping that, just as

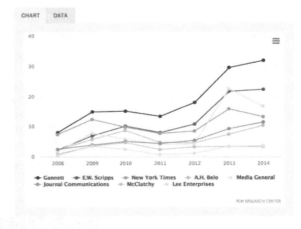

FIGURE 4.2 U.S. NEWSPAPER COMPANY STOCK PRICES

http://www.journalism.org/media-indicators/newspaper-company-stock-prices/
Source: SEC filings.
Note: Stocks prices as of December 31 of each year at close.

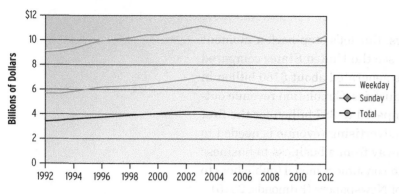

FIGURE 4.3 **NEWSPAPER CIRCULATION REVENUE**

Source: http://www.stateofthemedia.org/2009/chartland.php?id=1000&ct=col&dir=&sort=&c1=0&c2=0&c3=0
&c4=0&c5=0&c6=0&c7=0&c8=0&c9=0&c10=0&d3=0&dd3=1

1997

The Wall Street Journal implements a paywall and gains 200,000 subscribers in the first year.

audiences became accustomed to paying for satellite TV and radio, they will be willing to pay for newspaper content.

Another option to grow revenue that is not dependent on advertising is to charge subscribers separate or combined fees for print, tablet, smartphone, or online editions.

And still another initiative is to use crowdfunding to support a newspaper or special investigative reporting stories. For example, the *San Francisco Chronicle* used crowdfunding to support a multimedia project about immigration policies and the high-tech industry. It used Beacon, a journalism crowdfunding site whose investors match reader donations dollar for dollar. In another example, a Dutch entrepreneur used crowdfunding to raise $1.3 million in just 1 week to start an investigative reporting news site called *De Correspondent*.

Change in technology also impacted the industry and the traditional way of raising revenue. As the number of consumers who get their news from a mobile device increases, newspapers redesign their news for diverse platforms such as tablets, e-readers, and phones. Also, newspapers encourage readers to return to a news story to read others' responses to their comment or to add information. They also encourage readers to share news stories with their friends on Twitter and Facebook.

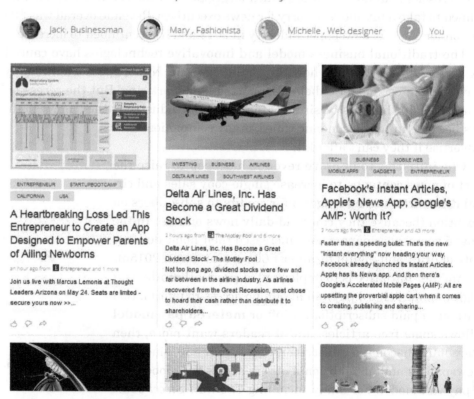

NEWS AGGREGATOR Many of the stories on News360 came from other news organizations. The site also generates original news.

Most news stories originate from traditional news organizations employing professional journalists. However, technology also brought about **news aggregates**—and suddenly people were reading news, but not from the original source. These aggregates copy news from news organizations and reformat it to attract readers to their sites, and place advertising around it. Thus, the aggregate attracts the audience and advertising dollars, whereas the news organization that paid the reporter for the original story receives nothing for its efforts. News organizations now demand and receive payment for their articles that are found elsewhere online.

> **News aggregates** take stories from the original news sources for display on their own sites, hoping to attract audiences. Most do not pay the originators, who should be paid and referenced.

CONTENT: WHAT IS NEWS?

With all of the new options on where and how to get news, people are spending more time with news than they have in about a decade.

Defining News

"Man Bites Dog!" For years news has been defined for many as what is unusual, striking, even sensational. Remember, the Penny Press, new journalism, and yellow journalism all strove to capture people's attention with large, shouting headlines, photos, and sensational topics—even with muckraking and investigative reporting.

Editors look for news that has certain clear characteristics. It involves many people (magnitude) and is recent, unusual, personal (human interest rather than institutional), critical of things that need to change (rather than supportive), linked to familiar places and cultures (rather than distant, unfamiliar ones), and often tragic in the sense of reporting disasters. These news elements were first observed in a study of Norwegian papers in the 1960s (Galtung & Ruge, 1965) and have been confirmed in many studies and in several countries. About 2.5 billion people worldwide read a print newspaper. In the United States, print news is still the most common way to read a newspaper, although newspaper digital audiences reached a new high of almost 180 million users (NAA, 2015).

News Elements

As you look over a newspaper, you would see that all of the stories have one of three purposes—to inform, to educate, or to entertain. But what stories to cover is often a news judgment call because so many issues and events happen in a community, state, and the world. News judgment means journalists consider news values or elements when deciding to cover a story: (1) timeliness—did it happen recently or just now, (2) magnitude or impact—what size of the population is affected, (3) proximity—news that happens closer to home is often more interesting than what happens in a town across the globe, (4) prominence—who is involved, (5) unusualness—is it something that is irregular or odd, and (6) conflict—is it a person struggling with themselves, nature, or another person.

Most stories are of two kinds: (1) hard news—the who, what, where, when, why, and how about something that just happened, such as an accident, and (2) soft news—a feature or human interest story that does not have time elements. These are stories about hobbies, history, and how-to's, for example.

Editors group similar news stories into several distinct sections that serve different audiences: international news, national news, local news, editorial and commentary, sports, business, lifestyles, entertainment, comics, and classified advertising. Sections make it easier for newspaper readers to navigate to these specific interests. *USA Today* is widely credited with accelerating this trend with its sections: News, Sports, Money, and Life. Newspapers try to build overall circulation by providing something for everybody and to increase targeted audiences for advertising.

Print and online newspapers vary a great deal in the sections they emphasize, usually depending on the geographic area they cover and their news focus.

- *National newspapers* report on international news, national news, editorials and commentaries, business news, lifestyle, and entertainment news of a general nature.

- *Metropolitan dailies* usually focus more on regional and local news, lifestyles, entertainment, sports, and comics. They have more local ads for such businesses as supermarkets, auto dealers, and real estate.

- *Local weekly newspapers* go even further toward local news, such as **hard news** and **soft news** or human interest (feature) stories that do not have immediacy, shopping information, and ads, and sometimes are the town's number one booster.

Online newspapers narrow these headings further. For example, "sports" can be subheaded into college and high school teams. "Opinions" usually includes social media—editorials, columnists' blogs, letters to the editor, readers' blogs, and readers' uploaded photos and videos. Some online newspapers program "top picks" of comments, photos, and videos based on reader's votes. Whereas at one time, reporters rarely heard from their readers, they now enjoy readers' immediate feedback on their stories and comments that sometimes add to the story, offer follow-up story ideas, or correct inaccuracies immediately.

Types of Newspapers and Their Audiences

Newspapers come in different platforms, but they also differ in their range of content. There is a considerable, growing audience for community newspapers covering local and entertainment news. The sections below explain the different types of U.S. newspapers according to their audiences, no matter if the news is a print or digital edition. They are explained next.

Dailies. Newspapers (printed and digital) published at least 5 days a week are termed *dailies* and can be national, metropolitan, or suburban. Top-tier daily newspapers experienced a 22 percent increase in weekday and Sunday circulation from 2012 to 2013. But then circulation fell for dailies overall about 3 percent in 2014 (Pew Research Center, 2015). Many people consider television to be their immediate news source, although better-educated audiences tend to rely more on newspapers and the Internet. They use the radio and television to hear about an event or issue and then turn to print or online newspapers for more in-depth information.

There are several types of dailies: national, metropolitan, suburban, and local. Most national dailies are metropolitan newspapers distributed by

> **Hard news** is the immediate coverage of recent events, such as accidents and crime.

> **Soft news** stories can be covered or published at almost anytime.

1982

USA Today national daily launched

TABLE 4.1 Newspapers: Circulation at the Top 5 U.S. Newspapers Reporting Monday–Friday Averages

STATE	NEWSPAPER NAME	TOTAL AVERAGE CIRCULATION
DC	*USA Today*	4,139,380
NY	*The Wall Street Journal*	2,276,207
NY	The *New York Times*	2,134,150
CA	*Los Angeles Times*	690,870
NY	*New York Post*	497,878

Circulation averages for 6 months ended September 30, 2014.
Preliminary figures as filed with alliance for audited media—subject to audit.
Source: Alliance for audited media.

satellite to multiple locations. For example, *USA Today* began with the intent of covering the country and now has a global combined print and digital readership of 7 million and combined circulation of 4 million. (The newspapers with the highest circulation can be seen in Table 4.1.)

Although most newspapers have a print and digital versions, some very successful national (and international) dailies are digital only—not connected to a legacy news organization. Some of these have made the list of the 50 top news websites. For digital-only news websites, *Huffington Post* leads the way with 100,000 **unique visitors per month**. Almost all of the top 10 digital-only news websites (except CNET.com) experience more visitors using mobile devices than desktops. (See Figure 4.4.)

> **Unique visitors per month** is the measure of how many different people visit the site within a month. A visitor can make many visits to the site, but is counted once. (It is the computer origination that is counted and not the person.)

Usually when a daily newspaper dominates a city, it tends to be sustainably profitable. They are profitable usually because they share content and management costs with other newspapers within their newspaper chain. Sometimes, however, instead of reinvesting back into the local newspaper, the profits from one newspaper might go to a fledging newspaper in another town also owned by the chain.

> **Shoppers** are free to readers and are supported by advertisers. Content sometimes includes news stories, but advertising is the main objective.

Newspapers continue to operate in the black; however, metropolitan newspapers have experienced some difficulties because many readers have moved to the suburbs and shifted to national dailies and local dailies or weeklies. Thus, suburban areas have increasingly grown with industry, business, and entertainment.

Consequently, as many towns grow in economic importance, local dailies and weeklies (suburban—or community—newspapers) have risen in importance and gained in numbers and circulation. In response, many of the metropolitan dailies added suburban sections and publish regional editions, such as the San Fernando Valley and Orange County editions of the *Los Angeles Times.*

Weeklies. Other newspapers include specialized weeklies, **shoppers**, and other publications. These local papers are not as affected, as national and metro dailies, by the ups and downs of the national economy because they serve a local market—and are less dependent on national advertising. Local businesses run ads

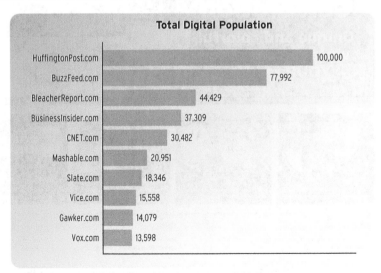

Total Digital Population

HuffingtonPost.com	100,000
BuzzFeed.com	77,992
BleacherReport.com	44,429
BusinessInsider.com	37,309
CNET.com	30,482
Mashable.com	20,951
Slate.com	18,346
Vice.com	15,558
Gawker.com	14,079
Vox.com	13,598

FIGURE 4.4 **TOP DIGITAL-NATIVE NEWS ENTITIES**

http://www.journalism.org/2015/04/29/digital-news-audience-fact-sheet/

5,000 STORIES A DAY Bloomberg produces general and specialized news online and in newspapers, magazines, radio, TV, and apps for news bureaus in 73 countries. (http://www.bloomberg.com/company/bloomberg-facts/)

in the local paper because of the focus on consumers and shoppers who are more likely to visit their stores and businesses in town.

Most weeklies—published fewer than four times a week—cover communities or rural areas that are too small to support a daily. About a third of weekly papers also cover the suburbs.

The Alternative Press. The alternative press is another form of weekly paper that is usually in tabloid form. The alternative press covers topics that the mainstream press can't or won't cover. Different types appear in many areas, including opinion weeklies, fashion or entertainment-oriented weeklies, such as the *Austin Chronicle* that is given away at music stores, bookstores, and other locations. These free weeklies are supported by advertising and cover dining out, movies, live concerts, and local events. Some cities also have political weeklies, and yet others have ethnic or minority group-oriented weeklies that focus on news and events within a particular community, and which add diversity to news coverage.

News Wire Services and Other Newspaper Sources. Many news service organizations—traditionally called *wire services* (see page 108)—contribute to newspaper content. International and national stories are taken directly from the news services or are combined with local reporting to put a unique local angle on international or national news.

THE FUNNIES King Features, of the Hearst Corporation, is one of the largest syndicates in the world, supplying news organizations with comics, crossword puzzles, editorials, and other nationally distributed features.

As you read earlier, the AP was the first wire service in America and it is still the leading national news service. For international news, the AP competes with Agence France-Presse (the oldest wire service in the world), Reuters (headquartered in London), the Interfax News Agency (headquartered in Moscow), and several other global news agencies.

Dozens of other news services, including those run by major newspaper chains, such as Gannett, or major metropolitan newspapers, such as the *Los Angeles Times–Washington Post* News Service, distribute stories written by their own reporters to other newspapers that subscribe to the service. Other news services not directly affiliated with newspapers, such as Bloomberg, gather news and write stories about specialized topics, such as finance or the environment.

POLITICS, THE INTERNET, AND SOCIAL MEDIA

Political campaigns discovered the power of the Internet and social media; they fanned the flames of passion among activists. A benchmark was the initially wildly successful Democratic primary campaign of Howard Dean in 2004 that was driven in part by passionate young bloggers, who created a buzz of political excitement, raised millions of dollars, and organized a grassroots campaign of house parties, street canvassers, and phone callers.

President Obama was the first politician to successfully leverage social media in his 2008 and 2012 campaigns with his AMA (Ask Me Anything) on Reddit to reach young voters and minority populations. Hillary Clinton and Jeb Bush announced their 2016 presidential nominations on Snapchat and Instagram for the 2016 election. Still others have used social media to raise millions of dollars (Green, 2015).

As you consider the numbers below, you can see that the Internet and social media have a great impact on spreading news and information that affects society and culture within the global village.

Internet

- 3.175 billion Internet users (half of the world's population)
- 367 million websites
- 300 million registered domain names (6 million added in the first quarter of 2015)

Social media

- 210 billion e-mails sent daily (80% are spam!)
- 152 million blogs
- 347 registered users on LinkedIn

- 646 million people on Twitter; 284 are active users
- 58 million tweets per day
- 500 million people on Facebook
- 468 million people on China's Wechat
- 22 percent of teenagers log on to Facebook more than 10 times a day
- 4.2 billion videos watched per day on YouTube
- 3.25 billion hours of video watched per month on YouTube
- 70 percent of YouTube users are outside the United States
- 100 million monthly users on SnapChat
- 300 million users on Instagram
- 70 million photos and videos are sent daily on Instagram
- 70 million users on Pinterest

Mobile Social Media

- 541 million mobile social media users
- 1 million mobile social users added per day

Numbers vary according to sources:

Social Media Today (2015). http://www.socialmediatoday.com/social-networks/kadie-regan/2015-08-10/10-amazing-social-media-growth-stats-2015

Bullas, J. (2015). Social Media Facts and Statistics You Should Know. http://www.jeffbullas.com/2015/04/08/33-social-media-facts-and-statistics-you-should-know-in-2015/

statisticsbrain.com/social-networking-statistics

Still other news syndicates supply subscribing news organizations with comics, crossword puzzles, and editorials by national columnists, all popular staples of newspapers. The King Features Syndicate, a subsidiary of the Hearst Corporation, is the largest. Syndicators employ the cartoonists and the editorial writers or make distribution arrangements with writers' "home" newspaper organizations. They then resell the funnies and commentaries to other newspapers on a contractual basis.

Citizen Journalism and Citizen News Sites

In addition to newspaper websites, citizen journalism sites and citizen news sites have emerged. If the site has professional journalists writing the news, then it is termed *citizen journalism*. If those contributing are not professional journalists, then a more appropriate term for the websites is *citizen news*.

These sites emerged for two reasons: (1) The cost to begin an online news site is relatively cheap and (2) private citizens or professional journalists feel that their town is not being covered as well as it should be by other news sources. Citizen journalism and citizen news sites have taken on a special importance in developing countries or countries that do not have a free press. In countries where authorities control the traditional news outlets, such as in the Middle East, people turned to citizen journalism and citizen news sites on the Internet for accurate information about Arab Spring movements and backlashes. In these countries, people felt they could trust the news that other citizens witnessed and could see what was happening from the photos and videos uploaded from phones.

MEDIA *LITERACY*

CHAIN OWNERSHIP AND CONGLOMERATES

Family-owned newspapers were once common in the industry—and many still exist, especially in local or regional markets. However, many family-owned newspaper organizations have become large, publicly traded companies, such as The McClatchy Company (with 30 daily newspapers), that buy up newspapers in order to obtain a **local market monopoly,** while pursuing national horizontal integration of newspapers across the United States. Some companies then consolidate their newspapers with other types of media outlets— broadcast, digital, mobile, and other publishing properties. Some mergers put newspapers into vertically integrated groups to share content with their radio, television, website, and mobile holdings.

> **Local market monopoly** occurs when one company owns (controls) the media in that community.

As with most industries, the media landscape is fluid. Let's take for example the Gannett Company, which began in 1906. It owns 92 U.S. daily local newspapers, including *USA Today*, and connects with 100 million unique U.S. digital news consumers. Its U.S. assets are valued at $9.2 billion. It also owns 160 U.K. daily local newspapers and about 640 nondaily news products. It has more than 31,500 employees.

In 2014, Gannett split into two companies, retaining the Gannett name for its publishing and related digital assets and Tegna for its broadcasting products.

Gannett recently bought the Journal Media Group. When the dust settles from this sale, it will add about 15 daily newspapers, 18 weeklies, and several other types of publications to Gannett's portfolio.

Only a year before, E. W. Scripps bought Journal Communications and they placed the newspapers in one basket (renamed Journal Media Group) and the broadcasting entities (retaining the E. W. Scripps name) in another.

Here is the first point: several large media companies recently have split their publication and broadcast companies into two groups. The second point is that now all of the newspapers from three large media companies—Gannett, Scripps, and Journal Communications—are under one roof . . . Gannett. This consolidation might have an effect on the type and quality of news read by people across the country.

Newspaper chains and media-consolidated companies, such as Gannett, own news-related businesses. There are also companies—called conglomerates—that own seemingly unrelated businesses. For example, media conglomerate News Corporation, owned by Rupert Murdoch, has holdings in every type of media internationally, as well as books and films and other entertainment businesses. Media critics worry that news might become biased to further an owner's other interests.

A recent trend is for private owners to buy newspapers when prices have lowered. They decided newspapers were a good investment and wanted to improve the journalism in their communities. For example, investor Warren Buffett bought his Omaha hometown newspaper and 63 other Media General newspapers with the result of reviving the news media conglomerate. The *Columbia Journalism Review* website (cjr.org/resources) offers a guide on who owns the major media companies.

LOCAL NEWS MONOPOLIES

Most U.S. cities are served by one newspaper. The result is a local monopoly that has political, economic, and social effects. Politically, the one newspaper is likely to reflect a single editorial perspective, although other local media may reflect alternate viewpoints. Economically, newspaper choices available to both advertisers and readers are reduced, which can lead to higher subscription and advertising rates. Socially, readers are all depending on the one newspaper for accurate information to lead productive lives. Sometimes people won't ever know what the newspaper doesn't report.

Traditionally, owning more than one media organization within one market was prohibited because it did not produce a diversity of voices whose opinions could be heard. However, in the 1980s, the Reagan administration relaxed restrictions on horizontal integration in the belief that the role of government should be reduced so that competition could thrive. As a result, major newspaper group owners have steadily acquired more newspapers. In 2008, the Federal Communications Commission (FCC) decided to allow companies to own newspapers and broadcast outlets in the same city, as long as the company was able to show that local news coverage would improve as a result. The federal court overturned the decision, not because of its merits, but because not enough time was given for public comment before the ruling was made. Local cross-ownership is now back in court. Many people do not realize they are getting their news from the same parent company. For example, the largest newspaper group in the United States, Gannett, now owns 88 daily newspapers and about 850 nondaily publications, in addition to its 23 TV stations and online and digital properties.

Joint operation agreements (JOAs) have been one solution to the problem of excessive concentration. When competing newspapers cannot survive

Joint operation agreements (JOAs) allow competing newspapers to share resources while maintaining editorial independence.

economically, they can negotiate an agreement with each other to share facilities, production costs, administrative structure, and advertising while attempting to maintain editorial independence. That negotiated limit on competition was permitted by the Newspaper Preservation Act of 1970. Seven cities maintain two newspapers through JOAs.

In Detroit, for example, the liberal *Detroit Free Press* and the more conservative *Detroit News* have a JOA. They share facilities and keep their writers separate.

PROFESSIONAL AND AMATEUR NEWS SITES

Entrepreneurs sometimes see a niche in topics or in the community that they feel is not covered adequately, if at all. Most of these sites have hyperlocal news—that is unique to their communities. They try to fill this niche with a news website, mainly because it is easier to start an online newspaper than a print one. Some of these niches are filled with social media sites—citizen journalism sites (with professional journalists offering context and meaning to news) or citizen news sites (often nonprofessionals blogs and videos) that also compete for advertisers.

News consumers should know the difference (media literacy) in these news websites. Professional journalists are trained to research information, verify sources, and report stories in ways meaningful and helpful to their audiences. Many untrained citizens simply repeat what someone has said (gossip) without verifying tweets or quotes—and then call it "news." When news sites are run by nonjournalists, however well intentioned, there is a danger that the credibility of the news will be undermined by these amateur efforts.

DOMAIN NAMES

The Internet grew by 6 million domain names overall in just the first 6 months of 2015! Such a proliferation of news and information! Many news organizations now include the domain name of .news to highlight their credibility. But don't be fooled by .news! With 10,000 registrations of .news within the first week of availability, it appears that a lot of people are buying it.

FREEDOM OF SPEECH AND THE FIRST AMENDMENT

Newspapers have been far more protected in freedom of speech than have electronic media, such as radio and television. There have been few attempts in the United States to limit freedom of speech or of the press.

For instance, during the 1950s, the anti-communist campaign of Senator Joseph McCarthy resulted in many authors being blacklisted (many were falsely accused of being Communist sympathizers), which prevented them from publishing books or writing for Hollywood films and television. However, McCarthy steered away from directly attacking newspapers, including how they covered Communism (perhaps because he needed press coverage). Freedom of the press has enabled journalists to take unpopular stands. It tends to protect journalists in the United States from outside pressure to avoid certain stories. But in many other countries, journalists face outright pressures—their stories are censored, they are fired, or they are threatened or even killed. The International Federation of Journalists, composed of journalists from more than 100 countries, works to defend press freedom and social justice (ifj.org). The Committee to Protect Journalists (cpj.org) keeps a tally of the number of journalists detained or killed in Iraq and other countries. Another international organization, Reporters without Borders, tracks the degree of freedom and censorship of the press—through print or the Internet—in different countries (en.rsf.org).

ETHICS

Journalists know their stories are scrutinized by thousands of readers. They know their stories need to be accurate—from the correct spelling of people's names to placing the information in the appropriate context. Readers use the information from news outlets to make the good decisions that lead to productive lives—from paying taxes to voting to making real-estate purchases—so journalists need to get it right.

The accuracy and objectivity of information has long been a primary consideration of journalists and of their news organizations. Accuracy means fair and balanced information when gathering, organizing, and presenting the news. Journalists strive to be objective by reporting without favoritism or self-interest. It means avoiding stereotypes and unsubstantiated allegations. The ethical treatment of a news story is a question of credibility for media organizations that can affect their success at all levels from economic survival to perceived prestige. Accuracy and objectivity are professional obligations that are treated in more detail in Chapter 17.

Thousands of reporters do their jobs well. However, the nature of the news business exposes the reporter who is a "bad apple." Journalists who get it right are rarely named, but those who have become unethical are often publicized. In recent years, **plagiarism, fabrication,** and **anonymous sources** have gotten reporters in trouble. Sometimes, inexperienced journalists use quotes and wording from online sources or press releases and fail to attribute the sources. This is considered plagiarism. Reporters also try to avoid using anonymous sources because they place doubt in a reader's mind as to why the person can't stand up for what he or she is saying. When a person speaks to a reporter on the condition of anonymity, the journalist can use that as a lead to find someone who is willing to be named.

When newspapers make an error, they correct it immediately online or acknowledge it with a correction in print somewhere near where the error appeared or in a standard corrections box the next day. Substantial errors, particularly those that may have damaged the reputations or careers of the persons covered, are acknowledged in follow-up stories or in a letter to readers from the editor.

News organizations have a social responsibility to the public to present news accurately. In addition, ethical lapses are bad business. Numerous retractions are bad for business because readers go elsewhere for the news, and then there are fewer audience members to sell to advertisers.

Plagiarism is using someone else's ideas and work without citation.

Fabrication is information that is made up instead of emerging from facts.

Anonymous sources are people who give reporters information but do not allow the publication of their names.

ICP/AGE Fotostock

VERIFY! Twitter is a quick and easy way to get information. It is sometimes so quick that the information has yet to be verified—unless it is from a trained journalist.

Most news organizations have codes of ethics (see Chapter 17), which set them apart from other news and information sources and sites. Journalistic ethics standards require very careful checking for accuracy. One of the reasons that websites for well-known newspapers are important news and information sources for Internet users is that they continue to offer a high level of accuracy compared with many other sites that are not so careful (see Chapter 17). But increasingly, blogs provide an important check on the accuracy of mainstream journalism.

PUBLIC'S RIGHT TO KNOW VERSUS INDIVIDUAL PRIVACY

Privacy issues revolve around a conflict between the public's right to know something and the right of private citizens to keep it to themselves. The media treat public figures differently than private citizens. However, many questions remain about just how closely public figures can be scrutinized before the boundary of ethical behavior is crossed. Some journalists disregard the adulterous affairs of a public official, whereas other critics reason that if a marital promise is broken then it points to personal character and potentially broken promises to constituents.

Libel. Freedom of the press is not absolute, even in the United States. The publication of libel, defamation, and the invasion of privacy are not protected by the First Amendment. Libel and slander refer, respectively, to printing and to making false statements about private citizens that might damage their reputations. Writing true things about someone is not libel (see The Colonial and Revolutionary Freedom Struggles, page 104). Libel, however, is handled differently for private and public individuals. For example, tweeters who write nasty things about their relationships may find themselves facing a libel suit from a "significant other," whereas similar nasty comments can be made about public figures, such as the president.

Laws against libel are supposed to protect the reputations, welfare, and dignity of private citizens. Public figures, such as media professionals, celebrities, and public officials, are not generally protected against libel on the theory that they have chosen to act in the public sphere and not remain private citizens. This is because the U.S. legal policy balances libel concerns against the watchdog role of the press, which is to expose corruption or incompetence on the part of officials or public figures. When people take a public position and seek publicity for their views, then libel against them is also harder to prove. They have become public figures.

Tabloid Journalism. Sensational supermarket **tabloids**, such as the *National Enquirer* ("Enquiring Minds Need to Know!"), whose headlines you read as you stand in the grocery store checkout line, have questionable methods and stories. Contrary to journalism ethics codes, tabloids are known to pay their sources for information, and sources often will falsify information or exaggerate in order to be useful.

Celebrity blogs, such as Perez Hilton, and paparazzi are not considered journalists, mostly because they do not follow codes of ethics. Paparazzi usually are photographers who intentionally invade the privacy of celebrities, in an effort to snap a photo to sell to magazines, such as *Globe* ("Bill Is Not

Tabloids are newspapers focused on popular, sensational events.

Chelsea's Father!") and *ok!* ("Justin Bieber and Selena Gomez Get Intimate in Two Instagram Videos").

BEING A GOOD WATCHDOG TODAY

Investigative reporting became a hallmark of the newspaper profession in the 1960s and 1970s with Vietnam and Watergate, and students flooded into journalism schools. Today, the watchdog role has spread from major national newspapers and websites to smaller local newspapers and community blogs. Investigative journalism is practiced in all corners of the globe. For example, as a result of a story called "Stock Option Abuses" by *The Wall Street Journal,* 130 companies and 60 top executives were under federal investigation for rewarding themselves illegally through stock options. Blogs have expanded the investigative role by adding to the number of watchdogs. That incident showed two things about blogs as watchdogs: many of these blogs are partisan and run by people driven by political passion. Blogs are a part of a partisan media system that serves as both watchdog and agenda-setter for the less partisan press. Conservative bloggers often turn up material that then appears on conservative radio talk shows, then in cable talk shows, then Fox News, and then perhaps the national press. Similar patterns can be seen on the liberal side. The movie *Spotlight* also showed the power of the press to expose and right a wrong for the good of individuals and society. It portrays *Boston Globe* reporters in 2001 who investigated allegations of the sexual abuse of 80 boys by a former priest and the cover-up of sexual abuse within the Roman Catholic Church.

Journalists argue that their "watchdog" role is to be critical, to hold people and institutions responsible for their actions, especially while other people, such as politicians, companies, and their public relations staff, are pushing only "good" news about their policies or institutions. Furthermore, reporters argue that watchdog journalism is in fact what sells news; the public wants to know what their local government is doing, how any wrongdoing affects them, and how the situation can be improved.

NEWS EDITORS AND GATEKEEPING

Newspapers perform important functions for audiences. Some newspapers that focus on government policy, such as the *New York Times,* pride themselves on having an influential readership and on sometimes shaping policy debates with their articles. *The Wall Street Journal* focuses on reaching the business elite but aims at government policy makers too. The *Christian Science Monitor* (csmonitor.com) offers internationally oriented news. The *Los Angeles Times,* especially its calendar section, serves the film, music, and television industries. Readers look to these newspapers in part to tell them what is important in these areas.

Editors do several things that require human intuition and creativity. First, they perform a *gatekeeping* function: they tell you about important issues and events happening in the world that you ought to know. Thus, you avoid the frustration of reading more of what you already know. Second, newspapers and magazines can make intelligent suggestions about new things that you

STOP & REVIEW

1. What are the main sections and content of newspapers?

2. Is there still a mass audience for newspapers?

3. What are the concerns about monopolies in the news industry?

4. Can social media counter these concerns about monopolies since more people can comment on stories and news events and issues?

5. What are the main ethical issues for newspaper reporters?

may be interested in beyond what you already know. This helps you avoid the claustrophobic narrowness of interests implied by Negroponte's idea of a "Daily Me," that is, a newspaper customized exactly to our own specific interests.

By definition, however, gatekeepers must make choices about the issues and events covered. Not all of the infinite number of things that happen every day can be reported, nor all points of view: there simply isn't the space nor the resources. Some social media provide a check on the gatekeepers. For example, major news organizations were slow to report the killing of Trayvon Martin by a neighborhood watchman and began to pay attention only after a major outcry on Facebook and Twitter.

Most people who want news and information about their community or the world continue to prefer the classic editing and gatekeeping functions that a good newspaper provides, whether that newspaper appears in print or digital. With so many people on the Internet writing their thoughts and opinions, it is hard to separate fact from fiction. With all of the events and issues in a community or internationally, professional journalists determine what audiences would want to know, check facts several times over for accuracy, find varying points of view to provide a comprehensive story, and follow up on that issue or event. They help audiences understand what is happening in the world around us.

SUMMARY&REVIEW

WHAT ESTABLISHED THE PRECEDENTS FOR PRESS FREEDOM IN COLONIAL AMERICA?

The colonial press was often critical of British governors. In a key case in 1733, John Peter Zenger published a newspaper critical of the British governor of New York. Zenger was jailed for criminal libel. Despite British legal precedent to the contrary, Zenger's lawyer Andrew Hamilton successfully argued that the truth of a published piece was a defense against libel.

WHAT WAS THE PENNY PRESS? WHAT LED TO IT?

By 1800 most large cities had at least one daily, but circulation was limited to the political and business elite. By 1830, new technological inventions made possible lower-cost papers aimed at a broader audience. More people were learning to read, public education was expanding, wages were increasing, and more people were gathering in cities. Benjamin Day launched the first low-cost daily, *The Sun*, in 1833. It sold for only a penny.

WHAT WAS MUCKRAKING?

In the early 1900s, crusading newspapers turned their attention to exposing scandals and corruption in government and among industry cartels. Muckraking contributed to several acts of legislation designed to reform various industries for the good of society.

WHAT ARE THE DIFFERENCES BETWEEN NEW JOURNALISM AND YELLOW JOURNALISM?

After the Civil War, the new journalism covered stories that would interest the average person: divorces, police news, scandals, disasters, and features about prominent personalities and social events, such as weddings, deaths, and parties. Sensationalism, with exciting illustrations, large headlines, elaborate descriptions, and exaggerated stories initially spiraled into the yellow journalism of Hearst, Pulitzer, and Bennett in the late 1800s, although some of it is still very much alive today.

WHEN DID NEWSPAPERS PEAK AS MASS AUDIENCE MEDIA?

The efficiency of newspaper printing increased rapidly and coincided with the peak of the newspapers' monopoly as a mass medium by about 1920. The newspaper industry had grown larger than its advertising and circulation could support. In addition to other print publications, motion pictures and the phonograph began to vie for people's attention and money. Newspapers' status would be challenged again by radio in 1927, by television in the 1950s, and by the Internet today.

WHAT WAS THE IMPACT OF WATERGATE ON AMERICAN JOURNALISM?

Woodward and Bernstein went against the tide and dug into a presidential cover-up story that ultimately led to Richard Nixon's resignation from the presidency. This story is pointed to as a test of courage and tenacity, exemplifying the watchdog role of the press and investigative reporting.

WHAT ARE THE MAIN RECENT TRENDS IN NEWSPAPER DELIVERY TECHNOLOGIES?

Newspapers were often delivered directly in cities and in bulk along railroads and shipping lines. In the 1990s, delivery by the World Wide Web became an alternative for "newspaper" delivery. Today, print news is increasingly delivered to e-readers, tablets, and handheld devices that replicate the look of a newspage.

WHAT IS THE IMPACT OF THE INTERNET ON NEWSPAPERS?

Newspapers can now reach more audiences through the World Wide Web. However, readers have more access to more news online. Newspapers must now compete for readers with a rapidly increasing variety of websites, such as other online newspapers, wire services, search engine news links, citizen journalism websites, and social media such as blogs, online commentary, Facebook, YouTube, and Twitter.

WHAT ARE THE MAIN NATIONAL DAILY NEWSPAPERS?

The Wall Street Journal is a specialized business paper with a broad general readership. The *New York Times* specializes in interpretation of the news and focuses on media and business. *USA Today* carries shorter news items and more entertainment. National dailies have responded to a public interest in national and international news and have been able to reach national audiences at an affordable price by using new technology for satellite delivery to primary plants. Almost all of them contain ads.

HOW IS THE NEWSPAPER BUSINESS MODEL CHANGING?

Newspapers depended on advertising—and most still do. They would sell audiences to advertisers; the larger the audience, the more the newspapers can attract and charge advertisers. However, more newspapers are now charging for content by raising subscription prices (for print and digital) and putting up pay walls for nonsubscribers. The metered pay model allows nonsubscribers to read only 10 articles on the news site and about three on the news app. If readers want more, they have to become subscribers. Thus, news organizations are becoming more reliant on circulation revenue.

WHAT ARE THE MAIN SECTIONS AND CONTENTS OF NEWSPAPERS?

The national newspapers stress international news, national news, editorials and commentaries, and business, with some lifestyle and entertainment news. Metropolitan dailies usually focus more on local and regional news including local lifestyles, entertainment, sports, and comics. Many weeklies focus almost exclusively on local events, shopping, and entertainment.

WHAT IS THE IMPACT OF NEWSPAPER MOBILE APPS ON NEWSPAPER WEBSITES?

More people enjoy reading their news from mobile apps (phones and tablets). The look and feel of the digital appear more like the traditional print newspaper that they are comfortable reading at leisure. Many consumers prefer the traditional design to that of the website they access with a computer. They also like "turning" the pages rather than clicking on links. With mobile news apps, more people are spending more time reading news and getting it from more sources than before.

WHY ARE THERE CONCERNS ABOUT CONSOLIDATION IN THE NEWSPAPER INDUSTRY?

A number of formerly competitive newspapers have entered into joint operation agreements to share facilities, costs, administrative structure, and advertising while attempting to maintain editorial independence. However, the lack of competition and the nature of the joint operation may well reduce independence and diversity in editorial points of view. Chain ownership may similarly reduce local independence and standardize editorial and reporting approaches across the country. Cross-ownership at the local level between newspapers, radio, broadcast, cable, and satellite television is also a concern, particularly when newspapers owned by chains are also part of media cross-ownership.

SHOULD WE WORRY ABOUT CONGLOMERATES?

Large corporations that own many companies other than newspapers might have a tendency to make purely business decisions that affect journalistic ethical standards. A conglomerate that has entertainment holdings might use the newspaper to promote its other businesses.

WHAT FIRST AMENDMENT ISSUES AFFECT PRINT MEDIA?

Freedom of the press for newspapers has been limited at times by concerns about libel, defamation, and invasion of privacy, but within the media and courts, freedom of speech has usually been the dominant principle.

WHAT ARE THE MAIN ETHICAL ISSUES FOR NEWSPAPERS?

The main ethical issues for newspapers revolve around accuracy, fairness, and balance. Journalists must also consider each case separately to help the most number of people while incurring the least harm, such as in weighing the public's right to know with individual privacy.

THINKING CRITICALLY
ABOUT THE MEDIA

1. What is the proper role of a free press in a democratic society?

2. Go through your local newspaper—in print, on the Internet, or mobile device—and describe the objective of each section. How do local newspapers differ from national ones in content?

3. Why do most people prefer getting their news from a traditional news organization (whether in print or digital) with an editor than searching online or reading a blog?

4. What does it mean for journalists to be the watchdogs?

5. What is news for you? And what should be news?

KEY TERMS

abolitionist (p. 80)

anonymous source (p. 105)

backpack journalism (p. 88)

blog (p. 91)

conglomerate (p. 86)

convergence (p. 89)

corantos (p. 77)

dateline (p. 77)

diversity (p. 79)

fabrication (p. 105)

hard news (p. 98)

joint operation agreements (JOA) (p. 103)

libel (p. 78)

local market monopoly (p. 102)

marketplace of ideas (p. 78)

metered pay model (p. 95)

muckraking (p. 85)

new journalism (p. 82)

news aggregates (p. 97)

news industry business model (p. 95)

objectivity (p. 85)

partisan press (p. 79)

paywall model (p. 95)

Penny Press (p. 80)

plagiarism (p. 105)

scoop (p. 82)

seditious speech (p. 79)

shopper (p. 99)

social responsibility model (p. 86)

soft news (p. 98)

tabloid (p. 106)

teletext (p. 90)

unique visitors per month (p. 99)

videotex (p. 89)

wire service (p. 81)

yellow journalism (p. 83)

MindTap

Test your knowledge with online printable flashcards and online quizzing.

MindTap Log on to the MindTap Communication for *Media Now to* access a variety of additional material, including this chapter's e-book, learning objectives, comprehension quizzes, videos, and more!

MAGAZINES

LEARNING OBJECTIVES

After studying the topics in this chapter, you will be able to:

1 Give at least one example of the impact of muckraking on political or social reform.
2 Compare the different economic strategies used in the magazine publishing industry to target a mass or segmented audience.
3 Discuss how technology has changed the magazine business.
4 Define the measurements of audience, circulation number, and pass-along rate.
5 Understand intellectual property and copyright issues.

HISTORY

Early Magazines

Magazines began to develop in Great Britain in the 1700s. They carried fiction and nonfiction in varying degrees, depending on the readership. The first was the British *Gentleman's Magazine* of 1731, whose editors deliberately left news to the newspapers and focused on elegant and amusing writing about literature, politics, history, biography, and criticism (Riley, 1993). This formula still characterizes much of magazine content: humor; fiction; and essays about politics, literature, music, theater, and famous people.

The first American magazines debuted in 1741 in Philadelphia, the nation's first center for magazines. William Bradford's *American Magazine* lasted for 3 months, whereas its competitor, Ben Franklin's *General Magazine and Historical Chronicle,* was printed 3 days later and lived for 6 months. Publishers tried to popularize several other short-lived magazines prior to the American Revolution, but all were limited by too few readers with leisure time to read, high costs of publishing, and expensive distribution by horse-drawn coaches.

During the American Revolution, magazines became more political. For example, Thomas Paine edited *Pennsylvania Magazine,* which urged revolution. Despite the emphasis on politics, many magazines in

MAGAZINES are available in print and digital formats, found at newsstands and on smart devices.

iain Masterton/Age fotostock/Superstock

the 1700s were called **miscellanies** and appealed to a small, far-flung, and diverse audience. After the American Revolution, magazines took a while to succeed economically. Magazines were given no cost break in postal rates until 1794 (Riley, 1993), so few magazines were widely read or long-lived until the 1800s (Tebbel, 1969).

The fledgling American publishing industry was given a significant economic boost by the first U.S. Congress with the passage of the Copyright Act of 1790. This legislation gave authors and their publishers exclusive rights to their publications for a period of 14 years (renewable for an additional 14 years). During that time, anyone who wished to reproduce the work would have to make a payment, called a *royalty fee,* to the copyright holder for the use of the work.

As the 1700s drew to a close, American magazines were aimed at the better-educated and wealthy elite and a small but growing middle class. Publishers took up political causes, siding with Federalists (promoting a strong central government, a federal system) or their opposition (wanting a state-oriented, decentralized government). The political organ of the Federalist movement, *Port Folio,* was the first magazine to achieve substantial national circulation and contained essays such as Alexander Hamilton's "Federalist Papers," promoting the passage of the Constitution. A formidable anti-Federalist magazine, the *National Magazine of Richmond,* was one of the few magazines published outside the dominant publishing centers of Philadelphia, Boston, and New York.

In the early 1800s, there was a new trend toward "literary miscellanies," such as the *Saturday Evening Post,* whose editors moved from reproducing European literature to popularizing American writers. They covered weekly events, history, politics, art, reviews, travelogues, short stories, and serialized fiction. "Special miscellanies" focused on specific topics and audiences. Sarah Josepha Hale's *Ladies' Magazine* of Boston was the first successful American magazine targeted toward women and was soon followed by *Godey's Lady's Book.* By the 1840s, magazines shifted their attention toward broader and more sustainable mass audiences.

During the Civil War era, magazines began to have a much greater impact on public life. Several magazines grew to fame for their coverage and illustrations dramatizing scenes of the war. Magazines such as *Harper's Weekly* created an important new form of publication, the illustrated newsweekly. During the war, talented correspondents quickly sketched battle scenes that were sent back home to the magazine for artists to fill in with detail. Then **woodcuts** were quartered so that different parts of the scene could be carved by different artists simultaneously and put back together, so the illustration could be published with its news story as soon as possible.

> **Miscellanies** were magazines with a wide variety of content.

MindTap®
Start with a quick warm-up activity.

> **Woodcuts** were used to make illustrations by carving a picture in a block of wood, inking it, and pressing it onto paper.

North Wind / North Wind Picture Archives

THE CIVIL WAR ILLUSTRATED The vivid illustrations of Civil War action in *Harper's Weekly,* like these images in woodcuts of the attack on Santa Rosa Island and of Mathew Brady's photograph of Capt. S. F. DuPont, attracted large readership in the 1860s. To examine larger and more woodcuts in this issue, see www.sonofthesouth.net.

MEDIA THEN··· MEDIA NOW

1440
> Gutenberg introduces movable type printing press to the West

1741
> First American magazine published

1790
> Copyright Act gives authors and publishers rights to their works

1846
> Rotary press speeds printing for mass publications

1879
> Postal Act lowers rates for mailing magazines

1950s
> Magazines experience competition from television for advertisers and audiences

1906
> Pure Food and Drug Act results from muckracking by Collier's magazine

1923
> Time magazine introduced

1990s
> Magazine-like pages and sites proliferate on the Internet

1998
> Digital Millennium Copyright Term Extension Act ratified

MindTap

Read, highlight, and take notes on the complete chapter text in a rich interactive online platform.

1741

First American magazine published

America Reads

As the U.S. postal system improved, methods of transportation became reliable, and as more people appreciated literature as an important form of knowledge and entertainment, magazines grew into a major mass medium in the 1800s.

Magazines benefited particularly from a major change in their delivery system. The Postal Act of 1879 clarified that magazines were second-class mail and were given a special, lower rate for distribution. Within 40 years, the number of magazines grew almost sevenfold, to 1,800 (Riley, 1993). Today's mail classifications have changed, and magazines are now grouped under the Periodicals class of mail.

Many students today would not recognize a magazine of the 1800s. Most were octavo sized (a little larger than 6 × 3 × 9 inches) with matte (nonglossy) pages. Covers had ornate, illustrated woodcut borders and the table of contents, listing titles and authors, was centered in the middle. By the late 1800s, the flowing borders and the table of contents gave way to elaborate artistic drawings surrounding the magazine's name. Color and more sophisticated drawings surrounding teasers about content were new innovations in the early 1900s. And as reliance on advertisers grew, so did the number of pages devoted to ads. Many magazines charged about $250 for full-page ads, which were grouped together in the front and back of the periodical, separately numbered, and often bound together as a pamphlet that could be lifted out of the book. *Harper's New Monthly Magazine* (April 1894) cost 35 cents, whereas the average factory worker's wage was 5 to 20 cents an hour. A sample of the content shows illustrations, including one by Frederic Remington; a story by journalist Richard Harding Davis; vignettes; poems; history; political events and issues; and a "monthly record of current events."

By the twentieth century, most Americans were literate and could afford small luxuries, such as magazines, which were cheaper than ever before. They had more leisure time to read, as both the agricultural and industrial economies developed, and their interest in civic affairs, the arts, professional matters, and politics boomed. New **genres** appeared—investigative magazines, digests, **news magazines,** and pictorial magazines. An increasing sense of openness and freedom in the press expanded the number of topics acceptable to magazine readers. By the early twentieth century, popular "pulp" fiction magazines, named for the cheap, pulpy paper they used, began to push the bounds of social acceptability with sensationalism—police stories, romance, crime mysteries, scandals, science fiction, and fantasy.

> **Genres** are distinctive styles of creative works. The term is also used to represent different types or formats of media content.

> **News magazines** are weekly periodicals with coverage (text and visual) on current news events.

> **Muckraking** is investigative journalism that "rakes off the muck"—dirt and filth—to expose corruption and scandal.

Muckraking

In the late 1800s and early 1900s, magazines began to overtake newspapers in investigative reporting and crusades for reform. Much of this investigative reporting, known as **muckraking,** appeared in *McClure's* and *Collier's,* nationally circulated and inexpensive magazines that reached millions of readers and had a great impact on public opinion. The term refers to reporters being willing to stir up and sift through the unpleasant aspects of public life that most people ignore and to identify and publicize misdeeds by public figures. Magazine journalism looked for crusading reporters who could report and write controversial, striking stories that would draw in a mass audience.

In 1918, during the Progressive Era (which ran from 1890 to the end of World War II), reform politicians, unions, rural associations, and magazine and newspaper reporters protested the power of big business and the conservative politics of the parties in power. Reformers pushed for more social, economic, and political justice, like the regulation of food and drug purity, child labor laws, a shorter workday, a minimum wage, job safety rules, reduced political corruption, and government regulation of

Bettmann/Corbis

MUCKRAKER In the early twentieth century, Ida Tarbell gained prominence as one of the leading magazine writers by exposing the abuses of the Standard Oil Company.

NEWS MAGAZINES

The news magazine genre was born in 1923 when Henry Luce and Briton Hadden started *Time* magazine. Its success led Thomas Martyn (a former foreign correspondent for *Time*) in 1933 to launch *Newsweek*. Then, Time Inc. founder Henry Luce bought *LIFE*, a general-interest magazine in print since 1883, because he wanted the rights to the name. He went a step further and turned *LIFE* into a weekly news magazine that focused on photojournalism.

LIFE met the public's desire for a photographic report of the world with pictures of the week's events and fairly short news analyses, creating a visual style of journalism. Almost a century later, competition for advertisers and audiences from an upstart mass medium with moving pictures—led to the first closing of *LIFE* in 1972 and, after several revivals, a final closing in 2007, although some special issues continue to be published. No doubt the proliferation of colorful photos and well-designed pages on the Internet also influenced those decisions.

The Pew Research Center annually studies the major types of news media. For example, of the most prominent news magazines in 2012, four increased their combined print and digital subscription rates (*The Economist, The New Yorker, The Atlantic,* and *The Week*), one stabilized (*Newsweek*), and one decreased by 1 percent (*Time*). Single-copy sales at the newsstand dropped for all of the titles. Ad pages also declined except for *Newsweek*. However, digital circulation sales rose for all of the news magazines except *Time*, which remained the same as the prior year.

Contrary to the other news magazines, *The Week* does not do in-depth reporting but collects and summarizes (aggregates) the reporting of recent news events from other publications. It was started in 2001, and continues to grow. When

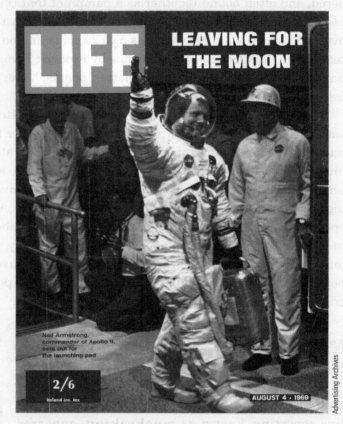

LIFE — **LEAVING FOR THE MOON**

Neil Armstrong, commander of Apollo 11, sets out for the launching pad

2/6
Ireland inc. tax

AUGUST 4 · 1969

Advertising Archives

A PICTURE IS WORTH A THOUSAND WORDS The dynamic photojournalism of *LIFE* magazine pioneered a visual approach to the news that was later copied by television.

The Week launched an iPad app early in 2012, online traffic rose 71 percent, according to Nielsen NetView. The content is different from the print. About 30 new stories daily motivate readers to return frequently. Print subscriptions rose 4 percent and overall circulation (single-copy purchases and subscriptions to both print and digital) rose 4.4 percent, second in the news magazine group only to *The Atlantic*, with a 4.7 percent increase.

1950s

Magazines experience competition from television for advertisers and audiences

big-business excess. Editor Ida Tarbell, from *McClure's,* wrote a meticulous muckraking exposé that was devoured by the public on the unprincipled rise of Standard Oil Company under John D. Rockefeller's unethical business tactics. The 19-part series is still considered a hallmark in investigative journalism, and it is listed as fifth out of the top 100 influential works in American journalism, according to New York University (http://www.infoplease.com/ipea/A0777379.html).

Muckraking often led to landmark reform legislation in the first decade of the twentieth century. The Pure Food and Drug Act of 1906 resulted from an article in *Collier's* called "The Great American Fraud" by Samuel Hopkins Adams. The Mann Act, which prohibited transportation of women across state lines for immoral purposes, resulted from an article in *McClure's,* titled "Daughters of the Poor," by Burton J. Hendrick. And Upton Sinclair's *The Jungle,* a book about Chicago slaughterhouses, led to the Meat Inspection Act.

The term *muckraking* has now lost its crusading political meaning and today refers more to the investigation of sexual scandals and other "dirt" on public figures. However, contemporary journalists continue to target corruption and abuse of power with a crusading spirit that often results in positive change. Some current magazines—*The Nation* and *Mother Jones*—still specialize in muckraking journalism. Many Web magazines and blogs have also continued this tradition with commentary and opinion.

Most magazines did well even after television became popular. It was common for about 10 magazines to be artistically lined up on the coffee table in everyone's living rooms. And life was good—until the Great Recession of 2007. People who were strapped financially considered magazines as a luxury and circulations fell. Businesses cut advertising budgets and ad pages decreased. Five years later, the downward trend finally leveled off and subscriptions increased as the economy improved and magazines got a better handle on how to produce increasingly popular magazine apps for tablets. The *Ladies' Home Journal* is an example of an older, successful magazine with a narrow, and loyal, targeted audience. It holds on tightly to 12th place in circulation among the top magazines. Its staff has been imaginative and creative throughout the decades to compete with numerous other women's magazines and other media, such as radio, TV, streaming movies, DVDs, websites, and mobile devices.

STOP & REVIEW

1. Why and how did magazines develop?
2. What was the role of the print media in the Civil War?
3. What was *muckraking*?

Magazines Target Specialized Audiences

Magazines started out as publications for the elite—those who had money to buy a magazine, education to understand it, and time to read it. News magazines still attract elite audiences who are older, better educated, and wealthier than the average person.

Overall, however, magazines became general-interest publications to a mass audience as more people could afford them. After competing with television for mass audiences, magazines targeted specialized audiences—ages and interests—and have prospered as a whole through the years.

Doug Houghton / Alamy Stock Photo

READY TO RIDE Magazine publishing thrives on very specialized audiences, like car enthusiasts who want to keep up with the latest trends.

In 1950, there were 250 magazines in publication (Alsop, 1997, p. 929). Magazines today number more than 20,700—the highest number recorded by the National Directory of Magazines.

New magazines are launched at an average of two a day in the United States, with many folding by their second year (http://consultingandresearch .wordpress.com). Survival rate has improved recently. For example, 870 new magazines were launched in 2012 (and about the same number in 2013) with an 85 percent survival rate in their first year, the highest survival rate recorded. Of these new magazines, about 185 had a publication rate of four or more times a year (quarterly, monthly, weekly, etc.).

Recent decades have seen a proliferation of more specialized magazines for even narrower audiences. This trend has only accelerated. Today there's a magazine to cover almost every hobby, occupation, and interest, from canoeing to dairy farming (see Table 5.1).

TABLE 5.1 New U.S. Magazine Launches by Interest Category

NEW MAGAZINES BY INTEREST CATEGORY	
Crafts/games/hobbies/models	23
Special interest/lifestyle	19
Metropolitan/regional/state	18
Popular culture	15
Sports	13
Epicurean	11
Military/naval	10
Home	9
Children's	8
Ethnic	8
Automotive	8
Men's	7
Fitness	7
Women's	6
Fashion/beauty/grooming	5
Art/antiques	5
Fishing and hunting	5
Comic technique/comics	4
Motorcycles	4
Literary/reviews/writing	4
Gay/lesbian	4
Music	4
Gaming	4
Politics	3
Computers	3
Bridal	3
Health	3

(Continued on next page)

Travel	3
Pets	3
Business	2
Entertainment	2
Teen	2
Equine	2
Religion	1
Photography	1
Camping/outdoor recreation	1
Parenting	1

Source: http://www.magazine.org/sites/default/files/MPA-FACTbook2013-f-lo.pdf, p. 83.

TECHNOLOGY TRENDS

Printing Since Gutenberg

You learned in Chapter 3 about the printing revolution that was started with the invention of the printing press by Johannes Gutenberg around 1440.

The invention of the first rotary press was a significant advancement in printing. It improved upon the process of cylinder presses, and later used rotating drums in 1846. Unlike previous presses that printed on single sheets of paper one sheet at a time, rotary presses used rotating drums of type to print on both sides of large, continuous rolls of paper. Typesetting remained a slow, manual process until linotype machines were introduced, which cast entire lines of type from molten lead instantly.

Printed illustrations had been a staple of magazines since the Civil War (1861–1865), but only a few publications could afford them because they required the painstaking hand carving or engraving of wood or metal master plates. Lithography speeded the printing of illustrated pages by replacing engraving with a type of chemical etching. Photoengraving transformed illustrated publications by chemically etching images onto the surface of metal plates through a photographic process, a vast improvement over handmade lithographs. After World War II, offset printing was introduced, so an entire page of print, complete with illustrations, could be photographed and the photographic image transferred to a smooth metal plate with chemically etched images that could be inked and printed.

Publishing in the Information Age

At first, computers were put to work assisting typesetters, automatically hyphenating and spacing the type on each line. In the 1970s, computers replaced typesetting machines by transferring text directly to photographic film that in turn was transferred to metal printing plates. The computerization of the layout and paste-up process further simplified printing, as did the digitizing of photographs so that they could be edited and placed on a page electronically. Now companies produce magazines with **computer-to-plate** technology.

As more power and speed were packed into desktop computers, software enabled users to lay out pages on a personal computer and scanning became

Computer-to-plate technology transfers page images composed inside a computer directly to printing plates.

WANTED! WRITERS AND EDITORS!

Books and magazines have one of two purposes—to inform or to entertain—or both. Their content is mostly in the form of words and visuals.

In this section, we will concentrate on writers, authors, and editors in the book and magazine industries, although these businesses also include visual communicators, sales personnel, and promotion experts, among other professionals.

A wonderful aspect of being a journalist, writer, author, or editor is that—depending on your employer and the organization—you can write at home all day in your Captain America pajamas, or work at the office in your new "Dress for Success" suit, or gather information in the field in your Abercrombie-distressed jeans. The Internet and communications software have made other options, such as freelancing, feasible as self-supporting professions.

Most writers and editors major in journalism, communication, or English. Journalism majors learn how to write fact-based, nonfiction stories. They learn how to gather information through making observations, interviewing sources, researching documents in print or online, and thinking critically. They also learn how to organize and present their information, as they consider the story angle, the audience, and the medium.

Some writers are generalists and can write well about many subjects because of their good research and writing skills. Others are specialists who have perhaps minored or gained expertise in an additional area, such as the environment, international affairs, medicine, technology, science, business, sports, or fashion.

The best way to break into the business is to work in student media while in college or job shadow a professional. A good way to get ahead is to do several internships while in school.

Internships can help beginners understand the field and find out what else they need to know to be successful.

Writers and authors put together the story, usually in narrative form, for a magazine or book. Writers and editors must master grammar, punctuation, spelling, and word usage.

Editors plan the theme of a magazine and choose appropriate writers. They also review the completed stories. Book editors review proposals and make decisions to hire particular authors. Copy editors and proofreaders go over the completed works with a fine-toothed comb to make sure that every letter is in place and that every word conveys the desired meaning.

If you do well as a writer or editor for a publishing company (books, magazines, news), then you've begun to establish a good track record. Their editors will continue to contact you for additional projects.

It's a competitive market, so you need to be good. The Bureau of Labor Statistics (bls.gov) expects the profession of writers and authors to grow 15 percent and editors to increase at the pace of the national average of 8 percent. Many are self-employed. Although the phone and the Internet allow writers and editors to work from anywhere, major media and entertainment markets are located in Boston, Chicago, Los Angeles, New York, and Washington, D.C. The average salary for a writer or author is $66,000, with the highest 10 percent earning about $110,000.

Probably earning more than the average magazine writer is Jess Cagle, who was an entertainment journalist for *People* magazine and is now the editorial director for both *People* and *Entertainment Weekly* magazines. Cagle graduated from Baylor University, in Waco, Texas, with degrees in journalism and Russian.

> **Desktop publishing** is the process of editing, laying out, and inserting photos to design and display a page using a desktop computer.

cheaper. By the late 1990s, **desktop publishing,** inexpensive photocopying, high-speed printing, and the publication of magazines in virtual form lowered the barriers to entry into the magazine business. Now, anyone with a personal computer can produce books, magazines, flyers, and posters.

Digital Publishing

The magazine industry migrated to the Web and then tablets and smartphones, similar to most former print-only publications. Adding multimedia, such as videos, additional photos, slide shows, audio, and animation, attracts readers to articles they might not have read otherwise. As magazine websites decrease, e-readers, tablets, and smartphones (see Chapter 11) are increasing the popularity of magazines and many publications are creating mobile apps for readers on the go. More than 90 percent of adults read a print or digital magazine. And some are shedding the print for digital only. This group grew almost 85 percent from 2012 to 2013. Good news for magazine publishers is that, as people are introduced to digital magazines, they are increasing their time spent with all types of magazines. About 90 percent of college students read a magazine in the past month. Publishers look forward to introducing you to more magazines in the future.

And, perhaps surprisingly, the advent of electronic cash registers and bar codes has transformed the publishing industry. For book publishers, bar-code scanners changed how inventory is tabulated and best-seller lists are compiled, by automating records instead of polling clerks, as in the old days. Another form of bar code, the QR (quick response) code, those squares with jumbles of tiny square dots in popular magazines, activate interactive ads and editorial features when scanned with a smartphone.

INDUSTRY

The Web reaches out to everyone. Publishers can target readers on another continent and consumers enjoy reading international publications. Major industry trends also include corporate consolidation, improvements in magazine circulation and advertising, book and magazine specialization, audience segmentation, and convergence with other digital media.

Ownership Changes from Individuals to Conglomerates

New magazines, both conventional and Internet based, spring up constantly. Most of them peter out rather quickly or are acquired by larger groups, which can provide them with marketing, publicity, advertising contracts, and better circulation prospects. However, the magazine industry is also one of the media areas where a new entrant or competitor can best break in by appealing to a new segment of the market that is not yet served by other magazines. For instance, *Rolling Stone* went quickly from a small counterculture or "hippie" magazine in 1969 to a widely read rock music and counter-lifestyle magazine in the 1970s to the most popular mainstream music magazine today.

If you want to see the up-to-date numbers and the colorful covers of new magazines, go online to Mr. Magazine's website (www.mrmagazine.com). About 270 magazines were launched in the first four months of 2016. Of those, 61 plan to be published regularly and the rest are "specials," with simply one issue.

STOP & REVIEW

1. Why did magazines move from attracting general audiences to targeting smaller audiences?
2. How did the rotary press affect printing?
3. How did desktop publishing influence the industry?

TABLE 5.2 Top Magazine Companies

COMPANY	NUMBER OF MAGAZINES	COMBINED CIRCULATION FOR ALL MAGAZINES	TOP MAGAZINE	TOP MAGAZINE'S CIRCULATION	MAGAZINE REVENUE 2010	PERCENTAGE OF REVENUE FROM MAGAZINES
Time Warner	19	32,582,300	Time	3,298,390	$3.68 billion	13%
Hearst Corporation	19	30,037,000	Good Housekeeping	4,341,430	$2.27 billion	unav.
Meredith Corporation	19	27,652,800	Better Homes and Gardens	7,617,840	$763 million	70%
Advance Publications	23	18,668,300	Glamour	2,353,860	$2.96 billion	41%
Reader's Digest Association	12	14,456,500	Reader's Digest	5,560,050	$665 million	100%
Rodale	7	7,866,980	Prevention	2,874,120	$376 million	100%
American Media	14	5,810,480	Shape	1,568,060	$369 million	93%
Source Interlink	7	5,196,130	Motor Trend	1,135,090	$335 million	unav.
Wenner Media	3	4,236,160	Us Weekly	2,009,310	$603 million	100%
The Newsweek Daily Beast Company	1	1,519,490	Newsweek	1,519,490	unav.	unav.

Source: http://stateofthemedia.org/media-ownership/magazines/

The same groups of popular topics for new print launches in recent years continue to be crafts/games/hobbies/models and special interest/lifestyle (see Table 5.1, p. 118)

Although anyone can start a magazine, companies with big bucks have the ready resources to make a new magazine successful quickly. Many of these companies are **conglomerates.** For example, Time Warner owns 19 magazines whose revenues total $3.7 billion. Their combined circulation puts Time Warner at the top. Yet, only 13 percent of the company's revenue is from its magazines (see Table 5.2, p. 122). The other 87 percent comes from its filmed entertainment, cable networks, and other publishing holdings that might also appear online (see Chapter 9). Conglomerates are geared to be profitable, and they can create synergies (such as cross-promotion or multiple usage of content) with their other holdings.

> **Conglomerates** are big businesses or corporations that own seemingly unrelated holdings. They are made up of diverse parts from across several media industries and are involved in multiple areas of business activity.

ECONOMICS

The magazine industry continues to lure entrepreneurs, and many are successful. About 150 print magazines have flourished for more than 50 years, and about 47 magazines have prospered for more than a century. Many magazines start up and close every year. The Association of Magazine Media and Mr. Magazine are two online sources that keep track of the magazine industry's number and type of new magazines and audiences.

Magazines target either **segmented** or **mass audiences.** But to be profitable, they strive for the largest possible audience they can reach within their potential target—or market—group, and they still follow such economic rules as economies of scale.

Magazines want to report a large **audience** to advertisers. Magazines with large audiences can charge more for advertising because more people will see the advertisement. Audience is made up of the **circulation** number (subscription and single-copy sales) multiplied by the number of people who have seen a copy of the magazine. This second number is called the **pass-along rate**—how many people who read the same copy sitting in the doctor's office or on a bus, for example. Advertisers compare audiences when deciding to advertise in different magazines, online or print publications, radio, or TV. The audience formula for magazines is the following:

Circulation (average number of copies) × Readers per copy = Audience

Some advertisers, such as deodorant companies, want the largest exposure possible because everyone is a potential customer (shot-gun approach). Others that sell exercise machines, for example, would prefer to advertise to a narrow (health care) audience that will pay attention to their product and not waste money advertising to other segments of the public who don't care about their product.

Magazine revenue comes from advertising, subscriptions, and single-copy sales. Overall, about 60 percent comes from advertising, 30 percent from subscriptions, and the rest from single-copy sales. The mix of revenue from these sources varies greatly among different kinds of magazines.

Most **consumer magazines** depend on subscriptions and advertising. Subscriptions account for almost 90 percent of total magazine circulation. Single-copy, or newsstand, sales accounted for the rest (MPA, 2011, p. 14). However, single-copy sales are important: they bring in more revenue per magazine, because subscription prices are typically at least 50 percent less than the price of buying single issues. Further, potential readers explore a new magazine by buying a single issue; all those insert cards with subscription offers are included in magazines to encourage you to subscribe. Some magazines are distributed only by subscription. Professional or **trade magazines** are specialized magazines and are often published by professional associations. They usually feature highly targeted advertising. For example, the *Columbia Journalism Review* is marketed toward professional journalists and its few advertisements are news organizations, book publishers, and others. A few magazines, like *Consumer Reports,* strive for objectivity and therefore contain no advertising.

Advertising is a crucial source of revenue for most magazines, and the competition for ads is very intense. For most consumer magazines, ads are a far more important source of revenue than subscriptions, but the magazine must reach the right audience for the advertiser. For example, in the computer and telecommunications industries, many magazines like *Network World* are sent free to professionals who make decisions about purchasing computer programs, equipment, or services that the magazine might advertise. A magazine's decision to cater to such subscribers convinces advertisers, with high-tech equipment to sell, to place their ads in that magazine.

Segmented audiences are consumers that can be grouped together because of specific demographics or special interests such as hobbies or politics.

Mass audience is a large, broad audience interested in a variety of general topics.

Audience is the number of readers of a magazine.

Circulation is the number of copies distributed to the public, for a price or free.

Pass-along rate is the number of people who see a single copy of a magazine.

Consumer magazines are magazines that contain general-interest topics.

Trade magazines are magazines that are targeted toward a particular profession.

In some magazines, ad pages almost equal the number of editorial pages (see Table 5.3). If ad pages frustrate you, just remember that without advertisers, your magazine might cost more. Some readers find advertising pages informative. Just ask your roommate.

Circulation and Advertising Trends

The age of the mass-marketed magazine is still with us. Some consider *AARP The Magazine* a mass circulation magazine because its stories touch on all topics, from money matters to weight loss to affordable cities to celebrity news. *Reader's Digest, National Geographic,* and *People* are among the leading magazines distributed through the conventional magazine channels of yearly subscriptions and newsstand sales (see Table 5.4).

The recent Great Recession combined with free information on the Internet took a bite out of the magazine industry. Lack of advertising revenue—not a lack of readers—is generally the reason magazines close. Also, magazines

TABLE 5.3 Editorial and Advertising Pages

YEAR	% EDITORIAL	% ADVERTISING
2012	55.0	45.0
2011	54.8	45.2
2010	54.1	45.9
2009	56.0	44.0
2008	53.8	46.2
2007	52.9	47.1

Note: Sunday magazines excluded.
Source: Hall's Magazine Reports, 2013 (chart found at http://www.magazine.org/sites/default/files/MPA-FACTbook2013-f-lo.pdf p. 93).

TABLE 5.4 Top 15 Consumer Magazines by Paid Circulation

PUBLICATION	TOTAL PAID & VERIFIED 6 MONTHS ENDING 12/31/2013
AARP The Magazine	22,274,096
AARP Bulletin	22,244,820
Game Informer Magazine	7,629,995
Better Homes and Gardens	7,615,581
Good Housekeeping	4,348,641
Reader's Digest	4,288,529
Family Circle	4,092,525
National Geographic	4,029,881
People	3,527,541
Woman's Day	3,311,803
Time—The Weekly Newsmagazine	3,289,377
Ladies' Home Journal	3,225,863
Sports Illustrated	3,023,197
Cosmopolitan	3,015,858
Taste of Home	2,975,929

Source: Audit Bureau of Circulations (chart found at http://www.auditedmedia.com/news/blog/2014/february/us-snapshot.aspx).

must vie with other media, such as newspaper, television, radio, and online media, for advertising dollars. Then, advertising revenue is split among magazines, and that means fewer dollars for both new and established magazines. New magazine titles appear digitally and in print every year to share the total "pie" of advertising revenue. Fortunately, when the economy turns upward, the size of the total pie usually grows again, making room for new publications.

Distribution and Marketing

Consumers get their magazines by subscriptions or at retail outlets, such as supermarkets, drugstores, and bookstores. Readers often subscribe to a magazine by returning the magazine's inserts (postcards, bind-ins, tip-ins, magna strips!) and a quarter of subscribers buy their subscription online. And let's not forget the ever-popular school and club fund-raisers that sell magazine subscriptions.

Single-copy or newsstand sales do not make a lot of money for publishers, but they increase the paid circulation rate that they can sell to advertisers. Visibility on the newsstand rack also confirms the popularity of the magazine to current subscribers and advertisers and it may entice new subscribers who bought a single copy on an impulse.

A crucial link between publishers and retailers is magazine wholesalers and distributors. Distributors have a great influence on getting a magazine to a particular store or newsstand and placing it in a visible location to reach the public. A few publishers find it more efficient to do their own research and promote themselves directly to stores, bypassing distributors. Some retailers, such as Walmart, also bypass distributors to pick the magazines they think will attract their customers. Other stores simply take what the wholesaler delivers, because some wholesalers do their own market research or the staff to do selective ordering.

CONTENT: GENERAL INTEREST AND SPECIAL INTEREST

North American publishing houses churn out almost 7,400 consumer magazines (see Figure 5.1). Companies define and count "magazines" differently. Whereas some are subscriber based and somewhat general interest ("consumer magazines"), others are free with a group membership fee for a specialized interest. For example, the top magazines are *AARP* and *AARP Bulletin* (see Table 5.4, p. 124). They appear in the mailboxes of people who are paid members of the American Association of Retired Persons. What might also help to keep *AARP* on top is that there are not as many senior-citizen magazines competing for similar audiences as there are for health/medicine magazines. Thus, a magazine niche, such as health, might

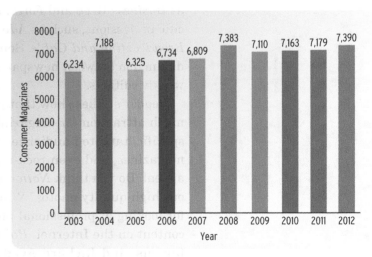

FIGURE 5.1 **MAGAZINE PUBLISHING INCREASES**

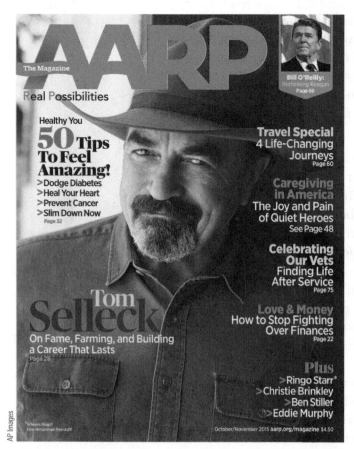

AP Images

NO. 1 AARP is the top consumer magazine. It contains different types of articles for a mass audience.

experience shake-outs when audience circulation and economic support by advertisers are divided among too many magazines.

Generally, magazines have several advantages as *segmented* media. Although they are somewhat constrained by limited newsstand space, magazines can continue expanding into more specialized topics and treatments until they no longer find audiences large enough to be worthwhile. Also, their formats and economic base are more flexible. A small-circulation magazine can still be profitable if those it reaches are interested enough in its contents to support it or if that audience is important to specific advertisers. Many magazines don't need to compete. There are lots of college alumni magazines, each with a different audience. Your college wants to reach only its alumni, in the hopes they will continue to feel connected to the university, and perhaps offer donations and scholarships to benefit students like you.

Magazines (and books) can perform an important set of communications functions for elite audiences. Political activists are served by a variety of magazines ranging from the liberal, such as *The Nation* (founded in 1865), to the conservative, such as the *National Review* (started in 1965). Intellectual magazines, such as the *New York Review of Books,* try to set the stage and agenda for academic and political debates on various issues, often by reviewing books that they hope will help shape those debates. Some government policy-oriented magazines, such as *Foreign Affairs,* pride themselves on having an influential readership and having their articles sometimes affect policy debates.

Similarly, magazines and trade journals can meet the needs of business audiences by providing information about professional development, specific business areas, and current economic trends. Some business magazines, such as *Business Week* and *Fortune,* are fairly general, whereas others cover specific professions, such as *Advertising Age, Columbia Journalism Review,* and *Broadcasting and Cable.* Some trade publications, such as *Variety,* blur the distinction between newspapers and magazines by publishing both daily and weekly editions.

Reader studies show that photos in both articles and advertisements hold much attraction for magazine readers. Visual magazines serve much more specific, targeted audiences. Bridal magazines, fashion magazines, sports magazines, and even rock-music magazines depend a great deal on visual appeal. Do you think *National Geographic* or *Brides* would sell as well without high-quality photos? While reading print magazines, most readers prefer looking at professional photos and images to looking at the same visual content on the Internet. *Rolling Stone* made photographer Annie Leibovitz famous, and Richard Avedon gained fame from his photos in fashion magazines.

It is still too early to tell, but the popularity of magazine apps might be shifting the economic landscape for the print version of magazines.

Redefining the Role of Magazines

As magazine publishers compete with an ever-expanding array of media that provide many options for readers, publishing executives must reflect on what they do best in comparison to other media. Magazines offer high-quality imagery for artwork, photos, and advertisements, which remains key for many industries and readers. And they can offer greater depth than radio, TV, or even newspapers, so people still depend on magazines such as *The Economist* for comprehensive coverage of news and *Rolling Stone* for music news.

To remain competitive, magazines must accommodate the needs and wants of audiences and the times. Celebrity print magazines, such as *People* and *Us Weekly,* are no longer at their peak. Meanwhile, celebrity blogs such as *Perez Hilton, TMZ,* and *Gawker* are some of the most popular blogs on the Internet, and they've got photos, gossip, and attitude. They also continue to gain advertising and hits. Celebrity magazines are holding their own, incorporating blogs and video into their online presence. Whereas celebrity blogs are mostly gossip, magazines have in-depth, objective stories and the resources for better journalism.

The challenge for magazines now is to be an interactive app for a mobile device, computer tablet, or e-reader, such as the iPad, Kindle, or Nook. A digital magazine has to offer more than simply replicating the printed magazine, especially when the app costs the same as the printed version.

1990s

Magazine-like pages and sites proliferate on the Internet

STOP & REVIEW

1. How are audiences measured and why is this important?
2. How are magazines distributed?
3. What is wrong with copying a picture of your favorite movie star from an online magazine to your Web page? (You need to read the next section to answer this question!)

MEDIA *LITERACY*

INTELLECTUAL PROPERTY AND COPYRIGHT

Copyright issues have become key points of contention for print media. In recent years, publishers of magazines and academic (research) journals have cracked down on students who use material that has been copyrighted. In the digital age, it is all too easy to copy someone else's work and paste it into a class assignment or research article. This is plagiarism. Any ideas and words that originated elsewhere should be attributed and cited. Publishers are increasingly concerned about the number of "borrowed" images, photos, sections of text, and headlines from printed and online newspapers, magazines, and books. Because publishers and authors are determined to collect royalties from such reproduction and use, new **intellectual property** rules have changed as electronic distribution increases. If you copy a photo of your favorite movie star onto your website from a magazine, by law, whoever holds the copyright—the photographer, her photo agency, or the magazine itself—would like you to pay for the use of the photo. After all, they had to pay the celebrity and the photographers for the photo shoot and foot the bill for travel, rental of the set, and lighting and camera equipment.

Intellectual property is a creative work of art, writing, film, or software that belongs to a legally protected owner.

Individual authors and photographers have rights to their intellectual property during their lifetimes, and their heirs have rights for 70 years after the creator's death, so any publication less than 125 years old has to be checked for its copyright status. The duration of copyright protection has increased steadily over the years; the life-plus-70-years standard was set by the Copyright Term Extension Act of 1998, which increased the 50-year limit established by the 1976 Copyright Act (see Chapter 16). Supporters of such legislation like to defend these increases with tales of starving writers and their impoverished descendants, but in reality the beneficiaries are more likely to be transnational publishing conglomerates. And note that copyright laws serve a dual purpose. In addition to protecting the rights of authors so as to encourage the publication of new creative works, copyright is also supposed to place reasonable time limits on those rights so that outdated works may be incorporated into new creative efforts. Therefore, the extended copyright protection frustrates new creative endeavors such as including poetry and song lyrics on Internet sites.

SUMMARY & REVIEW

WHY AND HOW DID MAGAZINES DEVELOP?

In 1741, the first U.S. magazines appeared—William Bradford's *American Magazine* and Benjamin Franklin's *General Magazine*. During the American Revolution, many magazines took a more political tone. Few magazines were popular or long-lived during this time. They covered weekly events, politics, and art and contained reviews, travelogues, short stories, and fiction; they were aimed at an educated elite. By the 1820s, magazines of more general interest, such as the *Saturday Evening Post,* began to appear. The number of magazines increased during the Civil War, and they began to reach wider audiences. The Postal Act of 1879 made distribution cheaper.

WHAT WAS THE ROLE OF PRINT MEDIA IN THE CIVIL WAR? HOW DID THE WAR AFFECT THE MEDIA?

Books and magazines affected the issues debated that surrounded the Civil War. *Uncle Tom's Cabin,* for example, is a book widely credited with helping influence northern U.S. opinion against slavery. Several magazines, such as *Harper's Weekly,* grew to fame during the Civil War as a result of their print coverage and their illustrations, which dramatized scenes of the war. Illustrations became prominent tools of magazine journalism. Circulations grew.

WHAT ARE THE MAIN COPYRIGHT ISSUES FOR PRINT MEDIA?

A major issue in print media is the photocopying of copyrighted material. The Copyright Term Extension Act of 1998 extends the period of protection to the life of the author plus 70 years. Many newsletters and new electronic publications borrow images, sections of text, and headlines from newspapers, magazines, and books. Publishers and authors want to collect royalties in return for such use. As electronic distribution increases, new intellectual property rules have been developed.

WHAT WAS "MUCKRAKING"?

Muckraking characterized the period around 1900, when crusading magazines exposed scandals and corruption in government and among industry cartels.

WHY DID MAGAZINES MOVE FROM ATTRACTING GENERAL AUDIENCES TO TARGETING SMALLER AUDIENCES?

Magazines continued to serve a broad audience up through the 1950s, when both their photojournalism roles and entertainment functions were undercut by television. In order to survive the competition from TV, magazines re-invented themselves into publications with specialized content that would attract smaller audiences who would pay for information not readily found elsewhere. These publications would also attract advertisers who knew that people interested in a particular topic would also be interested in their products. Now, instead of addressing a broad mass audience, magazines increasingly focus on specific demographics and interest groups and on audiences particularly interested in politics, hobbies, and other subjects.

HOW DID THE ROTARY PRESS AFFECT PRINTING?

Printers could only print one sheet of paper at a time, which was labor intensive and time consuming. The rotary press used drums that rotated against each other to print on both sides of continuous roles of paper.

HOW DID DESKTOP PUBLISHING INFLUENCE THE INDUSTRY?

At one time, only people with large financial backing could start a magazine (or printing company) because the large printers were expensive and labor intensive. After desktop publishing was introduced in the 1990s, almost anyone with a computer and a printer could print and make multiple copies of pamphlets, newsletters, books, and magazines. People can start their own small businesses without a huge investment of capital. Can you imagine your life without your computer and a printer?

HOW ARE AUDIENCES MEASURED AND WHY IS THIS IMPORTANT?

Most magazines are supported significantly by advertising. Magazines can charge advertisers more money for exposure to larger audiences. And, advertisers want to know how many people will see their ads. Audiences, circulation and pass-along rates are important measurements.

HOW ARE MAGAZINES DISTRIBUTED?

Readers receive magazines regularly by buying a subscription (print or digital) or they can pick up a single print copy at retail outlets. Of course, audiences can also read some magazines online. After magazines are printed, they move from the publisher to a distributer or wholesaler to the retailer. Sometimes the stores and publishers communicate directly and bypass the distributor. Certainly, a distributor is not needed for online magazines.

WHAT IS WRONG WITH COPYING A PICTURE OF YOUR FAVORITE MOVIE STAR FROM AN ONLINE MAGAZINE TO YOUR WEB PAGE?

It probably cost the magazine a lot of money to get the photo for their website. Nonetheless, the photo belongs to whoever paid for it. It certainly doesn't belong to anyone who comes along and copies it. Copyright laws prohibit people from passing off other people's work as their own or for their own use without permission from the copyright holder, who might charge for its use.

THINKING CRITICALLY
ABOUT THE MEDIA

1. How has the content of magazines changed over time, and why?

2. How do conglomerates affect print publishing? Are there positives and negatives associated with conglomerates?

3. How is recent technology changing the way print media is produced, distributed, and read? Is this a good thing?

MindTap®

Test your knowledge with online printable flashcards and online quizzing.

KEY TERMS

audience (p. 123)	mass audience (p. 123)
circulation (p. 123)	miscellany (p. 113)
computer-to-plate (p. 119)	muckraking (p. 115)
conglomerate (p. 122)	news magazine (p. 115)
consumer magazine (p. 123)	pass-along rate (p. 123)
desktop publishing (p. 120)	segmented audiences (p. 123)
genre (p. 115)	trade magazine (p. 123)
intellectual property (p. 127)	woodcut (p. 113)

MindTap® Log on to the MindTap Communication for *Media Now* to access a variety of additional material, including this chapter's ebook, learning objectives, comprehension quizzes, videos, and more!

RECORDED MUSIC

LEARNING OBJECTIVES

After studying the topics in this chapter, you will be able to:

1 Review the evolution and diversification of musical genres that occurred concurrently with the technological innovations that increased sound fidelity.
2 Review the impact of digital recording and marketing on the diminishing role of the music industry as gatekeepers.
3 Analyze the music industry's ongoing struggle to restrict digital piracy by introducing increased copyright protections, subscription streaming services, and digital downloading.
4 Follow a new band or musical act from signing a record deal to promotion and distribution of a new album, according to the corporate music industry model and an independent label model.
5 Summarize the technological changes in recording music that occurred from the debut of the phonograph to the introduction of digital recording.
6 Assess at least one advantage and disadvantage of using the Internet as a marketing, promotion, and distribution tool to increase music sales.
7 Understand better how genres in media develop, based on the example of how music genres have changed in the U.S.

HISTORY: FROM ROOTS AND RECORDS TO SOUNDS IN THE CLOUD

The roots of today's popular music can be traced to earlier musical traditions. Hip-hop rhythms have roots in drumming in African religious ceremonies. African-American gospel music took root in the nineteenth century and is still performed today by groups like the Kingdom Heirs. White gospel spread from churches to country-and-western recordings with such songs as "Rock of Ages." Appalachian folk songs, such as

RECORDED MUSIC provides much of the soundtrack of our lives, both new sounds like Adele and classic sounds like the Beatles, as the music industry faces challenges from iTunes and Internet radio.

Sascha Steinbach/Getty Images

MEDIA THEN··· MEDIA NOW

1877
> Thomas Edison introduces the speaking phonograph

1940
> Frank Sinatra becomes the first modern teen music and radio idol

1981
> MTV music channel appears on cable TV

1982
> CDs revolutionize "record" sales

1999
> Napster introduces Internet music file sharing

2003
> Apple introduces iTunes and iPod, and legal Internet sales of music take off

2011
> Digital music sales are over half of U.S. music industry sales

2015
> Online streaming dominates music listening

MindTap
Start with a quick warm-up activity.

A nickelodeon is a phonograph or player piano operated by inserting a coin, originally a nickel.

Acoustic is a sound that is not electronically amplified.

"I'll Fly Away" on the *O Brother Where Art Thou?* soundtrack, are still often recorded, with many younger artists now recording similar music and calling it Americana. Delta blues songs, like Robert Johnson's "Crossroads," were turned into hits by 1960s–current blues guitarists like Eric Clapton. Cajun music is performed by the Cajun All-Stars. Mexican border *rancheras* (love songs) and *norteño* (border) music by Los Tigres del Norte are big hits with many U.S. Latinos.

Some of the earliest printed materials were song lyrics and musical notations. A sheet music industry dates back to the late nineteenth century. Songwriters, not performers, had a more central role and were more widely recognized. Rather than waiting until a performer made the music popular, people flocked to buy the latest sheet music of well-known composers or lyricists, such as ragtime great Scott Joplin and march composer John Philip Sousa.

The Victrola

During the late 1800s and early 1900s, in an attempt to reproduce music for the public, inventors created mechanical devices, such as music boxes and **nickelodeons.** Thomas Edison developed the first **acoustic** recording and playback technology in 1877, a "phono-graph." In 1906, the Victor Talking Machine Company introduced the home **Victrola.** People liked listening to recorded music in their homes, so the phonograph quickly became a widely used medium.

Early Recorded Music

The home Victrola introduced more people to new kinds of music more rapidly than ever before. The notion of popular music caught on, as writers and composers began to discover what kinds of music most appealed to a mass audience. Jazz, such as New Orleans Dixieland, became popular in the 1920s and 1930s. So did show tunes from talking movies, such as Al Jolson's songs from *The Jazz Singer* (see Chapter 8). Blues was popular among African-American audiences but did not cross over to other audiences much at that time (Romanowski & George-Warren, 1995).

Big Band and the Radio Days

Radio had an immediate impact on recorded music, like the impact of television on cinema attendance later. When people could first hear live music at no cost on the radio, they bought fewer records. As radio took off in the late 1920s, record and phonograph sales dropped by almost half. That produced a panic in the record industry similar to its reaction to Internet music downloads. Gradually, however, listeners bought their own recordings of music they had heard. In fact, the recording industry began to rely on radio to promote recording artists, and the performers they heard on the radio began to be more important than the composers of the music.

Because early recording technology had not achieved very **high fidelity,** and because radio fees for recording artists had not yet been worked out, music was primarily broadcast live. Networks introduced the most popular groups and orchestras to the entire country. Radio stimulated a demand for a variety of musical genres, ranging from classical to country and western, making big stars out of singers like Bing Crosby and Hank Williams.

Big Band Music and the World War II Generation

The most popular music in the 1930s and 1940s was the "big band" sound. Developed from jazz, it was the pop music of its day. Band leaders Glenn Miller and Tommy Dorsey put together orchestras that introduced a number of singers, such as teen idol Frank Sinatra, who led pop music into the 1950s.

Record sales had dipped and some predicted the death of the phonograph, but Sinatra's appearance helped revive record sales. Wherever he went, he was pursued by hordes of screaming teenage girls. Mass production had kept record prices down around a dollar, making records fairly affordable, and the fans began asking stores for the latest Sinatra record. The idea of

1877

Thomas Edison introduces the speaking phonograph

Victrola was the trade name for an early phonograph.

MindTap

Read, highlight, and take notes on the complete chapter text in a rich interactive online platform.

High fidelity is accurate reproduction of natural sound.

NOW HEAR THIS The phonograph, pioneered in 1877 by Thomas Edison, helped create the technological base for the music recording industry.

Frank Sinatra becomes the first modern teen music and radio idol

> **Gospel** music derives from white and black southern church hymns.

> **Blues** came from music by black slaves in the South, which was characterized by specific chord progressions and moods.

> **Bluegrass** came from white music in the South and Appalachia, building on Irish and Scottish instruments and traditions.

music stars and fans echoed the movies and built a powerful industry force that still exists today with stars like Taylor Swift or Beyoncé.

New Musical Genres

National radio networks featured the pop music of the day: big bands, light classical music, and movie and show tunes. However, important developments in musical genres were happening in regional recording companies and radio networks. A network of southern stations carried the Grand Ole Opry and bluegrass acts, such as the Carter Family, featured on recording labels that served largely southern audiences. These new music genres built on the main regional musical traditions of American music, such as southern **gospel, blues,** and **bluegrass.**

They also reflected the popularity of western music and singing cowboys in the movies, like Gene Autry, who began to sell enough records to interest major recording labels. Genres blended too. The combination of bluegrass, gospel, western, and western swing eventually became known as country and western, led by singers like Hank Williams. It followed southern migrants north as they looked for jobs in the industrial Midwest. A recording industry for this music grew up in Nashville, where the Grand Ole Opry was broadcast. National music labels like Capitol and RCA began to pick up country stars and project their music far beyond the South and Southwest.

The blues followed African-American migrants from the South to Chicago and New York, where a harder, electric blues developed in the 1940s and 1950s. Small, independent labels developed new artists and new audiences who had not been served by major record labels or network radio. Chess Records in Chicago, for example, carried a number of blues and rhythm-and-blues artists who were played only on what were called "black" stations back then, although one of their artists, Chuck Berry, finally broke the color barrier and introduced black rock to white audiences. The movie *Cadillac Records* (2008) tells a fictionalized version of the Chess story.

Blues greatly influenced rock and roll. Rock bands of the 1960s, Cream and the Rolling Stones, did versions of Chicago blues songs by Muddy Waters and Howling Wolf (see Media & Culture: Black Music: Ripped Off or Revered?, page 135). Gradually, blues and gospel songs were blended with elements of pop music into new genres, such as rhythm and blues (R&B), which produced artists like Ray Charles. Black music was originally considered "race" music by the recording industry, which did not target it to white audiences for most of the 1930s, 1940s, and 1950s. R&B initially served a largely African-American audience in the early 1950s, but some of its artists, like rock-and-roll pioneers Chuck Berry and Little Richard, were playing music that white audiences saw as part of the rock and roll they liked. But even in the 1960s, guitar great Jimi Hendrix started on the black music circuit until he made his breakthrough with a white backup group in Britain.

Hulton Archive/Archive Photos/Getty Images

WHAT I SAY Ray Charles blended gospel and R&B to create soul music and cross over into pop stardom.

BLACK MUSIC: RIPPED OFF OR REVERED?

What happens to cultures when one group "borrows" music from another? For some, like African Americans, it seems that other people have long ripped off their musical traditions and ideas, even ridiculing them in the process. For example, many white Americans in the 1920s and 1930s enjoyed seeing Al Jolson, who performed in blackface, doing his versions of African-American jazz and blues, but they would not have listened to black singers doing their own songs. Many African Americans felt insulted by the whole idea of a white man doing their music in blackface, and black musicians were restricted to performing their own music in media and venues aimed at African Americans. Thus, white musicians appropriated the music of another group. Some black musicians did eventually benefit from the exposure given to their music, but many died in poverty and obscurity.

Henry Diltz/Historical/Corbis

VICTIM OR IDOL? Blues musician and songwriter William James "Willie" Dixon wrote songs that were covered by many popular white artists, including The Rolling Stones, Bob Dylan, and The Doors.

The tradition of white covers of black music continued in the 1950s and 1960s with Elvis, the Beatles, and the Rolling Stones doing covers of Black blues, rhythm and blues, or soul songs, usually selling far more records than the original artists. The Rolling Stones were pleased that their music made U.S. audiences more aware of their own blues artists, but thought it was ironic.

Now, black hip-hop and rap musicians are very popular. However, white artists like Eminem, "borrowing" their genres, still sometimes make more money. Critics like Herman Gray have argued that black music performed by white people lacks authenticity, a sense of the context in which it was created. Certainly a critical issue for an artist like Eminem, performing in a genre that came from and is still predominantly performed by African Americans, is whether both black and white audiences consider his music and performance authentic enough to be worth listening to.

A largely positive interpretation of such trends would be that such musical "borrowing" is a natural part of an ongoing process of cultural hybridization. Examples might be Eminem, who was produced by an African-American rap artist, or a black fusion musician like Jamaican reggae singer Shaggy, who can blend rap, reggae, and white pop ("Angel of the Morning") into a song like "Angel." In this view, African-American and white American music have been mingling, to the long-run benefit of both, for hundreds of years.

Hybridization also applies to other U.S. and regional cultures. For example, regaettón, started as "Reggae en Español" in Puerto Rico, spread among Latino audiences and went mainstream in the United States in 2004. It has since achieved worldwide popularity.

Rock and Pop History

People like to debate the origins of rock and roll in the early 1950s and what was the first real rock song. Rock built on a variety of roots, **hybridizing** them into a blend that gradually took on an identity that people could call a new genre. Rocks deepest roots were in blues, like Big Mama Thornton's version of "Hound Dog" (that Elvis later **covered**), but country, western swing, and rockabilly all fed in, too.

> **Hybridizing** genres or music blends different traditions into a new form.

> **Covers** are artists' performances of others' songs.

A blend of jump-blues and western swing produced "Rock Around the Clock" in 1954 by Bill Haley and The Comets. It was the first rock record to become a hit and register loudly in the national consciousness. Elvis covered a song, "That's All Right, Mama," by blues singer Arthur "Big Boy" Crudup that some think was the most important song in getting widespread acceptance of rock. Elvis first emerged on Sun Records, one of the first labels that produced blues, country, and rock records, launching not only Elvis but also Johnny Cash.

The young "rock" radio-listening and record-buying audience gradually turned to R&B and soul music as it gave rise to the Motown sound of the Supremes and the Temptations, which was a major part of the pop music of the 1960s. Rock was still somewhat unified as a genre until the late 1960s, with Motown; English groups including the Beatles and the Rolling Stones; and heavy rockers, such as Led Zeppelin and Jimi Hendrix, all known as "rock" (Limmer, 1981).

The recording industry began to rely on radio more than ever as a promotional device to make the public aware of new music and to help the recording industry sell records. The relationship got a little too close when record labels bribed **disc jockeys (DJs)** to play their records, a practice known as **payola.**

> **A disc jockey (DJ)** is a radio station announcer who plays records and often emphasizes delivery and personality.

> **Payola** occurs when record companies give bribes to DJs to get their records played.

The Record Boom and Pop Music

Technological innovations revitalized the recording industry and had an impact on radio as well. In 1947, magnetic tape improved sound fidelity, reduced costs, and made editing easier. This enabled the recorded music industry to produce the music of more artists less expensively and with better quality. In 1948 and 1949, Columbia introduced the large 33 1/3 rpm long-playing (LP) record and RCA introduced the smaller 45 rpm record (rpm stands for revolutions per minute). The 33 1/3 rpm LP albums prevailed for albums, whereas the faster-spinning 45 rpm records dominated releases of single songs (Sterling & Kittross, 2002).

For a while, the limits of the 45 rpm single had limited pop songs to under 6 minutes. Radio also preferred shorter songs. Some producers, like Phil Spector, managed to pour entire symphonies of densely layered production into a 2- to 3-minute single, like "River Deep, Mountain High" by Ike and Tina Turner, but by the mid-1960s, many found the format very constraining. Bob Dylan blew it apart in 1965 with a 6-minute hit, "Like a Rolling Stone." The Beatles, together with their producer, George Martin, were creating increasingly elaborate arrangements with multiple segments and layers of instruments, as on songs like "Penny Lane." The concept album, like *Sergeant Pepper's Lonely Hearts Club Band,* strung together a number of cuts that were still mostly short enough to fit standard 2- to 3-minute song radio formats. However, the Beatles, Dylan, and others steadily pushed toward longer songs that allowed more complex ideas and arrangements. Another strong new direction that expanded rock's horizons came from singer-songwriters like Dylan, who scandalized folk purists by strapping on an electric guitar and doing rock albums like *Highway 61 Revisited* (1965).

The Rock Revolution Will be Segmented

After 1970, both recording companies and FM radio stations began to diversify into distinct rock and pop formats, such as album-oriented rock (Bruce Springsteen), Top 40 (Michael Jackson), rock oldies (Chuck Berry), heavy metal (Led Zeppelin), adult contemporary (Linda Ronstadt), R&B/urban

(Funkadelic), disco (KC & the Sunshine Band), and country and western (Tammy Wynette).

Rock and pop's diverse roots fed further diversification into a number of branches or subgenres, which produced new radio formats, as can be seen in Figure 6.1. By the 1990s, dozens of subgenres had descended from 1960s rock, pop, and soul roots. Several early rap groups, like Public Enemy, did a number of songs clearly designed as political commentary to challenge ideas about the relations between black youth and the police. The continuing formation of smaller recording labels gave expression to musical subgenres and the subcultures that enjoyed them. Some musicians, like Dr. Dre, turned into producers and label owners. This was enabled by technological developments that lowered the price of recording tapes, records, and CDs.

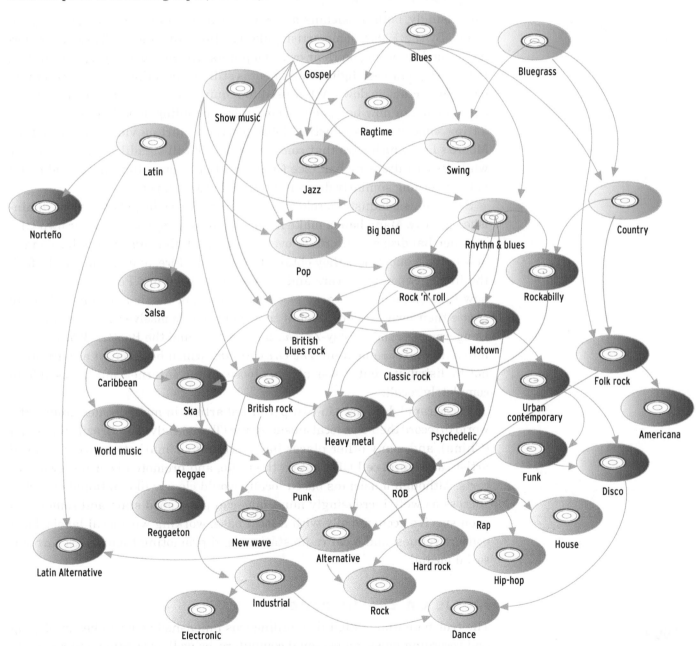

FIGURE 6.1 **THE EVOLUTION OF POPULAR MUSIC GENRES** A wide variety of popular U.S. music genres have evolved from roots in Latin music, show music, gospel, blues, and bluegrass.

In 1982, a new round in the recording format wars began with the introduction of compact disc recording. Some were not very impressed with the shiny new discs at first, finding their sound rather harsh and brittle. But the recordings were more compact and relatively immune to dust and scratches compared to LP phonograph records.

By the late 1990s, CDs had pushed vinyl 33 1/3 record albums and cassettes off the record store racks (although some listeners persisted in their love of vinyl, spawning a comeback of sorts for LP records). Retail CD distribution also moved to the Internet, in online music stores and catalog sellers that sold recordings on websites for delivery through the mail.

1982

CDs revolutionize "record" sales

Digital Recording

Increasingly, both musicians and music consumers record music in digital forms. By the 1990s, some artists, like Fat Boy Slim, did professional performance and recording on their own computers. The number of people recording music using low-cost digital equipment is still skyrocketing as music-recording equipment costs go down. What used to require specialized mixing and effects equipment can now be done on computers, including shooting music videos, letting some stars, like Justin Bieber, get their start on video channels. Like Moore's law, which says that computing power will steadily double in power while its cost drops by half (see Chapter 10), it seems that digital audio and video recording similarly drops in price and grows in power.

So the music industry's role as gatekeepers over who gets to record diminished greatly. Many bands make money by touring and selling their own CDs and merchandise at concerts or over the Internet. Consumers also have many new options about how they obtain, buy, record, store, and mix music. In fact, the line between producers and consumers is blurring. People at home can now take elements or tracks of various pieces of music and remix them to create their own versions, even if they don't see themselves as musicians. DJ Dangermouse remixed Jay-Z's *The Black Album* and the Beatles' *White Album* into a new mix or mash-up, *The Gray Album,* which he received a court order not to distribute, but it was already loose on the Internet and impossible to completely recall.

These rapid decreases in cost permitted artists in many locales around the world to record their own local music. Austin (Texas), Salvador (Brazil), Shanghai (China), and many other places have local music markets in which a local artist can record, sell CDs, get on the radio, and promote his or her own concerts. Although musicians based locally would clearly like national or global success as well, increasingly musicians can get a good start and sometimes even survive economically with a local base, working with local labels, local concert venues, and local radio stations and promoting themselves through social media.

Music on the Internet

1999

Napster introduces Internet file sharing

The true potential of digital recording was unleashed as users began playing and recording music on personal computers, as well as sending and receiving music over the Internet. In 1999, Shawn Fanning started Napster, a file server that let people exchange songs as MP3 digital music files via the Internet.

TWENTY ONE PILOTS AND THE HARD WORK OF MUSIC

Music is hard work. Like most media work, getting in, becoming full-time, and staying on top is hypercompetitive. As the music business changes with technology and media industries, music careers have become more complex and multilayered. It is not enough to get a record contract and make some hits. Bands have to work very hard. A Columbus, Ohio band, Twenty One Pilots, seems likely to be the hardest working band in 2016; they will do 85 shows in their world tour, culminating in two nights at Madison Square Garden. That sounds like success, but it is no surprise that their 2015 hit, which reached the number four spot in the Billboard top 100, is named "Stressed Out." Since record sales are now uncertain, given the high degree of piracy, or illegal copying of music, musicians are thrown back more on making a living by performing and touring. Recordings are still crucial, however, for gaining attention to a band or singer.

Twenty One Pilots became much more successful, and in demand for shows, after that hit single in 2015. The song sounded good, in part because they had been playing together, working up material, and polishing it in concerts. One good historical example is how important a couple of years playing lots of shows together in England and Germany was to the early success of the Beatles. Their first recordings sounded fairly polished because they had played together thousands of hours already. Constant playing also helps nurture songwriting. The Beatles played lots of pop and R&B standards, even on their first few records, as they gradually matured into writing more of their own material.

YouTube has been crucial for Twenty One Pilots, with "Stressed Out" getting 50 million views. As a two-piece group they use extensive recorded backing sounds, but may add more group members to add to the live synergy they get in concert. They use costumes for dramatic effect and find that the visual

Kevin Winter/Getty Images

HARD WORK PAYS OFF
The members of the rising Ohio band Twenty One Pilots have to work hard, tour constantly, and have dramatic, entertaining YouTube videos to make it in the music business.

element is key to their popularity. Making their music personal has also been key to their success. Their new album is a concept piece about a character from their stage show named Blurryface, who represents the lead singer's own anxieties about how he looks, which resonates with young audiences. This move toward greater interactivity with fans is something that is rising both in the indie music world. Although there is already a lot of fan fiction about them, they avoid reading it. Even at the peak of the music industry, few artists made a lot of money in music. Twenty One Pilots aren't counting on even a hot single to make money. They are a good example of both hard work and the multiple ways musicians make money these days.

The term *social media* was not in wide use back then but that's what Napster and other file-sharing sites to follow were since they shared content uploaded by users. The problem for the music industry was that they were nearly all illegally "shared" files that were not of the users' own making.

The recording industry preferred the term *stolen* to *shared* since they saw music sales declining. In 1999, the music industry sales peaked at $23.7 billion, but dropped to $15 billion in 2014 [Solsman, 2016 #4722].

2003

Apple introduces iTunes and iPod, and legal Internet sales of music take off

THE TALENT Taylor Swift has become such a major star that she can defy the push toward streaming music, holding her recent album off services like Spotify to push more album sales.

Copyright is the legal right to control intellectual property. With it comes the legal privilege to use, sell, or license creative works.

2011

Digital music sales are over half of U.S. music industry sales

In 2000, the Recording Industry Association of America (RIAA) began to file lawsuits to force "free" music exchanges like Napster to shut down and followed with suits against individual users. Artists also went to court. Prince sued The Pirate Bay, a notorious download site based in Sweden, in an effort to stop free downloads of his recordings. Another popular file-sharing site, MegaUpload, was closed down in 2012 when government officials in several countries arrested its managers but tens of millions are still downloading music through file-sharing sites based on BitTorrent. Also in 2012, RIAA worked with the film industry to get legislation passed through the U.S. Congress that would have required Internet service providers and search engines to block sites that carried **copyright**-protected material without permission. The online community rebelled, including a one-day shut down by Wikipedia, and forced the industry to rethink that plan.

The record industry very slowly moved to create a system for letting people get music online for a charge. In 2003, Apple broke ground by creating a pay download service, the iTunes Music Store, and followed up with its popular iPod players. Steve Jobs of Apple was the first to present a convincing package of technology and price, and persuaded the music industry majors to go along. Apple initially charged $0.99 per song, but a downloaded song could be copied only onto a limited number of devices. Frustration with copy protection standards led to selling songs free of copyright protection. In 2008, Apple surpassed Walmart to become number one in all record sales, online or off. A number of companies, like Amazon, now are offering similar download stores, with comparable features and cooperation from the music industry. Download sales are still one of the two main sources of digital profits for the music industry. In 2013, the dominance of online download stores, like iTunes, continued to grow to 40 percent of all sales, while physical store sales dropped to 16 percent. Worldwide, digital and physical sales were equal in 2014, but the trend to digital was moving fast.

The other main source of revenue for the music industry is subscription music services like Spotify, which are stand-alone services that are supported by a combination of advertising and monthly fee services. The industry now derives 32 percent of its digital revenues from such services. Others, like Pandora, let you create your own channels by suggesting music based on what you already like. Using computer algorithms that examine patterns among users to see that, for example, people who like Neko Case also like Gillian Welch, Pandora then makes suggestions for you.

Other services offer unlimited downloads that are packaged together with other services that customers are used to paying for, like mobile phone subscriptions. Both Google and Apple introduced options to let users store and stream their own music onto computers, portable players, and smartphones from Internet servers in "the cloud" (see Technology Trends, page 142). Some of these have pre-programmed services, like Internet radio. Apple acquired Beats

Music and reconfigured it and iTunes to be Apple Music. It is betting heavily on its new streaming services and "radio" stations like Beats One (see Chapter 7).

The big news in 2015 was music streaming, which nearly doubled (Sisario, 2016). CD sales declined 11 percent in 2015, down 82 percent from their peak in 2001. Digital downloads of albums declined 3 percent, while downloads of individual tracks declined 12 percent (Sisario, 2016). A few blockbuster album sales in the United States grew, largely thanks to stars such as Taylor Swift and Adele, reflecting the continuing importance of blockbuster hits (Christman, 2014). To keep sales high, both those stars refused to put their new music on services like Spotify.

Global music sales increased, and global digital revenues were up by 8 percent, particularly strong in emerging markets. Revenues from music subscription services and sales of digital single tracks and albums; managing live performances; and licensing music to television, film, and video games, like "Guitar Hero," have been increasing in general but so far haven't quite replaced CDs as the cash cow of the industry, still 46 percent of all global sales, less in the United States. The music industry (46%) and videogames (52%) are ahead of all others in making revenue from digital sources, but they have also lost more to unlicensed digital traffic, too—a 33 percent decline in the value of the global recorded music industry, 2004–2014.

The music industry also claims it is losing a great deal of licensing revenue to video services like YouTube, which offer a great deal of music while using copyright loopholes to pay low royalties (IFPI, 2016). Since music revenue has dropped by almost half from 1999 to 2014 despite new sources like concerts and live performances, Internet and mobile phone services, global markets, and publishing (licensing, digital platform use, Internet radio, TV, and film soundtracks), the music industry is desperate to find new or increased revenues from services like YouTube. (See Figure 6.2.)

Social media continue to impact the music industry in new ways. Facebook Music helps popularize new music by linking tunes from your friends' music services and hosting fan clubs and profiles of performers. Top acts like Lady Gaga communicate with their faithful fans through Facebook and Twitter. Aspiring stars are finding that they can launch careers and push album sales through social media without the backing of either a major

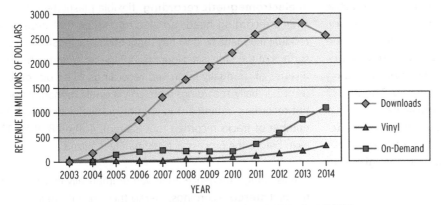

FIGURE 6.2 SOURCES OF REVENUE FOR THE U.S. MUSIC INDUSTRY While overall revenue is down considerably, downloads are still profitable for the music industry, on-demand or streaming is rising rapidly and vinyl has made a slight comeback.

1. How did music genres evolve from earlier music traditions?

2. What are the major genres and traditions that fed into rock and roll?

3. How did record/CD sales and radio affect each other over time?

4. What led the segmentation of rock into subgenres since the 1960s?

5. What is the impact of MP3s, Internet music downloads, streaming services, and video services like YouTube on the recording industry?

label or extensive concert tours. For example, singer-songwriter Lana del Rey became a sensation in 2012 after posting a music video on YouTube and generating buzz on Twitter and Facebook. That is now the mainstream for new stars.

TECHNOLOGY TRENDS: LET'S MAKE MUSIC

The first music recordings were purely analog. With Thomas Edison's phonograph of 1877, sound waves were recorded as indentations on a spinning cylinder covered with malleable tinfoil. Analog records and tapes lasted almost 100 years (see Technology Demystified: From the Victrola to AAC). Digital CDs seemed revolutionary at first, but what really reshaped music are computer-based technologies, from GarageBand (for Mac) or TrackAx (for PC) for cheap recording and remixing, to the Internet for distribution, and iTunes, iPods, and Spotify for listening.

New Digital Formats

Music recording technology and computer media converged rapidly. Recordable CDs and DVDs were equally at home in the CD bays of personal computers and stereo systems. But files of music data can also be stored on a computer's hard drive, and many laptops don't even have a CD drive anymore. For most of our readers, your laptop, tablet, or smartphone is also now your stereo, with

Technology Demystified

FROM THE VICTROLA TO AAC

The wax and foil cylinders used in early recordings were replaced by more durable flat gramophone disks first invented in 1882 by Emile Berliner (Brinkley, 1997). In the early twentieth century, the hand cranks gave way to electric motors. In later electronic equipment, movements of the stylus, or "needle," generated an electric current that was amplified and sent to the speakers. There the current activated an electromagnet attached to a vibrating membrane inside the speakers that reproduced the original sound waves. In 1948, two recording formats still found today were introduced. The 33 1/3 rpm LP records held 23 minutes of music per side. The 45 rpm records held up to about 6 minutes to a side. Both new formats used better needles and amplification to achieve improved sound that was thought of in the 1950s as high fidelity.

In the recording studio, modern microphones all employ a thin membrane that catches the sound waves. The "condenser mics" found in recording studios have a pair of thin,

electrically charged flexible metallic plates inside. As the sound waves press against one of the plates, its vibrations push electrical charges back and forth between the plates, creating an electrical current that matches the sound.

In **electromagnetic recording,** flexible plastic tape passes over a recording head, an electromagnet that imparts a residual magnetic field to tiny magnetic particles stuck to the surface of the tape (see Figure 6.3). Tape recording permitted a series of gradually improved recordings to be put onto a record. Initially, recordings were only a single monaural track, but recording equipment in studios gradually increased the number of tracks recorded to 2 (stereo), 4, then 8, then 32, even before the process was ultimately digitized.

The listening experience improved dramatically in 1956 with the first **stereo** recordings. Stereo tricks us into hearing the musicians as though they were sitting in different chairs in front of us, whereas the previous monaural recordings made it seem that all the sounds were coming from the same point.

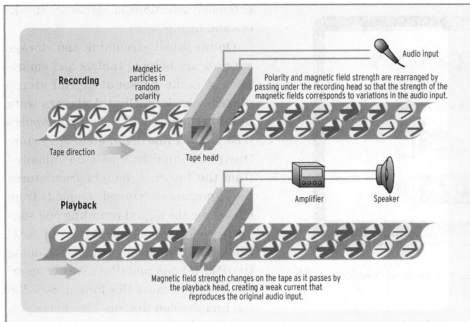

FIGURE 6.3 AUDIO RECORDING Music is stored in tiny magnetic particles on the surface of audio tapes.

Source: http://www.billboard.com/biz/articles/news/digital-and-mobile/5855162/digital-music-salesdecrease-for -first-time-in-2013

Stereo adds the illusion of depth to the music. To accomplish the illusion, we divide the music into two separate sources, or tracks, and replay them so that they are heard over different speakers.

CDs arrived in 1982. As we noted in Chapter 1, CD recorders convert sound waves into the 1s and 0s of computer data. During playback, another laser shines on the surface of the disc, but the light is scattered when it hits the pits, turning the laser's reflection off for a brief moment. This pattern of "lights on" and "lights off" regenerates the computer data and, eventually, the original sound (Benson & Whitaker, 1990) CDs faithfully reproduce the entire range of sound frequencies audible to the human ear and are less vulnerable to dust and scratches than earlier recording media. They also provide more capacity than the previous recording media. Now Beethoven's Ninth Symphony fits on one side of a CD. In fact, the size of the CD was set so that it could fit the 74-minute playing time of Beethoven's "greatest hit."

However, in devising the standards for CDs, certain compromises had to be made to limit the amount of digital information required to record a song, such as limiting the number of computer bits per sound sample. Online music file standards such as **MP3** (short for Motion Picture Expert Group-2 audio layer III), **AAC** (advanced audio coding), and WMA (Windows Media Audio) make further compromises in sound quality to reduce file sizes. Although the details vary, the basic trick they all use is some form of audio compression, which removes redundant information that the listener does not perceive. For example, when you turn up the volume of your iPod to drown out background noise, you "mask" (no longer perceive) the unwanted noise. That's because when two sounds of approximately the same pitch occur simultaneously, we perceive only the louder of the two. Audio compression uses computer algorithms to filter out the sounds that we would not perceive anyway so that the resulting music can be digitally encoded using fewer bits with acceptable (e.g., "near" CD quality) results.

CD quality, let alone "near" CD quality, is not enough for some audiophiles who crave the "warmth" of analog recording. That is why vinyl records are making a comeback. However, the aging recording equipment that presses the vinyl platters is falling apart, limiting their reach. "Lossless" digital services that use triple or quadruple the number of bits normally found in streaming music files are trying to make an impact, such as Deezer and Tidal (baked by rap legend Jay-Z). However, user acceptance has been limited to say the least, possibly because so many of the low-fidelity earbuds in use make it difficult to detect a difference compared to near CD quality.

ISALES Apple's iTunes store leads the way in legal music downloads and has surpassed Walmart to be music's main retailer.

> **Electromagnetic recording** is a method of storing information as magnetized areas on a tape or disk.

> **Stereo** is splitting recorded sound into two separate channels.

> **MP3** is a sound digitization and compression standard, short for MPEG-2 Layer 3.

> **AAC** is advanced audio coding.

extensive selections of accessory speakers and headphones.

Online music streaming and storage services are helping tablets and smartphones make personal digital stereo players obsolete. Digital players were first introduced in 1998, but soon Apple's iPod product line dominated. They store "near" CD-quality music downloaded from the Internet, bought from stores like Amazon or "ripped" (copied) from CDs using the digital recording and storage formats known as **MP3** and **AAC** (the default for Apple products including the iPod, iPhone, and iPad). We say "near" CD quality because this format uses digital compression that does not make perfect reproductions but sounds almost as good to the listener and takes up only a tenth of the space to store. Attempts to market CDs with superior sound quality, Super Audio and DVD Audio, were failures because the average listener couldn't detect an improvement over conventional CDs. These days, recording studios emphasize volume over fidelity, the better to blast the ears of iPod, iPhone, and iPad users and drown out background noise. Beats headphones with strong bass now have the prestige that very good stereo speakers once had.

Sinking the Pirates

Widespread "sharing" or "piracy" of MP3s online led to the development of the music industry's secure digital music initiative. This made it possible to encrypt (or scramble) the music so that only paying customers of industry-backed online music services can download it. Consumer reaction was so poor that eventually Apple, Amazon, and others eliminated copy protection standards like FairPlay and now sell digital music downloads without restrictions.

Technology is also aiding the music industry trade association RIAA as it tracks music piracy online. The RIAA uses a library of digital fingerprints that it says can uniquely identify music files that have been traded online as far back as 2000. Such fingerprints can separate those who copied their own CD into MP3s on their computer from those who downloaded a fingerprinted version of a file that has been identified as in circulation on file-sharing Internet services. The industry hopes to use these fingerprints in their (so far unsuccessful) attempt to promote new laws that will make it possible to automatically block the transmission of pirated recordings over the Internet.

MUSIC TO GO Digital music players like the Apple iPod or iPhone allow users to play AAC recordings and travel with tens of thousands of songs in their pockets.

Streaming and Cloud Music Services

Is it time to think about throwing your iPod onto the same trash heap as your old CD player? Now music fans can enjoy unlimited access to a huge music catalog on services like Spotify or Apple Music or to their own music by storing it on a "cloud." That is the term used for storing (legally purchased) music on the Internet so that it can be downloaded or streamed to any device you wish, whenever you want (see Chapter 10). Apple's iCloud, Google Play, and Amazon Cloud Drive let users store music they purchase online plus music they upload from their own collections into what is called a cloud locker, a music archive on a remote server that lets you play your own music through a variety of devices. High-speed wireless networks (see Chapter 11) offer the capacity for speedy downloads and smooth streaming, including music stored on the new cloud services, as well as streaming services such as Spotify.

Social Music Media

Social media on the Internet, such as Facebook and YouTube, are changing music promotion. Now bands and distributors and independent musicians push music through YouTube, Facebook, Bandcamp, SoundCloud, and Twitter. YouTube is currently seen as the most effective place to promote new music, but Facebook users can link to groups, promote lists of what they like, and let their "friends" know what they are listening to. Spotify works through Facebook to do the same. Music blogs let listeners find new music and musicians promote theirs.

THE RECORDING INDUSTRY

New digital technologies seem to allow many more new entrants in music recording, music production, and distribution. However, economic and regulatory changes have also encouraged unprecedented concentration of the ownership of most of the major players (in terms of hits, sales, and profits) all across the music industries. So the music that is such a part of our culture has largely been controlled by "the suits," the men and women in business suits who run the record industry. However, some former outsiders, like Dr. Dre or Timbaland, have forced their way into the inside by becoming successful producers and managers. And in an age of fewer blockbuster hits, stars who can still sell lots of CDs or downloads, like Taylor Swift, have more power than stars used to.

The key elements of the recording industry are the talent (the songwriters, singers, and musicians), the producers, the recording studios, the recording companies and their various labels, the distributors, independent promoters, and retailers. Also important to musicians' success are their managers and arrangers. Despite the fast-paced developments in digital music, most musicians still hope to get a contract from a record company to make money. Unfortunately, the road to riches is lined with traps set by the suits who charge the bands for marketing and concert promotions and retain the rights to the music. So more and more singers and groups try to make it on their own.

MUSICIANS, MOGULS, MUSIC IN EVERYTHING ELECTRONIC

As the music business changes with technology and media industries, new careers open as others close. There is as much room as ever for singers, musicians, arrangers, composers, and directors, but like most media work, getting in, becoming full-time, and staying on top is hypercompetitive.

There were about 173,000 musicians and singers, making an average of $24,000, and 82,000 music directors and composers employed in the United States in 2014, making an average of $48,000 (U.S. Occupational Outlook Handbook, 2016). Slower-than-average growth is expected in both occupations because of cutbacks in publicly funded music organizations like opera companies and symphonies. However, online promotion and distribution of music is expected to create more demand for performers.

Jobs for the recording industry are declining, as technology permits more people to record their own music at home. However, there is still a niche for high-end recording, and there is actually a proliferation of small studios in more cities, using the new low-cost equipment but promising a better sound than people can create for themselves. There are also new jobs in designing sound and applying music to film, television, games, websites, and all kinds of interactive media. Placing music in these venues is increasingly important to musicians and the music industry, so work in these interfaces is growing.

Music careers tend to show the importance of connections. Many people follow family or other connections into the industry. Mick Jagger, who co-produced *Vinyl*, a 2016 HBO mini-series about the music industry, helped his son, James, get a part as the lead singer of a punk band in the show. Some start in radio, then move to music promotion, producing, writing songs, or recording. Some, like Carrie Underwood, a communication graduate from Northeastern State University, paused her education to take a successful shot at fame as a singer on the television talent contest *American Idol*. Work in college radio often pays off in experience and connections, as does work on music videos. Producing your music video and putting it on YouTube works for some, as it did for Rebecca Black with "Friday," in 2011, but her parents had deep enough pockets to pay for high-quality recording, so connections still matter, even if the barriers to entry are a lot lower these days.

Scott Dudelson/Getty Images

GET PAID Singers like Vince Staples are part of "the talent" that keeps the music industry going.

The Talent

Groups form at a local level. There are tens of thousands of aspiring local groups and singers throughout the United States. For example, the college club scene in Chapel Hill, North Carolina, spawned Ben Folds Five, and the local scene in Portland, Oregon, produced the Decemberists. Such acts perform locally, try to get concert or dance bookings out of town, become better known, and make a recording to circulate to record companies or sell directly through the Internet. Many move to larger, more competitive locales more frequented by record company scouts, such as Los Angeles, Nashville, and New York. A number achieve regional status as traveling acts that circulate in a state or region. A few are discovered and make it big, but most break up, whereupon the more talented musicians form new groups and move on. Talent scouts from record companies are always looking around college towns, festivals like South by Southwest (Austin), and concert circuits for new acts, but competition is fierce. So, many groups who don't get or even seek record contracts also sell or distribute their own music at concerts and over the Internet.

Recording Studios and Record Companies

It used to be that recording companies would bring promising acts into the recording studio, where engineers and arrangers could capture their music on tape for an album or a single. Recording studios are now relatively cheap to create and can be found in most cities of even a few hundred thousand people. Aspiring groups can increasingly cut or record a set of digital tracks or CD locally for $500–$600, or less. Others cut and edit their own CDs and online music files on personal computers or even iPads. That music won't reflect professional producers' assistance with arrangements, but with it a group can look for more club dates and promote its recordings on the Internet as MP3s or AAC music files. They can also promote their music to talent scouts from record companies or sell their tunes directly to the public.

However, recording companies are still important gatekeepers; they often still decide who gets distributed and promoted nationally on the radio, in social media, in concerts, and in record stores. The most visible to musicians are artists and repertoire (A&R) executives, who search for, spot, recruit, and nurture talent.

Three big companies dominated the music industry: Sony, Universal, and Warner Music Group. A former major, EMI, declined and was broken up in 2011, with parts sold to Universal and Sony, so now there are three. Warner was sold to a new conglomerate (Access Industries). Music group ownership has been volatile in the face of declining CD sales, and the rise of streaming services, as the EMI breakup and Warner sale show. However, these companies still dominate distribution in the United States and the world. Industry figures worry that reducing four ownership groups to three may reduce competition in recording, distribution, and music publishing in ways that are not good for consumers or artists (Billboard, 2011).

Recorded music is very much an international industry. Sony is a Japanese company, which recently bought BMG, Arista, and RCA from the German BMG. The French company Vivendi bought the Universal Music Group. Foreign owners have not pursued different kinds of musical content from domestic owners. All the majors have operations in a number of countries where they develop local and promote global artists, much more than do global conglomerates in film or television.

Some of the major recording companies have a number of separate labels, each with a separate image and intended market segment. Sony Music Entertainment has the Columbia and Epic labels; Warner Music Group (formerly owned by Edgar Bronfman, Jr., now owned by Access Industries) has Rhino, Elektra, Warner, Sire, and Atlantic; and Universal Music Group (owned by French media conglomerate Vivendi) has Island, Def Jam, Capital, and Geffen. Independent distributors had 35 percent of the U.S. market for album sales in 2015,

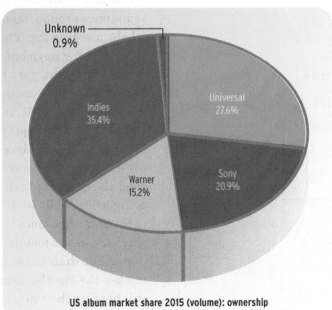

US album market share 2015 (volume): ownership

FIGURE 6.4 BIG THREE MUSIC GROUPS' SHARE OF U.S. MARKET While a consolidated three big global music groups dominated U.S. album sales in 2015, indie labels or individual musicians sold over a third, more than any single big music group.

compared to 28 percent for Universal, 15 percent for Warner, and 21 percent for Sony (Figure 6.4, page 147; Nielsen, 2016).

Recording companies decide which songs to promote via social media, Web promotions, radio, billboards, and print ads. The labels' first copy costs for new CDs or digital tracks are often high, starting with recording, mixing, and producers' costs, not to mention the huge salaries they pay "the suits." Labels also often have to pay an independent promoter to get a song on the radio, and they also have to pay producers, directors, and crews to do a music video that will make it onto cable music channels or be a hit on YouTube. All that can cost millions, so the labels are often tempted to slow or even stop promoting a group that is not an immediate big hit, and maybe even cancel the group's contract. With the outsize financial success of Taylor Swift, Adele, and Beyoncé in recent years, the music business is now as dependent on a few global mega-hits as the film industry.

Rather than going with majors, many groups increasingly go with independent labels, which came back strongly in the 1990s. An independent label is one owned by someone outside of the three majors and can vary in size from tiny (three or four employees) to medium size (50 or so employees). Some independent labels work on very low promotion and profit margins so that they and a group can make money after selling as few as 25,000 copies, compared to the millions required for a major label hit. So, most tend to see the promotion of a band as a long-term project. And some see file sharing as an ally, a way for people to hear about new groups on their labels, who then often buy the CD or a legal download. As in the movie industry, there is an increasing synergy between indie labels and music producers. If a new group on an independent label does well, it may be picked up for distribution by one of the big three, either by striking a deal with the indie label or by buying out its contract. Social media are helping musicians and audiences find each other through, or sometimes around, labels. Related new forms of distribution, like net or digital labels, are growing. They help musicians sell music either by download or by CD, accepting payment via PayPal or credit card.

1981

MTV music channel appears on cable TV

An important part of the promotion of the most promising groups with national potential used to be making a music video for MTV. When MTV came on the scene in 1981, it had great influence on which records become popular and even what gets played on radio stations. However, YouTube has supplanted MTV as the main place people see music videos. *American Idol* has launched several hit singers, such as Carrie Underwood and Kelly Clarkson, and strengthened the careers of others. Soundtracks to television shows, like *Empire,* can become hits, as its soundtrack was number one on R&B and hip-hop charts.

Radio has become less central to music promotion now that YouTube, the playlists on our mobile players, or recommended playlists on Spotify are more important than those on local radio stations. In 2015, Universal decided to release the Beatles catalog on Spotify to ensure that younger listeners were still hearing their music (Heine & Swant, 2015). A controversial and expensive part of music promotion to radio stations is independent promoters. These promoters are hired by record companies to convince radio stations to play new records. There have been several scandals involving *payola,* or bribes, from promoters to station managers or program directors, to play songs, which led to calls for reform of the business of promoting music to radio stations.

Music Distribution

The music companies distribute recordings in a variety of ways. Some stores, like Walmart, deal directly with record companies. Big-chain record stores, like Tower, once dominated this retail business, but Tower went bankrupt, and huge general retailers, such as Walmart and Best Buy, grew in importance. Now they have been bested by iTunes, which is being surpassed by streaming companies like Spotify.

The once conventional music store model is dying in most places. Mass retailers like Walmart lost 16 percent of their music sales in 2013, and chain stores like Best Buy lost 20 percent, while nontraditional CD sellers like Starbucks or concert venues rose 2 percent. The increasingly dominant form of distribution is the purchase and download of music over the Internet from online stores, such as the iTunes Music Store or Amazon, which sold 40.6 percent of music in 2013 (Christman, 2014). An emerging business model treats music as a loss-leader as part of a scheme to sell hardware. Apple nets only a few pennies per iTunes song after paying the record label and credit card processing fees. But they profit enormously from their iPod, iPhone, and iPad hardware sales, which are driven by iTunes sales. Amazon took a different approach when it started selling its Kindle Fire for slightly less than it cost to make in 2011, assuming the tablet, tightly integrated with its online store, would drive Amazon content sales and profits.

The combined effect of all these competing forms of distribution, plus the continued growth of illegal file sharing, has been a decrease in CD sales. So, the 10- to 12-track album as the dominant mode of music sales is declining even though digital album sales are now increasing and there has been a small uptick in vinyl record sales. But the single, the forgotten champion of the 1950s and 1960s, is back, in digital download form instead of 45 rpm records. However, as digital sales of both tracks and albums level off and decline, the music industry is pinning more of its hopes for revenue on streaming services.

Streaming services were a fairly marginal part of overall music consumption until 2011, but they have now begun to realize some of the industry's hopes for a substantial new revenue stream. Labels, performing artists, and writers get very small payments each time a song is played on Pandora or Spotify but those small sums add up quickly as such services become more popular, even though most people listen for free, in return for listening to ads, or for nominal subscription fees. Similar small revenue streams come each time someone plays music that they have placed in a cloud-based music service, like iCloud, Google Music, or Amazon Cloud. Since these systems are now promoted heavily by three of the strongest technology firms, their use and importance to musicians and labels is likely to grow significantly. In potentially the most significant move of all, Google is trying to figure out more ways to make YouTube pay off. Artists already get exposure from YouTube, but if the platform moves in a subscription direction, at least for some channels, then artists or copyright holders might make money as they do from Pandora, and perhaps a lot more.

Music Industry Associations

The RIAA and other trade associations function as the industry's lobbying and legal arm. The American Society of Composers, Authors and Publishers

(ASCAP) represents more than 550,000 songwriters, lyricists, and music publishers. Broadcast Music Incorporated (BMI) has more creative artists and publishers, with over 700,000 affiliates. Both help artists collect royalties from live performances by others, radio plays of recorded music, Internet radio, elevator music, use in commercial sound channels for stores, and other ways in which music gets played. ASCAP and BMI both monitor music play on media, collect royalties from media, and distribute them to artists. For songs covered by others, on every album with at least 10 tracks, the music publishers representing the authors of the songs earn 7.5 cents per track, which they distribute to the writers with whom they have agreements.

A number of alternative ways of looking at artists' rights to and benefits from their music are developing. Some artists, like Phish or the Grateful Dead, were very accepting of fans' recording and sharing concerts, assuming that people will buy tickets and CDs anyway. Others, like Dispatch, saw record companies as something to avoid and see Internet file sharing and music blogs with Internet downloads as good ways to market and sell their music. One idea was the Creative Commons, in which artists make their music available, not only for simple download and listening but also for sampling and mashing-up. These artists' idea is that music is to be shared, sampled, and reworked to spur creativity, and they also sell music directly through net labels that often use Creative Commons licenses. Other artists, such as the Eagles, are trying to use the "termination rights" clause of the DMCA to recover ownership rights to their own compositions. However, other artists are unwilling to risk that and have lined up behind RIAA's efforts to restrain file sharing (see Sharing or Stealing?, page 162).

(see Sharing or Stealing?, page 162)

STOP & REVIEW

1. How has the digitization of recording formats affected the industry?

2. What is the relationship between recordings, labels, and major music companies?

3. What is the impact of record clubs and major retailers like Walmart on the music industry? What about online retailers like iTunes? Streaming services like Spotify?

4. What copyright challenges are raised by Internet music technologies?

World View

HOW MUSIC CROSSES BORDERS

Music is one of the main instances in which American audiences are widely exposed to cultural products from outside the United States. English rock and pop have had a strong presence since the 1960s, so much so that many American listeners take it for granted, along with music from Canada and Australia. Some musicians, like Canadian Neil Young, moved to the United States and became part of the U.S. scene. Others, like the Beatles or Rolling Stones, toured the United States to promote their music but continued to live elsewhere. Musicians from other English-speaking countries also had an easier time breaking into the U.S. market, even when they sing in a notably different dialect, like that of Jamaica (calypso, reggae, ska, dance hall). A number of other musicians have also learned to sing in English to break into both U.S. and global markets. Scandinavian artists like Abba and Björk became familiar this way. So music is one of the best examples of how the United States is part of a transnational Anglosphere, or English-speaking world, in culture (see more on transnational cultural-linguistic markets in Chapter 18).

The broad genre of world music represents a relatively serious music industry effort to market singers and groups that are often extremely popular in their home markets into the United States. Some examples have included bossa nova and samba from Brazil; Celtic music from Great Britain, Ireland, and France; various African genres; and other Latin American and Caribbean music, along with Balkan, Greek, and others.

MEDIA LITERACY

WHO CONTROLS THE MUSIC?

One of the most important issues to understand, in order to be media savvy or literate, is who makes the decisions on music: who to record, distribute, and promote. The music industry seems large and diverse, with dozens of recording labels. However, how large and diverse is the group of people making content decisions? How is that changing with technology, industry, and other changes?

RECORDED MUSIC IN THE AGE OF THE NEW MEDIA GIANTS

The music business has never been regulated in the same way that broadcasting traditionally was. Most of the major film studios—Warner Bros., Disney, Columbia, and Universal—were once involved in the music recording and distribution business. However, the music business is now seen as less profitable than some other media businesses, so a number of sales and mergers have taken place, resulting in three giant companies: Sony, Universal, and Warner. Fewer firms are making key decisions, which might raise concerns about monopoly. But other companies, based on new technologies, like Apple Music or Spotify, represent new giants in the business that challenge the centrality of the main labels.

Antitrust concerns are also raised by two other segments of the music industry that have a direct impact on aspiring musicians as well as their fans: concert promotion and concert ticket sales. Both are dominated by Live Nation Entertainment, a spin-off of Clear Channel Communications. Live Nation owns over 130 top live music venues, including the House of Blues in 12 cities; operates dozens more; and manages top performers including Madonna, U2, Shakira, and Jay-Z. Live Nation dominates ticket sales as a result of a 2010 merger with Ticketmaster, although regulators insisted that the firm license its software and open up competition in concert ticket sales as a condition for approving the deal.

SHARING OR STEALING?

Reuse of copyrighted music has been a major issue for the recording industry. When artists record a piece of music written by someone else, whether for direct sale or for broadcast, they have to obtain permission and usually pay a royalty, a fee charged for use of the writer's intellectual property. Some well-known court cases have been fought over whether an artist used another's basic melody. For example, Robin Thicke claims that he did not plagarize the tune for "Blurred Lines" from an old soul song by Marvin Gaye, "Got to Give It Up," but Gaye's family and estate are suing him in court over it. This problem has been accentuated with the rise of sampling in hip-hop and rap music, music **mash-ups**, and multimedia, where artists record and reuse

> A **mash-up** combines several audio and/or video segments or tracks into a new creation.

bits, or samples, of existing works. Courts decided in 2004 that any sampling requires getting permission and paying royalties.

Distribution of music over the Internet raises another copyright and intellectual property problem. Virtually flawless digital recordings can be transmitted over the Internet for recording on a cellphone, hard drive, digital tape, disc, or recordable CD. Technical solutions were sought to prevent illegal copying and transmission, while permitting the legal sale of music over the Internet, but most copy protection was dropped by 2008. Internet sites, such as those using the BitTorrent protocol, allow users to swap high-quality digital files that contain music. Much of the music being swapped between computers is copyrighted, and swapping those songs can be considered piracy—violation of the copyright of the artists or recording companies who own it. So as a listener, you have a legal dilemma when you turn to the Internet and MP3s to look for diversity of music. By looking for new talent on the Internet, you can help new bands get around the gatekeeping of the music and radio industries, but if you only listen to their MP3s and don't buy their CDs or legal downloads, or listen on media like Spotify or Pandora that pay royalties, they won't survive.

According to RIAA, which represents the music industry, the association also began to sue individual downloaders—more than 20,000 by 2008—and settled suits with 3,900 of them. It proved sufficiently controversial that RIAA discontinued their policy of prosecuting downloaders. Nonetheless, it appears that file sharing is beginning to decline in favor of other forms of free online music such as Spotify or Pandora. However, the industry was concerned enough about continuing piracy issue to press in 2011 for new laws, which were opposed by Internet industry groups and users, to the point where the proposed laws were withdrawn in Congress. The recording industry turned to a system of monitoring BitTorrent and other sites of copyright violation, then issuing warnings through the Center for Copyright Information (see Chapter 16).

PITY THE POOR, STARVING ARTISTS

In their struggle against file sharing, a favorite tactic of the RIAA has been to call attention to the plight of poor, starving artists whose livelihoods have been ruined by illegal downloading. Other, less established artists see downloading as a way to break through the creative stranglehold that the industry has on new acts and reach the public on their own terms.

And it is comical that the industry should accuse music fans of starving the musicians when the industry itself has been bleeding artists dry for years. Rock-and-roll veteran Courtney Love "did the math" for the suits a few years back at an RIAA gathering. She pointed out that after paying for record manufacturing and promotion fees, a band with a hit record gets only a modest middle-class income, not the riches that aspiring musicians imagine. Punk original Johnny Rotten had to work for two decades to pay back what he owed his record company, after such "creative accounting," and only succeeding by using income from television commercials to pay back what he owed (McGuinness, 2015).

What's more, you don't even own your own songs. Standard industry practice is to have the artist sign over the rights in their first recording contract.

The Copyright Term Extension Act further empowers the media giants at the expense of the artist. Would your garage band like to record its own rendition of some song that would now be public domain under the old act? A hit from 1935, Depression-era hits like "The Good Ship Lollipop" might strike a resonant chord today. You can't use it under the current copyright laws.

Artists disagree on how to deal with record companies. Most just sign on and hope for the best. However, some are exploring their options. Many groups go to independent labels because no big label wanted to sign them or because the typical profit split (50/50) with indies is better than with the majors. But some groups create their own label or go to a smaller one to keep more control or get a better deal in terms of revenue sharing. For example, the Rolling Stones were one of the most famous rock groups of the 1960s but they only made much money after starting their own label in the 1970s. Independent labels, those that are not owned by the big conglomerates, are growing, although many get bought up by major labels. Many of these independent labels are actually distributed by major recording companies, but not all.

GETTING DISTRIBUTED MEANS GETTING CREATIVE

Both recording artists and record companies are grappling with the Internet, which has toppled established techniques for promoting talent and marketing music sales. One novel approach was Radiohead, which released *In Rainbows* for digital download on its own website, asking fans to pay what they thought it was worth. Although many downloaded it for free, it garnered so much publicity that it doubled the sales of Radiohead's previous two albums.

One new means to promote music to very specialized interests is Internet radio. Latino rappers, among others, use Internet radio to reach people who aren't necessarily concentrated into large, easily identified geographic areas for conventional radio coverage. As Internet radio takes off, recording companies have demanded that webcasters pay royalties for recorded music they play. Two industry groups, the Digital Media Association (DMA) and the RIAA, agreed in 2003 to a proposal for royalty fees that Internet radio services must pay record companies for webcasting their songs. That was first administered by the nonprofit SoundExchange. It collected royalties on behalf of recording copyright owners and featured artists for noninteractive digital transmissions, including satellite and Internet radio (see Chapter 7). However, this system was challenged in a number of lawsuits. Currently, the Library of Congress collects fees from statutory Internet radio licenses at rates decided by three judges on the Copyright Royalty Board.

Recording companies are finally beginning to get a bit more creative about distribution over the Internet.

NOT FOR SALE IN PERSON Radiohead released their album *In Rainbows* on the Internet first, letting fans pay what they wished for it.

Warner Music is experimenting with some relatively unknown acts by signing them to a digital-only label. It will release their songs through services like iTunes and Rhapsody, where its digital sales have grown considerably. They hope signing acts with small but established audiences will earn the company a profit on digital sales alone. This also lets them avoid the costs of the conventional distribution model: making a music video, paying music promoters to push the songs to radio stations, and advertising.

Some new distribution groups, such as Netlabel, are springing up. EMusic started an online music service that will give independent musicians a new option. The site will sell music from over 3,000 independent labels, a total of a half-million tracks. It may help fans locate small, obscure, and eccentric music; help musicians find their fans; and grab a chunk of the more than $2 billion in revenues generated annually by independent music labels. Another kind of alternative is a company called ArtistShare. Bypassing labels, distributors, and retailers, ArtistShare sells discs over the Web and turns over all the proceeds (minus a small fee) to the artist.

Some have hoped that the Internet would provide a meaningful counter-force to the music industry giants. That is beginning to happen, with artists like Lana Del Rey selling music and branded merchandise online on their own, through social networks, or through new net labels such as those found at www.netlabels.org.

MUSIC CENSORSHIP?

The record industry had some self-censorship up through the 1960s. To get on the Ed Sullivan Show in 1964, the Rolling Stones changed the lyric "let's spend the night together" to "let's spend some time together." Even in the late 1960s, FCC rules against obscenity and indecency restrained many radio stations from playing songs with lyrics like Jefferson Airplane's "up against the wall, mother f**ker." But many major rock groups carried by big labels began to use graphic language and explicit themes. This spread from rock to rap and hip-hop, so that quite a bit of the most popular music by the 1980s had some explicit lyrics. However, many songs over the years have had a word or two changed, blurred, or dropped in versions for radio, airplay, MTV, or other music video channels, in television or film soundtracks.

Congressional hearings in 1989 resulted in warning labels on record and CD covers, but their effectiveness has been questionable. In fact, many music sellers noted that music labeled with warning stickers sells faster, and sells at a higher volume, to both children and adults. In part, lyrics that might be considered problematic were very pervasive. In fact, even more challenging artists, like Rick Ross, whose lyric in rapper Rocko's hit, "U.O.E.N.O.," seemed to describe using the drug "molly" for a date rape, are now widely distributed and played on the radio. However, the climate for acceptance of rough lyrics can change. Ross's lyric received widespread criticism on social media and by the National Organization of Women, leading Rocko to drop the lyric and Reebok to drop Rick Ross from an endorsement deal.

The concentration of power in top retailers was apparent when, starting in 1997, Walmart refused to carry certain recordings that it considered offensive, including all CDs with parental advisory stickers. Walmart has some reason for caution. It was sued by parents over a CD by rock group Evanescence that contains swear words (Freemuse, 2007). Some artists now change lyrics in order to ensure that major chains, like Walmart, will carry them.

GLOBAL IMPACT OF POP MUSIC GENRES

Rap and hip-hop have flowed quickly and widely out into the rest of the world, where many people are listening to U.S. hip-hop and rap artists like Kanye West. This type of music is popular in a wide variety of countries from China to Mozambique, so much so that some people are worried about musical homogenization as hip-hop and rap replace earlier imports, like U.S. rock and local music. Clearly, this wave has sunk in. The authors have heard people singing or humming along to hip-hop in Brazil, Denmark, France, Mexico, Mozambique, and Taiwan. U.S. hip-hop dominates among imported music in many countries.

For many, however, the big story is not Chinese kids listening to Lil Wayne, but Chinese kids and others doing their own hip-hop and rap. A remarkable number of countries are producing their own rap or hip-hop, and local versions tend to do much better on the local charts than the imports. Many musicians also see rap as an appropriate music of protest to use in their own circumstances. Moroccans living in France listen to rap from home to feel less culturally isolated or to protest their living conditions in France. A Brazilian documentary, *Little Prince's Rap Against the Wicked Souls* (2000), showed a local rap group cheering on a vigilante who took on drug gangs when the police didn't act.

Some critics insist that hip-hop and rap reflect a specific urban African-American culture and history, so other cultures' appropriations of them would be a new form of cultural imperialism, homogenization, or Americanization. For example, the original film *Black Orpheus* (1959) introduced Brazilian samba and bossa nova to the rest of the world, so many Brazilians were shocked when a remake, *Orfeu* (1999), featured as much Brazilian hip-hop as samba. Many others see hip-hop and rap as just another global musical genre to be appropriated and localized. For example, well-known Brazilian samba and pop musician Caetano Veloso defended the use of hip-hop in *Orfeu* as highly appropriate for dramatizing issues in Brazilian slums and a good fit for the adaptability of Brazilian culture (2002). Analyzing this as musical hybridity, it seems that cultures have never been static. They always take in new forms and ideas (Pieterse, 2004). Rap itself is a hybrid with many roots, particularly from Africa. So it fits well with the ongoing diaspora of African musical traditions across the globe, which previously nourished rock and samba, among many others.

SUMMARY & REVIEW

WHAT KIND OF MUSIC INDUSTRY EXISTED BEFORE THE PHONOGRAPH?

Music was performed live for audiences. It was also printed as sheet music and sold for home performance. The phonograph made casual listening easier and increased the sizes of audiences for music.

WHAT WERE THE MAIN ORIGINAL TRADITIONS IN POPULAR MUSIC?

Blues is an African-American musical tradition based primarily on guitar and distinctive plaintive lyrics. Gospel originated as southern Protestant religious music. Country music developed from English, Scottish, and Irish roots with similar instrumentation and ballad forms.

HOW DID RADIO CHANGE THE MUSIC INDUSTRY?

It further increased the reach of musical performances. It also increased the size of the audience to a truly mass audience and emphasized performers over composers. It created national audiences for music but also permitted regional genres—such as country and western and blues—to evolve.

HOW DID RADIO BROADCASTING AFFECT THE RECORDING INDUSTRY?

At first, the recording industry's sales fell off, as people moved to purchase radios instead. Over the long run, the recording industry came to rely on radio to make people aware of artists and recordings that they could purchase.

HOW HAVE THE MAIN MUSIC GENRES EVOLVED?

The most popular genres in the 1920s were probably big band music, jazz, country, blues, classical, Broadway tunes, and gospel. From those evolved rhythm and blues, soul, and rock and roll, which have fragmented and further evolved into contemporary genres like hip-hop, rap, metal, modern rock, alternative, and so on.

HOW DO COMPACT DISCS WORK?

Whereas phonographs reproduce analog sound from grooves in records, CDs reproduce sound digitally, from 1s and 0s recorded as pits on the CD surface. The digital signal is then reconverted to the analog form and sent as electrical impulses to the amplifier and then to the speakers.

HOW IS THE INTERNET AFFECTING MUSIC DISTRIBUTION?

Some artists are now releasing music over the Internet to increase their audience and promoting it through social media.

Internet users are also exchanging copyrighted music files over services like LimeWire, leading record companies to fear that they are losing control over the business. Record companies and recording artists have sued both MP3 exchange services and Internet radio stations to get better compensation.

WHAT ARE THE KEY COMPONENTS OF THE RECORDING INDUSTRY ORGANIZATION?

They include the talent (the singers and musicians), the recording studios and technical producers, the recording company, the distributors, and retailers. Recording studios are diversifying, as cheap digital systems based on computers let small studios and even individuals record music too.

WHAT ARE RECORD LABELS?

Labels of record companies are particular names for a group of recordings, which usually represent a consistent type of music. One company may own several diverse labels.

HOW ARE RECORDINGS DISTRIBUTED AND SOLD?

Music companies decide which albums and songs to promote through radio, billboards, newspaper and magazine ads, music videos, music video services like YouTube, and online services like Rhapsody. The record companies distribute recordings in a variety of ways, including rack jobbers, retail music stores, big-chain stores, Internet stores or catalogs, record clubs, download services like iTunes, and streaming services like Spotify. The big three are Sony, Universal, and Warner, which have over 80 percent of the U.S. market.

WHAT ARE THE LIMITS ON FREEDOM OF SPEECH IN RECORDINGS?

The record industry practiced some self-censorship up through the 1960s. But after that, major rock groups carried by major labels began to use more graphic language and explicit themes. Congressional hearings in 1989 resulted in warning labels on record and CD covers, but their effectiveness has been questionable, since even more challenging artists are now widely distributed and played on the radio.

WHAT ARE THE MUSIC COPYRIGHT ISSUES?

Issues include making sure that artists get reimbursed for radio and Internet play and trying to forestall piracy of digital recordings over the Internet.

THINKING CRITICALLY

ABOUT THE MEDIA

1. How does the history of popular music help us understand where music is going as a business? As artistic statements? As politics?

2. What can other media industries learn from the challenge digital media and Internet distribution created for the music industry?

3. Has large-scale listening to black music by white audiences helped race relations?

4. Does the drive by the music industry to discover the next big hit keep other interesting music from being discovered?

5. Is the American music scene too fragmented? Or is it a good thing that people listen to just what they want?

KEY TERMS

AAC (p. 143)

acoustic (p. 132)

bluegrass (p. 134)

blues (p. 134)

copyright (p. 140)

cover (p. 135)

disc jockey (DJ) (p. 136)

electromagnetic recording (p. 142)

gospel (p. 134)

high fidelity (p. 133)

hybridizing (p. 135)

mash-up (p. 151)

MP3 (p. 143)

nickelodeon (p. 132)

payola (p. 136)

stereo (p. 142)

Victrola (p. 133)

MindTap®

Test your knowledge with online printable flashcards and online quizzing.

MindTap® Log on to the MindTap for *Media Now* to access a variety of additional material, including this chapter's ebook, learning objectives, comprehension quizzes, videos, and more!

RADIO

LEARNING OBJECTIVES

After studying the topics in this chapter, you will be able to:

1 Compare the economic structures of the American radio industry's advertising-driven model with the British radio's public license fee model.
2 Describe how the 1996 Telecommunications Act impacted radio station ownership.
3 Summarize the technological changes that occurred in radio broadcasting, from AM through FM and HD broadcasting.
4 Compare the radio programming strategies used by noncommercial and commercial radio stations.
5 Discuss how a radio format clock changes to reflect the interests of its audience throughout the day.
6 Analyze the influence of audience research and ratings in the competitive radio marketplace.
7 Examine the impact of new forms of Internet radio like Pandora or Apple's Beats 1 station on existing broadcasting or satellite radio station and networks.

HISTORY: HOW RADIO BEGAN

Save the *Titanic:* Wireless Telegraphy

In 1896, Italian inventor Guglielmo Marconi created a "wireless telegraph" that used **radio waves** to carry messages in Morse code. This was the first practical use of radio. Marconi employed his business flair to establish the Marconi Wireless Telegraph Company, setting up a series of shore-based radio stations to receive and retransmit telegraph signals to oceangoing ships, where telegraph wires could not reach. His company also manufactured and operated the radio equipment and dominated radio in Europe and the United States in an early example of global **vertical integration.**

In 1912, the wireless telegraph played a pivotal role in the *Titanic* disaster. The British ocean liner struck an iceberg and sank suddenly in the North Atlantic. It sent radio distress calls, tapped out in

NEWS REPORTERS such as NPR's Bob Edwards are one of the forces that keep radio an important national information medium.

CHUCK KENNEDY/KRT/Newscom

MEDIA THEN··· MEDIA NOW

1896
> Marconi develops the wireless telegraph

1906
> De Forest invents vacuum tube

1920
> Frank Conrad starts KDKA in Pittsburgh

1926
> RCA starts NBC Radio Network
> AT&T pulls out of broadcasting

1949
> DJ era of radio begins

1960s
> FM stations increase, go stereo, target segmented audiences with different formats

1996
> Telecommunications Act sets off radio station merger frenzy

2010
> Pandora and other Internet radio services take off

Morse code over the Marconi wireless system, relayed to radio operators in New York.

Not only was radio crucial to saving many passengers, it became central to reporting about the disaster, riveting people on both sides of the Atlantic. This attracted public attention to the fledgling technology—so much that the U.S. Congress took note and placed radio licensing under the supervision of the Department of Commerce in the **Radio Act of 1912,** beginning **regulation** of the airwaves.

Regulation of Radio

A number of inventions began to come outside Marconi's company, such as the invention of the vacuum tube in 1906 by De Forest. It permitted continuous sound wave transmission and reception, beyond the on/off transmission that had sufficed for the transmission of coded messages in wireless telegraph systems. This led to disputes over control of the technology through **patents**. During World War I, the U.S. Navy accelerated radio technology by intervening in patent disputes between Marconi and other early inventors, standardizing the technologies. After the war, Marconi tried to buy U.S. patents to consolidate a U.S.–European communications monopoly, but the U.S. government opposed

MindTap®

Start with a quick warm-up activity.

Radio waves are composed of electromagnetic energy and rise and fall in regular cycles.

Vertical integration is when a company with the same owner handles different aspects of a business (within the same industry), such as film production and distribution.

Time Life Pictures/Pix Inc./The LIFE Picture Collection/Getty Images

BEFORE MP3s Early radio broadcasted Morse code, not music. Here Marconi, at left, receives the first transatlantic signal.

1896

Marconi develops the wireless telegraph

1906

De Forest invents vacuum tube

Radio Act of 1912 first licensed radio transmitters.

Regulation is government restriction or supervision of privately owned activity.

A **patent** gives an inventor the exclusive right to make, use, or sell an invention for 20 years.

1920

Frank Conrad starts KDKA in Pittsburgh

Frequency is the number of cycles that radio waves complete in a second.

Licenses grant legal permission to operate a radio transmitter.

foreign control of a technology so crucial for military purposes. The navy still held temporary control over radio technology and assets. It proposed making radio a government operation. A negotiated settlement forced Marconi, an Italian citizen, to sell his American assets to General Electric (GE), which set up a new company, Radio Corporation of America (RCA), with American Telephone & Telegraph (AT&T) and Westinghouse, to develop the radio business in the United States. GE, RCA, and AT&T set up a patent pool in 1920 because none of them owned all the patents to make completely functioning radio transmitters or receivers (Streeter, 1996).

Broadcasting Begins

Frank Conrad, a Westinghouse engineer, began the first regularly scheduled radio broadcasts in the United States in 1920, attracting interest and newspaper coverage. A Pittsburgh department store sold radios to pick up Conrad's broadcasts. Westinghouse realized that regular radio broadcasts could help sell radios, so it opened station KDKA in Pittsburgh. Retail stores started radio stations to promote their goods. Newspapers saw news potential; schools and churches saw educational possibilities. With so many rushing into radio, the Commerce Department was asked to combat **frequency** interference, so it issued hundreds of **licenses** in 1923.

Two visions of radio probably determined its future. In 1916, David Sarnoff, then commercial manager of American Marconi, wrote a prophetic memo to his boss. He proposed "a plan of development which would make radio a 'household utility' in the same sense as the piano or phonograph. The idea is to bring music into the house by wireless. . . . The Receiver can be designed in the form of a simple 'Radio Music Box' and arranged for several different wavelengths, which should be changeable with the throwing of a single switch or pressing of a single button." Sarnoff's memo was ignored, but he anticipated perfectly the physical form that radio would take within 10 years. Later, as head of RCA, he had a chance to help make this vision of radio and a similar vision of television a reality.

The second defining vision for radio—entertainment supported by advertising—came from AT&T's station WEAF, started in 1922 in New Jersey. Following the model of the telephone industry, AT&T charged content providers a fee for the use of its radio stations, based on how much airtime they used. This evolved into letting manufacturers sponsor programs to advertise their goods, and then into advertisers paying to have their ads carried on programs. WEAF broadcast the first "commercial." Advertisers immediately responded to the opportunity. Commercial broadcasting grew quickly.

By 1927, U.S. radio had attained a distinct shape. Privately owned stations were linked into networks that determined most of the program choices, focused on popular entertainment, heavily tilted toward music, and were supported by commercial advertising—a model it retains today. Some audiences contested this model, preferring a more populist form of radio (Razlogova, 2011), but overall the network model won out in gaining station affiliates and listeners. This had an enormous impact on U.S. culture as people became more aware of how those in other parts of the country lived. It also increased awareness of national issues; the experience of being a national audience inspired a feeling of being more of a nation (Douglas, 2004).

A number of strong economic interests came together to set this pattern. RCA and other radio manufacturers wanted to sell radio sets. They wanted the most broadly appealing content broadcast to sell more radios. Radio stations, and soon radio networks, discovered a way to make a great deal of money selling advertising. Networks arose to supply stations with the most popular entertainment in a way that spread costs across a number of stations. Advertisers saw a way to create a mass consumer public, turning people first and foremost into consumers by promoting their goods on the airwaves. This changed how Americans thought about money, careers, credit, and even where they wanted to live: country, small town, or city (Hilmes, 1997).

Radio offered advertisers direct access to the home. To increase the size of the audience for their ads, advertisers steered stations toward entertainment programs, which were more lucrative than news or education (Streeter, 1996). In the 1920s, regulators and the radio industry worried that audiences would reject radio if it carried too much advertising. However, people were so enthusiastic about the new medium that they accepted the ads without much objection, and a commercial advertising-based model was soon firmly entrenched (Barnouw, 1966). This quick shaping of radio by commercial interests laid down a pattern that other media followed, both in the United States and abroad. The global shape of broadcasting today reflects this then-unique arrangement of radio in the United States.

BBC, License Fees, and the Road Not Taken

In 1922–1923, the British sent a commission to the United States to study radio development. They observed a rush toward a radio industry dominated by musical entertainment and paid for by advertising. They saw that as a waste of the medium's cultural and educational potential. On returning home, they recommended a public radio monopoly oriented toward education and culture, financed by a license fee paid by listeners, and overseen by a board intended to keep it independent of both government and private interests, such as advertisers. This system, which became known as the British Broadcasting Corporation (BBC), was highly regarded for news, cultural, and educational broadcasting, although many find some of the programming elitist, dry, and stuffy. Globally, it represented one major alternative to the model chosen by the United States in the 1920s, particularly in Europe and Japan. Within the United States, it created an alternative idea of radio that eventually turned into the nonprofit public network, NPR.

SOS Distress signals from the *Titanic* called public attention to radio communication.

1926

AT&T pulls out of
broadcasting

Radio Networks

AT&T became the first broadcast network, as it used its phone lines to link several of its stations. However, the U.S. government and major electronics companies opposed AT&T's domination of both broadcasting and telephony (Sterling & Kittross, 2002). Thus, to keep its telephone monopoly, AT&T sold out to RCA in 1926 and agreed to act as a transmission medium for all radio networks on an equal basis.

1926

RCA starts NBC Radio
Network

Paying for Programming: The Rise of Radio Networks

RCA set up its radio network, the National Broadcasting Corporation (NBC), in 1926. Networking, linking of stations together to share programming costs, made each station cheaper to operate by realizing *economies of scale* (see Chapter 2). Competition came when the Columbia Broadcasting System (CBS) quickly put together a network to rival NBC's. Both networks had their own stations, called *owned-and-operated* stations, or **O&Os.** Both also began to attract a number of **affiliated** stations, which they did not own but which carried their network programs as well (Sterling & Kittross, 2002).

> An **O&O** is a TV or radio station that is owned and operated by a network.

> An **affiliate** is a station that contracts with networks to distribute their programming.

> **Chain broadcasting** is synonymous with a broadcasting network.

Early network radio programming in the 1920s and 1930s was focused on music but also included news, comedy, variety shows, soap operas, detective dramas, sports, suspense, and action adventures. Many radio performers came in from vaudeville-style theater, such as George Burns and Gracie Allen. Comic books lent heroes, such as Superman, to radio adventure shows. Pulp-fiction westerns like *Riders of the Purple Sage* fed into radio westerns, such as *Gunsmoke.*

Because recording technology had not achieved very high fidelity, music was primarily broadcast live. Recording artists and companies were also initially unwilling to let radio play their recorded and copyrighted music until a royalty system was devised to compensate them. Networks introduced the most popular groups and orchestras to the entire country, which reinforced their appeal and power. The major pop music of the day included big band, light classical music, and movie and show tunes. Eventually, however, radio also stimulated a demand for a variety of musical genres, ranging from classical to blues, gospel, country, and western.

Radio Network Power

There was concern that the radio networks were abusing their power in one-sided dealings with their affiliated stations and with the on-air talent. The FCC's (Federal Communications Commission) 1941 **chain broadcasting** ruling prohibited the networks from forcing programming on affiliates and put the networks out of the talent-booking business. The FCC also forced NBC to sell off its second network, which became the American Broadcasting Corporation (ABC).

AND NOW, LIVE FROM NEW YORK! Early network radio like this early game show, *Pot-o-Gold,* was all live, but also very popular and eagerly supported by advertisers like Turns.

Network radio remained strong through World War II. Money spent on radio ads doubled, surpassing expenditures on newspapers. Radio was the paramount information medium of the war. Internationally, the use of radio for propaganda purposes frightened many people and stimulated research into the power of mass media over their audiences.

CBS radio reporter Edward R. Murrow broadcasted memorable live reports from London during World War II (1939–1945), dramatically covering the German bombing of London. His reports conveyed vivid, realistic, and often highly moving word pictures. He emerged as one of the most credible and admired newsmen in the CBS news organization (Edwards, 2004) and helped network radio, particularly CBS, achieve preeminence as a source of news.

Competition from Television

After 1948, television exploded across the United States (see Chapter 8). Radio was quickly and adversely affected. Many nonmusical broadcast programming genres, from news to westerns to soap operas, moved to television.

Radio networks saw their own parent corporations, such as RCA and CBS, refocus their energy on new television networks. They were entranced with both the audience and the advertiser response to television, seeing it as an even more profitable medium than radio. So their radio networks were left to struggle to try to find new niches and functions. Promising new radio technologies like FM were left undeveloped for decades as radio's parent networks focused all their energies on television.

> **Formats** are radio label content aimed at a specific audience.

> **Playlists** are the songs picked for air play.

Networks Fall, Disc Jockeys Rule

As television's popularity skyrocketed and it became the main source of mass entertainment nationwide, network radio began to slip. Audience attention, especially during the prime evening hours, moved to television. Advertising followed programs, like the popular western *Gunsmoke,* and audiences to television. Stations began to leave the networks, and network revenue dropped even more. Radio station management explored new ways to attract a more local audience.

Radio advertising shifted from a national to a local focus and began to rely on cheaper, more localized **formats,** such as recorded music, news, and talk. Success began to depend on the talent of each station's own announcers, on their ability to find the right music mix for their local market. Programming strategies organized around a **playlist** of music and focused on a particular genre or audience.

New radio formats featured rhythm and blues (R&B) and rock and roll. Disc jockeys (DJs) played records aimed at

THIS IS THE WOLFMAN HOWLIN' ATCHA! DJs like Wolfman Jack characterized radio from the 1950s to the 1980s.

DJ era of radio begins

Top 40 is a radio format that replays the top 40 songs heavily.

1960s

FM stations increase, go stereo, target segmented audiences with different formats

local audiences. So although many records became national hits, local music, such as bluegrass in the South, blues in Chicago, and country and western in rural areas, all helped stations thrive that catered to those local needs.

Todd Storz probably invented Contemporary Hit Radio (CHR), or **Top 40**, in 1949. He wondered why radio could not be more like a jukebox, playing the hit songs that young people really wanted to hear the most, over and over. Top 40 was the dominant radio format from the 1950s until the early 1970s. It played a mix of rock and roll, pop, Motown or soul, and some R&B.

The FM Revolution

Just as film companies looked for new technologies to compete with television, so radio companies developed FM to revive radio in the 1960s. FM has *high-fidelity* sound, but a short range—within the line of sight of the radio transmitter. That allows for more stations in each market by reducing interference with stations in nearby markets that use the same frequency. Since each market could have at least 15 FM stations, there was a tendency to focus on segmented audiences with more specific formulas and formats. Both FM and 33 1/3 rpm records moved into *stereo* sound (two separate, coordinated channels of music). By the mid-to-late 1960s, many popular groups were recording songs much longer than the 2- to 3-minute cuts typical of Top 40 AM radio, but which were fine for new formats on FM.

In the 1970s, "rock" radio split into Top 40, new wave, heavy metal or heavy rock, punk, soul, funk, and disco. The 1980s and 1990s added formats for alternative, industrial/techno, new age, ska, reggae, rap, and hip-hop. These stations gave expression to musical subgenres, the audiences that enjoyed them, and the advertisers that coveted those subcultures. Subcultures like punks, skaters, or hip-hop not only listened to different music, but also consumed very different clothes and shoes, so marketers could more easily target them via specific radio formats.

Some targeted FM radio formats, such as classical, jazz, or album-oriented rock, took advantage of the musical quality of FM's higher fidelity and new stereo capability. Much of the audience was also interested in improved sound quality, because high-fidelity stereo systems were becoming much more popular, and that had a decisive appeal for discerning listeners (Jones, 1992). FM came to dominate the radio industry. By 1979, FM stations drew over half of the audience, and their share was growing steadily.

Local DJs Decline: A New Generation of Network Radio

Though radio was characterized by local operations in the 1970s and 1980s, new forms of network radio began to emerge in the 1990s. Some stations bought into centrally produced program formats distributed via satellite. Large radio ownership groups began to act like the radio networks of old, looking for economies of scale from centralized program production.

To meet the demand for interesting music, news, and talk programs on dozens of FM and AM stations in each market, a number of outlets began to produce programs for **syndication.** Conservative talk radio pundit Rush Limbaugh developed a network of stations that carried his syndicated program.

Syndication is the rental or licensing of media products.

Other companies began to offer complete radio formats, such as the "Bob FM" format (random hits from several decades) on syndicated distribution. Advertising, the DJ's patter, and even "local" traffic and weather were increasingly broadcast from a distant location using local information. Regionalization became the dominant trend. One of the largest ownership groups, Clear Channel, dismissed dozens of local DJs in its stations in small markets, replacing them with regional or even national voice talent who voice "local" stations to reduce costs.

Changes in ownership limits established in the **Telecommunications Act of 1996** permitted radio station groups to acquire many more stations and grow much larger. The new regulations lifted national caps on how many stations a group could own but limited ownership within local radio markets, depending on the size of the market. As a result, thousands of stations changed hands in a few short years and ownership consolidated.

Clear Channel Communications was the largest ownership group that emerged. In a number of local markets, stations belonging to just two or three groups controlled 80 to 90 percent of radio ad revenues. That peak of concentration raised both policy questions and internal management problems. Clear Channel never became as profitable as anticipated, so it sold off over 400 stations from a peak of 1,100. After rebounding from the Great Recession in 2010, radio advertising sales have stabilized at about $17 billion per year.

With the return of advertising dollars, group owners are again on a buying spree. Clear Channel is adding stations again and is challenged by Cumulus Media. Cumulus is also challenging Clear Channel's talk show king Rush Limbaugh with new hosts, including Geraldo Rivera and former presidential candidate Mike Huckabee. Internet and mobile phone music apps (see Chapter 6) revenues rose from 2009 to 2013, so Clear Channel and others have invested in new media as well, like Clear Channel's iHeartRadio online radio and app.

1996

Telecommunications Act sets off radio station merger frenzy

> **The Telecommunications Act of 1996** is federal legislation that deregulated radio ownership rules and the communications media. It opened the U.S. telecommunications industry to competition.

New Genres: Alternative, Rap, and Hip-Hop Radio

Radio stations, particularly in FM, have continued to change or modify formats to follow the evolution of music genres and audience interests. For example, rap and hip-hop became prominent in the "urban" radio format. Rap, hip-hop, and contemporary R&B artists like Beyoncé have given African-American artists perhaps their highest visibility in pop music and Top 40 radio since Motown in the 1960s.

Latino artists have created a strong rap and hip-hop tradition of their own, which has fed into new musical genres and radio formats like reggaeton, mixing elements of hip-hop, reggae, and various Latin genres. An increasing number of Spanish-language rap format radio stations are a good example of how music genres grow and

ONLY ROCK N' ROLL The Rolling Stones are one of the bands that launched album-oriented FM radio in the 1960s.

Neal Preston/Historical/Corbis

subdivide, closely followed by radio formats. Some artists start in a smaller format, and then move to more widespread formats, as Latino artist Cypress Hill did when he moved from Latino to hip-hop stations and gained greater overall hip-hop radio popularity. Rap and hip-hop have also spread internationally, so raperos and reggaeton singers in Mexico now create music that flows back into the United States and vice versa. For example, a new radio format called "Spanish Contemporary" includes salsa and other Caribbean music, Mexican norteño, and Latin alternative.

2010

Pandora and other Internet radio services take off

Radio in the Digital Age

Satellite radio offers hundreds of more channels than terrestrial broadcasters, which are limited to 20 to 30 FM channels and a dozen or so AM channels in most American cities and towns. The two companies that dominated satellite radio, XM and Sirius, merged their operations in 2008. They hoped that by making exclusive deals with star announcers like Howard Stern, they would pull listeners from conventional broadcasts. Broadcasters worried that satellite radio would lead to a decline in both number and variety of local radio stations. However, after several tentative years, satellite radio is just now growing in the number of listeners and in revenue, finally turning a profit with over 24 million subscribers in 2013, which increased 7 percent by 2015. Much of Sirius' success comes from listeners in cars, so it may be threatened by the current push to put Internet connectivity into cars, so drivers would have many more new choices in Internet radio.

Internet radio is growing faster and is one of the few growth areas in radio advertising sales. Internet radio includes online streaming off existing stations, their network program sources (like NPR), and Internet-only stations and music services like Pandora and Spotify. Web radio networks list thousands of Internet radio stations. They cover mainstream pop artists and include many of the familiar formats of commercial radio, like country and western or adult contemporary. Thousands of local radio stations feed their programming to the World Wide Web through sites such as iHeartRadio (operated by Clear Channel) in an effort to reach out-of-town listeners and people at work. But there are many "Internet-only" channels that cannot be found on the air, playing things much too specific or offbeat to ever get on the air. According to Pew, over 53 percent of Americans over 12 listen to online radio networks, while 91 percent still listen to broadcast radio on a weekly basis (Vogt, 2015).

When radio stations offer Internet streams, it can boost the number of listeners they have, but any who tune in from outside the station's local broadcast market do not support the prevailing broadcast radio business model that depends on local ad sales. **Podcasting** is also a threat in that it lets almost any individual create audio programs that can be downloaded onto digital devices. Podcasting had its first breakout hit with *Serial* in 2014. The current digital trend is Internet radio apps for smartphones and tablet computers, offered by Clear Channel, Pandora, Spotify, Apple, and others. Pandora and last.fm are music discovery services that suggest new music to you based on what you have listened to or say you like. Spotify lets you play what you want, but also offers suggestions, and includes friends'

Podcasting is recorded messages or audio programs distributed through download to computers, iPods, or other portable digital music players.

playlists. A listener in rural Iowa who wants gospel-flavored Latino hip-hop probably won't find it on the local airwaves but can easily do so on Web-based stations, like podcasts, or perhaps even a smartphone app. However, podcast and app listeners, users, and subscribers to the new "cloud" music services like Spotify (see Chapter 6) all threaten the traditional radio broadcast model in that they can subtract music fans from the radio advertising base in the local markets where their listeners live. Social media also pose a continuing threat to the conventional broadcast model, since people often embed links to music, often on YouTube or Spotify, in social media posts. The music file-sharing craze that rocked the music industry (see Chapter 6) was an early social media phenomenon that predated the rise of social networking services like Facebook and continues today. Now music fans can share their favorite tunes with their Facebook friends, bypassing CD retailers and iTunes as well as their local radio stations. YouTube is another social media threat to radio broadcasters following a deal that was struck between its owner, Google, and music publishers that allows advertising to run alongside music videos on the site. Meanwhile, both new artists, like rappers Mac Miller, and established stars, like Beyoncé, are finding that they can promote their music through social media and distribute it online without the benefit of radio airplay. Beyoncé released her 2013 self-titled album, songs and videos, directly to iTunes, announced it to her 8 million Instagram followers, and sold 365,000 copies on the first day without resorting to conventional radio promotion strategies.

YOU'RE ALL WE NEED Despite changes in technology to play and deliver music, new genres like reggae-ton and hit music by popular artists like Rihanna are still what draw people.

Nonetheless, broadcast radio continues as an enjoyable and even indispensable medium for millions of listeners, from those who want the hits to those who want the news from NPR: 91 percent of Americans listen at least once a week. Although traditional FM radio revenues increased in recent years, AM radio revenues have slipped in the past few years and some new smartphones and consumer electronics interfere with AM signals. There has even been discussion about reallocating the AM radio band to mobile Internet applications. Congress is trying to protect AM radio as audiences dwindle by changing current rules requiring them to reduce their transmitter power after sunset (a measure that protects stations from interfering with one another). Another tactic is to hobble the competition, such as by lobbying the FCC for rules that prevent satellite radio from transmitting local traffic information and supporting extra copyright fees on Internet radio. At the other extreme, broadcasters lost their campaign to limit extremely local low-power radio stations, and there are currently about 800 on the air in the United States. Broadcasters are also banking on an innovative new digital offering of their own, high-definition (HD) radio, and there are over 2,200 HD radio stations already in operation, or about 15 percent of all radio. Stay tuned (to the next section) for more on that.

STOP & REVIEW

1. How did advertising come to dominate radio economics?

2. What kind of regulation was necessary for radio to develop technically?

3. What kinds of programming characterized radio networks in the 1930s and 1940s? Why did they decline?

4. How did radio formats change after the decline of radio networks?

5. How did music genres of the 1960s and 1970s and FM radio affect each other?

6. Why did radio station ownership concentrate in the 1990s?

7. How do new technologies like Web radio, smartphone apps, and podcasts affect broadcast radio?

TECHNOLOGY TRENDS: INSIDE YOUR RADIO

From Marconi's Radio to Your Radio

Radio was the first wireless communications medium, but the others that followed, including broadcast television and cell phones, follow the same basic principles of *electromagnetism* that Marconi harnessed in the nineteenth century. If you are interested in how things work—or are curious about the radiation that pulses through your head when you hold your cell phone to your ear—then be sure to read Technology Demystified: Fun with Electromagnetism?

High-Definition Radio

High-definition radio (formerly known as digital audio broadcasting) transmits audio that has been converted to computer data, as in a CD recording, over the air from earthbound radio transmitters to special digital receivers. This increases the quality of the sound and makes radio signals less susceptible to fading. Near CD-quality sound is the result, leading to the "high-definition" label, borrowed from high-definition TV. The digital signal also includes information about the music so that listeners may set their radios to "seek hip-hop" if they so desire and see the name of the station and the tune they are listening to on their display. The digital signals can also pack additional channels of information, such as news updates and alerts about travel and weather conditions.

While HD radio has been on the air since 1997 in Europe, it has been slow catching on in the United States. To protect their vested interests, radio stations insisted that the new service be transmitted in the same frequency band and on the same channel (the approach is called "in band, on channel") as their current stations, while maintaining the conventional analog service, which

Technology Demystified

FUN WITH ELECTROMAGNETISM?

You may remember a demonstration by your fifth-grade teacher; we'll call her Ms. McGiver. She showed you how you could make an ordinary iron nail into an electromagnet by winding a wire around it and connecting it to a battery, remember?

Then Ms. McGiver sprinkled some iron filings on a piece of cardboard, reconnected the electromagnet to the battery, and showed you that she could move the filings around the surface of the cardboard by passing the magnet under it. This proved that electromagnetic fields are invisible and act at a distance without any physical medium to convey them, just as a radio transmitter affects the antenna on your radio from miles away.

Then she hooked up a coil of wire to a meter that measured electric current and moved a magnet back and forth through the middle of the coil. As the magnet moved, the needle on the meter twitched, showing that a changing magnetic field made an electric current flow in the wire. This is what happens inside your radio antenna and also in the playback head of a tape recorder, converting a magnetic field back to electricity

Like the waves of water, radio waves rise and fall in regular patterns, called "cycles." The number of cycles that the waves complete in a second is their frequency and is measured in **Hertz (Hz)**. We refer to the height of the wave as its amplitude, and the phase refers to the point in the cycle at which we begin. In water, we can splash by either forcing our hand down on the water's surface, creating a "trough," or by bringing our hand up from below the surface, creating a "crest." The spectrum is a means of classifying electromagnetic radiation according to its frequency. The sounds made by our stereos and our iPods are between 20 and 20,000 Hz, the range of frequencies that can be heard by the human ear.

The radio frequencies used in our consumer electronics devices are organized into bands. For example, AM radio is in the high-frequency band; VHF television (channels 2–13) takes its name from the very-high-frequency band—that's also where FM radio is located. Similarly, UHF is the ultra-high-frequency band. Cell phones and satellites use yet higher-frequency bands.

Communication channels are assigned according to the frequency of their carrier waves. But additional frequencies clustering around the carrier are needed to encode the audio or video information, and the more space we have for each channel, the more information we can transmit. The total range of frequencies needed is the bandwidth of the channel. AM radio channels are 10,000 Hz, compared to 100,000 Hz for FM radio and 6 million Hz for television. Some parts of the spectrum are better than others. For example, the AM radio spectrum is highly desirable because waves can travel thousands of miles, whereas FM signals can barely peep over the horizon.

AM (amplitude modulation) means that the sound information is carried in variations in the height, or amplitude, of the radio wave. In an AM radio system, the electric current that comes out of a microphone or an electronic recording device is combined with a high-frequency electromagnetic carrier wave that corresponds to the frequency of a particular radio channel that can be found between 535 and 1,705 kHz. For example, the carrier wave is 540,000 Hz if you have your radio tuned to 540 on the AM dial. The combined wave is amplified and fed into a radio transmitter, which is essentially a giant electromagnet. The combined electromagnetic wave induces a weak electric current inside your radio antenna. Then the carrier frequency is removed and the original audio is recovered, amplified, and sent to the speakers (see Figure 7.1).

In **FM (frequency modulation)** radio, the sound information is carried by variations in the frequency of the radio wave around the central carrier frequency, which is 101,700,000 Hz if you are tuned to FM 101.7. Compared to AM, FM has a greater frequency range and less static, so stereo broadcasting was begun in the FM band (88–108 MHz). The FM channels are wide enough so that two slightly different versions of the broadcast can be carried. These are electronically combined inside your receiver to produce the two separate signals you hear in your left and right speakers.

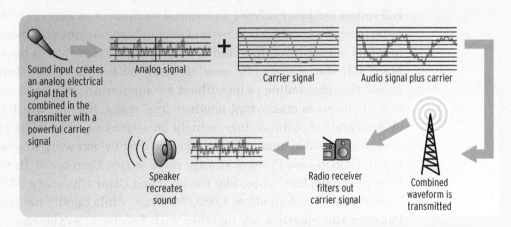

Sound input creates an analog electrical signal that is combined in the transmitter with a powerful carrier signal

Analog signal

Carrier signal

Audio signal plus carrier

Speaker recreates sound

Radio receiver filters out carrier signal

Combined waveform is transmitted

FIGURE 7.1 HOW AM RADIO BROADCASTING USES RADIO WAVES The announcer's voice is converted to electricity by the microphone. This electrical signal is then combined with a powerful, high-frequency carrier signal and transmitted to the home receiver. The receiver filters out the carrier and recreates the original electrical analog signal, which the loudspeaker converts back to sound energy.

took several years to perfect. Digital radio allows stations to broadcast several different channels within the same frequency space. NPR stations have taken the lead in many areas, broadcasting a classical music channel in addition to their regular programming, for example.

Satellite Radio Technology

Sirius transmits music via satellite to compact receivers via wafer-shaped antennas that can be placed on the roof of a car, bypassing earthbound radio stations entirely. Local *repeaters* mounted on the tops of buildings and hills operate in the same frequencies as the satellites and enable Sirius's signals to be available even if the view of the satellite is blocked by buildings or mountains.

Internet Radio Technology

In 1995, hobbyists, ad agencies, and regular broadcast stations began to create full-time Internet radio stations. Near CD-quality stereo can be had if you have a fast enough network connection. Internet streaming technologies make it possible to listen to programming in real time instead of downloading and saving prerecorded files. *Podcasts* are MP3 digital files (see Chapter 6) that can be downloaded to your smartphone, iPod, or tablet so that you can listen to talk, news, music, or whatever someone with a computer, microphone, and software wants to create. A variety of radio stations now broadcast on the Internet, some through websites, some through apps on smartphones and tablets.

Weighing Your Digital Radio Options

HD radio stations are slowly becoming more available and may take off now that HD radios are being offered as original equipment in new cars. Home satellite radio receivers boasting hundreds of channels are an option, although they carry monthly subscription fees and are not quite as portable as terrestrial radio. Many HD stations are also available now on Internet radio. Internet "appliances" that play online radio without a computer are available, and the spread of Wi-Fi hotspots makes that another "free" option through which to access tens of thousands of stations. Increasingly, smartphones and tablets are displacing dedicated portable music players like the iPod by accessing free online streaming and "cloud-based" music storage services (see Chapter 6). Branded streams through smartphone apps, like Pandora and Clear Channel's iHeartRadio, are also growing. Pandora offers 1,000,000 songs, while Spotify has over 20 million. Pandora and Spotify work together with Facebook, so you can see what your "friends" are listening to. So, unlike what they say in radio, don't *stay* tuned!

INDUSTRY: RADIO STATIONS AND GROUPS

Radio in the Age of the New Media Giants

Radio lives in a contradictory time of countervailing trends. New digital technologies seem to allow many more new entrants in radio, broadly defined, although they have also led to the dominance of digital music by Apple iTunes.

However, economic and regulatory changes also encouraged unprecedented concentration of the ownership of a few major players (in terms of hits, sales, and profits) all across the radio industry.

Radio stations were once owned by many kinds of individuals and small groups. After the 1996 Telecommunications Act deregulated ownership, concentration of station ownership in the hands of new, nonlocal groups increased dramatically (Table 7.1). The goal for these large groups has been to achieve national coverage. The largest of these, Clear Channel, boasts that it offers potential advertisers as much national coverage via its radio stations as do television networks. Groups can now own multiple radio stations in a single market, too, so they can offer an advertiser exposure on several different formats, such as country, classic rock, and urban contemporary that accumulate a large audience that no single station can boast.

Regulations in the 1996 Telecommunication Act permitted increased **cross-ownership** across industries. So Cox (cable), Disney (film and television), and others acquired radio station groups, too. Most of the major film studios were involved in the music-recording and distribution business. Regulations in effect until the 1980s prevented those studios from owning broadcast stations or networks, or vice versa. Now, as studios like Disney acquire television networks, such as ABC, they also get involved in the radio business, integrating broadcast distribution with their existing music production, an example of vertical integration. Some ownership groups, like Clear Channel, Townsquare, Entercom, Emmis, and Cumulus Media, are based primarily in radio, which reflects horizontal integration more than the kind of vertical integration represented by Disney or CBS (see Chapter 2).

> **Cross-ownership** occurs when one firm owns different media outlets in the same area.

Inside Radio Stations

Radio stations vary greatly in the size and complexity of their staff. However, they all have to take care of certain basic functions: administrative (payroll, accounting, purchasing), technical (engineering, transmitter operation, maintenance of FCC logs), programming (local, news, music playlists, network or syndicated programs, promotion of programs), and sales (local sales, relations with national and regional sales firms). Traditionally, most of these were done locally with at least a small staff. However, with the growth of ownership groups and the supply of programming by centralized services, most of these functions are done by a centralized group staff, which covers a number

TABLE 7.1 **Top Radio Industry Ownership Groups**

RADIO GROUP	NUMBER OF STATIONS OWNED IN 2015
Clear Channel	850
Cumulus Broadcasting (purchased Citadel Communications)	505
Townsquare Media	325
CBS Radio (purchased Infinity Broadcasting)	117
Entercom	120

Source: Ownership group corporate sites.

of stations across a state or region or even the national market. That has radically reduced the number of jobs available in radio.

In an independent station, the manager oversees planning, audience development, ratings, and sales. The program director supervises the air sound, playlists, DJs, and announcers. A music director plans the playlists. Producers are usually required for talk shows and drive-time shows. Many stations also have a news director. Someone has to keep the station on the air, so there needs to be an engineer on duty. Commercial stations have a sales manager and an advertising sales staff. The advertising sales staff was crucial for selling local advertising. However, at network stations, most of these jobs have been consolidated on a regional basis. Over the years, Clear Channel fired dozens of local DJs, sharing popular shows across radio stations instead. Even "local" weather is often remotely announced by someone hundreds of miles away.

When it comes to working with national advertisers who might want to sell national spot ads in the local market, that function is delegated to *advertising rep* (short for "representative") firms. The representatives work on behalf of radio stations to sell ads to national advertisers, although large radio station groups are heavily involved in this as well. Radio is third in local advertising revenue, after direct mail and local television, slightly ahead of local newspapers (Fratrik, Boland, & Ducey, 2015).

Syndication (see Chapter 2) is an important factor in the radio industry. Syndicators produce programming for resale to other media outlets. For example, Sean Hannity, who started as a talk show host on WABC in 1997, was syndicated to other stations in other markets in 2001, and is now a streaming radio host through Clear Channel's iHeartRadio service.

Noncommercial Radio

Commercial radio dominates, but many stations are licensed for noncommercial formats and purposes. They tend to focus on news, education, classical music, jazz, independent rock, a variety of ethnic immigrant music, and public affairs. Many are owned by universities or other educational groups, although quite a few are owned by foundations, local nonprofit groups, churches, and others. **Low-power** FM licenses now offered by the FCC only to nonprofit and government organizations are increasing the diversity of noncommercial radio through many community groups. Most noncommercial broadcasters are FM stations, typically at the lower end of the dial. Most AM licenses were granted before the FCC started reserving a few licenses in each market for educational and noncommercial groups.

Public broadcasters are roughly one-third of all noncommercial stations, compared to a larger number of student-run stations at universities, and a smaller number of religious stations. Most depend on a mix of government, institutional, and listener support. Many public stations tend to focus on news and public affairs programs. Some public stations program music that is not commercially profitable, depending on the market. Over a third of public stations program a great deal of classical music; others

Low-power stations have more limited transmission power and cover smaller areas than regular FM stations.

Public broadcasters aim to serve public interests with information, culture, and news.

NEWS REPORTERS such as NPR's Bob Edwards are one of the forces that keep radio an important national information medium.

program jazz and, on many college stations, folk, indie rock, noncommercial rap, and so forth. A number of noncommercial stations also program to religious audiences or in languages spoken by too few local residents to support commercial broadcasting. Some large cities may have several noncommercial stations. Before 1990, public radio stations tended to depend quite a bit on program support from the Corporation for Public Broadcasting and financial support from federal and state governments. Since 1990, the funding for those national resources has been steadily cut back, so public stations have come to depend more on their sponsoring institutions (including many colleges and universities), other supportive local institutions, local sponsors, and direct contributions from listeners. However, as much as NPR listeners dread local stations' pledge weeks, appeals to local listeners have often been very successful, now producing as much as 90 percent of some affiliates' revenue, so NPR is more fiscally solvent and independent of national government program support than is PBS TV.

GENRES AROUND THE DIAL

Radio Formats

Rigid musical programming formats dominate many stations. They focus on an hourly cycle of music, advertisements, station promotions, short news items, traffic reports, and weather reports. We can visualize this hourly cycle as a **format clock** in the shape of a record (see Figure 7.2). This hourly schedule shows the DJ when to play certain kinds of music, when to read a news item, when to play prerecorded ad spots or promotions (promos), when to read ad copy, and when to bring in another announcer for news, weather, sports, or traffic.

Format clock is an hourly radio programming schedule.

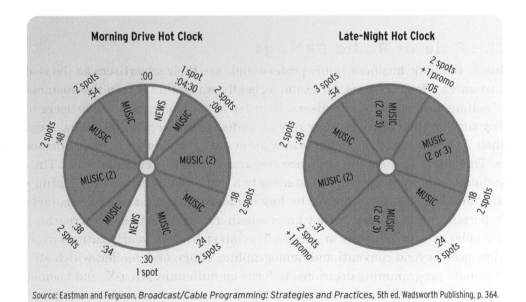

Source: Eastman and Ferguson, *Broadcast/Cable Programming: Strategies and Practices*, 5th ed. Wadsworth Publishing, p. 364.

FIGURE 7.2 CLOCK CONCEPT OF FORMATS Radio programmers and DJs often use a clock concept to program what will be played in an hour: music from different lists, spots or ads, news and weather, and so on.

Source: Eastman and Ferguson, *Broadcast/Cable Programming: Strategies and Practices*, 5th ed. Wadsworth Publishing, p. 364.

This hourly schedule often includes just enough news, sports, weather, and talk to meet the audience's general interests, but focuses on music. The key programmer, therefore, is the music director (or the station's music format consultant) who selects the music that fits into the various parts of the hourly schedule to capture and hold the audience's attention. The music director creates a playlist of songs, organized by categories. A typical Contemporary Hit Radio (CHR) station has a playlist of a few top songs that might be repeated almost hourly at various points on the clock, interspersed with a few songs that are rising in popularity and a few others that are fading but still popular. Depending on the station or network, the DJ either plays exactly what the music director specifies or picks songs within a fairly narrow range. For stations that use syndicated program services or among stations owned by national groups, music selection is often centrally decided. Although the format clock is most associated with Top 40 radio (or CHR in contemporary terms), similar repetitive patterns may be found at country and western, urban contemporary, and even classical stations.

The format clock is no longer followed as religiously as it once was. For example, many stations have turned to a menu of talk and humor lightly interspersed with music during the morning drive-time hours, while focusing more on music later in the day. Others vary their music blocks to provide "thirty continuous minutes of commercial-free music" or "twelve in a row" in hopes of attracting audiences during commercial breaks at other stations.

These blocks may be commercial free but not *promotion* free, as radio stations seem to be constantly promoting themselves. The various on-air contests, station identifications, listener call-ins, dedication lines, and concert promotions are a vital part of radio programming, too, to build listener loyalty and get them to put that station on the preset buttons of their car radio or the equivalent on their mobile apps or computer.

The Role of Radio Ratings

Inside the radio business, many professionals see their advertisers as the real customers. Clear Channel, for example, boldly states that it is in the business of selling audiences to advertisers. In order to persuade those advertisers to buy time on their stations, they rely on audience research to show how large their audience is and, more important for many advertisers, who the audience is. This kind of pragmatic audience research is called a **ratings** study. They estimate how many people are listening to a station at a certain time. Ratings also break down the audience by key demographics that are particularly important to advertisers, so they know whether the people their ad is reaching are older or younger, male or female. The latest Nielsen yearly ratings overview goes beyond conventional demographics of age and gender, which still dominate programming decisions, to focus on millennial, Gen-X, and boomer age groups, as well as African-American and Latino audiences (Nielsen, 2014).

In 50 of the largest radio markets, Nielsen Audio uses electronic meters that radio listeners carry with them, called *portable people meters,* that automatically record the stations they come in contact with during the day while working, playing, or driving. Eventually, the company hopes to replace paper diaries in all of the 279 markets it tracks nationwide. Through its electronic

Ratings measure the proportion of television households that watch a specific show or how many people are listening to a radio station.

meters, Nielsen Audio now examines all manner of radio listening, broadcast, online, and through apps; considers programs such as Pandora as well as conventional radio stations; and plans to follow listening across many kinds of devices in different spaces and places. However, the electronic meters have dramatically lowered the ratings of stations that target minority groups, probably because Nielsen has a difficult time retaining African Americans and Hispanics in their panels. Also, the meters show that listeners tend to tune out DJ chatter between songs, leading to efforts to cut back on talking between records, including announcements of the song that just played.

Ratings can be crucial for establishing the importance, or more specifically the commercial attractiveness, of a new format or audience group. For example, whereas Latino audiences are now majorities in many cities, in others with much smaller Latino populations, it is not clear whether there are enough people interested in Latino music to attract advertisers and justify a commercial station focusing on them. In this kind of case, audience ratings research can help show whether a new station has a viable audience. Good ratings in one city for a new format, like "jammin' oldies" or "Jack," may lead other commercial broadcasters to try the format. Poor ratings may lead to long-standing stations or radio personalities undergoing radical changes. Many both inside and outside the industry are frustrated with the power of ratings.

Music Genres and Radio Formats

Increased competition for audience segments has also increased the importance of research. When deciding which music format to adopt, stations increasingly rely on consultants who try to determine which new format or format variation is likely to draw the biggest audience. This is becoming increasingly true of large ownership groups who own up to half a dozen stations in a single market. They use research carefully to avoid overlap in the audiences that they reach and to ensure that they reach the audience segments that are the most attractive to their advertisers.

In fact, stations are frequently targeted to some audience groups that are smaller than others but sufficiently attractive to advertisers so that both advertisers and radio programmers prefer to focus on them. This is apparent in Table 7.2, which shows that although Top 40, or Pop Contemporary Hit Radio, draws the third highest national share of radio listening, it has fewer stations than several other formats, including news/talk, country, religious, contemporary Christian, variety, adult contemporary, and all sports, most of which have lower listening shares nationwide. Similarly, urban adult contemporary has the eighth highest share, but fewer stations than most other formats, since its audience is concentrated in larger markets served by fewer stations. However, in specific local or even national advertising markets, the audiences for those other formats may well have greater purchasing power and be much more attractive to advertisers and, hence, to programmers. Some formats, like religion, are carried on commercial stations because of the interests of their owners rather than ratings.

Music genres evolve with their audiences, and many radio formats have changed quite a bit in the past decade. For example, starting in the late 1990s, many stations went to an "alternative rock" format "Jack," a supposedly

TABLE 7.2 Radio Formats' Popularity versus Share of Stations, 2013–2015

FORMAT	2015 AUDIENCE (%)	2013 AUDIENCE (%)	2013 # STATIONS
Country + New Country	15.2	14.2	2,893
News/Talk/Info/Personality	10.6	11.4	3,984
Pop Contemporary Hit Radio	8.0	8.2	1,012
Adult Contemporary + Soft AC	7.6	8.1	1,390
Classic Hits	5.5	5.2	883
Classic Rock	5.6	5.2	944
Hot Adult Contemporary	5.3	4.7	810
Urban Adult Contemporary	4.3	4.1	336
Contemporary Christian	3.5	2.9	1,691
All Sports	3.3	3.1	1,274
Urban Contemporary	3.2	3.0	274
Rhythmic Contemporary Hit Radio	3.0	3.4	370
Mexican Regional	2.6	2.9	550
Active Rock	2.0	2.1	356
Adult Hits	1.9	2.2	395
Album Oriented + Mainstream Rock	1.7	2.0	336
Alternative	1.8	1.9	614
Oldies	NA	1.8	831
Classical	1.5	1.4	823
Spanish Contemporary + Hot AC	1.3	1.5	224
All News	1.3	1.4	93
Religious	1.3	1.3	1,739
Album Adult Alternative	NA	1.1	508
Variety	NA	1.0	1,579
Gospel	NA	0.7	454

Source: Nielsen, *State of the Media: Audio Today,* How America Listens, 2015, p. 14.

random mixture of 1970s through 1990s rock hits. This format deliberately reached across a number of audiences for earlier, more targeted formats, like classic rock. "Jack" managed to bring in both younger and middle-aged audiences, thus reaching an interesting breadth of people for its advertisers.

This section has discussed mainly FM formats. Because of AM's broader signal reach, many stations in sparsely populated smaller towns adopt a format that is broad based, middle-of-the-road, such as country-western, talk, religious, variety, or oldies (e.g., classic rock, classic hits). So, AM accounts for many of those stations in the numbers in Table 7.2. In fact, as FM reaches further into more towns, and Internet radio carries more kinds of music, AM has gravitated more toward local news and talk radio.

Talk Radio

Over twice as many AM stations have a news/talk/news personality format as on FM. Thus, music is not the only game on radio. All-news stations and news talk formats are on the rise. As stations specialize, news, talk, weather, and sports information/talk grow in importance. A number of audiences are strongly attracted to news, sports, and talk, so station owners and advertisers who wish to pursue that audience tend to consider using this format. The news and talk general area is subdivided into a number of niches. Some stations do 24-hour news and weather. Most of those are national network news stations, but very few do primarily local news. Many stations carry nationally syndicated talk shows, such as those of Rush Limbaugh, Laura Ingraham, Glenn Beck, and others.

On the AM band, sound quality is not quite as high as on FM, so many AM stations emphasize news, talk, and sports

SYNDICATED Political talk personalities like Rush Limbaugh have become one of the mainstays of AM radio.

to take advantage of that. A mixture of talk and music has also proven very successful, particularly during morning commute hours (6 a.m. to 10 a.m.). Morning shows on major stations increasingly reflect a more chatty drive-time format, on both AM and FM. As the syndicated talk formats gain more of an audience, many FM stations that had focused on music find themselves changing to talk formats because they draw a more lucrative audience.

National Public Radio

Many public stations get much of their programming from a few key national sources: National Public Radio (NPR), Public Radio International (PRI), American Public Radio, and, for a few, the Pacifica Network. NPR is a growing source of news and news talk radio to more than 27 million Americans and provides an afternoon news program called *All Things Considered,* a morning news program called *Morning Edition,* and other programs to a large group of affiliated public stations. Government funding and listener support provide the majority of NPR funding, but some foundations and corporations offer funding for the certain kinds of programming and news that interest them.

Radio Programming Services

The economics of radio programming changed in the 1990s to favor centralized, syndicated, or networked programming. A number of different sources exist from which to choose. Many stations now subscribe to national, regional, or state networks for news and sports (including the regional networks on which college sports are broadcast). Syndicated radio programs most widely listened to are now news and talk: Rush Limbaugh, Sean Hannity, and others.

Music-oriented stations also carry syndicated programs, such as concert specials or Top 40 hit countdowns. Many also switch away from music in drive-time hours when a mix of local weather, traffic, and news or talk is most appealing.

STOP & REVIEW

1. What kinds of radio networks exist now?

2. How are radio formats related to music genres?

3. What are the target audiences for some of the main radio formats?

4. Why does the concentration of radio ownership cause concern?

5. What copyright challenges are raised by Internet radio and podcasting?

For an increasing number of station owners, locally programmed stations are a risky venture. Many stations buy complete, packaged music services such as "Jack" and "Bob" designed by outside experts who look at the prospective audience, consider the format options, and evaluate what has worked in similar markets. The 1960s-style DJ who picked his own records is almost extinct, eliminating quite a few entry-level jobs in radio.

A variety of radio programming services is available. The most complete are satellite-based networks that deliver news, music, and other entertainment and even sell national advertising. Those are the easiest options for an owner, who simply affiliates with a network and carries its programming, like old-fashioned network affiliates. Format syndicators provide a full music program but do not sell commercial ad time for the station or provide news or other information services. Full-service automation started with formats like "Classic Gold" and "Great American Country," by Drake-Chennault in the 1970s, but became much more popular when a wave of mergers swept the radio industry in the 1990s. Nonlocal owners were less likely to feel that they knew the peculiarities of the market and more likely to rely on relatively safe, nationally standardized formats. Locally programmed automation systems became cheaper; for example, a fully programmable system that handles up to 300 CDs, as well as tape machines for commercial and announcement inserts, costs under $10,000. Interestingly, some suppliers of syndicated shows and automated formats, like the Ambient music supplier, Hearts of Space, also sell streaming access plans to individuals, thus blurring the business of supplying formats to stations and music "channels" to individual subscribers.

Your Media Career

LOCAL DJS DECLINE BUT OTHER FORMS OF RADIO RISE

Jobs in the radio industry are strongly affected by the trends discussed in the chapter. DJ and announcer positions are slumping as broadcast stations use syndicated program services. Centralized sales and management also reduce the availability of some jobs; however, new jobs have been created by satellite and Internet radio in these areas and others. Changing news talk formats also create jobs.

Many small radio stations (38%) employ less than five people, but most jobs are in companies of at least 50 employees (Occupational Outlook Handbook, 2014). There are jobs in program production, news, technical, sales, and management. At small stations, jobs are less specialized and employees often perform several functions. On-air positions are the most visible jobs in broadcasting. There are about 52,000 employed as announcers in the United States, making an average of $29,000, with little or no growth expected in the next decade due to continuing consolidation in the radio industry. A bachelor's degree and an internship are typical entry requirements to get in back of a mic. The majority of employment opportunities are in front of the microphone rather than behind it: most managers start their careers in advertising and sales. There are actually more sound and broadcast engineers, over 117,000, better paid at an average of $43,000 because all radio stations are required to have a local engineer, even if he or she is only monitoring automated equipment, carrying completely prerecorded or piped-in programming.

MEDIA *LITERACY*

THE IMPACT OF THE AIRWAVES

One of the most important issues to understand, in order to be media savvy or "literate," is who makes the decisions on radio content. Radio seems very diverse, with dozens of stations in most areas. However, how large and diverse is the group of people making key radio content decisions?

WHO CONTROLS THE AIRWAVES?

The FCC is supposed to use a "public interest" standard for reviewing and renewing licenses, but that has proven too vague to provide a basis for denying license renewal to misbehaving broadcasters. For example, Howard Stern's indecency violations did not result in the denial of license renewals for any stations, the resulting fines were just "the cost of doing business," but it made them nervous, and he moved to satellite radio, whose content is not regulated by the FCC.

In the past, the FCC created rules about ownership, **concentration of ownership** and cross-ownership, obscenity and indecency in radio content, and the role of networks and affiliates. The Telecommunications Act of 1996 eliminated the national limits regarding ownership. Under the 1996 Act, a single owner can own up to eight radio stations in a market with 45 or more commercial radio stations. However, such limits have been challenged in the courts, but the FCC has cracked down on arrangements for selling advertising on multiple stations, known as joint sales agreements.

> **Concentration of ownership** occurs when several kinds of media or many outlets of the same kind of media are owned by a single owner.

CONCENTRATING OWNERSHIP, REDUCING DIVERSITY?

Fewer radio station owners than ever are local residents of the areas their stations serve, which presumably limits their ability to understand local interests. Fewer owners are minorities or female. Fewer stations are programmed locally because **group owners** often supply programming from a central source. The local stations are automated and play just the prerecorded programming.

> **Group owners** own a number of broadcast stations.

The counterargument is that concentrated ownership may actually provide more format diversity. When one group owns six to eight stations in a market, it will target each one at a different interest group.

What is more problematic is that news and information content lack genuine local input or diversity. This seems to go against the principle of maximizing localism that has, in theory, guided FCC licensing decisions since the 1934 Communications Act. A poignant case in point was a train accident in Minot, North Dakota, in 2002. Local residents tried to call the radio station to warn residents to evacuate, only to discover there was no one "there" at the remotely controlled "local" station. Some FCC commissioners are concerned now that the decline in AM radio may threaten some of the few stations in most markets that are locally programmed. (Music-oriented FM stations are more likely to be nationally networked than variety-oriented AM stations.)

What many community groups object to is precisely the decrease in local control and local input that the growth of groups like Clear Channel seem to imply. Enough individual citizens and groups complained to their congressional representatives that Congress instructed the FCC not to change the cross-ownership rules, and the FCC decided not to fight to change them. On the other hand, the FCC did vote to permit increased cross-ownership of newspapers and television in the same cities (see Chapter 16 for more information on how this process works).

Extensive horizontal integration may not even be in the interest of the owners. At its peak in 2006, Clear Channel owned 10 percent of all stations, but it took in about 20 percent of the overall advertising revenue and attracted about 25 percent of total listeners nationwide, which seemed to give it considerable advantage. It also took a lot of flack from critics, took on debt, and saw profits stall. So Clear Channel spun off its concert promotion business and sold over 400 stations in smaller markets to focus on its core business and markets. It still has over 850 stations. The second largest radio ownership group, Cumulus, has increased its numbers and now has 530 stations. So horizontal integration is still an issue regulators have to consider.

So, the bottom-line question amounts to this: is there enough diversity on radio *for you?* If the answer is no, you can join the Media Reform campaign (www.freepress.net). And you do have options from satellite or the Internet. If those are still not enough, then start your own radio station on the Internet. Internet radio providers like VosCast will put your station on the net for a few dollars a month and tell you how to share in advertising revenues, although you will have to pay royalties on the songs you play (see "Who Owns the Music?"). Don't do it to get rich, though, because it won't happen. Do it for the love of your own unique genre of music and, just perhaps, the joy of hearing your own voice on the radio.

YOU CAN'T SAY THAT ON THE RADIO

Freedom of speech continues to be a focus for radio broadcasting. In contrast, the recording industry has traditionally been lightly scrutinized. It has been considered analogous to publishing in that it doesn't involve use of a scarce public resource, such as the airwaves; it has a large degree of competition, and exposure to recorded music is, in principle, entirely voluntary.

Radio has been more closely scrutinized under the rationale that the airwaves are a scarce resource to be used in the public interest. The FCC has standards restricting **obscene speech** or **indecent speech.** Up through the 1970s, certain words could not be used, and broadcasters were held responsible even for call-in programs to make sure that prohibited language was not broadcast. The late comic George Carlin developed a comedy routine in that era about "Filthy Words," which featured words you couldn't say on public airwaves. Those prohibitions were challenged in court (see Chapter 16), but the FCC still restricts speech that is considered indecent—that is, that uses

Obscene or indecent speech depicts sexual conduct in a way that appeals to sexual interests in a manner that is "patently offensive" to community standards, and lacks serious artistic, political, or scientific value.

graphic language pertaining to sexual or excretory functions. The FCC prohibits such language during daytime and evening hours but has made the late-night hours between 10 p.m. and 6 a.m. a "safe harbor" for more explicit kinds of speech. Despite the prohibition, shock jocks, such as Don Imus, routinely violate the rule, are fined, and consider paying the fine a cost of doing business. Thousands of radio stations play music by stars whose lyrics probably also violate those rules, but music has been less scrutinized by the FCC than comedy or commentary. Others wonder whether the definition of indecency should be expanded from talk about sex and excretory functions to racial slurs and sexism. In 2007, Don Imus was suspended from his show after protests over his use of a racial slur against black players on a college women's basketball team. In 2012, Rush Limbaugh caused a national scandal and lost several advertisers for calling a birth control advocate a "slut" on his syndicated radio show.

CAREFUL WHAT YOU SAY The FCC controls indecency on radio, but not YouTube. Stars like Justin Bieber have used profanity and uttered racial slurs in videos. While the government has no legal mandate to control this, the visibility of such speech often brings its own sanctions in terms of public censure and criticism.

WHO OWNS THE MUSIC?

Reuse of **copyrighted** music, syndicated talk shows, and other intellectual property has been a major issue for the radio industry. The licensing of recorded music for play over the radio is complex. Copyright law requires payment for performance of work copyrighted by an artist, including the playing of a recording over the radio. Two main music-licensing groups—the American Society of Composers, Authors and Publishers (ASCAP) and Broadcast Music Incorporated (BMI)—serve as intermediaries between songwriters or other copyright holders and radio stations (although not the recording artist, since they don't receive performance royalties from radio). These two traditional groups have been joined by the Radio Music License Committee, which represents radio stations in negotiations with ASCAP. Radio stations get licenses for the music listed by the music-licensing group in return for a fee, usually 1 to 2 percent of the station's gross income. ASCAP or BMI then pays the copyright holders according to how often each song is played.

> **Copyright** is the legal right to control intellectual property. With it comes the legal privilege to use, sell, or license creative works.

Things are different for Internet radio, however. Internet radio stations are required to pay both songwriters and performers, at a rate higher than satellite or terrestrial radio, requiring a fee per song for each listener. In 2010, the Copyright Royalty Board set a gradually increasing fee (which for 2016 is 17 cents per 100 plays on free, ad-supported services and 22 cents on subscription-based platforms in 2015) for each use of copyrighted songs. The recording industry sees this as a new revenue stream to replace declining CD sales (see Chapter 6). After vehement complaints, separate settlements were reached for small and noncommercial webcasters.

SoundExchange is an industry-backed organization that collects royalties for record labels and artists. Pandora and other companies negotiated a compromise in 2009 that distinguishes between paid streaming services and large and small free services. Some of these negotiated agreements are about to expire and will have to be renegotiated. For example, SoundCloud just negotiated a new agreement with Universal. All pay an initial streaming fee; then different-sized operations have choices between paying fees per song played and flat percentages of their revenue, after they have established profitable revenue streams. Internet radio was to pay higher fees than satellite radio, but challenges by Pandora and others led to arbitration by the Copyright Royalty Board, an official U.S. government system of three judges, which now adjusts copyright fees for both satellite and Web radio.

SUMMARY & REVIEW

WHAT WERE THE KEY DEVELOPMENTS THAT LED TO RADIO BROADCASTING?

Marconi pioneered radio as a form of two-way communication. The development of the vacuum tube by de Forest was crucial. It permitted continuous soundwave transmission and reception, beyond the on/off transmission that had sufficed for transmission of coded messages in wireless telegraph systems. Other crucial developments included better microphones, amplifiers, tuners, and more powerful transmitters.

WHAT CAUSED THE RISE AND FALL OF THE ORIGINAL RADIO NETWORKS?

The main radio networks were put together by David Sarnoff at RCA/NBC and William Paley at CBS, who saw potential to make and sell radios, as well as to sell advertising. During their high point, network radio relied largely on music but also carried news, sports, comedy, variety shows, soap operas, dramas, suspense, and action adventures. Many of those genres moved to television after 1948. After television coverage and audiences began to grow, around 1948, network radio also began to lose much of its audience to television. Some of the types of entertainment it had relied on worked better for the mass audience with a visual component on television. Radio came to rely more on music, which could be programmed locally by DJs playing records.

WHEN DID FM RADIO BEGIN TO INCREASE IN IMPORTANCE? AND WHY?

FM radio offered stereo and higher fidelity. It began to increase as more receivers became available in the 1960s. It also prospered as FM stereo became widely available and appreciation of music

quality increased among the audience, making FM the main radio medium for music.

WHAT KINDS OF RADIO NETWORKS EXIST NOW?

New ownership and programming syndication groups, such as Global Digital and Clear Channel, created new networks around popular syndicated shows, such as Rush Limbaugh's. Large ownership groups like Clear Channel use a number of nationally programmed formats, which are the main new networks. NPR also emerged as a significant news and public affairs programming service, linking most of the nation's noncommercial, or public, radio stations.

HOW IS THE INTERNET AFFECTING RADIO?

Many radio stations are now transmitting their music, news, and other programs over the Internet to reach new audiences, both in their regular coverage areas as well as in distant ones, but some stations may have to close because of an inability to pay royalties to record companies and recording artists. Internet-based services, like Pandora and Spotify, increasingly integrated with other services, like Facebook, and now also compete with radio.

WHAT ARE RADIO FORMATS?

A format is a particular radio programming strategy oriented around a playlist of music and focused on a particular genre or audience. Common examples are Contemporary Hit Radio/Top 40, R&B/urban contemporary, and country. Radio formats have followed the segmentation of the audience and fragmentation of music genres.

Radio programming became decentralized as local stations pulled away from networks in the 1950s. DJ-driven formats like Top 40 or Contemporary Hit Radio dominated. New formats evolved on the increasing numbers of FM stations in the 1970s and 1980s. With the rise of large ownership groups and talk radio, centralized program service providers created a new form of network.

On FM, the main formats now are news/talk, country, contemporary Christian, religious, variety, adult contemporary, sports, classic rock, Contemporary Hit Radio, oldies, classical, hot adult contemporary, Spanish, alternative, and urban contemporary. AM stations tend to emphasize news, call-in talk shows, and talk and sports. AM stations also tend to serve smaller towns and rural areas, where the population is less dense.

WHAT ARE THE KEY COMPONENTS OF RADIO INDUSTRY ORGANIZATION?

The main elements of industry organization are national ownership groups, like Clear Channel; national music program services; national business services, like ratings organizations; and local stations. Affiliates in broadcasting are stations that contract to use the programming of a network and to share advertising and advertising revenues with it. Networks also have O&O stations. Group owners own a number of broadcast stations. Sometimes group owners provide these stations with common programming, as a traditional network would. New kinds of networks are emerging that provide programming for stations for a fee or for shared advertising. Companies can provide ready-made programming for dozens of formats.

WHAT WAS CHANGED BY THE COMMUNICATIONS ACT OF 1934?

The Communications Act of 1934 defined the broadcast band, standardized frequency designations, and created a more powerful regulatory body, the FCC. The FCC devised more systematic procedures for granting radio licenses and rules on transmitter power, height, and frequency use. The FCC imposed rules about ownership, concentration and cross-ownership, and the role of networks and affiliates.

WHAT WAS CHANGED BY THE TELECOMMUNICATIONS ACT OF 1996?

The Telecommunications Act of 1996 changed FCC rules about station ownership limits. It eliminated previous station ownership limits. For radio, there are no national limits, and local ownership caps increase with market size. This considerably increased concentration of ownership, which raises issues about content diversity, localism, and minority ownership.

WHAT ARE THE ISSUES INVOLVED IN CONCENTRATION OF RADIO OWNERSHIP?

A few large ownership groups now own as many as half of all stations in many cities. This clearly reduces the localism of ownership, which may then reduce responsiveness to local interests. Group stations are increasingly programmed at a distance, including programming of "local" news. Diversity of both music and news may well be reduced, although ownership groups claim that they actually increase the diversity of music formats available in a market.

WHAT ARE THE LIMITS ON FREEDOM OF SPEECH IN RADIO BROADCASTS?

Up through the 1960s, certain obscene words could not be used, and broadcasters were responsible for ensuring that they were not used. Those prohibitions were successfully challenged in court, but the FCC still restricts speech that is indecent. The FCC prohibits such language except during late-night spots that are a "safe harbor" for more explicit speech. Satellite and Internet radio are essentially unregulated in their speech.

THINKING CRITICALLY

ABOUT THE MEDIA

1. How does the history of radio help us understand how Internet radio, podcasting, and other audio media are going to develop as commercial forms? As artistic forms?

2. The United States was the first country to turn radio into a commercial medium. What does that tell us about how new media will develop in the United States? How might they be different elsewhere?

3. Does obscenity on radio need to be more tightly controlled? Justify your answer with examples from radio history.

4. What might justify new regulation to break up large radio groups and make radio a more local medium again?

5. Do you think broadcast radio still plays a positive role in helping people like you learn about new music? If not, what if anything should be done about it?

MindTap®

Test your knowledge with online printable flashcards and online quizzing.

KEY TERMS

affiliate (p. 162)

AM (amplitude modulation) (p. 170)

chain broadcasting (p. 162)

concentration of ownership (p. 179)

copyright (p. 181)

cross-ownership (p. 171)

FM (frequency modulation) (p. 170)

format (p. 163)

format clock (p. 173)

frequency (p. 160)

group owners (p. 179)

Hertz (Hz) (p. 170)

indecent speech (p. 180)

license (p. 160)

low-power station (p. 172)

O&O (p. 162)

obscene speech (p. 180)

patent (p. 160)

playlist (p. 163)

podcasting (p. 166)

public broadcaster (p. 172)

Radio Act of 1912 (p. 160)

radio waves (p. 158)

ratings (p. 174)

regulation (p. 160)

syndication (p. 164)

Telecommunications Act of 1996 (p. 165)

Top 40 (p. 164)

vertical integration (p. 158)

MindTap® Log on to the MindTap Communication for *Media Now* to access a variety of additional material, including this chapter's e-book, learning objectives, comprehension quizzes, videos, and more!

FILM AND VIDEO

MOVIES LIKE STAR WARS that are powerful enough to frame how we think about ourselves now converge and cross over with books, music, and video games. This power is exemplified in fans who gather at events like Comic Con.

GV Cruz/WireImage/Getty Images

LEARNING OBJECTIVES

After studying the topics in this chapter, you will be able to:

1 Discuss the influence of silent films on film genres, production techniques, and narrative formulas.

2 Weigh at least two advantages with two disadvantages of vertical integration in the 1930s Hollywood studio era film industry.

3 Give at least two examples of how the film industry responded to new competition from television in the 1950s.

4 Summarize three strategies that the modern movie industry has employed to remain profitable in the competitive digital market.

5 Define the following special effects terms: *rear projection*, *front projection*, *compositing*, *matte*, *postproduction*, and *nonlinear editing*.

6 Describe the role of each individual involved in the movie-making process, including studio executives, producers, writers, guilds, talent, distributors, and audience members.

7 Understand the role of indie production versus studio production in today's film industry.

HISTORY: GOLDEN MOMENTS OF FILM

The early years of film were marked by experimentation with content and forms, major technological innovations, and disputes over who could use, control, and benefit from the inventions. The first challenge was to capture motion on film. The next trick was to find a useful way of recording and showing events in motion.

Thomas Edison invented the first functional motion picture camera in 1888 (see Technology Trends: Making Movie Magic, page 197). The French Lumière brothers came up with the idea of projecting movies on a screen. Most early films simply showed short black-and-white, silent depictions of actual events in motion, such as horse races. *The Great Train Robbery,* made by Edwin S. Porter in 1903, was the first story film and was very popular. At first, audiences ducked when the train robber's gun fired into the camera.

Edison and Biograph, which had somewhat superior camera and projector technologies, pooled patents to establish a single motion picture standard. They tried to collect a fee from every new film.

MEDIA*THEN*···
MEDIA*NOW*

1888
> **Edison develops the motion picture camera**

1906
> **The Kelley Gang (60 minutes, produced in Australia) is the first feature film**

1927
> **The Jazz Singer *is the first "talkie"***

1946
> **At the peak of the film box office, 90 million people attend the movies weekly**

1948
> **Television competes; major studios have to divest their theater chains**

1968
> **MPAA movie ratings are introduced**

1977
> **Star Wars *highlights focus on big-budget blockbusters***

1995
> **Toy Story *is first major-release computer-generated film***

1997
> **DVDs are introduced**

2007
> **Netflix streams films over the Internet to an increasing number of devices**

2010
> **Avatar *is the highest-grossing film of all time, breaking 3-D into the mainstream***

2015
> **Star Wars: The Force Awakens *shows the continuing power of film franchises***

> **Netflix revives indie film market**

1888

Edison develops the motion picture camera

Feature films are story films, usually over one and a half hours.

Independent producers started to use bootleg equipment and moved their operations far away from the dominant companies in New York. They chose Hollywood, California, for its weather and space for studios. The industry became centered in Hollywood after 1915, and the earlier companies lost their control.

A number of films claim the title of being the first **feature film.** It seems to be *The Kelley Gang,* a 60-minute film produced in Australia. There were at least four feature-length films made in the United States in 1912. The early film that created the most controversy came in 1915, when film director D. W. Griffith released the controversial drama *Birth of a Nation*. He used well-produced out-door battle scenes, close-ups, and cuts between different simultaneous sequences of action, such as the threat to an imperiled heroine and the rescuers riding to save her, to increase dramatic tension. It was the most popular film in the United States for more than 20 years. However, the film, set during and after the Civil War, featured antiblack Ku Klux Klan members as its heroes and was used by the Klan as a recruiting film. Although the film was revolutionary in form, it was racist in content and was boycotted by the NAACP in its initial release. Concerned it would incite violence, several states banned the film, an early instance of film censorship. In the 1920s, the industry started self-regulation (see Violence, Sex, Profanity, and Film Ratings, page 208).

How to Use Images: Silent Films Set the Patterns

Hollywood has had several "booms" or "golden ages" of prosperity, artistic success, and widespread cultural impact. These booms have later been followed by "busts," when the film industry lost parts of its audience to newer media technologies. The first golden age was silent film, from 1903 to 1927.

Silent films established classic genre formulas for telling stories with images and motion that are still followed today. Because producers of silent films had to rely on visuals, with only brief written dialogue added in still frames, these films were oriented toward action, dramatic visuals, and lavish sets. *The Great Train Robbery* featured crime, action, and suspense, and *Birth of a Nation* showed battles, chases, and historical scenes. The genres they relied on are alive and well today in action-adventure (*Marvel's The Avengers*) and historical costume dramas (*Twelve Years a Slave*). Table 8.1 describes the major silent and early sound film genres.

MindTap

Start with a quick warm-up activity.

MindTap

Read, highlight, and take notes on the complete chapter text in a rich interactive online platform.

1906

The Kelley Gang (60 minutes, produced in Australia) is the first feature film

TABLE 8.1 **Early Film Genres**

SILENT FILM GENRES	EARLY SOUND FILM GENRES
• Westerns, such as *The Great Train Robbery* (1903)	• Crime dramas, with cops, gangsters, and violence, such as *Little Caesar* (1930)
• War movies, with battles and character conflicts, such as Abel Gance's epic silent *Napoleon* (1927)	• Animation, such as *Snow White and the Seven Dwarfs* (1937)
• Horror, including the original *Dracula, Nosferatu* (1922)	• Screwball comedies, with glamour and light humor, such as *It Happened One Night* (1934)
• Romances, love stories such as *The Sheik* (1921)	• Character studies, such as *Citizen Kane* (1941)
• Physical comedies, with car crashes and pratfalls (such as the *Keystone Cops* shorts) or facial expression and body language (such as Charlie Chaplin and Buster Keaton films)	• Detective movies, with complex heroes, or antiheroes, such as *The Maltese Falcon* (1941)
• Historical costume dramas, with fictionalized plots, such as D. W. Griffith's *Intolerance* (1916)	• Suspense, such as Fritz Lang's *M* (1931) • Monster movies, such as *King Kong* (1933)
• Documentaries, such as *Nanook of the North* (1921)	• Horror movies, such as *Dracula* (1931)
• Action-adventure, such as Douglas Fairbanks's *Thief of Baghdad* (1921)	• Musicals, such as *Flying Down to Rio* (1933)
• Melodramas and serials, such as *The Perils of Pauline* (1914)	• Film noir, "dark," skeptical films, such as *Double Indemnity* (1944)

Setting Up a System: Stars and Studios

From their new base in California, several **major film studios** developed a strong industrial production capability, producing movies almost on an assembly line, leading critics to complain about cultural industries that mass-produced culture (Horkheimer & Adorno, 1972). Studios developed their own complete teams of actors, writers, directors, technicians, and equipment that enabled them to produce large numbers of successful feature films.

Film studios discovered that certain actors and actresses could attract viewers no matter what the movie was about. The **star system** was born. Rudolph Valentino (*The Sheik,* 1921), Lillian Gish (*Intolerance,* 1916), Mary Pickford (*Madame Butterfly,* 1915), and Charlie Chaplin (*The Gold Rush,* 1925) became such attractions that their names appeared above the title of the film on theater marquees.

Even silent, early movies were visually powerful enough to create both adoration and controversy. Some movies in the 1920s shocked audiences with sexual themes, partial nudity, and depiction of a fast urban life, as in *The Jazz Age* (1929), where both men and women "partied" hard. Stardom made the private lives of these early movie actors more visible, and some stars' lives were scandalous to many viewers. The industry decided to impose self-censorship before it was censored by outsiders. In 1922, the studios created the Motion Picture Producers and Distributors of America, known as the Hays Office after the former U.S. postmaster general who was put in charge of it. It created voluntary content guidelines, the **Motion Picture Code.** The Catholic Church, B'nai Brith, and National Education Association all pushed for a production code that forbade scenes that portrayed "crime, wrongdoing, evil, or sin" in a positive light. Hays soothed public complaints but imposed a tough internal censorship that bridled the creativity of industry writers, directors, and actors (Knight, 1979).

1927

The Jazz Singer is the first "talkie"

FILM LEGENDS Stars were important to the success of the film medium. Douglas Fairbanks and Mary Pickford (bottom row) were so big that they started their own studio, United Artists (with Charlie Chaplin and D. W. Griffith).

How to Use Sound: Look Who's Talking

Attempts were made almost from the beginning to make the moving pictures talk. The studios and movie houses were initially reluctant to invest in sound technology because it was new and expensive. Eventually, Warner Brothers made the commitment to develop sound technology and created *The Jazz Singer* in 1927. It featured two sections of recorded music and included singing that was synchronized with the film so that the singer's lips moved when they were supposed to. It also had a little bit of recorded dialogue, which fascinated the audience. Unfortunately, *The Jazz Singer* also reflected American racism of the time: rather than featuring an African-American performer, the film used white singer Al Jolson playing the jazz singer in "blackface," dark makeup that made him look like a negative parody of an African American.

Talkies ended the golden age of silent movies. Acting became less stylized, since plot could be carried by dialogue, not just by expression and gesture. Studios suddenly had to become skilled in the use of sound effects and music. Some actresses and actors did not have the vocal quality or more subtle acting skills to survive, as illustrated in the classic *Singin' in the Rain* (1952). Talkies required an influx of new talent, such as Fred Astaire, from vaudeville and Broadway, who talked, sang, and danced. Because audiences liked talkies, they made even more money for the producers of the movies. In a few years, nearly all films had sound.

New genres arose that emphasized the advantages of sound (see Table 8.1, page 187), showing one of the ways technology and culture interact. A new golden age of movies created extravagantly produced musicals, with lavish visuals, dancing, and singing. A series of films by the elegant dancing team Ginger Rogers and Fred Astaire, starting with *Flying Down to Rio* in 1933, put music and motion together.

Comedies became more verbal, with jokes and sophisticated bantering added to the silent repertoire of slapstick and sight gags. Several comedy subgenres were created to play with sound. The zany comedies of the Marx Brothers, such as *A Night at the Opera* (1935), poked fun at authority. Screwball comedies, such as *It Happened One Night* (1934), featured Clark Gable and other big stars in elegantly set and clever but silly stories of romance.

Sound, dramatic visuals, and action were combined in increasingly complex genre formulas that often addressed concerns of the day. Crime stories, such as *Little Caesar* (1930), reflected a real-life increase in organized crime that grew with the prohibition of alcohol. Another genre was detective films, such as *The Maltese Falcon* (1941), directed by John Huston, which featured Humphrey Bogart. A key genre variation was the **film noir,** "the dark film," such as *Double Indemnity* (1944), which tended to be more skeptical, even cynical, and had antiheroes instead of the simpler heroes of earlier films. Suspense and mystery stories, such as Alfred Hitchcock's *The 39 Steps* (1935), constituted another major genre. Historical epics were another: *Gone with the Wind* (1939) continues to be a classic. War films, like *All Quiet on the Western Front* (1930), became a staple. World War II was such a pivotal experience for many Americans that films based on it, like *Valkyrie* (2008), persisted as a genre long after the war was over. By the late 1960s and 1970s, the growing negative public reaction to the Vietnam War changed the nature of war films to a more critical view, with films like *Apocalypse Now* (1979).

Similarly, the western became another means for exploring the American myth and American character. Director John Ford created a number of classic westerns. They gradually changed from the optimistic, positive view of cowboys and cavalry soldiers exemplified by *She Wore a Yellow Ribbon* (1949) to films such as *Cheyenne Autumn* (1964), which began to consider the perspective of Native Americans as "good guys," with a different slant on the American conquest of the West.

The Peak of Movie Impact?

The cultural impact of movies in the United States, and the world, in the 1930s and 1940s was extraordinary. Most people—especially young

> **Talkies** are motion pictures with synchronized sound for dialogue.

> **Film noir** comprised the "dark," moody American films of the 1940s, often focused on detectives or similar themes.

BEYOND DISNEY Director Chuck Jones (1912–2002) added many innovations and a wry sense of humor to animation at Warner Bros. *One Froggy Evening* (1957) was one of many films he created.

people—went to the movies weekly if their families could afford it. One ticket got you into the movie house and you could stay all day, watching the double-feature films as many times as you'd like. Going to the movies meant watching a *newsreel*—visual news of the world before television news—serial dramas, and cartoons sandwiched before and between the feature films. Audiences waited all week to see what would happen next to Flash Gordon or other heroes of the serials. Although the Depression (1929–1939) kept some people away, most tried hard to find a couple of dimes for the movies, and collectively bought about 70 million tickets a week. Hollywood provided a form of escapism that helped people forget their troubles. The pure fantasy of *The Wizard of Oz* (1939) and the antics of Shirley Temple and *The Three Stooges* are enduring examples of brilliant 1930s escapism. American movies also went international. Other audiences were intrigued by the modern U.S. life they saw on-screen, and studios pushed exports very hard, often aided by the U.S. foreign policy. The studios had joined together as the Motion Picture Export Association of America (MPEAA) in the 1930s and had taken control of much of the international film distribution business (see Chapter 18).

The Studio System: The Pros and Cons of Vertical Integration

Movies made a lot of money. As profits went up and movies became a successful business, a merger wave took place. The Great Depression killed off many small producers and nearly 5,000 independent movie theaters (Gomery, 1991). This strengthened the economics and control of a few big studios, and it concentrated production decisions in the hands of very few studio executives, a reality that came to be known as the **studio system.**

By 1930, a fairly stable pattern of studio organization emerged. There were five major studios: Paramount, Loews/MGM (Metro-Goldwyn-Mayer), Warner Brothers, Fox, and RKO. These studios owned their own distribution chains of movie theaters, as well as extensive production facilities. They relied on teams of stars and directors who made movies together for them. They developed both prestigious feature films and **B movies,** which were cheaper and not as prestigious but made consistent profits as the second feature at local theaters. Control over production, distribution, and exhibition enabled studios to make sure that their movies were distributed and played widely, but it constituted a form of **vertical integration** that ultimately drew the attention of federal regulators to the concentration of power in the studios. The studios of that time provide an interesting parallel to our current system, where deregulation

1946

At the peak of the film box office, 90 million people attend the movies weekly

The studio system in Hollywood emphasized key stars as a way to promote studio films.

B movies are cheaply and quickly made genre films.

Vertical integration occurs when a company with the same owner handles different aspects of a business within the same industry, such as film production and distribution.

in the 1980s and 1990s has permitted extensive vertical integration to emerge again between film studios, TV, and cable channels, like Disney.

Each studio also had its own distinctive style. Paramount was the most profitable and powerful studio, with over 1,000 theaters, employing proven directors such as Cecil B. DeMille (*The Ten Commandments,* 1923) and stars like crooner Bing Crosby and comedian Bob Hope. Loews/MGM sought prestige with new Technicolor musicals, but it also made a lot of money with B movies such as the *Tarzan* adventures. Twentieth Century Fox combined two studios, developed new stars such as Betty Grable, and also made money with documentaries including *March of Time* and *Movietone* newsreels. Warner Brothers promoted comedies, genre films such as Errol Flynn's *The Adventures of Robin Hood* (1938), and cartoons starring Bugs Bunny, Elmer Fudd, and Daffy Duck. RKO produced some quality films, notably *King Kong* (1933), Fred Astaire and Ginger Rogers musicals, and *Citizen Kane* (1941), but made most of its money from its movie houses and from cheaper, more predictably profitable B movies.

Several minor Hollywood studios of the 1930s and 1940s are still major players: Universal, Columbia, and United Artists. These studios struggled back then because they did not control their own distribution and exhibition networks. They also made most of their money with B movies. Another two studios were even smaller: Monogram and Republic. Republic was famous for a time for cowboy movies, launching John Wayne, and as a producer of action serials, whose cliffhangers and action sequences have been liberally borrowed by the likes of Steven Spielberg in his *Indiana Jones* movies.

The studio system peaked in 1946–1948. World War II ended the economic limits imposed on movie production by the Great Depression. After the war, returning soldiers and sailors joined the masses of people attending the movies weekly. The year 1946 was the peak of audience exposure and financial success for **theatrical films** in the United States. Around 90 million Americans went to the movies every week to see features such as *It's a Wonderful Life* (1946). In 1947, the U.S. film industry **grossed** $2.4 billion, a figure that sank to $1.3 billion by 1962 (in 2010 dollars), reflecting competition from television (Mast & Kawin, 1996).

Film Faces Television, 1948–1960

As World War II veterans started families and moved to the new suburbs, far away from the downtown movie theaters, film attendance declined. Worse yet, after 1948, television quickly cut into Hollywood's theatrical box office receipts. The film industry suffered a severe, concurrent blow to its theater-based revenues. The government had become concerned with the **concentration of ownership** in the Hollywood system. In 1948, the government ordered studios to get out of at least one aspect of film business: production, distribution, or exhibition. Studios challenged the decision, but the U.S. Supreme Court confirmed it (*United States v. Paramount Pictures,* 1948).

John Springer Collection/Historical/Corbis

BEST FILM EVER? Orson Welles's *Citizen Kane* popularized a number of filmmaking techniques, including new camera angles and types of shots.

Theatrical films are those released for distribution in movie theaters.

Gross is the total box office revenue before expenses are deducted.

1948

Television competes; major studios have to divest their theater chains

Concentration of ownership occurs when several kinds of media or many outlets of the same kind of media are owned by a single owner.

The four biggest studios—MGM, Warner, Paramount, and Fox—struggled to readjust after selling off their theater chains. Ironically, this forced divestiture of theatrical distribution took place at a point when studios were losing their dominance. Almost every small town went through the shock depicted in *The Last Picture Show* (1971) as thousands of small-town theaters disappeared. Hollywood responded with suburban drive-in movies and then, in the 1970s, shifted to new movie houses in shopping centers.

The film industry began to realize that if it couldn't beat television, it had better join it. Disney started producing programs specifically for television, such as *Disneyland*. Warner Brothers and Paramount made much of their money in the 1950s and 1960s by producing series and distributing movies for television (Gomery, 1991). The TV networks began to order most of their programs from film studios or independent producers since it was cheaper to buy programming from companies that were already geared up to create it than creating new studios (Sterling & Kittross, 2002). Later, television networks were forced to buy most of their programs from the studios because of government rules that limited how much network programming the network itself could create or own (see Chapter 9).

After 1961, movies were more common on television, as *Saturday Night at the Movies* (NBC) topped the ratings. Television networks have been using movies strategically ever since to compete with each other. Airing movies became an important way for UHF independent stations, PBS stations, and basic cable channels to compete with network TV programs.

As audiences got used to television, Hollywood responded by pushing a couple of long-overlooked technological innovations. Although Technicolor had been invented in the silent era, it spread slowly with films such as *Gone with the Wind* and Disney cartoons. By the early 1960s, nearly all films were in color. Another technology aimed at competing with TV was wide-screen film. Cinema-Scope had been developed in the 1920s, but it took hold only under encouragement from the head of the Fox studio in the early 1950s. Studios embraced the new wide-screen idea, but outfitting theaters with new screens proved expensive and time consuming.

Moviepix/Getty Images

Archives du 7e Art/Marvel Enterprises/Photos 12 / Alamy Stock Photo

SPECTACLE Big-budget, big-screen historical epics such as *Ben Hur* were Hollywood's answer to competition from television in the 1950s. As *The Avengers* showed, they continue to work today. Looking at all-time worldwide box office receipts, the big-budget fantasy epic spectacle, *Avatar* (2009), leads with $2.8 billion, followed by the historical epic, *Titanic* (1997), with $2.2 billion.

Hollywood tried to compete with TV by mounting lavish, big-budget spectacles such as *Ben Hur* (1959). It also capitalized on more controversial material than TV could offer: sex in the James Bond thriller *Goldfinger* (1964) or social issues like racial prejudice in films like *Guess Who's Coming to Dinner* (1967). European films like Frederico Fellini's *La Dolce Vita* (1960) also flourished in the U.S. art house and campus circuits with similar material.

By the 1960s, independent producers gained more of a role in producing movies for studios to distribute. Film studios began to spend much of their own time producing series for television. The studio system died due to changes in technology and the new industry competition that built on it.

Studios in Decline

Although movie studios suffered in the 1950s and 1960s, only RKO went out of business. Most changed hands. Most struggled through lean years with few hits and fat years when a hit saved the day; *The Godfather* (1972), for example, made Paramount an unprecedented $1,000,000 a day for its first month.

Warner and Columbia Pictures made television series. Universal was acquired by MCA and also went into television production. United Artists capitalized on distributing movies, such as John Huston's *The African Queen* (1951), for talented independent producers. Disney moved into the studio ranks with animated films and its Buena Vista production and distribution company, which produced family fare epitomized by *Mary Poppins* (1964).

Independent producers gained more power as several things happened to American movies. Audiences changed, becoming younger, more cosmopolitan, and more interested in the kind of sensation and social observation they saw in imported European films. The values and current interests of teenagers and college students began to dominate films (Mast & Kawin, 1996). New directors pushed into Hollywood, some from 1960s underground films, some straight from film school, and some from TV commercials. These new directors transformed traditional Hollywood genres, often by increasing the use of sex, violence, and social controversy, as did Francis Ford Coppola (*The Godfather,* 1972). Writer/directors, or **auteurs,** like Woody Allen (*Annie Hall,* 1976) created more offbeat, personal films, some of which turned out to be major commercial successes. Much of their innovation came from a new form of an old Hollywood practice, borrowing successful ideas from Europe, like the sexier, more personal, and artistic films of the French New Wave. These films experimented with cinematography and styles of storytelling, and pushed the edges of content.

Films became more political and topical. For instance, although *M*A*S*H* (1970) was set during the Korean War, it was filled with the antiwar sentiment many Americans harbored about the

> **Auteurs** are directors who also see themselves as artists. They want to control all aspects of their production, often writing, sometimes shooting or editing, their films.

Paramount/ THE KOBAL COLLECTION AT ART RESOURCE, NY

GODFATHER REVIVES THE BOX OFFICE Coppola's *Godfather* films revived Hollywood audiences with violence, costume drama, and innovative production and editing.

Vietnam War. *Taxi Driver* (1976) explored the underside of city life, whereas *The Graduate* (1967) explored the angst of growing up in the suburbs. Films reexamined American archetypes, such as the hardbitten film noir detective, in movies like *Chinatown* (1974).

Rebellion against the strict morality that had inspired the Hays Office was part of the change American society underwent in the 1960s. The Hays Office itself closed down in 1945, although the code technically remained in force until 1966. Meanwhile, local censors were muzzled by free speech rulings from the U.S. Supreme Court. Movie producers continually pushed the limits of what was acceptable, which led to new calls from concerned parents that raised the specter of government censorship. Instead, the industry again opted for self-regulation, this time in the form of content ratings administered by the Motion Picture Association of America (MPAA).

Even as films seemed to turn inward to focus on American culture in the 1960s and 1970s, they were still selling very well abroad. Exports continued to help keep Hollywood profitable throughout the 1950s and 1960s.

Blockbusters *Jaws* (1975) and *Star Wars* (1977) are usually regarded as the turning points in a return to spectacular, big-budget *blockbusters,* which began a new golden age. Steven Spielberg and George Lucas rediscovered that film has a visual intensity well beyond that of television, especially in the darkened movie house with a big screen and thundering sound. Action sequences, striking landscapes, and special effects became competitive advantages for movies. As sophisticated Dolby and Surround Sound systems emerged, intense sound also characterized the movie theater experience. Thus, film took advantage of new technologies to create a more intense viewing experience than television could provide.

For **first-run distribution** to movie theaters, most films were increasingly targeted at the 15- to 24-year-olds who still went out to film theaters. Still, blockbuster movies such as *Lord of the Rings* (2001) or *Forrest Gump* (1994) could ensure a studio's financial health for years by reaching a wide audience, even though they were more expensive. Filmmakers hurried to take advantage of the latest special effects, often raising costs. The star system also returned with a vengeance, which also raised film costs since stars such as Tom Cruise could get over $20 million for a film.

1977

Star Wars highlights focus on big-budget blockbusters

First-run distribution for film productions is made specifically for movie theaters.

Universal Pictures/Photos 12/Alamy Stock Photo

MONSTER HIT Digital effects, like these virtual dinosaurs in a live action adventure film like *Jurassic World* (2015) are part of how big budget films keep audiences coming back for more.

Hollywood Meets HBO

By the late 1970s and early 1980s, the film industry took increasing advantage of cable TV and rented videotapes as new distribution channels. Home Box Office (HBO), launched in 1975 (see Chapter 9), initially relied almost exclusively on feature films for its content. Cable channels like WTBS concentrated on old films, as did independent TV stations, usually on UHF.

These developments helped the film industry regain some of the revenue that it had lost to network television in the 1950s and 1960s.

Videocassette recorders (VCRs) and DVDs diffused very quickly to become the primary means of watching movies in the home. The spread of video rentals ultimately contributed both to the blockbuster phenomenon and to audience segmentation. Whereas many people rushed to rent the latest hit movie on DVD, others went straight for Japanese animation, old cowboy movies, old *Star Trek* episodes, or whatever else captured their attention. Similarly, many B movies or indie films now go straight to Netflix or Amazon Prime, where loyal fans are waiting for yet another raunchy guy buddy comedy or low-budget horror film.

By the 1970s, made-for-TV movies also became increasingly common. Movies could be turned into TV or cable TV series if they were popular, as was *M*A*S*H* (1970). Made-for-TV movies often did surprisingly well against other movies and series. Audiences and revenues for cable channels in the 1990s were so large that made-for-cable movies, like *Dillenger* (1991), also became increasingly common on channels such as HBO and TNT. Basic cable networks scheduled over 100 original films in 2009. In 2011, Hallmark's two channels alone produced 32 original cable films.

Movies Go Digital

New technology and market forces continue to transform the movie industry. Home video had become a driving force, with revenues from rentals and direct sales of videos and DVDs outstripping box office receipts two to one, but that income dropped sharply as new forms of digital distribution emerged and consumers tightened up their discretionary purchases during the Great Recession of 2007–2009. At the same time, the cost of producing major films skyrocketed as producers raced to outdo each other with spectacular computer-generated special effects. In hopes of spreading those costs over larger audiences, the industry began to internationalize both its ownership—which now included foreign owners such as Sony Corporation and Rupert Murdoch—and its audiences. Moviemaking at the major studios began to gravitate more toward genres (e.g., science fiction, action-adventure) that could translate and export well across cultures.

There was also a revival in independent filmmaking outside the major studios. Some directors, like the late John Cassavetes, had survived as independents for years. Many others followed in their footsteps. Computer technology for editing and high-quality, low-cost digital cameras drove down the cost of producing "small" or indie films and offered the prospect of a renaissance in filmmaking apart from the financial pressures of the blockbuster mentality that gripped Hollywood. It helped that some inexpensively made films, like *Once* (2006), also made considerable profits. But the idea of **independent film** is relative. The most successful recent indie film was *The Silver Lining's Playbook* (2012), which made over $132 million, but it was produced for $21 million. Some prefer to use the independent label for much smaller films.

About 400 independent feature films are made each year, often starting as film school projects and sometimes funded through relatives' credit cards. (One of the authors overheard one of his film students debating the wisdom

1997

DVDs are introduced

Independent (indie) films are films not made by the major studios.

2007

Netflix streams films over the Internet to an increasing number of devices of maxing out all his cards to make his movie just last week.) These films circulate at film festivals around the world, hoping to strike gold. The indie film world depends on both economic and technological ups and downs. Financing initially dried up after the 2008 economic recession. Studios picked up fewer indies for theatrical distribution. However, the recent expansion of digital distribution and even production by Netflix, Amazon, and others has created new possibilities. In 2015, almost 100 of the 124 feature films shown at the Sundance Film Festival were picked up for some form of distribution, most in the new digital channels, who outbid studios for some films. The amount of money invested in producing indies is huge, more than that invested by either the studios or Netflix (Leipzig, 2015). But beware, much of that is lost, as the large majority never get distributed.

Faced with mushrooming costs as well as competition from video games, the Internet, and digital television for the young movie-going audience, the motion picture industry confronts significant challenges in the digital age. The studios are battling with their stars, directors, and writers over the proceeds from digital rights to their productions. To battle piracy of first-run films, thought to cost the industry billions each year, in 2008 the industry began offering legal Internet downloads of some films on the same day as DVD releases. That trend continues as DVDs, like music CDs, lose the position as the central money-maker for the industry. In the meantime, Netflix is bringing more movies into living rooms, even as some movies are being pulled back from its collection, since studios think they are not making enough money from new low-cost distribution like Netflix and Redbox film rentals. That pushes Netflix toward increasing distribution of television shows and its own original productions, which may be counterproductive for the film industry, too.

To draw audiences into theaters, the studios rely more and more on blockbusters, particularly in the summer season, and "franchise films" such as *Iron Man* and *Spider-Man*. The summer of 2015 had scheduled sequels in the franchises for *Batman*, *The Avengers*, and others. All were expensive, and less than half made a lot of money, so some think this industry formula is wearing thin, but the industry seems to be doubling down on it, putting more money into potential blockbusters while making fewer mid-size films and funding or distributing fewer low-cost indies, which are shifting to electronic channels like Netflix. After all, the big news of late 2015–early 2016 was *The Force Awakens*, the latest installment of the *Star Wars* saga/franchise that had topped box office records for the United States.

The studios also increasingly rely on the revenue generated by higher priced ticket sales for 3-D and IMAX screenings of popular films. Hollywood majors rushed to produce more 3-D and IMAX format films following the success of *Avatar* (2009), and reworked some existing new films to screen in 3-D, like Disney's *Beauty and the Beast* (2012). However, by 2013, both revenue and attendance for 3-D films were down, as was overall film attendance. So as with many previous film technological developments, 3-D helps some films but is not a permanent solution for film competition with other media. The industry also continues to internationalize: for example, a Chinese theater exhibition group bought the U.S. theater chain AMC in 2012, in part to get better access to new exhibition technologies like IMAX and 3-D.

2010

Avatar is the highest-grossing film of all time, breaking 3-D into the mainstream

STOP & REVIEW

1. What was the studio system?

2. Which were the main studios?

3. What were some of the main silent film genres?

4. What genres came in with talking films? Which were prominent in the 1930s and 1940s?

5. Why did studios want to own their own distributors and movie theater chains? Why did federal regulators force the studios to divest themselves of their movie theater chains in 1948?

6. How did the movie industry compete with television?

SAVING NATIONAL PRODUCTION OR THE NEW CULTURAL IMPERIALISM?

It worries many countries that Hollywood films tend to dominate their viewing screens. Hollywood films can take up to 90 percent or more of screen time in many countries, perhaps even more of video streaming and DVD rentals and sales. So countries are increasingly anxious to find ways to increase national production. (For more on the history of why U.S. films have tended to dominate, see Chapter 18.) However, many other countries are beginning to produce more films that do well at home, including national blockbusters like *Fetih 1453,* a Turkish film showing their heroic ancestors conquering Constantinople. A number of national blockbusters sometimes play well in the United States, like some recent Chinese and Korean dramas, which also do well in global export.

One phenomenon that is blurring and perhaps also partially solving the issue is an increasing tendency for Hollywood to participate in complex coproductions with other countries—for example, the *Lord of the Rings* films that were shot in New Zealand. A UNESCO (2003) study cited coproductions, such as *Lord of the Rings,* as an example of how Hollywood films dominate, but are they in fact Hollywood films? The basis for the films is J. R. R. Tolkien's novel trilogy of the same name, which the author seems to have originally intended as a mythology for Great Britain, his home country *(The Letters of J.R.R. Tolkien,* 1981). Critics such as John Garth (2003) argue that the story and some of the characters come directly from Tolkien's experience in the British Army in World War I. The director, the main screen story adapters/writers, the special effects people, and a number of actors are from New Zealand. The films were shot and edited in New Zealand and the special effects were created by a New Zealand company, Weta Workshop, which has become a major global special effects house. Most of the lead actors were British or American. Financing and distribution came from Hollywood.

One can argue whether the sensibility is essentially that of a Hollywood blockbuster. Fans of the books have scrutinized the films closely to see if the original story has been overwhelmed, and opinion from them is mixed. The films have helped create a burgeoning film industry in New Zealand. Other films made there include *The Adventures of Tintin* (2011) and the films based on British author C. S. Lewis's *Chronicles of Narnia* series.

A number of other current examples abound. After the recent success of a number of Mexican films, directors, and writers, Hollywood is actively looking in Mexico for scripts, directors, and actors for coproduction. The same is true with Hong Kong, India, and Brazil. Critics in those countries are wondering whether some of their best and brightest are being seduced into making films that are directly co-produced using Hollywood money and formulas, or less directly borrowing Hollywood formulas to eventually gain global distribution by Hollywood distributors, who control global distribution. However, other critics and viewers are happy that Hollywood money, distribution, and formulas are facilitating the revival of filmmaking by national directors.

One way of looking at this is as a new wave of U.S. cultural imperialism with U.S. ways, financing and distribution, if not literally U.S. movies, continuing to dominate the world (Miller et al., 2005). Or one can view it as a complex globalization where the United States and other countries interact with each other, even though the United States still tends to dominate the overall output and flow of films.

Source: Humphrey Carpenter (ed.). *The Letters of J.R.R. Tolkien.* Boston: Houghton-Mifflin, 1981, p. 144. John Garth. *Tolkien and the Great War: The Threshold of Middle-Earth.* Boston: Houghton-Mifflin, 2003. Toby Miller et al. *Global Hollywood 2.* London: BFI, 2005. UNESCO. Convention for the Safeguarding of the Intangible Cultural Heritage. Paris: UNESCO, 2003.

TECHNOLOGY TRENDS: MAKING MOVIE MAGIC

Eadweard Muybridge's first motion picture of a galloping horse used a rather unwieldy recording system—the horse's hooves triggered trip wires on 700 still cameras to yield a mere 60 seconds of action. Edison's *kinetograph* in 1888 was a close relative to his phonograph (see Chapter 6), in that the pictures were recorded a frame at a time on a hand-turned revolving cylinder with a light-sensitive surface. Soon the cylindrical photographic plates gave way to strips of the newly invented Kodak film.

Edison's *kinetoscope* was the first playback mechanism for the masses—but for only one viewer at a time. The Lumière brothers originated the movie projector in 1895 by shining a light through the strip of picture transparencies and enlarging the pictures with an optical lens. If the frames were changed fast enough (20 frames per second was about right, later increased to 30 per second), the viewer had the sense of continuous motion. This was because the afterimage of each frame persisted just long enough for the next frame to appear.

Apart from some advances in film processing and developing, basic motion picture technology did not change much over the next 25 years. The actors' words appeared printed on the screen, not spoken, and a live organist played theme music in the theater.

Movie Sound

The first successful talkie was *The Jazz Singer* (1927). AT&T Bell Labs scientists synchronized a record with the film. Soon a way was found to record the sound on an optical track right on the film. A *photoreceptor* picked up variations in the light shining through the sound track and reproduced them as weak electric currents that were fed into an amplifier and then the movie theater's speakers. The current Digital Theater Sound (DTS) systems hearken back to the old AT&T system, except that digital CDs hold the sound and are synchronized with the images via digital codes printed on the film, yielding multichannel digital surround sound. Surround sound systems have proliferated in home theaters to simulate the sound of the theater experience.

Special Effects

Early audiences were easy to fool with simple stop-action effects. If you showed them a magician climbing into a box and closing the lid, stopped the camera long enough for the magician to exit, and then restarted the film to show an empty box, early moviegoers were convinced that the magician had magically escaped. (*Hugo* [2011] shows how some of these early effects were done.) Later, the actors were filmed against the backdrop of another film projected from behind. This technique, called **rear projection,** gave the impression that actors in the studio were really paddling a boat in the rapids or engaging in other dangerous stunts; many a model train and toy boat were sacrificed to simulate real-life cataclysms.

Modern special effects are often traced back to the 1933 classic *King Kong*. The big ape was actually an 18-inch furry doll with movable limbs that were painstakingly moved one frame at a time. When Kong grabbed our heroine, Fay Wray, she was filmed in the clutches of a life-sized mock-up of a giant gorilla's arm. *King Kong* was the first film to use a technique called **front projection.** When our heroine appeared struggling on the top of the Empire State Building, a building model was shot with a miniature movie screen on its roof, onto which pictures of the real Fay struggling were projected. *King Kong* also

Rear projection effects have images projected behind performers who are in the foreground.

Front projection lets actors be photographed in front of an image so that they appear as part of it.

relied heavily on the already familiar rear projection, as well as a technique in which live actors were filmed against a neutral backdrop and then *composited* with a background shot of, say, a charging dinosaur. The background was *matted,* or blacked out, in the areas where the actors would appear so that the two images could be superimposed. Stop-action, **compositing, mattes,** and scale models are still the staples of many special-effects sequences today. For example, look at the production documentaries that are included on DVDs such as *The Lord of the Rings: The Fellowship of the Ring* (2001), which has a particularly extensive set of "making of" documentaries.

The Digital Revolution

The computer has taken over in special effects. *Star Wars* (1977) used computer-driven cameras to construct multilayered space battles. In an update of Muybridge's pioneering technique, computer-controlled still cameras shot the spectacular slow-motion action scenes in *The Matrix* (1999). In 1995, Pixar Animation's *Toy Story* became the first full-length computer-animated hit film. No one had to draw each frame, or cell, of animation as in all previous animated movies.

Increasingly, computer-generated monsters and sets are filling in for scale models. Sometimes computer images stand in for real actors in dangerous action sequences, such as the "people" falling off the *Titanic* (1997) as it slipped beneath the waves. The waves were computer-generated too. "Green screen" techniques allow actors shot against green backgrounds to be digitally inserted in live-action scenes or computer-generated backgrounds. Computer effects were also what made it possible for makers of *The Lord of the Rings* to use the motion capture technique, in which motion sensors were attached to a live actor to create motion for the character Gollum, but then change his appearance to something much less human. James Cameron's film *Avatar* (2009) pushes computer special effects in another dimension. A number of major characters exist only as computer animation, but seem real (see Technology Demystified: Entering the Third Dimension, page 201). Studios are starting to create 3-D scans of actors so that the day may come in which movies are made by manipulating their computer images instead of by directing real actors.

Special effects are glitzy, but the real computer revolution in Hollywood is taking place behind the scenes, during the **postproduction** process, when films get their finishing touches. Film editing used to involve unspooling miles of raw film footage and manually cutting and splicing to make a master copy. Now the filmed sequences are transferred to computer media where they can be accessed at random and spliced with the click of a mouse—a process known as **nonlinear editing.** Not only is this faster, but it also allows the editor to be more creative in playing "what if" in the editing suite.

Celluloid film itself is becoming obsolete with the advent of digital cameras that record high-quality images directly in

> **Compositing** is merging several layers of images that were shot separately.

> **Mattes** are background paintings or photographs that are combined with performers in the foreground.

1995

Toy Story is first major-release computer-generated film

> **Postproduction** includes editing, sound effects, and visual effects that are added after shooting the original footage.

> **Nonlinear editing** uses digital equipment to rearrange scenes to make the master copy.

PA Images/Alamy Stock Photo

THE HUMAN DIMENSION. Special effects that use motion capture technology add new realism to computer generated characters, their movements, and their expressions.

digital formats—with no chemical film processing required. In fact, they don't call it "filming" anymore; now it's "image capture." George Lucas's *Attack of the Clones* (2002) was the first major production to use **digital video** for image capture. Now it is increasingly common in animated films like *Tintin* (2011).

Now that computers have become involved in all aspects of moviemaking, "desktop" filmmaking is fast becoming a reality. Small groups of talented people can shoot films in digital video and edit them on personal computers with off-the-shelf software and without Hollywood actors, directors, cameras, sets, or key grips. Digital filmmaking lowers costs, opening the film industry to student filmmakers and diverse artistic visions. The Internet is beginning to serve as a distribution mechanism for digital filmmakers, removing the last analog stop in film production and perhaps also the last financial barrier to the solo film artist-auteur. In fact, we already have virtual film studios, such as Pixar Animation Studios, started by Steve Jobs, cofounder of Apple Computers. Pixar has become known for its various hit movies, like *Frozen* (2013) produced entirely with digital animation inside computers, starting with the *Toy Story* series.

Movie Viewing

Movie producers have always tried to stay a step ahead of the competition by offering an aesthetic experience that cannot be duplicated by its competitors, so look for bigger screens and ever more sophisticated digital sound systems. The old movie projector is being replaced by new digital light processors (DLPs) that show digitized movies stored on compact discs. DLPs have microchips with millions of tiny mirrors on their surfaces. The mirrors are adjusted thousands of times per second to reflect tiny dots, or pixels, of red, green, and blue light onto the movie screen. Digital cinema was initially slow to catch on, in part because the projectors cost several times what conventional ones cost, and the DLPs have lower resolution, about 1,300 lines compared to 4,000 lines for conventional film. But that is changing fast. Some of the new digital films have 4,000 lines of resolution, 48 frames per second speed to improve the quality of images in motion, and increasingly clear surround sound. *The Hobbit* is an example of these new production image and sound standards. The industry mandated a changeover to digital projection in 2014, which threatens any small movie theaters whose owners do not have the $150,000 required to convert to digital projection.

There were over 38,000 digital screens in North America in 2014, and that number is increasing rapidly, with under 2,000 nondigital screens remaining. The same is increasingly true in the rest of the world, which is now 51 percent digital. Many of those are also converting to 3-D. The number of IMAX theaters is also growing, including the conversion of traditional screens in multiplexes. They feature films shot in a special large image, high-resolution format, very large immersive screen technology, and very high-quality sounds. IMAX screens are also prized venues for 3-D movies, such as *Avatar*.

Although the movie theater may never die, movies are increasingly viewed in the home with digital technologies, including DVD, digital video recorders (DVRs), and digital streaming. Sony's Blu-ray high-definition DVDs are the current home standard but have not fully displaced regular DVDs. However, overall DVD player penetration has begun to decline in U.S. households.

On the Internet, a download movie battle is looming to rival the fracas over music downloads. BitTorrent scatters fragments of large, often illegal video files across multiple computers, making it faster to "share" the lengthy files. Pay services such as Netflix, Amazon, and iTunes provide legal alternatives. With around four-fifths of all U.S. Internet homes now on broadband connections, movie streaming and downloads have all but eliminated home video stores. Another growing home video option is the video-on-demand service offered by cable companies. Unlike conventional pay cable services, these allow viewers to start and stop—and rewind or fast-forward—the movie as they please. The copy protection technology embedded in video-on-demand movies make it impossible to copy movies during the first 90 days after their release, opening a new "window" during which first-run films are distributed directly to the home earlier than the current 90-day window for DVD sales.

Another consumer option is to purchase digital copies of films, which are placed in a cloud locker (a secure spot on a remote server), like the iTunes and

STOP & REVIEW

1. Who developed the basics of film camera and projector technology?
2. How does movie sound work?
3. How was movie image quality improved?
4. How have special effects in film developed?
5. What will be the impact of high definition and 3-D on film technology and business?

Technology Demystified

ENTERING THE THIRD DIMENSION

Stereopsis. That's the term for the magic behind 3-D movies like *Avatar*. It is an optical illusion, a trick that our eyes play on our brains that makes our brain think we are looking at a 3-D object when in fact we are looking at a 2-D picture. The trick is to send two, separate, flat image views of the same object to the brain at the same time. If the two views are taken from slightly different angles so that they appear to be about two and a half inches apart (the distance between our eyes), then our brain is fooled into thinking that it sees the object in three dimensions.

There are a variety of methods to induce the illusion, and the trick has been used for amusement for quite a long time. A favorite parlor pastime in the 1800s was to peer at side-by-side still images taken from slightly different camera angles through a viewer that held the mages at a fixed distance in front of the eyes. The early 1950s witnessed a 3-D movie craze that had audiences peering at cheesy horror flicks with names like *Bwana Devil* and *Creature from the Black Lagoon* through cardboard glasses with filters that sent different images to the left and right eyes. *Avatar* and other 3-D movies of the current day use high-tech active glasses with side-by-side liquid crystal displays (LCDs) in place of lenses. The two LCDs alternate between being open and closed and are synchronized with the images on the screen via radio transmitters in the theater. The images on the screen alternate between the left eye image and image as seen from the right

eye but that happens so quickly that, thanks to persistence of vision, the two images register on the brain at the same time and are blended into a 3-D illusion.

But there is a lot more film magic behind *Avatar* than the 3-D illusion moviegoers experience in the theater. Old-fashioned 3-D movies from the *Bwana Devil* era were shot with two synchronized cameras positioned side by side and two and a half inches apart. Both images were projected on the movie screen and integrated into a single image inside the viewer's brain. Save for a few sequences, there were no cameras in the studio when *Avatar* was made. The actors' movements were recorded by motion capture suits that recorded their body movements and facial expressions. This trick has been around for a while, for example, in making an animated Tom Hanks in *Polar Express*. *Avatar* producer James Cameron integrated the digital image of the characters with a 3-D image of the virtual environment of Pandora generated in real time so that he could see the 3-D world as he directed the movements of the actors. If he didn't like the way the scene came out, he could remake it from an entirely different angle after the actors were gone by moving the point of view around inside the virtual space. Generating the alternate left and right images for the 3-D version was a simple matter of shifting the point of view slightly, by about two and a half inches.

Source: Anne Thompson. (2010, January). How James Cameron's Innovative New 3D Tech Created Avatar. Popular Mechanics. Available: http://www.popularmechanics.com/technology /industry/43394BB.htm

Amazon cloud music services described in Chapter 6. Another approach is to wrap film and television delivery (and profits) into the cable industry strategy for "TV Everywhere," like the way large numbers of people use HBO Go to view popular films and series on other devices, when authorized by their cable subscription (Chapter 9).

THE FILM INDUSTRY: MAKING MOVIES

The Players

Today, the film industry is a high-volume mixture of large and small players that continue to shift and evolve. There are eight major film producers: the old-time studios—Columbia, Fox, MGM, Paramount, Universal (Comcast), and Warner Brothers—along with Buena Vista (Disney) and TriStar (Sony). A few of these (e.g., Disney and Universal) are part of vertically integrated *conglomerates* (see Chapter 3) that dominate video and film production and distribution. Each has tended to produce 15 to 20 movies per year, combining for about one-fifth of the over 700 feature films released annually in the United States (MPAA, 2015). In contrast, at the height of Hollywood's fame in 1946, the major studios each produced 40 to 50 movies every year.

Today the major studios invest an average of about $66 million per film, plus an average of $36 million in advertising per film, and they spend a high overhead to keep the studio organizations running. Top actors and directors further drain profits by demanding a percentage of the profits. A big name like Johnny Depp can earn an additional $50 million on the "back end" of a successful film in addition to the $20 million he makes "up front" just to appear. So the stakes are high and the pressure to produce big hits is enormous.

One "new" studio, DreamWorks, started by Steven Spielberg in 1995, has been successful in animation, but struggled in other areas, leading to concerns about its survival. With the *Shrek* and the *Madagascar* series, DreamWorks became the main competitor to Pixar Studios in popular animated films, but it has declined in the last few years. Pixar had primarily worked as an animation production group distributed by Disney. It became part of Disney in 2006, with Pixar executives like John Lasseter taking the lead of the combined animation operation. Several other new studios, Magnolia Pictures, Weinstein Company, and Lionsgate now often produce more feature films per year that the "majors."

Independent Filmmakers

Most films (77% in 2014) are now being produced outside the studios (MPAA, 2015). However, although many independent films are being produced, fewer are being distributed. Almost 600 films were released in North America (i.e., Canada and the United States) in 2014 (MPAA, 2015). Many films go directly to video distribution and many simply never get released at all. So for indie directors, particularly students, getting distribution is the primary goal. Furthermore, financing through studios and other sources has declined, so indie production is also declining.

Still, there are some independent film companies, like Tom Hanks's Playtone and Drew Barrymore's Flower Films. These are not to be confused with an extensive, much less formal network of independent filmmakers.

These indies usually produce films for much less than the major studios or the major independent production companies, often only a few million dollars. A classic pattern is that new filmmakers eke out a hodgepodge of financing for their first film. Once new filmmakers have their first feature film, they can try to get it shown at a variety of festivals. There are both national festivals, such as the Sundance Festival in Park City, Utah, and regional festivals, such as South by Southwest in Austin, Texas. Various organizations run specialized film festivals, presenting film series focused on LGBTQIA (lesbian, gay, bisexual, transgender, questioning, intersex, ally), Jewish, and Asian content, for example, or by filmmakers belonging to these cultural groups. Sundance has become crucial to indies, as have new distribution technologies like streaming. Companies like Netflix bought most of the indie feature releases at Sundance in 2015, reestablishing a major for indie films.

The Guilds

As the 2007–2008 Writers Guild and Screen Actors Guild strikes showed, the craft guilds in Hollywood still wield a great deal of power. Whereas television can shift programming to unscripted reality shows, films require writers. Editors, lighting, sound, and many other technical guilds are also important. However, one reason so many productions have fled to other countries is to get around guild rules and labor costs, so Hollywood has responded by offshoring many jobs too.

Film Finance

Films are financed in a variety of ways. In the United States, one of the ways Hollywood retains its power is in its control over finance. Nearly any film with a budget over a few million dollars tends to be at least partially financed by the major studios, which often sets them up for control over distribution and other decisions as well. Netflix and other streaming companies like Amazon Prime are beginning to move in to this role. Sometimes other kinds of investors are drawn into film projects, but the risk of expensive failure for any given film tends to scare away those who are not committed to the business for long term. Outside the United States, national governments, regional governments like the European Union, and sometimes even states and cities all help finance movies through direct investment, tax incentives, cooperation with production needs for locales, extras, and so on. The rising costs of moviemaking and distribution have tended to keep Hollywood central, even to the financing of major film projects in other countries. However, now Hollywood studios themselves are looking for financial partners, with states like Louisiana, which offer subsidies and tax credits for productions that locate there, with governments in places like China and Europe, as well as with production and finance groups in places like India with their own thriving film industries. These can be crucial in attracting or keeping a production, as when Maryland cut a deal in 2014 to keep Netflix's *House of Cards*.

Film Distribution

Films have traditionally been distributed in a series of **windows** of time linked to specific channels. The classic distribution for a major film used to

Windows are separate film release times for different channels or media.

be theatrical distribution; international theatrical distribution; pay-per-view; pay cable; DVD rentals and sales; paid downloads through iTunes or Amazon; streaming through Netflix, Amazon, or Hulu; network exhibition; basic cable networks; and finally syndication. All the domestic steps have an international parallel. Netflix and Amazon have begun to change this system, sometimes releasing films on streaming at the same time as theatrical release, but theater chains have boycotted some of these attempts.

All the windows are compressing to reduce effects of piracy. Films now tend to be released almost simultaneously in the United States and abroad, to limit piracy. In 2012, one of the biggest blockbusters of the year, *The Avengers,* was released first in several overseas markets for that reason. DVD, pay TV, online streaming, and other releases have also been moved forward in the United States, and online distribution is moving up to meet the DVD release dates to try to get legitimate copies into markets as soon as pirate copies arrive. Fights are looming between theaters, which want to keep a privileged first window, and studios and others who want to get the movies out into other channels or windows as soon as possible. In general, there are many more film distribution options now than in the heyday of studio control. Many films not seen as worth the promotional costs for theatrical release go straight to video for distribution in stores, on cable, and streaming on Netflix.

Revenue from theatrical distribution of films has recovered and stabilized after the Great Recession of 2007–2009, despite some spectacular box office flops, like *The Lone Ranger* (2013). Over 60 percent of the North American population went to the movies in 2014. U.S. moviegoers attend the movies an average of four times a year (MPAA, 2015). However, movie going has shifted to audiences under 40. They are particularly affected by word of mouth and electronic discussion, so some movies like *The Lone Ranger* (2013) now tank earlier after their openings, due to poor word of mouth. Audiences might wait to see the movie on DVD or Netflix.

However, movie theaters are still growing in number. There were fewer than 18,000 screens for films in the United States in 1980, but just over 40,000 in 2014, 84 percent in multiplexes. 38,000 of them have digital projection, two-fifths of those 3-D. The push toward 3-D has increased revenues by an average of about $3 per film, split between theaters and distributors. However, both production costs and theaters equipment costs have gone up with 3-D.

International audiences steadily became more important to the Hollywood bottom line. In 2013, international film distribution was 70 percent of total receipts (international [$25.0 billion] and United States/Canada [$10.9 billion] at the box office), and growing.

DVD sales have declined significantly in the past few years, although most people preferred to watch movies at home. Declining DVD sales worry studios, since that had been their largest source of revenue for years. They hope to replace it with new forms of digital sales. Paid downloads, like on iTunes and Amazon, continued to grow, as did electronic sell-through or digital HD and video on demand.

Both rentals and sales of DVDs are declining while films on broadcast or cable remain popular. The rising trend is toward streaming films on

STOP & REVIEW

1. How do independent filmmakers differ from studios?

2. What is currently the typical distribution cycle of a film?

3. What has been the effect of home video on the movie industry? What has challenged home video?

4. What is the current effect of streaming and other digital channels?

platforms like Netflix or Amazon. More specialized streaming services like the Sundance Doc Club create new venues for more specific tastes like documentary films.

Career Profile

Spike Lee grew up in Brooklyn and started out with a B.A. in Mass Communication from Morehouse College. He went for an MFA at NYU, making a student film, *Joe's Bed-Stuy Barbershop:We Cut Heads,* that got enough attention to be featured in Lincoln Center's new directors festival. He made his first major feature, *She's Gotta Have It* (1986) for $175,000 in two weeks. It made $7,000,000 and really launched his career, which was cemented by *Do The Right Thing* (1989), which was nominated for an Academy Award. He has gone on to make a number of films and become known as both a passionate sports fan and a strong advocate of African-American interests.

Your Media Career

YOU OUGHT TO BE IN PICTURES

Unlike some media areas, the film industry is still growing. Film production continued to grow through the 2007–2009 recession and is rebounding. Furthermore, film is consumed through an increasing variety of media, opening new opportunities in the field. One of the first apps for the iPad was a Netflix viewer, for example. So film production, distribution, and related jobs should continue to grow as the economy regains growth.

Film employment is notoriously unstable. Everyone from camera operators, editors, special effects team, and sound technicians to actors, producers, and directors are temporary workers on short-term production projects and do not hold steady jobs. Full-time employment in other fields, a "day job," may be necessary to support you at least in the early stages of a film career.

There are about 80,000 actors and 104,000 producers and directors, primarily in motion pictures, but also in performing arts and television. The industry is centered in New York and Los Angeles, although thousands also work in regional production centers like Austin and New Orleans. Slower-than-average growth is expected in these occupations over the next decade, although demand to fill new online channels with entertaining content could improve the picture. Aspiring actors face especially keen competition for low wages.

The median wage is $20 an hour, which would work out to $40,000 a year in the (unlikely) event of full-time employment. But few other occupations have $20 million per appearance at the top end of the pay scale! Cameramen or cinematographers and editors make an average of $52,470. Directors and producers have median salaries of $69,100 a year. Also needed are people with training in scriptwriting, animation and special effects, visual design, sound design, set construction, etc. Many of those entering the film industry have university degrees in media-related fields or fine arts academy training, but many break into the business on the basis of talent, luck, or connections rather than formal training. There are a wide variety of entry points, including internships with production companies and employment in craft and service occupations involved in film production. However, opportunities to enter the business through live theater productions are declining due to cutbacks in public arts budgets.

There are also a significant number of people who work for film production or distribution companies in other roles such as writers and marketers. Yet others work for talent agencies and for a wide variety of service companies, from caterers to animal handlers, which film producers need.

Source: Bureau of Labor Statistics. (2015). *Occupational Outlook Handbook.* Available: http://www.bls.gov/ooh/

TELLING STORIES: FILM CONTENT

Film is centered around storytelling, the creation of striking and memorable narratives that draw people in to spend steep ticket prices to see them, often repeatedly.

Team Effort

Creating filmmaking is an ensemble or group effort. Although audiences tend to think of movies in terms of which actors star in them, filmmaking is probably more driven by directors, producers, and writers, as well as visual designers, photography directors, music directors and designers, film editors, special effects people, and casting directors. Even less obvious but just as critical are script readers, development executives, market researchers, focus group services that examine ideas and plots, studio finance people who package various sources of money together, marketing strategists who plan promotional campaigns, and release strategists who assemble theaters so that films can open "big" and gain momentum that carries them into DVD sales, streaming, and so on.

Many people add to the substance of a film's contents. A memorable, award-winning film, like *Avatar* (2009), is based on strong performances, innovative use of special effects, and strong directors like James Cameron, who pushed and worked on the film for almost 20 years. But it also depends on a good script, the casting of less-well-known actors, striking visual design, original cinematography, memorable music, sound effects, and the central role of the director in orchestrating all of these processes and the people who perform them. Although the number of Academy Awards may seem endless, it is interesting to think about how all these people contribute creative elements to the final film content. The complexity, organizational, and financial demands of putting all these people and their roles together in a finished film is one reason that the Hollywood studios dominated film production for so long and are still central to the production of most major films, performing most of the business, finance, and marketing functions that give the artists budgets to work with.

Most often, the controlling hand on film production and storytelling is the director. Sometimes, however, directors are simply hired to oversee a process envisioned by a producer, who typically lines up the financing, story developers, scriptwriters, director, and sometimes major stars. The most memorable films usually reflect the artistic vision of a director who selects and directs the people who actually act, shoot the film, create the special effects, and so on. The most strongly creative directors often write or cowrite the scripts or story concepts for their films.

Many films start with a writer's draft film script, which is circulated among studios, producers, directors, and even leading

Jeffrey Mayer/WireImage/Getty Images

GROUP EFFORT Although it's the famous actors and directors who are glorified during awards shows, making a movie is an ensemble process involving the creative talents of many people.

actors, looking for interest. Thousands circulate, hundreds get optioned for a serious look, but few get made. Sometimes scripts emerge as films with remarkably little change. More often film scripts go through revisions, including the addition of other writers, and are often changed substantially by directors on the scene of production or in the final editing.

Finding Audience Segments

The history section of this chapter describes the earlier genres that laid the foundation of current moviemaking formulas. These are still present, but an explosion of new film genres began in the 1950s and continues today as filmmakers experiment with new ways to attract audiences. Table 8.2 lists several more recently evolved film genres.

New genres proliferate in search of audience segments. However, the basic ones are the kinds of genre categories that you find labeling the aisles of video stores or on Netflix's website: comedy, drama, action, horror, science fiction, classics, family, western, animation, documentary, and foreign. These genres continue to dominate, as filmmakers blend classic genres to reach very broad audiences both in the United States and abroad. The blockbusters favor genres in which big budgets and special effects can be used to best advantage: action-adventure, crime, horror, drama, and science fiction. Those are also the genres in which the United States has the greatest export advantage in world film markets, although filmmakers based in other countries increasingly fill many of these genre niches in their own countries or regions, with national blockbusters like *Fetih 1453* (the heroic conquest of Constantinople from the Turkish point of view) and compete with the United States in some genre niches as well. For example, Disney has prominently imported and distributed the films of Hayao Miyazaki, like *The Wind Rises* (2013).

Film content has become more diverse in part because film audiences have become more diverse. However, films are often still made to maximize the box office earnings of the initial theatrical distribution (Table 8.3). The initial box office is what gives a film its "buzz," its momentum. Thus, studios still tend to make movies for people who go out to the movies. This makes the typical

STOP & REVIEW

1. What movie genres are most dominant now?
2. How are films targeted to audience segments now?
3. Why were film ratings developed? What are the pros and cons of ratings?
4. How has audience segmentation changed film production?
5. What copyright and piracy problems does the film industry face?

TABLE 8.2 Current Film Genres

- Vampire movies, such as *Dracula* (1931) or *Twilight* (2008)
- Spy stories, with gadgets and action, such as James Bond in *Goldfinger* (1964) or *Spectre* (2015)
- Romantic comedies, with varying degrees of sex, such as *Pillow Talk* (1959) or *Brooklyn* (2015)
- Science fiction, such as *Forbidden Planet* (1956) or *The Martian* (2015)
- Slasher movies, such as *Friday the 13th Part VII* (1998) or *Saw 3D* (2010)
- Zombie movies, such as *Night of the Living Dead* (1968) or *World War Z (2013)*
- "Black" movies, such as *Superfly* (1972) or *Straight Outa Compton* (2015)
- Spanish-language movies, such as *El Mariachi* (1992) or *Pan's Labyrinth (El laberinto del fauno)* (2006)
- Coming-of-age movies, in which teenagers discover things about themselves, such as *The Breakfast Club* (1985) or *Divergent* (2014)
- Antiwar movies, such as *Apocalypse Now* (1979) or *The Green Zone* (2009)
- Sword and sandal movies, with heroes and muscles, such as *Conan, the Barbarian* (1982) or *Hercules* (2014)
- Disaster movies, such as *The Towering Inferno* (1974) or *Gravity* (2013)

TABLE 8.3 Top 10 Worldwide Movie Earners of All Time

FILM	STUDIO, YEAR	DIRECTOR	BOX OFFICE GROSS (IN MILLIONS)
Avatar	Fox, 2009	James Cameron	2,788
Titanic	Paramount, 1997	James Cameron	2,186
Star Wars: The Force Awakens	Buena Vista, 2015	J.J. Abrams	2,040
Jurrasic World	Universal, 2015	Colin Trevorrow	1,670
Marvel's The Avengers	Buena Vista, 2012	Joss Whedon	1,519
Furious 7	Universal, 2015	James Wan	1,516
Avengers: Age of Ultron	Buena Vista, 2015	Joss Whedon	1,405
Harry Potter and the Deathly Hallows: Part 2	Warner Bros., 2011	David Yates	1,341
Frozen	Buena Vista, 2013	Chris Buck, Jennifer Lee	1,276
Iron Man 3	Buena Vista, 2013	Shane Black	1,215

Source: http://boxofficemojo.com/alltime/world/

movie theatergoer, who is younger and more tolerant of sex and violence, disproportionately influential in decisions about what kinds of movies are made.

Increasingly, filmmakers are relying on social media to help them create buzz. Facebook "likes" and Twitter tweets quickly get the word out about a new release faster than conventional word of mouth ever could. Producers enlist their stars to tweet about new releases and post on their Facebook pages as well as create Facebook pages for their movies that users can "like" and refer to their friends. These social media strategies build on the enthusiasm of teens and young adults for social media.

MEDIA LITERACY

FILM AND YOUR SOCIETY

The film industries are embroiled in a number of policy and social issues that affect how they conduct business and the kinds of content they create.

1968

MPAA movie ratings are introduced

> **MPAA** (Motion Picture Association of America) is a trade organization that represents the major film studios.

VIOLENCE, SEX, PROFANITY, AND FILM RATINGS

For years, one of the most powerful forces in the entertainment industry has been the **MPAA.** The Motion Picture Association of America, composed of the major film studios, has been a significant player in American culture and politics, even though its members, the large studios, only produce about one-fifth of U.S. feature films now.

After years of debate and what seemed to be an increase in the number of movies with profanity, explicit sex, and violence in the 1960s, the MPAA instituted a rating system in 1968 to give people an idea of what they might encounter in a film to avoid outside regulation by letting people make more informed choices. After some further modifications over the years, the **MPAA ratings** categories are as follows:

MPAA ratings are part of a movie-rating system instituted in 1968.

G—For all ages; no sex or nudity, minimal violence

PG—Parental guidance suggested; some portions perhaps not suitable for young children, mild profanity, non-"excessive" violence, only a glimpse of nudity

PG-13—Parents strongly cautioned to give guidance to children under 13; some material may be inappropriate for young children

R—Restricted; those under 17 must be accompanied by parent or guardian; may contain very rough violence, nudity, or sex

NC-17—No one under 17 admitted; generally reserved for films that are openly pornographic, although some mainstream films receive this rating

Many people have debated the appropriateness and utility of these ratings. Some argue that as a form of industry self-censorship, the ratings violate freedom of speech for filmmakers. Others argue that, as with music lyric advisories, the ratings simply excite the interest of younger viewers. Many observe that the restrictions imposed on teenagers by R and NC-17 ratings are not enforced by theaters whose managers are aware that teens are the main moviegoers. Indeed, enforcing the rule would be hard; in multiplex movie theaters, people under 17 often buy a ticket for a PG movie, and then go into an R-rated one. There is also category creep. Films that might once have been rated R now squeak through with a PG-13. Many people would like to distinguish what some call "hard R" movies, like *Saw 3D* (2010), which feature gruesome violence or torture, from other R films. But NC-17 films don't tend to do well, so filmmakers resist accepting that rating and tend to change only as much as they have to get an R rating from MPAA reviewers (Figure 8.1).

The ratings system has allowed filmmakers to continue to produce films with sexually explicit and violent content, because they can argue that audiences are alerted to avoid such material. Ratings have not decreased the numbers

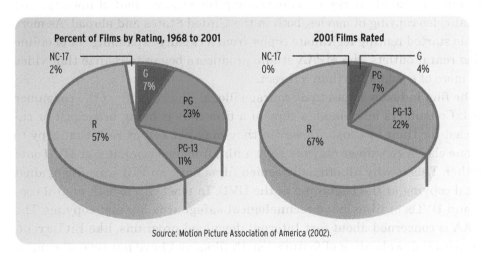

Percent of Films by Rating, 1968 to 2001

NC-17 2%
G 7%
PG 23%
PG-13 11%
R 57%

2001 Films Rated

NC-17 0%
G 4%
PG 7%
PG-13 22%
R 67%

Source: Motion Picture Association of America (2002).

FIGURE 8.1 **FILM RATINGS** The number and proportion of R-rated films has grown to over half.

of violent or sexual films. From 1968 to 2008, 58 percent of all films have been rated R, down slightly to 52 percent in 2013. However, most top-grossing films have been PG or PG-13 (mpaa.org). In 2013, 15 of the top 25 films were PG-13 and six were PG or G (MPAA, 2013). Movies are usually rated R for profanity, nudity, or sex, whereas PG-13 movies are often by far the most violent in amount and intensity. Starting in 2007, MPAA also includes the incidence of on-screen smoking as a factor in the ratings. One study shows that parents care most about shielding their children from scary violence, whereas MPAA film raters seem to care more about guarding against sex or profanity. Although many parents have expressed appreciation for the ratings, which give them something to work with in guiding children's viewing, they say the ratings are not dependable because they are not consistent from movie to movie.

We suspect that many of our readers are enjoying their newfound freedom to watch R-rated films, but in a few years many will be in the role of "concerned parents" themselves, wondering how to shield children from excessive sex and violence. The movie ratings are one option. Another is technologies like ClearPlay that automatically edit out sex and violence in DVDs as they are played back, by simply skipping over time codes on the disc that correspond to the offending material.

VIEWER ETHICS: FILM PIRACY

Illegal use of copyrighted intellectual property has been a serious issue for the film industry (also see Chapter 15). Film industry estimates of financial losses to studios and other film copyright holders resulting from illegal copying or piracy are in the hundreds of billions of dollars, both in the United States and abroad, although many critics do not find those estimates credible.

Films have been relatively easy for many people to copy ever since videotape technology came into wide use in the 1980s, and the introduction and early popularity of VCRs unnerved the movie industry, which feared that illegal copying or piracy would keep people from paying for either a movie ticket or a video rental. The MPAA initially tried to suppress the diffusion of videotape technology, fearing massive piracy. When that attempt failed, the MPAA put a great deal of energy into demanding the enforcement of laws against illegal video copying of movies, both in the United States and abroad. As more people started renting legitimate copies from a rapidly expanding set of online video rental outlets, the MPAA studio producers began to realize that video was more of a gold mine than a threat.

The film industry hopes to discourage illegal film copying at the consumer level. Consumers may make a copy of a film that is being broadcast or cable-cast for their own use. However, they may not sell or rent that copy to anyone else. A consumer may not copy a film from one computer or DVD onto another. This is why all officially copied films have an FBI warning against illegal copying at the beginning of the DVD. In most cases, both digital copies and DVDs of films have technological safeguards against copying. The MPAA is concerned about fast Internet download programs, like BitTorrent, that permit downloading of feature-length films and have put several similar networks out of business. However, the most recent MPAA effort to restrict online trading and downloading, a proposed bill in the U.S. Congress called the

PIRATES vs 007. James Bond may be able to stop world domination by the bad guys, but Hollywood has not stopped world piracy from eating up a large percentage of it's potential revenue.

Stop Online Piracy Act (SOPA), was seen as too intrusive into online freedom and was fought down in Congress by an online campaign that had been pushed hard by computer and Internet industry interests.

The big issue in piracy is illegal copying by people who intend to sell or rent the illegal copy. This practice defrauds copyright holders of rentals or sales that they might otherwise have from potential consumers who rent or buy the illegal copy instead of the legal one. Only legal copies provide royalties to the copyright holders, compensating them for the expense and work that went into the movie. Thus, the film industry, via the MPAA, has pushed law enforcement officials both in the United States and abroad to enforce copyright laws by pursuing large-scale, commercially oriented pirates. Those who are illegally copying films on a large industrial scale are the ones principally targeted by enforcement efforts and the Center for Copyright Information (see Chapter 16).

> **Stop Online Piracy Act (SOPA)** was an antipiracy initiative by the film and music industries, defeated in 2011 because it seemed to limit Internet rights.

Media & Culture

FIGHTING THE ANTI-PIRACY WAR HERE AND ABROAD

The MPAA has had remarkable success in getting many governments to crack down on film piracy abroad. The U.S. government has helped apply pressure on other governments to enforce the existing international copyright agreements. Nearly all governments have signed the Berne Copyright Convention, which covers video piracy.

Protecting intellectual property that exists in digital form is hard since it is easier to pirate digital material because a computer can be used as the main copying tool and can "share" movie sites over the Internet. The movie theater is another front in the antipiracy war. Films now include flashing colored dots that carry identifying information about the print so that the studios can track down pirates who surreptitiously tape first-run movies at the multiplex. Other technologies, including night vision goggles, are used to look for hidden cameras in the audience on premiere nights. Google is also perfecting a "video fingerprinting" technology that makes it possible for computers to spot copyrighted material. Avast, movie pirates!

SUMMARY&REVIEW

HOW HAS MOTION PICTURE TECHNOLOGY DEVELOPED?

Thomas Edison invented most of the major components of the camera, whereas the Lumière brothers in France discovered the principle of projecting light through transparent filmstrips. Film has been improved by increasing the number of frames or images per second, making the image wider, and adding color. Special effects developed from mechanical models, as in the classic *King Kong* (1933), have become more sophisticated and ultimately replaced by computer-generated images. The superimposing of images and the use of background mattes have also been made more sophisticated by computers. Digitization changed not only effects but also image capture (cinematography), editing, and, increasingly, projection.

WHAT WERE THE STAR SYSTEM AND STUDIO SYSTEMS?

Rudolph Valentino, Lillian Gish, and Charlie Chaplin were such attractions that their names appeared above the name of the film on movie marquees. The studios rose on the basis of this star system, using the stars' popularity to promote their movies.

The studio system consisted of production companies that employed the complete set of facilities and people required to make and distribute movies. The major movie studios grew by developing a stable of actors, writers, and directors who worked for them over a period of years. The main Hollywood studios were United Artists, Paramount, MGM, Fox, Warner Brothers, Universal, Columbia, and RKO. The major film producers are still the old-time studios—Columbia, Fox, MGM, Paramount, Universal, and Warner Brothers—along with Buena Vista (Disney) and TriStar (Sony). Independent film companies work alone or with majors. Individual independent filmmakers, or "indies," usually produce more films but for much less money than the majors—often a few million dollars. Indie films are still primarily distributed by the majors.

WHAT WERE SOME OF THE MAIN DEVELOPMENTS IN FILM FORMS AND GENRES?

D. W. Griffith pioneered using a large-screen, well-produced outdoor battle scenes, moving shots, feature-length films, and close-ups. The silent film genres included westerns, war movies, science fiction, romances, physical comedies, and historical costume dramas.

Talking pictures created a sudden change, starting with *The Jazz Singer* in 1927. Acting became less overstated and stylized. The actors' voices and the use of sound effects, as well as music, became important. Talkies required an influx of new talent, which came mostly from vaudeville and Broadway. A number of new genres, such as musicals, film noir, and others, took advantage of both technology and studio system possibilities. The basic current genres are the categories you would find in video stores or on Netflix: comedy, drama, action, horror, science fiction, classic, family, western, animation, and foreign.

HOW DID HOLLYWOOD AND ITS FILMS CHANGE AFTER THE ADVENT OF TELEVISION?

The film industry was closely tied to theatrical chains, and television quickly cut into their revenues. As small theaters closed all over America in the 1950s, the film industry began to realize that it couldn't beat television. Disney started producing programs for television in 1954, and other studios followed. All began to license films for showing on television, and many eventually produced made-for-TV movies. By the 1960s, the power of the movie studios was declining. Independent producers gained more of a role in producing movies, and film studios began to spend much of their time producing TV series. Movie channels like HBO provided an important new distribution channel for films, while cable channels and streaming channels commission new made-for-cable films, as well as distributing films not picked up by major studios.

WHY WERE FILM RATINGS DEVELOPED? WHAT ARE THEIR PROS AND CONS?

After years of debate and what seemed to be an increase in movies with explicit language, sex, and violence in the 1960s, the MPAA instituted a ratings system to give people an idea of what they might encounter in a film. Some critics argue that as a form of industry self-censorship, ratings violate freedom of speech for filmmakers. Others argue that the ratings simply draw the interest of younger viewers. The restrictions on teenage viewing of films rated R and NC-17 are often not enforced by theaters, because teens are the main moviegoers.

THINKING CRITICALLY

ABOUT THE MEDIA

1. How does the history of film help us understand how movies will develop as they interact or converge with parts of the Internet, like iTunes distribution or Netflix?

2. How does learning the forms and history of film help us understand how other visual, narrative forms, like video games, are going to develop as commercial forms? As artistic forms?

3. What would be the most effective response by the film industry to keep it from being hurt by piracy in the way that the music industry has been?

4. Does violence in film need to be more tightly controlled? Please justify your answer with examples from film history and from controversial films like the *Saw* series.

5. Do you think that the impact of special effects and other technology on films is positive? Do the new tools help or harm storytelling in film?

KEY TERMS

auteur (p. 193)	Motion Picture Code (p. 188)
B movies (p. 190)	MPAA (p. 208)
compositing (p. 199)	MPAA ratings (p. 209)
concentration of ownership (p. 191)	nonlinear editing (p. 199)
digital video (p. 200)	postproduction (p. 199)
feature film (p. 186)	rear projection (p. 198)
film noir (p. 189)	star system (p. 188)
first-run distribution (p. 194)	Stop Online Piracy Act (SOPA) (p. 211)
front projection (p. 198)	studio system (p. 190)
gross (p. 191)	talkies (p. 189)
independent (indie) film (p. 195)	theatrical film (p. 191)
major film studios (p. 188)	vertical integration (p. 190)
mattes (p. 199)	windows (p. 203)

MindTap

Test your knowledge with online printable flashcards and online quizzing.

MindTap Log on to the MindTap Communication for *Media Now* to access a variety of additional material, including this chapter's e-book, learning objectives, comprehension quizzes, videos, and more!

TELEVISION

LEARNING OBJECTIVES

After studying the topics in this chapter, you will be able to:

1. Given the number of televisions and the number of households watching a television show, calculate the share and rating of a specific television show.
2. Assess the impact of Federal regulations and laws dating back to the 1930s on television today.
3. Summarize various economic models of television programming, according to genre and distribution technology.
4. Contrast the basic economic models for commercial and basic cable networks, premium cable stations, and public broadcasting.
5. Describe at least four of the programming strategies employed by the television industry to increase ratings and maintain audience interest.
6. Take an informed position on the social issues related to television today.

HISTORY: TV EVOLVES

When Television Was New

Television was once the new medium of its day and it might be said that it is rapidly becoming a new medium once again. However, the basic business models and practices, genres, and audiences of television that were developed in radio (Hilmes, Newcomb, & Meehan, 2012) and during TV's early years continue to shape what we see today even as "television" expands across a variety of screens.

For example, consider the basic economic model of television: Why are there ads? Netflix does not need them, so why does CBS? Television could have been created as a public service, paid for by taxes on TV sets, the model that Great Britain adopted. Or, television could have developed as a monthly pay service, beginning with the first cable systems in 1949. In the United States, the Federal Communications Commission (FCC) endorsed the commercial model from radio when it authorized

9:41 AM

Main   TV   Movies   Qu

Featured   Most Popular   Recently Added

American Dad!
Tears Of A Clooney
Season 1 : Ep. 23 (21:54)

Modern Family
Truth Be Told
Season 1 : Ep. 17 (21:36)

Parenthood
The Deep End of the Pool
Season 1 : Ep. 3 (43:13)

Spaced

Handout/MCT/Newscom

TABLET TV is one of many new options for viewing discussed in this chapter that change and challenge conventional television networks.

TELEVISION AND THE DAYS OF OUR LIVES?

If films are larger than life, television seems more intimate, the very stuff of our daily life. Television seems to influence our daily routine more than any other medium. In the 1950s, people began to eat their dinners off TV trays so that they could watch the tube during dinner.

Anthropologists observe how people see television as an essential part of their daily lives, and television programmers have tried hard to see that this continues. Some of the more successful television genres, talk and reality shows, play up this connection to daily life, looking in on the daily lives captured on the screen of MTV's *16 and Pregnant*.

This focus on daily life in television studies corresponds to changes in social theory. Social and cultural theorists, from Fernand Braudel to Anthony Giddens, have focused our attention on how people live their daily lives and how it reflects the choices they make. Scholars like David Morley look at the patterns of daily life to see how television is affecting us and whether we are accepting or rejecting its messages. Feminist scholars, like Charlotte Brunsdon, look at how women watch soap operas to resist and cope with the pressures on women in society.

Television is, or at least was, often the source of some of the main narratives of our lives, the topics we talk about with our friends, family, and coworkers. Horace Newcomb called television a cultural forum, one of the places where important forces like race and gender, and issues like fear of terrorism or crime, get discussed in very broad ways.

Bettmann/AS400 DB/Corbis

TV DINNER Television has had a profound influence on our daily routines since the 1950s.

At another level, Raymond Williams talked about the flow of television—that television is not just a series of discrete programs, but more of a continuous flow of experience. Both academic and industry researchers try to understand how television holds the audience over from one program to another (Williams & Williams, 2003). Since the 1950s, television programmers have been pushing the message: "Don't touch that dial." They hope that if we really like *NCIS*, we will also stick around to watch what comes next. But the natural flow of television declined with the remote control, ended with the enormous multiplication of channels brought by cable and satellite television, and is now totally defeated by the DVR and streaming video online.

---

commercial television stations in 1941, the same year that TV's technical standards were established by the National Television System Committee.

Thus, government regulation of television has long played a role in the evolution of the medium. The basic premise of government regulation, then and now, is to manage a scarce resource: the limited channel space available in the communications spectrum. At first, the imperative was to expand the number of TV channels available over the air. As television sets became available to the public after the end of World War II, demand for TV channels grew so fast that the FCC put a "temporary" freeze on new stations in 1948 while it came up with a plan to expand viewing choices for everyone. However, the technical issues surrounding the introduction of color television complicated the plan, and the freeze dragged on until 1952 (Sterling & Kittross, 2002).

1941

Commercial TV begins in the United States

MindTap®

Start with a quick warm-up activity.

1952

FCC Sixth Report and Order defines TV service

MEDIA THEN··· MEDIA NOW

1927
> Philo Farnsworth develops electronic television

1941
> Commercial TV begins in the United States.

1948
> First TV news on NBC

1951
> I Love Lucy debuts

1952
> FCC Sixth Report and Order defines TV service

1953
> KUHT, the first PBS station, goes on the air

1961
> FCC chair calls TV a "vast wasteland"

1967
> The Public Broadcasting Act is passed by Congress

1972
> FCC lifts ban on urban cable TV systems; HBO pioneers pay TV

1987
> Fox Network goes on the air

1996
> The Telecommunications Act relaxes media ownership rules

1998
> Broadcast networks fall behind cable

2009
> U.S. digital TV transition goes into effect

2014
> Netflix surpasses HBO

2016
> Television spectrum auction

> **VHF** is the very high-frequency television band, channels 2 to 13.

The 1952 FCC rules, the Sixth Report and Order, expanded the **VHF** (very high frequency) television band (channels 2 to 13), opened 70 new **UHF** (ultra-high frequency) channels, and set aside channels for educational broadcasting.

We still hear today of the Big Three television networks (ABC, CBS, and NBC; FOX came along a generation later) whose primacy was an unintended consequence of the FCC's early actions. Only VHF stations prospered because those signals are stronger and because the FCC did not require UHF tuners in all new TV sets until 12 years later, so that UHF stations had an inherently weaker appeal to advertisers. Most cities had only three VHF channels available. Radio pioneers David Sarnoff at NBC and William Paley at CBS (see Chapter 7) put the talent and sponsors developed by their commercial radio networks at the disposal of early television producers, leaving competing networks and independent stations at a disadvantage. By the mid-1950s, television was the leading advertising medium in the United States, ahead of radio, newspapers, and magazines.

UHF stands for ultrahigh frequency, channels 14 to 69.

So, instead of a bounty of viewing choices for all, the FCC's actions ultimately had the effect of limiting almost everyone's choices to three networks that still lead prime time ratings and television advertising decades later.

Many of the latest trends in television have a "back to the future" ring to them, harking back to the 1950s. Today we fill social media with buzz about television shows, but that is nothing new. Early television was also a "social medium" of sorts, as television owners invited their family and friends over to share the novel viewing experience and relived moments from top-rated shows in conversations the next day.

Advertisers sponsored entire shows that they named after themselves (e.g., *The Kraft Television Theater*) and filled with plugs for their brands. Today, when a sponsor's products appear during the scripted portion of the show, we call those program placements.

1948

First TV news on NBC

That period is called television's "Golden Age," a tribute to quality dramas such as Rod Serling's *Twilight Zone* series (that may still be found on YouTube .com today). Now we seem to be in a second Golden Age, with hundreds of scripted series available across broadcast, cable, and streaming television outlets. From the early days, television news shaped the public agenda, beginning with the first regularly scheduled TV news program on NBC in 1948. In one of television's finest moments, CBS news correspondent Edward R. Murrow exposed Wisconsin Senator Eugene McCarthy's anticommunist "crusade" of the early 1950s as a campaign of innuendo and half-truths.

Into the Wasteland

The quality dramas and penetrating public affairs programs of television's early years raised hopes that the new medium would elevate culture and public debate, help educate the young and inform the citizenry, similar to the hopes pinned on the Internet 50 years later. Instead, much of what came forth was ordinary, commercialized, uninspiring, and even harmful.

The first Golden Age died as audiences expanded and **ratings** ruled (see Figure 9.1 and Media & Culture: Going by the Numbers, page 218). The broader audience didn't appreciate the highbrow drama anthologies as much as the well-educated, urban, East Coast early adopters had. Sponsors wished for more upbeat lead-ins to their snappy commercial jingles. Advertising practices changed so that sponsors could purchase short "spots" rather than entire programs. This focused attention on "buying" audiences by the thousand (the **cost per thousand** [CPM]), and programs that appealed to refined, but uncommon, tastes had prohibitively high costs on that basis.

MindTap

Read, highlight, and take notes on the complete chapter text in a rich interactive online platform.

Ratings measure the proportion of television households that watch a specific show, or how many people are listening to a radio station.

Cost per thousand is how much a commercial costs in relation to the number of viewers who see it, in thousands.

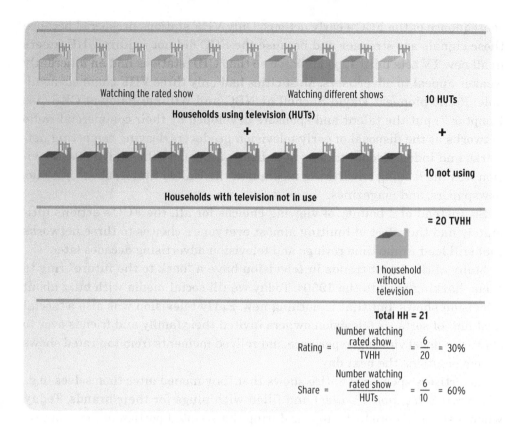

Watching the rated show   **Watching different shows**   **10 HUTs**

Households using television (HUTs)

+   +

10 not using

Households with television not in use

= 20 TVHH

1 household
without
television

Total HH = 21

$$\text{Rating} = \frac{\text{Number watching rated show}}{\text{TVHH}} = \frac{6}{20} = 30\%$$

$$\text{Share} = \frac{\text{Number watching rated show}}{\text{HUTs}} = \frac{6}{10} = 60\%$$

FIGURE 9.1 **HOW RATINGS ARE COMPUTED** Ratings are computed by dividing the number of homes watching a show by the total number of TV households. Shares are computed by dividing by the number of households using TV at a particular time.

*All Other TV includes independents, Pay Cable, FOX/WB/UPN/PAX Affiliates, PBS, and all other cable.
Note: NHI Quarterly NTAR. All shares are based on the sum of total U.S. HH delivery (not HUT) for total day.

1951

I Love Lucy debuts

LUUUUUUCY! Comedienne Lucille Ball was a popular star in TV's Golden Age and a pioneer female executive behind the scenes.

Ratings are one-half of the formula for economic success in television; low production costs are the other half. Situation comedies, or sitcoms, cost less than drama or variety shows, and the 1951 hit *I Love Lucy* proved their appeal. Cheaper still were quiz shows that eliminated scripts and professional actors—we call them reality shows today—and those shot to the top of the ratings in the mid-1950s. Television executives also turned to Hollywood for more efficient, but also less original productions. Western movies were popular then, and television producers recycled sets and unemployed actors from westerns to produce shows like *Maverick* on the cheap.

Television's power to offend audiences and degrade culture as well as to entertain and enlighten became evident. The children of the early 1950s suffered an epidemic of broken limbs as they jumped from garage roofs while attempting to imitate TV's Superman, incidents that led to the first congressional hearings about the effects of television on children. A few years later, greedy sponsors rigged popular TV quiz shows to improve their ratings, causing a national scandal. In 1961, FCC Chairman Newton Minow called American television a "vast wasteland" of mediocre, uninformative programs.

Television continued to have golden moments. The whole nation seemed to watch together as events like the Kennedy–Nixon presidential debates,

Kennedy's funeral, the Vietnam War, and the moon landing unfolded in the nation's living rooms. Entertainment programs from that era also left their mark. *All in the Family* focused on the clash between generations and exposed racial bigotry, whereas the *Mary Tyler Moore Show* offered positive images of professional women. *Roots,* a blockbuster miniseries about the passage of African Americans in the United States, sparked renewed pride in African origins and interracial dialogue.

Washington to the Rescue?

So the question for regulators in Washington became how to balance the good that television could do against the cultural damage it could inflict. Perhaps the Big Three's *oligopoly* (see Chapter 2) had to be broken, beginning with their stranglehold on television production. In the 1970s, regulators acted to push the networks out of the **syndication** business through which they profited from reruns of popular shows. Regulators also closed the 7 to 8 p.m. time slot to network programing and limited the amount of entertainment programing the networks could produce in-house.

Television units associated with major film studios began to profit from syndication and the early evening filled with cheap-to-produce **first-run syndication** shows like *Wheel of Fortune.*

However, quality, uplifting, and informative programing was still difficult to find. Why not directly regulate content, at least that which was potentially harmful? As the nation's inner cities and college campuses erupted in violence in the late 1960s and early 1970s, a finger of blame was pointed at the thousands of hours of violent programs served up by the Big Three each year. In 1975, the FCC pressured the networks to institute a Family Viewing Hour from 8 to 9 p.m. That policy collided with the First Amendment rights of broadcasters and was soon struck down by the courts, however (see Chapter 16), dooming even modest efforts to improve commercial television programing through government action.

Paul Schutzer/Time Life Pictures/Getty Images

THE NATION WATCHED The first ever televised presidential debates between Kennedy and Nixon demonstrated television's power to inform the public and impact the nation's culture.

Bettmann/Corbis

TOP RATED The *Roots* miniseries was one of the top-rated TV shows of all time and pioneered a new genre, the miniseries. Top-rated shows like the Super Bowl attract larger audiences today but reach a lower percentage of TV households than top shows of the 1980s.

1961

FCC chair calls TV a "vast wasteland"

Syndication is the rental or licensing of media products.

Another approach to breaking the Big Three's oligopoly was to provide a noncommercial alternative. The FCC's Sixth Report and Order allocated hundreds of channels nationwide for noncommercial educational TV. The first such station, KUHT in Houston, signed on in 1953 but funding was a problem. The Public Broadcasting Act of 1967 established the Corporation for Public Broadcasting (CPB) to finance programming from federal tax funds, followed 2 years later by the Public Broadcasting Service (PBS) to distribute programs to public stations. PBS added some new viewing choices, notably

Media &Culture

GOING BY THE NUMBERS

Since 1950, the Nielsen Company has been a force in television audience measurement with technology that automatically records when the television set is on and the channel to which it is tuned. The households that participate in ratings studies are randomly selected so that every home has an equal chance of being included. This makes the sample statistically representative of the population from which it is drawn—all U.S. television households.

Figure 9.1 (see page 218) shows how television ratings are calculated. A television household is any home with a (working) television set, and there are about 116.4 million in the United States. An HUT is a Household Using Television; about 60 percent of all TV households are usually HUTs during prime time. A rating is the percentage of all television households tuned in to a particular program. Each rating point thus represents 1 percent of the total, or about 1,164,000 households. A share is the percentage of HUTs watching a program: thus, it is based on only the homes actually watching television at a particular time.

Advertisers perform an additional computation to arrive at the CPM. They multiply the rating by the number of households each rating point represents and divide that into the cost of buying a commercial spot in the corresponding program. So, if 60 Minutes has a 10 rating, that translates into 11.6 million television households, or 11,600 lots of 1,000 homes each. If a 30-second spot on 60 Minutes costs $94,000, we divide that by 11,600 and arrive at a CPM of $8.10. Generally, advertisers select the programs that have the lowest CPM.

The old-style meters that recorded only household-level viewing by recording channel tuning on the TV sets in use have given way to people meters in large markets. The 25,000 people meter families are prompted by a flashing red light to push buttons on a box to indicate who is in the room at that moment. Conventional meters have been phased out in 56 local markets that Nielsen monitors continuously and have been replaced with local people meters, which are included in the national sample. Meanwhile, paper diaries to record viewership are still mailed out in some 105 smaller local markets in the months of November, February, May, and July, about 300,000 diaries in each of these months. You may have noticed that the programs are a little better and the local news stories are a little more sensational during those "sweeps months" as broadcasters compete for attention in the Nielsen homes. In 45 mid-sized markets with the older set meters Nielsen guesstimates the demographics of the viewers based on household and viewing characteristics.

The accuracy and validity of ratings is a growing concern. Only about a quarter of all the homes contacted participate in diary, and viewers in people meter homes, especially young children, tire of pushing buttons during the 2 years they remain in the sample. The ratings of shows starring minority characters also do poorly in people meter homes even though the proportion of African-American and Hispanic households in the people-metered sample closely matches the national percentages of these groups. However, measuring viewership across television, personal computer, tablet, and smartphone screens is a challenge. Nielsen is striving to keep up with the new media environment. Nielsen now provides ratings of individual commercials as well as the TV shows they appear in and includes delayed digital video recorder (DVR) playbacks in its data. In 2014, Fox dropped Nielsen ratings for its stations and signed with Rentrak, a company that compiles viewership data from set top boxes in cable TV homes, a change that Nielsen followd in 2016. In 2015, Rentrak merged with comScore, an Internet audience measurement company, in an effort to develop multiscreen viewing data.

children's programming like *Sesame Street* and British imports like *Upstairs, Downstairs*. However, those wholesome alternatives failed to attract audiences on the scale of violent cartoons and popular crime shows offered by the Big Three.

New Media to the Rescue?

Today, streaming Internet video is widely regarded as a disruptive new media technology but it harkens back to new media of the 1970s. The new media of that decade established new economic models, telecommunications infrastructure, and audience habits that presented a new path out of the wasteland of the Big Three oligopoly and made way for the streaming video of today.

Cable television spread as cable operators picked up broadcasts from major market TV stations and relayed their signals to smaller communities. However, these distant signals threatened local independent UHF stations, so the FCC ruled that cable systems **must carry** all nearby broadcast signals and initially banned cable from the 100 largest major markets. The FCC reversed its ban on urban cable systems in 1972 and mandated that new systems have at least 20 channels, the same year that pioneering **pay TV** network Home Box Office (HBO) was established. HBO's carriage of the Ali–Frazier boxing match was the first pay program distributed via satellite and through local cable systems to home viewers, in 1975.

Basic cable channels were filled with new distant signals such as WTBS from Atlanta, and others like ESPN available only on cable were supported by a combination of advertising sales and monthly cable subscription fees. With new channels and the lure of pay cable revenues, large cable companies that owned multiple cable systems—**multiple system operators (MSOs)**—contended for cable franchise rights in the top 100 cities. The MSOs laid thousands of miles of wires to connect homes to their networks, wires that would one day deliver broadband Internet service to our homes. In the 1990s, **direct broadcast satellite (DBS)** operators DirecTV and the Dish Network emerged as alternative television delivery systems that transmitted satellite signals directly to the home for a monthly fee.

Surely, the new wealth of channels should provide enough variety to silence TV critics, but "fifty-seven channels and nothing on," as sung by Bruce Sprinsteen, became their refrain. Rather than exiting the wasteland, cable TV seemed to expand it by amplifying old program formulas (i.e., drama, movies, sports, news) to entire channels and further recycling old reruns of the Big Three. And, free of the indecency rules that broadcasters had to live by, original cable programming featured steamy music videos, nudity, and profanity that raised new concerns about the effects of television on children.

1967

The Public Broadcasting Act is passed by Congress

1972

FCC lifts ban on urban cable TV systems; HBO pioneers pay TV

> **Cable television** transmits television programs via coaxial cable or fiber.

> **Must carry** is the policy that requires cable companies to carry local broadcast signals.

> **Pay TV** charges cable customers an extra monthly fee to receive a specific channel.

Everett Collection

BROADCAST KNOCKOUT The big fight between Muhammad Ali and Joe Frazier was the first national pay event from HBO. Cable TV changed the industry in much the same way that Internet television is changing it today.

1987

Fox Network goes on the air

1996

The Telecommunications Act relaxes media ownership rules

1998

Broadcast networks fall behind cable

It was not until the turn of the century that cable started to produce quality original content like *The Sopranos* with themes and characters that conventional network television did not offer.

The first home videocassette recorders, or VCRs, appeared in 1975, and video stores spread like wildfire in the 1980s. It was feared that home video would lure people away from cable, but many viewers just added rented videos to their existing entertainment options. Video rentals provided a second alternative to the advertising-supported "free" TV model of the Big Three networks, a model that would later give Netflix its start as a mail order video rental provider. For the first time, VCRs also liberated viewers from the tyranny of the network television schedule, allowing them to watch what they wanted, when they wanted.

The Big Three in Decline

Some 25 years after television was first declared a "vast wasteland" of repetitive programming from the Big Three, the conditions were at last right for new broadcast networks to emerge. The Big Three weakened as they changed owners in the mid-1980s and the new bosses slashed staff to improve profitability (Auletta, 2010). Cable TV must carry regulation extended the audience coverage and economic viability of UHF stations, and the FCC increased the number of TV stations one corporation could own from 7 to 12. In 1987, that made it feasible for Australian media magnate Rupert Murdoch to create the Fox network built around a collection of major market UHF stations. Rules prohibiting networks from producing and syndicating their own entertainment programs were lifted. That encouraged more new networks and *vertical integration* of networks with movie studios, like Murdoch's Twentieth Century Fox. Warner started the WB network, and Viacom built UPN around stations it owned (these were merged into The CW in 2006). For Spanish-speaking viewers, there was Univision. They were joined in 1998 by Pax TV (later calling itself Ion Television).

The new networks largely imitated the Big Three, even further pushing the bounds of good taste with offbeat family comedies like *The Simpsons* and sexy youth-oriented shows. But still, broadcast network ratings declined. The list of top-rated shows of all time, exclusive of sports, has not had a new addition since the early 1980s (see Table 9.1). In 1998, for the first time, the Big Three attracted less of the daily viewing audience than ad-supported cable networks

TABLE 9.1 The Top TV Shows of All Time (Excluding Sports)

RANK	PROGRAM	NETWORK	RATING	SHARE	DATE
1	*M*A*S*H Special* (Last Episode)	CBS	60.2	77	2-28-83
2	*Dallas* (Who Shot J.R.?)	CBS	53.3	76	11-21-80
3	*Roots Part VIII*	ABC	51.1	71	1-30-77
4	*Gone with the Wind–Part 1*	NBC	47.7	65	11-7-76
5	*Gone with the Wind–Part 2*	NBC	47.4	64	11-8-76

Source: Nielsen Media Research-NTI. Retrieved from http://fbibler.chez.com/tvstats/misc/all_time.html

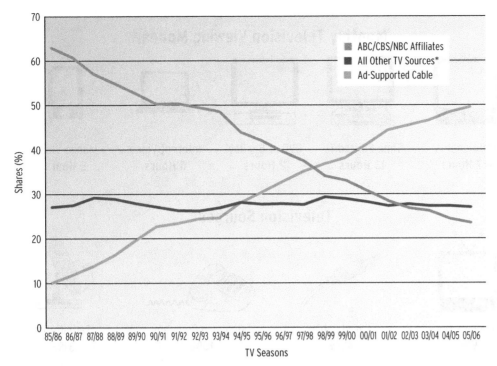

*All Other TV includes independents, Pay Cable, FOX/WB/UPN/PAX Affiliates, PBS, and all other cable.

Note: NHI Quarterly NTAR. All shares are based on the sum of total U.S. HH delivery (not HUT) for total day.

FIGURE 9.2 **BIG THREE AT THE CROSSROADS** The share of prime-time TV audience held by cable networks surpassed the Big Three for the first time in 1998. Broadcast network shares have continued to decline since then.

(Figure 9.2). Only profits from the networks' owned-and-operated (O&O) kept them afloat. The Telecommunications Act of 1996 further relaxed media ownership rules and triggered a merger binge that married broadcast networks to cable television, music and print publishing, Internet enterprises, and movie studios.

Television in the Information Age

Television as it was known in the heyday of *I Love Lucy* is dead. Interrelated changes in technology, audience behavior, and economics continue to transform the television medium (Auletta, 2014).

Playbacks from DVRs and videos streamed from Netflix, Amazon, and Hulu onto iPads, smartphones, and Internet-connected flat screen televisions have replaced the big box in the living room (see Figure 9.3, page 224). Less than 10 percent of the U.S. homes receive television the old-fashioned way, off the air, through an antenna.

Viewing habits are changing rapidly. Shows like *The Walking Dead* draw up to two-fifths of their audiences from DVR players in the week following their original airing. On the other hand, social media boost live ratings of sporting events and *Keeping Up With the Kardashians* as millions tweet about them in real time each week.

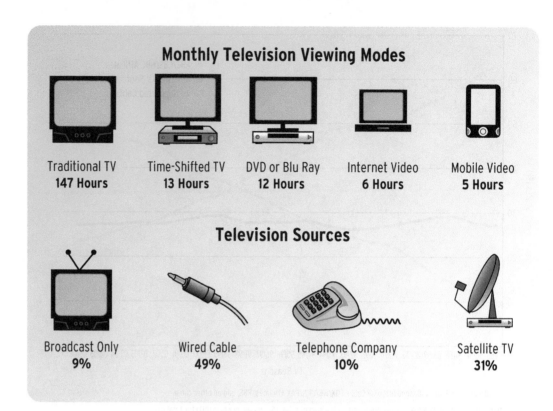

Monthly Television Viewing Modes

Traditional TV	Time-Shifted TV	DVD or Blu Ray	Internet Video	Mobile Video
147 Hours	**13 Hours**	**12 Hours**	**6 Hours**	**5 Hours**

Television Sources

Broadcast Only	Wired Cable	Telephone Company	Satellite TV
9%	**49%**	**10%**	**31%**

FIGURE 9.3 **TV ANYWHERE, ANYTIME, ANYPLACE** TV-viewing patterns are shifting away from traditional TV received over the air with an antenna.

Source: Nielsen (2013). The Cross Platform Report: A Look Across Media. Available: http://www.nielsen.com/us/en/reports/2013/a-look-across-media-the-cross-llatform-report-q3-2013.html

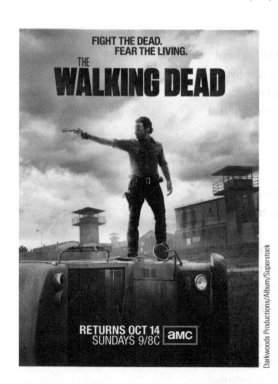

CABLE TV HIT Popular shows on cable TV networks like AMC's *The Walking Dead* score ratings that rival those of hit shows on broadcast television networks.

Some viewers are turning off conventional television distribution channels altogether. YouTube videos often have more viewers ("visitors" in the language of Internet audience measurement) than top-rated shows on conventional television. In 2014, Netflix's revenues surpassed HBO's for the first time in the battle for pay TV supremacy even as HBO started its own streaming service. *Cord cutters* are those who abandon cable, broadcast, and satellite services in favor of *over-the-top* viewing of streaming videos through Internet connections (i.e., on top of the Internet infrastructure), including original productions like *Orange Is the New Black* from streaming video provider Netflix. *Binge* viewers run their own streaming television marathons, sometimes purposely avoiding the first-run broadcasts and the commercials embedded in them.

The airwaves that carry conventional television broadcasts are also under attack from competing mobile technologies. The FCC organized a spectrum auction in 2016 with the aim of consolidating UHF channels and opening up new spectrum space for smartphones and other mobile devices. Over the next few years, many TV stations are expected to shift to new channels, other stations will channels with each other, while others may leave the air entirely. Participation in the 2016 auction was voluntary, but the event was a reminder that broadcasters do not own the spectrum they use and in the future the public interest could be served by devoting yet more space to mobile services (see Media Literacy, page 244).

With all of the new viewing options, have we at last exited the wasteland of mediocre broadcast network television? Television appears to be having a new golden age. Repetitive, cheaply produced reality shows like *American Idol* that dominated network television in recent times are making way for more thoughtful programs. In the 2015–2016 season, there were over 400 scripted television series under production across broadcast, cable, and Internet providers. Many explored novel and challenging subject matter well outside the mainstream of conventional network television.

STREAMING THREAT Original productions by streaming television services, such as Netflix's *Orange Is the New Black* entice cord cutters and binge viewers, trends that threaten advertising-supported broadcast television.

High-profile live sports events and awards shows are the last refuge for the conventional broadcast network model that exposes a large, captive, general audience to advertising spots. The 2016 Super Bowl broadcast had the third largest television audience of all time, but it did so with a rating of only 49 percent compared to 60 percent for the final episode of *M*A*S*H*, a former record holder from 1983. Also, the Super Bowl dwarfs the audiences for prime-time network television offerings that have dipped into the single digits. Thus, the huge football audience ironically provided further evidence of the decline of the conventional network television business model. Meanwhile, 4 million watched a free video stream of the game from CBS, perhaps fortelling the future evolution of big event television.

The economics of advertising-supported TV channels are threatened by diminishing audiences, widespread commercial skipping while watching DVR playbacks, and the emergence of Internet advertising as a dominant advertising vehicle. Advertising sales account for only about half of the revenue for CBS Television, for example (Auletta, 2014). These changes force conventional television broadcasters to seek new sources of revenue.

Rights fees paid by Netflix and other streaming video sites and by international broadcasters for reruns of network television shows add to CBS's bottom line. Another revenue source is the CBS All Access streaming service that carries episodes of the network's current shows and also old favorites, including all the original episodes of *I Love Lucy* and other old favorites. Broadcasters pressure cable operators to increase **retransmission fees** for the right to carry their channels, often threatening to remove their stations from local cable systems on the eve of major sporting events as a bargaining tactic. CBS reportedly is paid $2 per month per subscriber in retransmission fees in major markets where it owns its own stations. Television networks are reversing the long-honored practice of compensating their affiliates for carrying network

2014

Netflix surpasses HBO

2016

Television spectrum auction

> **Retransmission fees** are monthly per-subscriber fees that local broadcasters charge cable companies for the right to carry their programs.

programs. Now they are demanding that the affiliated stations they don't own pay fees to the network or a share of the retransmission fees for the privilege of carrying network programs.

Advertisers still value broadcast television for its ability to reach a broad, if dwindling, audience. There is a potential upside for advertising revenues when networks begin charging advertisers for the extra audiences attracted through DVR playbacks during the week following the initial broadcast. Network television could get a further ratings boost when Internet streaming videos of their shows are added to the ratings, provided they can curtail ad skipping online and improvements in TV rating systems can track them. However, a future in which all TV is pay TV and streaming Internet video replaces conventional broadcasting is also possible. Stay tuned for further developments.

Technology Trends: From a Single Point of Light

1927

Philo Farnsworth develops electronic television

All television pictures are formed by a single point of light that races back and forth and up and down the television screen so fast that it fools the eye into seeing a full moving image. This approach was originally designed for analog TV sets but digital receivers use it, too, with some refinements (see Technology Demystified: Inside HDTV, page 228).

Whether analog or digital, TV thus uses the same optical illusion exploited by motion pictures (see Chapter 8): *persistence of vision.* Inspired by the rows made by tractors moving back and forth across potato fields in his home state of Idaho, Philo Farnsworth invented an electronic scanning system in the 1920s, and he is often credited, at least in American textbooks, with inventing television. In 1941, the National Television Systems Committee (NTSC) set the technical standards that defined the analog television service in the United States and much of the rest of the world for the next seven decades. By today's standards, NTSC video was low quality, with the equivalent of only 525 lines of vertical resolution, and also rather "square-ish" with a ratio of screen width to screen height of only 4 to 3, the aspect ratio.

Digital Television Is Everywhere

The original goal of digital television was to improve the viewing experience by making the picture seem clearer and wider and sound better. Broadcasters hoped that these improvements would revive their profits by drawing more viewers, much as color television had when its use became widespread in the 1960s. However, digital television is having a much wider impact than its original advocates may have bargained for as it spreads to Internet-connected "smart" TVs, tablets, and smartphones.

Digital video that matches NTSC's quality and aspect ratio is now called *standard-definition TV (SDTV),* whereas

Bettmann/Getty Images

NEW MEDIA OF 1922 Philo Farnsworth demonstrates his invention, the electronic television set, that became a fixture in homes worldwide in the 20th Century.

high-definition television (HDTV) provides pictures suitable for large-screen home theater systems. Both forms are called *digital television*. Satellite television, digital cable services, video discs, and DVRs all use digital forms for transmission or storage as well. HDTV more than doubles (to 1,080) the number of vertical scan lines, widens the picture to match the 16 to 9 aspect ratio of movie screens, and adds six-channel "surround sound." Digital television also brings with it *multicasting*—that is, transmitting up to four standard-definition signals simultaneously within the space formerly occupied by a single conventional analog channel. These are designated as subchannels. For example, WNBC Channel 4 in New York City transmits an all-news service on Channel 4.2, whereas Channel 4.1 is the designation for its primary broadcast service.

The digital television transition completed in 2009 forced viewers to buy either a digital television set or a digital converter for their old analog sets. In the transition, most viewers bought flat-screen *liquid crystal display* (LCD) or plasma televisions. Old-fashioned televisions with bulky picture tubes collect dust in closets and clog landfills, but are no longer found at consumer electronics stores in the United States.

The HDTV standards were developed with over the air broadcasts and cable TV in mind. However, the adoption of wide-screen digital receivers and digital cable connections also made **streaming video** delivered through high-speed Internet connections popular. Internet-capable television sets, sometimes called *smart TVs*, have built-in apps that connect directly to online video websites like Netflix and Hulu, as can tablet computers and smartphones. However, anyone with a high-speed Internet connection can experience streaming video by downloading the app that plays the videos. On free sites like YouTube, the software is built into the latest browsers (HTML5, see Chapter 10), although at others you have to pay a monthly subscription fee, including the YouTube Red subscription service. Inexpensive wireless devices like Google's Chromecast beam video streams from your personal computer to your "stupid" digital TV if you don't have a "smart" one. Some DVRs and video game consoles can also hook you up to streaming content. All told, streaming video accounts for half of all Internet traffic during peak evening hours.

If you want live TV, however, streaming is still in its infancy. First-run network television programs are not "posted" on sites like Hulu until a day or more after their initial broadcast. For about $50, you might purchase a digital TV tuner accessory for your tablet or Smart TV to pick up off-the-air signals. Slingbox streams live programs from your cable TV set-top box to you anywhere on the Internet but you still need to pay for a cable subscription. Cable companies and broadcasters offer TV Everywhere service that allows paying customers to stream live (or only slightly delayed) content through Internet connections. However, users have to

> **High-definition television (HDTV)** is digital television that provides a wider and clearer picture than standard television.

2009

U.S. digital TV transition goes into effect

> **Streaming video** converts video to continuous streams of data for transmission over the Internet.

Kevork Djansezian/Getty Images

INTERNET TV Apple is among the several computer and Internet companies that want to offer video distribution systems that will compete with broadcasters and cable companies. Here Apple president Tim Cook shows off Apple TV.

INSIDE HDTV

Television pictures are an optical illusion generated from a single point of light racing back and forth across your TV screen. In old-fashioned sets with cathode ray tube (CRT) screens, the light is produced by a beam of electrical charges that are "shot" from an electron gun at the rear of the picture tube. When they hit the inner surface of the tube, they cause the coating on the inside of the tube to give off a glow. The more electrons that hit the surface at a given instant, the brighter the glow. The electron beam sweeps back and forth in successive rows to create each full-screen picture from top to bottom, one pixel, or picture element, and one horizontal line at a time. In conventional analog sets, that feat was duplicated 30 times per second. Each frame of the picture was made up of 525 lines, but that is divided up into two sets (or fields) of 262 and a half lines, and the two halves of the picture are combined, or interlaced, to complete the picture.

CRT sets are outdated now, but standard-definition digital sets replicate the same picture creation process with new flat-screen display technologies, whereas high-definition sets improve the clarity of the picture by increasing the vertical resolution to 1,080 lines. Digital televisions employ two different scanning methods, 1080i (the "i" is for "interlaced") or 1080p ("p" is for "progressive"). The latter is the scanning method used in computer monitors and is said to produce a better picture and works better with high-definition DVDs.

There are several digital TV technologies from which to choose. LCD screens have three tiny, lightweight solid-state devices at each pixel that control the flow of light through miniature red, green, and blue filters. Flat-screen plasma displays have three miniature fluorescent lights located at each pixel that are activated by grids of invisible wires running across the screen. For the home theater crowd, digital light processing (DLP; see Chapter 8) technology has made its way into consumer video projection systems. Another projection system option is LCOS (liquid crystal on silicon). OLED (organic light-emitting diode) screens are the latest; they are a fraction of an inch thick and have low power consumption and high-contrast pictures. They are already found in smartphones and are being introduced into huge, lightweight television screens that can hang on the wall like a picture frame.

Behind the wider and clearer picture lies a complete change in the way television programs are made and transmitted to the home compared to analog TV. The output of the camera is digitized using the same basic techniques of sampling and quantizing we learned about in relation to music CDs in Chapter 1. But video contains a lot more information than audio, so the information is sampled much more often than for musical recordings. Our eyes are less sensitive to color information than they are to light and dark (luminance), so the color components are sampled less frequently.

Next, the signal must be cut down to a size that can be transmitted over a standard TV channel. This is done by removing redundant information within and between frames of the television picture. The compression uses a process called *MPEG-2*, after the Motion Picture Expert Group that developed it. (The MP3 music files on the Internet reflect the audio portion of this standard.) The picture comes out of the MPEG encoder chopped up into hundreds of chunks, or packets, that make up each frame of the picture.

The next step actually adds to the length of each packet by appending data that help detect and correct errors that may occur during transmission. The data stream modulates a carrier signal in much the same way that a modem sends data over a phone line (see Chapter 11). Back in the studio, early TV cameras used the image orthicon picture tube ("immy" for short, the origin of the "Emmy" designation for awards in television excellence, incidentally). Modern TV cameras use solid-state components called *charged-coupled devices (CCDs)* to make pictures, instead of glass tubes. In CCD cameras, each pixel is represented by a miniature solid-state component that converts light to electricity. The electrical voltages associated with individual pixels are transmitted one at a time according to a fixed scanning pattern. Color cameras separate the incoming light from the scene into three separate color components, each with its own CCD.

authenticate themselves with passwords and subscriber ID numbers to view. Eventually, live streams may be available from local broadcasters, like the CBS All Access service offers from participating stations.

New TV Horizons

The latest Ultra HDTV (UHD) sets are selling quickly, but should you buy one? The 4k version of UHD offers four times the number of pixels as conventional HDTV sets and even newer 8k sets will have eight times as many. That makes the picture appear clearer and more life-like, matching the clarity of the so-called retina displays on the latest smartphones. Wall-sized, curved OLED screens spanning 20 feet or more can give you an immersive feeling of being inside the picture.

However, there is very little UHD content available currently. Netflix started UHD streams in 2014, but those require very fast Internet connection speeds and new TV sets with high-efficiency video coding (HEVC) built-in chips. Live events in UHD, such as the Superbowl, are many years in the future since they would require significant upgrades of cable TV networks to reach a true mass audience.

THE ULTIMATE TV? Ultra High Definition TV receivers offer sharper pictures than today's HDTV sets and curved screens that immerse the viewer in the scene.

Many early UHD adopters fail to see much difference compared to "plain old" HDTV unless they are equipped with high dynamic range (HDR) software that enhances the colors as well as the resolution. These are marketed as Ultra HD Premium sets. So, try before you buy to see if the extra cost is worth it and to make sure that you are not one of those who is nauseated by immersive display technologies. The idea of "talking back" to your TV and having it respond is nothing new. In the 1970s, Time Warner experimented, and failed, with an interactive cable system called "Qube." Emerging interactive TV ideas combine television with the Internet. One new option is the ability to make TV commercials "clickable" by moving a cursor over objects that appear on the screen so that viewers can call up information or order free samples for the products they see. Social media are proving to be a way to attract and hold a highly involved audience. Video chatting while viewing is another option now. Video conferencing applications like Skype are available on smart TV sets and social media services like Vine are promoting video interaction.

The integration of computer and television technology also makes the TV remote obsolete. Cell phone and iPad apps can take the place of conventional remotes. Video game manufacturers are licensing their motion-sensing controllers, like Microsoft's Kinect, to TV manufacturers so that gestures can be used to change the channel. Voice recognition is being added to smart TVs. That will bring channel-changing technology full circle back to the 1950s when voice commands were first used in early TV homes: "Junior, go over and switch the channel to Ed Sullivan." The latest Apple TV includes the Siri voice recognition application familiar to iPhone users. Siri supports advanced searches by title, genre, and favorite actors and will even translate what actors with thick British accents just mumbled.

UHD will require upgrades to Internet and cable TV connections in many U.S. homes. While Netflix and Hulu can be enjoyed over 3 megabit connections,

UHD content requires 20 megabits, to which tens of millions of U.S. homes do not have access. Telephone companies like Verizon are up and running in many cities with fiber optic systems (FiOS) that offer expanded channel capacity along with high-speed Internet connections. Google is building fiber optic networks in select cities, boasting connections that are 100 times faster than anyone else's. The cable industry is responding with a high-speed technology called *DOCIS* (Data Over Cable Service Interface Specifications) 3.0 that makes it possible to receive multiple HDTV video streams simultaneously.

Video Recording

UHD programing also pushes against the limits of video recording technology, a continuing problem with new video technology. Magnetic audiotape was introduced in the late 1940s, but television contained so much more information than audio that mountains of tape would have to move across the recording head at impossible speeds. The key development that paved the way for the home VCR was *helical scanning*. It stored video tracks on a slant (imagine cutting up tape into short segments and pasting them together slantwise), so the length of the tape could shrink to manageable proportions. VCRs are analog devices and few have survived three waves of digital video recording innovations that have followed.

DVD players store compressed, digitized video on higher-capacity versions of the familiar audio compact disc (see Chapter 6). HDTV recording requires improved laser and video compression technologies to put movie-length high-definition features on a single disc, up to 50 GB in all. In 2008, the "format war" between Blu-ray and the competing HD DVD standard ended with Blu-ray the winner.

DVR systems cross a VCR with a computer hard drive, continuously storing compressed digital video as it is transmitted. The TiVo brand name is often associated with these, but most of them are now being rented by cable TV and DBS companies rather than sold. Although few people ever mastered the intricacies of programming their VCRs, the DVR interfaces are easy to learn and the machines can "remember" the shows you want saved. DVRs also make it possible to skip the commercials, a feature that threatens the existence of both commercial broadcasters and basic cable or satellite channels. Not surprisingly, the DVRs distributed by cable companies, who profit from selling local ads in cable channels they carry, lack the commercial-skipping feature.

What's next in home video recording? High-capacity Blu-Ray DVD players capable of storing UHD content are beginning to appear. But, do we still need video recorders? Video-on-demand services offered by cable and satellite companies and streaming video Internet services like Netflix and Hulu aim to make home recording technologies obsolete. The percentage of U.S. homes with DVD players has already started to decline. Videos of weddings and birthday parties are routinely recorded on smartphones and tablets and stored on computers or uploaded to "the cloud" (see Chapter 10). So do we still need a stand-alone device for recorded videos?

Video Production Trends

Over the years, cameras have steadily shrunk in size for easy portability. Rugged portable cameras (and, increasingly, videos shot by viewers on digital cameras and smartphones) have greatly expanded coverage of live events from the studio to floors of political conventions to the helmets of football players. Electronic news gathering (ENG) systems transmit the news footage back to the studio via remote microwave antennas mounted on mobile vans. Other footage arrives in the newsroom via satellite, and the incoming digital video files are stored on video servers, which are massive computer disc drives. Reporters and news editors view the files and compose and edit stories while sitting at computer workstations that are linked to the video server through local area networks that interconnect all the computers in the newsroom.

These systems take advantage of digital film production techniques (see Chapter 8) that have been adapted to television. *Nonlinear editing* had a great impact on video production by speeding up postproduction and lowering costs. Digital graphics, special effects, and computer animation are also becoming routine. For example, many TV stations have virtual news studios in which the reporters perform on an empty stage and computer graphics fill in the set. Digital production techniques are migrating from specialized studio equipment to personal computers so that what once required a professional editing suite can migrate to an ordinary desktop. YouTube Tools (which you can easily find by Googling, naturally) and other free or low-cost applications enable you, our reader, to produce your own streaming videos.

STOP & REVIEW

1. What was TV like in its first Golden Age?
2. How did cable television develop?
3. Why is network television in decline?
4. How has digital technology impacted television?

INDUSTRY: WHO RUNS THE SHOW?

The changing fortunes of media empires have brought about shifts in the ownership of the major national broadcast television networks. These are the CBS, NBC, ABC, and Fox networks. Note that we continue to call them "broadcast" networks even though less than 10 percent of U.S. homes now receive them exclusively over the air instead of through cable, satellite, or streaming video services. The media conglomerates (Viacom, Time Warner, NBCUniversal, Disney, and News Corp) that dominated television in the first decade of the century have largely come undone, with only Disney remaining intact. In 2011, Comcast, the largest cable television operator in the United States, bought NBCUniversal. To pump up their stock values, Viacom, Time Warner, and News Corp split their media holdings to separate their slow-growing and debt-laden businesses from their faster-growing, more profitable ones. The national broadcast television networks are still regarded as valuable assets and integrate production, distribution, and public exhibition functions, but are generally placed in the slow-growth categories as audiences for conventional broadcast network fare continue to shrink.

Local television stations continue to attract investments from *group owners* who can profit from integrating management and advertising sales across multiple properties. Recently, low interest rates on the loans media companies take to finance their acquisitions, a recovery of the advertising market, and new revenues from retransmission fees paid to stations by cable operators have fueled a TV station buying binge. For example, the Tribune Company, a firm with a long and storied history in print as publisher of the *Chicago Tribune,* decided to spin off its troubled newspaper operations and buy local TV stations instead.

Other major players participate in one or two aspects of the television industry. For example, Sony Corporation produces TV shows through its Sony

Pictures division, has international satellite TV channels, and manufactures television and video equipment. Discovery Networks owns a stable of cable channels, including Discovery Channel and Animal Planet. A+E Networks runs the Lifetime, A&E, and History cable channels, among others, and is a joint venture of the Hearst Corporation and Disney. Capitalizing on the streaming video trend, new players like Apple, Microsoft, Google, Netflix, and Amazon are entering the television business with vast financial resources and their own plans for Internet television, video "apps" for tablets and smartphones, and video production and distribution.

VIDEO PRODUCTION

The way television programs are produced varies somewhat according to genre. Each reflects a slightly different economic model.

Entertainment. Production companies hire directors, actors, and technicians, and shoot and edit television entertainment programs (see Your Media Career: Video Production). However, much of the talents, both behind the camera and in front of it, are not full-time employees of either the networks or the production companies. Rather, they are hired on a project-by-project basis. Actors, directors, screenwriters, and other creative minds in the television business belong to labor unions, called *guilds* (e.g., the Writers Guild and the Screen Actors Guild), which negotiate the basic terms of employment with the production companies.

The networks contract with production companies for the rights to first runs of the shows, and typically pay fees that cover two-thirds to three-fourths of the initial production costs. The production companies may profit from the syndication rights by selling them in off-network syndication. For example, each episode of *The Simpsons* is worth about $4 million in syndication fees when rerun on local stations. Most network entertainment programs are now either produced in-house or co-owned by the networks themselves. The rest are usually purchased from production companies associated with other national television networks that have gobbled up the many independent producers that once thrived in Hollywood.

Reality shows represent a different economic model. By using amateur actors and doing away with scripts and elaborate sets, reality shows can be produced at far lower cost than scripted dramas or situation comedies. Reality shows also economize by using nonunion labor and paying production staff members about half the salaries they might command if they worked on unionized, scripted programs.

Not all the new program ideas go to network television, though. First-run syndication programs are rented to network O&Os, network affiliates, cable networks, and independent stations. Each of the major broadcast networks has subsidiaries that produce

PRODUCTION COSTS Leading actors for top-rated scripted series like *NCIS* bid up their salaries over time and can make them unprofitable to continue producing.

Eric Mccandless/CBS Photo Archive/Contributor/Getty Images

programs for first-run syndication, but others are associated with movie studios (e.g., Sony Pictures, producers of *Wheel of Fortune*) or major television group owners. A new niche is opening for programs produced for digital television subchannels, for example, Live Well Network, a channel dedicated to health and lifestyle programs.

Network News. News programs are journalistic endeavors, and we refer the reader to Chapters 4 and 16 for a discussion of those aspects of news production. We should point out that television journalism differs from print journalism in several important respects. Due to the nature of the medium, television news stories are often reduced to "sound bites" and short video clips that lack the in-depth reporting found in leading newspapers. The visual nature of the medium introduces a serious bias toward prioritizing stories that contain a gripping visual element: "If it bleeds, it leads," as the saying goes. Critics argue that the ratings-driven nature of the television business also causes television news to avoid controversial stories that may alienate viewers and to pander to the interests of sponsors.

Here we consider the news in the context of other types of television programming. News programs have little value in syndication, so their producers have to make all the money during their first run. The Big Three produce the evening news and magazine shows like *60 Minutes* through their own in-house news divisions. The networks cut many of their correspondents, and cut back on investigative reporting to reduce costs during multiple rounds of mergers and acquisitions. Now they rely more on footage supplied by local network affiliates, foreign television networks, independent "stringers," and even amateur video caught on smartphone cameras. CNN contends with the Big Three (and specifically CBS) as the network of record by building its own international news operation, and Fox News now draws bigger audiences than CNN by targeting a political niche audience—a strategy copied by MSNBC.

Local News. Most programs produced by local television stations are either newscasts or magazine-format shows. Local news is a major profit center, accounting for nearly half of all station revenues on average, so much so that local stations run an average of 5 hours of news a day (Waldman, 2011). Stations profit from the news because it is popular both with local audiences and with local advertisers and the revenues go directly to the local station—they are not shared with the network or a program syndicator. The news expansion has also been fueled by the ready availability of news footage, including that obtained from networks via satellite, as well as what comes from the station's own local electronic news-gathering capacity ("Live! From News Chopper Five!") and cell phone footage submitted by viewers. Production costs have declined over the years as equipment has become cheaper and news staffs have contracted, although those cost savings are easily erased by the purchase of news helicopters, weather radars, and HDTV camera equipment.

ColorBlind Images/AGE Fotostock

AFFILIATE PROGRAMMING Local affiliates of major TV networks also produce their own programming—most notable are the local news shows. Local news is a major revenue source for local TV stations.

Sports. Who produces the Super Bowl? Is it the NFL? No, but the networks can't just walk into the stadium and set up their cameras; they have to buy the rights to the broadcasts from the sports leagues and pay dearly for the privilege. For example, ESPN pays the National Football League $1.1 billion a year just for the rights to *Monday Night Football*. ESPN can still profit by further increasing the affiliate fees paid by cable operators, already the highest in the business. The same was not true for ABC television, which had only advertising fees—and declining ratings—for the broadcasts. That's why *Monday Night Football* moved to ESPN in 2006.

Public TV. Most PBS programs are produced by PBS stations in Boston, San Francisco, Los Angeles, New York, and Washington, D.C. Independent producers, notably Sesame Workshop (the producers of *Sesame Street*) and the British Broadcasting Corporation (*Masterpiece Theater*), account for the rest, some through coproduction agreements with PBS stations. The CPB funnels taxpayers' money to fund PBS programming. PBS now follows a centralized programming decision-making model, not unlike the commercial networks, under which programming executives in Washington decide which series to develop and air nationally on PBS stations. Producers depend on a mix of funding from CPB, PBS member station contributions, corporate **underwriting**, public contributions, and foreign network co-sponsorship. Contributing corporations and foundations are acknowledged in underwriting credits, those on-air announcements that express appreciation for financial support and describe what the donors do, but aren't commercials—not really.

Cable Production. National cable networks follow the same content acquisition strategies as the national broadcast networks, but local production is rather limited. Many cable systems produce their own **local origination** programming. The most elaborate operations resemble television stations, producing local news and sports for advertising-supported channels that are programmed by the cable operator. These are sometimes organized at a regional level to spread production costs across multiple cable systems. Most cable systems also maintain **community access** channels over which the operator has no direct control. Employees of the local educational or governmental institutions create the programs, or they are sometimes made by individuals who want their own cable show and staff their own productions. Community groups subsidize these local productions, whereas franchise fees paid by the cable operator to the municipal franchise authority finance the facilities used to produce them. However, several states, such as Texas, have now eliminated local public access by restricting the right of municipal franchise authorities to require operators to pay for them.

National Television Distribution

Television programs are distributed nationally by either networks or syndicators. Broadcast and cable networks differ somewhat in the ways they finance national distribution.

Commercial Networks. CBS, NBC, and ABC have been joined by Fox, The CW, MyNetworkTV, Ion, and Univision. These eight commercial broadcast networks all develop and schedule programs for national audiences, distribute them to their local affiliates via satellite, and profit from the sale of spots to national advertisers.

> **Local origination** means created within the community by the cable operator.

> **Community access** means created by community residents without the involvement of the cable operator.

VIDEO PRODUCTION

The producers and directors described in Chapter 8 often complain about the interference of "the suits," the studio and network television executives who oversee their projects. "We have some notes," they say as they hand the producer a tattered script covered with yellow stickies (or these days, Microsoft Word comment boxes). "You mutilated my work" is one often-heard complaint from the producer. Perhaps you would rather be one of the suits. Actors, producers, and directors account for only about one-third of the professional employment in the industry. Here we will go a little further behind the scenes to look at some of the more plentiful occupations we can find there.

There are more suits, people employed in the industry as business and financial managers, than actors, producers, and directors combined, reflecting the "bottom line" focus of the industry. These are occupations that students prepare for by majoring (or double majoring) in business, finance, accounting, marketing, or public relations.

There are also more film and video editors and camera operators than actors (employed ones, at least). There are about 33,500 film and video editors and 25,400 camera operators nationwide. Picture yourself working under a deadline to get the latest film clips from a war in the Middle East or a protest in your home town edited in time for the evening news. Most of these jobs are in large metro areas, including New York, Atlanta, and Los Angeles, although many of the entry-level television jobs are in much smaller markets. Median annual wages are about $57,000 a year for editors and about $48,000 ($9,000 less) for camera operators. College training in film and video production courses can help land an entry-level job. However, competition is keen due to the large number of students who wish to enter the industry. Rapid growth is expected for film and video editors in the next decade as new media develop content for mobile and digital platforms. The growth in opportunities for camera operators should be much slower than average due to automation and a trend toward combining reporting and editing roles in broadcasting.

Career Profile: Robert Iger

Not all of the top-level "suits" in Hollywood have backgrounds in finance or business administration. Robert "Bob" Iger, the chairman and CEO of the Disney Corporation holds a Bachelor of Science in Television and Radio from Ithaca College. He started out as a local TV weather announcer and worked his way up at ABC television over the years, becoming president of the network in the 1990s. He continued in high-level positions after Disney bought ABC in 1996 and took the top job in 2011. His annual compensation is over $40 million, a good year's pay for a TV major!

Sources: *Bureau of Labor Statistics (2011). Career guide to industries, 2010–2011 edition, motion picture and video industries. Bureau of Labor Statistics (2014). Occupational Outlook Handbook, 2014 edition, film and video editors and camera operators. Retrieved from http://www.bls.gov/ooh/media-and-communication /film-andvideo- editors-and-camera-operators.htm*

The traditional, advertising-supported broadcast network model is no longer profitable. The Big Three and Fox each generate several billion dollars in network advertising revenues per year, but profits are drained by huge payments for sports rights, production fees for entertainment shows, and multimillion-dollar salaries for on-air talent, plus the same taxes and routine operating expenses that all media firms incur (see Chapter 2). Network TV losses are offset by profits from other lines of business, including their cable networks, their

O&O stations, syndication fees, and the sale of programing to new media outlets like Netflix and Hulu. Shares of the retransmission fees that local affiliates of the networks charge cable operators are growing sources of revenue.

Basic Cable Networks. Over 400 basic cable TV networks are delivered via satellite, either to local cable systems that redistribute them to their customers or directly to the home via DBS operators Dish and DirecTV. Media conglomerates like Comcast control many of the leading cable channels. Basic networks derive their revenues from national advertising sales and affiliate fees. The **affiliate fees** are paid by cable operators, on a per-subscriber basis (these range from $7 per month per subscriber for ESPN to a few cents per month for C-SPAN). Many basic networks also make local advertising spots available that local cable systems sell to local advertisers. The largest basic cable networks (Table 9.2) are found on virtually all cable systems where they are usually part of basic cable offerings purchased by all customers. There are about six dozen regional basic cable networks (e.g., Madison Square Garden Network, New England Cable News).

Premium Services. HBO is the largest premium cable TV network. Along with its companion network, Cinemax, it reaches about 29 million subscribers through cable TV providers and another million through HBO Now, its stand-alone online subscription service. In terms of revenues, Netflix became the number one premium television service overall in 2014, although it is not counted as a premium *cable* service even though it reaches most homes through high-speed Internet connections provided by cable television operators. Showtime and Starz/Encore are the other leading pay networks. Pay TV networks derive their revenues exclusively from affiliate fees. With only one revenue stream, these fees are substantially higher than for basic services. A small cable operator might charge subscribers $10 per month for HBO and pay half of that back to HBO. Large cable MSOs have the market power to negotiate discounts,

> **Affiliate fees** are monthly per-subscriber fees that cable programming services charge local cable operators.

TABLE 9.2 Top 10 Cable Networks*

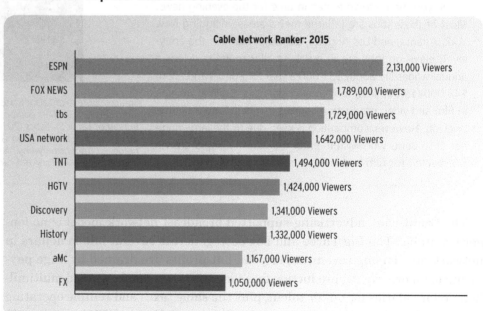

Cable Network Ranker: 2015

ESPN	2,131,000 Viewers
FOX NEWS	1,789,000 Viewers
tbs	1,729,000 Viewers
USA network	1,642,000 Viewers
TNT	1,494,000 Viewers
HGTV	1,424,000 Viewers
Discovery	1,341,000 Viewers
History	1,332,000 Viewers
aMc	1,167,000 Viewers
FX	1,050,000 Viewers

*Prime-time live plus same-day viewing averages for 2015, all persons aged 2+.
Source: Nielsen TV Ratings.

so they may pay HBO only about half of what the small cable company does and keep the rest of the subscriber fee as profit. Pay-per-view programming is also delivered by cable TV systems through satellite and is financed by affiliate fees, predicated on the number of pay-per-view orders.

Netflix and HBO Now are premium online services that cut out the cable operator in the middle and keep all of the monthly fee for themselves. Other premium online services, like Hulu, have a mixed model, combining advertising revenues with monthly subscription fees. Genre-specific online services are beginning to emerge for sports and movies.

SYNDICATED Longtime syndicated hit *Wheel of Fortune* is licensed directly to local TV stations. It is an example of first-run syndication in that its episodes were not previously seen on network television.

The Kobal Collection at Art Resource, NY

Public Broadcasting. PBS is careful not to call itself a network, but it performs many of the same functions, notably developing and distributing a lineup of programs nationally via satellite. There are no advertising sales, but PBS does funnel money to national program development.

Syndication. Local stations fill out their schedules with syndicated programming, particularly during the daytime and the 7–8 p.m. time slot during which broadcast networks are barred from scheduling their programs. These include first-run syndication programs, licensed directly to local stations, and off-network syndication, reruns of programs that previously aired on network television.

Syndicators obtain the rights for programming and then license the programs to local stations. Syndication is increasingly dominated by the major broadcast networks and their affiliates (e.g., *Wheel of Fortune* is owned by Sony but is distributed in the United States by CBS Television Distribution), but affiliates of lesser media conglomerates, such as Hearst Entertainment Distribution, and independent companies also play a role. Stations may pay for the programs outright (*cash*), pay a reduced price and show some advertisements or commercial spots arranged by the syndicator (*cash plus barter*), or pay nothing but give the syndicator more commercial minutes to sell to national advertisers (*barter*). Syndication contracts have an exclusivity clause so that only one station per market will have the right to show a particular program, although sometimes the rights are sold simultaneously to national basic cable networks. Many of these deals are made at the annual convention of the National Association of Television Program Executives (NATPE), which functions as a bazaar for syndicated programming.

Local Television Distribution

Local distribution of television was once the exclusive province of the local TV station. Now, cable television and satellite systems also play a role. A television station is an organization that holds a federal license to create or organize programs for a specific community and transmit them on its assigned channel. There are currently about 1,400 local commercial TV stations nationwide, and they may be categorized according to their ownership arrangements and relationships to national networks.

Group-Owned Stations. Many stations are operated by companies with multiple broadcast properties, called *group owners*. Group owners benefit from economies of scale in management, programming, and advertising sales. To prevent monopolization, limits were set on the number of stations one group could own. Currently, no ownership group may own stations that reach more than 39 percent of the television audience among them. That's according to the way the FCC counts coverage, in which UHF station coverage is cut in half, but when UHFs are fully counted, the Ion Media group reaches over three-fifths of U.S. households (McAvoy, 2011). *Duopoly,* that is, ownership of two stations in the same market, is permitted in large markets but not in smaller ones, and triopolies are prohibited. *Local management agreements* also allow group owners to manage local stations they do not own on a contractual basis. Cross-ownership rules that would allow one company to own both a newspaper and a television station in the same market remain under review as of this writing.

The four major broadcast networks are also group owners. Their O&O stations are concentrated in major markets where they are major profit centers for their parent. The largest group owners in terms of the number of stations are Media General, with 98 stations, and the Sinclair Broadcast Group, with 128.

Network Affiliates. A common misconception is that the broadcast TV networks own all their local outlets. However, aside from the network O&Os, which currently represent about 100 stations in all, local distribution of network programs is carried out by *affiliates*. These are individually owned or group-owned stations that have contractual arrangements with a network to show its programs locally.

Network affiliation is desirable because of the ratings draw of network prime-time shows. Local stations profit from the sale of local ad spots that run during network programs. A little over half of station revenue comes from local ads, including those placed in locally produced or syndicated programs as well as the local ad availabilities in network shows. The other half of the revenue comes from ads placed through the station by national and regional advertisers. These are arranged through *rep firms* that act as intermediaries between local stations and advertisers based in other cities.

Network affiliation has been especially profitable over the years because the Big Three paid their affiliates to take their shows, a practice called *affiliate compensation.* Now the networks are starting to charge the affiliates for programming, either as a flat fee or as a percentage of the retransmission fees that local stations collect from cable TV operators, and bidding wars have erupted among group owners for the right to represent the Big Three in major markets. Local stations also hope to profit from selling ads on their new digital subchannels that are part of the HDTV transition.

Independent Stations. Independent stations are not affiliated with any network. Independents buy most of their programming from syndication services and sell their advertising in the local, regional, and national spot markets.

Relatively few independents remain now that there are eight national networks in operation.

Down at the Local Station. Local stations vary in size from a couple of dozen employees to several hundred, depending on the size of the market they serve. Regardless of size, all commercial television stations have a common set of key roles (Table 9.3) organized around the basic tasks of obtaining and transmitting programs that will attract audiences and, with them, advertisers.

The program director arranges contracts with networks and syndicators and is responsible for filling the overall broadcast schedule. Local news programs are an important source of profits and so account for most of the local programming resources. Stations employ news directors, assignment editors, news writers, on-air personalities, and remote camera crews to produce their news shows. Promotion managers draw audiences with on-air promotions ("Plane crash coverage, live at 11!") and use advertising, public relations, and their websites to make the station more visible in the community.

Advertising sales are the lifeblood of every commercial television station. The sales director manages a staff of account executives who make sales calls to local advertisers. They carry rate cards that list the charges for advertising according to the time of day and length of the commercial spot. The sales director also contracts with a rep firm to sell blocks of commercials through national and regional advertising agencies. The traffic manager makes sure the commercials air at the proper times. Stations contract with Nielsen Media Research to provide ratings data that they use in their sales presentations. Large stations employ their own research directors who analyze the ratings and conduct local market studies, such as evaluations of local news anchors.

TABLE 9.3 Local Television: Key Personnel

JOB TITLE	JOB DESCRIPTION	HELPERS
Station Manager	Responsible for overall management, financial performance, planning, community relations	All other managers, front-office staff of secretaries
Chief Engineer	Keeps station on the air, monitors FCC standards	Transmitter engineers, studio technicians
Program Director	Selects and schedules programs, negotiates for syndicated programs	Syndicators
Promotion Director	Plans and directs on-air and off-air community promotions	Graphic artists, copywriters
News Director	Responsible for local news programs	Assignment editors, writers, announcers
Production Director	Produces the station's programs	Producers, directors, production crew
Sales Manager	Sells advertising time	Account executives, national rep firms
Director of Finance	Controls the station's finances, monitors the budget	Accountants and bookkeepers
Research Director	Analyzes and compiles reports on ratings, commissions local research	Ratings services
Traffic Manager	Schedules commercials	Advertising agencies

Source: Sherman, B. L. (2007). *Telecommunications management: Broadcasting cable and the new technologies.* New York: McGraw Hill.

STOP & REVIEW

1. What are the major U.S. television networks?

2. Why is it hard to make a profit from ad-supported network television? How do networks stay in business?

3. What is the relationship between television networks and their affiliates?

4. How do the economics of broadcast television production differ from those of cable channels?

Underwriting is corporate financial support of public television programs in return for a mention of the donor on the air.

Stations also employ engineers to keep the station on the air and maintain the transmitter and studio equipment. The finance department keeps track of revenues and expenses for the benefit of the station manager, who has overall responsibility for the profitable operation of the enterprise.

Noncommercial Stations

There are over 350 public television stations. There are community stations that rely on individual and corporate contributions and educational stations, usually affiliated with local colleges or universities that also receive funding from state or local governments. PBS stations must pay for the programming they receive from PBS and also for any syndicated programs. In place of the advertising sales force found in commercial stations, public stations have managers in charge of staging on-air membership and auction drives and soliciting contributions from private individuals and local foundations. They also seek corporate **underwriting** of local and national programs.

Television Advertisers

Advertisers spend about $25 billion a year on television network advertising and another $25 billion on cable networks. There are several basic types of TV advertisers with differing needs. National advertisers sell general consumption items, such as soft drinks. They buy blocks of advertising time from national broadcast networks during the *up-front* season. That's the time each spring when the networks sell time on the next season's shows. Time that is not sold then goes into the *spot* market and later into the *scatter* market, for last-minute ad sales. National spot advertisers and regional advertisers sell products with more limited geographic appeal, such as winter tires. They buy spots through advertising rep firms from both network affiliates and independent stations. Local advertisers, such as automobile dealers and supermarkets, buy slots in locally produced shows or those allocated by the networks to their local affiliates during network programs.

GENRES: WHAT'S ON TV?

As we know from Chapter 2, *genres* reflect a negotiation between the artist and the audience as to what is engaging or entertaining. In television, advertisers and network accountants are very much parties to that negotiation, however. Throughout the history of television, genres evolved to pursue audiences that interest advertisers and also in response to the changing economics of production.

Broadcast Network Genres

With the passing of *American Idol* in 2016, the proliferation of reality shows is waning, and scripted comedies like *New Girl* and dramatic series like *The Walking Dead* are making a comeback. Almost anything that appeals to 18- to 49-year-olds who are especially beloved by advertisers stays on the air, but with hundreds of scripted programs appearing across broadcast, cable, and streaming channels there is something for (almost) anybody.

Examples of each of the main television genres, along with their early television ancestors and predecessors in other media, are shown in Table 9.4. The table also shows some of the major genre variations. For example, dramas may be subdivided into medical, legal, and police dramas. Other variations hinge upon the interplay of plot and character development. In many sitcoms, the characters are static and only the situations change from week to week (e.g., *Modern Family*), whereas in others the characters continually develop and stories revolve around their interactions (*Mad Men*). In yet others, the weekly stories are woven into continuing plot lines (e.g., *Grey's Anatomy*).

Television genres continue to develop over time in response to changes in audience tastes and original creative ideas. Now television is becoming increasingly globalized as television networks look for creative formats from around the world that can be adapted in many countries. For example, *The Biggest Loser* was developed by The Shine Group, a British company recently acquired by Fox.

What's on Cable?

Cable networks elevated counterprogramming to an art form by chipping away at the network prime-time audience with specialized target audience programs. The Weather Channel follows the programming clock model found in radio, scheduling recurring segments at the same time each hour. General audience cable channels such as USA Network maintain a balance of programming intended to attract a broad audience throughout the day, translating the broadcast television

LOOKS LIKE A NEW GENRE Combine a cop show with a hospital show and you get a forensic investigation show, like *CSI*. New shows often combine elements from previous hits in an effort to define new winning program formulas.

TABLE 9.4 **Prime-Time Television Genres**

GENRE	ORIGINS	EARLY EXAMPLE	CURRENT EXAMPLE	GENRE VARIATIONS
Situation Comedy	Radio comedy skits, "screwball" movie comedies	*I Love Lucy*	*The Big Bang Theory*	Family, workplace, buddy
Drama	Live theater, radio and movie dramas	*The Twilight Zone*	*Grey's Anatomy*	Crime, medical, law, romance, soap opera
Action-Adventure	Radio serials, westerns, gangster movies	*The Lone Ranger*	*The Blindspot*	Detective, science fiction, western, police, horror
Reality	Radio quiz shows, movie documentaries	*Queen for a Day*	*Dancing with the Stars*	Talk shows, home video, singing & dancing competitions
Movies	Live theater, vaudeville	*Monday Night at the Movies*	*Turner Classic Movies*	TV movies, miniseries
Game Shows	Radio quiz shows	*21*	*Jeopardy!*	Quiz, celebrity guessing games
Newsmagazine	Newspapers, radio news, movie newsreels	*See It Now*	*60 Minutes*	Newsmaker interviews

daypart strategy to cable, in which genres vary over the course of the day to match the audiences that are available at different hours.

Cable is well known for niche channels dedicated to particular interests or groups of viewers, or *narrow casting*. Narrowcasting works for cable but not for broadcasters because advertising-supported cable networks supplement their income from affiliate fees paid by local cable systems. And advertisers will pay a premium if the audience includes a high proportion of viewers interested in their products. For example, a computer company may find a higher concentration of potential customers viewing a cable TV show about computers than among viewers of a broadcast situation comedy. Genre channels extend particular genres to occupy entire full-time channels, for instance, CNN (all news) and ESPN (all sports). As the channel capacity of cable systems climbs, the genre channels diversify into subgenres. For example, the "news" category includes channels dedicated to regional news (Northwest Cable News), local news (NY1 News), sports news (ESPNEWS), entertainment news (E! Entertainment Television), and business news (CNBC).

Other channels are built around audience characteristics; they are target audience channels. For instance, Black Entertainment Television schedules movies and original series featuring black performers to target African-American viewers. Women (WE), children (Nickelodeon), and Hispanics (Univision) are among the other demographic target audiences. Others might better be described as lifestyle channels. Their programs are aimed at people who share a common interest or way of life, on channels for people who enjoy the outdoors (the Outdoor Channel) as well as for homebodies (HGTV).

PBS Programming

PBS stations are not as ratings driven as commercial television, but they still need audiences to attract donations, corporate underwriters, and voter support for continuing government subsidies. PBS stations focus on cumulative (or "cume") ratings that reflect program viewership over a week or a month. This gives PBS the freedom to specialize in different genres from commercial broadcasters. Documentaries, highbrow cultural programming, and drama anthologies could not survive on network television but pull in enough occasional viewers to keep public broadcasting viable.

Programming Strategies

The underlying assumption of program scheduling has long been that television viewing is a deeply ingrained habit and that most people, most of the time, sit (or lie) down to watch television as opposed to specific programs. Thus, the key to ratings success is to be the least objectionable choice among the many programs offered at a particular time of the day.

Program executives build ratings by maintaining a consistent flow of viewers from one program to the next, and the tactics they use fill a colorful vocabulary—*hammocking, stripping, tent-poling,* and so on (Eastman, 1993). They may schedule programs in blocks of the same genre (e.g., edgy cartoon family comedies *The Simpsons* and *Family Guy* back to back) that appeal to the same audience segment. They will lead off a time block or lead into a promising new show with a proven show like *NCIS* in hopes that the weaker that follow will inherit the audience. A new show's chances can also be improved by following it with a highly rated, established show like *Grey's Anatomy* as a *lead out,* or by inserting it between two strong shows, which is called *hammocking.* If there aren't enough established programs for that, a strong show may be placed between weaker ones, which is called *tent-poling.* Local stations rely on *stripping,* running the same program in the same time slot every day of the week, and *checkerboarding,* rotating programs in a particular time slot.

The competitors try to disrupt audience flows. *Stunting* includes changing the time slot or length of a program, adding high-profile guest stars, running intensive promotions, or scheduling specials to make some of the viewers "flow" away from their usual programs and disrupt established viewing habits. Programmers may go *head to head* with the competition by scheduling a program in the same genre as the competitor's, such as running a police drama opposite *CSI.* Or they may *counterprogram* with an offering from a completely different genre that caters to a different audience, such as going against *Monday Night Football* with a sensitive drama. In this light, PBS might be seen as a counterprogramming network.

Media &Culture

DIVERSITY IN TELEVISION

On-screen and behind-the-screen diversity are logically related. It takes diverse people to make diverse images. So we ask: how diverse is television ownership and television employment?

Females and minorities are drastically underrepresented in the ranks of TV station owners and board memberships, and minority television station ownership is declining. The FCC once had rules to encourage minority ownership, but these were abolished by federal courts as imposing racial quotas. According to FCC data, minorities own controlling interests in only 3 percent of the nation's full-power TV stations, even though they comprise 38 percent of the total U.S. population. Women own 6.3 percent of all full-power TV stations even though they make up 51 percent of the population (FCC, 2014).

Minority and female broadcast ownership is slowly improving over time, but barriers remain. Consolidation in the television industry leaves women and minorities behind, since they do not enjoy equal access to financing for station acquisitions. Ownership of cable television channels received a boost from a condition attached to Comcast's purchase of NBCUniversal to develop minority-owned cable channels, such as the Aspire network, owned by Magic Johnson. However, the FCC's current equal opportunity rules require only monitoring of minority employment and outreach efforts for minority applicants, and minority groups complain that the FCC has not applied the rules when evaluating TV station license renewals.

Various groups have been historically underrepresented in front of the camera, sometimes leading to threats of boycotts by groups like the NAACP. The casts of prime-time programs are still predominantly white and male and many groups, including Asian Americans, Native Americans, lesbian-gay-bisexual-transgendered persons, and Arab Americans are both underrepresented and misrepresented on television (see Chapter 15).

Diversity in television matters. First, all of society benefits from diverse points of view and one of the best ways to guarantee that is to have owners, managers, producers, and performers drawn from all segments of society. Second, children take their cues from television. Seeing a predominance of white males in powerful TV roles may give minority and female children the mistaken impression that it is their "place" in society to be subservient and submissive. Broadcasters respond that they are in the business of entertainment and making money, that it's not their job to cure all of society's ills. However, this ignores the prominence of television and also, perhaps, the broadcasters' obligation to operate in the public interest.

Streaming video services and DVRs that offer up programs whenever and wherever audiences choose further disrupt the strategies of network television programmers. Time-honored programming customs like fall preview week, summer rerun season, and sweeps months (when the rating services conduct studies in all TV markets) are also eroding as more markets are monitored for television ratings continuously throughout the year. No longer is the flow of audiences from show-to-show dictated by the schedules of handful of television networks. With program scheduling no longer the potent audience builder it once was, new strategies are needed. Chief among them are uses of social media to generate "buzz" about programs such as by planting stories in Twitter, running online contests, offering online chats with star performers, and encouraging viewers to reach out to social media friends during the program.

STOP & REVIEW

1. Why are reality shows being replaced by scripted shows?
2. What are the major threats to broadcast television?
3. How can we clean up violence and sex on television?
4. How diverse is television ownership?

MEDIA LITERACY

OUT OF THE WASTELAND AT LAST?

Today there are hundreds of viewing options—hundreds of thousands if we count the Internet—where once there were only three. Perhaps we are in a new Golden Age with many new quality options. Still, we can ask what we as viewers, consumers, and voters can do to improve television?

THE NEW TELEVISION HEGEMONY

The influence of giant media firms is limited by a law that prevents any entity from owning TV stations that reach more than 39 percent of all TV households. The restrictions are to prevent excessive **horizontal integration** that might limit the diversity of content, especially the news. **Vertical integration** also limits diversity by giving cable and network television corporations power over both what is produced and how it is distributed. Thus, both horizontal and vertical integration in the television industry could contribute to the hegemony of ideas (see Chapter 2). We might ask whether television hegemony is still a pressing issue in a rapidly changing new media environment.

Perhaps it is. The Big Three (and now CNN) still cover basically the same stories, with similar footage, and with a similar slant. The Fox News Channel, MSNBC, and the many online news sources are alternatives, supporting the "diversity through abundance" argument. However, the senior management and boards of trustees for all of these news sources, as well as the print media, draw from the same stratum of society as the Big Three do, a group that is well represented by families from the top 1 percent of the income distribution, the group that dictates the hegemony of ideas. Also, our online tweets, likes, and vines often take their cues from conventional media organizations and their online extensions. With the exception of radical extremist content, one

Horizontal integration is the concentration of ownership by acquiring companies that are all in the same business.

Vertical integration is the concentration of ownership by acquiring related companies in the same general field.

could argue that that same basic hegemony of ideas is perpetuated, or at least not vigorously contested, in online venues.

How to guarantee diversity? We could require television to cover controversial issues or give advocates of opposing views the right to reply. The Fairness Doctrine (see Chapter 15) once required it, but in 2000, the Supreme Court struck it down. Diversity of ideas might be improved through rules assuring more diverse ownership of television stations (see Media & Culture: Diversity in Television), but those rules also have been eliminated and never did apply to new media. How can we break free of the smothering embrace of the Big Media? Political economists tell us that the problem is with the capitalist system, which promotes "bigness" in media corporations and "sameness" in content, but changing the system is a tall order. We can try writing Congress. We can do a Google search for the House Subcommittee on Telecommunications and the Internet, but our message will probably get through only if we live in the congressional district of one of the subcommittee members and contributed to his or her last campaign. And the policies governing both conventional television and new Internet media are the subject of intense lobbying by powerful industry groups like the National Association of Broadcasters that will drown us out.

So to make our voices heard, we might support advocacy groups like Fairness and Accuracy in Reporting (on the left) or the Media Research Center (on the right). Another strategy is to "vote with our touchpads," choosing sources of news and entertainment that are not dominated by Big Media. Or we could switch off our TVs and amuse and inform ourselves with our smartphones, or even talk to someone. That revolution will not be televised.

IS IT TIME TO CUT THE CABLE CORD?

Cable television gets very low marks from consumers for customer service and ever-rising prices, and as a result cable subscriptions are declining as consumers defect to satellite TV and the Internet. In technology trends, we saw how easy it is to cut the cable TV cord in favor of streaming Internet video, so why not? The main drawback is missing out on live programing, especially major sporting events, but that is why they have sports bars. Or, if you supply the pizza, someone you know will provide the Super Bowl.

The true extent of cutting the cable TV cord in favor of streaming video from the Internet appears to be still in single digits nationwide. However, many viewers are cutting back on pay cable channels and downgrading their cable service to lower levels to economize. Beware, streaming video services are poised to raise their fees to cover the rights fees charged by network owners and to fund original productions. Anyway, cord cutting won't free many of us from Big Cable's grip since cable companies also have a large share of the high-speed Internet market.

IS TELEVISION DECENT?

Janet Jackson's "wardrobe malfunction" during the 2004 Super Bowl halftime show sent a shock wave through the executive suites of the broadcast networks. In the wake of the public outrage that the incident caused, CBS was forced to pay half a million dollars in fines and Congress raised the fines. However, in 2012, the Supreme Court overturned fines for the Super Bowl incident and other examples of "fleeting" indecency on the grounds that the FCC had not properly notified broadcasters of its rules governing fleeting indecency (see Chapter 15). By now, broadcasters have been duly notified that occurrences of fleeting indecency are subject to fine, but the FCC is considering changing its policy so that they are not.

Broadcasters complain that it's not fair that they are subject to decency restraints but cable and Internet providers are not. The rationale for that policy is that broadcasts enter the household unbidden, over the public airwaves, whereas viewers must pay to receive cable. With either cable or satellite subscriptions now in over 90 percent of U.S. homes, this argument is getting a bit shabby.

If we see something on television that offends us, we can file a complaint with the FCC electronically (at http://www.fcc.gov/complaints, then look for "obscene, indecent, and profane broadcasts" under the Broadcast Television Consumer Guides). Don't expect an immediate response, though. The FCC waits until the courts have dealt with legal appeals to "clear" its backlog of complaints, a process that took 8 years in the case of the Super Bowl wardrobe malfunction. And if our concern is that there is already too much censorship on television, there is no easy way to register that sort of complaint with the FCC. For that, we might lend our support to free speech advocacy groups such as the American Civil Liberties Union.

CHILDREN AND TELEVISION

How to keep TV sex and violence away from children? Usually, regulatory efforts run up against the First Amendment and its protection of free speech, so industry self-regulation has been the inevitable outcome. However, self-regulation has never been effective in the long run. Broadcasters question the validity of research about the effects of television (see Chapter 14) and insist that it is up to the parents to mind their own children. To help parents do their part, the Telecommunications Act of 1996 required a V-chip that enables viewers to block programming, via an electronically encoded system that works off voluntary content ratings supplied by the broadcast networks. If anyone finds cable indecent, they can either choose not to subscribe or buy lock-out devices that will screen out indecent channels. However, less than 20 percent of parents actually use the V-chip, and only about half consult TV ratings to decide what children can watch (Rideout, 2007).

An alternative to censorship is to ensure a supply of educational children's programming; this was the objective of the Children's Television Act of 1990. However, the FCC wrote rules broad enough to allow *The Flintstones* to be counted as educational. After years of quibbling over what was "educational" and what was "specifically designed for children," a quantitative standard of 3 hours per week of children's programming was set (Kunkel, 1998). However, industry follow-through has been unenthusiastic and has not met the spirit of the rules, and perhaps not even the letter of the requirements.

The Parents Television Council (www.parentstv.org) continues the effort to reform television. At this point, the most effective action is to take advantage of the self-regulatory tools that Congress put in place. The FCC has a guide to using the V-chip and parental lock-out devices on its website (www.fcc.gov/parents). A grade-school curriculum, Student Media Awareness to Reduce Television, has been formed, which is aimed at reducing exposure to television (notv .stanford.edu). However, today's parents are more likely to be concerned about what their children are doing online than when watching television.

WILL PUBLIC TELEVISION SURVIVE?

The fate of public television hangs in the balance every year when Congress approves the annual appropriation for the CPB, currently $445 million. Critics question the need for federal funding of public broadcasting amid the abundant sources of educational, children's, and cultural programming provided by the marketplace through cable television and the Internet.

PBS defenders suspect the real target may be the public affairs programming on PBS that conservative pundits claim has an excessive liberal bias even though many observers agree that diversity in the points of view presented there has increased in recent years. Other woes come from within the PBS community. KCET in Los Angeles abandoned the national programming pool after finding that it could no longer afford to pay its dues and other stations are considering their own withdrawals or closing down completely.

The changing television environment further challenges the survival of public television. When *Sesame Street* defected to HBO in 2016, that deprived PBS viewers, including the low-income and minority children whom the program was originally designed to benefit, of a signature program. With the end of the popular *Downton Abbey* series, public broadcasting is searching for new quality shows to justify its existence. However, Britain's BBC can no longer be counted on as a source for those programs now that BBC has its own cable channel in the United States and many of its shows are streamed online. Public stations taking advantage of the 2016 television spectrum auction could leave some areas without coverage, and PBS fans are more reliant on over-the-air reception than most viewers.

CAN BROADCAST TELEVISION SURVIVE?

What is more important to you? Your smartphone or your television antenna? The answer to that question highlights a threat not only to public television but also to commercial broadcasting. The television spectrum auction of 2016 aimed to consolidate the UHF band to free up space for mobile services. The auction was voluntary and the channels that entirely disappeared mostly served fringe audiences for foreign language, religious, and classic television programs but some PBS member stations disappeared as well. That certainly reduced the diversity of television but did not affect the vast majority of viewers who have those viewing options through cable TV or the Internet.

Those of us who have watched streaming video on our tablets or smartphones, especially those who have sampled CBS Television's All Access live feeds of local stations, may well wonder why broadcast television is still needed at all. Broadcasters might find that appealing since they would then enjoy the same two streams of revenue that basic cable networks due, one from paying viewers and the other from advertising. To preserve localism, why not just connect local TV stations directly to cable head ends and provide streaming versions that will include local news and weather? That would free up the VHF spectrum, which is even better suited for mobile communication than UHF.

The problem is that low-income families and PBS fans could be disenfranchised, although both groups do seem to have an affinity for smartphones (see Chapter 11). Changes in the Universal Service rules governing telecommunications (see Chapter 16) to include smartphones and broadband Internet access also address gaps in access to news, educational, and public affairs content.

TELEVISION NEEDS YOU!

If you think television is still a vast wasteland, why don't you do something about it? Why not make your own TV show and post it on YouTube or one of the dozens of other websites that welcome user-made videos? The basic steps are a snap: sign up for a YouTube or Vine account, and click the video upload button. Using either your smartphone's camera or a webcam (now selling for under $20), you can upload the videos without any special software. Just turn on the camera and start talking, dancing, or doing something mildly disgusting. It is true that many popular YouTube videos have professionals and many hours of preparation and postproduction behind them. Still, that makes them an excellent way for aspiring video stars, producers, and directors to showcase themselves.

SUMMARY & REVIEW

HOW DID THE BIG THREE NETWORKS DOMINATE TV?

NBC, CBS, and ABC brought their programs, stars, audiences, and advertisers with them from radio. During the FCC freeze, most cities had only one or two stations, and NBC and CBS were the top affiliation choices.

WHAT WAS THE GOLDEN AGE?

Early network television featured variety shows, drama anthologies, and quality public affairs programming seldom seen today. Top actors and writers based in New York tackled serious dramas. Shifting audiences, creeping commercialism, Hollywood production values, and quiz show scandals spelled the end of the Golden Age.

HOW DID VIEWING CHOICES EXPAND BEYOND THE BIG THREE?

FCC Chairman Newton Minow called television a "vast wasteland" of bland programming in 1961. CPB and PBS were established to provide an alternative source of programming. Regulatory measures limited the amount of television programming that the networks could produce and own. Independent UHF stations began to prosper and the FCC opened up the major cities to cable television. That paved the way for pay services like HBO and advertising-supported basic channels like WTBS.

HOW DID NEW TELEVISION NETWORKS DEVELOP?

In 1987, Rupert Murdoch started the Fox television network. Cable TV helped Fox, since most Fox affiliates were independent UHF stations, which cable brought to most homes with excellent picture quality. Fox also pursued younger viewers beloved by advertisers. The WB, UPN (later combined into The CW), and Ion networks followed.

WHAT IS THE IMPACT OF CABLE ON BROADCAST TV?

The proportion of viewers who tune in to prime-time broadcasts from ABC, CBS, and NBC has declined dramatically in recent decades. Cable households are heavy viewers of television, and over half of viewing in cable households is now devoted to channels available only on cable.

HOW IS NETWORK TELEVISION CHANGING?

The advertising-supported broadcast television model is under attack from changing viewing habits and new technologies that give viewers more control over where and when they watch and shrink broadcast network audiences. The networks are searching for new financial and programming models involving digital distribution technologies. The retransmission fees paid by cable operators to local television stations and rights fees paid by websites and overseas networks increasingly sustain network television.

WHAT IS DIGITAL TELEVISION?

Television completed the transition to digital broadcasting in 2009. HDTV sets display sharper, wider pictures. Broadcasters also transmit SDTV pictures on digital subchannels. New digital options are appearing, including DVRs, video-on-demand systems, and television distribution through the Internet and cell phones.

WHERE DO COMMERCIAL TV PROGRAMS COME FROM?

Companies owned by the major broadcast networks dominate the production of network television and cable programs, the production and distribution of first-run syndicated programming, and the syndication of off-network reruns of network programs. Lesser media companies and a dwindling number of independent producers and syndicators account for the rest. National broadcast, cable, and satellite networks transmit programs to the public. The broadcast networks own their own stations (O&Os) in major markets and rely on affiliates to broadcast them elsewhere. Cable channels reach the home through local cable television systems.

WHAT ARE THE MAIN TELEVISION GENRES?

Sitcoms, dramas, action-adventures, movies, news, and reality shows are the main genres in network prime time today. Genres that appeal to 18- to 49-year-olds predominate, as that group is highly valued by advertisers.

WHAT ENCOURAGES DIVERSITY IN TELEVISION?

Horizontal and vertical integration in the television industry threaten the diversity of ideas. Limits on television station ownership and on cross-ownership of media have been relaxed over the years. Companies can now also own or manage more than one station in a single market. Policies that encourage minority and female ownership and employment in the television industry, or that mandate fairness in the coverage of important issues, can also increase diversity.

WHY CAN'T THEY CLEAN UP TV?

The First Amendment frustrates efforts to censor violent or sexual content, so industry self-regulation is ultimately the only option. Cable has even fewer restrictions than broadcast TV on the premise that parents can simply discontinue their subscriptions or purchase lock-out devices if they find its content objectionable.

THINKING CRITICALLY
ABOUT THE MEDIA

1. Are we coming out of the TV wasteland at last or getting lost in it more deeply than ever before? Explain your opinion.

2. How do you assess your options for future TV viewing? If you had to buy a TV right now that would meet your needs in 2018, what would you buy?

3. If the conventional network TV model is in fact dying, what do you think should replace it?

4. How does television fit into your entertainment diet? What do you rely on it for?

5. Pitch your idea for a YouTube video. Think about what would make it appeal to 18- to 34-year-olds since that is a group that advertisers prize. Make it good if you want to be discovered by Hollywood!

MindTap®

Test your knowledge with online printable flashcards and online quizzing.

KEY TERMS

affiliate fees (p. 236)

basic cable (p. 222)

cable television (p. 221)

community access (p. 234)

cost per thousand (p. 217)

direct broadcast satellite (DBS) (p. 222)

first-run syndication (p. 220)

high-definition television (HDTV) (p. 227)

horizontal integration (p. 244)

local origination (p. 234)

multiple system operators (MSOs) (p. 222)

must carry (p. 221)

pay TV (p. 221)

ratings (p. 217)

retransmission fees (p. 226)

streaming video (p. 227)

syndication (p. 219)

UHF (p. 217)

underwriting (p. 240)

vertical integration (p. 244)

VHF (p. 216)

MindTap® Log on to the MindTap Communication for *Media Now* to access a variety of additional material, including this chapter's e-book, learning objectives, comprehension quizzes, videos, and more!

THE INTERNET

LEARNING OBJECTIVES

After studying the topics in this chapter, you will be able to:

1 Trace the development of the Internet from a Cold War weapon to a global medium for information, entertainment, and social interaction.

2 Identify current trends that threaten the ideal of the Internet as a global community, open to all.

3 Describe how Web pages are transmitted and displayed on your computer using TCP/IP protocols.

4 Assess how new computer and Internet technologies are transforming what we see and do online.

5 Provide an answer to the question, "Who governs the Internet?"

6 Discover new ways to protect your online privacy, safety, and security.

HISTORY: SPINNING THE WEB

The forerunners of the Internet date back to the hot and cold wars of the past century. John Vincent Atanasoff of Iowa State University invented the electronic computer in 1939 on the eve of World War II. During World War II, the British secret service developed an all-electronic digital computer (named *Colossus*), conceived by computer pioneer Alan Turing, to crack Nazi secret codes. ENIAC, the original general-purpose computer, was enlisted in the Cold War that followed, running calculations for the first hydrogen bomb. The SAGE air defense system, dating from the early 1950s, introduced **modems** to feed warnings of approaching Russian bombers (which never came) into the first **wide area network (WAN).** The first **local area network (LAN)** linked computers at the Livermore, California, atomic weapons laboratory.

The Internet was originally developed to continue weapons research at Livermore and other labs even if civilization was wiped out in a nuclear war. It was then called *ARPANET* and was funded by the U.S. Department of Defense. Anyone who has ever struggled with

VIDEO RULES THE INTERNET
YouTube shows like *Smosh* and other streaming videos now account for the majority of the traffic on the internet.

Source: Youtube

MEDIA THEN··· MEDIA NOW

1939
> John Vincent Atanasoff invents the computer

1972
> The Internet is born

1977
> Apple II computer is introduced

1991
> The World Wide Web is born: Tim Berners-Lee creates HTML and the first browser

1995
> The Internet opens to the public

1997
> The term weblog is coined

2001
> Wikipedia is founded

2004
> Facebook is invented

2006
> The first "Tweet" is published

2012
> IP Version 6 is launched

2015
> U.S. Internet use declines

> Net Neutrality rules adopted

1939

John Vincent Atanasoff invents the computer

Modems (modulator-demodulators) convert digital data to analog signals and vice versa.

Wide area networks (WANs) connect computers that are miles apart.

an Internet connection will appreciate its famous first words, in 1969. The operator typed "L ... O ..." (trying to tell the person at the other end to *log in),* but the system crashed before the message could be completed!

The Web Is Born

The reinvention of the Internet for you and me involved bringing computer technology to the desktops of average users. The experimental Alto computer, developed by Xerox Corporation in the early 1970s, was the first personal computer. It boasted a mouse, a graphical user interface, and a high-speed LAN connection called *Ethernet,* invented by Bob Metcalfe.

The first commercially available personal computer, the Altair, inspired a young computer hacker from Seattle by the name of William Gates to write a programming language for it and to found Microsoft Corporation. It also inspired young Steve Jobs to build the first Apple II in 1977. In 1984, Apple's Macintosh introduced high-resolution graphics and multimedia to personal computers. Apple's HyperCard software popularized the *hyper-text* concept, the "linking" function that connects the Web. Today's social media trace back to the first *bulletin board systems* (BBSs) of 1978 to exchange e-mail, post opinions online, and share information (Rafaeli & LaRose, 1993).

The year that stands out for the "birth" of the Internet is 1972, for several reasons: ARPANET had its first public demonstration, e-mail was first introduced, and the network acquired its name and essential character (Cringely, 1998; Leiner et al., 2009). The basic rules, or protocols, for communication between networks were established, and these evolved into the **transmission-control protocol/Internet protocol (TCP/IP).** Internet pioneer Jon Postel contributed the system of naming and numbering addresses on the Internet.

A widening user base of college professors helped push the Internet out of the embrace of the Department of Defense as connections to major universities were added. An e-mail system for university professors (BITNET) and a popular discussion group system (USENET) grew at the same time. These networks were merged under the National Science Foundation (NSF) in 1986 to form NSFNET

In 1991, Tim Berners-Lee of the CERN laboratory in Switzerland wrote the **hypertext markup language (HTML)** and the first Web browser to solve the problem of transporting text documents across different computer systems. That was the birth of the World Wide Web.

Many of the Internet properties and pioneers that have since become household names got their start in the mid-1990s as entrepreneurs realized there was money to be made from the rapidly growing online population. The operation of the Net was turned over to commercial providers in 1995 and the Internet craze was soon in full swing, fostering a cultural and economic phenomenon that became known as the *dot-com boom.* Amazon.com started that year as an electronic bookstore before it evolved into an online mega-mall. Internet auction house eBay also made its mark that year as a marketplace for oddball collectibles, such as the Pez candy dispensers sought by the wife of its founder. Yahoo!, the brainchild of two grad students from Stanford, began a year earlier as an online search engine before being supplanted by Google (the work of two other Stanford grad students, Sergey Brin and Larry Page) and evolving into an advertising-supported portal. In 2000, the dot-com boom gave way to the dot-com bust as investors soured on Internet stocks, online consumers tired of the novelty of clicking on banner ads, and the general economy weakened.

Reining in the Net

The cultural impact of the Internet was also taking shape. On the positive side, many found the Internet to be a venue for social connections, engaging in public debate, learning about political candidates, finding a good deal on products and services, and exploring pleasant diversions. The Internet did not always live up to the promises of "Internet evangelists," however, who touted it as the cure for isolation, poverty, ignorance, political oppression,

GOOD JOB Apple pioneered the personal computer in 1977 with the Apple II, which featured a floppy disk drive.

Local area networks (LANs) link computers within a department, building, or campus.

MindTap°

Start with a quick warm-up activity.

1977

Apple II computer is introduced

1972

The Internet is born

Transmission-control protocol/Internet protocol (TCP/IP) is the basic protocol used by the Internet.

Hypertext markup language (HTML) is used to format pages on the Web.

THE FATHER OF THE WEB Tim Berners-Lee originated HTML and gave us the Web.

1991

The World Wide Web is born: Tim Berners-Lee creates HTML and the first browser

1995

The Internet opens to the public

and boredom. Governments around the world began to consider how to control an international medium that evaded their laws and challenged national media systems, the beginnings of a movement that now threatens the existence of the Internet 20 years later.

Content restrictions became an issue as the Internet collided with the cultures of diverse nations. In the United States, a portion of the Telecommunications Act of 1996, the Communications Decency Act, was written to ban "indecent" material, such as images of naked female breasts, from the Internet. That law was ruled to be unconstitutional, but efforts continue to restrict sexually explicit material in the United States (see Media Literacy: Getting the Most Out of the Internet, page 279). Enduring online horror, including child molesters stalking children (cyberstalking), teens harassing one another (cyberbullying), online gamers destroying their families (Internet gaming addiction), and identity thieves trolling for private information, began to emerge. Parents came to regard the Internet, rather than television, as the number one media threat to children (Common Sense Media, 2006).

Political communication across borders is also problematic. France apparently has no problem with breasts but tried to ban material considered politically obscene, such as online sales of souvenirs from Nazi Germany. China bans online criticism of its government and pro-Tibetan websites by blocking dissident Web pages and monitoring public Internet cafés. North Korea prohibits nearly all Internet access to prevent its citizens from learning of the world beyond their borders. In the wake of the 9/11 attacks, it became evident that the terrorists used the Internet to coordinate the plot, to raise funds, and to help recruit new members to their cause.

Intellectual property (see Chapter 16) also became an issue. Countries, such as the United States, with strict copyright protections, were alarmed to find that other countries with more lenient statutes became havens for file-sharing services that supported massive copyright piracy. Thousands of U.S. college students were threatened with lawsuits from the recording industry as a result.

Access to the Internet, as well as its content, also became an issue. Some argued that instead of curing poverty, ignorance, and isolation, the Internet perpetuated them. Gaps opened in access by minority, low-income, and rural families (NTIA, 1995). Developing countries in Africa, Asia, and South America were left further behind in the development of a global information economy for lack of access (Castells, 2004).

Frustrated by the difficulty of enforcing their own laws and customs beyond their borders, governments began calling for international oversight and an end to U.S. control. The ruling bodies of the Internet, notably the

Internet Architecture Board and the Internet Engineering Task Force (IETF), gradually expanded to include international representatives. ICANN (Internet Corporation for Assigned Names and Numbers) was formed as a nonprofit private corporation to oversee the assignment of Internet addresses (called *domain names*) and to develop new ones.

The Rise of Social Media

Although Facebook quickly became the leading name in social networking after its introduction in 2004, pioneering efforts began back in the 1970s. GeoCities began hosting personal Web pages in the mid-1990s, many of which resembled the social network profiles of today, and SixDegrees.com users could create profiles and lists of friends. The advent of blogging (in 1997) and Wikipedia (in 2001) were other milestones in the evolution of **social media** (Curtis, 2011).

Facebook, Twitter, YouTube, Flickr, Wikipedia, and the rest follow the **Web 2.0** model. First popularized in the years after the dot-com bust, Web 2.0 websites ask that we, the audience, provide much of the content and promote them to our family and friends. Advertising and public relations practitioners began hoping to "go viral," meaning that their pitches were picked up by users of social media and spread like a virus through the Internet. Affordable and easy-to-use audio and video production technologies lowered the barriers to entry (see Chapter 2) to the point that anyone with a computer and a digital camera could aspire to be a media star with thousands of followers. On Twitter, Vine, and Snapchat, a few words will do.

Facebook is fast becoming the new king of the media by acting as a portal to news and entertainment as well as social interaction for its users, and by becoming a major force in online advertising. But Facebook is no longer the sensation it once was among young adults now that their parents, grandparents, and employers are looking in. Some are turning to more restricted social media venues like Everyme and Google+ and ephemeral options like Snapchat and Vine that do not leave permanent tracks, or at least are not supposed to.

The impact of social media is boiling over into the real world. Political movements across the globe use them to organize protests against repressive governments. Facebook and Twitter played key roles in the rebellions that swept through North Africa in 2011 and in the Occupy Wall Street movement in the United States. Repressive governments fight back; for example, the Egyptian government effectively turned off the Internet in an effort to suppress a democracy movement, and Iran tracked down dissidents who used the Internet to organize anti-government demonstrations. Closer to home, conventional approaches to campaigning were upset in the 2016 presidential election cycle as candidates used Twitter and Facebook and voter profiles gleaned from Internet user data to attract supporters. In 2015, Americans were stunned by murderous attacks perpetrated by terrorists who were apparently radicalized through social media.

Old Media in the Internet Age

Let us briefly recount the changes that the Internet has brought in conventional media that we examine elsewhere in this text. The Web has had a disruptive influence on conventional media. Google is the new king of the media,

2004

Facebook is invented

> **Social media** are media whose content is created and distributed through social interaction.

2001

Wikipedia is founded

> **Web 2.0** are Internet applications in which users can provide content as well as consume it.

2006

The first "Tweet" is published

MindTap®

Read, highlight, and take notes on the complete chapter text in a rich interactive online platform.

surpassing television and cable networks, newspaper chains, and magazines as the number one vehicle for advertising. Craigslist siphons off classified ads that were once the lifeblood of print newspapers. Music file sharing ravaged the business plans of the music industry and paved the way for Apple's iTunes, Pandora, and Spotify to revolutionize music distribution. Tablets drain revenues from magazine publishers and video producers who find that they have to cut deals with the likes of Apple, Amazon, and Hulu to get their digital products seen. Facebook has evolved into a portal that many Internet users enter daily and never leave, subtracting eyeballs and advertising revenues from online content providers. Movie and video game rental outlets and small bookstores have been closed by the thousands, no longer able to compete with the convenience and prices of online distributors. Netflix competes head-to-head with Home Box Office to be the leading pay TV service.

Many conventional media outlets are adopting the philosophy of "if you can't beat them, join them." Some newspapers and magazines have transformed to online-only publications or smartphone apps, for example. Nearly a million books are available for Amazon's Kindle e-book. Legal music services supported by ad sales or subscription fees have the blessings of major record labels. Television networks establish their own streaming services and count on rights fees from online providers to stay in business. Millions of hours of videos are available for streaming online, so many that video traffic already accounts for the majority of the online content that consumers access and could account for as much as 90 percent in a few years (Cisco, 2015).

That is not to say that old media are dead: Analog vinyl records and books printed on paper are making comebacks as niche products, for example. However, online digital media possess some distinct advantages. Online media can be consumed almost anywhere, any time over a variety of devices, including the smartphone in your pocket. The new media can fatten their revenues from global markets, witness Facebook's 1.5 billion users, and Netflix's expansion into 130 countries. Internet-based media companies also know a lot more about their audiences than conventional media do by compiling vast databases of user behavior that have value to advertisers and help online media produce original content with predictable appeal.

Reinventing the Internet

In its short history, the Internet has been repeatedly reinvented: from a Cold War weapon, to a medium of scientific exchange, to a public information resource, to an online shopping plaza, to a conduit for social interaction, and to a digital home amusement center. The Internet continues to be all of those things, but where is it headed? The once-prevalent Internet ideal of a global community, open to all, is under attack from bad behavior in several quarters.

Corporate domination is one possibility. We could trade the hegemony of Big Media conglomerates like Disney and Viacom who ruled our first (i.e., television) screen for the hegemony of Big Data companies like Alphabet (as Google is now known), Apple, Amazon, Facebook, and Netflix who would like to rule the second (computer) and third (smartphone) screens. Government regulators are trying to keep the playing field level. A proposed merger between Comcast and Time-Warner Cable was shot down

2015

Net Neutrality rules adopted

over concerns that the deal would concentrate ownership of too much of the U.S. broadband Internet market. However, in 2016 Charter Cable's acquisition of Time-Warner Cable was approved, further concentrating ownership of broadband cable networks in the United States. In 2015, the FCC issued a landmark net neutrality decision that aims to prevent Internet service providers like Comcast and Charter from providing preferential access to their subsidiaries and business partners.

A more subtle problem with corporations in control is that they tend to erect walls around the Internet content: Social media apps, like Facebook, snatch eyeballs away from conventional media and the Web alike. Although the front door to Facebook can be reached through the Web, once inside users are in a "walled garden." Content is still delivered over the Internet, but not through our Web browsers, and it is "off limits" to search engines. Once inside, we are a captive audience subject to the whims of the owner of the garden and his ever-changing privacy policies and business alliances. Facebook and other social media are part of the growing *deep web*. That term refers to the Web content that is hidden behind pay walls or user log-ins where search engines and inquiring minds cannot easily find it.

Criminal behavior is another threat. Deeper still is the "dark Web," consisting of clandestine sites like Silk Road where illegal drug transactions are arranged and stolen files of credit card numbers are exchanged among international rings of cyber criminals. Dark websites are hosted on hidden servers, their content is protected by **encryption**, and their Web addresses are circulated only among the criminals. Terror groups solicit other forms of criminal activity in the name of their causes, complete with do-it-yourself bomb-making instructions. Some of the criminals are apparently sponsored by nation-states that organize online raids on the commercial and military secrets of other countries and dabble in sabotage. This raises the specter of cyberwarfare that could cripple the Internet and the global economy that relies on it. In 2016, the United States launched a campaign cyberattacks aimed at disrupting communications and operations of Islamic militants. This could bring the Internet full cycle back to its origins as a weapon of war.

Encryption is used when a message is written in a secret code.

Nations, including the United States, are behaving badly online in other ways that affect the future of the Internet. Two years after a massive Internet surveillance program by the U.S. National Security Agency was exposed, a European Union court ruled in 2015 that the agreement governing the flow of data between the European Union and the United State was invalid. Demands grew louder to place governance of the network in the hands of international bodies. Broader representation in Internet governance could be a good thing, but it also might result in more nations following the example of China, which severely restricts access to political and religious content, and embolden nations that temporarily turn off the social media to stifle protests.

There is a technology challenge from mobiles. Social media, and indeed all Internet-based services, face competition from "third screen" mobile applications (see Chapter 11), leading Facebook to acquire the WhatsApp mobile messaging service and to move aggressively into mobile social networking. There will soon be a glacial shift in the user paradigm as the majority of Internet traffic originates from mobile devices rather than from personal computers (Cisco, 2015). Mobile apps may spawn innovators who could someday push

2012

IP Version 6 is launched

aside the social media giants of today. However, mobile apps also further conceal and fragment information that was once freely available inside walled gardens. How will we "like" that?

Here is a curious trend: Internet use in the United States has started to decline. At the peak, three-fourths of Americans age 3 or older used the Internet, but that number has fallen in the latest national survey conducted by the Census Bureau (NTIA, 2015). Perhaps the bad behavior of criminals, corporations, and governments is having an impact? We should not ignore our own bad behavior, either: cyberbullying, trolling, partisan screeching, and oversharing online may be driving users away. Others may be turned off by hacker attacks, privacy invasions, incessant advertising intrusions, or the cost of cable Internet "bundles" and smartphone data plans. However, it may also be that when asked whether they use the Internet or not, some respondents to the government surveys do not realize that when using social media and other apps on their smartphones they are actually using the Internet. We will try to clear that up in the next section.

TECHNOLOGY TRENDS: METCALFE'S AND MOORE'S LAWS

When *are* you using the Internet? Technically, any time you use a device or application that transmits information using the packet structure specified by the TCP/IP protocol (see Technology Demystified: Inside the Internet), you are on the Internet. That includes surfing the Web, of course, but also checking social media apps on your smartphone, watching Netflix on a smart TV, playing video games online, and, in most cases, talking to someone or texting them from your mobile.

So, the Internet protocol is taking over all types of electronic communication. We can attribute that to Metcalfe's Law, credited to Internet pioneer Bob Metcalfe, which states that the value of network is proportional to the square of the number of users. This drives continual Internet technology growth and also explains the sometimes explosive popularity of new Internet applications like Vine. So, the value of the Internet rises as it becomes more universal, both in terms of the number of people who use it and the number of applications those users take advantage of.

Internet Trends

The future of the Internet is shaped by changes in network transmission technology that move those packets at ever-higher speeds, by the software that runs Internet applications, and by changes in the rules, or protocols, that are used in Internet transactions.

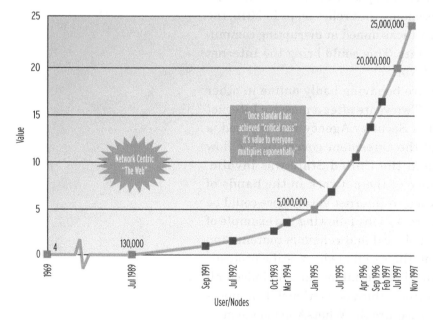

FIGURE 10.1 METCALF'S LAW The popularity of the Internet grew explosively after it reached a critical mass of about 5 million users. New applications continue to follow this curve.

Technology Demystified

INSIDE THE INTERNET

To understand trends in Internet technology, we need to recall that there are many varying patterns of communication, or **protocols**, that are the basic building blocks of Internet applications. Over 100 protocols are associated with the Internet, known collectively as *TCP/IP*. Some of the protocols that are readily apparent to Internet users include:

- *Mail:* The simplified mail transfer protocol (SMTP) is used for sending e-mail between host computers on the Internet. The post office protocol (POP) connects users to their mail servers. The listserv protocol governs electronic mailing lists (listservs) that "broadcast" e-mail to special-interest groups.

- *File transfers:* The file transfer protocol (FTP) governs how electronic documents and computer programs are transmitted across the Internet, such as when Web pages are uploaded to a Web server. The **hypertext transfer protocol (http)** handles file transfers over the Web.

- *Locators:* The domain name service (DNS) translates Web addresses that people use (such as http://www.msu.edu) into the addresses that the Internet uses (such as 35.9.7.102).

- *Document display:* The hypertext markup language (HTML) governs the display of Web pages on the screen.

Several of these protocols work together when you go surfing on the Web. Web pages are stored as files on Web servers connected to the Internet. The servers may be ordinary personal computers running special software that lets remote users access the data, but that makes for very slow downloads. Large commercial sites use high-powered computers connected to high-speed lines so that they can store gigabytes of data and serve thousands of users at once. The Web page files include HTML tags that your browser software (e.g., Chrome) uses to display the text and graphics on-screen (see Figure 10.2).

When you request a Web page by typing its *uniform resource locator* (URL) into your browser or by clicking on a hyperlink, the DNS protocol translates the address of the Web page you ordered into the numerical form of the address and sends the request out to the Internet through connections supplied by your Internet service provider (ISP). The request is formatted using the http.

Your request is a short message, but the Web page you receive in return may be quite lengthy, and that could tie up both the server and the network connection. So, before sending your requested page to you, the server breaks it up into a number of *packets* of about 1,500 characters (or about 12,000 bits) each. (This paragraph has about three-quarters of that many characters, including the spaces.) If you are downloading a music or video file, the computer data for those are also broken up into packets. One second's worth of music for your iPod takes up about six packets' worth of data, for example. The server appends a header with dozens of bits of information that indicate how many packets are in the message and the sequence number of each packet, along with the result of a mathematical calculation that is used to check each packet for errors that might occur during transmission. The rules for doing all that are specified in TCP.

The packet of data and the TCP information are then placed in a digital "envelope" that has your Internet address (known as your *IP address*), the address of the server, and instructions about what to do about packets that get delayed for some reason. That is done according to the *Internet protocol* (IP). Taken together, these two sets of rules are referred to as *TCP/IP*.

Then the TCP/IP packet is sent to a network switching device called a *router*. Routers are like postal clerks. They check the IP address on each packet and select the best path for it through the Internet backbone network. Along the way, the packets pass through several routers, and some packets may be diverted to alternate routes depending upon which path is the least congested at a given moment. The TCP/IP packet containing the requested Web page is ultimately directed to your ISP's router, then into the ISP's network, then to your home Internet connection, and finally into your own computer. You may need a router, too, if you have multiple Internet users in your home who all want to be online at the same time or if you connect through a wireless Wi-Fi connection.

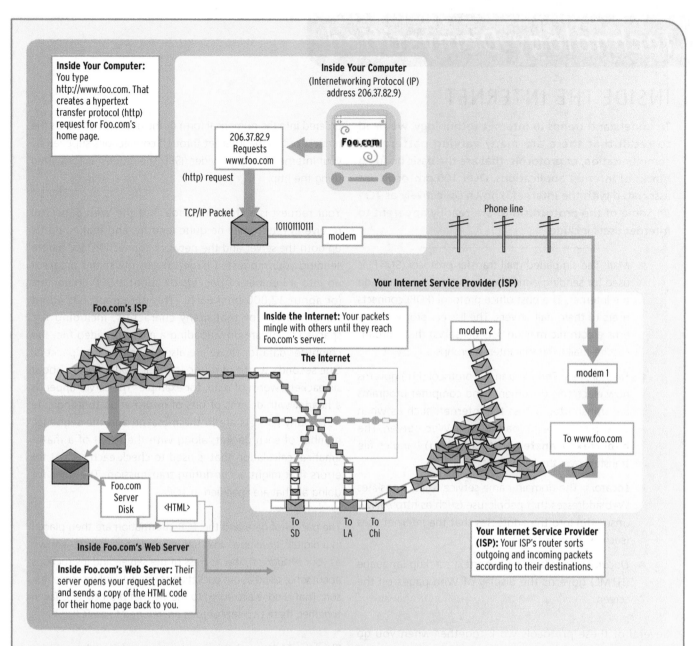

Inside Your Computer: You type http://www.foo.com. That creates a hypertext transfer protocol (http) request for Foo.com's home page.

Inside Your Computer (Internetworking Protocol (IP) address 206.37.82.9)

Foo.com

206.37.82.9 Requests www.foo.com

(http) request

TCP/IP Packet

101101110111

modem

Phone line

Your Internet Service Provider (ISP)

Inside the Internet: Your packets mingle with others until they reach Foo.com's server.

The Internet

modem 2

modem 1

To www.foo.com

Foo.com's ISP

Foo.com Server Disk

<HTML>

To SD   To LA   To Chi

Inside Foo.com's Web Server

Inside Foo.com's Web Server: Their server opens your request packet and sends a copy of the HTML code for their home page back to you.

Your Internet Service Provider (ISP): Your ISP's router sorts outgoing and incoming packets according to their destinations.

FIGURE 10.2 INSIDE THE INTERNET Information is sent over the Internet using TCP/IP. The addressing and sorting functions are analogous to the post office's.

Your computer reassembles the packets according to the sequencing information (the TCP part), checks for errors, and requests replacements for any corrupted packets. Then all the addressing and sequencing information is stripped away, and the parts of the original HTML file are merged together and sent to your browser. The browser displays the page for you according to the instructions it finds in the HTML file. Then you see the Web page.

Protocols are technical rules governing data communication.

IP Version 6. An update to the basic Internet protocol, *IP version 6,* is quickly becoming dominant. It extends the length of Internet addresses so that more can be made. The older version 4 has "only" about 4 billion addresses, not enough to issue addresses in all of the world's major languages or to give your smartphone, car, TV set, and toaster their own IP addresses. Launched in 2012, Version 6 supports trillions upon trillions of addresses and smoother streaming of audio and video in the bargain. Major ISPs like AT&T and Comcast have made the transition, and if your computer runs Windows XP or Mac OS 10.0 or a newer operating system, there should be no problem at your end.

Cloud Computing. Google, Microsoft, and many other Internet companies are expanding their businesses beyond the conventional model that runs software programs from the hard drives of personal computers. For example, Google Drive is available on an as-needed basis through the Internet and lets you store and share your files there instead of on your computer's hard drive. Apple's iCloud, Microsoft One Drive, and Dropbox are other examples that have free versions. You no longer need a huge hard drive, just a simple computer with a screen, a keyboard, and an Internet connection, the design specification for Chromebooks. This is called *cloud computing*. A variety of business models are emerging: "micro-payments" to use the software by the minute or the hour, pay per usage, flat monthly fees, and advertising-supported cloud services.

Plug-ins. These are "helper programs" that work with browser software to perform a number of functions including playing audio and video (e.g., Windows Media Player and QuickTime), activating animations (Flash), or displaying documents (Acrobat). Some plug-ins are large programs that must be downloaded and installed before the features will work, but the more popular (and less proprietary) ones eventually get built into new versions of Web browsers.

Among the most popular is Flash (from Adobe). It turns your computer into a multimedia machine that can display high-definition streaming video in the same wide-screen format as HDTV (see Chapter 9). However, the late Steve Jobs never liked Flash and banned it from Apple's mobile hardware. HTML5 (described in the sections that follow) is replacing Flash on both desktop and mobile hardware.

Scripts. When you see a gray box that says "application loading," that means a Java program is downloading to your computer. Java scripts are written with a subset of the Java computer language. They also can change the appearance of buttons as your mouse "rolls over" them and perform other interactive tricks. At e-commerce sites, your credit card and order information is funneled to the Web store's computer with another type of interactive program, common gateway interface (CGI) scripts.

New Markup Languages. Also adding much "coolness" to the Web are variations on the basic HTML. XHTML ("X" for extensible) lets programmers define their own tags. Tags are the commands that tell your browser how to display the document, for example, where to locate a picture on the screen and how big it should be. XML is a "meta language" from which tags for specific applications can be made. For example, NewsML-G2 is an XHTML variation that standardizes the presentation of audio and video clips and interactive features alongside Internet news stories. RSS (Really Simple Syndication) is another form of XHTML that posts frequent updates from other websites (such as the current *New York Times* headlines) to a personalized reader page, like iGoogle.

YOUR SECURITY IS A LOCK Look for the https (at the beginning of the URL) and the lock icon next to the URL window to be sure that you are on a secure Internet connection.

XHTML is part of the development of the *semantic Web*. This development is designed to attach useful indexing labels to the content of the Web. For example, if we were composing a story in NewsML, we might have a tag that indicates that the content that follows is a video. Advanced semantic Web tags could identify the location and nature of the story and indicate that the headline is about a hurricane hitting the Central American country of Belize. Then it would become easier to organize information about Belize, or hurricanes, and incorporate that in compiling databases about Central American countries or global climate change even if we didn't use the specific search term *Belize* or *hurricane*.

HTML5. HTML5 combines semantic Web features with multimedia players. For the user, that means this new version of HTML plays videos, video games, and music files without having to download and launch plug-ins, making media consumption on the Web as convenient as tuning a stereo or a TV set with a remote control. New types of interactions with Web pages are possible, including the ability to drag and drop elements within a page, to draw objects on a page, to work offline with interactive applications, and to interact with forms in new ways, such as using slider bars. HTML5 is also for smartphones, with built-in geo-location capabilities. Browser software is still catching up with the full range of HTML5 capabilities, but many of the basic features like audio and video players are already standard. To test the capabilities of your browser, you can visit http://html5test.com/. As of this writing, Chrome and Opera have the best support. However, the new version was designed from the start to minimize conflicts with older HTML implementations, so your favorite websites should still work even if your browser is out of date.

Privacy Trends

Tracking. Some other Web technologies aren't so cool if you are concerned about your privacy. **Cookies** are the files that some websites deposit on visitors' hard drives. That's how sites recognize visitors and greet them by name without making them log in every time. But cookies can also track and collate information between sites without the user's knowledge, and third-party cookies placed by companies that monitor Web advertising may also do so without the user's knowledge.

Web bugs are tiny (one-pixel) or invisible (e.g., matching the background color of the Web page) images embedded in the HTML code. When your browser pulls them up, the server that stores the invisible images receives a notification. These bugs can follow your tracks inside a website and also track you to other Web pages. They can also extract codes from cookies stored on your computer that identify you uniquely at the sites you have registered. And your e-mail can be bugged too, letting the sender know when you open it and also if you forward it to someone else!

> **Cookies** are small files that websites leave on their visitors' computers.

However, even when no cookies or Web bugs are present, your privacy is not ensured. That's because the basic operation of the Internet protocol routinely uses your Internet address to route information. When you switch from one website to another, the site you leave receives information about where you are going, and the next one you visit also knows where you were last. The fonts you use and the version numbers of the plug-ins you use create electronic "fingerprints" that make it possible to uniquely identify each Web user.

Yet another privacy threat is **spyware** (sometimes also called *adware* or *malware*). These are programs that are downloaded to your computer when you install other applications from the Internet, such as music file-sharing programs. The spyware not only monitors your surfing behavior but in some cases also causes ads to pop up on your screen in the hopes of directing you to e-commerce sites.

> **Spyware** is malicious software that secretly sends information about your online activities.

Your online safety is also threatened by security "holes" in your browser or operating system software. These allow hackers to get access to personal information stored on your computer or to use your computer to launch spam or viruses at other users using robotic programs, or *bots,* for short. That is why it is crucial to update your browser and operating software and accept automatic update notifications promptly.

Network Technology Trends

At only 56,000 bits per second, the "high-speed" computer modem of decades ago is an obsolete slowpoke. How much speed do you actually need? Video streaming is the most demanding broadband application that most Internet users crave and 3 million bits per second is generally sufficient for the likes of Netflix and Hulu. However, 25 million bits per second is the new norm for broadband service established by the FCC.

Most homes in the United States get their broadband connections from cable television companies. *Digital subscriber line* (DSL) connections have caught up to cable modems in the race to wire the country for broadband connections capable of millions of bits per second. To keep up with all the music and digital video files that broadband users download, the connections in the Internet backbone are also being upgraded to fiber-optic cables that carry billions of bits per second. Telephone companies connect individual homes to fiber in some parts of the country that transmit hundreds of millions bits per second, too. Google is outdoing both cable and telephone companies with fiber-optic networks boasting speeds of 1 billion bits per second, but so far only in 15 locations. For rural residents out of the reach of cable TV and other high-speed networks, HughesNet and Exede beam Web pages via satellite.

The other network trend is wireless. Third-generation (3G) and fourth-generation (4G) cell phones (see Chapter 11) make it possible to check your e-mail and surf Web pages with your phone faster than current networks and to run two-way video conferences and watch high-definition television on your cell phone. *Wi-Fi* (more formally known as IEEE802.11) offers wireless broadband access from hotspots covering a growing number of college campuses, airports, Internet cafés, and homes. Newer versions of Wi-Fi offer speeds many times faster than cable modems and make it possible to move around town without losing your connection. Now you can become your own mobile hotspot through a device connected to your computer that will let your smartphone and other Wi-Fi-capable gear share a wireless connection.

Internet2 is a new, faster version of the Internet.

Further in the future, **Internet2** (not to be confused with Web 2.0) is a project involving more than 200 universities that conduct experiments with the next generation of Internet technology and give us a preview of more things to come at speeds of 100 billion bits (or gigabits) per second. The Gig.U project is a consortium of over 30 universities that aims to extend gigabit networks to neighboring communities. High-resolution medical imaging and instant downloads of high-definition movies are possible applications.

Computer Technology Trends

The continual reinvention of the Internet is influenced by advances in computers and their networks. According to Moore's Law, processing capacity in computer chips has doubled about every 18 months since the late 1960s (Moore, 1996). That is why new personal computers are obsolete as soon as they come out of the box.

Increasingly, the same technologies that we find in our computers are migrating to entertainment media and mobile devices. The iPod, iPad, and iPhone are basically computer hard drives or flash memory devices with a small computer display and a data connection. TiVo and other DVRs are computer hard drives with connections for your TV, and new smart TVs have built-in hard drives and computer operating systems (Chapter 9). The LCD displays and other "flat-screen" technologies (see Chapter 9) that we now use for TV were originally developed for laptop computers.

As you may have learned in your high-school computer class, the evolution of computers is traced through their *central processing units* (CPUs), where all the actual data processing takes place. Today's personal computers are fourth-generation computers with very-large-scale integrated (VLSI) circuits with millions of components each.

Future reinventions of the Internet are inextricably intertwined with new developments in the computers connected to it. In the past, the prevailing imperative was to continually make computers more powerful, but now there is a countervailing movement to make them simpler and more compact. The tablets and smartphones popping up in college lecture halls are part of the "less is more" scenario. So are the low-cost Chromebooks that are designed to provide fast Internet and e-mail access. As more applications and data move onto the Internet and from there to "the cloud," the amount

© Canadapanda/Shutterstock.com

LESS IS MORE? Stripped down personal computers that double as tablets take advantage of programs and cloud storage to minimize the bulk and cost of consumer machines.

of processing power and storage capacity needed in personal computers decreases. Continuing the trend, special-purpose computers might take over your office, living room, and kitchen—all connected through the *Internet of Things*. *Wearable* computers such as the Apple Watch and Fitbit are part of a new trend that will soon include "smart" belts, shoes, and underwear. Everyday objects from clothing to furniture to the products on your pantry shelf will have miniature sensors, identification tags, transmitters, and data processors that will connect them to the Internet or send text messages to your cell phone ("Dear Dale: The milk is sour and your jeans are, too!").

MORE IS BETTER? Microsoft's XBox is a home media server for broadband Internet content as well as a game console. Will tablets or media servers dominate home computing in coming years?

In the "more is better" case, multimedia computers add new sound- and video-processing capabilities until they become home entertainment servers sitting in the middle of a high-speed computer network that distributes entertainment and information throughout your home. Capacious hard drives store all of your iTunes, family pictures, and video downloads and retransmit them to all the rooms in your home. Your smartphone "talks" to your PC or your smart TV through wireless computer network technology. Advanced video game machines also fill the niche, playing Blu-ray movies and connecting to the Internet. Virtual reality displays (see Chapter 12) are leaving the lab for the living room and the computing power needed to run them may once again convince computer buyers that "more is better."

INDUSTRY: DAVID VERSUS GOLIATH

The Internet industry has several major sectors. Each industry sector has giant firms but also many innovative small ones that sometimes overturn the Goliaths with bold new ideas.

Alphabet (the holding company behind all Google properties) is the current Goliath, having dethroned Yahoo! and Microsoft. It is most visible as a search engine company, of course, but nearly all of its revenue comes from serving up ads on the Internet. That includes the ads that appear alongside their search results, the AdSense service that places clickable ads on other websites, and the display ads that are distributed across the Web through Google's Double-Click subsidiary (see Chapter 14). Google is also, among other things, a Web portal (Google News), a software publisher (e.g., Picasa photo editor, Chrome Internet browser, Android operating system for smartphones), a smartphone distributor (Nexus), a social networking site (Google+), an e-mail service (Gmail), and an online video distributor (YouTube). But watch out, Google. Facebook is gaining on you and somewhere out there a group of college students is working on The Next Big Thing.

STOP & REVIEW

1. What does Metcalf's Law predict?

2. What is TCP/IP?

3. What are the trends in Internet connection technologies?

4. What are some new Web technologies?

5. How do Web pages get to your computer screen?

Computer Toy Makers

The hardware sector includes makers of computers (further subdivided into supercomputers, mainframes, minicomputers, workstations, and personal computers), computer storage devices (such as disk drives), and their peripherals (such as printers and scanners). The Internet also relies on *servers,* the hardware that directs packets of Internet data to their proper destinations.

The market for consumer electronics is being transformed by changes in the way we use the Internet. In the U.S. personal computer market, Hewlett-Packard and Dell are the leaders. The two companies that started the personal computer trend, Apple and IBM, are now lesser players, and IBM's personal computer operation was sold to a Chinese company, Lenovo. However, personal computer sales are plummeting worldwide as users switch to tablet computers and smartphones. Hewlett-Packard and Dell are also the leading manufacturers of Internet servers, and those sales are rising as cloud computing replaces conventional computer networks.

Where Microsoft Rules

Software manufacturers develop applications for personal computers, an industry several times the size of another well-known "software" industry, motion pictures. Microsoft dominates personal computer operating system software (i.e., Windows) and many application categories, including word processing (Microsoft Word) and spreadsheets (Microsoft Excel), but Google Chrome is now the leading Internet browser. Until recently, software manufacturers resembled book publishers, in that sales were made through retail outlets that offer titles from many different publishers. Much of the software that winds up in the hands of consumers is bundled with computer hardware at the time of purchase. Increasingly, though, software is bought and downloaded over the Internet, an important component of electronic commerce. As part of the cloud computing trend, software products like Microsoft Office 365 can be rented by paying an annual subscription fee and are automatically updated to the latest versions as they become available.

A great deal of software is available as *freeware* or *shareware.* This is software, such as the Linux operating system, the Firefox Internet browser, and the Avast anti-virus program, for which the authors do not claim copyright protection, whose developers lack a sophisticated distribution network, or that pursue an alternative to the "pay up front" software business model. Some hope that users pay voluntarily. That means users can often download the software for free (from sites like download.com) and pay on the "honor system" later if they like it. In other cases, the software is free but the user may be asked to pay for documentation, enhanced features, or updates.

As for Internet browsers and plug-ins distributed for "free," they are still part of a moneymaking scheme. Their creators profit from the sale of other programs that make new content and the specialized software that runs the servers on the Internet. Google Drive is part of a larger scheme aimed at capturing more and more information from Internet users that can be used to support the company's advertising sales.

Internet Service Providers

Internet service providers (ISPs) connect users to the Internet and provide e-mail accounts. Telecommunications giant AT&T and cable TV giants Comcast (which operates under the Xfinity brand) and Charter Cable are the industry leaders and account for well over half of all U.S. Internet subscriptions among them. Some ISPs, such as AOL (acquired by telephone giant Verizon in 2015), create original content and so combine the roles of ISP and content provider (as described in the next section). Others, such as EarthLink (and thousands of small local providers across the country), are purely ISPs, in that they provide access but little in the way of content aside from portal pages that welcome their users with the news of the hour when they log on. ISPs usually lease high-speed connections to the Internet backbone from telecommunications carriers or local phone companies or are affiliated with companies that provide network connections of their own. Currently, there are more than 400 ISPs in the United States with national coverage and many more that cover local communities. Although many are still small local operations, giant telephone and cable companies dominate.

Internet service providers (ISPs) provide connections to the Internet.

Content Providers

Web pages are often made by in-house design departments. Some of the largest are the multimedia design departments at old media titans, such as Disney. But new media companies, such as Google and Amazon, have in-house staff, as do thousands of companies large and small that are not directly connected to the media business. Another model is to reformat content produced for the old media side of the business, as they do at the *New York Times,* but even that requires dozens of employees with Web design skills. Many newspapers or other old media firms create new or extended content for the Web and provide ways for readers to contribute both stories and commentary.

Thousands of independent design firms and Web developers also blend the creative talents of graphic design professionals with the technical skills of webmasters (see Your Media Career: Web Developer, page 288) and computer programmers. Interactive ad agencies are another source of Web creation expertise. Traditional graphic design, advertising, and public relations firms have entered the market, as have *Web hosting* companies that provide server space and domain names for clients and will design and maintain the site itself for an additional fee. There are also innumerable freelancers and independent contractors, including Web-savvy college students who want to earn some extra money, who

WHERE'S THE COFFEE? Internet cafés offer temporary ISP service and computer access for a fee. They are a poor substitute for home Internet access for solving the problem of the digital divide.

do Web design work for small businesses and nonprofit organizations. We also need to include the many sources, ranging from the National Weather Service to the author of the local elementary school lunch menu, that create the raw information that others shape into information services. If you have ever posted your own "home page" on the World Wide Web or created a Facebook profile, then you are a content provider.

Internet Organizations

Who runs the Internet backbone (officially known as the very-high-speed backbone network service, or *vBNS*), the network that connects ISPs, Web servers, and individual computers around the world? It is a not-for-profit, cooperative enterprise of major regional networks, such as the MERIT network in Michigan. The Internet is made up of high-speed digital lines that are leased by the regional networks from long-distance telephone companies. At the local level, the ISPs lease or own high-speed lines that connect their local users to the Internet. The larger national ISPs maintain their own high-speed networks, interconnecting with the rest of the Internet only at regional *network access points* (NAPs).

One of the most important issues is the assignment of addresses and domain names. ICANN was entrusted with this task. ICANN, a nonprofit California corporation that operates under a contract with the U.S. Department of Commerce, ultimately decides who gets the rights to domain names and charges an annual fee to the domain owners for the privilege. However, if you want the rights to www.Iluvhiphop.com, you don't deal directly with ICANN. Instead, you contact one of the hundreds of domain name registries (DomainsPricedRight.com in this case) that ICANN authorizes around the globe.

ISOC (the Internet Society) is a nongovernmental international membership society that promotes the orderly use and development of the Internet. It is modeled after the professional associations that college professors belong to—a throwback to when the Internet was a research network run by major universities. The World Wide Web Consortium (W3C) is an international membership organization that formulates and approves standards for the Web, such as HTML5. The Internet Architecture Board (IAB) is a committee within the ISOC that makes important policy decisions about operations and future developments. Its members are, for the most part, employees of large corporations (such as Microsoft) that have important financial stakes in the Internet. Technical matters are overseen by the IETF through its various working-group committees.

The concentration of such activities in the United States makes other nations, companies, and users nervous, so international organizations like the International Telecommunications Union have tried to assert more control over Internet governance, so far with little success. Efforts continue to globalize control of the Web. The United Nations established the Internet Governance Forum to further diversity, security, and education in the information society and convened the World Summit on the Information Society to address ICANN control, the digital divide, and other global issues surrounding the Internet.

WEB DEVELOPER

The Internet is fast replacing television and film as the new "glamour medium." In Chapter 9, we noted that some of the fastest-growing occupations in the television and movie Industries require computer skills. Here we will explore other computer-related jobs in the new media industry.

_____

Many programs in mass communication and journalism now offer courses in Web design. You can be the one who "saves the business" by creating or redesigning a Web page that drives a significant increase in visitors or "click throughs" to the online shopping cart. Unlike conventional media where the results are often weeks or months in the future, Web developers experience the excitement of getting instant feedback on their designs and have the capability of quickly responding to consumer reactions.

Web skills courses open the door to an occupation that currently employs over 148,500 in the United States with 27 percent growth expected in the next 10 years and median annual salaries of over $63,000. Mobile services and electronic commerce are pushing demand for web developers. That means there are more positions available and more potential for growth than in conventional media jobs. And computer "stars" like Mark Zuckerberg make much more money than media stars and similar wage differentials apply at all levels of employment.

Although some computer programming skill is required, there are many niches that graduates of mass communication and journalism programs can fill if they acquire Web skills. Web developers, sometimes also called Web designers, create Web pages from software applications like Dreamweaver and gather user feedback to refine the aesthetics and functionality of the Web pages they design. A background in photography, video, or graphic design can give our readers an advantage over computer science grads. With a little more technical savvy, Web developers can assume the responsibility of Web masters who monitor and troubleshoot the performance of the Web servers that distribute the content to users. With a little bit of programming skill—but not necessarily a computer science degree—Web developers can learn to program interactive applications using Java scripts or HTML5. Having learned the basics in college classes, Web designers can upgrade their Web skills through on-the-job training, free online computer programming courses, workshops, and community college computer programming classes that stress problem solving and logical thinking rather than math. Web skills can also be the door opener for internships and entry-level jobs across all media fields, and indeed across the entire information economy.

Source: Bureau of Labor Statistics. (2016). *Occupational Outlook Handbook*. Available: http://www.bls.gov/ooh/computer-and -information-technology/web-developers.htm

CONTENT: WHAT'S ON THE INTERNET?

The Internet has some characteristic forms of content that we have called *genres* in previous chapters. However, these concepts are still couched in the technical terms of protocols and domains.

The World Wide Web's content can be characterized according to the various domains that are appended to **uniform resource locators (URLs).** URLs are the jumbles of letters, "slashes," and "dots" that indicate the network addresses of content stored on Web servers. The last set of letters, such as the .edu at the end of your school's home page, indicate the *top-level domain*. Each country also has a top-level domain of its own (e.g., .us for the United States). Others, such as .edu and .org, reflect the basic types of institutions that own the addresses. ICANN opened up the top-level domain system to include domain names that use non-Latin letters, such as Arabic and Chinese. Over a thousand new top-level domain names are on the way, including .travel for the travel industry and .singles for online dating. Major corporations can apply for

Uniform resource locators (URLs) are the addresses of Web pages.

their own, such as .ford, and so can you, if you own a trademarked name and can spare $1 million to cover registration, consulting, and legal fees.

Each of the top-level domains has its own characteristic types of content, but .com is still where most of the "sizzle" is found (see Table 10.1). We'll begin by considering types of content that fit well with the conventional mass media functions of surveillance and entertainment introduced in Chapter 2, and then go on to consider some of the newer forms.

Electronic Publishing

Electronic publishing includes online versions of conventional print publications, as well as information published only on the Internet, but with a difference. Even formal "old media," such as the *New York Times* (http://www .nytimes.com), reorganize content for the Internet crowd (such as the online *Times's* blog section, with comments by reporters) and add links to other sites from inside newspaper articles, searchable indices of past articles, online forums, and multimedia extensions. The multimedia extensions include audio and video files and computer simulations. The online *Times* has additional links to local television listings not included in the printed version.

Likewise, magazine websites (see Chapter 3) like People.com post tidbits from their latest issues and interactive features for free and offer paid subscriptions online. Others are using the Web to extend their brand names in hopes of enticing new readers and advertisers. Now many magazines are introducing apps of themselves for tablet computers that enhance the conventional print experience with video and personalized content. Similar to Facebook, these are "walled gardens" that are not freely accessible through the Web and search engines. Online magazines are not limited to Big Media companies, however. There are thousands of amateur magazines, many covering aspects of popular culture. These used to be called 'zines (see Chapter 3) but now most prefer to call themselves *blogs*.

The online publications are crowding out the printed output of organizations. Corporate sites run by large companies (e.g., http://www.apple.com) publish information about themselves, their products, and their services that was

TABLE 10.1 Top 10 Web Properties*

RANK	PROPERTY	UNIQUE VISITORS (×1000)
1	Google Sites	247,075
2	Facebook	219,268
3	Yahoo Sites	202,498
4	Amazon Sites	192,702
5	Microsoft Sites	183,676
6	AOL, Inc.	173,528
7	Comcast NBCUniversal	146,611
8	CBS Interactive	143,593
9	Apple Inc.	140,492
10	Mode Media	135,307

*Desktop and mobile. Total U.S. home and work
Source: http://www.comscore.com/Insights/Market-Rankings/comScore-Ranks-the-Top-50-US-Digital-Media-Properties-for-November-2015

once distributed in paper product brochures, annual reports, and press guides. But many, including IBM (http://www.ibm.com), offer useful information to consumers and professionals in their fields of interest. Government information is growing in importance, with U.S. government Web pages among the most popular (http://www.usa.gov). For example, to see what is going on at the Federal Communications Commission, there is www.fcc.gov. All levels of government have a trend toward e-government so that citizens can find public information about everything, from where the fish are biting to how to file for unemployment. An increasing number of applications and transactions with government agencies can be completed online.

Entertainment

The sharing of music files on the Internet introduced millions of people to the concept of getting their entertainment through the Internet, for free. The practice has spread to print, video, and video games with two important differences: the content is increasingly "shared" by commercial enterprises and much of it is no longer free. Although file sharing (the entertainment industry prefers the term *copyright piracy*) continues, the question becomes not if we will pay for online entertainment but how.

Advertising-supported online entertainment at least preserves the illusion of being "free." Online entertainment attracts audiences in numbers that appeal to advertisers. YouTube is perhaps the best known with a mix of original amateur video and professional video clips that can draw more viewers than prime-time television shows. YouTube channels such as AwesomenessTV and Blip.tv produce regularly scheduled programming that compete with conventional cable and broadcast television. Other sites like Hulu.com specialize in TV series from Big Media companies such as NBCUniversal. There are thousands of ad-supported streaming radio stations in cyberspace. Clear Channel's iHeartRadio is among the leaders, offering links to hundreds of streaming music channels originated by the many conventional stations they own. Other services, like Pandora, customize music channels for individual listeners.

Pay entertainment services are beginning to dominate, including YouTube's subscription service. Some, following the iTunes model, require a payment for the purchase of music and videos that the users "own," although often with limits on making copies and reselling the product. Netflix is a well-known example, with a base of paying subscribers that exceeds that of popular pay cable channels, and it produces its own original content, such as *Orange Is the New Black*. The xfinitytv.com service from cable television giant Comcast (see Chapter 8) has a unique twist: the videos are "free" if the user subscribes to the level of cable television service on which the channel is carried—and is willing to enter their subscriber ID code whenever they want to view them. The "app" model is also becoming popular, in which the user pays a fee for using a downloadable application with a limited shelf-life, similar to yearly magazine subscriptions. Others, including Pandora and Spotify, lure users with the promise of free service but also charge for commercial-free premium services with advanced features.

However, a great deal of the video on the Internet is produced by ordinary users. That includes short "cute cat" and wedding videos posted on YouTube and Facebook. Peer-to-peer video shared in Vine, through Skype, and live video game feeds (see Chapter 12) also add to the total.

Online Games

Online games are another form of entertainment, but their intense interactivity puts them in a category of their own (see Chapter 12). As their name suggests, Massively Multiplayer Online (MMO) games engage large numbers of users in online play. *Massively Multiplayer Online Role-Playing Games* (MMORPGs) are elaborate multiuser communities inhabited by players who adopt roles in an online virtual environment. One, "World of Warcraft," had 12 million players worldwide at its peak, and tens of thousands may be playing online at one time.

So-called casual games are the most popular genre of online games. "Scrabulous" (now known as "Lexulous"), the online version of the Scrabble board game, became a major craze for early Facebook users. More recently, Clash of Clans and Candy Crush Saga have become sensations and are played with such intensity by some that "casual" is perhaps not an appropriate term for it. Many casual games are now distributed for a fee over the Internet as smartphone and tablet apps (see Chapter 11), but many *browser games* can still be played through your Internet browser, usually for free.

Online casino and poker games that allow real-world bets to be made were once the rage, but U.S. players were cut off when law enforcement cracked down on credit card payments to poker websites made through American banks. The U.S. Justice Department has ruled that online poker is legal if kept within state borders, so online poker is returning. However, some states are cracking down on fantasy sports websites like FanDuel, arguing that their daily games are a form of gambling.

Portals

Portals combine directories, interpersonal communication, and information into an all-purpose, customizable "launch pad" that users will visit first whenever they go on the Internet. Portals greet registered visitors by name and keep track of their favorite types of content.

Portal content is organized around familiar categories, such as news, entertainment, travel, computing, health, and personal finance. Interpersonal communication features include e-mail services, chat rooms, and discussion groups. Portals compete with one another with new customer services; some will keep track of appointments or remind you of anniversaries. In that respect, they fill the surveillance function (see Chapter 2), once the province of newspaper headlines and television news broadcasts, with a new personal twist. Advertisers see them as the Web's equivalent to the electronic mass media. Leading portal sites include Yahoo! and those of ISPs. Many portals scrape the news from traditional news sites without paying for the information (see Chapter 4). However, social networking sites now compete with conventional portals by offering news and sports updates of their own and Facebook has now dominates, to the extent that it is the only destination that many Internet users visit in the course of their days.

Portals are Web pages that users launch when they first log on to the Web.

Search Engines

Search engines match the words you type into the "search window" to seek information based on matches to the keywords supplied by website owners, the content on the website, and the behavior of other searchers who have looked for an item in the past. Google has emerged as the giant among search engines, with Yahoo! and Bing trailing far behind. Google is consistently one of the top 10 Web properties (see Table 10.1, page 258), so much so that turning up near the top of its search results is the key to success for many websites. The same queries posed to other search engines may have varying results because of the different ways in which the

INSIDE GOOGLE Giant "server farms" such as this one run Google's search engine and other Internet services.

engines search for keywords. Search engines also differ in how they look for keywords in various locations on a Web page, such as in the title of the Web page, how high it appears on the page, or the frequency in which the keyword appears. It also depends on how often the search engine's software or "bot" searches the Internet. Students everywhere especially appreciate search engines of databases, such as Lexis-Nexis, Web of Science, and ProQuest, which connect them directly to articles they can cite in their term papers, without a trip to the library. There are also specialized search engines for academic publications that can help college students with their term papers (Google Scholar), for still images (Google Images), and for moving images (YouTube).

Social Media

The term *social media* has become almost synonymous with Facebook and other social networking sites that replaced published albums of pictures of incoming college freshmen (known in the olden days as "face books") with interactive online profiles. Since just about all college students still belong to Facebook, there is little point in describing it further here. However, because our definition of social media (from Chapter 1) specifies content generated through social interaction, more of what appears on Facebook is not social media as the application evolves into a general-purpose platform to deliver news, entertainment, and advertising to its users.

SOCIAL NETWORKING Initially considered an idle pursuit, Facebook is an ideal medium to spur needed social change. In 2011, many Egyptians communicated through Facebook pages to collectively stand up to their oppressors.

MEDIA, THE INTERNET, AND THE STORIES WE TELL ABOUT OURSELVES

Not long after the Internet started being used by mass numbers of people in the United States, Jon Katz wrote in *Wired* magazine about the impact of the Internet on the presidential election of 1996. The main impact then, he wrote, was that the Internet had enabled all the fringe groups to find and reinforce each other. Fast forward 20 year and that appears to be even more true today; witness the confluence of anti-immigration groups during the 2016 presidential campaign.

In that regard, many thought that the Internet was the very essence of a new *postmodern* society. One of the main points of postmodernism is that society is gradually losing its big stories that almost everyone knows—its meta-narratives. Many of those meta-narratives were taught by parents, schools, and churches. Many people had common topics to discuss because most were exposed to the same few channels.

Postmodern theorists like Jean-François Lyotard (1984) observed that one of the primary reasons for the breakdown in consensus over the main stories guiding our society was the fragmentation of people's experience with media. As media proliferated, people had more choices, so fewer shared common sources of ideas. People listened to different music, listened to talk shows of very different opinions, read different novels, and watched television shows with different spins and focuses. Within universities and high schools, people argued furiously over what ought to be read and taught, so no one could assume that people had read the same things in their freshman English courses or their introductions to literature. So overall, even before the Internet, people were receiving increasingly wildly diverse ideas from fragmented media. Many of the postmodernists consider this rather liberating. With less uniformity of media, it will be harder for anyone

CULTURAL DIVERSITY OR FRAGMENTATION?
Michel Foucault, pictured here in West Berlin in 1978, is one of the originators of the postmodern school.

to exercise hegemony over ideas, to create and enforce an ideological consensus that limits freedom of thought. However, some sociologists, like Todd Gitlin in *The Twilight of Common Dreams* (1995), worry that the consensus necessary for addressing social problems is breaking down into factionalism and perhaps that accounts for the extreme partisanship that paralyzes American civic society today.

Other scholars are wondering whether this supposed fragmentation is taking place. Looking at the Internet, for example, Robert McChesney (2013) argues that since so much of the Web traffic goes to the same large corporate media sites, the Internet does not have much potential for really breaking down the hold of the main media on the audience. They see news and information on the Web dominated by the same faces with the same hegemonic intent (see Chapter 2).

Still, many familiar Facebook functions, including friending, tagging, wall posting, and liking as well as participating in discussion groups and social games like CityVille, are social media activities under our definition. New ways of social sharing are emerging, including the Facebook Live streaming video application for sharing important events, and unimportant ones, in real time. Facebook, You-Tube, Twitter, and Reddit account for three-fourths visits to social media sites in the United States among them (Statista, 2016).

The social media craze has reached such heights that it seems every major website is going "social." Online newspaper stories invite commentary from readers, while websites connected to popular TV shows solicit real-time user comments to stimulate viewer engagement. Links to Facebook and Twitter are popping up seemingly everywhere so that Web surfers can instantly react to what they are seeing. Social media versions of familiar online forms are also appearing. Digg creates lists of top news stories and entertainment offerings based on the votes of visitors. Kaboodle is a "shopping community" for dedicated shopaholics. Groupon provides discounts to groups of consumers who self-organize through social interaction at that website. Marketers can track the success of brands and celebrities by counting the numbers of Facebook friends, Twitter followers, and YouTube views they receive or by monitoring the words that are used in Twitter. Now there is a counter-movement away from social media that have been invaded by snooping parents and advertisers. Snapchat is popular precisely because it promptly deletes postings, leaving no tracks for snoopers to find. Everyme helps users define themselves differently for the different social groups in their lives (e.g., family, soccer buddies) rather than one profile that everyone sees.

Blogs

Weblogs, or *blogs* for short, are an older but still influential form of social media that are organized around special themes such as technology (Tech-Crunch) and celebrity gossip (TMZ) with the hope of attracting like-minded contributors. Although they are being somewhat upstaged by more recent forms such as Facebook discussion groups, commentary in the "blogosphere" has a growing impact on public discourse. Many are written by professional journalists in their off-hours. Among the most popular is *The Huffington Post,* with political chatter and original stories organized by political gadfly Arianna Huffington. Millions of Web surfers have their own blog, far too many to keep up with, but there are websites (like technorati.com) that index the latest postings from thousands of blogs. Tumblr and Blogger are popular social media sites that make it easy for you to start your own customized blog. Or if you have something serious to say in more than 140 characters but don't want to take on a full-time blog writing responsibility, the medium blog site might post your essays and rants for a wide Internet audience.

Electronic Commerce

E-commerce businesses that make sales directly to consumers are known as *b to c* (business to consumer). They follow the familiar catalog shopping model, except that the product information and order blank are online. These sites are what the retail trade calls *category killers:* they specialize in one line of products, such as children's toys (e.g., eToys). Others, like Amazon, imitate shopping malls by carrying many different types of products. Some are pure

1997

The term *weblog* is coined

E-commerce (electronic commerce) is the ability to buy and sell online.

e-tailers that exist only online. Many, like Walmart's, are online offshoots of brick-and-mortar retailers that are called *clicks-and-mortar* operations.

Other sites depart from the catalog shopping model. Services as well as products are sold online, with the Internet taking the place of the travel agent (e.g., Expedia), taxi driver (e.g., Uber), and the hotel clerk (e.g., hotels.com). Auctions such as eBay (sometimes called *c to c*, for consumer to consumer) let visitors bid on antiques and yard-sale items offered by other visitors. *Reverse auctions* like priceline.com let shoppers name the price, and sellers bid to meet it. Or shoppers can buy things from other people by tuning into newsgroups that specialize in buying and selling goods. Some e-commerce sites don't actually sell anything, but act as clearinghouses for comparative shopping information (e.g., http://www.autobytel.com for automobiles). Others have product directories, coupons, and buyer incentive programs.

By far the biggest category of e-commerce is one that doesn't want your business, unless you *are* a business. Business-to-business (or *b to b*) sites sell products to firms. There are also online shopping malls for business supplies and services, and some of the biggest corporations are organizing online bazaars for their suppliers and customers. The watchword is *disintermediation,* eliminating distributors that serve as intermediaries between manufacturers and their customers.

What Makes a Good Web Page?

Over 3 billion people worldwide use the Internet. Personal communication is the most common activity (see Figure 10.3). The amount of time we spend each day on the Internet is quickly catching up to the amount of time spent on

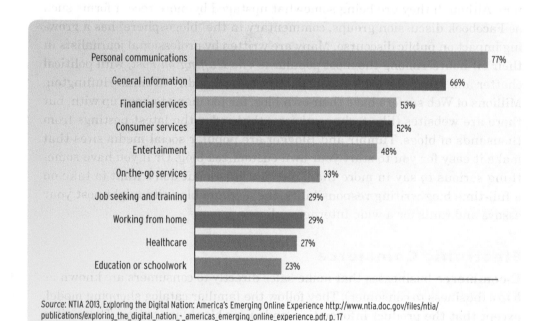

Source: NTIA 2013, Exploring the Digital Nation: America's Emerging Online Experience http://www.ntia.doc.gov/files/ntia/publications/exploring_the_digital_nation_-_americas_emerging_online_experience.pdf, p. 17

FIGURE 10.3 INTERNET USE BY THE NUMBERS Personal communication, general information, and financial services are the online activities that Americans rely on most.

television, partly due to the time spent on social networking sites but increasingly because of streaming audio and video consumption. Yet, most Web pages are viewed for less than a minute, so the question of what makes a good Web page that surfers will want to spend time with is still an important issue.

Some of the techniques thought to increase user engagement are borrowed from old media, including contests and giveaways (borrowed from radio), continual updates of content (à la the newsbreaks on network radio and television), and episodic storytelling (from television). Graphic designers adapt eye-catching colors and attractive layouts from magazine pages. Content counts, too, with Web surfers preferring short items (about a screenful) to lengthy articles. Portal sites borrow their basic "everything you need to start the day" strategy from newspapers. Other inducements to stick to e-commerce sites are drawn from retail promotions, including coupons, sales, and celebrity appearances. And if we can't beat TV, why not *be* TV? That's the premise of the various radio and TV services: to lengthen visits by streaming video and music videos.

There are other strategies unique to the Web that take advantage of the Web's interactive features. Many an Internet user has gotten hooked by playing online games, social networking, or even compulsively answering e-mail. Another strategy is personalization of content to individual users. In a sense, the website gets to know its visitors, responding to and even anticipating their needs. If you have bought anything from Amazon, when you log on, it frequently suggests book or record ideas, based on your previous purchases. Amazon follows up by sending you e-mail to tell you it has found something it thinks you will like. After establishing a personal relationship, visitors linger longer and return more often. Abandoning the site would incur the cost of reentering detailed personal information at a new portal, selecting from its content options, and waiting for it to learn our innermost desires by tracking our surfing behavior.

But perhaps the amount of time users spend at a site should not be the primary criterion for a "good" Web page. That reflects "old media" thinking tied to the need to deliver eyeballs to advertisers. What about good design as reflected by the winners of Webby awards (www.webbyawards.com) selected by Web design professionals? From that perspective, the key to having a good Web page is lots of empty white space (or blank dark space or gray space) with small print, intriguing video clips, and large graphic design spaces. Among media-related websites, the 2015 winners were *The New York Times* (in the news category), *The New Yorker* (magazines), KCRW (radio/podcasts), HBO GO (media streaming), Imgur (social media), and The Tonight Show with Jimmy Fallon (television). Another school of thought is that the amount of time spent on a page is an indication of bad design. *Usability* and human–computer interaction (HCI) researchers hold stopwatches on users and train cameras on them as they surf Web pages. They try to identify and correct confusing features that slow users down. Designing Web pages around tasks, giving all the pages in a site a consistent look and feel, supplying site navigation aids, and minimizing download times are key design considerations. In this approach, "cool" Web pages with artistic designs, unreadable text, and

GOOD DESIGN The *New Yorker* wins praise for attractive Web design among print media. Colorful graphics, attractive typeface, and an uncluttered style with lots of white space are the key ingredients.

STOP & REVIEW

1. List the major types of content on the Web.

2. What makes a good Web page design?

3. Who are the leading makers of computer hardware and software?

4. What is the difference between a content provider and an Internet service provider?

5. Who runs the Internet?

slow-loading videos that don't help users complete a well-defined task are poor designs. The HealthCare.gov website, as it was first unveiled in 2013, is the current champion of bad design, after it became a national scandal for slow response times and frequent session crashes. Some of the very same sites that win good design awards also show up on webpagesthatsuck.com, where the usability researchers have their say. But "uncool" designs with lots of text and buttons all over the place also tend to flunk their usability tests, so at least the designers and the usability engineers can agree on that.

MEDIA LITERACY

GETTING THE MOST OUT OF THE INTERNET

Earlier, we saw how bad behavior by big business, governments, hackers, and ordinary users is changing the course of the Internet. Here we look more deeply into those concerns and what you, the reader, might do about them.

DOES INFORMATION WANT TO BE FREE?

We don't hear so much about the problem of music piracy anymore. Piracy of copyrighted material devastated the record industry in the past decade. More recently, nearly all of the once-popular peer-to-peer music file-sharing sites like Napster and Lime Wire have been shut down, although entertainment industries still claim that such sites threaten their existence. However, YouTube and Spotify are more convenient options for getting free music online. Perhaps the pendulum has swung to giant media corporations who take advantage of their market power and hardball tactics to enrich themselves at our expense. Instead of treating Internet users as thieves, social media like Facebook treat their users like unpaid laborers, profiting from the content that users upload, without "sharing" the profits from advertisers with us. So, who are the real Internet pirates now?

Aside from their sheer economic might, **copyrights** and **patents** (see Chapter 15) are the most important tools that corporations have to control the Internet. The Digital Millennium Copyright Act of 1998 is a key weapon. It added an "anti-circumvention" provision that made it a crime to engage in activities like copying a copyright-protected music CD to a computer hard drive. Although the recording and motion picture industries lost a battle to enact sweeping anti-piracy legislation in the face of a massive online protest, they continue to urge Congress to give copyright holders the right to shut down websites that violate their copyrights and to prevent search engines from linking to the pirates.

The entertainment industry would prefer to limit distribution to secure sites like iTunes that can charge users for each copy. Another tactic is to cut off free access. Online news organizations would like those who repost their news articles to pay a fee. Yet others like cable and broadband Internet giant Comcast would like to see the cable television model in which content fees are bundled into a monthly service charge.

The ISP industry in which cable companies are dominant is another lair for would-be corporate pirates. Many of them actively oppose the new **net neutrality** policy that treats every Internet packet with equal priority and they are suing to undo the new rules. Internet providers would prefer to make deals like the one between Netflix and Comcast that compensates the cable company for providing improved access to its broadband networks. The costs will ultimately be passed on to consumers and pose a barrier to entry for potential Netflix competitors.

Copyright is the legal right to control intellectual property. With it comes the legal privilege to use, sell, or license creative works.

A **patent** gives an inventor the exclusive right to make, use, or sell an invention for 20 years.

Net neutrality means users are not discriminated against based on the amount or nature of the data they transfer on the Internet.

The FCC's new net neutrality rules forbid ISPs to block, slow, or prioritize traffic for pay and they apply both to wireline and mobile providers. The FCC also reclassified ISPs as *common carriers* (see Chapter 11), subjecting them to the same rules as telecommunication carriers such as ATT and Verizon. Common carriers must offer their services to all on an equal basis and there is the possibility, which the FCC promises not to pursue at this time, of rate regulation.

However, the growth in cable television subscription rates greatly exceeds the rate of inflation in the United States, while broadband Internet connections are much more expensive than in most advance countries. And, cable companies would like to impose usage-based billing on Internet service similar to that of some smartphone plans. More competition for Big Cable would help, either by encouraging private sector investors to enter the market, or by establishing public fiber-optic network utilities funded through municipal bonds. However, a myriad of municipal finance and network access rules would have to be swept aside to implement meaningful change. In the end, a fiber-optic infrastructure might prove to be a "natural monopoly" that only one provider can offer economically, in which case rate regulation might indeed be the only option.

Will information continue to be free on the Internet in the future or will it follow the pay TV or iTunes models? You, the reader, can be part of the solution by joining (i.e., by doing a Google search for) a movement called *Creative Commons*. Creative Commons advocates that authors opt into, or opt out of, specific copyright protections for their work. For example, you might allow all noncommercial use of your original work that you post on your Web page, or let others modify or sample from it—rights that are reserved by holders of conventional copyrights.

CLOSING THE DIGITAL DIVIDE

There continues to be a digital divide. For example, Caucasians are much more likely to use the Internet (75%) than African Americans (64%) or Hispanics (61%) (NTIA, 2015). The income gap is even wider. A total of 85 percent use the Internet in homes with annual incomes of $100,000 or more compared to 54 percent in homes with incomes under $25,000. Racial and income disparities in home Internet connections. combine to create a "homework gap" that limits the ability of children in minority and low income homes to complete homework assignments that are commonly available online in the nation's schools. The ability to use the Internet effectively once you have it is also an issue; some call it the second digital divide, whereas others refer to it as the knowledge gap.

The Obama administration made closing the gap a priority, pledging billions of dollars to put broadband in 90 percent of U.S. homes by 2020. To help bring that about, $7 billion was allocated through the American Recovery and Reinvestment Act of 2009 to upgrade broadband Internet networks and community computing facilities in schools and libraries. The FCC is redirecting universal service funds (see Chapter 12) that formerly subsidized telephone connections in low-income households to $9.25 monthly subsidies for Internet access, the Connect America Fund. However, given that broadband connections often cost over $50 per month, the subsidy may still not make broadband affordable enough in low-income homes. The FCC encouraged cable companies to institute the Connect2Compete program that offers low-cost computers, $9.99 a month broadband connections, and free computer training to families with children who participate in the free lunch program at school.

Unfortunately, the federal government's broadband stimulus program didn't provide the funds needed to keep the libraries open longer hours, which also contributes to the homework gap. So it's too early to conclude that the digital divide is going away. The danger is that as public institutions and political activism move online, the poor will be disenfranchised. In the long run, inferior Internet access will also mean inferior access to employment and educational opportunity, deepening the cycle of poverty that costs all citizens dearly, both in this country and worldwide.

CLOSING THE GAP Before the digital gap can close, more minority households will have to see scenes like this one, where families have personal computers in their homes (and tech-savvy children can teach their parents how to use them).

By some standards, all U.S. citizens are on the wrong side of a broadband gap. In terms of overall broadband penetration, the United States ranks a dismal 16th among 34 leading developed countries (OECD, 2014). By international standards, U.S. broadband service is also slow and expensive. Our readers can take direct action to close the digital divide themselves by helping classmates and relatives use the Internet more effectively. If helping others interests you and you have good computer skills, check out Geeks for America or the Intel Computer Clubhouse Network, volunteer organizations that provide computer support for nonprofit organizations and low-income communities, respectively. Or do a Google search for "computer volunteers" to find opportunities to help people in your area learn how to use computers.

GOVERNMENT: HANDS OFF OR HANDS ON?

Government intervention is one answer to threats of corporate abuse or class conflict. However, too much government control could destroy our Internet freedoms.

Governments like to tax what they control, which could retard the growth of the Internet. The taxation urge is strong at the state level, where e-commerce sales cut into sales taxes, which are the states' primary source of revenue, creating critical budget shortfalls in difficult economic times. Online stores are required to collect sales taxes on purchases made by customers in the same state, but that applies only to the state in which the Internet subsidiary has a physical presence. If you buy a product from an out-of-state website, you, the customer, are supposed to pay the appropriate sales tax to your own state. However, few people are that mindful, and thus far states have only gone after purchasers of big-ticket items. As of this writing, there is pending legislation that would allow states to collect taxes on out-of-state purchases made by their citizens, but without federal legislation retailer participation is voluntary.

It is tempting to look to the government for solutions to some of the social problems of the Web. For example, the Communications Decency Act was an attempt (although an unconstitutional one; see Chapter 15) to ban pornography sites on the Internet, while the Children's Internet Protection Act requires libraries and schools to filter out inappropriate content. The Child Online Privacy Protection Act restrains sites that obtain personal information from children. The CANSPAM law makes it a crime to send spam that does not have a legitimate return address. New laws are in the works to crack down on child molesters who prowl social networking sites.

However, too much government involvement could have frightening implications for our civil liberties. What preserves one person's sense of privacy, safety, or morality limits the freedoms of others. The USA PATRIOT Act, passed in the immediate aftermath of the 9/11 terror attacks, enlists Internet ISPs as government informers. The Homeland Security Act empowers government agents to sift through e-mail and Internet traffic logs to detect "patterns of terrorist activity." Government snooping broke into the headlines in 2013 when low-level security contract employee Edward Snowden revealed the extent of data collection from U.S. citizens and foreign leaders by the National Security Agency. Another issue is how long ISPs and search engines should keep files detailing our online activities. The U.S. government wants to keep them for years. The European Union, in contrast, limits the record keeping to a month or two and is seeking new rules that would require websites to justify and obtain explicit permission for all uses of personal data. The leading U.S. search engines keep data for 12 to 18 months.

And how will governments resolve conflicts that cross their borders? Efforts to stamp out smut on the Internet in America could undermine free-speech rights in other countries with more liberal mores. The Chinese government demands that search engines block searches related to that country's pro-democracy movement, a practice that Google complied with, since it threatened the company's ability to do business there. U.S. copyright protections are stronger (some might say excessive) compared to other countries.

Stronger European Union privacy laws are a standard that U.S. companies have to meet if they want to do business there. In 2015, a European court struck down the so-called Safe Harbor agreement that governed data transfers between the United States and the European Union. That was in response to revelations about the U.S. National Security Agency snooping on personal information held by U.S.-based Internet companies like Facebook and Google. A new Privacy Shield agreement was negotiated in 2016 that protects European citizens from snooping by intelligence agencies in the United States and places further restrictions on the transfer of personal information across the Atlantic by American companies such as Google and Facebook (see Chapter 16). Europe also provides a "right to be forgotten" that requires search engines to remove links to outdated or erroneous information about individuals. To implement that right, European citizens can only access Google through country-specific versions of the search engine (e.g., Google.fr in France) and are blocked from seeing the global version of Google that users in the United States access. Privacy advocates in the United States would like to see the same protections enjoyed by European citizens, for whom privacy is a fundamental right, on both sides of the Atlantic.

A new role for governments is the conduct of cyberwarfare. In 2013, hackers based in Syria attacked websites in the United States, including the *New York Times*. The United States considered going on the offensive by shutting down Syria's electrical power grid in retaliation. However, that could set a dangerous precedent. That is because the nation's economy is heavily dependent on the Internet and critical infrastructure systems, including the telephone network and the national energy grid, which are susceptible to attack. As of this writing, the United States military is engaged in a "cyberwar" on radical Islamic groups that aims to disrupt online recruiting and the flow of money that supports terrorism.

Global issues are even more intractable than national ones when it comes to "doing something," but remembering that "all politics are local," this is a case where campus activism might have an impact. Colleges and universities are ISPs and staunch defenders of freedom. So interested students might read their institutions' "acceptable uses" policies to see what issues are covered, such as who can snoop through your e-mail, and the length of time records are kept.

ONLINE SAFETY

Crime and fraud run rampant on the Internet. Many of us have fallen victim to **phishing** scams, also known as *social engineering*. The obvious scams are the e-mails purportedly from former officials of countries seeking our assistance in getting money out of their country. Others are harder to spot, such as when you get a legitimate-looking request from, say, someone who claims to be from the campus computer center who needs your password to investigate a security breach. More sinister are scams involving personal information snatched from the social networking sites, such as an e-mail requesting that you wire money to bail out a friend who has landed in jail while on vacation. Online thieves are waiting to plunder your account. Just visiting the links in phish mail could lead you to a Web page that downloads spyware or a virus. Or the "phishcatchers" may turn your computer into a zombie machine that attacks others or sends spam to everyone in your e-mail directory.

Our privacy is also at risk from intrusive commercial activities, such as from **spamming** and spyware. Internet users place themselves in the crosshairs of direct marketers who employ harvesting programs when they expose their e-mail addresses in chat rooms or social networking sites. Spammers may also share (i.e., sell) information to third parties. The software we download may also contain spyware that will report our online behavior and, in some cases, expose private information stored on our computers. Keyloggers are a growing threat. They are software programs that record all of our keystrokes (including passwords and credit card numbers) and send them to criminals. Internet cafés and other public terminals are popular sites of infection, but keyloggers can also be introduced on home computers by opening an e-mail attachment or visiting a website. Routine Web searching and surfing can put your privacy at risk, as well. The search terms we use and the cookies deposited on computers by commercial websites can be linked in the service of online advertisers. And anything we post in social media also makes us more vulnerable to hackers and marketers.

> **Phishing** is an online scam in which criminals pretend to be someone you trust in an effort to obtain money or sensitive information.

> **Spamming** is unsolicited commercial e-mailing.

Even if we go to great lengths to protect ourselves online, we are still vulnerable to identity theft when the computers of the companies we do business with are breached. The new credit cards with built-in chips will help to some extent, but what is really needed is the so-called *chip and pin* technology, adopted just about everywhere except in the United States, that requires a personal identification number (PIN) be entered to authorize each transaction.

But let's not blame criminals, negligent retailers, or government inaction too much. We, the users of the Internet, also have a personal responsibility to make the Internet safer. We each need at least three basic protections: a malware scanner to seek and remove viruses and other malicious software, a spam filter to detect unwanted e-mails, and a firewall to prevent unauthorized connections to your computer. So if you don't have all three, you are part of the problem. Most ISPs, including your college or university, offer these protections free of charge, but it is up to you to install them, use them, and update them. Your browser and operating system should also be set to receive automatic updates to plug security holes.

Beware of downloading protections from unknown sources, however. Some purported anti-spyware protections are spyware themselves! *Rogue anti-spyware* programs are the ones that pop up out of nowhere, informing you that they have scanned your computer and found numerous serious infections or illegal software, problems that they will fix if you just send them your credit card number. Some of them block the legitimate protections you already have and keep you from accessing websites where you can download software that will erase the rogues. So, close your browser right away and turn off your computer when you are offered a free scan. Consult reliable sources such as PC Magazine for reviews of legitimate protective software. The easy-to-remember passwords you use also pose a risk. Passwords should be at least 8 characters; include upper- and lowercase letters, numbers, and special characters (e.g., !@#$%). Also avoid common names, your college mascot's nickname, your favorite movie star's name, and any of the 10,000 most common passwords that you find on http://www.passwordrandom.com/most-popular-passwords. It is a good idea to maintain separate passwords for everyday use and for your bank account and to change them periodically. That is a lot of bother, so to help, there are *log-in encryption* (just Google those keywords) products available that will automatically generate and manage complex passwords for you. Another emerging technology is biometric verification systems that, for example, scan your fingerprints or facial features to make sure it's "really you" logging into your bank account.

Here are some other safety tips: Always look for the "https" at the top of the page and the lock icon in the browser frame before you send complete a credit card transaction or register at a site demanding personal information. Don't post your birth date or reveal your travel plans in Facebook since those lead to identity theft and "bail me out of this Turkish prison" scams. Think twice about posting pictures of your last keg party anywhere on the Internet, especially on Facebook. We can see you; so can online scam artists, and someday, prospective employers and your own children may see you, too. And by using cheap facial recognition software, police can take a picture of the real you participating in, say, a post-game college riot, and match it to your Facebook you.

STOP & REVIEW

1. What are the main public policies governing the Internet?

2. What is the digital divide?

3. What does net neutrality mean?

4. What are some of the major threats to privacy on the Internet?

5. How can you keep yourself safe online?

SUMMARY & REVIEW

WHAT ARE THE ORIGINS OF THE WEB?

The first electronic computers were developed during World War II, and forerunners of the Internet were developed to support nuclear weapons research. Today's Internet began in 1972 as ARPANET, a computer network using TCP/IP to transmit messages among defense-related research labs. It slowly evolved to serve wider groups of academic and organizational users before being opened up to all computer users in 1991. The World Wide Web originated with the creation of the HTML language in 1991.

HOW HAS THE INTERNET IMPACTED SOCIETY?

On the plus side, the Internet can contribute to meaningful social interaction and public debate. On the downside, it can be accused of replacing human interaction with superficial online chatter and cultivating hate. As an international medium, content and user behavior acceptable in one country may not be permissible in others. Pornography, intellectual property rights, political speech, and social inequality are among the issues raised by the spread of the Internet.

HOW HAS THE INTERNET IMPACTED CONVENTIONAL MEDIA?

The advertising, newspaper, and music industries have seen their conventional ways of doing business threatened. Old media firms are scrambling to create new revenue sources by either selling content online or developing new outlets like the Hulu video service. The popularity of social media like Facebook and Twitter poses a fundamentally new way of creating content that challenges old media models at their core—by having the audience create the content.

WHAT ARE SOME FUTURE DIRECTIONS FOR THE INTERNET?

One is to make personal computers simpler, perhaps yielding "a network of things" that will be found in many everyday devices such as TV sets and household appliances. The other direction is the design of more sophisticated multimedia computers with virtual reality displays that will replace all of the other communications media found in the home today. HTML5 integrates today's plug-ins and makes information more accessible. IP version 6 expands the number of people and devices connected to the Internet. Broadband speeds are increasing as new wireless and fiber-optic technologies become available. Tablet computers, smartphones, and cloud computing offer new options for mobile Internet services that are replacing the conventional personal computer paradigm.

HOW IS THE INTERNET INDUSTRY ORGANIZED?

Google has become the giant of the Internet through its search and ad-serving businesses, but is expanding into software publishing, hardware, and video. Computer hardware companies such as Hewlett-Packard and Dell make computers and network servers. Software companies such as Microsoft manufacture common computer applications. Content providers are the companies that create information for the Web and multimedia applications, whereas ISPs make the actual physical connections between the Internet and the home.

WHAT'S ON THE INTERNET?

Internet content can be defined in terms of the major varieties of protocols that are used, which include e-mail, file transfer, and document display. The Web is an example of the latter. Web pages may be categorized by their top-level domain names (such as .com and .edu) that are being expanded to include non-English languages and specialized domains for travel and dating applications, among many others. Social media, online games, e-commerce, and entertainment sites are the leading categories today, but new genres are continually emerging.

WHO RUNS THE INTERNET?

No one entity owns or controls the Internet or the Web. They are run by a patchwork of voluntary organizations, including the ICANN, the IETF, the W3C, and the ISOC. The high-capacity backbone that interconnects major Internet nodes is operated by long-distance carriers, and local connections to those nodes are handled by ISPs and local telephone companies.

WHAT SOCIAL ISSUES SHAPE THE INTERNET?

Most issues revolve around the control of the Internet. Some proposed policies are aimed at keeping the Internet open and diverse, such as by protecting individual privacy, preventing monopolization by corporate interests, providing equal access for all, and keeping it free of taxation or direct control by national governments. Net neutrality is the concept that users should not be discriminated against based on the amount or nature of the data they transfer on the Internet. Others would clamp down on cyberspace by restricting pornography, encryption, and hate speech or by strictly enforcing the intellectual property rights of copyright and patent holders.

THINKING CRITICALLY
ABOUT THE MEDIA

1. How should we reinvent the Internet for our benefit? For the benefit of society?

2. Watch your favorite TV program online. Or if you already watch it online, watch it in real time on a conventional TV set for once. Then, discuss the advantages and disadvantages of Internet TV versus broadcast television. Refer to "Diffusion of Innovations" (see Chapter 2).

3. What would be the best way to govern the Internet in the future? Why?

4. How do you explain the waning popularity of social media like Facebook among college students?

5. Analyze your online privacy and security practices, and outline a plan for making yourself safer online.

MindTap®

Test your knowledge with online printable flashcards and online quizzing.

KEY TERMS

cookies (p. 262)

copyright (p. 279)

e-commerce (p. 275)

encryption (p. 257)

hypertext markup language (HTML) (p. 254)

hypertext transfer protocol (http) (p. 259)

Internet service provider (ISP) (p. 267)

Internet2 (p. 264)

local area network (LAN) (p. 253)

modem (modulator-demodulator) (p. 252)

net neutrality (p. 279)

patent (p. 279)

phishing (p. 283)

portal (p. 272)

protocols (p. 259)

social media (p. 255)

spamming (p. 283)

spyware (p. 263)

transmission-control protocol/Internet protocol (TCP/IP) (p. 253)

uniform resource locator (URL) (p. 269)

Web 2.0 (p. 255)

wide area network (WAN) (p. 252)

MindTap® Log on to the MindTap Communication for *Media Now* to access a variety of additional material, including this chapter's ebook, learning objectives, comprehension quizzes, videos, and more!

THE THIRD SCREEN: SMARTPHONES AND TABLETS

LEARNING OBJECTIVES

After studying the topics in this chapter, you will be able to:

1 Comment on how government regulations have affected the development of communication technology over the years.
2 Assess the impact of the Third Screen on conventional mass media and personal computer-based Internet services.
3 Determine the social and technological changes that led to the emergence of the current mobile device and app marketplace.
4 Distinguish the capabilities of third-, fourth-, and fifth-generation smartphones.
5 Explain the relationship between the four major cell phone network providers and MVNOs.
6 Identify the relative advantages of location-based applications for users and mobile commerce providers.
7 Review the public policy issues that affect the affordability and privacy of mobile communications.

HISTORY: BETTER LIVING THROUGH TELECOMMUNICATIONS

What is the most exciting and life-transforming development in new media today? Isn't it your smartphone? (See Media & Culture: What My Cell Phone Means to Me, page 289.) Perhaps that should not be surprising since advances in the telecommunications infrastructure have had transforming impacts on the lives of individuals and

THE "THIRD SCREEN" With TV and computer screens as the first and second screens in our lives, the handheld third screen keep us in contact with our friends and relatives and brings us growing array of mobile entertainment and information options.

Krisztian Bocsi/Bloomberg/Getty Images

287

MEDIA THEN… MEDIA NOW

1844
> Samuel Morse introduces the telegraph

1876
> Alexander Graham Bell invents the telephone

1880
> Bell's photophone anticipates fiber optics and smartphones

1896
> Marconi demonstrates wireless telegraph

1921
> Graham Act calls for universal telephone service

1934
> Communications Act establishes the FCC

1962
> The first digital telephone network is introduced

> The first communication satellite, Telstar, is launched

1983
> Cell phones debut in the United States

1984
> AT&T forced to sell local phone companies

1992
> Was IBM's Simon the first smartphone?

2007
> The iPhone is introduced

2010
> The iPad popularizes tablet computing

> 4G cell phones are introduced in the United States

2016
> Virtual reality apps for smartphones

> Mobile ads catch up to personal computer ad revenues

MindTap

Start with a quick warm-up activity.

societies in the past. Today, smartphones and tablet computers are ushering in a new phase of our relationships with telecommunications networks, becoming the third screen (after personal computers and televisions) in our lives. However, the wireless networks of today were built upon the wireline networks of yesteryear that first defined the role of telecommunications in our world.

WHAT MY CELL PHONE MEANS TO ME

Throughout history, telecommunications have had transforming effects on the people who use them and the societies they live in. What impact do cell phones have on us and our culture? Why not ask college students about that? They are members of the first cell phone generation. Accordingly, we convened small groups of students to discuss the meaning of cell phones in their lives.

Many restated the obvious benefits that cell phone companies stress in their marketing campaigns: convenience, safety, and staying in touch anytime, anyplace. However, some of these take a unique twist in the lives of college students such as coordinating pit stops between cars while on road trips. The positive effects center on increasing social interaction and the ability to participate in more social activities. On the negative side, students were annoyed by repeated calls from people they didn't want to hear from, the increased pace of their social lives, and a loss of spontaneity due to overplanning. Some also found that their social interactions tended to become limited to the people they texted frequently.

Comments like these resonate with concerns about the effects of communication technology on society. One point of view is that Americans are becoming less involved in organized social activities, that they too often go "bowling alone," in the words of one social critic (Putnam, 2000). To the extent that cell phones stimulate and coordinate social activity, they could help reverse that trend. However, other critics fear that new media offer us too much choice in the content we consume and the associates we seek out, breaking our sense of living in a shared culture. If we limit our social contacts only to others with cell phones or those on our text messaging buddy list, that trend could accelerate. Whether cell phones ultimately improve or destroy social contact will, of course, depend upon which of these opposing tendencies becomes the dominant one.

The New Media of Yesteryear

The story of the **infrastructure** is the story of how diverse cultures create the means to communicate at a distance—the essence of telecommunication. The ancient Greeks and Romans had fire towers to carry messages from distant outposts of their civilizations. The Yorubas of eastern Africa had a network of drummers. The Anasazi people of the American Southwest "broadcast" fire signals from atop high plateaus in the twelfth century. In Napoleon's day, mechanical semaphore signal towers sent dispatches across France (Holzmann & Pherson, 1994).

All of the history-making networks mentioned in the previous paragraph are what we might now call "wireless." However, the early history of electronic telecommunications was dominated by *wireline* communication, before coming full cycle back to wireless in the current century. A review of that history helps us understand the technological and legal frameworks in which our smartphones operate today.

Samuel F. B. Morse's telegraph was an early forerunner of the Internet in 1844, when he tapped out the first words, "What hath God wrought?" Was that the first text message? If so, the text messages of the nineteenth century were just as powerful as those of today. Historian Daniel Czitrom (1982) called the telegraph wires "lightning lines" both for their speed of transmission and for their transforming effects. Together with the railroads, the telegraph made national economies and a national culture possible.

MindTap®

Read, highlight, and take notes on the complete chapter text in a rich interactive online platform.

The infrastructure is the underlying physical structure of communication networks.

1844

Samuel Morse introduces the telegraph

1876

Alexander Graham Bell invents the telephone

1880

Bell's photophone anticipates fiber optics and smartphones

Library of Congress Prints & Reproduction Division [LC-USZCN4-134]

LIGHTNING LINES The telegraph transformed communications in the business world in the late 1880s. Here telegraph wires span a busy New York City street.

The story of telecommunication in the United States is intertwined with the history of telecom giant American Telephone and Telegraph (AT&T). The story began one day in 1876 when Alexander Graham Bell called out for his assistant, "Mr. Watson, come here! I want to see you!" and the apparatus on his table relayed his words over wires to his assistant in the next room. In 1880, Bell would invent an early, if initially impractical, ancestor of the wireless phone he called the *photophone*. It transmitted voice wirelessly through the air over beams of light.

These nineteenth-century "new media" foretold those of today. With its combination of interpersonal communication and information services, wasn't the telegraph the Internet of the nineteenth century (Standage, 1998)? Much early speculation about the telephone centered on multichannel mass media functions like conveying news and music to the home (LaRose & Atkin, 1992). Early phones often had party lines shared by multiple users who occasionally joined in on the conversations, a forerunner of today's social media chatrooms.

The Rise and Fall of Ma Bell

Soon after the Bell Telephone Company was established in 1877, it acquired Western Electric, an electrical equipment-manufacturing firm, the third cornerstone of a **vertically integrated** monopoly that also included its local and long-distance networks. In its early years, the Bell Company ruthlessly used its **patent** rights to undercut its competitors and refused to interconnect competitors with its long-distance network.

Efforts to reign in AT&T's monopolistic bad behavior established the framework of government regulation that still oversees telecommunications and the Internet today. Under threat of an antitrust suit, AT&T promised to provide quality service for all, the principle of **universal service,** that was codified in the Graham Act of 1921.

The telephone slowly expanded from the circles of wealthy tradespeople and professionals who owned them at the turn of the twentieth century (Fischer, 1992). It became a "social network," thanks to the women who reinvented it as a medium of social exchange. It became a lifeline to rural families, which now felt less isolated, and along with the automobile, helped spur migration from the cities to the suburbs. It was something of a mixed blessing for women, though, because while it connected them to family and friends, it also confined them to their homes more than when they went out on social visits in person (Rakow, 1992).

During the Great Depression (1929–1939), AT&T continued paying dividends to stockholders (mostly Republicans) while laying off thousands of

---

Vertical integration occurs when a company with the same owner handles different aspects of a business within the same industry, such as phone manufacturing and phone service.

A patent gives an inventor the exclusive right to make, use, or sell an invention for 20 years.

1921

Graham Act calls for universal telephone service

Universal service is the principle that everyone should have basic access to telecommunication services.

1934

Communications Act establishes the FCC

workers (mostly Democrats). This placed communications policy on the agenda of Democratic President Franklin Roosevelt. The Communications Act of 1934 established the **Federal Communications Commission (FCC)** to regulate communications. It defined AT&T as a **common carrier,** a concept that is still being invoked today to preserve net neutrality on the Internet (see Chapter 16). This required AT&T and other telephone companies to offer service on an equal basis to all paying customers and prohibited them from having any financial interest in the content.

The FCC soon launched an antitrust investigation that dragged on for almost 50 years. It ultimately ended in the Modified Final Judgment (MFJ) in 1984, which forced AT&T to sell off, or divest, its local phone companies. The local exchanges were parceled into seven **regional Bell operating companies (RBOCs).** The AT&T of today was reassembled over the decades through a series of acquisitions and mergers that gave it control over local wireline service in the midwest, far west, deep south, and southwest. Verizon, covering the eastern seaboard from Virginia to New York, and CenturyLink, spanning western states from the Pacific Northwest to Minnesota and south to Arizona and New Mexico, are the other remaining holding companies. However, the wireless revolution has made those territorial rights to provide wireline service increasingly irrelevant.

NUMBER, PLEASE Before automatic switching, live operators completed all calls by moving plugs around their switchboard. They were replaced by electromechanical devices that automated the process.

Cutting the Wires

Practical wireless telecommunication dates back to Marconi's wireless telegraph of 1896. Radio was primarily a two-way communications medium for the first 25 years of its existence, before radio broadcasting dominated the airwaves. All of the messages were texts, transmitted in the Morse Code that wireline telegraphs used and such bulky equipment was required that only large oceangoing vessels, like the *Titanic,* had mobile radios.

The first land-based mobile radios through which voices were heard in the United States were two-way radios installed in Detroit police cars in the early 1920s. Mobile radios advanced rapidly during World War II as they became commonplace in tanks and airplanes. The first handheld personal communication devices also appeared on World War II battlefields, in the form of the walkie-talkie. They were the work of Canadian inventor Al Gross, who went on to pioneer an audio forerunner of today's chat services, citizens' band (CB) radio, and yet another form of texting, the telephone pager (Bellis, 2000).

Mobile telephones for personal use have been around since 1947, but early systems had only 23 channels. That meant years-long waiting lists for new customers and busy signals for subscribers. In 1975, the CB radio service

1984

AT&T forced to sell local phone companies

Common carriers provide service to all on an equal basis.

The Federal Communications Commission (FCC) regulates communication in the United States.

Regional Bell operating companies (RBOCs) are the local telephone operating companies that AT&T divested in 1984.

1896

Marconi demonstrates wireles telegraph

NOT FOR MY POCKET PHONE The first U.S. cell phone weighed 2 pounds, cost $4,000, and was known as "the brick." That's Martin Cooper, "the father of the cell phone," showing it off. Despite its weight and cost, it caught on with businesspeople on the move and became a status symbol that encouraged further adoption.

1983

Cell phones debut in the United States

> **The Telecommunications Act of 1996** is Federal legislation that deregulated the communications media. It opened the U.S. telecommunications industry to competition.

2007

The iPhone is introduced

2010

The iPad popularizes tablet computing

1992

Was IBM's Simon the first smartphone?

> **Smartphones** are mobile phones that can access the Internet.

opened up to general use and quickly became the first wireless communication craze. Movies like *Smokey and the Bandit* and hit songs on the radio popularized the new medium. The CB airwaves were soon clogged with "good buddies," imitating the slang of long-distance truck drivers. Still, many enjoyed sharing information about the activities of traffic police and doings at the local truck stop, popularizing this early form of social media.

The demand for mobile communications still mounted, prompting the FCC to reallocate TV channels 70 to 83 for a new type of mobile telephone service that gave cell phones their name, analog *cellular radio*. It became available in the United States in 1983. A second generation of digital wireless phones came along in 1995. The FCC declined to select a technical standard. Meanwhile the rest of the world settled on a European standard (*GSM*, short for *global system for mobile communications*) and enjoyed lower prices, wider availability, and more rapid innovation. This left the United States lagging behind the world in telecommunications for perhaps the first time since the invention of the telegraph. Perhaps deregulation would help the United States catch up to the world. Under the **Telecommunications Act of 1996,** restrictions that prevented telecommunications companies in one industry (e.g., wireline telephone) from entering other telecom industries (e.g., cable television) were relaxed. AT&T, Verizon, and a plethora of new entrants including Sprint and T-Mobile were free to compete with one another for cell phone customers. In the decades that followed, falling rates and expanding coverage meant that cell phones began to replace wireline connections. Telephones were transformed from a household utility to a personal communication device.

The Third Screen Arrives

Cell phones have completely replaced landline phones in nearly half of U.S. homes (see Figure 11.1). The introduction of Apple's iPhone in 2007 and the iPad in 2010 began to shift content once confined to computers, televisions, game consoles, and home video screens to mobile platforms. Mobiles have thus joined television (the first screen) and computers (the second screen) as the third screen that is widely viewed in the home.

As we have seen, Apple did not invent the cell phone or the **smartphone,** either, even though it may sometimes seem that way. The idea of adding visual displays to phones is nothing new. That dates back to AT&T's pioneering experiments with television in the 1920s— what we might call a video chat or a "vine" today. AT&T periodically announced from the mid-1960s onward that video phones were going to be "the next big thing," but they failed to catch on back then.

The first cell phone that we might recognize as a smartphone today was IBM's Simon, first introduced in 1992 with a touch screen, data and voice capabilities, and built-in "apps" including calendar, calculator, e-mail, and games. Simon was

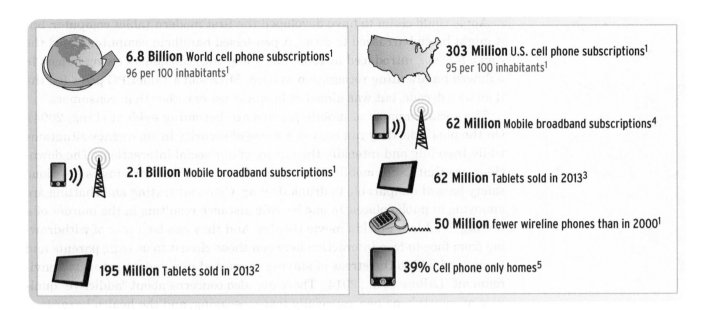

6.8 Billion World cell phone subscriptions[1]
96 per 100 inhabitants[1]

2.1 Billion Mobile broadband subscriptions[1]

195 Million Tablets sold in 2013[2]

303 Million U.S. cell phone subscriptions[1]
95 per 100 inhabitants[1]

62 Million Mobile broadband subscriptions[4]

62 Million Tablets sold in 2013[3]

50 Million fewer wireline phones than in 2000[1]

39% Cell phone only homes[5]

FIGURE 11.1 THIRD SCREENS AROUND THE GLOBE

Sources: [1]ITU (2014).Statistics. Available: http://www.itu.int/en/ITU-D/Statistics/Pages/stat/default.aspx. Based on 2012 data.
[2]http://techcrunch.com/2014/03/03/gartner-195m-tablets-sold-in-2013-android-grabs-top-spot-from-ipad-with-62-share/
[3]http://www.cdc.gov/nchs/data/nhis/earlyrelease/wireless201312.pdf
[4]http://mobithinking.com/mobile-marketing-tools/latest-mobile-stats/b#mobilebroadbandcountries[5]http://www.prweb.com/releases/
DRGTabletForecast/01/prweb10857238.htm

aimed at business users and was too heavy and bulky to catch on with consumers, though. Handheld personal organizers known as *personal data assistants (PDAs)* were introduced at about the same time, and some could be purchased with cell phone add-ons as extra-cost (and extra-bulky) options. Finnish phone manufacturer Nokia came out with a line of cell phones that added e-mail and address book functions in 1996, which we might also call the first smartphone. The Blackberry, first sold in 1999, deserves mention as the handheld telecommunications device that made mobile messaging a popular cultural phenomenon—and a personal obsession for many of its users (Reed, 2010).

HEALTH BENEFIT? Wearable monitoring apps like the Fitbit, shown here, have the potential to combat health problems like obesity—if users take advantage of the feedback and if the data supplied is accurate.

Apple could claim to have developed the first modern tablet computer, but it might be embarrassed to do so. A pen-based handheld computer called the *Apple Newton,* introduced in 1993, was a flop with consumers owing in part to a flawed handwriting recognition system. Microsoft's Tablet PC preceded the iPad by a decade, but was aimed at business users rather than consumers.

The social impacts of mobile phones are becoming evident (Ling, 2004). On the plus side, they can convey a sense of security in emergency situations while traveling and intensify the nature of our social interactions. The downsides are that using mobile phones to talk or text while driving is a serious safety hazard comparable to drunk driving. Constant texting and chatting are annoying in public places, in one horrific instance resulting in the murder of a texting fiend in a Florida movie theater. And they can be a way of withdrawing from face-to-face interaction between those closest to us (e.g., parents and teens) and add to the stress of staying connected in a gadget-saturated environment (LaRose et al., 2014). There are also concerns about "addictive" qualities of smartphone use, especially text messaging, and the health hazards of the electromagnetic radiation that leaks from them (see Chapter 15).

Media Face the Third Screen

The advent of the iPad, even more so than the iPod, iPhone, and Kindle before it, made media executives rethink the future of media distribution. The iPad screen is large enough to make it a viable video player and game device, as well as a music player for iTunes and a passable e-book reader. Many of the hundreds of thousands of "apps" made for the smartphones also play on tablets.

There is great interest in the media industry in apps that deliver versions of print publications to the device. Unlike Web publications that are open to anyone, apps create "walled gardens" that discourage users from surfing away as they read and make it difficult to hotlink into articles without viewing the ads that go with them. That way, publishers also keep possession of proprietary information about reader preferences and activity inside the app, an important resource for advertising sales. The market for mobile video is also promising. Nielsen Media Research (2015) estimates 133 million smartphone owners watch video on their phones each month. That's almost half the number who watch "regular" TV, although the amount of smartphone viewing still pales in comparison to conventional viewership. In 2016, the FCC auctioned off some of the spectrum occupied by broadcast television to make even more space available for mobiles.

Mobile media are making big media money and drawing large audiences. App sales are a big business, grossing $50 million a year. By comparison, that is more than the annual global movie box office. Mobile ads account for over $12 billion a year in ad revenues, and are growing fast (Internet Advertising Bureau, 2015), so fast that they surpassed advertising on conventional PC in 2016. Smartphones and tablets are also making inroads on online purchases, commonly called **m-commerce.** Mobile purchases are over $53 billion a year, and top-rated apps like Facebook draw over 100 million visitors a month (Palmer, 2015). Mobile advertising revenues are gaining on those from conventional personal computer platforms. Thus, before too long,

M-commerce means electronic shopping transactions completed with a cell phone.

Modems (modulator-demodulators) convert digital data to analog signals and vice versa.

STOP & REVIEW

1. Why did the government want to break up AT&T?

2. How has the structure of the telephone industry changed over the years?

3. What led to the development of smartphones?

4. What do we mean by "the third screen"?

5. How are mobiles affecting conventional media?

the third screens on smartphones and tablets may surpass both the first (television) and second (computer) screens at the center of commerce and culture in modern society.

TECHNOLOGY TRENDS: DIGITAL WIRELESS WORLD

Tracing today's technology back to its analog roots can help us better understand tomorrow's technology (see Technology Demystified: How Telephones Work).

From Analog to Digital

The basic way to transmit computer data is to turn on a tiny electrical voltage to represent a 1 and to turn off the voltage to represent a 0. For those few who still rely on dial-up Internet access, the **modem (modulator-demodulator)** converts digital pulses to signals that can be accepted and processed by the

2016

Mobile ads catch up to personal computer ad revenues

Digital subscriber line (DSL) sends high-speed data over existing phone lines.

Broadband refers to high-speed Internet connections.

Packet switching breaks up digital information into individually addressed chunks, or packets.

Technology Demystified

HOW TELEPHONES WORK

An appreciation of Morse's telegraph—and all of the electronic media that followed—begins by harking back to an experiment popular in many elementary schools. The teacher wraps a wire around a big iron nail and hooks the wire up to a battery. Then, she flips a switch that sends electricity flowing through the wire and the nail instantly turns into a magnet that can pick up other nails. When she flips the switch off, the nails drop dramatically back to the table. Telegraph keys turned the flow of electricity on or off, and the magnet caused a thin strip of metal to click up and down in telegraph offices many miles away. The pattern of clicks spelled out the letters of the alphabet in the Morse code. For example, the letter A was a short click (called a *dot*) followed by a long click (called a *dash*), analogous to the 1s and 0s of computer data.

When Alexander Graham Bell called out to Mr. Watson, the air pressure waves from his voice hit a flexible membrane. A short wire was attached to the membrane, and as Bell shouted, the wire bobbed up and down in a beaker of acid, varying the electrical resistance in the circuit in response to Bell's voice. That was the *variable resistance transmitter* that was the basis for Bell's patent. The wire was connected to an electromagnet in the next room, which tugged at a flexible steel reed in response to the varying current. As it vibrated, the steel reed generated air pressure waves that sounded like Bell's voice. The acid was banished after it ruined Bell's

trousers, but varying an electrical current in response to sound pressure waves is still the basic function of all microphones.

As early telephones spread, their many wires darkened the skies above major cities. This led to a technical trick called *multiplexing*. Early multiplexing systems combined telephonic conversations with high-frequency carrier waves to be sent over telephone wires, just as multiple radio channels are transmitted simultaneously through the air (see Chapter 7). Coaxial cable has a single, long wire running down its central axis and a second electrical conductor wrapped around it like a long metal tube. This arrangement keeps unwanted signals from entering the cable and also prevents the cable signals from leaking out and interfering with other communications.

The very first telephone lines were dedicated wires that connected two locations. Later, human operators manually completed calls by plugging patch cords to interconnect callers. Early automatic switches were close relatives of the jukebox. Mechanical arms rotated and jiggled up and down, touching tiny electrical contacts connected to subscribers' telephone wires. Telephone calls are no longer "circuit switched" from end-to-end as they were a century ago, however. **Packet-switching** networks employing Internet technology (see Chapter 10) are gradually taking over, although wireline telephone customers are still connected by a pair of wires to a local switching office that supports the legacy touch-tone and rotary dial phones still in use.

BLINKING LIGHTS Fiber-optic systems carry information at gigabit speeds with few errors. They are replacing coaxial cable and conventional copper phone lines in most wireline networks.

Fiber-optic systems use light instead of electricity to transmit information.

1962

The first digital telephone network is introduced

phone system as if they were sound. The **digital subscriber line (DSL)** transmits digital video as well as data and voice at the speed of millions of bits per second over standard telephone lines. DSL is a **broadband** technology, meaning that it transmits data at speeds of over 768 thousand bits per second.

Digital Networks

If we could redesign the cable TV and wireline telephone networks from scratch today, then we could make them all digital. Digital telecommunication began in 1962 with the introduction of a digital carrier system, known as a *Tl*. It converted voices to digital pulses and back again (see Chapter 1) and reconstructed a simulated voice for the listener on the other end. By taking turns transmitting short digital voice samples from multiple calls, 24 simultaneous conversations were combined on a single copper wire circuit. When used for data instead of phone calls, Tl lines carry 1.5 million bits per second.

That isn't fast enough anymore. The *laser*, invented at Bell Labs, held the key to practical fiber-optic systems by producing intense beams of pure, concentrated light. **Fiber-optic** carriers are ideal for computer data since they are immune to the electrical interference that plagues copper wire systems and thus are relatively error free. Their method for sending information, turning the light source on and off, is well suited to the 1s and 0s of data

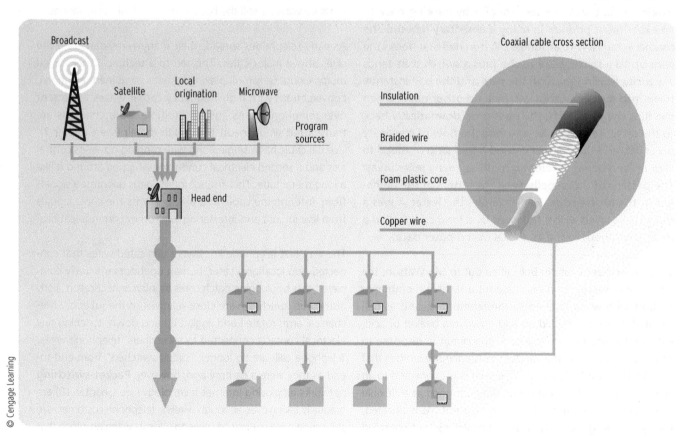

FIGURE 11.2 CABLE TV The cable head end feeds broadcast, satellite, microwave, and local origination signals into a coaxial cable distribution network of trunks, feeders, and drops in individual homes.

communication. Optical fiber signals travel hundreds of miles before they fade and have to be regenerated, further reducing errors.

Now telephone companies and Google are installing fiber-optic system connections directly to the home, offering data transmission speeds of up to 1 billion bits per second to home users. Cable TV companies are also installing fiber optics in their networks but they usually make the final connection to subscribers with a copper-based medium, the **coaxial cable** (see Figure 11.2) connected to **cable modems** inside the home.

Mobile Networks

Mobile communication uses techniques very similar to radio broadcasting (see Chapter 7) except that mobile services operate in different portions of the **communications spectrum** than broadcasters do and use far less powerful transmitters.

> **Coaxial cable** is the high-capacity wire used for cable television transmission.

> **Cable modems** connect personal computers to cable TV systems.

1962

The first communication satellite, *Telstar*, is launched

Technology Demystified

WHISTLING YOUR COMPUTER'S TUNE

To understand how today's digital networks work, we will backtrack to old-fashioned modems. Modems had to use the same sound frequencies that we use to talk, or whistle. We humans can transmit data, just not as fast. For example, to send a 1, whistle a high note (wheet). To send a 0, whistle a low-pitched note (whoot). Or we could make a loud whistle (WHOOT) for a 1 and a soft whistle (whoot) for a 0. (Try it! 1000001 = WHOOT, whoot, whoot, whoot, whoot, whoot, WHOOT—that's the letter A in computer talk!). If you whistle very quickly, you might reach 5 bits per second, although no human listener could keep up.

The trick is to transmit more than one digit each time we whistle. For example, we could make a loud, high-pitched note (WHEET) correspond to 00, whereas a soft, low note (whoot) would be 11 (and wheet = 01, WHOOT = 10). Now, we could whistle up the letter A as follows: WHOOT-WHEET-WHEET-whoot (we added an extra 1 at the right to fill out an eight-bit character, or byte).

Your local telephone company can use the same old phone wires to supply Digital Subscriber Line service, but the phone company installs a new computer card for your line in its central office. By transmitting multiple digits every time we change the signal, we attain speeds of up to 18 million bits per second, enough for several digital television channels. Cable modems work much the same, except that the frequencies they use are farther up in the electromagnetic

spectrum, well beyond the range of our hearing. The cable operator packs the data into unused television channel slots so that it travels to your home right alongside HBO.

Packet switching divides streams of text characters, video, or sound into chunks using the Internet protocol (IP) (see Chapter 10). Since IP is used, Internet telephony also goes by the name *voice-over IP*, or *VoIP* for short. By integrating voice communication and Internet access in the same network, it will eventually be possible to replace expensive telephone switches with cheap, generic packet-switching equipment

© Norman Chan/Shutterstock.com\

NEED FOR SPEED Cable modems offer fast Internet access, but you have to share the connection with your neighbors. DSL connections can be faster but only if users are near the telephone company's central office.

2010

4G cell phones are introduced in the United States

Mobile Evolution. Wireless telecommunications as we know them today are an outgrowth of World War II radar detection systems. Initially, wireless communications were **microwave** systems found at the center of the telecommunications network rather than at the periphery to carry bulk quantities of calls between cities. **Satellite** communication was inspired by science fiction writer Arthur C. Clarke who proposed that three microwave transmitters circling the planet could cover the globe if their orbits (*geosynchronous* orbits 22,300 miles high) were such that their rotation speed matched that of the earth. Communications satellites are essentially microwave transmitters launched into space, beginning with AT&T's *Telstar* satellite in 1962. However, the same principles apply if we put the transmitters atop tall towers, which is what mobile networks do.

The original mobile telephone service operated from a single central antenna in each city and handled only 46 simultaneous conversations at any time. This meant that the 47th caller did not receive a dial tone, which happened often as the subscriber base grew and multiple users contended for the limited number of channels. What was needed was a more efficient way to use scarce channel space.

Cell phones take their name from dividing large service areas into clusters of small zones, or *cells,* each only a few miles across (see Technology Demystified: How Your Cell Phone Works, page 300). The transmitters in each

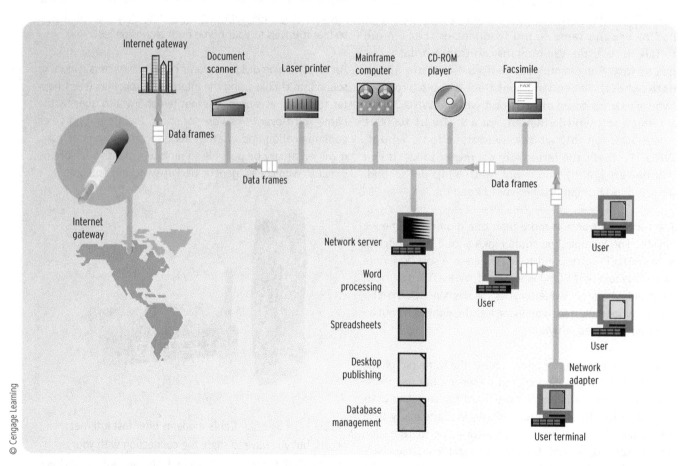

FIGURE 11.3 LAN Local area networks allow multiple users to share peripheral devices, such as printers, and to access software stored on a shared file server. Wireline LANs connect the offices on college campuses. Wireless LANs are a popular means of connecting multiple home computers to a single Internet outlet.

cell are relatively weak, so it is possible to reuse their frequencies in nearby cells without causing interference. As the user moves, the call is handed off to the next cell in the network and automatically reassigned to a new channel.

Cell phone technology has evolved through a series of generations, signified by the capital *G* that mobile providers use in their ads. The first-generation cell phones, the Advanced Mobile Phone System (AMPS), used analog transmission and are now extinct in the United States. Second-generation digital phones introduced the world to text messaging but are also on their way to the trash heap now.

Third-generation (3G) phones were the first to cross a telephone and a handheld computer, with a built-in Web browser and an e-mail service. 3G networks boast broadband transmission speeds of 1–3 million bits per second, enough to send full-color motion pictures through your cell phone, to download your favorite music and video files, and to surf the Web on handheld computers. *Fourth-generation (4G)* phones were introduced in 2010 and covered about four-fifths of the United States as of 2015, although network coverage and average speeds lag other advanced countries such as South Korea and Japan (OpenSignal, 2015). Telecom carriers around the world are adopting the *LTE* (short for *long-term evolution*) standard. The 4G phones treat both voice and data streams as packets of data like those on the Internet. They have theoretical download speeds of up to 100 million bits per second in a speeding car and up to 1 billion bits per second standing still, although actual speeds average only about 10 million bits per second in the United States. That is still enough to support high-definition television streams and video conferencing with our friends.

Wi-Fi. The **Wi-Fi (wireless fidelity)** hotspots that are cropping up everywhere are formally known as *IEEE802.11* (after the standard from the Institute for Electrical and Electronic Engineers that defines the service). Wi-Fi sends the Internet's TCP/IP packets through the air to wireless receivers at speeds of over 1 billion bits per second, so it is a broadband system. New Wi-Fi varieties are entering the market, some boasting the ability to move from one hotspot to another without losing the connection. Cell phones that use Wi-Fi networks, including the Wi-Fi network you may have in your home, allow you to make "free" telephone calls through your home computer connection or anywhere you happen to find an open Wi-Fi connection.

Bluetooth. The desktop version of wireless networking is called *Bluetooth* (named after a tenth-century Danish king with dental issues). It links your earpiece to your phone and your phone to your personal computer, or to wireless printers, scanners, and digital cameras. Early versions had a range of only about 300 feet and a top speed of 1 million bits per second, but advanced versions up the speed limit to 24 million. Bluetooth also connects your smartphone to the information systems that are quickly becoming standard on new automobiles.

Satellite. Voice calls using geostationary satellites like the ones used by satellite TV companies DirecTV and Dish aren't feasible because callers have to wait for the signal to make a 45,000-mile round-trip to the satellite and back. However, wireless voice and data service can also be provided by satellites that fly in low Earth orbit (LEO), a couple of hundred miles up. The lower orbits mean smaller and cheaper receivers with a small whip antenna

Third-generation (3G) cell phones have high-speed data transmission capacity for video and Internet.

Wi-Fi is short for *wireless fidelity*, a standard for wireless data.

HOW YOUR CELL PHONE WORKS

To imagine the structure of a cellular phone network, think of a honeycomb. It is made up of six-sided geometrical shapes (hexagons) arranged in neat rows. The hexagons are the cells, and in the center of each cell is a radio transmitter that "broadcasts" in the frequency range set aside for cellular radio service. The next time you ride an interstate highway, look for elongated pyramids alongside the road made out of metal tubing (they look a little like the Eiffel Tower) topped by triangular antenna arrays that look a lot like a wedge of cheese with beer cans stuck to their sides. Those are the cellular radio towers, and they are connected by wires with the rest of the public phone network through a mobile telephone switching office. Each tower has many different channels to carry calls, and those same channels can be reused at other towers that are one row of cells removed in the hexagonal pattern—that's what makes cellular radio much more efficient than the old mobile phone systems.

When you turn on your cell phone, it lets the nearest antenna know you are there. Then, when a call comes in for you, the system pages your cell phone, it rings, and if you answer your cell phone, it negotiates with the nearest cell site to determine which channel to put you on. Similarly, when you place a call, your cell phone requests a channel for you and transmits the number you send.

Each cell is only a few miles across, and in a speeding automobile you may cross a cell boundary every few minutes. When that happens, the cell you are leaving automatically "hands off" your call to the next cell, which assigns you a new channel so you can continue talking

Digital cell phones use digital compression to reduce the size of the channels that are required. This approach (patented by 1940s movie star Hedy Lamarr) scatters the digital fragments of your conversation over many channels but attaches an identification code to each one so that they may be snatched from the air and reassembled into a phone conversation.

4G systems break up our voice and data into packets and send them out on multiple, closely spaced channels, with the number of channels adapted to the type of transmission (e.g., voice or video).

Now 5G systems are being tested by telecom carriers around the world for introduction in the early 2020s. Like the generations that preceded them, the new phones will offer faster speeds, but the emphasis will be on more efficient use of the communications spectrum to support an expected explosion in wearable devices (see below) and wireless sensors embedded in household appliances and the urban infrastructure, including streetlights and sewer systems.

TOWER OF TALK Our smartphones connect through antennas like this one that are at the center of each of the "cells" in cellular telephone networks.

instead of a dish. Low-flying satellites constantly change their position, so dozens are needed to ensure coverage. Satellite phones have never been an economical option and so are mainly used by foreign correspondents and arctic explorers whose travels take them to places not served by terrestrial cell phone networks.

Locater Technologies. Your smartphone knows where you are and it lets others know, too. Another popular satellite technology is the *GPS (geo-positioning satellite)* system that locates your smartphone's position in the real world by comparing the strength of signals received from three or more satellites turning overhead. GPS features in smartphones also power turn-by-turn directions and locate you and your social networking partners. Wireless networks can also locate your phone by measuring the strength of your smartphone's signal at nearby cell phone towers, Wi-Fi nodes, or Bluetooth transmitters. *NFC (near field communication)* capabilities are being built into smartphones. These are short-range radio transmitters that allow you to send information, such as authorizing a credit card charge, by "bumping phones" with another NFC-equipped device but could also be used to detect your location in relationship to a product display inside a retail store. And if you are temporarily in a location with no satellite, cell phone service, or Wi-Fi signals, sensors in your phone can track the direction and speed of your movement. The ultimate goal seems to be to track our movements within inches, close enough to determine what we are staring at on the supermarket shelf.

More Smartphone Gadgetry. Apple no longer has an exclusive lock on combining voice recognition with artificial intelligence to enliven its personal assistant Siri. Its competitors include Google Now, Cortana (from Microsoft), Alexa (Amazon), and also Hello Barbie, a talking version of the popular doll. The digital assistants are also examples of "cloud computing" (see Chapter 10) in that requests are automatically relayed from a smartphone to a remote computer that processes the request and replies with a synthesized voice.

Wearable accessories monitor your heart rate as you jog or notify you that you have "sweaty palms," indicating that you are feeling anxious about the text message you just received from a significant other. Wristwatch phones and other forms of cell phone jewelry are yet other examples of wearables, although they are still rather bulky-looking and their touch screens are inconveniently small. But gadget makers are already working on cell phone implants that you could wear in you instead of on you, perhaps beginning with surgically installed headphones.

Virtual reality accessories are wearable visual displays that use smartphones to create immersive images of virtual environments. When they debuted in 2016, video games were the most eagerly awaited development (see Chapter 12) but educational and work-related applications are also anticipated. Instead of attending lectures, imagine learning about your career in journalism in a virtual reality environment simulating the newsroom of a major metropolitan newspaper! However, with text messaging already causing traffic fatalities, we shudder to think what mayhem wearers of virtual reality displays will cause. *Augmented reality* is perhaps more practical for mobile applications; it superimposes virtual images on the real-world environment. For example, instant facial recognition searches might pull up the Facebook pages of strangers you run into on the street.

Helen Sessions/Alamy Stock Photo

YOU'RE SO SMART
Smartphones are cell phones that can surf the Internet, play videos, and run video games. And make phone calls.

2016

Virtual reality apps for smartphones

PLACING YOUR CALL

Long-distance networks are monitored at network control centers like this one. Network engineers can intervene to redirect traffic when routes become overcrowded or damaged.

> **Mobile virtual network operators (MVNOs)** offer mobile services by leasing capacity from network owners.

STOP & REVIEW

1. What are the major types of digital data networks?
2. What are the important trends in mobile communications?
3. What is the difference among the generations of mobile services?
4. How can your smartphone's location be identified?
5. What does an MVNO do?

INDUSTRY: THE TELECOM MOSAIC

The telephone industry has an old media—new media transition in progress not unlike that found in the publishing and broadcasting industries. Here, the conventional wireline telephone industry is making a transition to a mobile communications industry as it converges with Internet technology. The infrastructure industry is a complex one, thanks to historic restrictions on the types of businesses that could enter.

The Wireline Industry

Telephone companies can be divided roughly into three categories based on the scope of the calls they carry: international, long distance, and local. *International record carriers (IRCs)* handle long-distance calls between countries. Once, this was the exclusive domain of AT&T in the United States, but now there are dozens of options. *Interexchange carriers* carry domestic long-distance telephone calls made between area codes (such as between Grand Rapids, area code 616, and Detroit, area code 313) and those completed within area codes that cross *local access and transport area (LATA)* boundaries. Verizon, the "new" AT&T, and Sprint are the leaders, but there are hundreds of smaller long-distance companies.

Local telephone service is the domain of the *local exchange carriers (LECs)*, including the three remaining regional operating companies (Verizon, the "new" AT&T, and CenturyLink) and hundreds of local independent phone companies as well as competitive local exchange carriers like Comcast that offer local and long-distance service over their cable networks.

The Wireless Industry

There are four competitors with national cell phone networks. AT&T and Verizon are the largest with over 100 million customers each, followed by T-Mobile and Sprint (FCC, 2015). The industry leaders also do business under wholly owned subsidiaries such as Virgin Mobile and Boost (both owned by Sprint) that target young adults. US Cellular, nTelos, and dozens of others are regional or local providers who own their own networks. Another 50 are "virtual" cellular carriers, called **mobile virtual network operators (MVNOs),** like TracFone Wireless that don't have networks of their own but lease space from the major carriers and resell it.

Cell phone manufacturers are part of the wireless picture, of course. Samsung and Apple are the world leaders in terms of market share (IDC, 2015). "Dumb" cell phones have their features programmed on the computer chips built into the hardware, but smartphones require software, and supplying that software is becoming an important part of the wireless industry. Smartphones have operating systems just as computers do. Nokia, Apple, Research in Motion (makers of the Blackberry), Google, and Microsoft have competing systems, but Google's Android is dominant.

The analogy to computer software extends to the many application programs, or **apps,** that are being developed for smartphones. Although the makers of the operating systems make their own apps, the apps craze has also spawned a cottage industry of more than 100,000 independent developers (see Your Media Career: Mobile Media Star).

CONTENT: THERE'S AN APP FOR US

No one has yet defined genres of smartphone apps, but some broad categories are beginning to emerge. Apps, in the sense of programmed features, also exist for conventional wireline phones and mobile "dumb" phones, although we are not used to thinking of them that way.

Your Media Career

MOBILE MEDIA STAR

The telecommunications industry that runs the third screen is not the best place for our readers to look for a career. Although it is one of the larger industries in the United States with over 800,000 jobs, overall employment is shrinking. Many of the careers offered are in installation and maintenance positions that don't require a college degree. The industry has a large number of customer service positions where many recent college graduates with interpersonal communication skills find employment, although these are relatively low-paying, with average pay of $39,000 per year. The upper ranks of the industry are filled with engineers and computer specialists (BLS, 2016).

However, a variety of interesting niches are opening up that offer ground-floor opportunities not unlike those in the Internet realm a decade ago. For example, students with advanced Web design skills might consider designing apps for smartphones and iPads. Magazine publishers are getting into the app business to repackage content for the mobile user. So even if you can't write computer code, there will be openings for those who can design a readable graphic layout. For those interested in video, producing and editing video content for mobile video channels is cited in the Occupational Outlook Handbook as a growth area for directors and producers (see Chapter 8). Advertising and public relations careers are another entry point.

Career Profile: Paul Scanlan

To prove our point, consider the example of Paul Scanlan, president and co-founder of MobiTV—a provider of video

services to leading mobile carriers—who graduated with a BA in communication from the University of Wisconsin and started out in telecommunications sales. In his case, an entry-level customer service job in the telecommunications industry was his springboard.

MOBILE TV MAN Paul Scanlan majored in communication at the University of Wisconsin and went on to head a mobile television company.

Source: BLS. (2016). Industries at a glance: Telecommunications: NAICS 517. Retrieved February 6, 2016 from: http://www.bls.gov /iag/tgs/iag517.htm.

http://www.mobitv.com/about/ corporate-overview /management-team/

Wireless Apps

Visits to the "app stores" were our starting point in an effort to define app genres. Some of the app categories at Apple fit neatly into the functions of the mass media that we discovered in Chapter 2. The surveillance (news and weather apps), values transmission (education), and entertainment (music and games) functions are well represented. No obvious category matches the interpretation function, but social networking and book apps might fill that niche. Conventional mass media such as newspapers and television were never ideally suited for some other vital functions that we have apps for, including navigation, making money, staying fit, being productive at work, or acting as a flashlight, but we can find many apps for them. Other categories are defined by what you like to do (e.g., lifestyles, favorite play activity).

Over 1.5 million active applications at the Apple app store existed at the time of this writing. Amazon, Google, Blackberry, and Microsoft have app stores of their own. Facebook is by far the most popular app, found on over three-fourths of all Apple and Android phones (see Table 11.1, page 304). Messaging apps [Facebook Messenger, Gmail, and Instagram] are well represented in the top 10.

New sensations continually sweep over the social media realm. Familiar apps like Facebook and Twitter lose some of their appeal as parents, college admissions deans, and prospective employers learn how to use them to monitor younger users. Social media offering unique features such as online photo albums (Pinterest and Tumblr), video (Vine), disappearing messages (Snapchat), and anonymous chatter (Kik and Yik Yak) become attractive as the second or third hourly social media check-ins. We are waiting for virtual reality social media apps to become the next big thing.

> **Location-based services** use information about the location of mobile phone users to tailor content to specific locations.

TABLE 11.1 Top 10 Smartphone Apps

APP	PERCENT OF SMARTPHONES
Facebook	77
Facebook Messenger	62
YouTube	61
Google Play	52
Google Maps	51
Google Search	50
Gmail	46
Pandora	44
Instagram	39
Amazon Mobile	39

Source: comScore Reports December 2015 U.S. Smartphone Subscriber Market Share. Accessed February 7, 2016 from:http://www.comscore.com/Insights/Market-Rankings/comScore-Reports-December-2015-US-Smartphone-Subscriber-Market-Share

Location-Based Services

As the name implies, **location-based services** vary their content according to where we are and add some interesting new dimensions to our favorite online activities. Google Maps represents this genre in the top 10 list, but there are many others. For example, Foursquare can create a map of where our online "friends" are in the real world in case we should want to talk to them face-to-face and Tinder will find potential dates near you. They can also provide helpful directions if we get lost or want to find the nearest restaurant in a strange city. Advertisers are excited about the prospect of location-based advertising and smartphones that can scan barcodes from billboards and in-store displays (see Chapter 14).

M-commerce is just starting to catch on in the United States, although it has been common in Europe and the Far East for years now. The many shoppers who bring their cell phones into stores to search the Web for deals at other retailers or to order out-of-stock sale items online represent one aspect of this trend. Smartphone apps that use their built-in cameras to scan barcodes make this an efficient shopping strategy. Electronic wallets that will let us pay for our fast-food meal by pointing and clicking our cell phone at the cash register are just starting to appear in the United States. Text-payment services will let you transfer cash to those who don't accept credit cards.

Wireline Apps

The oldest app of all, although apparently one going out of style, is the ability to talk to a real person. Basic local telephone service has the acronym *POTS*, for *plain old telephone service*. The POTS functions—dial tone, transmission, and switching—are unchanged since the 1890s. In the 1970s, computerized switching added options like touch-tone dialing and the features we take for granted on our smartphones, including call waiting, speed dialing, conference calling, call forwarding, caller ID, voice mail, automatic redialing of the last party we called, or the last party who called us. Wireline phone companies are beginning to imitate cell phone features, too.

MEDIA LITERACY

SERVICE FOR EVERYONE?

The main issues confronting society regarding the infrastructure industry still revolve around fulfilling the goal of the Graham Act: how to provide affordable service to all. What does that commitment mean in an era of wireless, digital telecommunications?

NO MORE FREE CELL PHONES

Until recently, the 2-year service contract with a "free" cell phone included was the norm in the cell phone industry. Your cell phone was "locked," that is, it could be used only on the network of the carrier that you bought it from for the term of the contract. Carriers locked their phones to recoup the cost of the phone that was offered "for free" or for a deep discount at the time you initiated a service contract. Buying your own phone at the full retail price or a cheap prepaid phone were the only options.

By 2016, all of the major carriers phased out the two-year contract and separated the charges for service and for the smartphone, now paid in 24 monthly installments. In the long run, you can economize by keeping your cell phone longer than 2 years and see your monthly bill drop by $20 or $30, if you can stand the shame of having an out-of-style phone. If you like the illusion of getting a "free" phone you can continue with that type of contract, but you won't be able to return to that option after you switch to the new plan.

CONSUMER ISSUES IN TELECOMMUNICATIONS

The Telecommunications Act of 1996 was intended to untangle ownership rules and line-of-business restrictions and let free market forces prevail for the benefit of consumers. The hope was that industry structure would remain fluid and that competition and continuing technological change would drive down prices. Whether it was policy or technology that was responsible, consumers do have many more options these days. Nearly everyone in the United States is served by at least two mobile phone companies and over 90 percent have four or more options, although rural and low-income areas are considerably less well served (FCC, 2015).

To sort through your cell phone options, there are online comparisons of services available in your area (e.g., http://www.wirelessadvisor.com and www.myrateplan.com). When signing up for a new plan, beware of the practice known as "cramming." That is when the customer service rep you place the order with signs you up for extra-cost services.

Thanks to an agreement between the FCC and cell phone companies, getting an unpleasant surprise when your bill arrives should not happen anymore. Carriers are supposed to notify you when you are getting near your monthly limit. You can also slash your phone bill by sending text messages and voice calls through data networks instead of the phone networks, through services such as Skype. And if you are worried about "maxing out" your minutes, you can also wait until you have a Wi-Fi connection to stream videos or music.

Cell phone theft is still a crime problem in cities. Cell phone carriers put stolen phones on a blacklist that prevents them from being reactivated in the United States, but stolen iPhones in particular demand high prices overseas where they can still be activated on foreign networks. Cell phone carriers have resisted selling new phones with a "kill switch" that will permanently deactivate them, possibly because they fear that will deter thefts to the point that it will cut into their lucrative cell phone theft insurance business. Some Android and the latest iPhones have a kill switch feature that will "turn your phone into a brick." However, that feature only works if you activate it and over half of cell phone users do not (Consumer Reports, 2015). Many have older software that lacks the feature. California and Minnesota require that new phones be sold with the feature activated, but Federal legislation is perhaps needed.

WHOSE SUBSIDIES ARE UNFAIR?

It has long been the practice to subsidize some phone uses at the expense of others. Before it was broken up in 1984, the "old" AT&T diverted revenues from long distance to subsidize local telephone service with the regulators' blessings. Now surcharges of 7 to 12 percent are tacked onto your long-distance bill to support local exchanges; they are sometimes called the regulatory cost recovery charge.

Some users are subsidized as a matter of social policy. Low-income households get special low phone rates, and homeless persons are being provided with cell phones to help them connect to employment and housing. Discount cell phone service with 250 free minutes a month is available for those who receive food stamp or participate in other federal programs for low-income households. The universal service fee that appears on phone bills also subsidizes phone service where costs are unusually high and connects schools, libraries, and hospitals.

There are some other charges you may wonder about. The emergency 911 charge should be self-explanatory: it is paid to local governments to maintain emergency call centers. If you see a Local Number Portability charge, that is to cover the cost of switching numbers from one phone company to another. An item for the Telecommunication Relay Service might also appear. That supports services that complete calls to hearing- and speech-impaired persons. State and local taxes are also tacked on, but these are used for public purposes other than telecommunications services.

WHO CONTROLS THE AIRWAVES?

Historically, licenses to use communication frequencies were awarded in competitive proceedings by the FCC to the companies that were best qualified to operate in the public interest (see Chapter 16). But now free markets are "in" and regulation is "out," and auctions have replaced competitive licensing. Less government bureaucracy is needed to monitor that system, and the proceeds from the auctions go into the public treasury, so theoretically they reduce the tax burden for all. However, the auction proceeds have been unpredictable and subject to speculation. Some "winning" bidders have been bankrupted by the exorbitant sums they paid, whereas other auctions have seen valuable spectrum space go for bargain-basement prices.

Auctions have also meant less government influence in achieving important social goals. The FCC wants to make the speed and cost of the U.S. infrastructure more competitive with that of other developed nations and expand the spectrum space available for smartphones and tablets.

Accordingly, in 2016, the FCC ran an auction for wireless providers to reallocate broadcast television channels. Television occupies some prime spectrum space where signals easily penetrate buildings. Also, the current channel allocations waste valuable space by leaving channels blank to prevent interference. However, the television stations we depend on for local news won't disappear. Rather, the channel allocations will be reorganized to move them closer together to free up space for wireless, and broadcasters will be compensated for their trouble.

911 EMERGENCY One of the fees built into our monthly phone bills supports emergency call centers like this one. The fees are set on a state-by-state basis but may be adjusted by local municipalities.

ALL OF OUR CIRCUITS ARE ... DESTROYED

An information society is inherently dependent on the functioning of its communications infrastructure. The September 11, 2001, terrorist attacks and Hurricane Katrina in 2005 demonstrated both the vulnerability and the resiliency of the telecommunications infrastructure.

The World Trade Center was a major hub for telecommunications. The falling towers destroyed telephone switching equipment serving 175,000 customers in lower Manhattan, cell phone and broadcast antennas atop the Twin Towers, and fiber-optic links in the Trade Center's basement that carried Internet traffic as far away as Washington, D.C. Still, emergency 911 phone service never went down, and portable cell phone towers were quickly trucked in to restore service near Ground Zero. AT&T technicians were able to open lines for outgoing long-distance calls with a few taps on their keyboards, and Verizon was able to quickly reroute local lines for use by government and emergency officials (Guernsey, 2001).

New Orleans residents were not so fortunate after Katrina hit. The floodwaters immediately knocked out the electronics for millions of customers, and more lines, including cell phone towers, continued to fail as their emergency backup power supplies ran out of gas. The Department of Defense was able to restore emergency communication links via satellite, but no one thought to stock extra batteries for the satellite phones that were supposed to provide coordination among emergency agencies. The result was chaos and a pointed reminder of how vital telecommunications infrastructure is to our civilization.

You and I can make these disasters even worse by immediately jumping on the phone to call our relatives, which just further overloads the networks. A helpful suggestion: next time use text messaging to let your family and friends know you survived. Texting puts far less strain on the networks we all rely on in emergencies. You will also start receiving emergency text messages about terror attacks, natural disasters, and child abductions from the president and local authorities as part of a new nationwide alerting system.

MAJOR HUB The 9/11 terror attacks disrupted phone service throughout the Northeast. Service was quickly restored, but the telecommunications infrastructure remains vulnerable to disasters and hacker attacks.

BIG BROTHER IS LISTENING

The 9/11 attacks also produced some changes in telecommunications surveillance laws. As any devotee of TV cop shows knows, law enforcement can listen in on phone conversations and read your e-mail only if they have a warrant from a local judge that establishes a probable cause for their search (i.e., probable evidence that a crime will be discovered). About 1,300 wiretaps a year are authorized in the United States for criminal investigations, mostly for drug-related crimes.

However, information about the time and destination of calls (sometimes called *trap-and-trace information*) is considered less private and is easier to obtain—law enforcement merely has to certify that it is needed for an investigation, with no hearing or probable cause required.

Digital technology complicated telephone surveillance. If the police tap an Internet connection, all they hear is computer noise, not "I'll send you the plans for the nuclear power plant next Tuesday." Copper wires are easy to tap since they radiate electromagnetic energy that can be readily intercepted, but fiber-optic lines are untappable without physically cutting into them. This led law enforcement officials to request—and receive—special access ports to digital networks in the telephone central offices. Under the Communications Assistance for Law Enforcement Act, they have special access to Internet provider networks, too, including those operated by colleges and universities. In the aftermath of the September 11 attacks, Congress passed the USA PATRIOT Act (see also Chapter 16), which significantly expanded the scope of surveillance. Trap-and-trace authority is extended to the Internet so that now law officers without a warrant can demand to see records of the websites you visited. The FBI and the CIA can conduct nationwide roving wiretaps without going through local courts or even naming specific suspects. The law seems to contain loopholes that would allow domestic law enforcement agencies to circumvent restrictions placed on them by claiming the search is covered by the Foreign Intelligence Surveillance Act, under which warrants are issued in secret. Similarly, national security agencies might circumvent the limits on them by obtaining information from domestic law enforcement agencies.

Although we all hope these measures will help crack down on terrorists, civil libertarians fear this legislation could usher in a future society, patterned after George Orwell's *1984,* that will routinely monitor the movements and words of all citizens. These fears were validated amidst an international scandal in 2013 when it was revealed that the U.S. government's super-secret National Security Agency (NSA) had been collecting phone records and cell phone location data on American citizens as well as foreign nationals.

PRIVACY ON THE LINE

So we can't be sure the government isn't listening in on our conversations, but can our nosy neighbors hear us? The Electronic Communication Privacy Act (ECPA) generally assures us that our wireline conversations cannot be tapped or recorded without our permission or legal authorization.

However, the issue of telephone privacy is a complex one, depending upon the technology we use and where we use it. If we use a cordless phone, we lose our legal right to privacy. That's because the frequencies that cordless phones use are in the easily accessible FM radio spectrum and are readily intercepted.

If we use a cell phone, the electronic transmission is protected even though older-model scanners can tune in. By law, newer scanners can't access the cell phone frequencies. That law was enacted precisely to preserve the expectation of cell privacy. But if we carry on our cell phone conversations in a public space, we may lose that expectation. In addition to being rude, we are making public utterances that can be intercepted and recorded, and a sensitive microphone might also pick up the voice of the person we are talking to through our handset.

A new privacy threat comes from cell phone locator services. Cell phone providers have been required to deploy technology that makes it possible to identify the location of cell phones within about 1,000 feet, so that emergency 911 calls can be traced back to their origin. GPS-enabled phones pin down your location even more precisely. Apple collects that data from its iPhones and iPads and reserves the right to share it with their business partners (i.e., sell it for profit); it says so in their "privacy" policy, and a court upheld their right to do so. Smartphone app proprietors are eager to turn location information into cash by selling it to advertisers. Mobile ads can both slow your phone down and deplete your monthly data allowance, so it is advisable to learn how to use privacy settings to manage which services have access to your location data. However, cell phone (and also e-mail) records have also become common items of discovery in divorce proceedings and civil suits. So, it's a good idea to erase your cell phone memory when you turn in your phone, by following the reset procedure in your user's manual.

On the plus side, the Federal Trade Commission has a Do-Not-Call list under the Telephone Consumer Protection Act, passed back in 1991. Now you can sign up online (just do a Google search for "Do Not Call" to find it) to have your phone number protected from telemarketing calls. Violators face fines of $11,000 per call. However, nonprofit organizations, pollsters, market researchers, and companies that you have a prior relationship with (such as your college's or university's alumni fund-raisers) are exempt. And if you respond to a mail solicitation to request "further information" about a product or service, that establishes enough of a prior relationship to invite telemarketers to call. Cell phones get special protection from an especially annoying privacy invasion, so-called robo calls containing pre-recorded messages from politicians and marketers. However, a loophole in the law deems that you give consent for robo calls if you respond to a request for your cell phone number. The Truth in Caller ID Act prohibits the use of phony caller IDs by telemarketers. However, telemarketers have learned to disguise their true identities by forwarding calls through foreign countries over the Internet, making it difficult for both consumers and the FTC to track down the offenders.

Another privacy option is to encrypt your calls. Digital cell phone calls are scrambled and some of them scatter pieces of your conversation across a wide range of channels, making them difficult to intercept. Add-on encryption systems (Google "cell phone encryption") are available. But anything that can be scrambled can also be unscrambled with a powerful enough computer, and the NSA has the computers that can do just that. Or, you can protect your cell phone with a password that will lock the phone after repeated attempts to open it. In a controversial case in 2016, Apple refused to help the FBI open an iPhone that was involved in a terror attack, claiming that user privacy was part of the Apple "brand." Ultimately, the FBI obtained access by exploiting a security flaw unknown to Apple, but that flaw afflicted only a small number of iPhones. Still, other iPhones might have other vulnerabilities so you cannot count on the Apple brand to hide your data. So ask yourself, what do you have to hide from the FBI?

STOP & REVIEW

1. What are some major categories of apps?

2. What are important mobile communication issues for consumers?

3. What are the main issues in spectrum allocation?

4. Who receives subsidized telephone service in the United States?

5. What are the threats to phone privacy?

SUMMARY & REVIEW

WHAT WERE THE ORIGINS OF TODAY'S TELECOMMUNICATIONS INDUSTRY?

Morse's telegraph and Bell's telephone were the first electronic communications networks. Bell founded the company that was to become AT&T. AT&T's effort to monopolize led to government regulation that shaped the entire telecommunications industry for decades. Important interventions included the Graham Act of 1921, the Communications Act of 1934, and the Modified Final Judgment of 1984 that forced AT&T to divest itself of the companies (RBOCs) that provided local telephone service, while retaining its long-distance network.

HOW DID MOBILE PHONES DEVELOP?

Before radio broadcasting began, the medium was used primarily for mobile wireless communication with oceangoing vessels. Although mobile telephone service dates back to 1946, early systems were plagued by insufficient capacity. In 1983, cellular radio service was introduced in the United States, expanding the capacity of mobile telephone networks. Consumer smartphones originated in the late 1990s, representing the convergence of cell phones and personal data assistants.

WHAT ARE THE IMPACTS OF MOBILE COMMUNICATIONS?

Mobile communication devices like the iPhone and iPad are the third screen, which, in addition to television and computer screens, offer a wide variety of entertainment and information services to their users. They are rapidly replacing conventional wireline phones and converging with Internet services to enable new forms of mobile transactions. Mobile media offer both threats and opportunities to the business models of conventional mass media.

WHAT ARE THE TRENDS IN DIGITAL NETWORKS?

High-speed DSL, coaxial cable, and FiOS have replaced the pokey telephone modems of yesterday. Virtually all types of communication, including our daily phone conversations, are being converted to digital formats that can be transmitted as Internet data through packet switching.

HOW ARE WIRELESS DATASERVICES EVOLVING?

3G cell phones made wireless Internet access commonplace. Wi-Fi is the location-specific wireless Internet technology found in coffee shops and home offices. Bluetooth is the short-range wireless option for cell phone ear pieces and wireless printers. 4G cell phone networks offer high-quality video including two-way video services.

HOW IS THE INFRASTRUCTURE INDUSTRY ORGANIZED?

Wireline telephone companies are categorized by the scope of service they offer: international, long distance, or local. There are four national mobile carriers: AT&T, Verizon, Sprint, and T-Mobile. MVNOs resell discount cell phone services. Companies that provide software and apps for smartphones are a fast-growing segment of the telecommunications industry.

WHAT ARE THE TRENDS IN TELEPHONE SERVICES?

Music downloads and television services are extra-cost options that are being popularized by smartphones connected to 4G networks. Smartphone apps fill a wide variety of entertainment, information, and personal productivity needs. Location-based services and mobile commerce are new categories of interactive applications unique to the third screen. Social media are rapidly moving to mobile platforms.

HOW DO TELECOMMUNICATION POLICIES AFFECT CONSUMERS?

A recent policy change encouraged cell phone operators to unlock cell phones and helped bring about the end of the 2-year service contract. Other efforts to increase competition in telecommunications services have increased the number of options available to consumers and have driven down prices in some instances. Government regulations subsidize basic telephone and Internet service for low-income families, rural residents, schools, libraries, and hospitals.

WHAT CHALLENGES DO TELECOMMUNICATIONS NETWORKS POSE FOR SOCIETY?

Society must decide how to allocate scarce resources, such as the communications spectrum, to competing interests. The growing reliance on the information infrastructure makes society increasingly vulnerable to technical disruption of telecommunications providers. Advanced digital technology also poses barriers to the legitimate electronic surveillance needs of law enforcement officials while at the same time raising the specter of excessive snooping on ordinary citizens.

THINKING CRITICALLY

ABOUT THE MEDIA

1. Are smartphones and tablets making PCs and TVs obsolete? Explain.

2. How has your smartphone changed your life for better? For worse?

3. Now that you can have a two-way wrist TV, what would you use it for?

4. Describe how a cell phone works so that a 12-year-old child could understand it.

5. What will your mobile phone be like in 2020?

6. What is the justification for taking spectrum away from television and giving it to mobile providers?

7. Now that you know your cell phone is a threat to your privacy, what will you do?

KEY TERMS

apps (p. 303)

broadband (p. 295)

cable modem (p. 297)

coaxial cable (p. 297)

common carrier (p. 291)

communications spectrum (p. 298)

digital subscriber line (DSL) (p. 295)

Federal Communications Commission (FCC) (p. 291)

fiber optic (p. 296)

infrastructure (p. 289)

location-based service (p. 304)

m-commerce (p. 294)

microwave (p. 298)

mobile virtual network operators (MVNOs) (p. 302)

modem (modulator-demodulator) (p. 295)

packet switching (p. 295)

patent (p. 290)

regional Bell Operating Companies (RBOCs) (p. 291)

satellite (p. 298)

smartphone (p. 292)

Telecommunications Act of 1996 (p. 292)

third generation (3G) (p. 299)

universal service (p. 290)

vertical integration (p. 290)

Wi-Fi (wireless fidelity) (p. 299)

VIDEO GAMES

LEARNING OBJECTIVES

After studying the topics in this chapter, you will be able to:

1. Summarize the changes in the video game industry that pushed games to mainstream adoption.
2. Determine whether video games are a threat to society or a scapegoat for its problems.
3. Comment on the impact of virtual reality, augmented reality, and artificial intelligence technology on game play.
4. Appraise the barriers of entry for amateur developers in the video game marketplace.
5. Discuss the difficulties that the video game industry has had in attracting female players and developers.
6. Explain what is meant by "serious games."

HISTORY: GETTING GAME

Opening Play

Gaming may seem like the newest of new entertainment media, but it is arguably the oldest. "Senet," dating back to 3000 BCE in ancient Egypt, involved a race to a finish line while overcoming various barriers and so shares key play elements with video games in the "Mario Brothers" series. Chess, a forerunner of strategy and role-playing games of our day, goes back over 1,000 years (Parlett, 1999). Early nineteenth-century war simulations played by Prussian army officers as well as family game room staples like "Monopoly" and penny arcade pinball machines are other forerunners of today's video games (Egenfeldt-Nielsen, Smith, & Tosca, 2008; Kent, 2001).

If we consider a **video game** to be one played on a television screen, then the first was "Chase," developed by inventor Ralph Baer in 1967. However, if we define video games as **digital games** played on a visual display created by a digital computer, then the honors might go (there are competing claims) to a tic-tac-toe game, "Noughts and Crosses," made by A. S. Douglas in 1952 (Winter, 2006), or the "Spacewar!" game created by Steve Russell and two other MIT students in 1962 (Kirriemuir, 2006).

Nolan Bushneil created an arcade version of "Spacewar!" called "Computer Space," which was the first widely available arcade video game. However, in a world full of gaming novices, it proved too difficult

Ethan Miller/Getty Images

VIDEO GAMES are changing fast as console games like "Call of Duty" give way to mobile games.

MEDIA THEN··· MEDIA NOW

3000 BCE
> Ancient Egyptians play Senet game

1967
> "Chase" introduced as the first video game

1972
> Pong popularizes arcade video games

1976
> Mattel introduces handheld games

1977
> Atari 2600 console popularizes video games in the home

1980
> "Dungeons & Dragons," first multiplayer Internet game

1982
> Trip Hawkins founds game maker Electronic Arts

1993
> Congressional hearings held over violence in video games

1999
> "EverQuest" popularizes MMORPGs

> The Sega Dreamcast is the first console to connect to the Internet

2006
> Nintendo's Wii is introduced

2016
> Virtual reality games become a reality

3000 BCE

Ancient Egyptians play Senet game

1967

"Chase" introduced as the first video game

> A **digital game** is a game in which a digital computer facilitates the game play.

> A **video game** uses a television or similar screen to display the game play.

to play in its time. The first turning point for video games was the release of a second arcade game made by Bushnell in 1972, an electronic version of table tennis called "Pong," triggering the first of many video game booms. Bushnell founded Atari to manufacture and distribute the coin-operated version, and the company became a dominant force in the first golden age of video games that followed (Kirriemuir, 2006). Coin-operated arcade games like "Space Invaders," "Asteroids," and "Pac-Man" popped up in bars and shopping malls everywhere over the next decade.

Home Game

Games entered the home to capitalize on the arcade game craze. The first home video game console, "Odyssey," went on sale the same year "Pong" hit the arcades. A glut of "Pong" imitations and the introduction of second-generation consoles led to the first great crash in the video game market in 1977.

The second generation included the Atari 2600 console that accepted cartridges that stored the games; it enabled consoles to play many different games, and players could add new titles as they pleased, the same basic model that continues with consoles today. This innovation also encouraged independent software developers like Activision to begin making cartridges for the best-selling consoles. Popular home games built on arcade hits of the day and introduced titles such as "Mario Brothers" that have become mainstays.

A popular arcade game, "Donkey Kong," also marked the debut of Nintendo in the American home market. Japanese game artist Shigeru Miyamoto created the Mario character (originally called "Jumpman") for

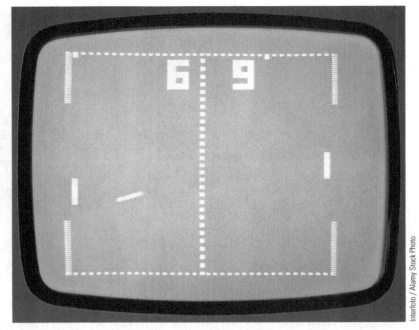

Interfoto / Alamy Stock Photo

YOUR TURN "Pong" was the first hit arcade video game. Together with versions made for home consoles, it launched the development of video games.

that game. However, a glut of consoles, a price war among console makers, competition from personal computers and independent developers, and hastily designed and unoriginal games led to a second great crash in the video game market in 1983. Notable among the failures was "E.T the Extraterrestrial," which, despite its tie-in to a blockbuster movie, was so hastily developed that it is sometimes cited as the worst video game ever made. The crash eventually forced all of the console makers of that era to sell out or go bankrupt (Kent, 2001). Many thought that video games were dead.

Personal Computers Get in the Game

The integration of video games with personal computers was a turning point in the development of both. The Commodore 64 personal computer featured color graphics and the same game controllers as the popular Atari game console. The Commodore inspired former Apple employee Trip Hawkins to found video game software maker Electronic Arts in 1982, a company that would go on to be the largest video game publisher.

By the end of the 1980s, personal computers had colorful displays and sound, and graphics options were available to make them viable game machines. Computer games became one of the main reasons for buying home computers.

"Dungeons & Dragons," a role-playing game initially played on paper with miniature figurines, inspired multiplayer games called *MUDs* (multi-user dungeon). Roy Trubshaw and Richard Bartle are often credited with developing the first one. A version was placed on ARPANET, the forerunner of today's Internet (see Chapter 10), in 1980, giving it a claim to be the first multiplayer game on the Internet (Koster, 2002; Mulligan, 2000).

1972

Pong popularizes arcade video games

MindTap

Start with a quick warm-up activity.

1977

Atari 2600 console popularizes video games in the home

1982

Trip Hawkins founds game maker Electronic Arts

1980

"Dungeons & Dragons," first multiplayer Internet game

MARIO MAKER Japanese video game designer Shigeru Miyamoto created the original Mario video game character. The "Mario Brothers" series is one of the best-selling games of all time.

1999

"EverQuest" popularizes MMORPGs

> **Massively multiplayer online role-playing games (MMORPGs)** are online games that thousands play at the same time in a virtual world.

1976

Mattel introduces handheld games

"MegaWars I" was something of a hit in the pre-Internet era. It was hosted by an early online service called *CompuServe* (Koster, 2002). Despite the crude graphics of early online games, the first reports of financial and family ruin related to excessive online gaming began to emerge. In 1993, a virtual "rape" was committed in an online role-playing game, drawing wide attention to the online gaming community phenomenon (Dibbel, 1993). "Quake" was launched in 1996 at just the time that the Internet was becoming a social phenomenon. But "Quake" was soon topped by "EverQuest," which opened for business in 1999 and quickly came to define the category known as **massively multiplayer online role-playing games (MMORPGs)** (Koster, 2002).

Gear Wars

Two years after the great crash of 1983, the third generation of home console systems kicked off continuing rounds of technological "one-upmanship" among console manufacturers to improve the speed and graphical richness of play that continue to this day. The Nintendo Entertainment System (NES) stood out with an innovative control pad in place of joysticks, and a new business model: Nintendo sold the game system at a loss but made profits on the software. Fourth-generation consoles of the mid-1980s featured built-in CD players to add video action to games (Kent, 2001). Fifth-generation machines with still faster, but overpriced, hardware were slow to catch on, but 3-D graphics revived play. Nintendo scored a hit with "The Legend of Zelda: Ocarina of Time," recognized by some as one of the best video games of all time (IGN Entertainment, 2010). The sixth round of console wars broke out in 1999 with a focus on higher resolution graphics and Internet gaming. It saw the introduction of the all-time console sales leader, the Playstation 2, as well as the entry of Microsoft into the battle with Xbox. Sony pushed gaming further out of the child's playroom and into the adult mainstream with titles like "Grand Theft Auto: San Andreas."

Game consoles generally stayed a step ahead of personal computers by incorporating advanced graphics and processor components. Still, PCs remained viable game machines with the addition of improved audio and CD-ROMs. "Doom" was a PC game that first popularized the first-person shooter (Kent, 2001). By the mid-1990s, computers were able to keep up with game consoles and, with the addition of sound and graphics enhancements and suitable controllers, could emulate the console game experience.

Handheld games also evolved over the years. They were pioneered by Mattel in 1976, and portable games like "Simon" (an electronic version of the childhood favorite Simon Says) became big sellers (Kent, 2001). The category took off with the release of the Nintendo Game Boy in 1989 that caused a sensation with "Tetris" and went on to sell over 100 million units worldwide (Edwards, 2009).

Games and Society: We Were Not Amused

Are games a threat to society? If so, the threat is nothing new. In twelfth-century Britain, chess was so popular that it was considered a moral hazard that undermined the development of youth (Riddler & Denison, 1998). Similar concerns emerged in the early 1980s as tales of marathon games starting during school hours led to local bans on arcade play during school time (Kent, 2001).

Another concern about video games has been the possible effects that the violent and sexual behavior they contain may have on children (see More Harmful Than TV? page 422). The first public outcry against video games was heard in 1976 with the release of "Death Race 2000," a racing game in which players earned points by running over people. Improved graphics in third-generation machines led to more graphic violence, notably in "Mortal Kombat." Concerns about the impact of violence on children led to congressional hearings in 1993 (Jenkins, 1999) and a rating system for video games that later evolved into the Electronic Software Review Board (Anderson, Gentile, & Buckley, 2007).

For a while, the game industry was praised for its efforts to police itself. However, calls for content restriction were renewed after the 1999 Columbine High School massacre in which two teens, reportedly obsessed with "Doom," gunned down 12 of their classmates (Kent, 2001). Each new release in the popular "Grand Theft Auto" series also provokes criticism for increasingly graphic displays of violent crimes and other antisocial behavior. The media seemed to reflexively assign blame to games for every outbreak of violence, although a direct link is difficult to establish (see Chapter 15). Something of a "smoking gun" was found in the case of Adam Lanza, the Sandy Hook Elementary School killer, who had a video game called "School Shooting" and various first-person shooter games on his computer. However, his visits to real-life shooting ranges with his mother might also have fed his violent fantasies.

Another recurring theme of game critics is the lack of games for girls and the sexual stereotypes that portray females as either victims or sex objects. Early video games were almost exclusively a male domain, raising concerns that girls would lag behind in an increasingly computer-oriented society. In 1996, "Barbie Fashion Designer" was the most successful game, demonstrating that there was a female market, although the stereotypical female pursuit featured in

MindTap

Read, highlight, and take notes on the complete chapter text in a rich interactive online platform.

WRITE TO CONGRESS "Mortal Kombat" was a hit title for third-generation machines. The gory violence led to congressional hearings about the effects of video games on children and to the establishment of the Electronic Software Review Board.

Arcade Images / Alamy Stock Photo

1993

Congressional hearings held over violence in video games

the game (i.e., fashion design) raised further concerns about the effects on the life aspirations of young girls (Cassell & Jenkins, 1998). However, games continue to be populated by female sex objects and victims and designed mainly by males (Kafai et al., 2008). The long-running "Gamergate" controversy highlights antagonism toward women in the gaming community and unwillingness to let criticism of sex roles in games "spoil the fun."

The New State of Play

2016

Virtual reality games become a reality

> **Virtual reality** is a computer-generated environment that immerses the user in a make-believe world.

Game software is a $15 billion annual industry in the United States. That's more than either the domestic network television or film industries. Gaming reaches deeply into society (see Figure 12.1): About two-fifths of U.S. residents play video games 3 or more hours a week. The average age of gamers is now 35, and 44 percent of the gamers are female (ESA, 2015).

The gear wars continue into the seventh (PS 3, Xbox 360, Nintendo Wii) and eighth generations (Wii U, Xbox One, and PS4) with consoles packing multiple processors running in parallel, capacious hard drives, broadband Internet connections, high-definition graphics, and voice and gesture controls. However, that may be game over for console wars and for the business model in which gamers buy physical copies of software for the latest game players. For the first time in 2014, sales of games in physical formats were outpaced by digital sales, including subscriptions to online games, digital downloads, mobile game apps, and social network gaming (ESA, 2015). Computer chip makers are planning to introduce higher powered technology for personal computers that could make consoles obsolete. **Virtual reality** games (see "Virtual Reality Enters the Game," below), introduced in 2016, required high-end computers to play. Also, there is a shift in progress to mobile games played on smartphones and tablets, rather than consoles or dedicated handheld game machines.

Console game fans also have rising expectations about production values of popular games, some of which might be described as interactive films with characters that seem like real actors. The latest in the "Call of Duty" series registered more sales in its first week than most blockbuster Hollywood films do in their entire run. As a result, game development budgets are soaring into the tens of millions and top game designers are being treated like Hollywood producers. A blockbuster mentality dominates the console side of the business that means fewer, more expensive games than in the past, and a tendency to produce reliable sequels of popular games rather than risky original productions.

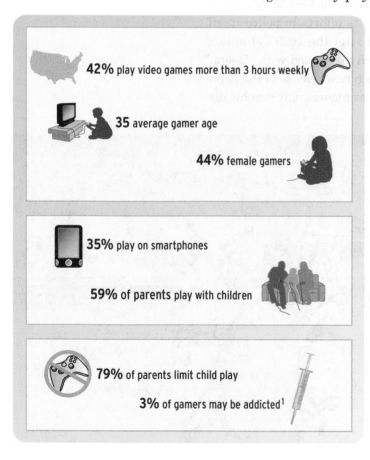

42% play video games more than 3 hours weekly

35 average gamer age

44% female gamers

35% play on smartphones

59% of parents play with children

79% of parents limit child play

3% of gamers may be addicted[1]

FIGURE 12.1 WHO'S GOT GAME?

Source: Except as noted, Electronic Software Association. 2013 Sales, Demographic and Usage Data. Available: http://www.theesa.com/facts/pdfs/ESA_EF_2013.pdf.
[1]Ferguson, C. J., Coulson, M., & Barnett, J. (2011). A meta-analysis of pathological gaming prevalence and comorbidity with mental health, academic and social problems. *Journal of Psychiatric Research*, 45(12), 1573-1578. Available: http://www.christopherjferguson.com/Video%20Game%20Addiction.pdf

The game apps, downloads, and social media games are inspiring new directions in gaming. One trend is toward relatively simple **casual games** like "Candy Crush Soda Saga" that can be played to conclusion in short periods of time. MMORPGs have been suffering from subscriber losses. This has led many, including long-running favorite "World of Warcraft" as well as upstarts like "Clash of Clans," to adopt a *freemium* model in which game publishers profit from selling premium features, advanced levels, or longer play sessions from inside games that are initially free to play. Ads placed in games and "crowdsourced" games developed with online contributions from prospective players are other new business models. There is also growing interest in watching others play games rather play them ourselves. YouTube channels, live feeds of game play through Twitch, and "e-sports" competitions are becoming a popular entertainment form in their own right. So as the popularity of gaming continues to fluctuate, its future direction continually evolves as rival gaming paradigms compete for screen time. Game on!

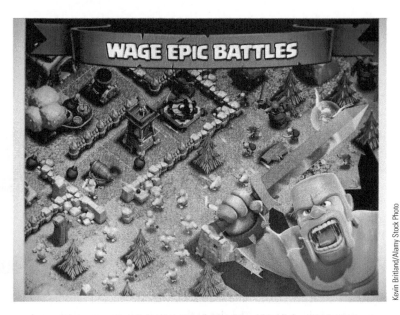

Kevin Britland/Alamy Stock Photo

MOBILE MAYHEM. Popular downloadable games for smartphones like "Clash of Clans" threaten conventional console games but also expand the market for video games to new groups of players.

> **Casual games** are informal games that can be completed in short periods of time.

TECHNOLOGY TRENDS: THE NEXT LEVEL

Generations

First-generation games like the home version of "Pong" had their programs hardwired into the consoles. The second generation was cartridge machines so that consoles could play a wider variety of games. Still, the games were hardwired inside the cartridges and therefore relatively expensive to produce, and the cartridges were not interchangeable between consoles. Graphics were limited to crude shapes and a narrow range of colors, whereas sound effects were mainly buzzes and beeps.

The gear wars that have played out over the past 40 years were largely defined by the number of computer bits that the central processing units of the game consoles could process simultaneously. For example, the third-generation NES was an 8-bit machine, whereas sixth-generation products like the Xbox upped the ante to 128. The latest consoles use multiple parallel processors that work in tandem. The number of bits is important because it determines the resolution of the graphics and the speed with which new images can be projected on the player's screen. Current game machines create high-definition images and so need to be especially powerful since both the size and the vertical resolution of the images have increased dramatically over early games designed for old-fashioned analog TV sets. Also important is the speed at which the game's central processing unit can move the bits in and out (the "clock speed" in computer technology terms) of the processor while implementing

STOP & REVIEW

1. What is the difference between a video game and a computer game?

2. Why did the video game market crash in the 1970s and again in the 1980s?

3. How have video games affected society?

4. How is the business model for video games changing?

SECOND GENERATION The Atari 2600 was the leading console of the second generation of video games. The slot at the upper middle accepted game cartridges so that players could build libraries of games.

1999

The Sega Dreamcast is the first console to connect to the Internet

> **Game engine** refers to the software components that govern the physical properties of the game world, interact with the user, and render images for the player.

instructions from the game software's **game engine** (see Technology Demystified: A Look Under the Hood at Game Engines).

Other game components have progressed over time as well. Graphics accelerators speed up the rendering of images so that games can instantly generate new images, including high-definition images in the latest gear, in response to controller input. Likewise, sound cards have advanced to provide stereo surround sound. The game storage medium is another defining characteristic, progressing from cartridges, to built-in computer memory, to CDs, DVDs, and Blu-ray high-definition DVDs. The latest consoles include high-capacity hard drives so that they can store not only games but also movies and other multimedia downloads so that they can function as home entertainment centers. Later generations of consoles also feature Internet connections, beginning with the Sega Dreamcast in 1999 (CNET, 2014).

Personal computers can be made into game machines as well. To do so, game fans either start with the most advanced personal computers on the market or else upgrade standard computers with high-end components, including the computer's central processing unit, graphics, and sound cards. Add a custom controller, a Blu-ray drive, headphones, and a big-screen HDTV and it might be possible to top the performance of the latest video game consoles. But that could cost several thousand dollars. Since console manufacturers sell their products for a few hundred dollars and hope to make money on the software, most gamers are content to enjoy the relative "bargains" offered by Microsoft, Sony, and Nintendo.

No More Consoles?

Why not just stream video games the same way we stream videos from YouTube and get rid of the consoles? OnLive will help you do that. An outgrowth of the cloud computing trend on the Internet (see Chapter 10), Sony's PlayStation Now, Twitch.TV, and other services allow players to get in the game without a console, streaming games through a browser plug-in or downloading them for a modest monthly fee. Smartphones, tablet computers, and Internet-connected TV sets are other console killers as more and more games are downloaded as apps rather than sold as game software in a box.

No More Button Pushing?

Joysticks were the popular controllers for first- and second-generation games, but players had to hold the base in one hand and push the joystick with the other, which felt unnatural. The NES's controller featured a

A LOOK UNDER THE HOOD AT GAME ENGINES

There's nothing magical about video game consoles; they are really just personal computers with high-end components. The video game magic that animates characters performing impossible feats in exotic settings in response to our every command comes from a collection of elements in the game's software generally described as the *game engine*.

The game engine is a development tool for game designers. It handles the basic functions that make the game operate, such as receiving user commands from the controller to record pulls on the trigger and running the graphical displays that keep track of the number of monsters killed. After computing and displaying your score, the game engine loads the image of the next monster and the dungeon it lives in and makes the monster move through the virtual environment. The physics engine makes the elements obey the rules of the physical world. It wouldn't be realistic if the monster walked through the torture rack in the middle of the dungeon (unless, of course, that is the monster's magical power), and the game engine governs interactions between objects to prevent collisions and overlaps. After you shoot the monster, you expect it to fall to the floor under the force of gravity (unless, of course, the monster lives in outer space), so the physical properties of the in-game environment are also determined by the game engine using parameters set by the game designer. Finally, the game engine renders the images

and sounds so that you can see the impact of your silver bullets on the monster, watch him fall, hear him scream, and watch him bleed. The artificial intelligence of games like "Grand Theft Auto" is also built into the engine. So if the dying monster turns to you and says, "Argh, couldn't we start by shaking hands," that's the game engine talking.

Game engines are thus somewhat analogous to personal computer applications like PowerPoint. They enable a range of basic functions (e.g., slide transitions) that are selectable (e.g., fade) and modifiable (e.g., slow fade) by the designer. However, the content (e.g., final project presentation) comes from the mind of the designer herself. In the case of video games, the content includes the characters and the environments they live in, and the shapes, lighting, colors, and textures that are used to construct them. These are created in separate programs such as Maya and 3DS Max and then imported as "assets" that can be summoned by the game engine.

Video game engines are reusable. As games become more complex and expensive to create, developers rely more on commercially available engines like "Unreal" that they can buy off the shelf rather than start from scratch with their own game engine. For the beginner, there are point-and-click game engines like "Torque Game Builder" and "Unity 3D" that require little computer programming.

---

cross-shaped pad that made it much more comfortable to navigate the game environment, although avid gamers sometimes developed calluses on their fingertips from using them. An astonishing variety of controller options are available. Some are built around specific games, including steering wheels, throttles, and brake pedals for auto racing games and small musical instruments for music games like "Rock Band." Dance pads and light guns are other popular controller accessories that transmit player actions to game software.

Or make your body the controller. Nintendo's wireless Wii controller was a significant innovation, sensing the natural gestures of the player and converting them to actions inside the game. Infrared transmitters, similar to those in TV remote controls, track the position of the controller, and another sensor keeps track of how fast the controller is changing its speed. A Bluetooth connection similar to those that connect "hands-free" cell phone earpieces relays signals from the handheld "nunchuk" to the game console. Microsoft's Kinect system uses cameras to track the player's motions and

2006

Nintendo's Wii is introduced

PUTTING YOU IN THE GAME. Virtual reality gear immerses players in game action and promises to transport users to a new level of excitement. When combined with motion sensing controllers and tactile feedback, VR comes close to reproducing real life experience.

to embed the user's "character" in 3-D environments. Rather than tracking a single motion with a device held by the player (e.g., waving the Wii wireless controller back and forth), a range of body motions are automatically translated into the game environment.

Touch screens are another controller trend found in the PlayStation 3DS, PlayStation Vita, and the Wii U controller. Tablet computers that use the entire screen as a controller are other examples. Wii U is equipped for near field communication, a technology that allows gamers to interact with figurines and real-world toys with built-in miniature radio transmitters.

Virtual Reality Enters the Game

Video games were originally developed as TV accessories and have made the transition to high definition, sometimes played across three screens simultaneously to enhance the experience. To revive flattened sales, the game industry would like to give you the thrill of immersing yourself in the game, instead of watching a two-dimensional image on a screen across the room.

You have probably enjoyed a 3-D movie by now (see Chapter 8), although you may have been annoyed, or even nauseated, by the glasses you had to wear. Portable video game players like the Nintendo 3DS Gameboy do away with the glasses by putting thin layers of lenses over the screen that direct images as viewed from slightly different angles to each eye, creating a 3-D effect. Another approach is to project images taken from slightly different angles into your left and right eyes through a head-mounted display unit.

The Pokémon Go™ smartphone app introduced millions to **augmented reality** in which the game world invades real life by superimposing game elements on real world images viewed in the smartphone screen. The Nintendo® app builds on the trend towards mobile gaming that replaces both conventional consoles and dedicated handheld game players in favor of ubiquitous mobile devices that can quickly drive adoption of new games through fun social media interactions. Other augmented reality devices like the Epson Moverio project images onto glasses, similar to the (now discontinued) Google Glass headset. Current products use smartphones to power the graphics. Microsoft's HoloLens promises 3D holographic images and will work wirelessly from any computing device, but a consumer version is still a few years off.

Instead of superimposing game images on the real world, **virtual reality (VR)** superimposes the real you in a virtual world. There are many options, ranging from Google Cardboard for a few dollars, to Samsung's Gear VR for about $100, to Oculus Rift (now owned by Facebook) for a few hundred dollars. Lower-end devices work through your smartphone. Google Cardboard,

Augmented reality
superimposes game objects on a real-world environment.

Chesnot/Getty Images News/Getty Images

perhaps better described as a viewer for 360 degree photos than "true" VR, is basically a foldable cardboard holder for your Smartphone that you hold up to your eyes. Gear VR provides a cradle for your smartphone in its headset. Top gear connects to personal computers (Oculus Rift) or game consoles (Sony's PS VR) to support fast-changing graphics as you turn your head.

In addition to the quality of the graphics, motion sensing technology is what defines the virtual reality experience. Basic VR devices rely on the limited-motion sensors that come with your cell phone, but give many users motion sickness when movements on the screen do not match our internal sensations. More sophisticated, less nauseating, systems track head motions precisely through external sensors, such as those found in advanced game systems. Microsoft is partnering with Oculus Rift to integrate its Kinect system into VR game play so that players can gain the illusion of moving around in the virtual world. The Xbox One version of Kinect reads lips, can recognize spoken commands, and tells if you are afraid by monitoring your heartbeat. It uses reflections from objects in the room made by fast-pulsing infrared light (invisible to the human eye but not the controller) that track you as you play and detects subtle changes in your motions and muscles so that it can, for example, estimate the force behind a virtual punch you throw at an in-game opponent.

Future VR enhancements will detect the emotional responses of players by analyzing their facial expressions and physiological responses. Games could pick up the pace as you play if they detect you are getting bored or turn down the action if you look overwrought. Sensor-filled wearable harnesses and full-body suits may track fine-tuned movements, such as those involved in throwing a spiral pass with a virtual football. The complete VR experience will extend beyond sight and sound to give us the tactile sensations of bumping and grinding through the craters of Mars or perhaps a whiff of a zombie's breath.

No More Rules?

Part of the fun of gaming is to conquer the tricks and traps of a new title. Having mastered them, the repetition is no longer as much fun and we begin to look forward to the new version. Wouldn't it be everlasting fun if the game continued to change by introducing new events and characters and never became entirely predictable? That is the promise of bringing **artificial intelligence (AI)** into the game. In the video game sphere, that means features that make the virtual characters operated by the game act as if they were human. For example, AI features in "Grand Theft Auto" series vary the police response and the weapons they use according to how "wanted" a character is. More advanced forms add new events to the game and the story evolves as you progress.

Ultimately, game characters might respond to your actions or spoken words with improvised actions of their own. If the characters learn from your behavior and make decisions that are not simply preprogrammed paths through the game, then they would achieve the status of "true" AI that is the goal of computer scientists. If you were confronting the artificially intelligent characters in an augmented reality environment, you might mistake them for real people, at least until you tried to shake their hands to introduce yourself.

Artificial intelligence (AI) is the property of an interactive medium that convinces users that they are interacting with a real person.

STOP & REVIEW

1. What distinguishes the different generations of video game consoles?

2. What is a game engine?

3. What is the difference between virtual reality and augmented reality?

GAMING ON THE GO The Pokémon Go smartphone exemplifies two trends that are transforming video games: mobile gaming and augmented reality.

INDUSTRY: THE GAME PLAYERS

The video game industry surpasses the music, network television, and movie industries in terms of total revenues and so is a significant entertainment industry in its own right. The major segments of the game industry include consumer electronics companies that make game gear, developers who design the games, publishers who manufacture the game software, and retailers who sell the games to the public. The relationships among these industry "players" vary according to the type of game **platform** involved: console game system, handheld, personal computer game, online game, or apps for smartphones and tablet computers like "Candy Crush Soda Saga" (ESA, 2015).

> **Platform** is a basic type or brand of game system.

Gear Makers

Sony is the current champion in the console sales game thanks to the introduction of a popular new version of its PlayStation console (PS4) along with the older PS3 and PlayStation Portable. Gear makers also include third-party manufacturers of custom controllers like Mad Catz Interactive and high-end game desktops like Dell Gaming's Alienware that speed up personal computer games. We must also count tablet and smartphone manufacturers such as Apple and Samsung since mobile gaming is stealing customers from consoles.

Game Publishers

Game publishers are analogous to movie studios and record companies. However, unlike in other media industries that we have examined, hardware manufacturers continue to have a central role in software manufacturing by retaining their own in-house game publishers. For example, Nintendo acts as its own publisher for its most popular titles such as "Wii Sports" and "New Super Mario Bros." and is the leading game publisher overall. Sony Computer Entertainment and Microsoft are also top publishers. The top independent publishers are Activation and Electronic Arts. In addition to developing its own games, such as "Need for Speed" and "Madden Football," Electronic Arts also distributes games made by third-party developers that it does not own, such as MTV Games' "Rock Band." Social network games are a significant presence in the game sphere, although the top social game publishers like King ("Candy Crush Soda Saga") and Supercell ("Clash of Clans") tend to come and go with each new hit game. Social games are converging with mobile games as publishers of popular social titles like King make app versions to follow social media users as they network on their smartphones.

The publishers make copies of games and historically have distributed them to consumers through one of three basic channels. The top-selling games of all time are those that came bundled with game consoles. Other console titles and personal computer games are sold (or rented) through retail outlets. Online games are purchased over the Internet from the publisher or through retail stores. Newer distribution channels have upended the console game market structure. These include games that can be streamed over the Internet, game apps that are downloaded onto smartphones and tablets, "free" casual games found on Facebook, and digital downloads of multiplayer games. The placement of ads inside games and the sale of virtual goods and premium features within online games are significant new sources of revenue for game publishers.

There is an important category of game software that every player uses indirectly, but that is not marketed to the general public: *game engines*. These are the programs that make the characters and objects in games move on the player's screen and do what they are supposed to, such as keep out of each other's way, fall to the ground when they are "killed," and cast shadows where they should (see Technology Demystified: A Look Under the Hood at Game Engines, page 321). For example, the "Unreal Engine" by Epic Games of North Carolina is a popular engine that has been used in over 200 games, including multiple titles in the "Star Trek," "Medal of Honor," and "Tom Clancy" series. Epic licenses its engine to developers, which means that it collects fees—sometimes millions of dollars per title—for its use. Game developers also license tools that assist with specific game and graphics features, such as music, lighting, and textures. A growing segment is *middleware* that packages a variety of tools needed for game development. However, dozens of engines can also be used for free, such as *OGRE*, a rendering engine that is found in several adventure and online role-playing games. "Unity" is a popular game-authoring system among students since it has a free version as well as tutorials and user forums.

Game Developers

Game developers create game software by combining the skills of graphic artists and computer programmers (see Your Media Career: Getting Paid to Play?). Like the movie studios of old, leading game publishers have their own in-house design studios. For example, Electronic Arts has game development studios at its headquarters near San Francisco in Redwood City, California, and some two dozen other locations around the world. EA, as it is known, has absorbed a number of other game developers such as Maxis (makers of "The Sims"). Like the movie studios of today, game publishers also distribute the productions of third-party developers who have varying degrees of autonomy from the publisher, similar to the function of music labels in the recording industry (see Chapter 6), ranging from wholly owned subsidiaries (like Maxis at Electronic Arts) to recurring informal partnerships.

There are also thousands of independent game developers. Like independent filmmakers or "garage bands," these are individual programmers or small teams that develop games that they hope will be picked up by major publishers. The Independent Games Festival (www.igf.com) is the showcase for top independent game developers. For example, "Joe Danger" was created by Hello Games, a team of four artists and programmers who had previously worked for major game developers.

Your Media Career

GETTING PAID TO PLAY?

Video game designer is one of the most exciting media professions today. What could be more thrilling than helping to create the entertainment industry of tomorrow, the games that everyone will be talking about? The opportunities are there. The U.S. video game industry directly employs about 42,000 people across 36 states, and game developer compensation averages about $80,000 per year overall (Siwek, 2014).

Game designer is a feasible occupational choice for our readers (Liming & Vilorio, 2011). For designers, undergraduate degrees in computer science are not required and a growing number of college media departments are offering specialties in game design. Game design aspirants might pick up computer programming on their own or seek out community college, technical school, or free online courses (like www .codeacademy.com) to get up to speed. One entry route for designers is to start as a play tester whose job is more formally known as *quality assurance* or *usability research*. In other words, you get paid for playing games and giving feedback to designers. Another entry path is to design informal games, the video game equivalent of the student film, to show off your design skills. Designers typically get their start with small game design companies. They progress through the ranks by adding to their portfolio, beginning with creating specific components for a new game (e.g., a more realistic explosion or a creepier monster), progressing to a "mission leader" for a specific level of a game, and finally assuming responsibility for the overall look and feel of a new

game. To advance through the ranks, designers must also be team players with excellent writing and project management skills and prove that they can work under pressure. Designers who make it to the top with major design studios can command six-figure salaries and stock options that make them millionaires while still young enough to enjoy it.

There are many other occupations in the gaming industry. Computer science degrees are required for programmers, of course. Artists, writers, and audio producers are other occupations that require specialized training. Video games are a big business, so just as in any other media field, there are plenty of openings for those with advertising, marketing, accounting, and management backgrounds.

The game industry is not all fun and games. It has been criticized for exploiting young programmers and artists. When the ship date for a new game looms, 60- or 80-hour workweeks are expected without overtime pay. A never-ending succession of "crunch times" can lead to rapid burnout. The good news is that frequent burnouts open up more opportunities at the entry level for the aspiring designer to get in the game.

Sources: Liming, D. & Vilorio, D. (2011). Work for play: Careers in video game development. Retrieved from February 11, 2016 from http://www.bls.gov/careeroutlook/2011/fall/art01.pdf

Siwek, S. E. (2014). Video games in the 21st century. Accessed February 11, 2016 from http://www.theesa.com/wp-content/uploads/2014/11/VideoGames21stCentury_2014.pdf

Some developers specialize in making assets that are assembled in games developed by others, such as characters or the settings in which the characters move. Both amateur and professional developers also show off their skills by crafting game **mods** that change game features, ranging from adding new weapons into first-person shooter games to complete makeovers that change the basic nature of the game play. With smartphones and tablets expanding popular game platforms, the market for relatively simple game "apps" has radically expanded the market for game creators and lowered their barriers to entry. Independent developers also have a new way to finance their creations without selling out to major publishers; they can *crowdfund* new games attracting small donations from game fans through Internet sites like Kickstarter.

> **Mods** are modifications to game play or game environments made by users and amateur game developers.

Selling the Game

Video games were originally distributed to users through coin-operated arcade machines and toy stores. Currently, console game retailing resembles the home video market, with specialized outlets like GameStop competing with "big box" retailers like Walmart and game rental operations such as GameFly. Many players also buy used games from the likes of GameStop or online from eBay and Amazon.com.

Online distribution is an especially important outlet for independent game developers. There are online distribution channels for independent games sponsored by each of the major game hardware manufacturers, the Xbox Marketplace, WiiWare, or the PlayStation Network. Other indies, as they are called, develop informal games (e.g., using Flash) that they distribute as freeware over the Internet or sell on eBay. App stores run by Apple, Google, Amazon, and others are revolutionizing how games are distributed and sold to smartphones and other portable wireless devices. Steam provides one-stop shopping for games across console, multiplayer, and mobile platforms for independent developers and major game studios, complete with community and cross-platform management functions for its users.

STOP & REVIEW

1. What are the major segments of the video game industry?
2. What do video game publishers do?
3. What are the different methods for distributing video games?

VIDEO GAME GENRES: RULES OF THE GAME

Although a big part of the fun of gaming is trying out the technology in the latest game consoles, there is more to it than that. What makes a game appealing to its players? In previous chapters, we examined media **genres** when trying to understand their appeal to their audiences. The same type of analysis can be made for video games.

> **Genres** are distinctive styles of creative works. The term is also used to represent different types or formats of media content.

The list of the all-time best-selling video games (Table 12.1) offers few clues beyond the obvious fact that Nintendo is still the all-time number-one game console maker. These figures include games that were distributed free with game systems, fattening the sales totals. The five Wii titles in the top 10 are arguably little more than demonstration programs for capabilities of the Wii console. Working with genre categories commonly used in the industry, we have a puzzle game, two sports games, a role-playing game, a racing game, three platform games, and a shooter game rounding out the list.

Beyond the top 10, a wider range of genres may be found, but there is not much agreement about what the main genres are and how many variations,

TABLE 12.1 Top 10 Best-Selling Console Video Games of All Time

RANK	GAME	CONSOLE	YEAR	GENRE	WORLD UNIT SALES (MILLIONS)
1	Wii Sports	Wii	2006	Sports	82
2	Super Mario Bros.	NES	1985	Platform	40
3	Mario Kart Wii	Wii	2008	Racing	34
4	Wii Sports Resort	Wii	2009	Sports	32
5	Pokémon Red/Green/Blue Version	Game Boy	1996	Role-playing	31
6	Tetris	Game Boy	1989	Puzzle	30
7	New Super Mario Bros.	DS	2006	Platform	30
8	Wii Play	Wii	2006	Misc	29
9	New Super Mario Bros.	Wii	2009	Platform	28
10	Duck Hunt	NES	1984	Shooter	28

Source: http://www.vgchartz.com/gamedb/

or subgenres, should be recognized. Since video games are often described as interactive movies (see Media & Culture: Video Game as Interactive Film?), it is tempting to draw on literary or movie genres, and indeed we can readily identify science fiction, horror, and action video games. However, many popular video games are so abstract that they have no plot, or narrative structure, and even games that use the settings, symbols, and themes found in popular film genres usually lack a plot in the conventional sense. But game genres borrowing from film or literature merely recycle the conventions of old media. Genre analysis should give us insight into the underlying appeal of the interactive medium rather than focusing on superficial aspects of themes and settings.

One possibility is to adopt the genres of 2-D board games, for example, race, space, chase, displace, and theme games (Parlett, 1999). Race games proceed in a linear fashion from start to finish with the object of being the first (or quickest) to reach the end. Games in the "Mario Brothers" series fall into that category. In this context, space games aren't set in outer space but rather involve aligning game pieces in a particular pattern, for example, "Tetris." Chase games are asymmetrical contests in which the goal of the player is to avoid capture, as in the "Grand Theft Auto" series. In displace games, the aim is to annihilate the opponent, which is also the goal of first-person shooter games like "Call of Duty." Theme games engage players in a simulation of a real-world activity, for example, "The Sims."

Another approach to defining genres is to focus on the types of interactions (e.g., capturing, fighting, driving, shooting) that users engage in while playing. Early games were often built around single types of interactions, but the complex games of today typically involve several types. For example, games in the "Grand Theft Auto" series include all capturing, fighting, driving, and shooting interactions.

Since genres reflect a negotiation between producers and audience, another way to characterize game genres is to ask what types of games are the most popular (See Table 12.2). By that standard, strategy, casual, and role-playing games account for nearly all the most popular titles.

TABLE 12.2 **Top Video Game Genres**

GENRE	EXAMPLE	% TOTAL SALES
Strategy	"Starcraft" "SimCity"	38
Casual	"Fruit Ninja" "Candy Crush Soda Saga"	25
Role-Playing	"Fallout" "Final Fantasy"	20
Shooter	"Call of Duty" "Halo"	6
Adventure	"Life Is Strange" "Minecraft Story Mode"	5
Action	"Grand Theft Auto" "Resident Evil"	2
Driving: Flight, Racing	"Need for Speed" "Mario Kart"	1
Other: Sport, Arcade, etc.	"Madden NFL" "Just Dance"	3

Source: Wolf, M. J. (2001). Genre and the video game. In M. J. Wolf (ed.), The Medium of the Video Game (Austin, TX: University of Texas Press), pp. 113–134.

Media & Culture

VIDEO GAME AS INTERACTIVE FILM?

A close relationship is emerging between video games and movies. Both are very visual media that provide an intense experience for their fans. Both media employ the latest visual and auditory technologies to deliver ever more intense experiences. And a blockbuster game generates as much revenue as a blockbuster movie.

Filmmakers have become interested in the narrative qualities of games, which some call "cyberdrama." So they might look at the image and character of Lara Croft in the "Tomb Raider" game the same way they look at her character in the movie and draw similar inferences about stereotypical attributes of females from both (Bryce, Rutter, & Sullivan, 2006). Other video game narratives resonate with those of popular films, telling stories that reinforce the hegemony of the dominant economic and cultural groups in society, for example, by reinforcing consumerism in "The Sims" or furthering the dominance of commercial media symbols while playing games spun off from "X-Men" or "Star Trek" (Crawford & Rutter, 2006) or reinforcing conventional sex roles (Cox, 2011).

Movie-style storytelling is beginning to find its way into games. "Heavy Rain" and "LA. Noire" are often cited as examples of advanced storytelling techniques. Artificial intelligence and the ability to interact through dialogue (captured through game consoles that recognize spoken words or read lips) might make for compelling interactions with game plotlines. A video game has already met the challenge posed by famed film producer Steven Spielberg, to create a video game whose story will make us cry: "That Dragon, Cancer" about a young boy dying of cancer is tear-inducing for its players.

Virtual reality technology is also finding its way into filmmaking, another path of convergence between game and film. The Sundance film festival's New Frontier program features films that combine storytelling with VR effects, such as the *Martian VR Experience* that puts viewers/players in the seat of a Mars rover to recreate moments from *The Martian* hit movie.

We might also distinguish genres from other characteristics of games such as their hardware platform (e.g., PlayStation or Wii; console, handheld, PC, or mobile app), mode (e.g., single player or multiplayer, first-person or third-person perspective), level of involvement (e.g., hardcore or casual), and visual setting (e.g., science fiction or horror). We could also focus on the player's role in making the version of the game that he or she creates through intricate feedback with the game system rather than specific actions (e.g., dodging or shooting). For example, playing a racing game like "Project Gotham Racing 4" requires players to keep their eyes glued to the screen and to continually manipulate the controller in an intense performance feedback loop. In contrast, "Sim City" requires the player to make well-considered interventions based on the integration of information gathered over several screens as the player's virtual world evolves. Distinctions like these can also define different genres of interaction (Apperley, 2006).

MEDIA LITERACY

SPOILING THE FUN: VIDEO GAME LITERACY

Now that video games are a significant medium in their own right, it is time to ask about their larger impact on society. The answers may not always be fun to think about.

BEYOND BARBIE

One of the enduring challenges to video game designers has been to develop games that appeal to females. In the early days, games attracted a largely male audience. An exception was "Centipede," an arcade game from the early 1980s that was the first to be popular among female players. Some attributed that to the female-friendly pastel colors, but the fact that it was designed by Dona Bailey, the only female programmer at Atari at the time, may have had something to do with it (Kent, 2001). Another notable exception was "Barbie Fashion Designer," released in 1996, which was a hit among girls and surged to the top of the sales charts that year.

Games are now about equally popular among males and females (ESA, 2015) but critics argue that games are still designed to appeal to straight white male players on both a superficial and also a very profound level. On the surface, many female game characters are excessively buxom, scantily dressed, and overly submissive. At a deeper level, the action of first-person shooters, the worlds game designers create, and the way characters are framed and carry themselves also reflect a male perspective on the world (Cox, 2011).

The Gamergate controversy raises awareness of sexism in games and in the industry that creates them. Some dedicated game fans respond that they are being unfairly singled out given that sexist images can be found in many forms of media content and women are underrepresented throughout the media industry, which is in fact the case (see Chapter 14). And, anyway, the feminist critics were just spoiling the gamer's fun. However, the controversy boiled over in cyberspace resulting in profane postings and death threats that are spoiling everyone's fun. One positive outcome of all the ugliness is that female characters who are not portrayed as sex objects are starting to appear as heroes in releases from major game studios, such as Joule in Microsoft's "ReCore."

MORE ADDICTIVE THAN DRUGS?

Game developers sometimes brag that their new game is "more addictive than drugs." Dong Nguyen, developer of the popular "Flappy Birds" game, caused a stir in 2014 when he withdrew it from circulation because he felt it was *too* addicting. There have been cases of people literally dying to play. In South Korea, there have been multiple cases of online game players dying from cardiac arrest after days-long sessions without breaks for food or water. In China, the government has set up hundreds of boot camps to wean game addicts from their habits. Less dire effects also concern parents. Excessive amounts of sedentary game play may increase the risk of *childhood obesity* (HHS, 2010), a major health problem of American youth. "PlayStation palms" is a form of repetitive stress injury that can result from manipulating game controllers for hours on end. Effects on the social development of children have received the most attention in the United States (see "More Harmful than TV?" below). Internet gaming disorder has been tentatively recognized as a mental disease by the American Psychiatric Association (APA, 2013). About 3 percent of gamers may be affected (Ferguson, Coulson, & Griffiths, 2011). Whether or not these are truly "addictions" in the same sense of an addiction to drugs (more properly known as substance abuse) or a pathological gambling problem remains a controversial issue (Petry, 2011). Studies of video game addictions are often surveys in which college students or schoolchildren are asked to identify symptoms (e.g., Lemmens, Valkenburg, & Peter, 2009) that might not pass the scrutiny of a trained psychologist examining the participants in person. Some of the symptoms, such as a preoccupation with the game, wanting to play more and more, and feeling irritable when unable to play, are familiar to many game fans but are difficult to distinguish from our recurring, but often temporary, infatuations with new forms of entertainment. Other indicators, such as losing sleep, concealing the amount of play from others, and dropping out of school or losing a job because of the game, suggest that gaming can be a serious problem.

FAMILY FUN? Or family wrecker? Excessive involvement in video games can take time away from school, work, family, and friends. In extreme cases, that could be termed an addiction. For most, games are just lots of fun, but for those who lose control of their gaming, it can be a life-endangering obsession.

Online gambling for real-money jackpots is also returning in the United States. That raises concerns about a well-known form of mental illness, problem gambling, which has a long history of destroying lives and wrecking homes under a crushing burden of gambling debt. Betting on e-sports such as "League of Legends" tournaments is in its infancy, but could grow into a major source of problem gambling, especially since the "sports" are loosely regulated and thus vulnerable to manipulation by gamblers.

Meanwhile, readers out there who may be wondering if they are game addicts should first note that having an intense desire for any activity is not the same as being addicted to it, even if the two are sometimes equated in everyday terms, as in "Yeah, I'm a game addict, I can't get enough of 'Grand Theft Auto.'" Another common misconception is that the sheer amount of game play indicates addiction when the question is really how much it interferes with other aspects of your life. So, if you can honestly say that playing "League of Legends" 40 hours a week is not putting you in danger of flunking the class you are reading this for (honestly, now), then you are probably not an addict. On the other hand, if 3 hours a week (about the time the average family spends) is making you fail your classes or neglect your real-world friends, you might have a problem. If that is the case, chances are your "addiction" is just a temporary infatuation. It has been found that most of those who were categorized as addicted to games in 1 year were no longer addicted a year later (van Rooij et al., 2011).

To get your gaming under control, you should think about ways you might spend more time in the real world, or use an in-game tool that helps you keep track of the time you spend and begin rewarding yourself for cutting down on the time you spend playing from one week to the next. If you can't bring yourself to do even that, think about seeing a psychologist. Remember, it is only in the game world that you get "extra lives."

MORE HARMFUL THAN TV?

Other concerns about video games arise from content that is heavily laced with violence, sex, and traditional sex roles. The ability of television violence, sex, and sex roles to have negative effects on children has been documented (but is also controversial, see Chapter 15), so seeing the same things in video games might also have harmful effects, might it not? Certain violent video games might be even worse than television, where there is usually a plotline that includes punishment for evil doers, whereas in many video games violence is an end in itself, leading to higher scores and new "lives." As we will see in Chapter 15, reviews of the research have been contradictory, but the latest one (Greitemeyer & Mügge, 2014) concluded that violent video games increase aggression and reduce positive behaviors such as cooperation and helping.

Recognizing the possible link between game play and antisocial behavior, the Entertainment Software Review Board (ESRB) provides helpful content ratings to assist parents when selecting games for their children. Like similar content-rating systems that have been developed in the movie, music, and television industries, these are examples of industry self-regulation in which video game developers voluntarily submit their games to ESRB for review. The ratings initially developed in response to a public outcry following the introduction of fourth-generation games like "Mortal Kombat" in the early

1990s that featured extremely gory graphics. Critics contend that the Adults Only (AO) rating is only given for sexual content, whereas extreme violence should perhaps also be limited to adults. As with movie ratings, the game ratings are effective only if retailers faithfully check the IDs of game purchasers, but studies by the Federal Trade Commission indicate that enforcement is lax. However, over two-thirds of parents check the ratings before buying a game and four-fifths report limiting game play of children (ESA, 2015).

It might help if laws were passed to prohibit sales of M-rated games to minors. However, a California law banning violent video game sales to minors was struck down by the Supreme Court on the grounds that game developers have free speech rights that include the right to make violent computer software. Also, the court did not find the studies proclaiming a link between video games and violence to be credible.

DANGER TO SOCIETY? Playing violent video games can stimulate aggression, but the extent of the effects continues to be a controversial topic.

SERIOUS GAMES?

"Serious games" might seem like a contradiction in terms. However, there is mounting evidence that video games have positive effects on their players and that there could be a considerable upside to exploring their educational benefits. Perhaps you would rather play "Media Now," the game, rather than read *Media Now*, the textbook? Of course you would, and that is a driving trend toward *gamification* in education, the idea that anything that can be taught would be more fun and more effective if it was a game.

Until now, the greatest interest—and greatest source of funding—for serious games has come from defense departments around the world. The generals have found that battle tank simulators are an effective way of teaching recruits how to operate complex weapons systems at far less cost than running (and occasionally running into) the real thing. The generals appreciate "silly" video games, too, since the interfaces of computerized weapons systems increasingly resemble video game controllers and there is evidence that playing action games like "Medal of Honor" can improve visual attention (Barlett, 2009), a useful skill for warriors. Also, if video game violence indeed does cause violent behavior, that might produce more effective killers for the military, a possibility that the Marine Corps explored by developing "First to Fight," a first-person shooter game used to train Marine recruits and sold as a commercial video game (Anderson, Gentile, & Buckley, 2007).

Serious games are proving themselves in more socially beneficial applications, however. Serious games can produce situated learning that immerses the player in personalized simulations of the real-world environments in which they will ultimately be expected to perform (Gee, 2003). For example, simulation games can help doctors master the art of saving lives (Rosser et al., 2007) and in some studies exercise games (or *exergames* as they are called) have shown evidence of reducing obesity in children (Lu et al., 2013). Generally, serious games are more educationally effective than conventional classroom instruction, especially when the instruction is personalized to the abilities or interests of the learner (Clark, Tanner-Smith & Killingsworth, 2015).

Others (e.g., Bogost, 2007) prefer the term *persuasive games,* maintaining that the procedures players follow in games have an ability comparable to verbal arguments to convince people to change their ways. In this view, any game can have a persuasive impact, even if it is not primarily designed to meet an educational objective. For example, the play2Prevent Lab at Yale University develops games to teach youth about the risks of drug abuse and HIV and uses rigorous testing methods to determine their impact.

Calling certain games "serious" doesn't give proper credit to other games that may be equally beneficial. There is mounting evidence that playing games just for fun can improve cognitive functioning (Latham, Patston, & Tippett, 2013), with "Tetris" often cited as a shining example. Educational games are a tiny segment of the commercial gaming market, and perhaps with good reason. Children soon tire of predictable educational game play, such as awarding points for each country correctly located on a map, issuing in-game awards, and promoting players to new levels. However, if we blend the geography lessons with the adventures of a cute childlike "Dora the Explorer," we might teach something while having fun, an instance of incidental learning (see Chapter 15). Meaningful lessons can also be built around games, such as "Minecraft," that were originally designed for fun but can be adapted to computer science instruction.

As for replacing traditional classroom instruction with video games, a major stumbling block is their considerable first-copy costs (see Chapter 2). If educators tried to match the production qualities of "Grand Theft Auto," then each video game "text" would cost tens of millions of dollars to produce. The textbook market is highly fragmented and local adoption decisions are complicated, so amassing the necessary economies of scale to offset the development costs is a daunting task. For introductory college courses in rapidly changing fields like the media, the frequent updates required of the material would yield games that would cost several times the price of a print textbook.

So, any savings resulting from employing serious games in schools might have to come from eliminating the teachers, the buildings the students gather in, the campuses the buildings stand on, or even the football stadiums that the alumni fill. Failing that, serious games might become economically viable by adopting lower levels of technology than popular commercial titles. But what fun would that be?

STOP & REVIEW

1. What are some ways to describe the genres of video games?
2. How can you tell if you have a video game addiction?
3. What are some possible negative effects of video games?
4. What are serious video games?

SUMMARY & REVIEW

HOW DID VIDEO GAMES DEVELOP?

Games date back to the ancient Egyptians. Today's games evolved from classic board, arcade, and war games. The first popular arcade video game was "Pong," and Odyssey was the first console for home games, both from 1972. The video game industry survived major busts in the late 1970s and the early 1980s. Game consoles have evolved over eight generations of games, each adding to the quality of images and game play and extending the market for games. Early online games were text based and have evolved into massively multiplayer online role-playing games of today.

HOW HAVE VIDEO GAMES IMPACTED SOCIETY?

Video game play now extends deeply into society, broadening its initial appeal to teenage boys to include female and adult players today. Excessive video game play can interfere with important life activities and may cause violent behavior and strengthen sex-role stereotypes. Alarming outbreaks of youth violence, such as the shootings at Columbine High School and Sandy Hook Elementary School, have been attributed to video games, although the link is impossible to prove conclusively.

WHAT IS THE STATUS OF VIDEO GAMES TODAY?

The video game industry is evolving. The console game industry is beginning to resemble the film industry with respect to the production values of games, their rapidly rising development costs, and their ability to make blockbuster profits for their publishers. However, console games compete with increasingly popular online games including inexpensive casual games available on social media sites. Games distributed over the Internet and through smartphones and tablets pose further competition to the console game market.

WHAT ARE THE IMPORTANT TRENDS IN GAME TECHNOLOGY?

The progression of game gear through eight generations of console games has been marked by the power of the central processing units built into the consoles, the technologies used to store the software, and the controllers that let users interact

with the games. Seventh-generation games pack parallel processors, high-capacity disk drives, and high-definition video discs. Motion-sensing technologies like the Xbox One are revolutionizing the gaming experience. Augmented reality and virtual reality aim to completely immerse gamers in game environments.

HOW IS THE VIDEO GAME INDUSTRY ORGANIZED?

Sony and Microsoft are the dominant console manufacturers. The manufacturers publish their own games, but independent game publishers, including industry giant Electronic Arts as well as hundreds of smaller publishers, are also in the game. Game development companies make the games and distribute them through major publishers, through developer exchanges run by the console makers, or online via the Internet. Multiplayer game publishers, online distributors, and social networking sites are alternative distribution channels for video games.

WHAT ARE THE GENRES OF VIDEO GAMES?

Conventional movie genres such as action-adventure and science fiction can be applied to video games, as can the genres of 2-D board games. The game industry uses its own categories, including strategy, role-playing, action, adventure, and shooter games. Other attempts to define video game genres focus on the types of user interactions involved.

HOW DO VIDEO GAMES AFFECT THEIR PLAYERS?

Some players become so deeply involved in playing their favorite game that they might fairly be termed addicts, and psychiatrists continue debating whether or not to classify game addiction as a mental illness. However, that applies only in extreme cases when severe life consequences, such as flunking out of school, are involved. Playing violent video games is a possible cause of aggressive behavior, although the research is controversial. Military commanders for whom aggression is a desirable behavior are using video games to train the troops. Serious video games have also proven effective in encouraging healthy behaviors and have the potential to improve upon conventional classroom instruction.

THINKING CRITICALLY
ABOUT THE MEDIA

1. Have developments in video games been driven by technology or by their users? Explain.

2. What impact has video game play had in your life?

3. Have you ever felt "addicted" to a video game? What made you feel that way?

4. How would you go about getting a job in the video game industry?

5. Debate the following statement: sexist video games should be banned for children.

MindTap®

Test your knowledge with online printable flashcards and online quizzing.

KEY TERMS

artificial intelligence (AI) (p. 323)

augmented reality (p. 322)

casual game (p. 319)

digital game (p. 314)

game engine (p. 320)

genres (p. 327)

massively multiplayer online role-playing games (MMORPGs) (p. 316)

mods (p. 327)

platform (p. 324)

video game (p. 314)

virtual reality (p. 318)

MindTap® Log on to the MindTap Communication for *Media Now* to access a variety of additional material, including this chapter's e-book, learning objectives, comprehension quizzes, videos, and more!

JOHN MACDOUGALL/AFP/Getty Images

GOVERNMENTS, COMPANIES, INSTITUTIONS, POLITICIANS, AND CELEBRITIES all strive to gain the goodwill of their audiences. It is the job of PR professionals to craft clients' images, from Volkswagen to Bill Cosby, through the media of mass communication.

PUBLIC RELATIONS

LEARNING OBJECTIVES

After studying the topics in this chapter, you will be able to:

1 Give examples of how historical figures or institutions used public relations strategies before the emergence of PR as a profession.
2 List new or traditional media tools used by modern PR practitioners.
3 Outline major elements of a successful PR campaign.
4 Review at least eight functions of public relations.
5 Identify different publics who are addressed by PR activities.
6 Given a major crisis, critique the response given by a company's or an organization's PR team.

PUBLIC RELATIONS YESTERDAY AND TODAY

The three main elements of public relations—informing people, persuading people, and integrating people with other people—are practically as old as society itself, according to Edward Bernays (1923), who penned the first book and taught the first college course on public relations. Of course, the means and methods of accomplishing these ends have changed as society has changed, but maintaining a mutually beneficial relationship with audiences, keeping up-to-date on appropriate skills and tools, and being an ethical professional are still the necessary components for successful practitioners.

HISTORY: CIVILIZATION AND ITS PUBLIC RELATIONS

For Bernays and historians of the practice, professional **public relations** has always gone hand in hand with civilization. Kings and warriors of ancient civilizations, such as Sumeria, Babylonia, Assyria, and Persia, were memorialized in storytelling, songs, poems, and other communications to promote their prowess in battle and politics.

MEDIA THEN··· MEDIA NOW

1900
> The Publicity Bureau of Boston is founded as the first public relations firm

1913
> Ludlow Massacre establishes the value of corporate public relations

1917
> Creel Committee formed to motivate public support for World War I

1923
> Edward L. Bernays publishes Crystallizing Public Opinion, *the first book on professional public relations*

1927
> Arthur W. Page hired at AT&T and becomes "the father of corporate communications"

1929
> Bernays and Fleischman stage Torches of Freedom march promoting women's independence and smoking

1947
> Public Relations Society of America (PRSA) founded

1984
> Four models of public relations practice identified by Grunig and Hunt

1989
> *Exxon Valdez* crisis becomes PR nightmare

2002
> Global Alliance for Public Relations and Communications Management, made up of international PR organizations, founded

2009
> Federal Trade Commission (FTC) proposes to regulate viral campaigns

2010
> Barcelona Research Principles developed to evaluate public relations success

2012
> PRSA replaces the 1982 definition of public relations to emphasize "mutually beneficial relationships"

In Egypt, much of the art and architecture (statues, temples, tombs) was used to impress on the public the greatness of nobles, priests, and scribes. In ancient Rome, Julius Caesar carefully prepared the Romans for his crossing of the Rubicon in 49 BCE by sending reports, such as "Caesar's Gallic Wars" (52 BCE), on his epic achievements as governor of Gaul.

Augustus, who succeeded Julius Caesar, is historically renowned for being a master at communicating with the public. He used money, among other communication devices, to spread information. On one side of a coin was his picture and on the other side was news, such as his military conquests, public works, and governing triumphs. The coins and news spread as his citizens and soldiers traveled and traded throughout Europe, Asia, and Africa.

Later, the teachings of Jesus and his apostles took center stage in the battle for religious dominance in the public mind. Once the Christian church took shape, it relied on eloquent speeches and letters, such as Paul's epistle to the Romans, to guide the faithful and win converts.

In the fifteenth century, new knowledge spread in new forms—such as translations of the Bible from Latin into everyday languages, mass-printed books, and newspapers. This created an explosion of public communications. By 1792, the National Assembly of France created the first government-run **propaganda** ministry. It was part of the Ministry of the Interior, and was called the *Bureau d'Esprit,* or "Bureau of the Spirit." It subsidized editors and sent agents to various parts of the country to win public support for the French Revolution.

Down through the ages, those in government around the world have continued to use public relations tools to win favorable public sentiment for both themselves and their legislative acts.

The American Way

Great documents of liberty crystallized the power of **public opinion,** including the Magna Carta—the thirteenth-century English charter of human rights and liberties that inspired the U.S. Constitution. England's rebellious American colonies produced a host of PR experts for fashioning the machinery of political change. Three of these influential statesmen, Alexander Hamilton, James Madison, and John Jay, are credited with winning public approval of the ratification of the Constitution by publishing letters they had written to the press in 1787 and 1788. These letters became known as the *Federalist Papers*. Other great documents produced by the founders of the United States—the Declaration of Independence, the Constitution, and the Bill of Rights—may all be seen as masterworks of public relations in addition to being masterworks of political philosophy and democratic governance.

No history of public relations is complete without mentioning the master of all nineteenth-century press agents and publicists, Phineas T. Barnum. Showman par excellence, Barnum created waves of publicity stunts and coverage that made his circus, "The Greatest Show on Earth," an irresistible draw in every city and town it visited after its inception in 1871. Barnum sent

> **Public relations** activities are intended to favorably influence the public.

MindTap

Start with a quick warm-up activity.

MindTap

Read, highlight, and take notes on the complete chapter text in a rich interactive online platform.

> **Propaganda** is the intentional influence of attitudes and opinions.

> **Public opinion** is the aggregate view of the general population.

Archive Pics / Alamy Stock photo

THE GREATEST SHOW ON EARTH More than 150 years later, P. T. Barnum is still celebrated for pioneering successful PR practices.

anonymous controversial articles to local newspaper editors to drum up curiosity about his traveling shows with the goal of selling tickets before his circus hit town. He also used his creativity and imagination to write articles and illustrative ads about his intriguing American museum in New York. His successful publicity for a midget named "Gen. Tom Thumb" (Charles S. Stratton) and his wife (Lavinia Warren Stratton) sent all of them to England, where the Queen met them, artists painted the "Little General's" portrait, and composers wrote songs about him. Barnum also made the "Swedish Nightingale," Jenny Lind, popular in the United States.

From Governments to Entrepreneurs

The rise of the Industrial Age was a terrific force, propelling the need for PR practitioners. Then after World War I, other factors came into play that cemented the PR profession: America was building a consumer culture, people were more engaged in leisure activities, and public opinion was a common topic—thanks to influential communication theorists, such as Walter Lippmann, John Dewey, and Harold Lasswell. Advertising and publicity not only became a mainstay in newspapers and magazines but also appeared in radio and movies. For example, efforts to influence public opinion about World War I appeared in films, newsreels, and cartoons at movie houses. From 1920, when the first commercial radio station went on the air, to the end of the decade, sponsored programming and advertising streamed into more than 10 million households.

Entrepreneurs came to recognize and need the skills of PR practitioners. Many industrialists were arrogant, and their dispassionate attitudes toward the public were epitomized in 1892 by the coldblooded methods of Henry Clay Frick in his attempt to crush a labor union in the Carnegie-Frick Steel Company's plant in Homestead, Pennsylvania. The employees' strike was ultimately broken and the union destroyed, with the help of the state militia. Physical force won the battle for immediate control, but public opinion, framed in the struggle of the workers, won the war (Cutlip, Center, & Broom, 1985). Industrialists quickly learned the value of combating hostility and courting public favor through professional public relations.

Corporate leaders also soon learned the value of practitioners who could drum up publicity in attracting customers and investors. Companies across America established press bureaus to manage the dissemination of news favorable to themselves and unfavorable to their competitors. The "battle of the currents" between Westinghouse (advocate of alternating current, or AC, power transmission) and Thomas A. Edison's General Electric (advocate of direct current, or DC, transmission) is one of the earliest examples of how public relations was first conducted in the United States by powerful economic interests. Using former newspaper reporters as their publicists, the companies competed for media attention, political influence, and marketing advantage.

Trade associations were quick to catch the PR fever in the late 1800s. The Association of American Railroads is thought to be the first organization to use the term *public relations* in its 1897 *Year Book of Railway Literature*. Certainly, the railroad barons used PR tools of the trade to expand the railroads across towns and countrysides.

By the early 1900s, charities saw the emergence of PR departments within their local, national, and international offices, and soon, most nonprofit enterprises of any significance had in-house PR departments and/or outside PR agency counsel. These operations were much smaller than those in the corporate world, but their role was equally important. They helped to communicate their organizations' purposes, practices, and performance with the goals of building public awareness, raising money, influencing legislation, recruiting volunteers, and otherwise currying public support for their interests.

Whether in-house or acting as an independent agency, public relations in the early 1900s had evolved from being individual press agents and publicists to counseling firms that offered their services as experts in the field. The nation's first publicity firm, the Publicity Bureau, was founded in Boston at the turn of the twentieth century, and the PR industry continues to experience robust growth more than a century later.

PR Pioneers in the Modern World

Ivy Ledbetter Lee was a forerunner of today's PR practitioner. He convinced companies to have open communication to the public and the media, whether the news was good or bad. He believed that business had to tell its story honestly, accurately, and openly in order to win public understanding and support. He developed a publicity policy of "the public be informed" in contrast to the infamous statement of financier William Vanderbilt, "the public be damned."

Sometimes, however, Lee helped his clients to appear more sympathetic than they were. For example, John D. Rockefeller, Jr., asked for Lee's advice in handling the so-called Ludlow Massacre, which began in 1913 in southern Colorado when some 9,000 miners tried to form a union to protest their substandard living and working conditions. In response, the Rockefellers hired a private militia and guards who set fire to the miners' tent city and, in a skirmish, killed several of the miners, 2 women, and 11 children. With the family name being pilloried across the land, the Rockefeller family turned to Ivy Lee for help. One of Lee's strategies was to have Rockefeller, Jr., visit the camps after the strike and stage photographs of him talking with miners. Rockefeller would appear in newspapers and magazines as a concerned owner who cared about the miners' quality of life. At another time, Lee advised the senior Rockefeller, whose questionable business ethics were being attacked by muckrakers such as Ida Tarbell (see Chapter 5), to publicize his charitable contributions.

1900

The Publicity Bureau of Boston is founded as the first public relations firm

1913

Ludlow Massacre establishes the value of corporate public relations

1917

Creel Committee formed to motivate public support for World War I

"I WANT YOU!" SAYS UNCLE SAM America's most famous poster is a prime example of a successful PR campaign for the war effort. The poster was illustrated by James Montgomery Flagg for the Creel Commission during World War I.

1923

Edward L. Bernays publishes *Crystallizing Public Opinion,* the first book on professional public relations

1929

Bernays and Fleischman stage Torches of Freedom march promoting women's independence and smoking

1927

Arthur W. Page hired at AT&T and becomes "the father of corporate communications"

Sometimes the allegiance to Lee clients took precedence over other "publics." For example, Lee was being investigated before his death in 1934 for his involvement with Nazi-owned businesses, but meanwhile, his efforts with the Red Cross in World War I were highly praised. He raised $400 million in donations, recruited thousands of volunteers, and catapulted the Red Cross's image as a relief organization.

In addition to Ivy Lee, other forerunners of public relations were Edward L. Bernays and his associate and wife, Doris Fleischman. During World War I, Bernays—who was a theatrical press agent at the time—joined the U.S. Committee on Public Information, also known as the Creel Committee, which was successful in selling war bonds and generally promoting the war effort. George Creel was a remarkable practitioner who was able to form public opinion through information vehicles such as movies, cartoons, photographs, newsreels, and other media. The famous Uncle Sam "I Want You" poster was commissioned under Creel's direction.

Bernays is credited with coining the term *public relations counsel* in his first book on the subject, *Crystallizing Public Opinion,* published in 1923. Bernays and Fleischman viewed public relations as an art applied to a science. They would find out what the public thought and liked about their clients and then go about highlighting those attributes. They went well beyond publicity in their roles as consultants to business, government, and not-for-profit enterprises.

One of Bernays and Fleischman's classic campaigns was the 1929 Torches of Freedom march, in which they chose 10 women to walk down Fifth Avenue smoking cigarettes: symbols of equality with men during a time when women were "allowed" to smoke only in their homes. With the press already alerted, the coverage helped to advance feminism while setting the stage for a surge in smoking by women. What the public and the press didn't know, however, was that Bernays was a consultant to the American Tobacco Company, whose director realized that profits could be doubled with women smokers. All the news reports showed women smoking his Lucky Strike cigarettes. Bernays and Fleischman continued to contribute to women's equality. They were members of the Lucy Stone League (an equal rights, suffragist group), and Fleischman was the first married woman to be issued a passport with her maiden name.

Whereas Lee, Bernays, and Fleischman were consultants with their own PR agencies, and Creel worked for the government, Arthur Page was a PR pioneer in corporate communications. American Telegraph and Telephone (AT&T) hired Page as the vice president of public relations, and he advised executives on how to respond to public opinion and the media. He believed that public relations was publicity, but it included what managers said and how they acted with the public. Further, he said that the PR staff's job was to ensure that company promises to the public were kept.

Public Relations Matures

Although several organizations were founded in the 1930s and 1940s to represent the interests of PR practitioners, the most successful was the Public Relations Society of America (PRSA), formed in 1947. Today, the PRSA remains the world's largest PR membership association with more than 22,000 professional members, primarily in the United States. The PRSA offers certifications, conferences, and seminars to its members and has an affiliated student organization (the Public Relations Student Society of America—PRSSA) on college campuses across the country.

By the late 1960s, public relations had matured into a professionally recognized enterprise, comprising in the United States several hundred PR agencies and more than 100,000 individual practitioners (not all members of the PRSA) in business, government, and nonprofit enterprises.

Part of the driving force for this growth was the great burst of global political turbulence concerning the Cold War and government. Another part was civil unrest where U.S. colleges and university campuses became hotbeds of social action concerning civil rights and the Vietnam War. They, too, had to pay attention to their publics.

Still another part was the burgeoning consumer movement that sought to protect the average person against unsafe products, unhealthy working conditions, unfair pricing, and other breaches, real and alleged, of the expanding social contract that said, in effect, "the customer is king." Corporations recast their credit agreements and instituted numerous other reforms to guarantee consumer rights and satisfaction.

In the 1980s and 1990s, business and government became the primary targets for initiatives aimed at curbing air pollution, water pollution, deforestation, and the general threat of ecological disaster caused by global warming and the destruction of the world's natural habitats. For example, when the *Exxon Valdez* tanker ran aground, spilling 11 million gallons of oil off the coast of Alaska, the environmental catastrophe sparked a PR calamity for the entire industry.

By 2000, global issues such as unfair labor practices and unrestrained corporate expansion and market control became lightning rods for public concern about the almost unbridled success and globalization of such megabrands as Walmart.

Today, as always, good PR practices are needed in reaction to national events: government press agents communicated Obama's decisions to send special operation forces to fight ISIS; personal PR agents desperately mended the image of presidential candidate Donald Trump; and they curried public favor of Chipolte products during outbreaks of *E. coli* and norovirus, to name a few. PR practitioners have their work cut out for them with the barrage of pet food recalls, toy recalls, auto recalls, and oil spills.

On the one hand, PR practitioners are chastised for not doing enough to persuade companies to come clean sooner about their deceptions. On the other hand, many have received praise for helping corporations, government

Bettmann/AS400 DB/Corbis

A NEW AUDIENCE PR pioneers Bernays and Fleischman started a campaign to attract women to smoking. If Amelia Earhart smokes Lucky Strikes, then all women should!

1947

Public Relations Society of America (PRSA) founded

1989

Exxon Valdez crisis becomes PR nightmare

GARY I ROTHSTEIN/UPI/Newscom

PR PERSONIFIED The president of the United States performs a PR function whenever he addresses the nation. So do presidential candidates.

agencies, and nonprofit organizations communicate with the American public and the world about crises, what happened and what to expect in the near future.

Global Public Relations

What began as mainly a U.S. enterprise in the early 1900s has grown to become a global enterprise with about 250,000 PR practitioners in the United States and about 100,000 practitioners worldwide.

Many of these practitioners in other countries belong to public relations professional organizations similar to the PRSA in the United States. For instance, the Public Relations Institute of Ireland (PRII) was formed in 1954 and has about 1,000 members. The Institute of Public Relations of Singapore (IPRS) was founded in 1970 and has about 300 members. In Nigeria, it is illegal to practice public relations if you are not certified and a member of the Nigerian Institute of Public Relations (NIPR), according to its website.

PR groups and organizations from various countries in 2002 joined together to form the Global Alliance for Public Relations and Communications Management to promote professional values across cultures and diversity. The worldwide organization has 43 group members from 33 countries, and continues to grow. In many regions, such as Guatemala, the recognized need for public relations as a profession is in its infancy.

2002

Global Alliance for Public Relations and Communications Management, made up of international PR organizations, founded

Members of the Global Alliance for Public Relations and Communications Management

- ■ *Europe:* EUPRERA, CPRA (Croatia), ERPA (Estonia), ProCom (Finland), DPRG (Germany), PRII (Ireland), FERPI (Italy), NCA (Norway), APCE (Portugal), DIRCOM (Spain), SACP (Sweden), HB (Switzerland), pr suisse (Switzerland), SPRI (Switzerland), CIPR (United Kingdom)

- ■ *North America:* CPRS (Canada), McMaster-Syracuse MCM (Canada), PRSA (United States of America), UF CJC (United States of America), USC (United States of America)

- ■ *Latin America:* CONFIARP, CPRPA (Argentina), ABERJE (Brazil), Duoc UC (Chile), CUR (Columbia), CICOM (Mexico), PRORP (Mexico), UAGRO (Mexico), USMP (Peru)

- ■ *Asia:* APRN, ULAB (Bangladesh), PRF (India), PERHUMAS (Indonesia), CPR-PK (Pakistan), IPRS (Singapore)

- ■ *Africa:* PRSK (Kenya), NIPR (Nigeria), PRISA (South Africa), ZAPRA (Zambia)

- ■ *Oceania:* PRIA (Australia), PRINZ (New Zealand)

- ■ *Other:* IABC, IPR

Source: http://www.globalalliancepr.org/website/content/members

TECHNOLOGY TRENDS: TOOLS FOR GETTING THE JOB DONE

The goal of PR practitioners is to foster positive communication between their clients and the public. This usually means getting favorable information about the client's image, product, or service to the public.

PR practitioners use a combination of tools, techniques, and media to reach different audiences. Years ago, the best way to communicate to the public was to get information placed as news content (instead of paying for advertising). This technique is still used today but is among an array of tools that bypass traditional media to go straight to the public. For instance, a traditional news release to a print or digital newspaper might get the message about a bank's lowered interest rates placed as a serious news article and read by adults who are 40 to 60 years of age. Yet, a funny and animated video on YouTube coincidentally about a new water bottle is likely to be seen by your younger sister or brother on his or her smartphone. Thus, practitioners must think backward from their goal. They think about the audiences they want to reach, the medium their target audience uses, the form (visual or text or audio) the information will take, the content of the message, and the tools and techniques used to get the message placed.

THE VOICE Many television shows with similar formats compete with each other. PR practitioners find the right combination of tools and media, such as Facebook, Twitter, YouTube, websites, and blogs, to reach their audiences.

See Table 13.1 for some of the many different tools that practitioners around the globe use to get their messages across to their target audiences. These tools might appear differently, depending on the medium in which they are placed—print or digital newspapers and magazines, radio, TV, websites, and mobile devices. Some of the tools are discussed below. Although this section discusses a practitioner's tools, the most important skills are still excellent writing for a variety of media and audiences, and research to understand audiences, clients, and the communication process.

Traditional Tools

Press releases and press kits have been the dominant PR tools since the 1900s and are sent to traditional news media.

Press releases, now more often called *news releases* (print, audio, video, digital), are written as news stories that include a client's image, product, service, campaign, or special event with a quote from a company representative. News releases are sent to multiple news outlets in the hopes that the story will be published and regarded as a news story by audiences. Journalists usually use the releases as ideas to investigate further and then write their own stories on the topic, localizing it for their audience. PR practitioners are happy the news release generated publicity if resulting story includes the client's name or quote.

TABLE 13.1 PR Tools

Advertorials	Letters to editors	Radio
Annual reports	Meetings	Satellite media tours (SMT)
Audiotapes	Mobile Apps	Seminars
Audiovisual presentations	Newsletters	Social media
Backgrounders	News releases	Speakers' bureaus
Billboards	News stories	Special events
Blogs	Novelties	Speeches
Brochures, flyers, circulars	Online media centers	Sponsorships
Computer demonstrations	Open houses	Streaming videos
Conventions	Opinion polls	Surveys
Games	Paid advertisements	Teleconferences
Editorials	Photographs	Trade shows
Electronic press kits	Plant tours	Tweets
E-mail	Podcasts—audio and video	Video conferences
Event sponsorships	PowerPoint presentations	Video news releases (VNR)
Exhibits and displays	Press conferences	VIP visits
Fact sheets	Press kits	Webcasts
Interactive news releases	Product placements	Websites
Legislative alerts	Public demonstrations	Workshops
Legislative testimony	Public service advertisements	

A **webcast** is a real-time event transmitted over the Internet.

Live stream is when the events are streamed on the Internet and watched as they are happening live.

On demand means that audiences can download podcasts whenever they want.

Press kits are more often now called *media kits* and are a collection of multimedia materials about the client. They include a cover letter, recent news releases, fact sheets, publishable photos, brochures, biographies, business cards, and other information in different formats for media use. All of this might be sent to news organizations as print material in a traditional folder or as digital information on flash drives, CD-ROMs, or zip files in an e-mail.

Many organizations no longer send press kits to news organizations. Instead, they invite journalists to visit the online press rooms on their website.

Online press rooms (sometimes called a media center or news room) have the same type of materials as a media kit and more—archives of news releases, speeches, articles, annual reports and publications, photos and videos, fact sheets, links to information online, and related supporting materials. They also have the names and contact information of company representatives available for questions or interviews. (Two examples are Girl Scouts of America: www.girlscouts.org/news/ and Shell Global: http://www.shell.com/media.html.)

Video and Audio Tools

Video news releases (VNRs) are the video equivalent of written news releases. VNRs are professional, ready-to-air videos that look like news stories and are sent to TV news organizations. They are health care, consumer, technology, travel, and business stories that would appeal to viewers and include interviews with their clients. When a VNR segment is added to the news lineup or incorporated into news websites, it appears to audiences as though it came from an objective reporter and not a PR practitioner representing a client. Many audiences object to the use of VNRs for this reason.

Webcasts are presentations that are streamed live (or **live streamed)** over the Internet. Essentially, it is the same as watching an event on television or hearing it on the radio as it is actually happening. PR practitioners use webcasts for streaming press conference or speeches to journalists or audiences who may not be able to make the event in person. The webcast may also be downloaded **on demand** later.

Podcasts are audio or video interviews with company executives or representatives that are stored online and can be downloaded anytime. Practitioners hope the topics are interesting to audiences while also promoting their new product or service—such as a new miracle drug for weight loss described by a pharmaceutical company executive.

Satellite Media Tours (SMTs) can be considered live virtual interviews. These are carefully choreographed events in which journalists interview a practitioner's client from remote locations. SMTs—perhaps with a book author to promote a new novel or an actress to discuss a new movie—are pitched to various news organizations weeks ahead so that bookings are lined up in advance. The PR practitioner has control of the message and has previewed the questions from the media. The client will sit in a studio for several hours, answering questions from a series of journalists who are live with the client for only a few minutes each. For example, the client might talk with a Buzzfeed journalist for 3 minutes and then answer questions from a Today Show host for 2 minutes. The stations can run the interview live, tape it for use later, or edit excerpts into a news program.

E-Mail and Texting Tools

E-mail has been a boon to all practitioners, who can reach out to their audience with information, calls to action, and requests to volunteer. However, many journalists regard PR e-mail as spam that fills their inboxes with unwanted communications.

Texting is used for immediate communication. For instance, the press secretary of a governor might text a particular reporter across a crowded room, asking if he or she would like to stay afterward for an interview.

Shell Global

NEWS YOU CAN USE PR practitioners put together online press rooms filled with various information in different forms about their organization or client in the hopes that journalists and others will use the material in their stories. Journalists reference their sources, so PR practitioners hope the website also will be promoted.

ZUMA Press, Inc/Alamy

LIVE WEBCASTS Governments and organizations have press conferences that are webcast live. The webcasts are posted on official websites and other places on the Internet. Journalists analyze and comment about press conferences using excerpts from webcasts.

Social media are major tools for communicating with, engaging, and supporting various publics. Blogs are a tool to directly communicate with a client's audience or to endorse a product or service. YouTube videos let the practitioner be in control of a message to millions of potential viewers. Twitter enables fast responses in crisis situations. And, Facebook can build relationships while showcasing a client. Other social media outlets that PR practitioners use include Facebook, Twitter, Snapchat, and any other social network that audiences use.

Some networking sites, such as Facebook, gather data about who read messages or watched videos. Other social media get your message to your target audience for you—free! PR practitioners, on behalf of clients, upload many of the videos on YouTube. Presidential candidates run portions of their campaign on YouTube. One message can be communicated to millions of viewers who send clever videos to friends, who send them to their friends, and so on.

Snowball effects happen when a small event or issue builds quickly.

If planned strategically, this **snowball effect** is a result of a successful PR viral campaign where users get your message to your target audience for you. Viral campaigns include online videos, games, photos, text, and verbal messages in social media that are easily passed along to others. For example, for the past 10 years, Doritos has reserved ad space during the Super Bowl for a winning fan-made video. And, the public can vote once a day for their favorite ad. Imagine the huge number of videos about Doritos that were produced and shared online in the hopes of winning $1 million and having their video aired on Superbowl Sunday.

PR Databases

PR databases help practitioners gather information about their clients from news sources and also disseminate information to large numbers of people. Online tracking and monitoring systems help PR practitioners examine what the media, competitors, and the public are saying about their employers or clients or track how well a special promotion is doing.

Companies such as Cision, Inc., sell their databases, software, and services to PR practitioners and businesses. Practitioners can then access Cision, Inc.'s database of 1.6 million media contacts of journalists and bloggers, distribute news releases to news organizations, monitor different media, and analyze and measure the success of their messages. BurrellesLuce is another company that sells databases, services, and software to PR practitioners. It recently partnered with blinkx so that customers can search 35 million hours of indexed audio, video, viral, and TV content for information about their client. CyberAlert is another company that monitors media for practitioners and businesses. It tracks 55,000 online news sources and 25,000 print sources, Twitter and Facebook (about 200 million blogs and 70,000 message boards and forums), closed caption of 2,200 TV news programs, and does speech-to-text talk of 250 radio programs.

Most PR practitioners send their news releases to PR Newswire and Business Wire. About 800,000 journalists regularly troll the PR Newswire site for news and information. In addition, there are scores of smaller databases targeted to specific media and audiences, such as Hispanic Americans, Asian Americans, Arab Americans, and African Americans.

2009

Federal Trade Commission (FTC) proposes to regulate viral campaigns

PR AND SOCIAL MEDIA

In order to know how to reach their publics, PR practitioners research what devices different audiences use to get their information and what sources they use. It used to be that audiences were easy to reach with local radio and three broadcast TV channels and local and national newspapers and magazines. Now, people also have satellite TV with hundreds of channels and use tablets, smartphones, and mobile apps to get their news online, visiting millions of different news and social media site, such as Facebook, Twitter, and YouTube.

What does this mean to a PR professional? You know the answer: you must make your message digital to be seen and heard. It doesn't matter if your company or client is local, national, or international.

The traditional tools (print, broadcast, events, conferences) are fast becoming the add-ons to the Internet for getting information noticed and communicating with others for relationship building. Traffic is in high gear for website content, social media, blogs, and interactive games, for instance.

PR practitioners and their clients have their own websites, blogs, Facebook pages, and also court other bloggers for publicity. Side by side with text and photo blogs are podcasts and video blogs and links to their social media.

Companies spend billions of dollars on personal reference or "word of mouth" campaigns that sometimes hits a great area in ethics. They hire celebrity bloggers to promote products and pay endorsers to roam from one site to another, posting comments from a seemingly objective viewpoint, which is unethical. The FTC now regulates viral campaigns and blogs in a way similar to the regulation of paid advertising and infomercials. Bloggers who do not clearly and conspicuously state that they are compensated for their endorsements would be held liable—and so will the paying company.

Social media is also sometimes a headache for practitioners because the public uses Facebook, YouTube, Twitter, blogs, and other social media to tell companies what they think, firing off thousands of messages before the company can react.

With the growth of PR firms into global entities, there has been a corresponding increase in promotion and publicity campaigns across national borders. Since English has increasingly become the default language for international business, cultural and linguistic barriers have become less critical when dealing with the business publics. However, if you can communicate in the local language and understand the nuances of its culture, then you can promote and publicize much more effectively to the local market.

In many ways, the trend toward more frequent cross-border and global PR initiatives is an important step forward in the evolution of cultural cooperation between and among different countries. But it is also a trend that could inflame tensions on issues such as cultural imperialism and world domination, particularly by the United States.

On the one hand, the U.S. government has pledged to keep social media channels open to foster pro-democracy movements in other regions. On the other hand, countries sometimes regard these efforts as unwanted intrusions in their internal affairs. For example, the Chinese government employs about 2 million people to monitor posts and block international social media such as Google, Facebook, LinkedIn, Wikipedia, YouTube, and even *The Wall Street Journal* and censor topics on Chinese sites. In Iran, state security uses online postings to track down protesters. In Russia, the government blocks sites with posts that voice opposing views, while it uses other social media sites to spread its propaganda campaign.

INDUSTRY: INSIDE THE PR PROFESSION

2012

In 2012, the PRSA established a new definition of public relations: "Public relations is a strategic communication process that builds mutually beneficial relationships between organizations and their publics" (prsa.org). Clients often ask PR practitioners to do advertising or direct marketing to the public,

PRSA replaces the 1982 definition of public relations to emphasize "mutually beneficial relationships" which are not central to the PR function, per se. These have different purposes and are different professions that require specialized expertise and knowledge for their execution. Clear communication with clients helps to avoid misunderstandings about expectations. Given the complexity of public relations and the vast array of skills and technology used in communications between organizations and their various publics, it's not surprising that different definitions of the practice of public relations abound.

PR Agencies and Corporate Communications

PR practitioners usually work in a PR agency or within a business organization (commercial company, nonprofits, foundations, etc.). The difference is the practitioner in a **PR agency** represents several clients and in **corporate communications** only one company.

PR agencies range in size from one person who freelances to gigantic global agencies employing thousands of PR experts who specialize in some aspect of public relations. Agencies contract with different clients to perform distinct roles for varying amounts of time—whatever the client needs—such as monitoring social media; writing, photographing, and publishing a monthly e-newsletter or annual report; doing videos; and handling special events, such as company anniversaries or celebrations or the introduction of a new product or service. The needs of the client or "account" will determine which PR experts are wanted—those who are skilled in new technologies, special events, speech writing or video, for example.

PR practitioners who work in a PR department within a corporation do corporate communications. In small companies, the PR department does **media relations** and represents the company to the public. In large companies, the in-house PR department might have two jobs: (1) media relations and (2) internal communications. For example, a national jewelry company would want to keep all of its employees who work within its several hundred stores across the country networked together and feeling as if they are a vital part of the company. So internal communications might include writing and designing employee newsletters, sending out birthday cards, visiting stores, shooting videos, holding contests, and maintaining an employee website.

Elements of Successful Public Relations

The practice of public relations is based first on research, including public opinion polls, surveys, questionnaires, interviews, focus groups, and traffic statistics from their Internet servers (called Google analytics, see Chapter 10) to measure trends and issues. Although it is a continuous process, PR research is conducted in three basic phases: (1) preparation, (2) implementation, and (3) impact (Broom, 2009). Successful public relations begins with a serious assessment of public attitudes. Without adequate background on the people you are trying to reach and how they think, it is difficult, if not impossible, to communicate effectively. More specifically, without research and evaluation, you cannot identify public attitudes for your client or design programs that will achieve your communication objectives.

Second, public relations is a detailed strategy, not a hit-or-miss proposition. And it must be managed well. You must oversee the many small tasks that,

PR agencies have multiple clients they represent.

Corporate communications refers to when a practitioner is employed by a single company to do its public relations work, rather than contract out the work to a PR agency.

Media relations focus on establishing and maintaining good relations with the media.

taken together, achieve the overall organizational objectives. A strategic plan begins with a written action chart that allows for changes and contingencies along the way, and it must have the seal of approval from top management. Timetables and deadlines are scheduled for needed media communications and publications, such as websites, newsletters and reports, VNRs, blogs, electronic and text news releases, speeches, presentations, and special events.

Third, public relations has the goal of fostering public support. The public might support a for-profit organization by purchasing products, investing in stock, or voting for or against specific trade regulations. Public support for a nonprofit organization might take the form of donations of money or materials, volunteer assistance, or paid memberships. For a government agency, it might mean legislative influence, taxpayer cooperation, or public participation.

An evaluation of the campaign is always the last step in a strategy: what worked? What didn't? Where did we miss? Metrics are needed: how many more volunteers/money/publicity pieces do we have now when compared to the start of the campaign? What was the cost, and how have we profited? Were the results worth the investment? You can see the process of a PR campaign in Figure 13.1.

The Barcelona Declaration of Research Principles was developed by an international organization and can be applied to measuring and evaluating public relations: (1) goal setting and measurement is important, (2) media

2010

Barcelona Research Principles developed to evaluate public relations success

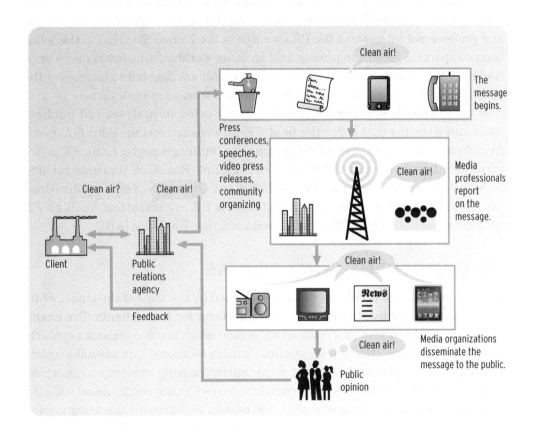

FIGURE 13.1 PR CAMPAIGN PR agencies organize communications events such as press conferences, speeches, and telemarketing campaigns to alert media organizations to important issues so that the subsequent media coverage will sway public opinion in favor of the client. Opinion polls and direct responses from the public provide feedback to the client and the agency.

measurement requires quantity and quality, (3) the value of public relations is not the same as advertising values, (4) social media can and should be measured, (5) measuring outcomes is better than simply measuring media results, (6) organizational/business results should be measured, and (7) research should be transparent and replicable (Grupp, 2010).

Professional Resources

An ever-expanding list of websites covering public relations continues to help practitioners with their skills, tools, and strategies. Included among these are www.online-pr.com (hundreds of listings and hyperlinks to PR, marketing, and advertising sites worldwide), www.prsa.org's Silver Anvil Awards (PR case studies and examples of award-winning campaigns), and www.iabc.com (networking internationally). Other websites encourage particular practitioners, such as www.womcom.org, whose membership is made up of women in communication. Still more online resources can be found for PR for different industries: entertainment, technology, hospitality, health care, event planning, press releases, software, education and training, and job consulting. You need it; the Web has it.

Although the PRSA has dominated the PR industry for most of its history, additional organizations have formed to serve particular specialties or groups within the profession. Some of these groups are the International Association of Business Communicators (IABC), the National Investor Relations Institute (NIRI), the Arthur Page Society, and Women Executives in Public Relations (WEPR). The Council of Public Relations Firms was established to represent the business and professional interests of the PR agencies in the United States. And there has been comparable growth in professional societies worldwide, as noted in the prior Global Public Relations section of this chapter. All are devoted to improving the practice of public relations and helping members succeed in their careers.

A bird's eye view of the PR industry is reflected in professional publications and websites that cover the field. These websites include *Jack O'Dwyer's Newsletter* (odwyerpr.com), *Bulldog Reporter* (bulldogreporter.com), *PR News* (prnewsonline.com), and *PR Week* (prweek.com). Research journals include *Public Relations Review* and *Public Relations Quarterly*. Some publications are automatic perks of being a member of a PR organization, such as *PR Strategist* published by PRSA and *Communication World* by IABC.

PR FUNCTIONS AND FORMS

Some of the forms of public relations are defined by the tools of the trade, while others are defined by the functions they perform for their clients. For examples, they might advise and counsel an organization's management regularly on communications affecting its publics ("media relations"), do special projects ("special events planning"), serve as an early warning system on emerging issues ("risk management"), or respond to crises ("crisis communication"). In addition, most managers prefer their PR person to represent the organization to the public and communicate with journalists. Important PR functions and forms are described in the list below. Some PR practitioners are generalists, doing everything for a client, while others specialize in an area.

Functions of Public Relations

- ***Publicity or media relations:*** Gaining press coverage through news releases, press conferences, and other materials

- ***Promotion or selling:*** Developing and disseminating print and audiovisual materials, arranging exhibits and displays, and providing promotional giveaways

- ***Community relations:*** Working with community groups and other key community interests that can influence public attitudes and public policies

- ***Government relations:*** Assisting or influencing state, local, or federal government action on problems involving legislation, regulation, and related activity

- ***Public information:*** Developing and disseminating print and audiovisual materials whose purpose is to inform, educate, and assist

- ***Special events:*** Planning and managing internal and external events, such as ground breakings, ribbon-cutting ceremonies, tours, and open houses aimed at attracting public attention

- ***Employee relations:*** Assisting management in informing staff at all levels about personnel policies and practices, labor relations, contracts, benefits, and other issues that involve the health and welfare of the labor force

- ***Risk management, Crisis communications:*** Identifying and helping to manage the big issues that affect institutional success, such as air and water pollution (the environment), foreign competition, ethnic diversity, plant closings or relocations, public censure, and corporate malfeasance

- ***Lobbying:*** Working with legislators and their legislative aides to influence the content and course of legislative action that affects institutional practices through contributions to political action committees (PACs), campaign contributions, and other direct assistance not included as part of more conventional government relations efforts

The Publics of Public Relations

PR activities are addressed to one or more of the many **publics** (or audiences) that can influence an organization's success (such as customers, employees, shareholders and donors) and the news organizations (such as local news outlets) and media they might use (such as newspapers and smart phones). Depending on the needs and interests of the institutions they represent, a particular list of publics could be extensive (see Figure 13.2). Multinational corporations deal with many publics, whereas the average nonprofit organization may deal with only a few. Normally, the publics are targeted with a mix of PR tools and techniques, many of which are used in conjunction with related, but independently developed, marketing, advertising, and human resources initiatives.

> **Publics** are the different audiences that PR practitioners communicate with as part of their daily work.

1. How did big business and muckraking figure into the evolution of public relations?

2. How did Lee, Creel, Bernays, and Fleischman differ in their functions and stakeholders?

3. During times of political turbulence and civil unrest in the 1960s, who had to pay attention to their publics, and why?

4. What PR tools go beyond the traditional press releases, pitch letters, and staged events?

5. What are some of the specialties or functions of public relations?

6. What are the key elements to successful public relations?

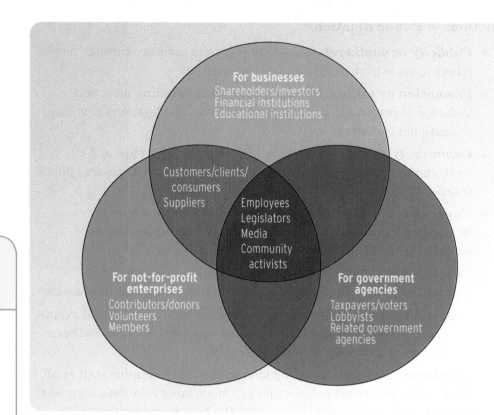

FIGURE 13.2 Examples of PR Publics. Businesses, Not-For-Profit Enterprises and Government Agencies have a variety of publics, and they have some in common.

Four Models of Public Relations

Different purposes of PR may follow different paths. One organization might want to simply get information to the public, while another one might want to hear from users of their products or services. PR experts James E. Grunig and Todd Hunt identified four models of public relations that define the relationship between PR practitioners and their publics. They also represent its evolution in the development of the profession (see Table 13.2).

The model of early press agentry is most commonly associated with P. T. Barnum's style of publicity. He used creativity and almost any means to attract audiences to his enterprises.

The public information model is what you often see in newspapers, magazines, radio, TV, or websites—it is information sent one way, from one source to

TABLE 13.2 Four Models of Public Relations*

MODEL	TYPE OF COMMUNICATION	PURPOSE
Press agentry/publicity	One way	To manipulate public opinion and behavior
Public information/journalism	One way	To disseminate information to the public
Two-way asymmetric	Two way	To persuade and find out how the public reacted
Two-way symmetric	Two way	To gain mutual understanding and find a win-win common ground

*James E. Grunig and Todd Hunt identified four models of public relations that also represent its evolution in their book, *Managing Public Relations*, published by Wadsworth in 1984.

many receivers. This is simply sending news and information about a company, product, or service out to the public. Although Ivy Lee is associated with this model, many PR practitioners work along these lines still today.

The third model of two-way asymmetric is likened to Bernays and Fleischman. They used various methods to influence public opinion and then tested to see if the methods worked. If not, they tinkered with the message or their methods and tested it again.

Bernays and Fleischman are also linked to the fourth model, two-way symmetric. They used social scientific methods to foster a mutual understanding of organizations and their publics. They wanted to know what audiences thought and how their clients could make improvements or help the public. No doubt, Bernays and Fleischman would have appreciated social media as an immediate and ideal way to communicate to, and receive feedback from, audiences. You can guess which model is ideal.

1984

Four models of public relations practice identified by Grunig and Hunt

Your Media Career

PR NUMBERS ARE STABLE

All leading corporations have PR departments of one sort or another. The same goes for major nonprofit organizations such as colleges, hospitals, and national charities. Various names for *public relations* are *public affairs*, *corporate communications*, and *corporate relations*. In specific industries, such as public utilities, you might find the terms *consumer affairs* or *community relations*; in nonprofit and government organizations, it might be *public information*, *public affairs*, or *marketing communications*. In addition, the function may be subdivided further to reflect specific areas, such as investor relations, financial relations, fundraising, charitable contributions, and media relations. Sometimes the subdivision may reflect specific skills, such as writers, videographers, bloggers, or social media managers.

While some PR experts are in corporate communications, others are in agencies, and still more are independent. Most in the industry are concentrated in areas where press services and other communications facilities are readily available and many businesses and trade associations have their headquarters, particularly in New York and Washington, D.C.

The top PR firm in the world is Edelman in New York with about 5,000 employees in more than 65 cities internationally and generating fees of more than $800 million. O'Dwyerpr.com ranks the PR firms in the United States. Holmesreport.com ranks PR firms worldwide and estimates that the top 10 firms together generated almost $5 billion in 2015.

There are more than 240,000 "public relations specialists" and about 57,000 "public relations and fundraising managers" in addition to still more who are self-employed, according to the U.S. Bureau of Labor Statistics (bls.gov). Specialist salaries average $60,000. And, the growth for specialists is about 15,000 new jobs, or the national average of 6 percent for most occupations, into 2024.

Most PR practitioners major in journalism, public relations, or communications and have some experience, such as an internship, while in school. Excellent writing for all media is expected, as well as other types of good communication skills.

Beginning practitioners start in the area of publicity and media relations, learning online tools, writing and editing news releases, mastering desktop publishing for layout and design of brochures, contacting reporters and editors, shooting photos and video, and generating press coverage. Seasoned practitioners are more involved with audience research; setting company policy, planning, and management; training executives to communicate with media; and other sophisticated issues, such as government relations and crisis communications.

MEDIA LITERACY

MAKING PUBLIC RELATIONS ETHICAL AND EFFECTIVE

Throughout history, PR professionals have faced the difficult challenge of performing their functions ethically while still meeting the needs of their clients. Here we examine some of the issues and case studies involved in keeping that balance.

PERSONAL ETHICS IN THE PROFESSION

Everyone thinks they are ethical. You have morals; your friends have morals. You know, however, that many people differ in the level of their principles because there were some pranks last year that you or your friends would or wouldn't join. So, not everyone has an equally high sense of ethical decisions and behaviors nor the guts to differ from group mentality. (But your family, friends, and business associates think they do.)

Most PR practitioners use good judgment and make ethical decisions. However, when a few disregard their inner conscience and do not think about the social consequences of their actions, then the public, their client, the PR image, and they themselves lose out. Their poor decisions attract media attention because of the massive domino effects that can occur; for example, employees may lose their jobs, stockholders may lose their hard-earned investments, or people may lose their lives.

Take the 2014 senate hearings that put General Motors (GM) in hot water. The company waited too late—after 13 deaths spread throughout a decade—to recall 2.6 million cars because of faulty ignition switches. The PR practitioners don't necessarily initiate the actions that lead to the fiascos, but they certainly play a major role in perpetuating the pattern of deception by downplaying the consequences when damages are done and become public.

In worldwide wrongdoing exposure, Volkswagen apparently felt it could cheat on international pollution emissions standards from 2009 to 2015. The carmaker rigged its cars to emit only a certain level of emissions when tested. Otherwise, the car emitted 40 times more, contributing to pollution, while saying its emissions were cleaner than U.S. regulations. After being found out, the company will spend more than $7.3 billion on refitting 500,000 affected VWs, Audis, and Porches. Its stock plummeted and it experienced almost a $2 billion loss within the last quarter of 2015. Some news reports indicated that 30 managers within VW knew for years about the discrepancy. For more than a year before the scandal broke, executives denied any wrongdoing.

Companies that remained silent appear uncaring to the public. It is the PR person's job to see potential problems that may result from a client's decision. Ethical PR practitioners counsel executives to take the high road in an effort to prevent a potential need for crisis management. Ethical practitioners also make commonsense decisions for the good of society.

Although there are accepted codes of ethics that guide the practice of public relations (see Chapter 17), the pressure on many practitioners to give unequivocal support to their employers' actions, even when those actions may be unethical and possibly illegal, remains a critical challenge for the profession. Other issues affecting public relations include personal and professional ethics, public interest, conflicts between private and public interests, professional development, and use of research and evaluation.

CRISIS COMMUNICATIONS MANAGEMENT

Good public relations has many benefits: greater sensitivity to public needs, increased credibility and accountability, stronger public identity, more favorable press coverage, improved employee morale, larger market share, increased sales, and better internal management, among other things. Bad public relations can exist as well, often because the PR people in charge do their jobs poorly or because they choose to work with companies or clients who do not see the public interest as a priority. In these cases, the relationship between the company and the public is not mutually beneficial.

Perhaps company executives allowed the production of faulty products, permitted pollution of the environment, ignored deaths caused by their products, or illegally manipulated the price of the company's stock. In these instances, PR practitioners have a hard job because they are called in to clean up the mess and deal with negative press coverage, public outrage, or regulatory punishment. Only a change in management policy or practice will truly make a difference. Using PR professionals to counsel management, help set company policy, and being proactive instead of reactive would prevent many problems from happening. If one cliché dominates PR thinking, it is this: "You can't undo something once it has happened."

A classic example of crisis communication is when the British Petroleum (BP) Deepwater Horizon oil explosion killed 11 people and wounded 17 more. It emptied 5 million barrels of oil into 4,200 square miles of the Gulf of Mexico and onto 320 miles of Louisiana coastline, threatening wildlife, fisheries, and tourism. It is still spending billions on cleanup. BP gave no apologies, denied responsibility, and pointed fingers at the makers of the rig and the foundation, and the government, for starters. It also wanted $11.8 billion in tax write-offs, claiming the cleanup as an ordinary business expense. This meant U.S. taxpayers would pay about 30 percent of the cleanup costs.

In crisis communication, people want to hear acceptance of responsibility, concern, and plans for rectifying the situation. After its gaffes, BP mounted PR campaigns that included social media and ads in newspapers

BAD PR The Deepwater Horizon explosion and BP's poor reaction is a pertinent example of how bad publicity can hurt major corporations.

Carolyn Cole/PhotoShot

and TV, telling Americans that BP would recapture the oil, clean up the ocean and land, and pay for the cleanup.

Chipolte has a continuous need for crisis communication. It has experienced eight outbreaks that included hepatitis, norovirus, *E. coli*, and salmonella from 2008 to 2015, in addition to earlier problems involving immigrant workers. Their PR practitioners work hard to gain a positive image to the public by having executives apologize in ads for the air-borne illnesses and reaffirming a commitment to food safety.

Some companies and their PR firms have established "dark" sites that can be uploaded at a moment's notice to serve as specialized press rooms should a crisis occur that requires an immediate response. Even celebrities can have dark sites, ready for uploading. For example, when celebrities die unexpectedly, publicists might use a dark site to launch a story and visuals that include details about the celebrity's life and career and special quotes from family members and other celebrities, as well as the circumstances of the death. These crisis-preventive sites can minimize media inquiries for basic facts about the situation and quell or otherwise control rumors.

PRIVATE INTERESTS VERSUS THE PUBLIC INTEREST

Often a natural tension exists between corporate interests and the public interest. This tension can be seen and heard daily in the press when corporations are charged with corruption, environmental pollution, undue political influence, and restraint of trade—in sum, with using their money, power, or influence in ways that compromise or undermine the public interest. In recent years, the agenda of issues has expanded to include critical social issues.

Simply by writing a story and putting a name in the news, the press gives coverage that can advance corporate interests—strong company earnings, successful government initiatives, and noteworthy charitable events. Much of the background for these and related stories, particularly in the business press, comes from reputable PR representatives with a journalism background who send news releases and pitch letters to editors and reporters suggesting angles that they and their publications or stations might take. These representatives also make countless phone calls to the media. They organize press briefings, press luncheons, and other "contacts" to stay in touch with editors and reporters for offensive as well as defensive purposes.

PR practitioners have to worry about what the public wants as much as what their employers want. Consequently, some live with a divided sense of self, whereas others choose clients with goals they appreciate. PR practitioners are both makers of messages and messengers. But most practitioners seem to relish their role despite its inherent difficulties. They understand the importance of the role that public relations plays in society, and they are willing to tolerate criticism in order to accomplish their goal.

The PRSA awards PR practitioners who have shown excellent judgment and skill on behalf of business, government, and nonprofit associations in a variety of categories including crisis management, community relations, issues management, public service, internal communications, and multicultural public relations. Winners of the Silver Anvil Awards can be found online at www.prsa.org/awards/silveranvil.

PROFESSIONAL DEVELOPMENT

Practitioners are continually retooling; their professional development and personal growth are always evolving. Clearly, there is a need for practitioners to become more sophisticated about how to use new technology for communications purposes. They also have to learn more about the basics of business, how it is structured, and how it is managed. Since many practitioners enter the field after majoring in journalism, or a related field, or after having worked in journalism and publishing, they should learn how corporations and small businesses operate. To communicate profit-and-loss issues for their clients, they need to get up to speed as quickly as possible.

There is a great concern in the field about maintaining the high standards in writing and critical thinking, which have been the foundations of the practice's success over the years. Senior practitioners, in particular, complain about how difficult it is to find employees who are strong, journalistically oriented writers.

There has been a growth in the numbers of local, national, and international PR conferences, seminars, and workshops. These meetings cover everything from the basics of public relations to trends and issues driving the management of organizational communications. The PRSA developed a Universal Accreditation program to judge an individual practitioner's understanding and knowledge. Conferences and accreditation open doors to jobs, promotions, and industry leadership. More generally, they underscore the public relations field's interest in improving the value of what practitioners do as communicators in the information society.

USE OF RESEARCH AND EVALUATION

A general criticism of the industry is that practitioners need to conduct more research on their audiences and increase their evaluation of the impact and effectiveness of their PR efforts. Although both activities are included in the traditional PR planning process, research and evaluation are still used scantily in helping define the goals of programs and activities and later in measuring their effectiveness. For example, Nielsen Media Research's SIGMA system has been a boon to VNR producers, allowing them to electronically track the number of stations that aired the VNR and report this information to clients.

Part of the reason for limited assessment is money. Most PR budgets allocate little money for anything beyond the essentials. These budgets focus largely on tactical, not strategic, thinking. To move forward in this area, practitioners integrate research and evaluation into their plans and budgets. They also educate top management on the value of research and development in designing and delivering more effective messages and programs.

Major research techniques in public relations include environmental monitoring (assessing the corporate climate), audits (evaluating an organization's standing with its publics), and readability studies (analyzing a publication's effectiveness). The Barcelona Declaration of Research Principles, mentioned in

STOP & REVIEW

1. What are four models of public relations?

2. Why is ethical behavior important in public relations?

3. What does it mean to be a PR professional?

4. How can some crisis communication emergencies be avoided?

5. What is the role of research and evaluation in public relations, and why is it important?

the Elements of Successful Public Relations section of this chapter, notes seven ways that research is used in different stages of a successful PR campaign.

In the absence of research and evaluation, public relations' effectiveness is compromised and the practitioner's credibility and accountability suffer. Unless you have the expectation of results and measure them, you will never really know whether you have succeeded. Clients or employers cannot rely on promises and recommendations, so you need to point to hard data substantiating the impact of your programs.

SUMMARY & REVIEW

HOW DID BIG BUSINESS AND MUCKRAKING FIGURE INTO THE EVOLUTION OF MODERN PUBLIC RELATIONS?

Muckrakers sought to improve society with their stories as they investigated and uncovered corrupt and unethical business practices. Modern public relations evolved in the late nineteenth century as large corporations sought to defend their interests in the arena of public opinion. The first independent PR counsel was established in the early 1900s. Ivy Lee was an early practitioner who worked to improve the image of the industrialists and German dictators of the late nineteenth century. Arthur Page worked to engage AT&T and the public in a mutually beneficial relationship, and Edward Bernays and Doris Fleischman are widely regarded as the originators of the current professional practice. Mass-persuasion propaganda campaigns during both world wars were also influential in expanding the scope and effectiveness of public relations.

HOW DID LEE (AND BERNAYS AND FLEISCHMAN), CREEL, AND PAGE DIFFER IN THEIR FUNCTIONS AND STAKEHOLDERS?

Ivy Lee, similar to Edward Bernays and Doris Fleischman, was a PR consultant who represented multiple clients (separately or simultaneously) and acted in their clients' best interests. Their employment was similar to that of being owners of a PR agency. Their stakeholders would be anyone who was a potential customer of their client's products. George Creel worked for the U.S. government (his one client) and his job was to promote positive public opinion about the war effort. The messages to the government's various stakeholders would be different, but would be anyone who was patriotic. Arthur Page did corporate communications for one company. AT&T's stakeholders would be investors, customers, legislators, employees, suppliers, and others.

DURING TIMES OF POLITICAL TURBULENCE AND CIVIL UNREST, WHO HAS TO PAY ATTENTION TO THEIR PUBLICS, AND WHY?

It is in the government's best interest to influence the public and to sway public opinion to support its decisions. (It should do more research to find out public opinion before making decisions!) A university promotes the safety of its campuses and educational benefits in times of student protests and marches to its stakeholders and employees and students.

WHAT PR TOOLS GO BEYOND THE TRADITIONAL PRESS RELEASES, PITCH LETTERS, AND EVENTS?

Expansion in the number of media outlets, especially online and mobile devices, has increased the opportunities for PR professionals to present their message to the public. Practitioners use VNRs to place PR stories in newscasts. Satellite networks and videoconferences afford new opportunities to deliver highly targeted press briefings. Multimedia news releases, website press rooms, blogs, podcasts, and tweets are also being applied in modern PR practice. Databases and online information services also help a PR practitioner plan and evaluate a successful campaign. Social media have given practitioners new opportunities to engage the public, without going through traditional media outlets.

WHAT ARE THE KEY ELEMENTS OF SUCCESSFUL PUBLIC RELATIONS?

PR campaigns succeed to the extent that they promote mutual understanding between the organization that sponsors the campaigns and one or more of the publics on which the organization depends to achieve its goals. Although it is a distinct function, public relations often relies on the successful execution of related pursuits, such as using social media, advertising, and marketing, for its campaigns to succeed. Evaluation and attention to ethical standards are two other key elements.

WHAT ARE SOME OF THE SPECIALTIES OR FUNCTIONS OF PUBLIC RELATIONS?

Most large organizations have their own PR departments, although they go by various names, including public affairs and public information. Other corporate communicators (PR) use their skills to connect employees and upper management. There are also thousands of independent PR agencies that supplement corporate PR departments or perform these services for smaller firms. Public relations may also be categorized in terms of functions, including media relations, promotion, community relations, government relations, public information, special events, employee relations, issues management, and lobbying. PR professionals are often members of such organizations as the PRSA and the IPRA.

WHAT ARE THE FOUR MODELS OF PUBLIC RELATIONS?

There are many models of public relations. Grunig's four primary models describe the evolution of PR practices through the years, all of which are still used today: (1) The press agentry/publicity model is the practice of one-way communication, telling the public almost anything to get them to act in a prescribed manner. (2) Public information/journalism operates by simply sending out information you want to convey to the public, through various media channels. You don't even check to see if they got the information. So this is also one way, and not really communication. (3) Two-way asymmetric is sending out information and then doing research to see if the public understands it in the way you intended. If not, then you might refine your methods. (4) Two-way symmetric is the most conducive for optimum mutual benefit. It involves researching the audience and finding out what is important to them and how they get their information, as well as evaluating how the public and the company see their relationship as mutually beneficial.

WHY ARE ETHICS IMPORTANT IN PUBLIC RELATIONS?

Ethical behavior—having high standards of principles and morals—is important in a person's private and social life.

Because the nature of the PR profession is to communicate with different publics, the actions and decisions of a practitioner and his or her client affect the public. Ethical practitioners make commonsense decisions. If you have to think twice about a decision, then your answer is probably evident, and you should go with what your gut tells you. Remember that there will be those who want you to explain your decision. When you disregard your inner voice of truth, then someone loses out and a domino effect occurs; eventual losses can be felt by the public, the company, perhaps its industry, the PR industry, and you. It will be hard finding a new job when the word is out about your bad judgment. And word will get out because a major component of PR is media relations. It is the media's job to tell the news.

HOW CAN SOME CRISIS COMMUNICATION EMERGENCIES BE AVOIDED?

Practitioners counsel executives as to right and moral decisions that are for the greater good. And, they show how these decisions ultimately benefit the company. Bad decisions that have a negative effect on the public ultimately waste time, energy, and money as the company and practitioner try to repair the public's bad feelings about the company. Sometimes bad decisions do not salvage a company and it goes under.

WHAT DOES IT MEAN TO BE A PR PROFESSIONAL?

Today's PR professionals hold college degrees in fields such as journalism, marketing, and mass communication. Also, more than 200 colleges and universities offer programs in the field of public relations. Practitioners seek accreditation from professional societies, such as the PRSA, and follow the society's voluntary ethical standards. They keep up to date by reading professional publications aimed at the PR field. They also participate in continuing education programs to develop their abilities throughout their careers.

WHAT IS THE ROLE OF RESEARCH AND EVALUATION IN PUBLIC RELATIONS?

Research helps PR practitioners improve the effectiveness of their activities, and evaluation helps them determine how effective they have been. Environmental monitoring, audits, readability studies, trend analysis, and evaluation activities, such as soliciting feedback from PR clients and publics, are examples of research and evaluation methods.

THINKING CRITICALLY
ABOUT THE MEDIA

1. Why and how has PR become a profession over the years?

2. Imagine that you are a PR practitioner hired to promote a shelter for homeless families. What steps and tools would you use and why?

3. Let's say a client wants to hire your agency. The only problem is that you don't agree with their ethics. What would you do and why?

4. Discuss if public relations has changed over the years in its primary purpose, or if it is only the tools that have changed.

5. Can you identify some organizations and public figures today who need public relations, and why?

MindTap

Test your knowledge with online printable flashcards and online quizzing.

KEY TERMS

propaganda (p. 339)

public opinion (p. 339)

public relations (p. 339)

publics (p. 353)

corporate communications (p. 350)

live stream (p. 346)

on demand (p. 346)

media relations (p. 350)

PR agency (p. 350)

snowball effect (p. 348)

webcast (p. 346)

MindTap Log on to the MindTap Communication for *Media Now* to access a variety of additional material, including this chapter's ebook, learning objectives, comprehension quizzes, videos, and more!

ADVERTISING

LEARNING OBJECTIVES
....

After studying the topics in this chapter, you will be able to:

1   Explain how the technologies of the Industrial Revolution ushered in the modern era of advertising.
2   Distinguish integrated marketing communication and viral marketing from conventional advertising.
3   Evaluate the impact of new media technologies on the evolution of advertising. Explain the importance of database marketing in targeting consumers.
4   Describe the functions within an advertising agency that combine to produce an ad campaign.
5   Outline the elements of a successful advertising plan.
6   List the strengths and weaknesses for each of the following advertising media: print newspapers, magazines, television, radio, Internet, and mobile media.
7   List at least five ways to persuade consumers to respond favorably to advertising.
8   Describe the possible negative impacts of advertising on society.

HISTORY: FROM HANDBILLS TO MOBILE ADS

The history of advertising is the story of how advertising professionals take advantage of the new media of the day to craft creative messages to entice consumers and to innovate with business models that serve advertisers better. The process continues today as mobile ads on our smartphones and tablets push aside "old media" like newspapers, magazines, television, and even desktop computers.

Advertising is often thought of as a twentieth-century phenomenon, but it is a creative art form that has existed for centuries. Signage on the walls of ancient cities of Greece and Rome marketed food and wine. Centuries later, town criers filled the streets of Europe to tell the citizenry about the "good deal" to be found "just around the corner." Pop-up ads and Twitter tweets are the advertising signs and cries of today.

The printing press was the hot new technology of its day when it was introduced in Europe in 1455 (see Chapter 3). It soon spawned a new form of advertising, the *handbill*. With this new medium, the message could be copied efficiently and distributed to many people

to where the flavour is.
Marlboro Country.

Marl

LOW TO MIDDLE TAR As defined by H.M.Government,
ET CARRIES A GOVERNMENT HEALTH WARI

Advertising Archives

AD ICON The Marlboro Man illustrates the power of advertising even when the product is harmful to consumers.

MEDIA THEN··· MEDIA NOW

1625
> First newspaper ads are printed

1704
> Boston News-Letter publishes first ad in America

1849
> Volney Palmer originates the term advertising agency

1865
> George Rowell founds first modern ad agency

1905
> Kennedy and Lasker redefine advertising as "salesmanship in print"

1911
> Lansdowne and Resor pioneer the soft sell

1926
> First radio ads

1941
> The first TV ad is broadcasted in the United States

1989
> Integrated Marketing Communications makes its name

1994
> The first banner ad appears on the Internet

2006
> Google becomes the leading advertising vehicle

2016
> Mobile ad spending exceeds desktop ads

1625

First newspaper ads are printed

> **Advertising** is communication that is paid for and is usually persuasive in nature.

1704

Boston News-Letter publishes first ad in America

in a relatively short time, and the content could be expanded to include detailed product descriptions and "special offers" to induce sales. Printing also enabled the first newspaper advertisements, which began around 1625 (see Chapter 5). Those were thus the ancestors of the newsfeed ads found in Facebook today.

Advertising in America

The earliest newspaper ads in America were classified ads published in the *Boston News-Letter* in 1704 (see Chapter 4) (Sandage, Fryburger, & Rotzoll, 1989). An example of advertising from the colonial period is the following ad, which appeared in Benjamin Franklin's newspaper, the *Pennsylvania Gazette*.

To be SOLD A Plantation containing 300 acres of good Land, 30 cleared, 10 or 12 Meadows and in good English Grass, a house and barn lying in Nantmel Township, upon French Creek, about 30 miles from Philadelphia, Enquire of Simon Merideith.

Benjamin Day's *The Sun* originated the concept of the mass circulation newspaper, or Penny Press, in 1833 (see Chapter 4). That transformed what today we would call the business model of advertising. From that point on, we see advertising emerging both as a form of persuasive communication, bought and paid for by the advertiser, and later as an economic engine with the potential to support the media enterprise financially.

EARLY PRINT ADVERTISING This ad for Cook's Virginia tobacco appeared around 1720. It is an early example of enhancing print ads with illustrations.

The Origins of the Advertising Profession

The business relationships between advertisers and media evolved as mass production expanded from local to regional to national markets and as the number and scope of advertising-supported publications grew (Sivulka, 2012). The complexity of the then-new print media gave rise to a profession of "go-betweens," the predecessors of today's advertising professionals.

The earliest advertising professionals were essentially advertising agents, who wholesaled advertising space on behalf of publishers. The best-known advertising agent from this era was Volney B. Palmer, who coined the term *advertising agency* in 1849. Palmer represented some 1,300 newspapers and originated the commission system, under which publishers paid a fee on completion of an advertising sale. Palmer also offered a wider range of services than other agents. He not only sold advertising space but also produced the ads, delivered them to the publishers, and verified their placement—all important functions of advertising agencies today.

In 1865, George P. Rowell, considered to be the founder of the advertising agency as we know it today, began contracting with local newspapers for a set amount of space and then brokered the space to clients. This arrangement made Rowell something of an independent "middleperson" who had to cater to both publishers and advertising clients. Rowell advised his clients on which newspapers to select for their needs.

Political propaganda also played an important role in the evolution of modern advertising. During World War I, advertising found its voice directed away from the materialistic needs of the average citizen and toward the good of the country as a whole. This campaign—in which advertising pioneer Albert Lasker played an important part—included activities designed to build public sentiment for the war effort as well as appeals to the home front to curtail unnecessary consumption and to "buy war bonds" instead. The success of the war bond drives convinced many of the power of advertising.

MindTap®

Start with a quick warm-up activity.

1849

Volney Palmer originates the term *advertising agency*

1865

George Rowell founds first modern ad agency

MindTap®

Read, highlight, and take notes on the complete chapter text in a rich interactive online platform.

The Rise of Broadcast Advertisers

Radio, the new technology of the early twentieth century, came of age as an advertising medium in 1926 with the formation of the NBC and CBS radio networks (see Chapter 7) that depended exclusively on advertising revenues. The creation of the radio networks gave national advertisers an unprecedented means of distributing messages to prospects across the nation simultaneously (Fox, 1984). Thus, radio gave advertisers advantages of broad scope and immediacy that are amplified by mobile advertising today.

Radio had two important limitations: it could not show pictures of the products and did not lend itself to detailed product descriptions. That created an opportunity for the growth of magazine advertising between the two world wars, a period that saw the birth and growth of mass-circulation magazines like *Time* and *LIFE*.

The first television ad was broadcast in 1941, but the years following World War II saw the explosive expansion of television as a new advertising medium, especially after the establishment of national television networks in 1948. Television quickly grew to compete with other forms of mass communication as the key creative medium for national advertisers. The combination of sight and sound gave advertisers the ability to demonstrate products to millions of viewers in a dramatic way.

Library of Congress Prints and Photographs Division [LC-US2C4-9850]

ADVERTISING GOES TO WAR During World War I, advertising turned from promoting consumption of goods to getting citizens involved in the war effort by buying war bonds. After the war, ad agencies applied techniques perfected during the war to mass market consumer goods.

Hard Sell Versus Soft Sell

The story of advertising is also the story of innovation with new advertising forms. At the turn of the nineteenth century, advertising copy was usually brief and hyperbolic, and most ads sought a *direct response,* in the form of a mail-in from the reader. New approaches were needed to rise above the clutter of screechy direct-response ads. A defining moment in advertising occurred in 1905 when John E. Kennedy, a copywriter working in partnership with Albert Lasker at the Lord & Thomas advertising agency in New York, redefined advertising as "salesmanship in print." This *hard-sell* approach to advertising as a mediated sales tool used persuasive techniques and introduced the "reason why" philosophy to copy preparation (Wells, Burnett, & Moriarty, 1995). Ads turned into lengthy arguments on behalf of the advertiser that were expected to prompt a delayed response that kicked in the next time the reader visited the store. The hard sell lent itself to print media and so declined as radio and TV became popular, although we still see it today in television informercials and on websites that boast at length about the features and specifications of their products.

The *soft-sell* approach was pioneered in 1911 by the first female copywriter Helen Lansdowne and her partner Stanley Resor at the J. Walter Thompson agency. Their ad for Woodbury Soap featured the slogan, "A skin you love to touch." Their approach took advantage of the newfound ability to print photographs and color illustrations (as opposed to labor-intensive hand engravings) of products. That made it possible to feature enticing and entertaining images of the product and an emotional rather than a rational appeal. The soft-sell became so prevalent by the 1980s that this period is often referred to as the **era of creativity**.

The Era of Integrated Marketing Communication

Although traditional advertising has long been the most common form of marketing communication, it no longer dominates the way it once did. For example, the 30-second prime-time network television advertising spot, which was the ideal vehicle for reaching a national mass audience for nearly 50 years, is in deep decline in the eyes of advertisers. The broadcast television audience has been fragmented by cable TV and drawn away by the Internet and video games, while viewers avoid ads and delay viewing with digital video recorders (DVRs) such as TiVo and streaming video services like Hulu. This has led to a new television advertising form—or rather a return to one that was prevalent in the late 1940s and early 1950s (see Chapter 9)—in which products are featured, or "placed," in the entertainment portion of the program. For example, during the 2014 Academy Awards broadcast, host Ellen DeGeneres transmitted a "selfie" from the stage using a smartphone manufactured by Samsung, one of the sponsors of the event.

Today, marketers choose from a wide array of media—from ads delivered to smartphones to those viewed before watching a streaming video. This situation recreates a phenomenon known as **integrated marketing communication (IMC)** a term originated in 1989. IMC involves the use of virtually all communication channels available to the marketer, not limited to advertising media. For example, in recent years, the ready-to-eat cereal industry has done more **sales promotion** (coupons, sweepstakes, sampling, etc.) than advertising. In the era of IMC, advertising media are not the only options, and the media used ultimately depends on the needs of the advertiser. Today, companies do not restrict themselves to advertising but instead try to find that combination of audience-focused advertising, **direct marketing**, public relations, and sales promotions that builds and sustains a relationship with the consumer to achieve their goals (Kitchen & Burgmann, 2004).

Advertising Now

What makes advertising both more exciting and challenging than ever now is the proliferation of new advertising media and business models. Technological innovations such as *ad servers* like DoubleClick (a subsidiary of Google) that

SOFT SELL iPod ads like this one stress the pleasure of using the product rather than rational arguments for buying it. A hard sell approach would list the specifications and price of the device and present verbal arguments for making the purchase.

In the **era of creativity,** advertisers emphasized entertainment as well as information.

1989

Integrated Marketing Communications makes its name

Integrated marketing communications (IMC) assures that the use of all commercial media and messages is clear, consistent, and influential.

Sales promotions are specific features like coupons that directly spur sales.

Direct marketing is a form of advertising that requests an immediate consumer response.

call up personalized advertisements to Web pages and e-mail alerts of new products and special offers from Amazon have ushered in a new phase of IMC. Now, advertisers seek to communicate and engage with consumers on an individual and ongoing basis in addition to reaching them through conventional mass media. For example, Procter & Gamble's award-winning 2015 Always #LikeAGirl campaign combined a documentary film, a Superbowl ad, and a Twitter hash tag to reach 85 million YouTube downloads, building awareness of sex-role stereotypes as well as P&G's relevance to a new generation of consumers. The Internet also provides the first global communication medium for advertisers. In the next section, we examine some of the technology trends that lend new sizzle to advertising, but there are three that stand above the rest: social media, mobile media, and the humble-looking sponsored links that appear at the top and sides of Google's search engine results.

Display ads appearing in social media are a fast-growing, multi-billion-dollar business, with Facebook racking up revenues that rival those of broadcast television networks. The strategy is **viral marketing,** to stimulate brand-related discussion and hope that others will carry it on, spreading word about the product like a virus to new customers. Social media campaigns don't always rely on the conventional ad agency model, such as the Pepsi Refresh campaign that generated online buzz by doling out $20 million in grants to charitable causes. Other social media campaigns rely on relatively low-cost promotional activities, such as creating fan pages on Facebook or organizing celebrity plugs in Twitter (basketball star LeBron James reportedly gets $125,000 per tweet, but Kim Kardashian is a bargain at $30,000). Marketers can get free advertising from "word of mouse" generated by consumers in online chat rooms.

> **Viral marketing** spreads ideas about products through chat rooms, blogs, social networking sites, or other Internet-based avenues.

Sponsored links helped Google become the number one advertising vehicle in 2006 and propelled the entire online advertising industry to double-digit annual growth at the expense of the Big Five traditional advertising media, notably network radio and local television. Behind the sponsored links is a revolution in the way that advertising is bought, sold, and evaluated: advertisers bid against one another in an auction for prime locations near the top of the results, paying anywhere from a few nickels to over $100 per click for their favorite search words. Search-based ads are changing the way that advertisers think about advertising and their ad agencies by making it possible to precisely target ads to consumers who are actively engaged in seeking information about products they might like to buy.

Leading global ad agencies (see Table 14.1) have had to add disciplines like *search engine optimization,* the art of getting their clients' websites near the top of Google's search results, to their skill sets. Search-based ads also give advertisers the ability to precisely measure the response to their ads through the analytic data Google provides them. *Big Data* is also capturing the attention of advertisers who compile huge files of proprietary consumer information from visits to their own websites and offline promotions, and combine that with consumer credit card transaction

TABLE 14.1 2014 Worldwide Revenue for Top Five Largest Ad Agencies

ORGANIZATION	HEADQUARTERS	WORLDWIDE REVENUE (BILLIONS)
WPP Group	New York	$19
Omnico	New York	$15.3
Publicis	Paris	$ 9.6
Interpublic Group	New York	$ 7.5
Dentsu	Tokyo	$ 6.0

Source: http://adage.coverleaf.com/advertisingage/20150504?pg=71#pg72

information and online behavior tracking to better understand and target consumers. Some large advertisers, including giant Procter & Gamble, are slashing their outlays to advertising agencies as they pursue online strategies that they find produce a better return on investment than conventional media buys placed through ad agencies.

Here is a quote often attributed to department store magnate John Wanamaker, one of the "fathers" of advertising: "Half the money I spend on advertising is wasted; the trouble is I don't know which half." If he were alive today, he might be to able tell which half that was, and that is the promise that drives growth in digital advertising (Figure 14.1). However, the same might be said for the video ads that that pop up on websites. Many of these are tiny, buried deeply inside websites, or are launched automatically so that they fail to attract the attention of visitors.

Aware of the dwindling attention span of the smartphone generation, thought to be about 8 seconds, advertisers are trying to capitalize on fleeting "moments" of attention, such as the time it takes to swipe a smartphone screen to view the latest alerts. Even more exciting to advertisers than interest-based search ads are location-based ads that appear on smartphones as consumers walk past a store or stroll down the aisles of a supermarket. In 2016, the revenue from mobile ads appearing on smartphones and tablets in the U.S. market surpassed the expenditures for "conventional" digital ads accessed through personal computers, even as total digital ad spending nearly matched television ad spending for the first time (eMarketer, 2016).

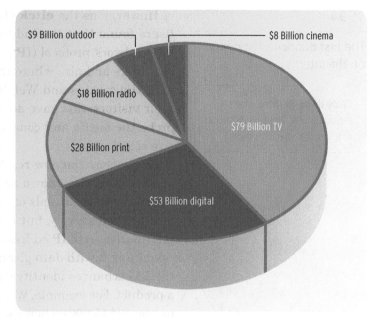

FIGURE 14.1 SLICING THE ADVERTISING PIE The total annual spending on advertising in the United States is $195 billion, with TV and digital accounting for almost two-thirds of the total.

Source: eMarketer (2013). US Total Media Ad Spend Inches Up, Pushed by Digital http://www.eMarketer.com/Article/US-Total-Media-Ad-Spend-Inches-Up-Pushed-by-Digital/1010154#0gXxUxcLlbejbSb;.9E

TECHNOLOGY: NEW ADVERTISING MEDIA

The technology of advertising has developed side by side with the technology of the mass media. We will not recount these developments here since they are covered in Chapters 3 through 12, but will instead focus on the ways in which information technologies transform conventional advertising forms and practices.

Advertising in Cyberspace

The banner ads that initially attracted the attention of advertisers to the Internet in 1994 took advantage of the basic hypertext linking capability of the Internet (see Chapter 10). By clicking on the narrow horizontal *banner* that appeared across the top of the page, consumers were immediately connected to the advertiser's website, where they could find more information, tempting product images, and, in some cases, the advertiser's own e-commerce site at which they could complete a sale.

2016

Mobile ad spending exceeds desktop ads

STOP & REVIEW

1. How would you describe advertising as a form of communication?

2. What role did the Penny Press play in ushering in the era of modern advertising?

3. How did wartime advertising influence the development of advertising?

4. How does the advertising of the early twentieth century differ from today's advertising?

5. What is integrated marketing communication (IMC)?

6. How are technological innovations the nature of advertising and advertising agencies?

Click-through rate is the percentage of readers who click on an ad to visit the advertiser's page.

However, as the **click-through rates** for banner ads plummeted, advertisers found that the hidden gold of the Internet was buried deeper, in the internetwork protocol (IP), which tells website owners the Internet addresses of visitors and also where they surfed from and where they go next. Together with the cookies and Web bugs (see Chapter 10) that websites use to track their visitors, this gave advertisers an unprecedented ability to identify and probe the media and consumption habits of individual consumers on a massive scale.

Advertisers can now reach consumers efficiently through a system of online ad networks, also known as *ad servers,* such as DoubleClick and OpenX. They partner with thousands of websites to display Internet ads that reach millions of users collectively, but that also target each individual user. By collating information from IP addresses, cookies, Web bugs, and online transactions and combining it with data gleaned from public records and credit card purchases, the ad exchanges identify website visitors who are likely prospects for buying a product. For example, Web users who divulged their age (say, 21) and annual incomes ($45,000) when they registered at a website and who recently read a new car review in the *New York Times* might be tagged as targets for ads for entry-level autos. Ad servers collate the demographic information (deposited in a cookie on the user's hard drive that can be opened and read by the ad server) with the surfing patterns collected by the *Times.* The next time the user opens the *Times* home page, he or she might see an ad for a new Honda Civic inserted in the home page, whereas prospective sofa buyers will see an ad for furniture. The ad servers are also responsible for many of the pop-up ads that we find annoying when they open on top of (or underneath) a Web page we are trying to reach.

Google's sponsored links show advertisements that are specific to the keywords, or *adwords* as Google refers to them, typed into its search engine. Advertisers bid for pride of place through a simple online interface that suggests an initial cost per click, reports the traffic that results, and suggests a higher bid when an ad has fallen too far down the page to be seen by most visitors to the Google search engine. If you subscribe to Google's Gmail service, you may also see sponsored links appear next to the e-mail messages, like the one Mom sends explaining that she can't send you money because she ran out of checks. Google analyzes keywords in the e-mail so that you might, in this fictitious example, see a sponsored link to a money-wiring service that accepts credit cards.

Through its AdSense program, Google analyzes key words in the discussions of participating blogs and other participating content providers, posts relevant advertisements in them, and shares 68 percent of the ad revenues with the content providers. For example, a blog about college football might attract a beer advertisement. Unlike the simple search ads that appear alongside Google search results, these ads can include graphics, audio, and videos. Some blogs have been extremely successful in generating advertising revenue. For example, the eHow website earns $500,000 a month in AdSense revenues by featuring items like "10 Tips for Dressing like a French Girl."

Google and Facebook have automated advertising buying with online *ad exchanges* that operate in real time with computerized instructions from advertisers or their agencies. Through the exchanges, advertisers can bid for the exact number of clicks or display ad impressions they want from a precisely defined target audience. This helps advertisers take advantage of the rich streams of data gleaned from tracking users online to identify target audiences.

Advertisements are popping up everywhere in cyberspace. The Internet Advertising Bureau has some two dozen standard options so that Internet ads now fill more of the Web page and may appear in the middle of pages instead of at the top and bottom margins. Animated ads play audio and video clips or feature graphics that sometimes literally leap across the page. *Intermercials* (ads appearing before the ISP connects to the Internet) and *buttons* (miniature banner ads) are other recent developments. *Floaters* are similar to pop-ups, but they use Flash animations (see Chapter 10) and are immune to the pop-up blockers many Internet users have to evade pop-up ads. Ads also appear in RSS (Really Simple Syndication) feeds, text messages that crawl at the bottom of popular websites with updates of the latest news, weather, and sports.

Social Networking: Advertisers' New Frontier

Advertisers value social networking because they believe that learning about products from our online associates is more believable and hence more effective than conventional ads. Because Facebook users provide rich demographic information, such as age, sex, and geographic location, as well as information about their life interests, "likes," important events, and media preferences, and also yield detailed information about their online activities, the social networking site is an advertiser's dream. In its efforts to attract more advertising dollars, Facebook is expanding its smartphone business and injecting video ads into its news feeds.

Media & Culture

COLLEGE STUDENTS RULE THE MARKETPLACE

The 18- to 24-year-old college student crowd is one of the favorites of advertisers. They set trends. They have discretionary income, both theirs and their parents. Although this group is one of the smallest U.S. demographics, 22 million compared with the 80 million baby boomers, they are vastly influential.

Marketers and demographers haven't decided yet what to call the generation that the current crop of college students belong to. They are too young to be millennials, also known as Generation Y, who were born between 1977 and 1994 by most accounts. Since today's students grew up after the invention of the Web (in 1991) and after the Internet opened to the general public (in 1995, see Chapter 10), they are sometimes referred to as "digital natives."

The annual American Freshman Survey provides some insights into the new generation (Eagan et al., 2015). At this point in their lives, they express relatively liberal social values. One-third identified themselves as "liberal" or "far left," more than in recent years and nearly equal to the Baby Boomers who entered college in the early 1970s. They are highly involved in volunteering and community service and politial activism grew markedly compared to preceding freshman classes. They have high regard for their academic ability, co-operativeness, and drive but relatively little for their artistic ability, popularity, and—surprisingly—computer skills. Biology, nursing are their top major choices, and three-fourths plan to obtain a degree beyond a bachelor's. In terms of media use, about three-fifths said they spent less than 3 hours a week watching TV, but more than half spent 3 hours a week or more on social networks during their last year in high school.

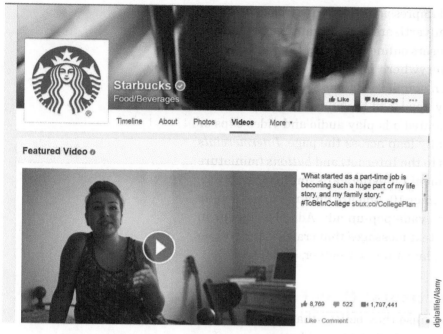

SOCIAL MEDIA ADVERTISING Companies like Starbucks have embraced social networking sites like Facebook, where they can freely invite users to "like" them. When an advertisement shows up on a page, it will also indicate which of your friends "like" that company.

Twitter allows a group of celebrities, bloggers, and regular Internet users to send advertisers' commercial messages to their personal contacts and sells access to its Trending Items list. Ad.ly is the social-media advertorial clearinghouse company most celebrities use to get paid to tweet. YouTube, the video-sharing website and a subsidiary of Google, has also become an advertising revenue generator. The website places advertisements with and around partner videos and splits the revenues with the creators.

Mobile Ads: The Newer Frontier

Smartphone ads are the next big thing in the advertising world because of their ability to reach consumers when they are in the neighborhood of a fast food franchise or standing in front of a retailer's product display. For example, Google owns AdMob, an ad server that inserts ads in Web pages and apps seen on smartphones that stimulate "click through" to the advertiser's website and AT&T's ShopAlerts notifies users about special offers when they pass near a participating retailer. Foursquare adds social media to the equation, with the ability to locate Facebook friends and Twitter followers in the real world while generating awareness of special offers from local merchants and national brands connected to the places where their social media relations "check in." The latest trend in mobile ads is to take advantage of "moments"; for example, the moment that a user located in the bar district enters a search for "taxi," an ad for Uber (or alcohol abuse counseling) might pop up. Ads delivered via the Internet to personal computers have similar capabilities, but smartphone ads achieve much higher response rates, at least while the novelty lasts.

A variety of technologies can be used to track smartphones, including built-in geo positioning satellite (GPS) receivers and triangulation with nearby cell phone towers (see Chapter 11). Once inside a store, near field communication chips can be added to in-store displays to track you and detect what you are looking at. Some day, the chips may be embedded in the products themselves to tell advertisers what you are interested in enough to pluck from the shelf.

Bar codes are another fast-growing facet of mobile advertising. Smartphone apps use the devices' built-in cameras to scan bar codes to automatically display product information and consumer reviews, download electronic coupons, show videos, or dial a live operator without having to type or search for information. The technology makes conventional print ads interactive by printing small blocks of black-and-white squares called a QR (*Quick Response*) code next to each featured item. They can also be embedded in outdoor billboards and in-store advertising displays to make them into interactive, location-based advertising tools.

They Have Our Number

The Internet is only one aspect of information technology that creates new ways of building relationships between consumers and brands. **Database marketing** makes this possible on a grand scale; it is part of the Big Data trend that is revolutionizing market research and advertising. One need not look further than a local grocery store for a starting point of database marketing. When we customers apply for discount cards or check-cashing privileges, we fill out a questionnaire giving personal information (address, occupation, income, product preferences, and so on) that is stored in a database along with a record of our purchases. The warranty cards we send in and the extended warranties we purchase when purchasing consumer products are also fodder for database marketers.

> **Database marketing** is used when advertisers store information about consumers so that they can personalize messages.

The information we supply is aggregated into national databases and then resold by *data brokers* like Acxiom and Equifax. Data brokers combine point-of-sale data with records of our credit card purchases; information gleaned from public birth, real estate, voting, and driver's license records; and data about our online activities. The brokers sell our information to ad agencies and advertisers, who in turn add the information in their databases where they match it to personally identifiable data generated by their customer service hotlines and websites. So, if a consumer regularly buys chocolate chip cookies but does not purchase the cookies during a grocery shopping trip, the checkout counter transaction might generate a coupon for the cookies.

Database marketing relies on a process known as *data mining,* or the ongoing compilation and analysis of pertinent data for the purpose of updating marketing strategies as consumer needs evolve. Data mining enables much more targeted advertising, even individual targeting. For example, a newspaper or a cable television company experiencing declining subscriptions might add information purchased from a data broker to its own customer database to identify high-value customers most likely to cancel subscriptions and then use direct mail to target them with special discount offers.

E-Commerce

E-commerce harkens back to the early days of advertising when a direct response from the customer was the goal. Direct marketers have long experimented with their appeals to find the best ones before launching new campaigns. E-commerce websites and online advertisers generally take direct marketing a step further by experimenting in real time with content strategies and marketing approaches to find the most effective ones. For example, when introducing a new design for a website landing page or an online display ad, an e-commerce site can direct randomly selected visitors to a version featuring either a 10 percent off promotion or a free shipping offer and directly compare the sales that result.

Some e-commerce proprietors still rely heavily on spam, or unsolicited commercial e-mail using addresses harvested from unwitting users who post them on Web pages. In the United States, the **CAN-SPAM Act** outlaws this practice.

> **CAN-SPAM Act** regulates commercial e-mail.

Nonetheless, spamming survives, often including Web bugs (see Chapter 10) in the e-mails that automatically notify the sender if the message has been opened, signaling a gullible prospect to be included in future spam campaigns. Legitimate spammers (yes, they do exist) use *permission marketing techniques* in which the consumer consents to receiving e-mail when registering at a website or activating a product warranty. In contrast, illegitimate spammers send their messages from countries that don't have anti-spam laws. Spam persists because it is free to send, so that a response rate of a few one-hundredths of 1 percent—"male enhancement" spam for men and fashion spam for women are among the most effective—is enough to make spamming profitable.

Advertising Everywhere

Hardly a week goes by without an announcement about a new way to reach consumers with advertising. Ads reach our ears in podcasts, satellite radio stations, and Internet radio streams. Advertising reaches our eyes through ad spots in streaming videos online, in product placements embedded in the programs we watch, through smartphone apps, and in movie theaters. Video games also include product placements, such as Adidas billboards that ring the stadiums in sports games, as well as interactive ads that, for example, make it possible to order pizza from within the game. Another trend is to make ads into a game; for example, McDonald's *Big Mac Farm Challenge* is an *advergame* that shows children how ingredients fresh from the farm go into their hamburgers.

That oldest form of advertising, the outdoor sign, is also undergoing a high-tech makeover. Digital imaging technology imposes signage onto stadium and arena walls that does not exist outside of the television screen, the same basic technique that superimposes a visible first-down line on the screen for football fans. Electronic message boards place billboard-like ads in malls and other indoor venues. Tri-face or revolving signs give more advertisers the chance to promote themselves in sports arenas. The same technology that makes it possible to project ads onto sports arena billboards during telecasts also makes it possible to project images onto dummy boxes of cereals posing on the breakfast tables in family sitcoms. Some day your DVR might insert ads customized for the viewers: boxes of Grape Nuts for seniors, Cocoa Puffs for young families. The cost of computer chips that can synthesize the human voice is dropping quickly, raising the specter of the "talking cereal box" shouting advertising slogans at us as we walk down the supermarket aisle or reminding us (or our smartphone) to stock up when the box is half empty.

INDUSTRY: INSIDE THE ADVERTISING INDUSTRY

Someone must identify the need for an advertising message—and foot the bill for the campaign that results. This initiator is the advertiser. Then the message must be created. Here the responsibility may either be retained by the advertiser or be subcontracted to an advertising agency. Next, the message must be placed in one or more of the **advertising media,** each of which has its own organizational form and structure. **Research organizations,** data brokers, and online data analytics providers then help all concerned evaluate

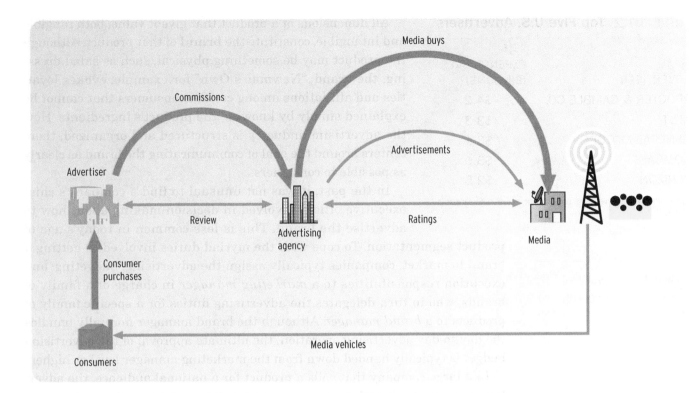

FIGURE 14.2 HOW ADVERTISING WORKS Advertisers pay commissions to agencies to create ads, and then review their work. Advertising agencies buy time on media and place ads according to ratings data. The media reach the public with the ad, and they buy the advertisers' product (or not). Consumer purchases resulting from the ads finance the next round of ad buys

and measure the target group, the message content, and the media vehicles under consideration. You can follow the development of an advertising campaign from the moment of its conception by an advertiser to its presentation to the public by examining Figure 14.2.

What makes the advertising industry so exciting is the dramatic interactions among these players and the competition between ad agencies and media outlets. The agency's creative staff may work for months on a concept for a new advertising campaign, only to have it shot down in a client meeting. Advertisers periodically fire agencies, even those who have been with them for decades, when their ad campaigns no longer produce the desired level of sales. Then competitions are held among agencies, sometimes ending in a "shoot-out" in which finished commercials are pitted against one another. Increasingly, advertisers and their agencies make dramatic changes in their purchases of advertising time based on audience trends revealed by media researchers, such as moving spending away from local TV and toward the Internet and mobile. Market researchers and data miners periodically chime in with findings that seem to shout "This changes everything!" and force advertisers and agencies to rethink their approach.

Advertisers

The top categories of advertising expenditures are retail, telecommunications, automotive, financial services, and medicine and remedies. In 2013, $157.4 billion was spent on advertising in the United States. Leading national companies such as Procter & Gamble and General Motors lead the list of major advertisers (Table 14.2).

TABLE 14.2 Top Five U.S. Advertisers

ADVERTISER	2015 EXPENDITURES (BILLIONS)
PROCTER & GAMBLE CO.	$4.2
AT&T	$3.3
GENERAL MOTORS	$3.1
COMCAST	$3.0
VERIZON	$2.5

Source: http://www.businessinsider.com/10-biggest-advertising-spenders-in-the-us-2015-7

A **brand** consists of all the dimensions that identify and give unique value to a product or company.

All dimensions of a product that give it value, both tangible and intangible, constitute the **brand** of that product. Although the product may be something physical, such as salad dressing, the brand, "Newman's Own" for example, evokes loyalties and affiliations among certain consumers that cannot be explained simply by knowing the product's ingredients. How the advertising industry is structured and organized, then, centers around the goal of communicating the brand as clearly as possible to consumers.

In the past, it was not unusual to find a company's chief executive officer involved in decision making about how to advertise the brand. This is less common in today's age of product segmentation. To cope with the myriad duties involved in getting a brand to market, companies typically assign the advertising, budgeting, and execution responsibilities to a *marketing manager* in charge of a family of brands, who in turn delegates the advertising duties for a specific family of products to a *brand manager.* Although the brand manager normally handles the day-to-day advertising operation, the ultimate approval of the advertising budget is typically handed down from the marketing manager level or higher.

In a large company that sells a product for a national audience, the advertising process begins when the marketing manager and the advertising manager of the firm settle on the advertising goals, deadlines, and expectations for the coming year. The creation of the advertising message is generally not performed by the company itself but instead is delegated to an advertising agency (see Figure 14.1, page 369). An advertising agency can provide an outside, objective perspective that companies can't get internally. The advertising manager invites a number of agencies to make presentations and, when one is selected, acts as a liaison between the firm and the agency.

For a local retailer, the process is much simpler. Typically, the owner determines approximately how much to spend on advertising in the coming year, writes the ads, and arranges to have them placed in local newspapers, on local websites, or in other local media. This is not to say, however, that the selection of the target for the ad or the development of the message is any less important. It is just that the process unfolds on a somewhat lesser scale than in a national program.

Local retailers also take advantage of *co-op advertising support* from national companies. For example, a retail store that buys a product such as Colgate toothpaste gets an allowance for advertising from the Colgate-Palmolive Company. Ready-made print ads are also provided for the retailer to use. In other words, a good share of local advertising is actually paid for by national advertisers.

Although the positions of brand manager and advertising manager remain important in most companies, there is a growing necessity for all marketing employees to know something about advertising. For this reason, in some companies the vice president of marketing is often a person skilled in *marketing communication,* as are the marketing managers and brand managers.

Inside the Advertising Agency

Most major companies do not want to plan and produce advertising campaigns themselves. Their business is to produce and sell a product, be it tennis shoes, soft drinks, or dog food. Therefore, a variety of advertising agencies have grown up at local, national, and international levels to plan and produce ad campaigns for them.

Agencies are organizations of business people and talented individuals who create and place **advertising plans** (see Table 14.3) for their clients. Today, full-service agencies complete virtually all elements of an advertising campaign, including research, strategic planning, and generation of creative ideas for ads. These companies employ **account executives,** who act as liaisons between the agency and the client. They mobilize and coordinate all of the agency's work on the advertising campaign and are one of the entry points for careers in advertising (see Your Media Career: Becoming a Madperson).

Agencies are experiencing considerable change stimulated by both new technology and the trend toward efficiency. A decade ago, agencies handled advertising in traditional media such as newspapers, magazines, television, and radio. Today, clients insist that they have expertise in direct marketing, online advertising, sales promotion, and public relations so that they can implement all aspects of integrated marketing communication campaigns. The following sections discuss the major departments within a typical ad agency.

The Creative Department. A key element in the advertising plan is the creative strategy, or what the advertising will say in order to achieve the objectives of the campaign. Using the research data as a foundation, copywriters

> The **advertising plan** is a written document outlining the objectives and strategies for a product's advertising.

> **Account executives** are the liaisons between the agency and the client.

TABLE 14.3 Elements of an Advertising Plan

ELEMENT	PURPOSE
Situation analysis	Explains where the company is, how it got there, and where it wants to be in the future. It identifies relevant problems that must be addressed by advertising and gives a detailed description of the consumer and the product.
Objectives	The goals we want the advertising campaign to achieve. Most advertising plans include both business objectives ("Increase unit sales by 25,000 during the next year") and communication objectives ("Achieve 65% awareness of the product within the target market"). Objectives differ according to the nature of the product, competition, consumer demand, and available budget.
Target market profile	A description of those individuals most likely to purchase the product. The target profile usually includes demographics (the target's age, sex, ethnicity, and income) and psychographics. Psychographics are lifestyle descriptions of the consumer's attitudes, interests, and opinions.
Positioning statement	A short paragraph explaining how the company wants the consumer to perceive the product. Much can be communicated (price, quality, convenience), but what is the most important thing the advertising has to convey? For example, the message of Procter & Gamble's Always #LikeAGirl campaign was to convey that the company was relevant to pubescent girls.
Creative strategy	Describes the specific theme and approach of the advertising. In other words, the creative strategy is a description of what the advertising will actually look like. In national campaigns, the strategy contains a big idea or a fresh and interesting way to make a point about the product. The big idea for Little Caesar's Pizza is an animated Caesar character in a Roman toga who utters, "Pizza, Pizza!" in all ads to communicate that you always get two pizzas for the right price.
Media plan	Lists the communication vehicles that will carry the advertising. Should television be used? Why or why not? If Internet advertising is rejected, why? A good media plan ensures that a sufficient target audience is reached at an efficient price.

and graphic designers in the creative department begin work on a creative concept or "big idea." *Concepting* is the act of saying something in a unique way but at the same time ensuring that the message is "on strategy" with what needs to be communicated for the product to sell. A classic example is the campaign for Energizer Batteries featuring the battery-powered Bunny, whose power supply is so much better than competing brands that the toy seems to work endlessly. The creative concept is to show what appears to be a normal commercial for another product, and then the mechanical bunny rolls across the screen, interrupting the ad in an unexpected and humorous way. This campaign is a classic example of concepting in that it is both attention-getting and informative in terms of a unique product feature. More recent examples of great concepts include Chrysler's "imported from Detroit" campaign as well as the "priceless" ads by MasterCard.

A variety of creative professionals may be involved in the ad's execution: writers, artists, art directors, musicians, graphic designers, content or subject experts, and researchers. What emerges after a period of creative incubation is not a single clear-cut solution to all of the client's problems, but rather several executions, one of which will be able to survive the critical client review process. Once an execution gets approval from the client, the assignment is given back to the creative department for final production.

CREATIVE CONCEPT Memorable images like this classic ad for Marlboro cigarettes engage the audience. Successful ads help consumers remember the brand names but also may affect consumption behavior among vulnerable audiences, such as children.

> **Media departments** negotiate on behalf of the advertiser to buy space from media companies.

The Media Department. Meanwhile, the agency's **media department** is hard at work selecting media to carry the client's message, given the budget available. The account executive works constantly to keep all parties up to date on one another's progress. After the client and the media buyer approve creative and media recommendations, a specialist within the media department initiates negotiations with media suppliers for the purchase of specific media vehicles to carry the advertising message. In some agencies, the staff not only place the ads but also write them in the style needed by the media. It used to be that the media department dealt only with traditional media (e.g., television, radio, newspapers, magazines, and billboards). Today, new technologies are forcing media departments to consider new options, on personal computers, tablets, and smartphones.

Advertising Media

The main economic base of many American media is still advertising. For commercial radio and television stations, it is their most important source of revenue, whereas newspapers and magazines depend on a combination of newsstand sales, subscriptions, and advertising. In selecting media,

BECOMING A MADPERSON

The popular TV series *Mad Men* offered an inside view of the advertising world of the 1960s that is still somewhat relevant today. Agencies still make high-stakes pitches to advertisers and compete for their business. Creatives still work through the night to come up with just the right slant for a new campaign. Researchers still sometimes inspire the creative process and at other times smother it. Although the large firms have gotten even larger and more globalized, there are still many smaller agencies like the one we saw in *Mad Men*. Other things have changed: smoking, boozing, and philandering in the office are no longer acceptable. Women and minorities play a much more prominent role in all aspects of the industry than they did back then, although the industry still needs to make more progress in diversity. Digital production techniques and social media have been added to the marketing mix that agencies manage for their clients.

For the purpose of analyzing career opportunities, the Bureau of Labor Statistics (BLS, 2015a) combines advertising with public relations (see also Chapter 13). Over 473,000 people are employed in the industry and most jobs require a college education. A wide variety of occupations are represented in the industry, with sales, art design, and management accounting for most of these. As it was in the days of the "mad men" on TV, advertising is a glamorous industry and so there is keen competition at the entry level. Account management and media buying are common points of entry and an internship is a definite plus.

Employment prospects vary by the field of specialty. Jobs for advertising, promotions, and marketing managers are expected to grow at faster than average rate compared to the general economy over the next decade, with median pay of over $123,000 a year. The strongest demand is for managers who can handle digital media. In contrast, openings for advertising sales agents who work for media companies to sell space to advertisers are expected to decline slightly. That is in response to the trend toward automated digital advertising, which does not require a human sales agent (BLS, 2015b).

Layoffs are common in the advertising industry in response to downturns in the overall market for advertising and the loss of major accounts by individual agencies. However, in a capitalist economy, manufacturers will still need to market and advertise their products, whatever the future may hold.

Career Profile: Sarah Hofstetter

Sarah is the CEO of 360i, the leading digital advertising agency. She started with a BA in sociology and journalism from Queens College in New York and started her career as an editor for the *New York Times* syndicate. She moved into public relations and made her mark with Net2Phone, an Internet telephony company, before founding Kayak Communications, where 360i was one of her clients. Sarah is a recognized leader in the advertising industry, with many honors to her credit, including *Advertising Age*'s "40 Under 40." (Source: LinkedIn profile: Sarah Hofstetter. Accessed January 28, 2016.)

Sources: BLS (2015a). NAICS 541800 – advertising, public relations, and related services. Accessed January 29, 2016 from http://www.bls.gov/oes/current/naics4_541800.htm.

BLS (2015b). *Occupational outlook handbook*. Accessed January 27, 2016 from http://www.bls.gov/ooh/a-z-index.htm

advertisers consider whom they want to reach, what kind of message or information they want to communicate, and the costs of various media.

Advertisers try to reach the largest number of people in the target audience at the lowest possible price. The costs of various media depend on several factors: the size of the audience, the composition of the audience (age, wealth, education, etc.), and the prestige of the medium. In general, media with larger audiences can charge more for accepting and carrying advertisements. However, a smaller, more specifically focused audience can sometimes be even more valuable to an advertiser than a larger, more heterogeneous one. Comparisons among conventional advertising vehicles are made on a *cost per thousand impressions* (CPM) basis—that is, on the basis of the cost of reaching a thousand members of the target audience for the ad. This efficiency comparison is determined by dividing the cost of each ad by the size of the audience it delivers, in thousands.

Magazines continue to generate massive advertising revenue. Paid circulation numbers determine how much magazines can charge for advertising. Three of the most popular magazines for the college group, *People, Sports Illustrated,* and *Cosmopolitan,* command a high premium for four-color full-page ads, $300,000 each in the case of *People.*

The general goal is to try to reach the largest number of people in the target audience for the lowest dollar investment, but many other factors may also be considered, including the inherent characteristics of different media. Table 14.4 lists some of the strengths and weaknesses of various advertising media. The nature of the target audience also affects media selection. Often media advertisers want to reach a broad general audience. Some advertisers want to sell products, such as soap or soft drinks that might interest virtually everyone in a mass audience. Other advertisers might use a general-audience medium if it has a high impact on a particular group they want to reach. For example, although a very broad audience watches prime-time network television, ads are often placed there for products aimed primarily at seniors, such as denture adhesive cream. Television may reach a larger proportion of older people than any other audience segment. An advertiser that wants to sell athletic shoes to teenagers

TABLE 14.4 Strengths and Weaknesses of Advertising Media

MEDIUM	STRENGTHS	WEAKNESSES
Newspapers (printed)	Intense coverage Flexibility Prestige Dealer or advertiser coordination Permanent message	Short life Hasty reading Moderate-to-poor reproduction Aging audience
Magazines	Market selectivity Long life High reproduction quality Prestige Extra services Permanent message	Inflexible to coverage/time Inflexible to copy changes Low overall market penetration Wide distribution
Television	Mass coverage High impact Flexibility Prestige	Fleeting message Commercial wearout Lack of selectivity High cost
Radio	Audience selectivity Immediacy Flexibility Mobility	Fragmentation Transient quality of listenership Limited sensory input Fleeting message
Internet	Cost-efficient Personal Interactive	Loss of privacy Computer required
Mobile	Personal Location-based targeting Immediacy	Short attention span of users Limited screen space

will pick the television shows and radio stations that appeal selectively to teenagers.

New media are changing conventional media buying practices. As described in Technology: New Advertising Media (page 369), online advertising exchanges allow advertisers and their agencies to bid on ad placements in real time and to place ads automatically using their own computerized decision systems. Rather than evaluating and paying for ads on a CPM basis, advertisers can pay by the click and calculate the effectiveness of ads based on the purchases registered on their websites or completed at their retail outlets by consumers whom they have tracked both online and offline.

ARE YOU WATCHING? Nielsen Media Research compiles local and national television ratings via People Meters like this one. Viewers in Nielsen homes are expected to press buttons on the meter to indicate when they leave or enter the room in which the TV is running.

Advertising Research

Many people have the misconception that advertising is extremely powerful, but many campaigns are ineffective and even successful ones typically produce increases in sales of only a few percent. Few ads can penetrate the clutter to the point that consumers can remember them the day after seeing them, let alone be motivated to leave their homes or use their smartphone or iPad to make a purchase. That's where research comes in, to measure the effectiveness of advertisements and to evaluate their potential impact before expensive investments in advertising space are made.

Market researchers collect and analyze data about product sales and factors that affect consumer opinions about products. In the advertising agency, account executives depend on research analysts and account planners to provide in-depth consumer profiles and key information about the competition. In other words, they try to get into your head to obtain a deeper, more thorough understanding of what drives you to buy products.

Media research experts work for both the media industry and the media departments of the advertising agencies to give them information about patterns of exposure to the mass media. Nielsen Media Research, the supplier of TV ratings, is the best-known name in this field (see Chapter 9). Media research encompasses:

- Ratings for radio and television broadcasts
- Tracking online behavior
- Circulation figures for magazines and newspapers
- Profiles of the users of consumer products
- Media usage habits
- Qualitative studies that gauge audience reactions to specific media vehicles
- Reports on annual advertising expenditure levels of the leading national brands
- Copy tests that evaluate the effectiveness of ads under development

TABLE 14.5 Research Services and the Audience Data They Provide

MEDIUM	COMPANY	AUDIENCE REPORT CONTENT
National television	Nielsen Media Research Rentrak	Ratings for programs on national TV networks
Local television	Nielsen Media Research Rentrak	Ratings for programs broadcast by local TV stations
Internet	Nielsen/NetRatings ComScore	Assessment of online audiences
National radio	Nielsen Audio	Ratings for network programs by national radio stations
Local radio	Nielsen Audio	Ratings for stations broadcasting in the local market
Newspapers	Audit Bureau of Circulation	The number of newspaper copies sold
Magazines	Simmons/GfK MRI Research	Ratings for the top magazines in the United States

Examples of research companies and the audience information they provide are listed in Table 14.5.

Audience measurement studies are sufficient to tell us whether the advertising message is being exposed to a target group and roughly what numbers are involved, but it does not provide insights into how or why the advertising communicates successfully. For this purpose, we need a second dimension of audience research, one that enables the advertiser to talk directly with the target group. Because this research focuses on individuals and what "drives" them, it is often referred to as *motivational research*. Examples of this form of audience research include focus groups and mall intercepts.

> **Copy testing** evaluates the effectiveness of advertisements.

Another form of advertising-related research, **copy testing,** is used to assess the effectiveness of advertisements while they are still under development. For example, a test ad might be inserted in television programs in selected markets, and researchers might contact respondents by phone the day after it appears to determine whether they can recall seeing the ad. More sophisticated methods allow direct comparisons of ads by doing "split runs" of magazines in which alternative versions of the same ad are sent to different households. Cable television systems can also be used in this way to provide comparisons of alternative treatments for television commercials.

Advertisers and their agencies are beginning to abandon traditional forms of audience research that focus on representative samples of consumers in favor of databases containing information about actual consumption and media behavior. For example, log information from advertisers' websites can tell them where visitors came from and where they go after their visits and record their activity, including purchases, while on the website. When combined with demographic information obtained when the consumer registers at the site, these data provide a more reliable and valid picture of the effects of advertising than conventional research. Sifting billions of pieces of user demographic, clicking, and product purchase behavior for market research is part of the larger *big data* movement that aims to understand human behavior through the traces it leaves in the online world (see Chapter 15).

Advertising research is pushing into new media. Social media have spawned new ways of assessing advertising effectiveness. Facebook offers metrics that provide advertisers a word-of-mouth dashboard, "People Are

Talking About This." The dashboard counts the number of people who have liked a page, shared a post, or taken some action involving the brand in the past week. Nielsen Media Research has expanded into Internet, smartphone, and video game audience measurement and tracks mentions of television programs in social media. In 2013, Nielsen acquired the Arbitron radio ratings company, with plans to improve the measurement of online radio stations and ad-supported streaming music services. To keep up with the demands of online ad exchanges, Google and comScore are partnering to provide real-time audience data on leading websites. ComScore has also formed a partnership with Rentrak, a television rating service that uses data from millions of set top boxes, to provide integrated measurement of conventional and online viewing.

STOP & REVIEW

1. What are the steps involved in making an ad campaign, and who implements each step?

2. What does an account executive do?

3. What are the major types of marketing research?

4. What are the criteria for judging an effective ad?

5. How is Big Data changing the way audiences are measured?

CONTENT: ADVERTISING'S FORMS OF PERSUASION

Advertising must communicate important information about products (such as price, features, channel of distribution, and the like), but it also requires a creative way of stating these facts that cuts through the clutter of competing advertisements and gets the attention of consumers. All messages have an informational and an emotional dimension. Because advertising has to get the attention of audience members who are usually not interested in the message, how the message is conveyed is just as important as what is said. In this section, we look at advertising as a form of communication in terms of both its style and its content.

Mining Pop Culture

One way in which advertisers align themselves with consumers is through the art and entertainment of popular culture. By borrowing familiar symbols in the culture, advertisers promote consumer identification with the product. So, when Kia uses an old David Bowie song in ads for their luxury model, they hope to evoke memories of a long-ago junior prom to entice older buyers who can afford it, while they invoke a Lady Gaga song for their youth-oriented Soul model. Ultimately, advertising turns out to be a reflection of social and cultural norms due to a tendency and the necessity to communicate in the language of the familiar.

Consumer-Generated Content

In an effort to continue innovative ways of connecting with consumers, some advertisers are getting help from the very people they attempt to attract by using *consumer-generated content* (CGC) as a source for advertising ideas. Labeled the first social media Super Bowl, the 2012 game generated 11.2 million social media comments on sites such as Facebook and Twitter. The going rate for a 30-second TV ad was $3.5 million; however, a social media ad that was widely remembered likely cost the advertiser, Doritos, a mere $20. The ad emerged as a winner in the snack food's "Crash the Super Bowl Contest."

Relationship Marketing

In **relationship marketing,** advertisers and consumers communicate one-to-one through personalized media such as the Internet, direct mail, or the telephone. Companies use databases to personalize messages, with an emphasis on talking with consumers and "growing" them rather than sending out the same message to everyone. Credit card companies, such as American Express, often study the demographic characteristics and buying habits of each individual cardholder in order to identify specific products that fit specific lifestyles (such as life insurance, special hotel accommodations, luxury gift items, and the like). Relationship marketing is successful when brand loyalty is achieved. Social media ads convey the message that "people like you," especially your online friends who "like" the product, endorse it so it must be good for you, too.

Direct Marketing

Direct marketing differs from conventional advertising in that it concentrates the marketer's resources on the most likely prospects, rather than sending a message to a wide audience in the hope that at least some of the prospects will receive it. Direct marketing also has a quality of immediacy, because recipients of the message are asked to take direct action, such as placing an order over the phone or returning a printed order blank by mail. Although direct-marketing messages do not have the same glitz as mass media advertising, they do have two major advantages over other forms of advertising: (1) they can be customized to individual consumers, using personal forms of address and bits of personal information gleaned from computer databases, and (2) their effectiveness can be measured so that they can be continually fine-tuned.

Direct marketing encompasses a wide variety of communications media and includes e-commerce. It has long been popular with book publishers, record clubs, and magazines, but now it is coming into favor with a full range of advertisers. Direct-mail (junk mail) solicitations, catalog sales, and telemarketing are perhaps the most obvious forms of direct-marketing activities. However, anyone who has ever called a toll-free number to order the "the greatest hits of the sixties," redeemed a coupon clipped from the newspaper, or opened an e-mail spam has also responded to a direct-marketing appeal.

Anthony Harvey / Staff/Getty Images

INFOMERCIAL SO GOOD HE PUT HIS NAME ON IT Advertisers of products such as the George Foreman Grill, shown here being demonstrated by its namesake, promote direct sales of products through program-length TV commercials.

Infomercials are a form of broadcast direct marketing. These are program-length, made-for-television presentations whose sole purpose is selling the featured product or service. The infomercial concept has been taken to its logical conclusion in the form of entire cable networks devoted to hawking products through toll-free numbers—home shopping channels, such as QVC.

The direct-marketing industry relies on many of the same creative and media professions that advertising does, but it has some unique disciplines of its own as well. For example, there are firms that specialize in compiling and matching computerized telephone and mailing lists, others that specialize in assembling direct-mail packages, others that receive only toll-free calls, and others that just open return mail and complete (or fulfill) the orders.

Research also takes on a distinctive character in direct-marketing campaigns. Direct marketers are able to gauge the results of their advertising appeal, as well as the appropriateness of the media chosen, by counting the dollars in the cash register at the end of the day. This direct cause-effect measure allows the advertiser to try out various approaches and see their results immediately without resorting to the various media research services. Website proprietors are exceptionally well positioned to take advantage of this approach because they can get instant feedback from thousands of actual visitors and quickly generate alternative versions of their websites to refine their pitches. For example, Facebook conducted dozens of experiments to determine exactly the best shade of blue for their logo.

> **Infomercials** are paid television programs that promote a product.

Targeting the Market

Here are some ways in which advertising influences your actions, if you are in the target market:

Give New Information. This includes announcements by advertisers regarding new products or product improvements, sweepstakes or contests, and other items of a newsworthy nature. The government-funded advertising campaigns showing people the proper way to sneeze (into the crook of your arm, not your hand) during flu outbreaks is an example.

Reinforce a Current Practice. Advertisers who currently enjoy a dominant position in a product category and need to make consumers less receptive to competitive appeals are the primary users of this type of message. This is one of the most efficient uses of advertising, because it addresses the frequent users of the product who do not need to be convinced of its merits. In this case, the advertiser tries to increase **brand loyalty,** the propensity to make a repeat purchase of the product. Budweiser's annual SuperBowl ads are a good example, in that they reinforce product usage that is happening even as the commercials are playing to a national audience.

> **Brand loyalty** is the consumer's propensity to make repeat purchases of a specific brand of product.

Change a Predisposition. This approach is exemplified by the often annoying ads that take on a competing product head-to-head. It is also the most difficult type of ad to execute successfully because it needs both to address and to change the purchasing habits of those who regularly use a competitor's product. (Furthermore, the competitors often answer with their own campaign.) Advertisers tend to be satisfied when they succeed in raising brand awareness or the consumer's ability to identify the product. Pantene's shampoo ads that illustrate how their product reduces breakage of strands of hair compared to the "other brand" are examples.

TABLE 14.6 Consumer Needs Appealed to by Advertising

APPEAL	CONSUMER NEED
Achievement	Accomplish difficult tasks
Exhibition	Win the attention of others
Dominance	Hold a position of influence
Diversion	Have fun
Understanding	Teach and instruct
Nurturance	Support and care for others
Sexuality	Establish sexual identity
Security	Be free from threat of harm
Independence	Make one's own choices
Recognition	Receive notoriety
Stimulation	Stimulate the senses
Novelty	Do new tasks or activities
Affiliation	Belong or win acceptance
Succorance	Receive help and support
Consistency	Achieve order

Source: Settle, R. B., and Alreck, P. L. (1986). *Why they buy: American consumers inside and out.* New York: Wiley, 24.

Understanding Consumer Needs

> The **buying motive** explains the consumer's desire to purchase particular products.

Whatever communication approach is used, all advertising must appeal to a **buying motive** to be successful. Table 14.6 lists 15 consumer needs, or motives, to which most advertising appeals. The copywriter selects a creative approach that is unique and addresses some consumer need. For example, Dove is positioned as a life-changing beauty product, not a soap, and Southwest Airlines is presented as a vacation machine rather than an air carrier. The most effective advertising communicates the need clearly and repetitively.

Given all the advertising industry knows about you, your needs, your consumption patterns, your media behavior, and the forms of persuasion you are susceptible to, you might think it was a cinch to make an effective ad. However, there is no sure-fire formula for success. There is not even any agreement on what constitutes success: is it sales, market share, brand loyalty, brand attitudes, emotional impact, brand recognition, advertising recall, or top awards in industry competitions? Well-liked and memorable commercials are not always successful by other measures, however. A famous example from the 1980s featured a cantankerous senior citizen demanding to know "where's the beef?" in a nightmarish fast-food franchise's giant hamburger bun, spawning a catchphrase still in use today. Unfortunately, few consumers could associate the commercial with the sponsor, Wendy's.

THE CHANGING NATURE OF THE CONSUMER

> **Demographic segmentation** is based on social or personal characteristics, such as age, sex, education, or income.

How are consumers changing? This is the question that drives **demographic segmentation,** which categorizes people on the basis of the personal and household characteristics that the U.S. Census Bureau tabulates, such as age, sex, ethnicity, and income. Trends in these areas are very important to

EFFECTIVE CAMPAIGN? Flo the Progressive Insurance pitchwoman has become a popular icon. But is she effective? Could you name the insurance company she works for without looking at her apron?

advertisers. For most advertisers of consumer products, women between the ages of 18 and 49 are the primary target group; they make the most purchases in supermarkets and department stores.

Of all demographic variables, age, gender, and ethnicity are of considerable importance to marketers at the present time. Census data, for example, reveal a growing senior market. Still, children (aged 5–12) and teenagers (aged 13–17) are important segments for advertisers since they are impressionable consumers developing consumption and media habits that may last a lifetime. Males between 18 and 24 years are also highly prized, in part because they are so difficult to reach. College-age males are abandoning the traditional mass media in droves for the Internet and video games. In addition, advertisers are studying ethnicity as a demographic category. About 30 percent of the population belongs to an ethnic minority group. According to the Census Bureau, non-Latino whites will no longer be the majority population by 2042. The Latino-American population is the fastest growing, followed by Asian Americans and African Americans. These developments remind advertisers that consumer markets are not homogenous and that messages must be sensitive to the needs of emerging segments.

Importance of Diversity

Taking into account the diversity of consumer groups, some companies have an ethnic plan so that advertising is inclusive and relevant to all consumers. Inevitable diversity exists within target markets, and they shouldn't be thought of as a single homogeneous group. Consumers of Peruvian descent have different buying habits than those from Mexico, for instance. And, contrary to popular perception, not all Latinos prefer advertising in Spanish.

Before 1980, African Americans were rarely featured in television commercials (Dates & Barlow, 1997). Although African-American celebrities such as Bill Cosby began appearing in commercials by the 1980s, it remained evident that advertisers were using "black celebrities, but few black faces" (p. 93). In other words, despite the fact that African Americans are found in all professions from technical to managerial, advertising tends to reflect the stereotype that successful African Americans are often portrayed as athletes or popular music stars.

How advertisers portray women has also been controversial. Women are consistently underrepresented and are less likely to be depicted in professional occupations. Women also tend to be portrayed as taller and thinner than average, a practice that raises the question of whether advertising encourages a feeling of dissatisfaction with one's own body. Researchers disagree, however, about whether these images actually create unrealistic expectations for young women and cause body dissatisfaction (see Chapter 15).

Global Advertising

Technology and political change have given rise to a new business environment where international marketing opportunities abound. The Internet, in particular, makes it possible for businesses to reach foreign markets inexpensively; advertising is conducted online without high overhead costs. The global business climate is also the result of political initiatives such as the North American Free Trade Agreement (NAFTA), the General Agreement on Tariffs and Trade (GATT), and the World Trade Organization, which create new opportunities for international trade.

International advertising is expanding due to more aggressive competition from foreign businesses that create pressure on U.S. companies to explore international markets. Although international advertising requires knowledge of other cultures, many global campaigns are not clearly translated into various languages and cultures. For example, Dove's "Choose Beauty" campaign, which showed women from around the world entering a building through the "average" door but exiting transformed (implicitly after using the sponsor's product), through the "beautiful" door was applauded by some as empowering women but criticized by others as patronizing and manipulative.

STOP & REVIEW

1. What differentiates direct marketing from conventional media advertising?

2. What are the three basic ways that advertising can influence its target market?

3. Give examples of basic consumer needs and how advertising appeals to each.

4. What are the main demographic trends that advertisers should be aware of?

MEDIA LITERACY

ANALYZING ADVERTISING

Media literacy for advertising leads us to ask critical questions about the medium. How can consumers protect themselves and their families from harmful and deceitful messages? How can we avoid being drawn into a false set of values based on the consumption of mass-marketed goods?

HIDDEN MESSAGES

Almost 60 years have passed since the advertising critic Vance Packard (1957) published *The Hidden Persuaders,* in which he called attention to some of the more underhanded tactics advertisers and their agencies used to sell their wares. These involve hidden subliminal messages that supposedly unconsciously stimulated buying, such as embedding the letters S-E-X or images of naked bodies in pictures in magazine ads. The impact of subliminal messages and indeed their very existence remain controversial.

However, advertising clearly does send us messages that go beyond pointing out the merits of a particular product; it also promotes a materialistic way of life. That is, the long-term impact of advertising has been to reinforce a market economy and create a consumer culture in which the acquisition of goods and services is the foundation of values, pleasures, and goals in a capitalist society. Lifestyle advertising for alcoholic beverages, which often situates products in luxurious settings, is an example. The legitimacy of the capitalist system is reinforced by sending the message that wealth is the top priority, ignoring the inequities and environmental damages caused by the system and the health risks associated with alcohol consumption. It also leads people to think of themselves primarily as consumers rather than politically aware citizens.

It is estimated that the average consumer is exposed to some 5,000 advertisements each day (Pappas, 2000, p. 1). Some scholars express concern that this volume of advertising encourages false needs in consumers. Social critic Stewart Ewen (1976) argued that advertising creates an ideology of consumption by promoting a materialistic way of life. When advertising trades in the core function of a product (a shoe's comfort and durability) for a lifestyle appeal (shoe as a symbol of power or an affluent lifestyle), it promotes a culture of consumption in which consumers subscribe to the idea that problems can be solved by simply acquiring products (Featherstone, 1990; see Chapter 15). However, other observers have questioned whether advertising creates a consumer culture or is, rather, simply a by-product of our consumer impulses.

Black Friday and Cyber Monday exemplify consumerism and materialism. Black Friday, the day after Thanksgiving, is associated with traditional brick-and-mortar stores and is heralded as the ceremonial kick-off to the holiday shopping season between Thanksgiving and Christmas. It represents businesses moving from the red (loss) to the black (profit). Cyber Monday is the first Monday after Thanksgiving and has become the defining day of the holiday season for e-commerce sites.

In stark contrast to Black Friday and Cyber Monday, Buy Nothing Day is a day of protest against consumerism observed the day after Thanksgiving. The day was promoted by the Canadian *Adbusters* magazine (which helped launch the Occupy Wall

COUNTERADVERTISING Adbusters tries to counter the effects of consumer culture—but TV networks won't accept their ads. Long-term exposure to commercial advertising may make consumers believe that material goods are essential for their happiness.

Street movement in 2011). Never heard of it? That's not surprising, since the major television networks refuse to run advertisements paid for by the event's promoters. This is a case where you can take a stand by doing nothing, by staying home (and crafting homemade presents) in the days after Thanksgiving. You may also have ad blockers on your smartphone and a fast-forward button on your DVR at your disposal. However, if you enjoy advertising-supported media, then it is your *duty* to watch the ads and buy the products you see advertised on the day after Thanksgiving and every other day of the year!

PRIVACY

Citizens are often outraged about the sale of personal data to other companies, resulting in a mountain of unwanted postal mail and e-mail. For this reason, responsible companies engage in permission marketing, informing website visitors about how the information will be used.

The Internet raises database marketing to a new level that many consumers find deeply troubling. Over time, information can be matched across sites and identified with individual consumers, even those who are careful to avoid revealing personal information on the Web. Personal information can then be matched to offline databases of commercially available public information, such as auto registrations, marriages, births, and home sales. From the advertiser's perspective, this has the advantage of greater efficiency, limiting ad exposure to the most likely prospects and reducing duplicate exposures. Consumers could benefit, too, by receiving useful information about products and special price offers when they are actually in the market for an item. However, personalized advertising can also mean discriminatory pricing. For example, when Orbitz found out that Mac users spent more on hotel rooms than PC users, they started to send the Mac people ads for more expensive hotels.

Nevertheless, much to the excitement of advertisers and the chagrin of privacy advocates, innovation in the area continues to proliferate. For example, applications that use GPS capture information on your physical location and personal habits. Facebook advertisers have access to the user's profile information, as well as all of your "likes" and "shares," unless great care is taken in selecting among the site's many privacy options. Google shares personal information across all of its websites, including search, YouTube, Gmail, and the Google+ social networking site. For now, smartphone users are safe from tracking inside the apps they use, but online ad exchanges are hard at work on applications that will track us across PC, smartphone, and tablet platforms. And, if Facebook is your favorite app, your private information is already bought and sold through their ad exchange.

Online marketers assure your privacy by voluntarily subscribing to privacy seal authorities BBBonline and TRUSTe. However, these programs merely assure that the practices set forth in the website's privacy policy—including practices that invade consumer privacy such as selling information to third parties—are being followed.

If you don't want to receive personalized ads, many of the online safety tips listed at the end of Chapter 10 will also protect you against the prying eyes of advertisers, especially spam blockers, ad blockers (like Super Ad Blocker), browser privacy settings, and social networking options. You might consider maintaining a separate e-mail account for online shopping and website registrations, one you can dispose of when it becomes choked with spam. When asked to "opt in" to e-mail alerts for new products, don't do it. Protests also work. Facebook modified its plans to share the list of products you had bought recently with all of your online friends, following a storm of protest from its users.

The privacy-conscious consumer can also take advantage of industry self-regulation. New Web browsers have a Do Not Track option, although few advertisers honor it. The industry has its own approach it calls AdChoices (http://www.youradchoices.com/). If you click on a tiny blue triangle in an ad from a participating advertiser, that will block ads that are sent to you based on tracking your online behavior—although the tracking itself will continue. You can also request a list of the ad networks that are tracking you, and the number of those may surprise you. You can also send away the data brokers by opting out of their databases at http://www.stopdatamining.me

In the offline world, beware of sending in product warranty cards, applying for supermarket discount cards, and entering contests or promotions. Those put you in advertisers' databases. If you really want to avoid leaving tracks, pay cash whenever possible. All your credit card purchases go into commercial databases, too. To avoid telemarketers, put yourself on the FCC's Do Not Call list (see Chapter 11) and do a Google search for the Mail Preference Service offered by the Direct Marketing Association if you want to cut down on junk mail.

DECEPTION

To preserve their good names, most advertisers go to great lengths to avoid deceptive advertising. However, advertisers sometimes push their claims too far. For example, in 2016, the Federal Trade Commission (FTC) found that Lumos Labs, maker of the Luminosity "brain game," was making unsupported claims about the ability of the game to prevent dementia and imposed a multi-million dollar fine. Sometimes, however, deception is less obvious. The term *puffery* refers to the advertisers' practice of making exaggerated claims that can't be proven, such as "Best pizza on the planet." At which point should an advertiser be required to substantiate such claims? From the perspective of social responsibility, advertisers must also ask whether particular consumer groups are vulnerable to puffery (e.g., children and seniors) and assure that groups are not taken advantage of. If you have been deceived, the FTC has an online complaint form (http://www.ftc.gov/ftc/contact.shtm). Or you might start with your state's attorney general's or consumer affairs office. How can you decide if an ad is deceptive? One criterion is that it could mislead a reasonable consumer, such as you!

Deception in social media is a growing concern. Social media plugs by ordinary consumers are highly sought after by advertisers because they are believed to be more credible and effective than conventional advertising. However, if consumers aren't "liking" a product on Facebook enough, marketers can buy "likes" from offshore "click farms" where low-paid workers work their like buttons all day for pennies. Or if customers are not "following" a brand enough on Twitter, promoters can make it a highly visible trending item by paying Twitter $200,000 a day. Unscrupulous promoters have also been known to plant phony online reviews of new products (the going rate is $4 and up) or to discredit or remove critical reviews. In 2016, the FTC issued guidelines for so-called "native" ads that appear to be legitimate news stories that advertisers hope will be shared through social media. The guidelines ask that clear disclosures about the true purpose of the story be posted prominently, not buried at the bottom of the page.

Advertisers are themselves victims of deception in the form of *click fraud,* in which advertising exchanges charge advertisers for clicks that are generated by robotic computer programs instead of real people. These practices undermine the credibility of social media in the long run and are beginning to draw attention and hefty fines from law enforcement.

1-800-QUIT-NOW

© U.S. HHS

WARNING: Cigarettes cause fatal lung disease.

BRAND

20 Class A Cigarettes

FDA/Getty Images News/Getty Images

GRAPHIC WARNING The Food and Drug Administration proposed horrifying graphic images such as these for cigarette packaging to counter the effects of cigarette advertising.

ADVERTISING HARMFUL PRODUCTS

If claims about ineffective products are prohibited, what about ads for products that are harmful to their users, such as tobacco and alcohol? How can the industry get away with advertising them? And if their ads are legal, why don't we see ads for cocaine? The short answer is that alcohol and tobacco, unlike other harmful drugs, are legal products and businesses have a free speech right to advertise them in the United States.

However, those rights have limits. Cigarette ads have been banned on television and radio since 1971. Cigarette ads moved to magazines after that but are required to include warnings about health effects. A new law took effect in 2010 that prohibits tobacco companies from sponsoring events and from displaying their logos on clothing, such as T-shirts. The U.S. Food and Drug Administration proposed graphic warnings for cigarette packages, such as a picture of a cancerous lung, and a lengthy court case in which the tobacco industry claimed the warnings would infringe upon their free speech rights was decided in favor of the FDA. However, the agency ultimately gave up on the graphic labels it originally proposed and, perhaps leery of another long-running court challenge, has declined to put forward any new rules. Controversy surrounds advertising for so-called e-cigarettes that deliver addictive nicotine vapors to the lungs without the cancer-inducing smoky by-products.

There is concern that the products will encourage smoking of "real" cigarettes by impressionable youth and that ads promoting them should be banned. The e-cigarette industry argues that they are a tool for those who wish to discontinue smoking while maintaining their nicotine addiction.

Alcohol advertising has followed a different path emphasizing industry self-regulation rather than legislation. Thus, for many years, ads for hard liquor were not seen on television, but that was because distillers voluntarily withheld them, a self-imposed prohibition that ended in 2002. Beer ads have long been abundant and remain so today, but the industry voluntarily follows some guidelines about their content. For example, cartoon characters that might appeal to underage drinkers should not be used (although cute puppies and ponies as seen in Budweiser SuperBowl ads are apparently OK), the pleasurable effects of alcohol should not be emphasized, and irresponsible drinking should not be encouraged. Another voluntary standard prohibits marketing liquor to minors. The FTC guideline is that alcohol ads should appear only in outlets where at least 70 percent of the readers or viewers are 21 or older. To that end, publications like *ESPN The Magazine,* with significant younger audiences, have made an effort to create separate editions for subscribers under 21 that do not carry liquor ads. Potato chips and soda can also be harmful, especially to children. In an effort to curb an epidemic of childhood obesity, there have been ongoing efforts to require advertisers whose products have unhealthful levels of fat, sugar, and sodium to cease targeting children between the ages of 2 and 11. The food industry has blocked prior initiatives, but a new effort to limit junk food marketing in schools was launched in 2014.

CHILDREN AND ADVERTISING

Advertising for children can be harmful because children are a vulnerable audience who lack sufficient resources to make informed decisions about advertising appeals (Buijzen & Valkenburg, 2013). Exposure to ads in childhood can bias product perceptions into adulthood (Connell, Brucks, & Nielsen, 2014). Ads impact children's health as well as their consumer behavior: ads for unhealthy foods affect the eating habits of children (Boyland et al., 2016), contributing to a worldwide epidemic of childhood obesity.

Complaints about children's advertising should go to the Children's Advertising Review Unit (CARU). It is made up of industry professionals who promote responsible children's advertising and respond to concerns raised by consumers. Among the guidelines on www.caru.org, you will find injunctions against using children's program personalities and showing larger-than-life toys, as well as mandates for caveats such as "batteries not included," "some assembly required," and "part of a nutritious, balanced diet." Policy makers are particularly concerned with how well preschool children can explain the purpose of commercials and differentiate them from the entertainment portion of the programs. For example, children's advocates called for an investigation of the YouTube Kids application on the grounds that ads and content were mixed together in a way that violated the guideline that program hosts should not appear in ads. The number of commercials per hour that advertisers can include in children's programs is also limited. The FCC fined Nickelodeon for that offense.

STOP
&REVIEW

1. What are some of the main social criticisms of advertising?

2. What aspects of advertising should parents review with their children?

3. How are consumers protected from the excesses of advertising?

4. How can consumers protect themselves from unwanted or deceptive advertising?

Organizations such as the Center for Media Literacy and Citizens for Media Literacy encourage audience members to develop critical skills to analyze media at a young age. For their part, advertisers remind us that children have always had a desire for information about products available to them. Parental supervision also plays an important role in how children come to use advertising in everyday life.

SUMMARY & REVIEW

WHAT ARE THE MAIN EVENTS IN THE HISTORY OF ADVERTISING?

Advertising has been around in some form since ancient times. The rise of new media technologies are the most influential events ushering in the modern era of advertising. Newspapers, magazines, radio, television, and computers have played major roles in commercial communication by expanding the scope of audiences that are exposed to ads and adding new dimensions of sight and sound to advertising copy.

WHAT HAS BEEN THE IMPACT OF THE DIGITAL MEDIA ON ADVERTISING?

Computers, tablets, and smartphones allow advertisers to build databases and store information so that personalized messages can be addressed to individual users and highly specialized market segments. Database marketing and social media help build deeper relationships with consumers. Data captured from users of the Internet by data brokers supply detailed profiles of media usage as well as consumer behavior, providing an unprecedented opportunity to target advertising efficiently, but also threatening the privacy of users. Online ad exchanges, search ads, and mobile advertising are changing the advertising marketplace.

HOW ARE ADVERTISING CAMPAIGNS COORDINATED?

Marketing managers and brand managers who work for major advertisers budget and plan advertising strategies that will help them introduce new products or increase the sales of existing products. They work with an advertising manager to coordinate their companies' overall advertising efforts. Once a campaign is planned, they might contact one or more advertising agencies to execute the plan.

HOW ARE CAMPAIGNS ORGANIZED INSIDE AN ADVERTISING AGENCY?

The account executive is the liaison between the advertiser and the advertising agency staff. The account executive coordinates the activities of the creative department, which creates the ads, and the media department, which determines where the ads will be placed. Copywriters conceive of creative ideas and write the ads. The agency's media buyer negotiates with the media.

WHAT IS THE ROLE OF RESEARCH IN THE ADVERTISING PROCESS?

Advertisers rely on market research to understand the target market. In the agency, account planners ensure that there is a strong connection between research findings and the final advertising message. Researchers use data about who watches or reads media, but also use sophisticated breakdowns by audience segment and psychographics to target advertising. The Internet permits new, even more detailed forms of research and data gathering, but also raises potential privacy issues.

WHAT DIFFERENT TYPES OF COMMUNICATION DOES ADVERTISING USE?

Advertising is generally designed to achieve one of three basic goals: to provide new information (brand awareness), to reinforce a current practice (brand loyalty), or to change an existing predisposition. Advertising genres are further categorized according to the type of buying motive they appeal to. Advertisers have identified 15 needs, or buying motives, to which most messages appeal.

WHAT IS DIRECT MARKETING?

With direct marketing, the recipient of the advertising message is asked to make a direct and immediate response to the ad, such as by mailing in a printed order blank or visiting a website to place an order. Telemarketing, home shopping channels, infomercials, and catalog sales are other common examples. The popularity of direct marketing is increasing as the spread of interactive technologies such as the Internet and smartphones makes it easier to place orders in direct response to advertising.

HOW ARE ADVERTISING AUDIENCES CHANGING?

The number of seniors is growing, as are several ethnic groups. Advertisers in the future must have a thorough knowledge of diverse markets. The Hispanic market will be the largest ethnic group in the United States, in terms of both population and buying power. The African-American population is younger and growing faster than Anglo-Americans.

IN TERMS OF ADVERTISING, WHAT DOES IT MEAN TO BE MEDIA LITERATE?

Consumers must be aware of implicit messages and teach children critical thinking skills, such as understanding the distinction between the world presented by advertising and the real world. Consumers must also learn to detect deceptive advertising and balance their privacy rights with the benefits of personalized advertising.

THINKING CRITICALLY
ABOUT THE MEDIA

1. What were the most important developments that led to the advertising industry of today?

2. What target markets do you belong to, and what media should advertisers use to reach you?

3. Debate the following proposition: Facebook and Google will make advertising agencies obsolete.

4. Advertising receives substantial criticism, so let's accentuate the positive: what are the good things that advertising does for you and for society?

MindTap®

Test your knowledge with online printable flashcards and online quizzing.

KEY TERMS

account executive (p.377)	demographic segmentation (p.386)
advertising (p.363)	direct marketing (p.368)
advertising media (p.374)	era of creativity (p.367)
advertising plan (p.377)	infomercial (p.385)
brand (p.376)	integrated marketing communication (IMC) (p.367)
brand loyalty (p.385)	
buying motive (p.386)	media department (p.378)
CAN-SPAM Act (p.373)	relationship marketing (p.384)
click-through rate (p.370)	research organization (p.374)
copy testing (p.382)	sales promotion (p.367)
database marketing (p.373)	viral marketing (p.368)

> **MindTap®** Log on to the MindTap Communication for *Media Now* to access a variety of additional material, including this chapter's e-book, learning objectives, comprehension quizzes, videos, and more!

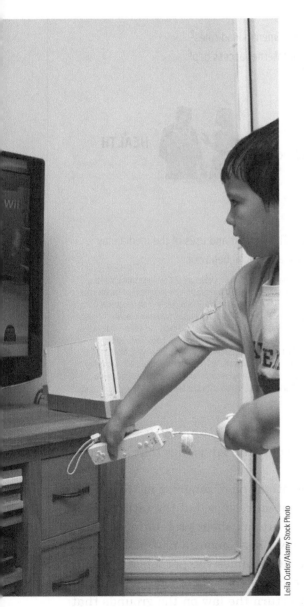

Leila Cutler/Alamy Stock Photo

VIDEO GAMES ARE FUN, BUT ...

Why do we spend thousands of hours
a year with the media, and what is the
impact on us and our society?

MEDIA USES AND IMPACTS

LEARNING OBJECTIVES

After studying the topics in this chapter, you will be able to:
1 Distinguish quantitative from qualitative research.
2 Differentiate inductive from deductive reasoning.
3 Compare the strengths and weaknesses of content analysis, survey, experimental, ethnographic, and big data research methods.
4 Define the following terms regarding experimental research: *generalizability*, *validity*, and *reliability*.
5 Given a question about media uses or impacts, determine the most appropriate theory to answer the question.
6 Summarize the scientific evidence about the effects of exposure to violent and sexual content in the media.
7 Assess the possible impacts of the media on well-being, community, political behavior, public health, and the economy.

BASHING THE MEDIA

"Media bashing" is a recurring ritual. It starts when critics point to new evidence of harmful effects in the endless stream of violence, sex, sexism, and racism that they see pouring forth from the media (see Figure 15.1). Talk shows and editorial columns buzz, and congressional hearings are held. The media industry representatives play their part when they criticize the research, blame the parents, say it's not their job to fix society, retreat behind the First Amendment (see Chapter 16), and promise to regulate themselves. What does the research really tell us, and how much can we rely on it?

Television and video games have been frequent targets for critics over the years. In 1954, the U.S. Senate held hearings about the impact of television on juvenile delinquency. But despite continuing concerns about the effects of television on children, industry self-regulation

CRIME

6 Violent acts/hour on prime time TV[1]
20% Children who are cyberbullied[7]

3% Video game addicts in the United States[3]
25% Children aged 10–15 who see online pornography[6]

SOCIETY

EQUALITY

15% Films with women in lead roles[2]
50% Rich–poor Internet access gap[8]

2,500 Smoking incidents in top movies[5]
$4.6 Billion Annual amount spent on fast food ads[4]

HEALTH

FIGURE 15.1 **MEDIA IMPACT RISK FACTORS** The content and uses of the media may contribute to crime, inequality, poor health, and undesirable social behavior.

[1]Federman, J. (1998). *National television violence study, vol. 3, Executive summary.* Santa Barbara: University of California Santa Barbara, Center for Communication and Social Policy; [2]Lauzen, M. (2014). It's a man's (celluloid) world: On-screen representations of female characters in the top 100 films of 2013. Available: http://womenintvfilm.sdsu.edu/files/2013_It's_a_Man's_World_Report.pdf; [3]Ferguson, C. J., Coulson, M., & Barnett Griffiths, J. (2011). Journal of Psychiatric Research, 45(12), 1573–1576. Available: http://www.tamiu.edu/~cferguson/Video%20Game%20Addiction.pdf; [4]*Fast food facts 2013.* Available: http://www.yaleruddcenter.org/fast-food-facts-2013-fast-food-companies-still-target-kids-with-marketing-for-unhealthy-products; [5]2012 data. *Smoking in the movies.* Available: http://www.cdc.gov//tobacco/data_statistics/fact_sheets/youth_data/movies/index.htm; [6]Ybarra, M. L. Mitchell, K. J., Hamburger, M., Diener-West, M., & Leaf, P. J. (2012). X-rated material and perpetration of sexually aggressive behavior among children and adolescents: Is there a link? *Aggressive Behavior,* 37, 1098–2337. Retrieved from http://dx.doi.org/10.1002/ab.20367; [7]Cyberbullying research center. Available at: http://www.cyberbullying.us/research.php; [8]U.S. Households with Internet access NTIA. (2015). Digital Nation Data Explorer. https://www.ntia.doc.gov/other-publication/2015/digital-nation-data-explorer

1954

U.S. Senate holds hearings on the relationship between television and juvenile delinquency

1993

Senate hearings on violence in video games

2011

U.S. Supreme Court rules that video games are protected speech under the First Amendment

remains the norm, including the voluntary parental advisories that appear at the beginning of TV shows.

Video game violence first attracted the attention of congress in 1993. That industry also responded with voluntary content ratings, but the ratings focus on sex, not violence, and video game stores are lax about prohibiting sales to underage customers. It seems every time we hear about a new mass shooting, the media run stories about violent video games the perpetrator might have played. California passed a law to prohibit the sale of violent games to minors, but an industry group sued to overturn the law on the grounds that it infringed on their free speech rights. In 2011 the Supreme Court agreed, in part because the justices were skeptical about the research. Meanwhile, children still play violence-packed games like "Call of Duty" and the shootings continue, but is there a connection?

MEDIA THEN··· MEDIA NOW

1898
> Hearst newspapers summon the United States to war with Spain with sensational headlines

1933–1945
> Nazi propaganda inflames the Holocaust and World War II

1954
> U.S. Senate holds hearings on the relationship between television and juvenile delinquency

1960
> Klapper's The Effects of Mass Communication argues for weak media effects

1961
> Schramm et al. publish Television in the Lives of Our Children

1965
> Bandura's bobo doll experiment demonstrates the effects of TV on children

1967
> Gerbner's first Violence Profile documents violence on television

1972
> U.S. Surgeon General reports on the relationship between television and violence

1985
> U.S. Senate hearings on pornographic music

1986
> Attorney General's Commission on Pornography

1990
> Children's Television Act mandates programs designed specifically for children

1993
> Senate hearings on violence in video games

2011
> U.S. Supreme Court rules that video games are protected speech under the First Amendment

How should we regard stories about the impact of media on society? Is the problem widespread, or have isolated incidents been magnified by sensational media coverage? Research might tell us if the incidents indicate a serious national problem or if they are merely anecdotal and help us to understand if it is the media content or other factors that provoke them. For example, how

MindTap

Start with a quick warm up activity.

> **Media effects** are changes in knowledge, attitudes, or behaviors resulting from media exposure.

MindTap®

Read, highlight, and take notes on the complete chapter text in a rich interactive online

> **Independent variables** are the causes of media effects.

> **Dependent variables** are the consequences, or effects, of media exposure.

many acts of copycat aggression would there be if violent video games were kept from the eyes of children? Are parents, poverty, mental illness, or gun ownership laws more to blame than the game publishers?

Media effects are changes in cognitions, attitudes, emotions, or behavior that result from exposure to the media. However, broader impacts on society, as opposed to individual effects, are also of concern to us. And some scholars do not see a cause-and-effect relationship between media use and human behavior. We will use the term *media impacts* in the broader sense to encompass these varying aspects of the complex relationship between media and society.

In this discussion, exposure to the media may itself be considered an impact, since the time we spend with the media affects our daily lives by reducing time that might be spent on other activities. For example, it had long been known that children spent less time socializing, playing, and reading because of the time they spend with television (Schramm, Lyle, & Parker, 1961).

STUDYING MEDIA IMPACTS

Media impact can be studied in a variety of ways. All the methods have strengths and weaknesses that we need to understand to evaluate their contributions to the debate over media and society. First, we will consider some of the contrasting general approaches to understanding media impacts; then we will consider five systematic methods for obtaining evidence of those impacts: content analyses, experiments, surveys, ethnographies, and Big Data.

Contrasting Approaches

Many social scientists begin with a theory based on the law of *cause and effect*. They derive, or deduce, predictions about media impacts from their theories of human behavior and culture and then test these predictions through observation. Their results either support the theory or refute it, which leads to new theoretical paradigms. Thus, they follow the *scientific method*. Mass media exposure is usually viewed as the "cause," or **independent variable.** Exposure to media content is seen as the trigger for mental processes and behaviors that are the "effects," or consequences of what people see and hear in the media. These effects—such as *antisocial* (e.g., violent) or *prosocial* (e.g., cooperative) behaviors—are called **dependent variables** (Wimmer & Dominick, 2014). Of course, if we are interested in the prior question of what causes media use or exposure, then media use becomes the dependent variable and the factors that may cause that use or exposure, such as gender, personality, and beliefs about the benefits of media exposure, become the independent variables.

Other scholars observe people's real-life interactions with media and with each other and then induce, or infer, theories about those interactions. These include most ethnographers and also many critical theorists. *Ethnographers* prefer to create theories close to the explanations people give for their own behavior, or at least based on their own careful observation.

Paul Lazarsfeld (1941), one of the pioneers in communications research, was the first to point out the difference between what he called *administrative research,* which takes existing media institutions for granted and documents their use and effects, and *critical research,* which criticizes media institutions themselves from the perspective of the ways they serve dominant social groups. Most of the research described elsewhere in this chapter, even that which results in "criticism" of the media for excessive sex or violence, falls into the administrative research category because it fails to critique the basic foundations of existing media institutions. Instead, critical theorists favor interpretive and inductive methods of inquiry drawn from such fields as history, feminist studies, cultural anthropology, Marxist political economic theory, and literary criticism (see Chapter 2).

Some social scientists use *quantitative* methods to enumerate their findings and analyze statistical relationships between independent and dependent variables. Other scholars infer the relationships from *qualitative* methods, such as by studying the symbols in media content or observing behavior in natural settings. Yet others believe it is important to combine both sets of methods and look for insights offered by both approaches and points of agreement between them.

NONVIOLENT? Football games don't "count" in studies of TV violence, but maybe they should. In this play, Jack Tatum (number 32) broke Darryl Stingley's back, paralyzing him for life. No penalty was called, but Stingley was definitely targeted by physical force initiated by Tatum.

Content Analysis

Content analysis characterizes the content of the media. Researchers begin with systematic samples of media content and apply objective definitions to classify its words, images, and themes. For example, what if researchers want to find out how much violence is in prime-time television shows? They could start with a sample of prime-time shows. Trained observers apply objective definitions of violence, such as "sequences in which characters are depicted as targets of physical force initiated by another character," compare notes to make sure that their definitions were consistent, and then tally the number of violent acts (Gerbner et al., 1994).

> **Content analysis** is a quantitative description of the content of the media.

Content analyses create detailed profiles of media content and identify trends in content over time. However, they cannot be used to draw conclusions about the effects of the media because the audience often perceives media in a different way than the researchers—or the producers of the content.

Content analysis is a time-consuming task, so researchers sometimes take only a limited sample (such as 1 week's worth of prime-time television shows) from major media outlets. That obviously doesn't reflect the full range of content that the audience sees. The definitions can be problematic, too. For example, if a character in a situation comedy slaps another character on the back (which might be interpreted to be a sequence in which a character is the target of physical force initiated by another character) and they begin laughing, is that violence? What if a character is hurt by a hurricane instead of another person? What about a football tackle? According to some definitions, these are violent acts; according to others, they are not.

One type of content analysis (quantitative) counts the acts, and another type of content analysis (qualitative) examines how the acts should be regarded.

Others draw even further back from the details of content to look at overall themes and narratives, trying to see the big picture that detailed content analysis might miss.

Experimental Research

> **Experimental research** studies the effects of media in carefully controlled situations that manipulate media exposure and content.

Experimental research studies media effects under carefully controlled conditions. Typically, a small group sees a media presentation that emphasizes one particular type of content. For example, preschool children are shown violent cartoon shows, and their responses are compared with those of preschoolers exposed to media that lack the "active ingredient," for example, nonviolent cartoons.

Experimental subjects must be *randomly* divided between these groups—such as by flipping a coin—to minimize the impact of individual differences among subjects. If they were not assigned randomly—if the children were simply asked to pick which kind of cartoon they would like to see—the aggressive children might volunteer for the violent ones, and the results would therefore reflect the nature of the children rather than any effect of the media content. The same goes for sex, age, social status, and other variables that might affect the outcome. The randomization process cancels out their effects by putting equal numbers of boys and girls, rich and poor, in each group.

Perhaps the most influential media effects experiments were conducted by Albert Bandura (1965) and his colleagues at Stanford University. They showed preschoolers a short film in which an actor behaved aggressively toward a Bobo doll, an inflatable doll the size of a small child with the image of a clown printed on its front and sand in its base so that it rocked back and forth when hit (today's children sometimes call them "bop dolls").

1965

Bandura's bobo doll experiment demonstrates the effects of TV on children

The children were randomly divided into groups that each had a different ending to the film: in the "model-rewarded condition," the aggressor received verbal praise and snacks; in the "model-punished condition," the actor was scolded and spanked; and in the "no-consequences condition," the film ended after the opening sequence.

After the show, adult observers watched the children in a playroom and many of the children in the model-rewarded and no-consequences conditions imitated the aggressive acts they had seen; those in the model-punished condition tended not to do so. The researchers concluded that the punishment the children experienced vicariously in the model-punished condition inhibited their aggressive behavior. However, the most important finding of the study was that the no-consequences condition also produced imitation. This suggested that mere exposure to television violence could spur aggressive responses in young children.

The value of such a carefully controlled design is that it rules out competing explanations for the results (such as the possibility that subjects who saw the violent endings were more violent children to begin with). Only the endings of the film (also known as the *experimental treatments*) were

GEOFF ROBINS/AFP/Getty Images

POTENTIAL HARMFUL VIOLENCE? Routine soccer plays like this are violent by our definition. They involve attractive role models and reward the perpetrator (here, with credit for a blocked goal shot), factors that Albert Bandura found to increase the performance of violent behavior among viewers.

varied among groups so that any subsequent differences among them (such as the beatings the subjects inflicted on their own Bobo dolls) could be attributed to the differences in the media content.

However, the small and unrepresentative samples used in experimental studies, which often consist of college students in introductory classes or the children of university professors, raise questions about **generalizability,** the degree to which the results apply to other populations and settings. The measures that are used (written responses to a questionnaire or highly structured experimental tasks) and the conditions under which the experiments are conducted do not reflect the real-world situations of ultimate interest, such as behavior in an actual child's playroom or on a school playground. This is the issue of *ecological validity*. More generally, **validity** is the degree to which research findings and methods reflect the true phenomena under study, without distortion. For example, college entrance exams are valid predictors of future performance in college only if those who score high on the exams also perform well in college later on. Or, to assess the validity of a paper-and-pencil measure of aggression, we might compare the results with observations of aggression on the playground.

A related concept is **reliability,** the degree to which our methods produce stable, consistent results. For example, if we readministered a college entrance exam or the aggression measure to the same group of students a week after the first administration, we would expect that the individuals with high scores at the time of the first assessment would also have high scores the second time around. Researchers have to provide evidence of both validity and reliability when reporting their results.

The experimental treatments may also be unrealistic. For example, in some studies of pornography effects, excerpts from several pornographic films are edited onto a single tape. The edited sequences may have more "action" than the original films, which sometimes intersperse the sex scenes with some token plot and character development. Moreover, experimental subjects, often recruited from first-year college courses, may be exposed to content that they might not normally see and view it in a lab setting unlike the real-world context where they might encounter it, and that might exaggerate the effects. One of the arguments in favor of inductive, observational methods is that they analyze people in their natural contexts and are perhaps more likely to catch the nuances of actual behavior with media.

Survey Research

Survey methods also play an important role in media research. For example, researchers interested in the effects of violent video games might administer a questionnaire to a random sample of U.S. schoolchildren (see Technology Demystified: The Science of Sampling). Media effects are inferred by statistically relating the independent measures of media exposure ("How many violent video games have you played in the last week?") to the dependent variable of interest (such as self-reports of violent behavior: "how many fights did you have last week?"). If those who play a lot of video games also get in a lot of fights, and those who do not play many video games are relatively nonviolent, we would say that the two variables are **correlated.**

Generalizability is the degree to which research procedures and samples may be generalized to the real world.

Validity is the degree to which we are actually measuring what we intend to measure.

Reliability is the extent to which a result is stable and consistent.

Correlated means that there is a statistical measure of association between two variables.

THE SCIENCE OF SAMPLING

Headline: Survey finds 10 percent hooked on social media. "How can that be?" you ask yourself, "*all the people I know are Snapchat junkies.*" The answer to this riddle is the key to the science of sampling. Clearly, one's circle of friends does not adequately represent the opinions of the entire country. Survey researchers could talk to absolutely everyone while conducting a census, but that would be prohibitively expensive. By using *probability sampling*, researchers can get accurate results with far fewer respondents. Telephone interviews are a popular way to conduct surveys, so let's see how sampling is done for them.

The ideal is to start from a complete *sampling frame*, a list that includes all members of the population under study. The other important point is to sample the list randomly, so that everyone on the list has an equal chance of being selected. We could cut up all of the phone books in the country, cull the duplicate listings, pack the individual listings in a giant revolving metal drum, and start picking numbers. That would take a drum the size of a cement mixer and would overlook the many homes with unpublished numbers or who use cell phones exclusively. It also leaves out people who moved since the last phone book came out, and they tend to be young, low-income, and minorities. Researchers, therefore, use *random-digit dialing* in which a computer generates random telephone numbers so that all telephone subscribers, including those with cell phones, have an equal chance of getting a call. To do so, they start with listed wireline telephone numbers or with cell phone exchanges and replace the last digits selected from tables of random numbers. By following this procedure, researchers can get an accurate response by contacting a relatively small sample, and they can estimate the precision of their findings and also the probability that they are in error. For example, a sample of 400 homes yields a 3 percent margin of error (or standard error as it is more properly known) for a question that 10 percent of the respondents say "yes" to; for example, "Are you addicted to the Internet?" That means the "true" proportion is likely to be somewhere between 7 percent and 13 percent, 10 plus or minus 3. If researchers replicated the survey many times to check its accuracy, the odds are that the results would fall within the range of sampling error 95 percent of the time. The beauty of this approach is its efficiency. A few hundred respondents can represent the opinions of the entire country.

However, to cut the margin for error in half in our example (to 1.5%), surveyors must quadruple the sample size.

These neat calculations overlook a messy problem with surveys, however: the growing number of people who refuse to cooperate with them. That's the problem of *nonresponse bias*. Cooperation rates have plummeted from 80 percent in early phone survey studies in the 1960s to under 10 percent recently, and telephone technology trends (e.g., caller ID and cell phone-only homes) point toward further problems with nonresponse bias.

Some researchers are turning to mail surveys, door-to-door interviews, and Web surveys instead. However, these techniques have their own sampling problems. Well-designed mail surveys can achieve superior response rates compared to phone interviews, but only by paying respondents monetary incentives that may bias the results. And the sad fact is that 20 percent of the adult population is functionally illiterate and can't read them. There is no comprehensive list of Web users and no efficient way to randomly generate e-mail addresses, so probability sampling is impossible there. Door-to-door interviewing still yields high response rates but cost 10 times as much as phone interviews. So, researchers have to economize by cutting their sample sizes, and that increases their sampling error.

JUST A FEW MORE QUESTIONS Many phone surveys are conducted from call centers like this one, in which survey takers read questions and record answers on a computer screen. That is known as computer-assisted telephone interviewing, or CATI for short.

Survey studies are often more generalizable than experimental studies because their samples may represent larger populations, such as all U.S. schoolchildren in our example. Even if the samples are not strictly representative of a larger population in a statistical sense, they may still add to our understanding of media effects. For example, instead of randomly sampling all U.S. schoolchildren, a very expensive undertaking, we might conduct our survey in several school districts chosen to include children from diverse backgrounds. By extending research to more realistic settings and more diverse populations than in experimental studies, surveys can increase our confidence in the generalizability of the findings. They can also account for a wider range of factors than just media exposure, such as peer pressure to play violent games and religious beliefs that discourage them.

However, survey research provides ambiguous evidence about cause and effect. In our example, it is possible that aggressive children like to play violent video games. In other words, a tendency toward violence causes the playing of video games instead of the other way around. It is also possible that both violent behavior and video game use are caused by some unexamined third variable, such as lax parental supervision. This is the sort of situation in which experimental studies or ethnographic research might help to sort out the ambiguities.

In media effects research, the most valid surveys are *longitudinal* studies that survey the same subjects repeatedly over a number of years. Huesmann et al. (2003) asked the parents of 8-year-olds to identify their children's favorite TV programs and asked the children's playmates to rate the children on their antisocial behavior. They recontacted the same families 5 and 10 years later and readministered the survey. If the youngsters who watched a lot of television are more violent as teens than those who watched relatively little television as children, then we can conclude that childhood television exposure does indeed encourage violent behavior later in life. If some of the teens in the follow-up surveys have subsequently reduced their television viewing but remain violent, we can rule out the competing explanation that "violent people like violent television." In other words, we can be fairly certain that television causes violent behavior and rule out the competing explanation that violent people like to watch violence.

However, very few survey studies are repeated over time; most are just "one-shot" studies that compare media exposure and behavior but ignore the direction of any causal relationship. Even longitudinal studies cannot account for the influence of all the possible variables the researchers might leave out, such as parental supervision, which might explain both violence and television viewing.

Ethnographic Research

Ethnography is a naturalistic way of looking at the impacts of communications media. It adapts the techniques anthropologists use—*participant observation* and interviewing—to look at cultures in a holistic way. Ethnography places media in a broad context of media users' lives and cultures. It emphasizes observation over time, usually at least 6 months, so that researchers can see how people respond to changes in their environment, like the media they use.

> **Survey studies** make generalizations about a population of people by addressing questions to a sample of that population.

> **Ethnography** is a naturalistic research method in which the observer obtains detailed information from personal observation or interviews over extended periods of time.

Marmaduke St. John/Alamy Stock Photo

A HOUSE OF MIRRORS Focus groups are conducted in front of two-way mirrors that let researchers observe and film the proceedings. Groups are a common tool of both ethnographic and market research where they are valued for letting participants respond in their own words. Their limited samples and group dynamics may produce misleading results.

For example, Danah Boyd (2014) combined years of interviews and visits with teens to examine the life of teens in the age of social media.

Focus groups are another way of capturing people "in their own words" through guided group interactions. A group of 6 to 12 people is gathered in a conference room and led by a skilled moderator as they explore a topic of interest to the researcher. Behind a two-way mirror sit researchers equipped with microphones and TV cameras taking in every word. These are free-flowing but guided discussions that produce long transcripts rather than neat statistical tables. Social scientists use them to explore new research topics and to help generate questions for surveys.

Ethnographers also use them to produce the raw data needed to formulate inductive theories of media processes, for example, to understand the information needs of minority and low-income Internet users. Media developers use them to see how people react to new programs or new media prototypes.

Like all types of research, focus groups have their flaws and cannot offer a comprehensive answer to every question. With focus groups, it is sometimes hard to find participants, even when recruiters offer substantial monetary incentives. The members of the targeted group, for example, fathers with teenage daughters, who show up for the interview in no way represent the general public, but do give some idea about the opinions or behaviors of fathers with teenage daughters. The other problem is group dynamics. A good moderator can generate profound insights and must skillfully steer away from individual participants' unique concerns that most people would never reach on their own. Sometimes a strongly opinionated individual will dominate a group. Focus groups on the same topic are repeated until the researcher hears the same general comments from the different groups.

Ethnographers use unstructured or semi-structured interviews as an alternative to survey research. Surveys make it possible to compare many people through standardized questions, but they may impose response categories (e.g., multiple-choice answers) on the respondents. That approach yields standardized responses that are easy to tally, but does the forced choice reflect what the respondent really meant to say? Ethnographers let the participants respond in their own words and then they can ask follow-up, in-depth questions of the participants. Sometimes an in-depth interview will draw unexpected causal connections in that one person's life. Ethnographies can yield in-depth information about a particular place at a particular time, but they do not permit much generalization. Although ethnographers try to record information so thoroughly and accurately that others would reach the same conclusions from their data, such reliability, or reproducibility, may be hard to achieve.

Big Data

Looking for patterns of human behavior amid huge databases, referred to variously as *Big Data* or *predictive analytics* is a new twist on ethnography. This approach employs quantitative analysis of the piles of digital data about us available from credit card transactions, public records, and traces of our online behavior. The computer programs that make recommendations for you in Netflix and Amazon are examples. These programs compare you with others with similar tastes to see what they like and calculate whether you might like it, too.

Social science researchers and commercial researchers alike have begun to probe data stored on Internet servers to supplement or even replace the conventional research methods examined above. For example, thousands of real-time tweets made during the 2014 World Cup competition were content analyzed by a computer, rather than by human coders, to track the emotional effects of the televised matches (Yu & Wang, 2015). That approach is similar to the sentiment analysis that Nielsen Media Research uses to create social media ratings of the "buzz" about popular television programs, which supplement Nielsen's ongoing survey research studies. Another study examined exactly which forms of Facebook use most affect our psychological well-being by correlating server data about Facebook activities, such as status updates, with subjective judgments of social well-being obtained from surveys (Burke, Marlow, & Lento, 2010). Experiments employing big data techniques are commonly used by website proprietors to gauge the effectiveness of new website designs and special offers by comparing results among randomly selected samples of visitors. In an experimental study of nearly 700,000 Facebook users, the proportion of positive items in the participants' newsfeeds was manipulated to see if it had an effect on their moods (it did).

These examples highlight both the strengths and weaknesses of big data techniques. Big data can be drawn at minimal cost from large and diverse groups and even entire populations of interest (e.g., all Facebook or Netflix users), as opposed to the small samples of college undergraduates that are the subjects of a great number of conventional media research studies. Big data advocates like to point out that server data capture "actual behavior," rather than often inaccurate self-reports; for example, our shaky recollections of how much time we spend on Facebook. However, the big data approach is limited to the behavioral traces people leave behind so if we are interested, for example, in the impact of Facebook on loneliness (as in Burke, Marlow, & Lento, 2010), we have to use surveys to ask people if they feel lonely or else concoct a proxy measure of loneliness from the behavioral traces that are available (e.g., the percentage of communications that our "friends" don't respond to within an hour). And, if researchers are interested in a more general phenomenon, such as the effects of social interaction on loneliness, the Facebook data are obviously limited just to users of that particular service. Also, very few websites (Twitter is a rare exception) offer researchers open access to data where scholars can conduct independent investigations that are not subject to the approval of the company that owns the data.

Thus, the different types of research methods tell us different things. Content analyses often show that the media are filled with violence and sex,

1. What are some of the concerns about the impact of media on society that lead to "media bashing"?

2. Contrast the inductive and deductive approaches to studying the effects of the media.

3. What is the purpose of content analysis?

4. In what ways are experimental studies superior to survey studies? In what ways are they inferior?

5. What do ethnographers do?

6. What are the strengths and weaknesses of Big Data methods?

Uses and gratifications is the theory that media are actively selected to satisfy our needs.

for example, but tell us nothing about the actual effects on the audience. Experimental studies often find evidence of effects, even from extremely short exposures of 15 minutes or less, but cannot assess how other factors may reduce or enhance those effects in the real world. Survey studies use larger, more representative samples than experimental research but seldom reach unambiguous conclusions about the effects of media exposure. Ethnographic studies provide deep insights, but the results are sometimes too subjective and particularistic to duplicate. Big data expand the scope and reach of research studies but is limited by the types of data that are recorded on servers and restrictions on access to the data. It is important to explore these issues with a variety of different methods not only to find "what" happens but also to find or describe the "how" and "why." By *triangulating* (a concept from ethnography) across different forms of evidence, we can see if consistent patterns emerge. Triangulation might give us a more valid sense of how people behave with media and why.

THEORIES OF MEDIA USAGE

What medium will I choose today? A video game, an iPad, or a textbook? *Media Now* or *Introduction to Calculus?* You obviously picked *Media Now,* but why? To understand media impacts, we need to understand how the media work their way into our lives. Are we uncritical consumers of everything big media companies send our way, or do we actively select content? Theories of media exposure and use attempt to explain the processes we use to make our daily media consumption decisions.

Uses and Gratifications

The **uses and gratifications** perspective dominates thinking about media consumption behavior. This theory assumes an active audience (see Media & Culture: The Active Audience, page 410): Users actively seek out media that meet their needs for knowledge, social interaction, and diversion.

The various media satisfy differing needs. For example, interpersonal communication is one of the important gratifications that people seek from the Internet (Papacharissi & Rubin, 2000). Websites like Facebook that fulfill these expectations are thus likely to earn long visits and repeat viewings. Entertainment needs are more likely to be addressed by Hollywood films or television shows.

Uses and gratifications theory (Palmgreen & Rayburn, 1985) focuses on the match between the gratifications we seek and those we actually obtain from the media. For example, if check in to Facebook on our smartphone seeking to gratify a need for social interaction and find friendly wall postings from our online friends, we have obtained the gratification we sought and we are likely to visit Facebook again. If instead we are met by caustic comments from one of our online "frenemies," we might seek out other means to gratify our social interaction need, such as a face-to-face meeting with a real-world friend. According to this theory, we arrive at our media consumption decisions by performing a mental calculation in which we compare the gratifications we obtain with those we seek from all of the media alternatives available to us, taking into account all of the needs (e.g., for diversion, information, companionship) that are relevant to us at a given moment.

Our media behavior changes all the time because the gratifications we seek from the media are in a constant state of flux. We encounter new media that address new or different needs. New media provide new gratifications, such as interactivity and navigability (Sundar, Waddell, & Huang , 2015). Our life situation may change and with it the criteria we use to select the media. We also may seek out media to manage our moods (Zillmann & Bryant, 1985) or to fulfill aesthetic urges to appreciate works of media art (Bartsch & Oliver, 2011). At some stages of our lives, we may seek media that entertain; at other times, information may be more of a priority. And the different media vary with respect to the gratifications they provide us at different points in their own evolution. For example, television is associated with entertainment, whereas the Internet was more related to information seeking, at least before it turned into a source of streaming entertainment media. Social media add some unique media gratifications of their own to the list, as well as fulfilling entertainment, information seeking, relaxation, convenience, and time-passing needs associated with earlier media forms (Whiting & Williams, 2013; see Table 15.1).

Learning Media Behavior

Uses and gratifications theory parallels two general theories of human behavior, **social learning theory** (Bandura, 1986) and the *Theory of Planned Behavior* (Ouellette & Wood, 1998) to some extent, except that our expectations of the media are said to form around outcomes of media consumption behavior rather than the gratification of needs. The outcome could be the feeling of joy we experience after seeing the latest Brad Pitt movie. The next Brad Pitt movie that comes along may attract us, too, because we expect a similar outcome. Likewise, if we find his new movie boring, we may pass up the one after that altogether. Uses and gratifications theory would call that enjoyment a gratification; social learning theory calls it an outcome expectation.

In social learning theory, our observations of the experiences of others are also important. For example, if we hear "positive buzz" from people who've

> **Social learning theory** explains media consumption in terms of its expected outcomes.

TABLE 15.1 Uses and Gratifications of Television, the Internet, and Social Media

I WATCH TV...	I USE THE INTERNET...	I'M ON SOCIAL MEDIA...
Because it entertains me	Because it's easier	For social interaction
Because it's enjoyable	To look for information	To communicate
Because it relaxes me	To get information for free	To express opinions
Because it is a pleasant rest	Because it is a new way to do research	To share information
Because it allows me to unwind	Because it is enjoyable	To observe and surveil others
When I have nothing better to do	Because it is entertaining	

Sources: Rubin, A. (1983). Television uses and gratifications. *Journal of Broadcasting, 27,* 37–51; Papacharissi, Z., & Rubin, A. M. (2000). Predictors of Internet usage. *Journal of Broadcasting and Electronic Media, 44,* 175–196; Whiting, A., & Williams, D. (2013). Why people use social media: A uses and gratifications approach. *Qualitative Market Research: An International Journal, 16*(4), 362–369.

Media & Culture

THE ACTIVE AUDIENCE

Just how powerful are the media relative to their audiences? Some believe that the media have an enormous influence on audiences. For example, Adorno and Horkheimer (1972) saw powerful media propaganda as an explanation for the Holocaust and other brutal acts during World War II. And today, some see the media as powerful carriers of ideology that impose the interests of ruling groups on vulnerable audiences (Chomsky & Herman, 1988), such as by convincing young children that shiny toys are the key to happiness.

However, other scholars think the power of the media is limited by processes of *selective exposure, selective attention,* and *selective perception* that have been well studied by social scientists. However, this idea of a selective audience parallels a popular notion in **cultural studies** that media and audiences are both powerful. The communication process is a reciprocal activity involving the joint creation of meaning between the author or producer and the person who receives the message and makes sense of it (Croteau & Hoynes, 2013). Stuart Hall (1980) redefined encoding as creating a message with verbal, visual, or written codes or symbols that someone else decodes with her or his own understanding

of those codes. From this perspective, communication involves the exchange of meaning through the language and mages that compose the shared culture of participants. The receiver of the communication plays an active role, filtering messages through the lens of his or her own social class, culture, significant groups, and personal experiences (Morley, 1992).

One view of the audience reception process builds on the idea of reading. Media producers create *texts*. Here, "texts" includes radio programs, music, television shows, video games, and films, as well as printed texts. In this context, *reading* is not literally the reading of words but our interpretations of the media. Creators of media content have a preferred reading that they would like the audience to take out of the text. However, the audience might reject it, or negotiate some compromise interpretation between what they think and what the text is saying, or contest what the text says with an alternative interpretation (Morley, 1992). The audience response depends on what they, their family, and their friends already think about things. For example, a Republican Party member watching a Republican political ad might agree with it, a Democrat might disagree with it, and an independent might agree with part and reject part.

> **Cultural studies** is a branch of scholarship that argues that media and audiences work together to define culture.

seen a new movie, we may want to see it too. We also learn by listening to what others have to say about the media, including people in our daily lives and media critics.

Social learning theory also explains the avoidance of media, as in "I'd better not let Mom catch me playing another video game, or I'll be grounded." Here, the expectation of a negative outcome dictates usage. Media behavior is also determined by our own inner *self-regulation* (LaRose & Eastin, 2004): "I'm not going to binge on Netflix tonight because I am disgusted with how much of a couch potato I am." Much media behavior is governed by *habit,* in which we suspend active observation of our own media consumption and just automatically turn to the sports page or begin our day by checking our e-mail. In the extreme, self-control may fail those who repeatedly rely on media to relieve negative feelings (Tokunaga, 2015). This type of reliance results in what some have called *media addictions,* such as overindulgence in video games or attachment to smart devices. Another factor is our perception of our own competency to consume the media, or our *self-efficacy*. If you've ever put down a book thinking, "That's too deep for me," or covered your eyes during a gory scene in a horror movie, self-efficacy influenced your media behavior. Issues of self-efficacy can pre-empt certain kinds of media use, as when older people say they are too old to learn to use a computer.

Is it possible to become so deeply involved with our favorite media activity that it acts like an addictive drug? At times, they even transport us to an ecstatic state called *flow* where time seems to disappear (Sherry, 2004). There have been cases of people who were literally dying to play, who suffered heart attacks during marathon sessions with online games. The addictive qualities are sometimes openly touted by game developers who promise a "better high than drugs," by Webmasters who brag about making their creations more "sticky," and by network television programing executives who promote "must see TV." Previously (see Chapter 12) we learned that Internet gaming disorder has been tentatively classified as

WHERE DID THE TIME GO? Deep engagement in video games may induce a flow state in which time seems to disappear. Excessive game play can also steal time from important real-life activities.

a mental disease (APA, 2013). Most of us have probably been late to dinner or missed a social engagement at one time or another while absorbed in a game or some other online pastime, a possible symptom of a life-wrecking problem, if it happens consistently. If that is true of you, we recommend thinking about ways of restoring self-control. We will make you a deal: if you spend an extra hour reading *Media Now* that you would normally spend in social media, then you can treat yourself to an extra dessert tomorrow. Deal?

Computer-Mediated Communication

A great deal of the research on mediated interpersonal communication originated in organizational settings, where computer networks were used for all forms of electronic communication long before today's social media were invented. Hence, this field of study is known as *computer-mediated communication* and includes media that we may not immediately associate with computer networks, such as video teleconferencing, as well as others that are obviously mediated by computers, such as e-mail.

An important concept in computer-mediated communication is *presence,* "a psychological state in which virtual [i.e., computer-generated] objects are experienced as actual objects" (Lee, 2004, p. 37). *Social presence* refers to the experience of social actors through the social cues provided in various communication media. Text messages that consist only of printed words are said to have low social presence, which theoretically makes them suited only for routine exchanges of information. Two-way videoconferences have high social presence since they convey important social cues in voice intonations and facial expressions and live interactions flow in both directions.

These features supposedly make "rich" media channels with high levels of social presence more suitable than lean channels with fewer social cues for complex or ambiguous tasks like negotiating business deals. However,

STOP & REVIEW

1. Name three theories of media use.

2. What are the uses and gratifications of television, the Internet, and social media?

3. How do habits affect media use?

4. What is computer-mediated communication?

e-mail and texting are used for just about everything today despite their low social presence. How can that be? Even a "lean" medium like texting can be used effectively in tasks requiring social cues as parties learn about each other through repeated exchanges. Might social media like Facebook be even richer than real life, a form of *hyperpersonal* interaction (Walther, 1996)?

THEORIES OF MEDIA IMPACTS

Now that we have considered some theories about why people use the media, we can examine theories of the consequences of media usage for the individual (see Figure 15.2). There are many such theories. Here we highlight some that cut across media forms and that have influenced thinking about the relationships between media and audience behavior down through the years. Each of the theories that follows aims to explain the impact of media on members of society. However, our susceptibility as individuals depends upon our personality and demographic characteristics, our stage of life, and our social context (Valkenburg & Peter, 2013).

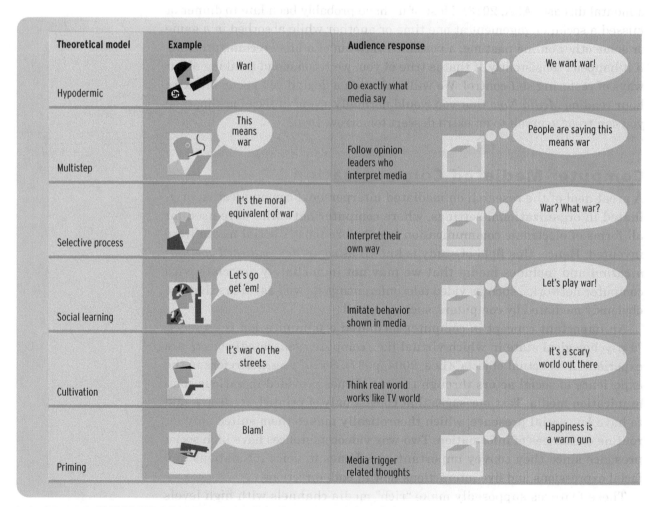

FIGURE 15.2 THEORIES OF MEDIA EFFECTS There are a number of alternative theories about how to understand mass media effects. Over the years, theories of strong effects have contended with theories positing weak effects. Currently we are in a "strong effects" period.

Media as a Hypodermic Needle

The United States was seemingly driven into war with Spain in 1898 by sensational coverage concocted by newspaper publisher William Randolph Hearst (see Chapter 4). His papers trumpeted so loudly the sinking of the U.S. battleship *Maine* in Havana Harbor and alleged atrocities by Spanish soldiers that the thirst for war became unquenchable (the *Maine's* sinking was later found not to be the work of Spanish saboteurs as Hearst's papers implied).

This event made the mass media seem extremely powerful—capable of swaying minds with the impact of a speeding bullet or a *hypodermic* injection—images that led to theoretical models of the same names (**bullet model,** or hypodermic model). Later, radio speeches by Nazi leader Adolf Hitler seemed to play a vital role in sparking the Holocaust of World War II. American film propagandists began the systematic study of the most convincing propaganda techniques. Experimental studies of **persuasion** begun during World War II identified the types of verbal arguments (e.g., one-sided versus two-sided appeals, and fear appeals versus reasoned arguments) that are the most convincing (Hovland, Lumsdane, & Sheffield, 1949).

The Multistep Flow

Survey studies of social influence conducted in the late 1940s presented a very different model from that of a hypodermic needle in which limited effects were instead perceived. For example, a **multistep flow** of media effects was evident. That is, most people receive much of their information and are influenced by the media secondhand, through the personal influence of *opinion leaders* (Katz & Lazarsfeld, 1955). The opinion leaders themselves are influenced by more elite media rather than everyday mass media channels. In the days of old when this phenomenon was first noted, social influence circulated through face-to-face communication within families, places of work, and civic associations.

Social media may amplify and speed up the flow of influence. During the 2016 presidential campaign in the United States, over two-thirds used social media or issue-based online groups to learn about the election (Gottfried et al., 2016). To use a current example, political opinion leaders might take their cue from the *Huffington Post,* an online newspaper devoted to political commentary for an elite audience. In the second step, the opinion leaders share their opinions with members of their immediate social circles—say, their followers on Twitter—but only after some modification and adaptation to the norms of that circle. The Twitter users they reach influence the social media users that they reach, and so on. Eventually, social influence radiates outward in society to people who never heard of the *Huffington Post.* But at every step in the process, social influence is modified by the norms of each new social circle it enters and by conflicting views that originate from other elite blogs as well as popular mass media sources, such as Fox News and CNN. The point is that although the media have some influence, the process of actual persuasion is primarily a social one.

Selective Processes

Another theme of the media effects studies that followed World War II was that the selective reception reduces media impact. Audiences exercise *selective exposure*: they avoid messages that are at odds with their existing beliefs.

1898

Hearst newspapers summon the United States to war with Spain with sensational headlines

1933–1945

Nazi propaganda inflames the Holocaust and World War II

The **bullet model,** or hypodermic model, posits powerful, direct effects of the mass media.

Persuasion is the use of convincing arguments to change people's beliefs, attitudes, or behaviors.

The **multistep flow** model assumes that media effects are indirect and are mediated by opinion leaders.

Thus, those who take the "anti" position in debate over the Affordable Healthcare Act are not likely to read a newspaper editorial advocating health insurance for everyone. Even when people expose themselves to discordant content, they distort it with *selective perception*. Thus, supporters of the healthcare act who watch a TV interview with one of its critics are more likely to find additional "proof" that their position is correct than to be converted to the other side. *Selective retention* means that people's memories are also distorted, so that months later someone may remember that her side won a healthcare debate when in fact her side was humiliated (Sears & Freedman, 1972).

In 1960, Joseph Klapper published an influential review of postwar research on the effects of the mass media. Klapper concluded that the media were weak, able to deliver only a few percent of the voters in an election, and able to gain only a few points' worth of market share for advertisers. Even these **limited effects** registered only at the margins, he said, primarily among the uninterested and the uninformed (Klapper, 1960).

Social media may facilitate passive selective exposure. For example, Google personalizes searches based on individual search histories so that the search results conservatives see for the topic "planned parenthood" may differ from those seen by liberals. Social media *recommender systems* automatically feed us stories that like-minded friends also like. The proliferation of online news sources and social media also make active selective exposure easier, helping us to find sites with the ideological slant we prefer or to click on stories that our social media friends "like" (Mutz & Young, 2011).

Social Learning Theory

Within a few years, Klapper's conclusions seemed unsatisfactory. In the 1960s, social critics cast about for explanations for mounting violence, political unrest, and a decline in public morality, especially among young adults. Television seemed a likely cause, because the young people belonged to the first "TV generation" that had grown up with the medium, and TV was loaded with images of violence and sex.

About the same time, a new theory of mass media effects, *social learning theory,* lent credence to these claims. Previously, we applied this theory to media consumption behavior, but it originally entered the field of mass communication research to explain the effects of television. The theory explained that viewers imitate what they see on TV through a process known as *observational learning*. The "rewards" that television characters receive for their antisocial behavior, including not just the loot from their robberies but also their very appearance on a glamorous medium, such as television, encourage imitation. On the other hand, when the bad guys on TV get caught and go to jail, this presumably inhibits viewers from imitating them. The more we identify with a character—the more it resembles us or someone we would like to be—the more likely we are to imitate his or her behavior. The Bobo doll experiments we examined previously and many others that followed validated this theory.

Cultivation Theory

Another explanation of media effects is that heavy exposure imparts a worldview that is consistent with the "world" presented in the media (Gerbner et al., 1994). According to **cultivation theory,** heavy television viewers are likely to

---

1960

Klapper's *The Effects of Mass Communication* argues for weak media effects

---

The theory of limited effects holds that the effects of the mass media on individuals are slight.

Cultivation theory argues that mass media exposure cultivates a view of the world that is consistent with mediated "reality."

be influenced by what is consistently shown in media, such as overestimating their own chances of being victims of violent crime, since it seems so common on television. For example, children who were heavy viewers of stories about child kidnappings were more frightened for their safety than those who watched relatively little television news (Wilson, Martins, & Marske, 2005). Their real-world experiences combine with the television worldview over time in a process called *mainstreaming*. When real-life experience confirms the media view (e.g., the viewers live in violent neighborhoods), the effect intensifies through the process of *resonance*. From this analysis, we project media effects. The viewers who adopt this distorted TV worldview might tolerate violence in their communities and families and in their own behavior because they see it as "normal."

Cultivation assumes that media systems like conventional broadcast TV deliver a consistent message to a mass audience. So, how can it apply to new media with their diverse messages and fragmented audiences? Supporters of the theory argue that as Big Media corporations extend their influence to the Internet, the new media will present the same worldview as the old. For example, by using Netflix to push downloads of *The Walking Dead,* the new media present the same message of unrelenting violence as the old. Video games cultivate perceptions of danger in the real world, although those effects may be limited to the specific situations that are similar to those encountered in the gaming environment rather than generating a generalized fear (Williams, 2006).

Priming

Priming theory is another theory (Berkowitz, 1984) in which the activation of one thought triggers related thoughts. Seeing the Roadrunner cartoon character bash the hapless coyote with a hammer makes us more likely to bash our little brother after the show, or so the theory goes. Incidental cues may unleash the aggression. The next time we see a hammer and little brother is standing near—look out! Children may store *scripts* about how to respond with violence that they learn from the media in long-term memory and then act out those scripts when a real-world event triggers that memory (Van Erva, 1990). The *General Aggression Model* (GAM; Carnagey, Anderson, & Bushman, 2007) integrates priming theory with social learning theory to describe how previously learned violent behavior may be triggered by thoughts, emotions, or physiological states provoked by media exposure.

> **Priming theory** states that media images stimulate related thoughts in the minds of audience members.

Agenda Setting

Agenda setting is a process through which public figures and important events help to shape the content of the media. Agenda setting theory also describes the effects of that process on the media audience: the rank ordering that the audience assigns to important issues of the day, the attributes of political candidates, and associations among key concepts tend to match the amount of coverage that the media give them (McCombs, Shaw, & Weaver, 2014). Originally conceived to explain the relationship between mass media news coverage and public perceptions, the theory can also account for other types of agendas, such as cultural or health topics. New media like Twitter have a symbiotic relationship with conventional mass media, sometimes leading and at other times following the lead of mass media news (Conway, Kenski, & Wang, 2015).

Catharsis

The *catharsis* hypothesis argues that media sex and violence have positive effects by allowing people to live out their antisocial desires in a mediated fantasy world instead of the real world (Feshbach & Singer, 1971). This theory was popular in the 1930s and 1940s before it was widely believed that the media were responsible for society's ills. The catharsis hypothesis resurfaced in a review of the effects of violent video games in which it was found that those who played video games for relatively long periods of time exhibited less aggression than those who played for relatively short periods (Sherry, 2007). However, it could also be that the longer people play, the more skilled and less frustrated and thus the less aggressive they become (Ferguson, 2009).

Critical Theories

Critical theorists question the theories used in media effects studies as well as the methods used (see Chapter 2). Critical studies of media impacts focus less on behavioral effects on individuals and more on how individuals and communities interpret media and, to some degree, on large-scale cultural impacts of media. For example, a critical analysis of John Hinckley's attempted assassination of Ronald Reagan in 1980 examined the way in which Hinckley "read" (or interpreted) a violent movie (*Taxi Driver*) and mingled it with his fantasies about actress Jodie Foster and former actor Ronald Reagan (Real, 1989). By noting that Hinckley committed his act of violence on the eve of the Academy Awards ceremony, Real wove an explanation of how the would-be assassin was trying to communicate his unrequited love for Foster. Does *The Force Awakens* glorify the military or is it a critique of militaristic society? The critical theorist is able to examine broad questions such as these about the relationship between culture and society that may elude the social scientist.

Note that in interpretations such as these, the ebb and flow of cause and effect between media and society is not a one-way street. In a sense, the media themselves are the "effects" of class domination or racial prejudice. For example, media might be used by their owners to assert, or make *hegemonic,* an idea that fits with their interests (see Chapter 2). People who own factories might want to make unions look bad. And unions may ally with politicians to create media messages that seek to limit owners' power. So, in this view, the media are a part of broader systems of economic exploitation and cultural interaction.

There is a split in critical theory between those who focus on political economy and ideology and those who focus on studies of culture. Among the former, researchers often argue for fairly powerful effects, since they assume that powerful media owners can assert their ideological interests in their media's content. Among the latter, rather than the term *selective perception*, critical cultural theorists speak of audiences that are active *readers* of media texts. Some focus on the role of the audience while others focus on a more qualitative, critical approach to media messages (Deacon et al., 2007). Some critical theorists speak of *group mediation* (Martín-Barbero, 1993) or *interpretive communities* of groups that are similar in education, occupation, wealth, and family background (Lindlof & Taylor, 2010), whereas other social scientists use the term *multistep flow* to describe the way in which social interactions affect perceptions of the media. Likewise, critical theorists have relabeled the SMCR model (see Chapter 1) the "linear model" or "transmission paradigm," in which messages are perceived as flowing in a manner that seems more unidirectional and clear than what critical theorists observe from their own studies.

Media and Antisocial Behavior

Antisocial behavior is contrary to prevailing norms for social conduct. That includes unlawful actions, such as murder, hate crimes, rape, and drug abuse, as well as behaviors that many members of society find objectionable even if they are not illegal, such as aggression, racism, sexism, drug abuse, and sexual promiscuity.

Violence

1972

U.S. Surgeon General reports on the relationship between television and violence

The effects of media violence are one of the most enduring topics in the annals of media effects research (Eastin, 2013). Riots in major cities in the late 1960s triggered national concern about the effects of television on violence, culminating in landmark studies sponsored by the U.S. Surgeon General. Those, in turn, led to a short-lived effort in the 1970s to limit violence in the early evening hours when children were most likely to be viewing. Effects on children are a special concern because youngsters have trouble distinguishing between the real world and the world of the small screen. To the child's mind, if Scooby-Doo recovers instantly from a bash on the head, then the same should be true for little brother.

Content analysis studies document the amount of violence. Beginning in 1967, George Gerbner conducted a series of content analysis studies to track the amount of violence on U.S. network television. Later research expanded the sample to cable TV networks (Federman, 1998) and found that three-fifths of all prime-time programs contained violence, and they averaged over six violent incidents per program per hour. They estimated that preschoolers who watch 2 hours of television daily witness 10,000 violent acts each year. Most of these involved "high-risk" portrayals that children are likely to imitate, such as violent acts committed by attractive characters in realistic settings in which no harmful consequences are shown. Children's television shows have even more violence than other programs, glamorize it just as much, and trivialize it even more (Wilson et al., 2002). Recently, attention has shifted to video games, which are packed with violent role models (Lachlan, Smith, & Tamborini, 2005) and the popular first-person shooter genre is saturated with violence.

1967

Gerbner's first Violence Profile documents violence on television

Hundreds of experimental studies, many patterned after Bandura's Bobo doll study described earlier, demonstrate that children can imitate violence they see, but do those effects persist outside the laboratory? Survey studies conducted in real-world settings also tend to show a relationship between violent behavior and viewership of violent television (Paik & Comstock, 2014). However, it is possible that violent people also like to watch violent programs,

CHILD'S PLAY? The effects of violent video games on aggressive behavior are highly controversial. Some reviews of the research find substantial effects, whereas others find none.

Leila Cutler/Alamy Stock Photo

so that it might be said that aggressive behavior causes viewing of TV violence rather than television causes real-world aggressiveness.

More convincing are longitudinal panel studies in which television viewing at one time is related to violence exhibited years later. Long-term panel studies (e.g., Huesmann & Eron, 2013) indicate that television viewing at an early age is related to aggressive behavior as well as to criminal convictions and developing an anti-social personality later in life (Robertson, McAnally, & Hancox, 2013). However, other longitudinal studies of TV violence have found no effects (Milavsky et al., 1982) or have yielded inconsistent findings over time (Huesmann & Eron, 1986) or across countries.

Thus, the findings are not entirely consistent across the thousands of studies of media violence that have been conducted over the years. Some reviews of the studies examining the effects of violent video games find evidence of major effects on aggression (Greitemeyer & Mügge, 2014), whereas others find little evidence that such effects exist (Kutner & Olson, 2008). Researchers disagree over the validity of the methods used in the studies and the interpretation of the findings (Ferguson & Kilburn, 2010). For example, many experimental studies focus on aggressive attitudes rather than behavior or use measures of violent behavior, such as administering blasts of loud noise, that have little in common with the real-world violent acts that are the real concern. Survey studies rely on often faulty memories about the amount of exposure to violent media. Also, the studies typically involve children and college students drawn from normal populations that do not frequently engage in violence.

Above all, there is the question of how socially significant the effect is: is it large enough to justify parental or public policy interventions?

Meta-analysis studies that review previous research and that quantify the magnitude of the effects can help answer that question. A recent review of such studies (Comstock, Scharrer, & Powers, 2014) found that the effects of media violence are substantial and consistent across both television and video game studies. The size of the effect is somewhat less than the relationship between cigarette smoking and cancer, but greater than the (negative) relationship between condom use and AIDs. However, other factors have a greater impact on youth violence, including family and peer influence, socioeconomic status, and substance abuse (U.S. DHHS, 2001). Still, these conclusions remain highly controversial. Significant effects are found in only about half of the experimental studies of television violence and might be at least partially explained away by genetic factors or exposure to violence in the home (Ferguson, 2009). And, there is no consistent evidence that the availability of media known for their violence affect community-level rates of violent crime (Ferguson, 2015).

So, after 70 years of debate and research, questions about the impact of violent media remain.

Concerned parents who may wish to err on the side of caution by protecting their children from media violence could benefit from warnings when violence is about to appear. Unfortunately the content labels supplied by television networks underrepresent the amount of violence in program content (Kunkel et al., 2002), and less than a third of parents fully utilize them, in part because they find that the ratings do not provide detailed enough guidance (Gentile et al., 2011). Moreover, the labels may not be effective unless accompanied by improved parental supervision or automatic content filtering. Simply labeling the programs as violent attracts more young viewers to the "forbidden fruit" (Bushman & Cantor, 2003). Parental intervention can make a difference. Providing brief negative evaluations of violent television characters (Nathanson, 2004) can reduce violence effects. Strict rules about the types of games children play may reduce their antisocial behavior; however, making negative statements about a child's favorite game may have the opposite effect (Martins, Matthews, & Ratan, 2015).

Prejudice

The media may also promote sexism, racism, and other forms of intolerance. Media portrayals encourage **stereotyping,** the formation of generalizations about a group of people on the basis of limited information. Stereotypes are harmful when they become rationalizations for treating others unfairly and when members of the groups to which they are applied internalize them. Media are generally very effective at creating stereotypes because they are sometimes the only source of information we have about other groups and because they often present a distorted view of those groups. Anonymous online communication may be particularly toxic since, in the absence of social cues, people magnify the smallest differences between themselves and "the other" to foment intergroup conflict (Spear & Postmes, 2015).

> **Stereotyping** is the making of generalizations about groups of people on the basis of limited information.

Since the 1970s, women have begun appearing in higher-status jobs and in somewhat fewer stereotypically female occupations on television. Still, they are more likely to be unemployed and less likely to have professional occupations than men (e.g., secretary and nurse; Signorielli, 2009; Signorielli & Bacue, 1999). The reinforcement of stereotypes begins with programs aimed at toddlers: *Barney and Friends* and *Teletubbies* portrayed the few female characters as caregivers and followers, whereas male roles included a wider range of possibilities (Powell & Abels, 2002). And the reinforcement continues through film and video game characterizations as toddlers grow into tweens and teens (Okorafor & Davenport, 2001; Williamson, 2007).

The Gamergate conflict between video game lovers and feminist critics of sexism in games (see Chapter 12) has renewed interest in the impact of sex role portrayals in games. Sex-role stereotypes are rampant in video games: women are seldom seen in general and usually appear scantily clad in sexy clothing when present (Downs & Smith, 2010). There is mixed evidence of the effects of sex-role stereotypes in games. In an experimental study, men exposed to stereotypical female characters in games had more lenient attitudes toward sexual harassment than a control group (Dill, Brown, & Collins, 2008). In a later experiment, women who adopted sexualized characters in video games tended to view themselves as sex objects (Fox, Bailenson, & Tricase, 2013). However, a longitudinal study of German gamers (Breuer et al., 2015) found that the overall amount of video game use had no effect on sexist attitudes. So, further longitudinal research focusing on the amount of exposure to games the most laden with sex-role stereotypes might resolve the conflicting findings.

How harmful are sex-role stereotypes? To the male viewer, stereotypes might make it seem acceptable to treat women as inferior. For their part, women may feel diminished because of their underrepresentation. Sex-role stereotypes in the media may have an effect on a wide range of outcomes including attitudes toward women and perceptions of the appropriateness of personality traits, occupations, and activities stereotypically associated more with one sex than with the other (Oppliger, 2007). Gender stereotypes can also make us dissatisfied with our own bodies. Exposure to media images that consistently portray slender female models and actresses may encourage unrealistic body images and lead to eating disorders among females (Tiggemann, 2014). As with violence effects, the impact of sex-role stereotyping might be counteracted by parental interventions that provide more realistic information, for example, pointing out that "lots of girls do things besides paint their nails and put on make-up" (Nathanson et al., 2002, p. 928).

The life aspirations of minority children are also affected by the limited media portrayals of minorities (Clark, 1972). Racially stereotyped portrayals persist on television; for example, African Americans are still more often portrayed as lazy, and Latinos as flashy dressers compared to whites (Mastro, 2008). Racially stereotyped television portrayals of minorities may lead white viewers to see minorities in more negative ways, such as making them more willing to perceive African Americans as criminals (Ford, 1997) or to vote against public policies aimed at ending racial inequality (Mastro, 2008). Highly sexualized portrayals of Hispanics and African Americans in primetime television are related to negative attitudes toward those groups in society at large, while exposure to minorities in professional occupations has a positive influence on racial attitudes (Tukachinsky, Mastro, & Yarchi, 2015).

Media stereotyping affects all groups in society. Adults over 60 years are relatively invisible on television, and when they do appear, they are portrayed as relatively powerless and sexless compared to younger characters (Lauzen, Dozier, & Reyes, 2007). Blue-collar families are underrepresented and often portrayed in a way that denigrates their lifestyles (consider *The Simpsons*). The same is true of homosexuals, persons with disabilities, the homeless, the mentally ill, and seemingly any group that deviates from a mainstream society dominated by professional, "straight," healthy, and wealthy white

FIRST LIGHT PRODUCTIONS/KINGS GATEFILMS/ The Kobal Collection at Art Resource, NY

UNDOING STEREOTYPES The success of female role models like 2010 Oscar winner Kathryn Bigelow may hold the key to reducing gender stereotypes in front of the camera as well as behind it.

males. We can easily summon to mind stock images of serious college students ("nerds" in media lexicon), billionaires, lawyers, and police that have little in common with their real-world counterparts. To some extent, the media cannot function without stereotypes. They are the "pictures in our heads" (Lippmann, 1922) that stories are made of, a type of conceptual shorthand that allows viewers to recognize characters immediately and connect with their situations.

It is when the negative stereotypes spill over from the flickering screens into our daily lives that they become a concern. In the midst of a continuing war on terrorism, there is the danger that we may be unduly influenced by media images of Muslims and Arabs as terrorists and warmongers. U.S. media contain many negative images of Muslims (Nacos & Torres-Reyna, 2007). Exposure to stereotypes of Muslims, such as portraying them as terrorists, is related to public support for policies that harm Muslims and to negative attitudes toward them (Saleem et al., 2015). Indeed, this situation is one in which the media images could be especially powerful. They highlight serious intergroup conflict in the starkest terms and strengthen stereotypes (Huesmann et al., 2012). These are conditions in which media stereotypes can have very corrosive effects.

Sexual Behavior

Sex in the media erupted as an issue in the 1920s, in the aftermath of a wave of Hollywood sex scandals. Hollywood imposed strict self-censorship standards that now seem ludicrous in retrospect: no cleavage, no navels, separate beds for married couples, no kisses longer than 4 seconds, and cut to the clouds overhead if sex is imminent. When Elizabeth Taylor said the word *virgin* in a 1954 movie, it caused a sensation.

Since then, producers and publishers have continually pushed the limits to reap financial benefits at the box office and the newsstand, so pornography continues to surface as a national issue. There were congressional hearings about pornography in music in 1985, which led to content ratings for recorded music. Two presidential commissions examined the impact of pornography on society, one (President's Commission on Obscenity and Pornography, 1970) finding that there was no effect and the second (1986) concluding that there was.

The past decades have seen a dramatic increase in highly explicit pornographic material through magazines, home video, movies, and cable television. Today, online sex is a growing concern. In a recent national study, about a fourth of children aged 10–15 years intentionally exposed themselves to X-rated material on the Internet, and exposure to violent pornography (although not exposure to nonviolent pornography) greatly increased the chances of engaging in sexually related aggression over time (Ybarra et al., 2012).

1985

U.S. Senate hearings on pornographic music

1986

Attorney General's Commission on Pornography

DANGEROUS IMAGES? The mix of sex and violence such as that on the HBO hit series *Game of Thrones* has been associated with increased chances of engaging in sexual aggression.

Among adults, the consumption of pornography is related to participation in extramarital sex and sex for hire, liberal sexual attitudes, promiscuity, prostitution, acts of sexual aggression (Wright, 2013; Wright, Tokunaga, & Kraus, 2016), and sexual harassment (Brown & L'Engle, 2009).

A growing cause for concern is "sexting," in which teens make their own pornography by taking pictures of themselves in various states of undress and share them via social media or cell phones. Although only about 2 percent of youth between the ages of 10 and 17 have sent pictures of that nature (Mitchell et al., 2012), the numbers are still alarming because parents, schools, and law enforcement officials treat the incidents as child pornography cases.

Is there a relationship between pornography and sex crimes in the real world? Sex offenders are likely to consume pornography before engaging in sex and are highly aroused by material that matches the nature of their criminal sexual activities. Among those who are at "high risk" for sexual aggression (e.g., men who are impulsive or hostile by nature), pornography exposure greatly adds to that risk. However, a link between the availability of pornography in a community and the incidence of sex crimes has not been established conclusively. The example of Japan is often cited, a culture in which sexual images in the media, including violent ones, are much more common than in the United States but sex crimes are far less frequent. That could be because of strict social norms against rape that inhibit the effects of pornography but also make victims reluctant to report it (Harris & Barlett, 2008).

The relatively mild sexual portrayals on broadcast television, in which sexual intercourse is at most strongly implied by showing "after" pictures of actors between the sheets, can also have harmful effects. Exposure to sexual content on television was found to be related to pregnancy rates during a study that followed a national sample of teens over 3 years (Chandra et al., 2008).

Drug Abuse

A lifetime ago there was concern that movies such as *Easy Rider* glorified the drug scene and contributed to illegal drug use among college students. The media generally bowed to these concerns, although perhaps only because drug films were not as profitable as those featuring violence and sex, and because distributors of illegal drugs cannot buy advertisements for them!

The abuse of legal drugs is quite another story. Cigarette ads have long been banished from television by law. Print ads can no longer glorify smoking by showing happy, glamorous people (or cuddly cartoon characters) puffing away; the Surgeon General's warnings about the hazards of smoking must be displayed; and there can be no imagery that obviously is designed to appeal to children. Hard-liquor distillers long avoided television (although this has changed), but beer and wine commercials are one of the leading sources of advertising revenue for television, as are ads for over-the-counter drugs. Restrictions on prescription drug ads have been relaxed so that they, too, can appear on television.

Advertisers claim that these ads do not boost overall consumption levels and affect only the relative market share the various brands enjoy. However, a comprehensive review of research about the effects of cigarette advertising concluded that cigarette ads may prompt both the initiation and the continuation of smoking (Capella, Webster, & Kinard, 2011). Public health officials are concerned that ads for the new "smokeless" e-cigarettes (see Chapter 14) will re-glamorize smoking and reverse the impact of bans on cigarette advertising on television (Fairchild, Bayer, & Colgrove, 2014). Advertising also plays a role in the initiation of alcohol consumption (Smith & Foxcroft, 2009). Critics have long contended that some of the ads are secretly targeted to young viewers through characters (such as the dashing Captain Morgan pirate character and Joe Camel) that are carefully crafted to appeal to impressionable young viewers at an age when they are vulnerable to initiating lifelong addictions. Revelations of secret cigarette industry marketing studies on children have shown that the critics were right.

Attention has turned to antismoking campaigns directed at teens and children. Campaigns from the national "truth" antismoking campaign that attack the motives of the tobacco industry have proven effective, but antismoking ads produced by the industry itself actually increase intentions to smoke (Davis et al., 2009). And ads that are highly critical of the industry are prohibited under the terms of a settlement with the tobacco industry that set aside billions of dollars for smoking prevention.

Tobacco and alcohol industry apologists like to argue that their products are legal and they have a right to advertise, even if some children get in the way. After all, fast food may be harmful. Why don't we ban hamburger commercials aimed at children? Maybe we should. Now some critics have begun to argue that like drugs, fatty foods are indeed addictive.

PROSOCIAL BEHAVIOR

Prosocial behavior is in a sense the opposite of antisocial behavior. It includes behaviors and positive qualities that we want to encourage in our children and our society: cooperation, altruism, sharing, love, tolerance, respect, balanced nutrition, contraceptive use, personal hygiene, safe driving, improved reading skills, and so on. We can also include in this list the discontinuing of antisocial behaviors, such as smoking, drinking, reckless driving, or unsafe sex. Prosocial media fall along a continuum based on the relative mixture of entertainment and informational content. They range from transmitting heavily sugar-coated, subtle messages to explicit, direct educational efforts.

Efforts to promote prosocial media are the flip side of "media bashing" that we outlined earlier. Instead of criticizing the media for sex and violence, only to have them retreat behind the First Amendment, why not encourage them to produce more wholesome and educational programs? The Children's Television Act of 1990 does just that. It mandates that programs designed specifically for children be aired as a condition for broadcast license renewals (see Chapter 16). After years of wrangling over just how much children's programming is enough, what "specifically designed for children" means, and even who children are, meaningful guidelines were finally passed in 1996 (Kunkel, 1998).

INFORMATION CAMPAIGNS

Information campaigns use the techniques of public relations and advertising to "sell" people on prosocial behaviors. They seek to achieve specific changes in their audience, such as heightening public awareness of a health or social problem and changing related attitudes and behaviors. They usually

STOP & REVIEW

1. Name three theories that contend that mass media have strong effects.
2. What are some of the factors that weaken media effects?
3. Do video games cause violence, or don't they? Explain your answer.
4. How do media stereotypes increase prejudice?
5. Identify three effects of pornography.

Prosocial behaviors are those that a society values and encourages.

1990

Children's Television Act mandates programs designed specifically for children

Information campaigns use the techniques of advertising in an attempt to convince people to adopt prosocial behaviors.

adopt an informal and entertaining style to attract an audience. Perhaps the most familiar manifestations of information campaigns are public service announcements, such as the recent campaign against texting while driving.

Information campaigns have a spotty record of success. Experimental studies show, however, that some campaigns do affect the awareness, attitudes, and behaviors of their audiences. Campaigns can succeed if they have clear objectives and sharply defined target audiences and if they find relevant ways to overcome indifference (Rice & Atkin, 2012). *Social marketing,* an integrated marketing communication approach to behavior change (see Chapter 14), combines media, interpersonal influence, and carefully managed efforts to introduce recommended products directly into the lives of the target audience. This approach has achieved considerable success in the health communication field (Wakefield, Loken, & Hornik, 2010). For example, in a safe-sex campaign, public service ads might be combined with posters in nightclubs and with volunteers who circulate on dance floors to distribute condoms. Success can also depend upon striking just the right chord with their intended audiences. For example, antismoking ads that emphasize the personal stories of the effects of smoking are more effective than others (Durkin, Biener, & Wakefield, 2009). However, habitual behaviors like smoking are generally harder to change through information campaigns than infrequent behaviors such as obtaining flu vaccinations.

Even when well designed, some information campaigns face too many obstacles to have much impact. Many rely on free advertising space (hence their appearance late at night) and consequently have difficulty reaching their audiences. The public interest groups that produce information campaigns too often expend all their resources in developing the media materials, leaving little for paid media placements directed to their target audience.

And not all information campaigns are effective to begin with. Advertising professionals who contribute their time in exchange for a chance to showcase their skills may not be familiar with scientific evidence about what works and what is needed to create successful campaigns. For example, health campaigns that emphasize social consequences and feature female sources tend to be effective, whereas those featuring emotional appeals or that rely on credibility of the sources tend not to be. It is important to tailor messages according to the involvement level of audiences as well as their age, gender, and race (Keller & Lehmann, 2008).

Other campaigns are worse than ineffective and can have unintended effects. For example, informing children about the risks of drugs can unintentionally make drug use seem more prevalent and therefore more socially acceptable. One widely touted drug education program, project D.A.R.E., was found to be ineffective at best (Lynam et al., 1999) and at worst may have encouraged drug use; it had to be redesigned.

Kayte Deioma / PhotoEdit

WE DARE YOU TO USE DRUGS Well-intentioned but poorly designed information campaigns sometimes unintentionally encourage the behaviors they hope to prevent. The D.A.R.E. antidrug program increased drug use when students learned that drugs were more prevalent than they had thought. The program had to be revised as a result of these findings.

In other cases, campaigns may have foggy objectives or uncertain target audiences, or they may have too many objectives, trying to satisfy multiple agendas ("We want users to stop using, potential users to stop thinking about it, and their parents to drum both messages into their children's heads"). Campaign developers seldom have the resources to fund the detailed research that goes into successful product commercials. Also they try to achieve much more than product advertisements, which merely aim to increase awareness of a brand name or a new product. Information campaigns often target deeply ingrained habitual behaviors, a goal that is generally unattainable through advertising alone.

Informal Education

Without a "captive audience" of classroom students, informal education efforts must artfully combine the elements of education and entertainment. The best-known example is *Sesame Street*. Since its inception in 1969, *Sesame Street* has proved to be a popular and effective means of readying children for school (Fisch & Truglio, 2001). However, *Sesame Street* is also an example of a phenomenon that plagues prosocial media—the unintended effect. *Sesame Street* was originally designed to close the gap in school readiness between minority and majority children. Unfortunately, it did just the opposite. Middle-class white children who watched the show learned more about "words that begin with b" than low-income minority children, and the knowledge gap (see page 430) between the two widened as a result (Cook et al., 1975).

What about the prosocial effects of entertainment media? Do couch potatoes soak up valuable information from TV quiz shows? Do children learn about cooperation by watching *SpongeBob SquarePants*? We call these effects *incidental learning* because they are side effects of exposure to entertainment. For example, in areas where the MTV show *16 and Pregnant* was heavily viewed and stimulated online discussion and information seeking, teen pregnancy rates dropped more than in areas where viewership was relatively light (Kearney & Levine, 2014). Internationally, a number of studies in Brazil, Mexico, India, and South Africa have shown that deliberate placement of plotlines in some operas and other serial entertainment encouraging smaller family sizes has had considerable impact over time—this approach has developed an entire approach to prosocial media called *entertainment education* (Singhal & Rogers, 2012).

Interactive media provide new venues for incidental learning. Prosocial video games can be effective in promoting desirable behaviors, such as cooperation, among children (Greitemeyer & Mügge, 2014). Many young Internet users engage in self-directed online research to learn about topics that interest them, often stimulated by their participation in online social media like Facebook (Ito et al., 2009).

Formal Education

The delivery of courses through the media is formally known as *distance education*. The new trend in distance education is putting courses on the World Wide Web, the virtual university. Overall, Web courses are at least as effective as classroom instruction and possibly more effective (Means et al., 2009).

However, there is wide variability in the effectiveness of distance education relative to classroom instruction: some online courses are more effective than the classroom, others far less so. With so many courses going online, either all or in part, the question becomes which forms of online coursework are most effective. For example, it appears that asynchronous courses that can be consumed at the convenience of the learner are more effective than synchronous courses even though the latter permit live interactions with the instructor (Bernard et al., 2009).

Online instruction could have a transformative effect on higher education that might someday eliminate many of our beloved alma maters as elite universities post online courses that are arguably "the best" and are also free. Stanford University offered a free online course about artificial intelligence that drew over 100,000 students. *Massive open online courses* (MOOCs) are generating massive interest in higher education circles, and consortia of major universities like Coursera, edX, and Udacity have formed to provide them. There is evidence that well-designed MOOCs are effective (Colvin et al., 2014), although research is in its early stages. Initial enthusiasm dimmed considerably when it turned out that less than 10 percent of students complete the courses, which too often have involved little more than viewing recordings of lectures with limited interaction.

There is growing interest in so-called "serious games" (see Chapter 12) that embed educational objectives in video games. Given the popularity of video games with learners of all ages, the ability of games to simulate real-world environments outside the classroom, and the way games can readily adapt instruction to the user, serious games are beginning to demonstrate their educational effectiveness compared to conventional instruction (Clark, Tanner-Smith, & Killingsworth, 2015).

The Impacts of Advertising

If the media have such mixed success in influencing behavior, why is there so much advertising? (For more on advertising, see Chapter 14.) The answer is that advertisers are happy to achieve rather limited impacts, at least when using conventional mass media. Most advertisers take our consumption behavior as a given. They merely seek to strengthen our *brand awareness* so that we think of their product when we are in the store and maintain *brand loyalty* so that we will keep coming back for more. At best, they hope to provide information that will sway the attitudes and purchase behavior among a small percentage of consumers and that those impacts will build slowly with repeated exposures to an ad campaign. However, conventional market research tools provide limited insight into the success of mass media advertising campaigns based on the demographic characteristics of audiences and the media and products they consume (Stewart & Pavlou, 2008).

Does advertising work? Even with these relatively modest goals, many mass media advertising campaigns are a flop. Sometimes they are outgunned by more powerful campaigns from competitors. Many other factors influence consumer purchases, including special promotional offers, the price of the product, its availability, the way it is packaged, and—let us not forget—consumer needs and the actual merits of the product. Any of these can negate the effects of the most polished advertising campaign. Sometimes the campaign is simply ineffective. Part of the problem lies with the way ads are tested. If they are highly memorable, they are deemed successful. Only much later do the advertisers find out whether they sold more hamburgers or athletic shoes.

It is unclear exactly how advertising works even when it is successful. The *hierarchy of effect* is a common notion in advertising research that states that purchase decisions follow a set series of steps: first comes awareness, then interest, then decision, followed by the action of actually buying the product. But there are many competing hierarchies, including some in which action comes first, as in the case of an impulse buy. One review of the literature concluded that none of the proposed hierarchies is especially compelling (Vakratsas & Ambler, 1999).

The impact of television advertising on young children is of great concern because most children first come into contact with the consumer society through TV. Young children have a difficult time understanding commercials. They confuse the commercials with the programs and react uncritically to advertising messages (Liebert & Sprafkin, 1988). Advertisers can exploit young viewers by using the hosts of children's shows to hawk their products, selecting deceptive camera angles to make tiny toys appear child-size. Sometimes, a new television show is really a big advertisement—part of a marketing campaign—where the characters of children's programs are dolls already on the store shelves waiting to be purchased. These shows prompt children to parrot advertising slogans to wear down their parents (Buijzen & Valkenburg, 2013). As we saw previously, advertising also plays a role in introducing children to harmful habits such as smoking and alcohol consumption.

Is advertising good for consumers in an economic sense? Overall, about 7 percent of what we spend on consumer goods goes into advertising (Shonfeld & Associates, 2012). In some product categories—cigarettes, beer, and soft drinks, for example—the advertising expenditures are considerably higher. When manufacturers establish brand loyalty, they can charge more for their products. However, advertising also makes consumers aware of alternative products and special offers, and it generally promotes competition, which helps to keep consumer prices down. However, ads are less of a bargain for advertisers than they used to be. The increase in sales stemming from increases in advertising is small, about 12 cents for every dollar spent on advertising, and has fallen to about half of what it was in the 1980s (Sethuraman, Tellis, & Briesch, 2011). In the critical view, many researchers are concerned about the larger social impact of advertising in locking people into a consumerist point of view and a lifestyle that

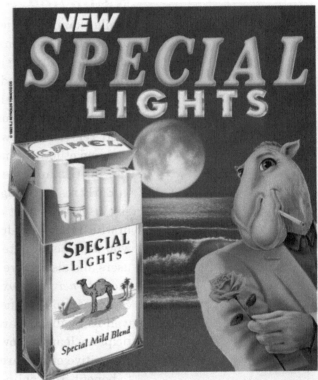

OLD JOE Cigarette advertising often influences impressionable minds and may encourage young children to acquire an unhealthy lifelong habit. The tobacco industry secretly marketed to children before the practice was uncovered and its effects on children were documented, resulting in new restrictions on cigarette advertising (which marked the end of Joe Camel's life).

has them spending money they don't have for things they don't really need (Jhally, 2000).

Online advertising and marketing forces a rethinking of basic questions about advertising effectiveness. In favor of advertisers, online search word advertising popularized by Google makes it possible to target ads to consumers who are in the market for a specific product, eliminating waste in advertising budgets. The effectiveness of an ad can be assessed with big data techniques by tracking purchases completed as a result of clicking through to the advertiser's Web page or recorded by check-out counter scanners or credit card transactions. In addition to conventional advertising sources, consumers turn to blogs, social media, product review sites, and other sources of online word of mouth (or *word of mouse* as is sometimes called) and these are proving effective. Positive online word of mouth, although not the overall volume of online comments, increases sales (Gopinath, Thomas, & Krishnamurthi, 2014) as does social media content posted by advertisers (Kumar et al., 2016).

Well-Being

While examining theories of media usage, we saw that people use the media to entertain and relax themselves and to dispel negative moods. Are the media effective in altering our sense of well-being, and for better or for worse? Previously we examined research about media usage that finds that people use television to entertain themselves and improve their moods, suggesting that the medium has a positive effect on our well-being. However, adults who limit their television viewing to a couple of hours a day suffer less from depression and other psychological maladies compared to those with normal levels of viewing (Hammermeister et al., 2005).

Early research suggested that the Internet caused depression among excessive users (Kraut et al., 1998). The researchers carried out a field experiment in which they introduced Internet access into homes and found that teenagers who were heavy Internet users exhibited more signs of depression than light users and also showed increased stress and loneliness. They called this finding the *Internet paradox,* meaning that a social technology, such as the Internet could lead to loneliness and depression. The negative effects on psychological well-being disappeared in a follow-up study, perhaps indicating that the participants learned how to use the Internet more to their advantage over time.

Positive effects are often found as well. Naturally outgoing extroverts tend to benefit from online interactions by making more friends, a "rich get richer" effect (Kraut et al., 2002), and can take good advantage of social networking sites like Facebook. However, inward looking introverts can also benefit by participating in anonymous online venues where their real-world self is not on display and where they feel comfortable engaging in interaction, so the poor can get (socially) richer, too. Older adults and members of stigmatized minority groups can also relieve loneliness and depression online (Amichai-Hamburger & Schneider, 2014). The effects of social networking on well-being have received particular attention. Among college students, Facebook use was positively related to self-esteem (Ellison, Steinfeld, & Lampe, 2007). A large-scale experiment that planted extra helpings of positive items in the newsfeeds of Facebook users elevated their moods compared to those who saw only the usual proportions of positive updates (Kramer, Guillory, & Hancock, 2014).

However, the impact of new media on psychological well-being remains controversial. Survey research suggests that Internet use is related to loneliness and decreased life satisfaction (Stepanikova, Nie & He, 2010). Uncontrolled, habitual Internet use may disrupt important real-life activities (LaRose, Kim, & Peng, 2010) and so-called Internet addicts tend to be depressed and socially isolated (Amichai-Hamburger & Schneider, 2014). The demands of staying connected to social media may induce negative moods (LaRose et al., 2014) and fear of missing out (FOMO) when not connected is negatively related to mood, life satisfaction, and fulfillment of psychological needs (Przybylski et al., 2013). Also, reading all the happy news from our Facebook friends may make us depressed about our own lives (Steers et al., 2014).

STOP & REVIEW

1. What is a prosocial media effect?

2. Name three forms of educational media.

3. How does advertising affect children?

4. In what ways do media affect our well-being?

UNDERSTANDING SOCIETAL IMPACTS

Here, we abandon the use of the term *media effects* at this point, since that is closely associated with social science research on the media and the individual, and instead consider broad "social impacts." Individual effects do not translate directly into broad social impacts and indeed different theories have been proposed to explain the broader implications of the media (see Chapter 2). In this section, we examine broader impacts on community, social equality, democracy, public health, and the economy.

SOCIAL INEQUALITY

One of the thorniest issues confronting society is inequality between social groups as defined by wealth, race, and gender. What are the roots of social inequality in society? As societies become more complex, they become more *stratified*—more divided into unequal social groups or classes (Braudel, 1994).

People may be categorized both in terms of their monetary wealth, or economic capital, and in terms of differences in their education and family backgrounds—their cultural capital (Bourdieu, 1984). Differences in both economic and cultural capital help perpetuate social inequality. As we saw in Chapter 10, gaps in Internet access still remain between income, racial, and education groups over time, a phenomenon known as the *digital divide*. We have seen that efforts to close the divide focus primarily on making up differences in economic capital by subsidizing computers and Internet connections in poor neighborhoods. Now there is growing concern about a second-level digital divide based on differential skill levels between better- and less-educated users (Hargittai & Hinnant, 2008). Low-income communities are also disadvantaged by lack of access to broadband connections that are necessary to take online courses and apply for jobs and social programs online (Dailey et al., 2010).

Equal access does not necessarily translate into social equality according to the *knowledge gap hypothesis*. The gap is between the information "haves" and the "have-nots." The information-rich "haves" are those with superior levels of education and access to libraries and home computers. The "have-nots" are the information-poor who have inferior levels of education and resource access and tend to be the economically poor as well (see Figure 15.3). The knowledge gap hypothesis states that the dissemination of information benefits both groups but that it will benefit the information-rich more, thereby widening the

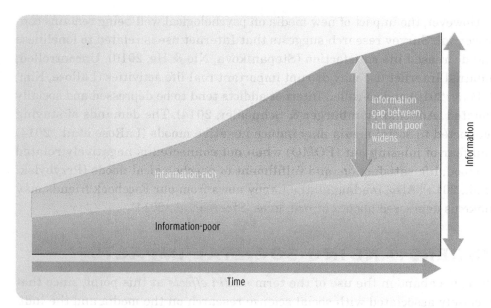

FIGURE 15.3 THE INFORMATION GAP According to the knowledge gap hypothesis, the introduction of new information technologies will help both the information-rich and the information-poor get richer, in terms of the information they possess, but the rich get richer faster, causing the knowledge gap to widen.

disparity between the two. Many studies have documented that information gaps are widened by the media (Hwang & Jeong, 2009), even by such well-intentioned efforts as *Sesame Street* that are specifically designed to close the gap. The gap is evident in disparities in Internet use between well-educated and less-educated Internet users. Those with a college education are twice as likely to search the Internet for information about health insurance or health providers or to obtain online job training as those with a high school education or less (NTIA, 2013).

The knowledge gap hypothesis suggests that efforts to close the digital divide (e.g., by placing computers in the schools or making e-mail available to all) will be at least partially self-defeating. That said, it will be difficult to close the knowledge gap short of changing the fundamental inequalities in society. One approach is community networking, which offers Internet access and content to disadvantaged groups through government agencies, schools, libraries, churches, or residential communities (Straubhaar et al., 2012). The premise is that community-based resources tailored to local needs by community members themselves will close the gap. The website www.digitalliteracy.gov has success stories and links to educational resources that can jump-start digital literacy education in your community. However, the substitution of Internet services for "real" public services may help justify cuts in public services while making the poor more reliant on a technology that they have difficulty accessing (Virnoche, 1998).

Community

What impact do media have on meaningful social relationships in our communities? Television usage may lower community involvement (Brody, 1990), and virtual communities on the Internet may displace face-to-face relationships (Stepanikova, Nie, & He, 2010).

Do you have social media friends who would support you with an employment recommendation or loan you money in a pinch? Internet researchers have focused on social support, often referred to as *social capital*, that derives from online interactions. That can come not only from strong social ties with family and close friends, known as *bonding* social capital, but also from weak ties such as with acquaintances and friends of friends, called *bridging* social capital. In a multinational survey study, Internet use was found to improve social contacts with family, friends, and colleagues (Amichai-Hamburger & Hayat, 2011). Those contacts matter: the number of Facebook friends was correlated to both bonding and bridging social capital in a study of Facebook users (Burke, Marlow, & Lento, 2010). However, people with adequate preexisting levels of social support are likely to benefit from online interaction, whereas those lacking adequate social support may become more socially isolated as a result of indulging heavily in online social interaction (Bessiere et al., 2008). Also, in-depth interviews with Internet users suggest that online relationships are a poor substitute for interpersonal relationships, lacking intimacy and the risks of real interactions (Turkle, 2011) and that the art of conversation seems to be getting lost (Turkle, 2015).

Social capital is also thought to accumulate through participation in civic organizations. The Internet paradox research (Kraut et al., 2002; see the Well-Being section, page 428) found that although initial impacts on individual well-being related to Internet usage disappeared over time, a negative relationship between Internet use and community involvement persisted. However, that was before social media. More recent research finds a positive relationship between social media use and civic involvement (de Zúñiga, Jung, & Valenzuela, 2012). If you participate in online movements through social media you might wonder if civic participation in the conventional sense of attending club meetings, joining bowling leagues, or marching in the streets is obsolete and if online activism is just as effective in accumulating social capital. A follow-up analysis of participants in the "Save Darfur" movement suggests that online activism is illusory in that the vast majority of participants neither contributed money nor recruited others (Lewis, Gray, & Meierhenrich, 2014). If you doused yourself as part of the "Ice Bucket Challenge" to encourage donations for Lou Gehrig's disease, you helped raise over $100 million to fight the disease. But, did you learn to trust the millions of other participants as a result? Social trust is supposed to be how social capital pays off (Putnam, 1995).

Democracy

Political campaigns often seem to have evolved into advertising campaigns, the candidate being the "product." The techniques of market research and mass persuasion have been applied with a vengeance to politics. The political caucus has given way to the focus group, the town meeting to the instant public opinion poll. The candidate with the wealthiest donors and biggest ad budget often wins. Can civic engagement through social media restore democracy as we might idealize it, with an informed and active electorate weighing the issues, debating among themselves, and making intelligent choices between the candidates?

What is the net effect of the political ads that glut the airwaves just before an election? The ads are most likely to impact those who are relatively unaware of an election and its issues, but are also likely to discourage highly aware voters from seeking other types of information (Valentino, Hutchings, & Williams, 2004). Still, political advertising expenditures are correlated to the share of votes that candidates receive in presidential elections (Gordon & Hartmann, 2013).Until recently, political communication researchers had largely given up trying to understand how to sway massive blocs of votes through persuasive argumentation, concentrating instead on more complex interactions between voters, the media, and political systems. For example, exposure to partisan media contributes to polarization on issues like global warming (Feldman et al., 2014). Political practitioners have turned to negative ads in the hope of cutting through voter apathy, but overall these are ineffective and may stimulate a lack of trust in government (Lau, Sigelman, & Rovner, 2007). Negative ads probably do not diminish voter turnout as once thought (Franz et al., 2008). Political advertising does the positive effect of stimulating discussion and civic participation (Cho, 2011).

The campaign coverage that appears in the media, including news stories, opinion polls, public appearances by the candidates, debates, and editorial endorsements, is inherently more effective than political advertisements. That is because authoritative media sources are generally more credible, or believable, than politicians, and credible sources are more persuasive. Also, recall earlier discussions (in Chapters 2 and 4) of the *gatekeeping, framing,* and *agenda-setting* functions of the mass media: their ability to define not only what the important issues are but also how to think about those issues. For example, in the 2008 presidential election, the media set the agenda for an Obama victory by emphasizing the economic failures of the preceding administration (Kenski, Hardy, & Jamieson, 2010). Debates have some impact on perceptions of the candidate's character but tend to only strengthen confidence in preexisting voting choices rather than change votes (Benoit & Hansen, 2004). However, the "spin" that the media place on the outcome of debates may affect voter attitudes (Fridkin et al., 2008).

The less important the election is, the more important the political coverage becomes. This is because voters are unlikely to be aware of candidates or issues outside of the presidential race and one or two other high-profile contests. Most Americans cannot name their own member of the House of Representatives, let alone the name of the challenger or the positions either candidate takes on the issues. Because people are naturally unwilling to vote for an unknown quantity, this often gives incumbents and candidates with names such as "Kennedy" and "Trueheart" a natural advantage. Issues have turned into TV "sound bites." In this vacuum, advertising can be effective in establishing name recognition. However, the effects of political ads in major campaigns may be obscured by the impact of other campaign activities. A study examining voters in media markets in "battleground" states in the 2004 presidential election but who lived in (non-battleground) neighboring states, and were able to see the commercials but not subjected to other campaign activities, revealed that campaign commercials are persuasive when considered in isolation from other campaign activities (Huber & Arceneaux, 2007).

The commonly held beliefs, attitudes, and misconceptions about the issues of the day are what we call *public opinion*. Like candidate preferences, public opinion is also shaped through interpersonal influence. The publicity attached to polls may help mold public opinion through a process called the *spiral of silence* (Donsbach, Salmon, & Tsfati, 2014). That is, when we believe that our opinions match the rising tide of public opinion—for example, when we view tweets that support our own opinions—we can comfortably post our own tweets. Conversely, when we sense that we hold an unpopular belief, a "red" voter in a "blue" state for example, we remain silent. Because one of the ways we gauge how popular our own opinions are is by hearing the same opinions voiced by others, a self-perpetuating cycle begins that eventually suppresses the less popular view.

KENNEDY WINS The first-ever televised presidential debates between John F. Kennedy and Richard Nixon are often credited as a decisive factor in Kennedy's 1960 election victory. However, debate performances seldom change votes.

Changes in the media landscape perhaps call for a reassessment of the effects of political communication. The power of the mass media to set the political agenda and frame the issues of the day (see Chapter 2) is perhaps diminishing. The popularity of partisan "red" media like Fox News (on the right) and "blue" MSNBC (on the left) and the accessibility of political forums of all political color shades in between may make it easier to maintain divergent views. This appears to foster political polarization by creating "echo chambers" as voters can immerse themselves in media environments that share only their own views (Bennett & Iyengar, 2008, 2010). However, many people do seek out political views that differ from their own in an effort to obtain understanding as well as consistency in their political world views (Holbert, Weeks, & Esralew, 2013).

Big data analysis is gaining new prominence in the political arena as attention turns from mass media advertising and conventional public opinion polling to data mining and highly targeted campaign pitches tested through rigorous experimentation (Issenberg, 2012). For example, researchers systematically vary the scripts used by campaign workers who go door-to-door before elections to see which versions result in higher voter turnout by a candidate's supporters. Detailed information provided by *data brokers* (see Chapter 14) makes it possible to identify potential swing voters using big data techniques and target them with just the right pitch over the telephone, in online ads, or personal visits by campaign staff.

Social media make it possible to seek out social groups that will support and even amplify unpopular opinions (Mutz & Young, 2011). Online political participation extends beyond the older, wealthier participants who take part in offline political activities (Jensen, Danziger, & Venkatesh, 2007). Social media use is related to civic and political participation offline as well as online (de Zúñiga, Jung, & Valenzuela, 2012). A big data analysis of millions of social media commentaries and news stories from 2012 found that social media activity on an issue often follows that in the conventional media but, in a reversal of the standard agenda setting effect (see Chapters 2 and 4), sometimes leads the conventional news media agenda (especially for social and law and order issues), and at times has an agenda of its own when topics mainstream media ignore "go viral" (Neuman et al., 2014). The number of tweets a candidate gets are also related to the number of votes they get (DiGrazia et al., 2013), although it is uncertain whether the tweets lead or follow the formation of voting decisions. However, the Internet is still not accessible to all; the digital divide (see Chapter 10) still persists among low-income and minority citizens. That limits its value as a medium of political communication, as a resource for political communication research, or as an electronic voting booth in a democracy.

The 2016 presidential primary season offered a glimpse into the future of electoral politics in a social media age, at once both exciting and concerning. The Sanders campaign raised funds for its TV ads almost entirely from thousands of small donations made over the Internet. The Trump campaign largely avoided conventional TV ad spending, benefitting instead on free news media coverage generated by the candidate's bombastic speeches, debate confrontations, and inflammatory Twitter postings. The Bush campaign, focusing on conventional TV ad buys financed by big donors, failed to gain any traction. The conventional media were there covering it all of course, but so were a legion of bloggers offering live images and instant commentary through their smartphones. The revolution won't be televised, but perhaps it will be streamed.

Public Health and Environment

Communications media affect physical health as well as mental health. Television viewing is associated with obesity in children (Tremblay et al., 2011) and video game play has a similar, but smaller effect (Rey-Lopez et al., 2008). The good news is that "active" video games with motion-sensing controllers that force players off the couch may be effective in attacking the child obesity epidemic, if children can be encouraged to play them (Baranowski, 2015).

Very low-frequency (VLF) radiation, the kind that electrical power lines emit, also poses a threat. At one point, EPA scientists concluded that VLF was as dangerous as chemical cancer-inducing agents, although this finding was overruled by EPA administrators. Computer video display terminals (VDTs) emit the same type of radiation, and some scientists suspect that this radiation causes cancer and miscarriages in heavy users. Overall the research is inconclusive on this point (Lim, Sauter, & Schnorr, 1998). Television sets emit the same magnetic fields, by the way, but not many people watch with the television in their laps.

However, if you watch streaming video with your smartphone or wireless tablet in your lap, that could be a matter for concern. Cell phones have been implicated in brain cancer, and health authorities in many countries advise against their use by young children. There is at best weak and conflicting evidence about the health effects of cell phone use, but that conclusion is based on studies that were done long before use reached the high levels of today (World Health Organization, 2010) and some countries advise caution, especially for children. In the United States, the Center for Disease Control advised caution on its website at one point, but later withdrew the warning. To be on the safe side, when selecting your next cell phone you might wish to compare its radiation to others and in the meantime learn about ways to reduce your exposure, such as using a headset or keeping the phone away from your body. And, do not put it under your pillow (http://www.ewg.org/cellphone-radiation).

There is clearer evidence of another public health hazard stemming from mobile phone and mobile texting. A study that analyzed videos of thousands of drivers in their cars found that texting while driving increased the risk of a crash by six times. However, simply dialing a number on a cell phone was the most dangerous distraction of all, increasing the odds of a crash by a factor of 12 (Dingus et al., 2016). As a result, in most states, it is illegal to text while driving a car or (do we have to say this?) when piloting a motorcycle or bicycle.

Up to a quarter of all computer users suffer *repetitive stress injuries*, mostly a result of poor posture, bad workstation design, and repetitive tasks, but also a function of work demands and psychological stress (Lim, Sauter, & Schnorr, 1998). Others get stress injuries from surfing the Web, playing video games, flipping the TV remote control, or composing texts with their thumbs (Annadurai & Danasekaran, 2015). Extreme cases force sufferers to resort to medication, surgery, and career changes. Computer labs run by high schools and universities combine many of the factors known to increase the risk of injury: nonadjustable work surfaces, chairs with no armrests or footrests, displays perched too high, and instructors applying stressful grade pressure.

The Economy

New media technologies in the workplace are impacting the economy. They are affecting both the quantity and the quality of work.

The Quantity of Work. Information technology improves *productivity* by eliminating employees. For example, nonlinear editing systems are a common productivity-enhancing feature wherever video is edited. Clips are stored and edited from computer disks, eliminating the time-consuming drudgery of moving forward and backward to particular sequences on a long spool of tape. So, more shows are edited per day with fewer editors—that's productivity.

That also means that we do not need as many video editors as we once did. This phenomenon is euphemistically called *job displacement* by labor economists. The United States has seen almost complete elimination of a blue-collar middle class in a single generation. Now millions of U.S. workers are part of the "gig economy," working as private contractors for Uber or selling things they make on Etsy, without benefits or long-term job security.

Artificial intelligence, expert systems, and information technology generally are threats to employment and may be suppressing wages and adding to income inequality (Brynjolfsson & McAfee, 2011). Computers that "think" as good as humans and perform useful tasks within the parameters of well-defined jobs, such as legal and financial analysts, but that do not command six-figure salaries or require days off can replace workers in many industries. In the short term, only a few jobs will be entirely automated out of existence, but the remaining jobs will change as specific tasks (including many of those performed by top managers) are automated (Chui, Manyika, & Miremadi, 2015).

Beware of *offshoring*—the use of advanced communication networks to link Americans to customer service agents and loan officers located in developing countries. These people generally work for a fraction of the salaries paid for comparable jobs in the United States. Many media-related jobs, including animation and documentary film production, are starting to move offshore. A new trend is *in-sourcing* that brings jobs back from overseas, but that also has a downside. To offset the higher labor costs in North America, the in-sourcers first redesign the production process so that it requires far fewer workers than when it was last based on our shores.

In the process, the old *corporate pyramid,* in which a few top executives command platoons of middle managers who in turn direct legions of rank-and-file workers, has toppled (see Figure 15.4). Information technologies have made it possible for top management to coordinate activities with far fewer middle managers, the *flattened pyramid.* Another model is the *core and ring,* in which the middle management is eliminated and rank-and-file workers are all contingent employees who are added or subtracted as conditions warrant. Then there is the *virtual corporation,* in which even top management is in constant flux, with networks of private contractors and temporary employees organized

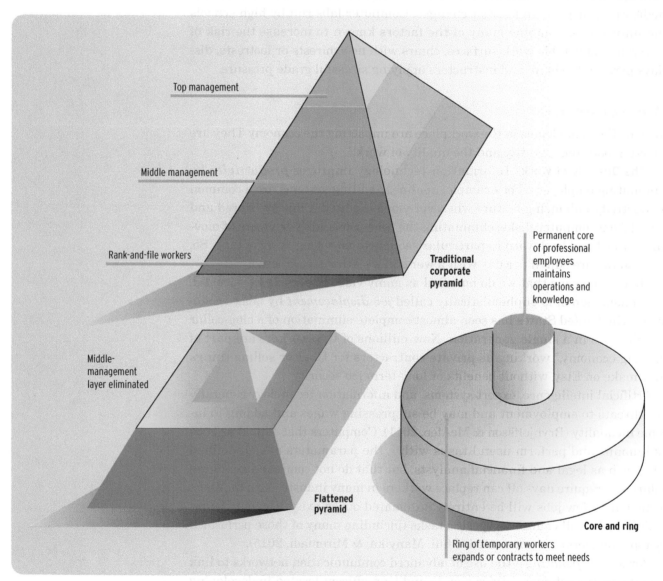

FIGURE 15.4 **EVOLVING CORPORATE STRUCTURES** The traditional corporate pyramid is being replaced by the flattened pyramid and the core-and-ring structure. In the process, layers of middle-management positions have been stripped away. New structures are more flexible but also dim prospects for job security.

for particular tasks and disbanded when no longer needed. Hollywood production companies have long followed this model, but it is spreading to many sectors of the professional service economy populated by artists, writers, Web designers, and computer consultants.

However, if information technology reduces costs and increases product quality, then there should be demand for more products and thus higher employment (Kilborn, 1993). For example, if super-high-definition television catches on (see Chapter 9), their costs will drop. Then Hollywood could fill hundreds of new channels with enticing super HD entertainment, and we would watch TV more and see more ads, creating demand for yet more channels and generating new employment in the television industry. Historically, fears about higher unemployment resulting from automation have proved unfounded, whether the "new technology" was the textile machinery of the 1790s or computers of the 1990s. However, information technology could disrupt the future as computer programs displace white-collar workers in law, health care, and finance (Brynjolfsson & McAfee, 2011). For example, if computerized recommender systems like Netflix are better at predicting what we like than humans are, why would there still be a need for network television programing executives?

But it isn't clear that all the investment in information technology actually improves productivity (Maes, De Haes, & Van Grembergen, 2011). Many high-tech investments never work quite right or incur hidden costs that sap their profitability. Economists call this the *productivity paradox*. Across the economy, it looks as if the benefits of information technologies used in businesses have been found mainly in the high-tech industries themselves.

Work Gets Worse. What will work be like for those who still have it? Today's college students will have several different careers in their lives, not just several different jobs in the same career path with different employers, which was once the normal pattern. And lifelong employment with one employer is a relic of the past. All of this insecurity could place downward pressure on benefits and wages, except perhaps for the highly skilled elite.

Information technology could reduce skill requirements, a process known as *de-skilling*. For example, if we wanted to increase the productivity of sports reporters, we might specify a set of standard lead sentences: "Things looked extremely [pick adjective] for the [city name] nine that day. The score stood [home team score] to [visiting team score] with but an inning left to play." Fire the writer, and hire a college intern to fill in the blanks using reports transmitted on the Associated Press newswire. Then we would hold a stopwatch on the intern to see how many game summaries she could write in an hour and replace her if she fell below the standard for the job. And this example is by no means far-fetched. StatSheet uses an artificial intelligence program to write sports stories for the Web and smartphones. This process is also known as *Taylorism,* after Frederick Winslow Taylor, the early twentieth-century efficiency expert.

Fordism, named after Henry Ford, introduced the assembly-line system, in which each employee performs a single, narrowly defined task over and over again. Taylorized and Fordized workers do not know how to "make" anything (such as a good sports story). Their knowledge is limited to one small task so that upward mobility is impossible. Only the owners and their white-collar managers (here, the sports editor) know how to organize those tasks to produce goods and services.

De-skilled workers can be paid less and replaced at will, a practice known as *post-Fordism.* Henry Ford was the first to pay rank-and-file factory workers a decent wage so that they could purchase the products that they assembled. Post-Fordism cuts pay to the point that workers can no longer participate in the consumer economy. In our example, the college intern might be paid so little (or perhaps be paid nothing—it's a media internship, after all!) that she could not afford an Internet connection to read her own sports stories on the Web.

Another dismal possibility is that skill requirements will be upgraded to the point that the current workforce does not possess them. This process is known as *up-skilling.* For example, many TV and film production specialists trained on analog technology cannot easily become a part of digital production teams because they lack the necessary computer skills.

Work Gets Better. But there are rays of hope, too, such as work decentralization. Computer networks make it possible to integrate the work of distant suppliers and far-flung backroom (or back lot) operations, moving them farther into the suburbs and rural areas. More employees can work where they want to live and avoid the stress of commuting and relocating at intervals. For example, the global nature of today's TV and film production industry, combined with traffic congestion, air pollution, and sky-high real estate costs in the Los Angeles basin, has prompted substitution of computer networks for travel in the industry. *Telecommuting,* defined as performing work tasks at home, involves about a quarter of U.S. workers. Climbing gasoline costs and environmental concerns about the "carbon footprints" of commuters encourage the practice. Telecommuting can potentially benefit workers by providing more flexible work hours that relieve the stress of child care and elder care responsibilities. However, telecommuting has not reduced work-family conflicts and instead has mainly expanded the number of working hours of salaried employees (Noonan & Glass, 2012) who do not get extra pay for overtime.

Re-skilling is another challenge. Overall unemployment remains high while openings for highly skilled workers in science and technology fields go unfilled, leading to calls to retrain workers for twenty-first-century jobs. However, retraining video producers to create digital special effects, for example, is not easily done. And the problem runs deeper than that in the United States. American workers, even college-educated ones, lag behind those in other developed countries in basic literacy and math skills (OECD, 2013).

Re-skilling has an upside, too: reassigning to current employees tasks that were formerly parceled out to specialized workers. The employee reclaims the role of the preindustrial craftsperson (Zuboff, 1984) as knowledge becomes the cornerstone for business and social relations (Bell, 1973). For example, desktop publishing puts print publication back within the scope of a single person sitting at a personal computer. Garage bands that produce their own recordings on their laptops and amateur YouTube channels are other examples. It hasn't been that way since the days of the medieval manuscript copyists. These changes rock the very foundations of industrial mass media by restoring control to the workers themselves. It is ironic that information technologies, the crowning achievement of industrial capitalism, may yet fulfill Karl Marx's prophecy. It was he, after all, who pointed out that capitalism creates the contradictions that inevitably lead to its own destruction!

STOP & REVIEW

1. What does the knowledge gap hypothesis predict about the effects of new information technologies?

2. What impact do social media have on social capital?

3. How are social media impacting the political process?

4. What are the health risks of communications media?

5. How do Taylorism, Fordism, and post-Fordism differ?

6. Give examples of jobs that have been de-skilled, jobs that have been up-skilled, and jobs that have been re-skilled.

SUMMARY & REVIEW

WHY DOESN'T SOMEONE "CLEAN UP" THE MEDIA?

Government control conflicts with the rights of the media to free speech. Media spokespersons question the validity of research that suggests the media's negative effects, and they argue that society's ills have deeper causes than mass media exposure. The media sometimes adopt their own guidelines. However, these are voluntary standards that are usually eroded by commercial pressures.

WHAT ARE THE MAIN APPROACHES TO MEDIA EFFECTS?

Media effects are changes in knowledge, attitude, or behavior that result from exposure to the mass media. In the deductive approach, predictions about media effects are derived from theory, and exposure to media content is treated as the causal, or independent, variable that leads to the effects, or the dependent variable. The inductive approach infers the impacts of the media, and theories that explain them are inferred from detailed observations in real-world environments.

WHAT ARE BASIC METHODS OF MEDIA EFFECTS RESEARCH?

Content analysis is used to characterize the content of media systems by enumerating the types of behaviors, themes, and actors that appear in the media, though such analysis cannot be used to make inferences about the actual effects of the media. Experimental research examines the relationship between exposure to media content and audience effects under tightly controlled laboratory conditions that make it possible to rule out competing explanations for the effects that are observed. Survey studies administer questionnaires to large representative samples of subjects to examine relationships between media exposure and media effects; they take into account a wider range of factors than experimental studies. In ethnographic studies, researchers maintain extended contact with subjects so that they can gain insight into social processes involving media systems. Their results, however, may not be generalizable beyond the specific communities they study. Big Data research analyzes large databases to identify patterns of human behavior related to media use.

WHY DO PEOPLE USE THE MEDIA?

People attend to media that best meet their needs and expectations. Through their interactions with the media and their observations of others, people learn expectations about the consequences of media use that shape their media behavior. Positive outcomes include learning new things, diversion, and social interaction. People may also wish to avoid media that they find boring or offensive or that they cannot enjoy because they lack the required skills. Media habits form when media are consumed without conscious intent.

HOW HAVE THEORIES OF MEDIA EFFECTS CHANGED?

Theories of mass media effects have evolved over the years. Early scholars believed the mass media could have immediate and profound effects on their audiences, after the fashion of a speeding bullet or a hypodermic injection. Later, researchers learned that the influence of the mass media is weakened by the intervention of social groups, via a multistep flow process, and by the audience's ability to selectively avoid, misinterpret, or forget content with which they disagree. Social learning theory describes how people can learn behavior from visual media, and cultivation theory shows how people's understanding of the world around them is shaped by media images. Priming theory focuses on the power of media images to activate related thoughts in our own minds. Critical theorists ask broader questions about the mutual relationship between media and society.

WHAT IS THE IMPACT OF MEDIA ON ANTISOCIAL BEHAVIOR?

Experimental studies have shown that even relatively short exposure to TV programs and video games featuring violence can provoke violent behavior in viewers, particularly young children. However, the long-term effects are still a matter of debate. Men exposed to violent pornography harbor more negative feelings toward women. Media also can reinforce sex-role and racial stereotypes that lead to sexism and racism.

WHAT IS THE IMPACT OF MEDIA ON PROSOCIAL BEHAVIOR?

Prosocial behaviors are socially desirable acts, such as cooperation, sharing, and racial tolerance. Information campaigns seek to convince mass audiences to adopt socially desirable behaviors. Although such campaigns are sometimes effective, they often suffer from poor planning and execution and from limited audience exposure. Furthermore, they must contend with resistance arising from social influence and selective perception among their audiences. Other varieties of prosocial media combine varying degrees of entertainment and educational content, ranging from distance-learning classes to incidental learning from entertainment programs.

WHAT ARE THE IMPACTS OF ADVERTISING CAMPAIGNS?

Despite the huge sums of money spent on commercial advertisements, their effects are relatively modest; they directly affect perhaps only a few percent of the audience. Those who are affected by advertisements are likely to be those who are relatively uninformed about or uninterested in the product or candidate to begin with. Interpersonal influence and selective perception act to reduce the impact of advertisements on most audiences. Still, that small percentage that is influenced can translate into millions of dollars in a successful advertising campaign. Social media afford new avenues for impacting attitudes toward consumer products.

DO THE MEDIA IMPACT WELL-BEING?

Although people use media to cheer themselves up, excessive use can be a problem. There is evidence of the positive impact of Internet use, and especially social media, in dispelling loneliness and depression. However, not all benefit equally. Some users may become more socially isolated by withdrawing from real-world interactions while social media primarily benefit those with strong offline social relationships.

HOW DO MEDIA AFFECT SOCIAL EQUALITY?

Information technologies do not benefit all groups in society equally. Minorities may be left behind in the transition to the information economy as the digital divide widens. The knowledge gap hypothesis predicts that efforts to improve the plight of the disadvantaged through improved access to communications media will instead result in widening the gap between rich and poor.

HOW DO MEDIA AFFECT COMMUNITIES?

The advent of the Internet has the potential for bringing about a situation in which everyone is our neighbor in a small, electronically mediated global village. The virtual communities that have formed on the Internet are an initial indication that new types of human relationships may be created and many can and do benefit from participating in social media. Social media can enhance social support and help to accumulate social capital. The impact of online community participation is controversial and many who engage in online activism may have only superficial involvement.

HOW ARE THE MEDIA AFFECTING POLITICS?

Conventional media advertising and candidate debates have limited effects on voter behavior, at least in high-profile elections. Campaign news coverage is influential especially in low-profile elections. Attack ads and partisan news coverage are polarizing influences on the political process. Social media may be influencing the overall public agenda and offering new avenues for candidates to raise money and reach voters.

DO INFORMATION TECHNOLOGIES CAUSE UNEMPLOYMENT?

Improvements in productivity brought about by applications of information technology have the potential to displace large numbers of jobs. Historically, new waves of industrial technology have increased employment in the long term, but the same might not hold true today. In the short term, many job tasks will be redesigned, and some jobs will be automated out of existence. Workers with obsolete skills may be forced to seek unstable "gig economy" employment.

DO COMMUNICATIONS MEDIA MAKE WORK LESS SATISFYING?

In some applications, information technologies increase the twin tendencies of Taylorism and Fordism, de-skilling work to meaningless, repetitive, assembly-line tasks. In the extreme, jobs become so degraded that workers no longer command a decent living wage, a condition called *post-Fordism*. In other instances, information technology up-skills jobs, displacing workers whose skills no longer match job requirements. However, information technologies can also be applied in ways that re-skill jobs, restoring work to a meaningful and dignified pursuit.

THINKING CRITICALLY

ABOUT THE MEDIA

1. What were the uses and gratifications of each of the media you consumed yesterday?

2. What would you say is the most important effect the media have had on your life?

3. Using the media effects theory of your choice, explain the likely effects of your favorite video game or TV program.

4. Does political advertising have a positive or negative effect on elections? Why is that?

5. What career path do you expect to have in the information society?

KEY TERMS

bullet model (p. 413)

content analysis (p. 401)

correlated (p. 403)

cultivation theory (p. 414)

cultural studies (p. 410)

dependent variable (p. 400)

ethnography (p. 405)

experimental research (p. 402)

generalizability (p. 403)

independent variable (p. 400)

information campaign (p. 423)

limited effects (p. 414)

media effects (p. 400)

multistep flow (p. 413)

persuasion (p. 413)

priming theory (p. 415)

prosocial behavior (p. 423)

reliability (p. 403)

social learning theory (p. 409)

stereotyping (p. 419)

survey studies (p. 405)

uses and gratifications (p. 408)

validity (p. 403)

MindTap®

Test your knowledge with online printable flashcards and online quizzing.

MindTap® Log on to the MindTap Communication for *Media Now* to access a variety of additional material, including this chapter's e-book, learning objectives, comprehension quizzes, videos, and more!

16 MEDIA POLICY AND LAW

LEARNING OBJECTIVES

After studying the topics in this chapter, you will be able to:

1 Give an example of a type of speech that is not protected by the First Amendment for each of the following: obscenity, defamation, plagiarism, invasion of privacy, and inciting insurrection.

2 Given a piece of copywritten media, determine whether its use falls under the guidelines of fair use for inclusion in a college term paper or creative project.

3 Justify governmental interventions into the media marketplace in terms of preserving competition.

4 Define *network neutrality*.

5 Distinguish vertical integration from horizontal integration and cross-ownership.

6 Give an example of the role that the following organizations play with regard to media regulations: the FCC, the Department of Commerce, NTIA, the judicial system, and Congress.

GUIDING THE MEDIA

The media play such a critical role in U.S. society that their right to contribute to public debate is guaranteed by the First Amendment of the U.S. Constitution. However, in a country where the media are in private hands, there is also potential for abuse of power by media owners. So, perhaps more than any other industry, the media are guided within a fabric of policies, laws, technical standards, and self-regulation. Communications **policy** reflects government and public consideration of how to structure and regulate the media so that they contribute to the public good. Industry trade groups and public interest groups monitor media performance and lobby the government to change communications policy. In the U.S. system of government, **laws** are binding rules passed by legislatures (e.g., the U.S. Congress), administered and enforced by executive power (e.g., Federal Communications Commission [FCC]), and adjudicated by courts (e.g., the U.S. Supreme Court). Policies are often turned into laws in order to make them legally binding. The Communications Act of 1934 and the Telecommunications Act of 1996 are the basic laws of the land for all communications media.

LAWMAKER As Speaker of the House, Congressman Paul Ryan influences the agenda for new laws governing the media.

AP Images/Andrew Harnik

MEDIA*THEN*··· MEDIA*NOW*

1791
> First Amendment ratified guaranteeing freedom of the press

1791
> U.S. Copyright Law protects the rights of authors to profit from their works

1865
> International Telecommunications Union forms to standardize telegraphy

1890
> Sherman Antitrust Act prohibits monopoly ownership

1921
> Graham Act codifies the universal access doctrine

1934
> Communications Act establishes the FCC

1957
> Roth v. United States *defines obscenity*

1986
> Electronic Communications Privacy Act extends wiretap protection to e-mail

1996
> Telecommunications Act updates regulation of telecommunications

1998
> Copyright Term Extension Act increases copyright protection to 70-plus years

2010
> Citizens United *decision lifts restrictions on political donations*

2015
> FCC sets net neutrality rules

Standards are technical characteristics, such as the number of lines on the television screen that must be agreed on for a technology to be widely manufactured and used. **Self-regulation** refers to the industry's own codes of conduct by which they monitor their own performance.

Some issues cut across all these media control mechanisms, for example, sex in the media. The FCC has rules—a policy—against using indecent language on radio and television. Congress established fines for violating those standards by passing a law. In addition, the 1996 Telecommunications Act required a *V-chip* system to help people screen out objectionable content, a technical standard. And then there's the television rating system, a system of self-regulation.

> **Policy** is a public framework for structuring and regulating media, so they contribute to the public good.

> **Laws** are binding rules passed by legislatures, enforced by the executive power, and applied or adjudicated by courts.

COMMUNICATIONS POLICIES

Policies governing free speech, privacy, intellectual property, competition, diversity, access, technical standards, and spectrum allocation form the basic framework guiding communications media in the United States. Policies continue to evolve as society confronts new conditions that call for collective action (see Figure 16.1).

MindTap

Read, highlight, and take notes on the complete chapter text in a rich interactive online platform.

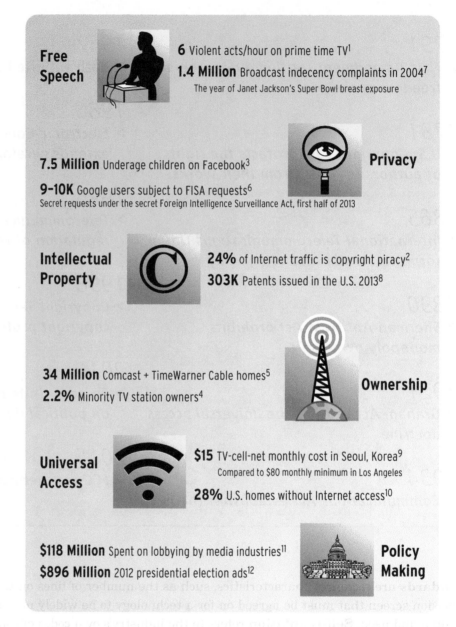

Free Speech

6 Violent acts/hour on prime time TV[1]

1.4 Million Broadcast indecency complaints in 2004[7]
The year of Janet Jackson's Super Bowl breast exposure

7.5 Million Underage children on Facebook[3]

9–10K Google users subject to FISA requests[6]
Secret requests under the secret Foreign Intelligence Surveillance Act, first half of 2013

Privacy

Intellectual Property

24% of Internet traffic is copyright piracy[2]

303K Patents issued in the U.S. 2013[8]

34 Million Comcast + TimeWarner Cable homes[5]

2.2% Minority TV station owners[4]

Ownership

Universal Access

$15 TV-cell-net monthly cost in Seoul, Korea[9]
Compared to $80 monthly minimum in Los Angeles

28% U.S. homes without Internet access[10]

$118 Million Spent on lobbying by media industries[11]

$896 Million 2012 presidential election ads[12]

Policy Making

FIGURE 16.1 COMMUNICATION POLICY TALKING POINTS Facts and figures like these spark communication policy debates.

[1]Federman (1981); [2]Netnames. Available: http://copyrightalliance.org/sites/default/files/2013-netnames-piracy.pdf; [3]Consumer Reports. Available: http://www.consumerreports.org/cro/magazine-archive/2011/june/electronics-computers/state-of-the-net/facebook-concerns/index.htm; [4]FCC Report on Ownership of Commercial Broadcast Stations. Available: http://www.fcc.gov/guides/ownership-report-commercial-broadcast-station-form-322; [5]NCTA. Available: https://www.ncta.com/industry-datc; [6]Google. Available: http://googleblog.blogspot.com/2014/02/shedding-some-light-on-foreign.htm; [7]Federal Communications Commission. Available: http://transition.fcc.gov/eb/pip/ComplStatChart.pdf; [8]U.S. Patent Office. Available: http: www.uspto.gov/web/offices/ac/ido/oeip/taf/us_stat.htm; [9]New America Foundation Available newamerica.net/publications/policy/the_cost_of_connectivity_2012; [10]NTIA. Available: http://www.ntia.doc.gov/dat; [11]Opensecrets. Available: https://www.opensecrets.org/lobby/top.php?indexType=i&showYear=2012; [12]Washington Post. Available: http://www.washingtonpost.com/wp-srv/special/politics/track-presidential-campaign-ads-2012/

Freedom of Speech

The most fundamental U.S. policy regarding the content and conduct of media is the **First Amendment** to the U.S. Constitution that was included in the Bill of Rights ratified in 1791. It establishes **freedom of speech,** both in person and over media, as a basic requirement for a free society. In Chapter 4, we recounted how this principle developed during the American colonial period and the Revolutionary War that followed. The First Amendment seeks to preserve a **marketplace of ideas** in which different voices could compete for attention.

The First Amendment says:

> Congress shall make no law respecting an establishment of religion, or prohibiting the free exercise thereof, or abridging the freedom of speech, or of the press; or the right of the people peaceably to assemble, and to petition the Government for a redress of grievances.

Some kinds of speech are not protected by the First Amendment: defamation, obscenity, plagiarism, invasion of privacy, and inciting insurrection.

Defamation. Defamatory statements (**libel,** if it is written, or *slander,* if it is spoken; see Chapter 4) are untrue declarations about private citizens that might damage their reputations. Libel is information that is false or is intended to damage the reputation of the person being libeled. U.S. legal policy balances libel concerns against the *watchdog role* of the press, which is to expose corruption or incompetence by officials or public figures. Journalists often have to decide whether a certain kind of story about individuals or certain treatment of individuals is ethical (see Chapter 17). Celebrities, politicians, and other public figures do not have the same protections as private citizens. To constitute libel against a public figure, false statements of fact have to be made knowingly and with malice.

Even if you do not work for a media organization, you have to be concerned about defamation, especially when you are online. If you post a scathing review of a product or criticize a company for its plundering of the environment, you might find that you are the target of a libel suit. Corporations are resorting to libel laws to curb "bad buzz" about their products and company reputations online. Truth is the ultimate defense in defamation suits, but it can prove costly to arrive at the truth in a court of law.

Social media are the new battleground for defamation litigation. If you insult someone on Twitter or post a negative product review on a website, can you be sued? Does insult-laden discourse on Twitter make tweeting that someone (like actor James Woods, in a current case) is a "cocaine addict" an acceptable hyperbolic opinion rather than a libelous statement of fact? There are many conflicting court rulings on these topics as free speech issues in social media settings wind their way toward the Supreme Court.

1791

First Amendment ratified guaranteeing freedom of the press

The First Amendment to the U.S. Constitution guarantees freedom of speech and of the press.

Freedom of speech is the idea that speech and media content should be free from government restriction.

Marketplace of ideas is the concept that the truth and the best ideas will win out in competition.

Libel is harmful and untruthful written criticism by the media that intends to damage someone.

Philippe Lopez/AFP/Getty Images

FREEDOM OF THE PRESS The First Amendment protects the publishers of stories such as Edward Snowden's revelations about U.S. government spying that made news worldwide. But the Hong Kong newspaper shown here would not enjoy the same freedom if it revealed secrets about the Chinese government.

Political Speech. Some nations give people who have been criticized a *right of reply*. That principle has seldom been applied to U.S. print media, because they are numerous and tend to balance each other's excesses. However, the Radio Act of 1927 assumed that the First Amendment goal of promoting a diversity of viewpoints needed regulatory assistance in the case of radio, where only a few could have direct access to the airwaves. This principle is still applied to political debates, where all major candidates must be allowed to participate.

A far thornier issue has been paid political advertising, where richer candidates' financial resources give them greater access to the airwaves. There, two principles have evolved. First, stations cannot refuse a candidate's advertising, although stations can refuse to run ads by advocacy groups. Second, stations have to sell advertising time at their lowest rate to candidates. Congress has attempted several times to limit campaign financing abuses; it most recently tried to clamp down on "bundling" of small donations by Washington lobbyists. But loopholes have always emerged. In 2010, the Supreme Court's Citizens United decision lifted restrictions on political donations (which mostly go into campaign advertising) and in 2014 abolished overall caps on the amounts individuals can contribute directly to political candidates, although the amount a donor can give directly to any one candidate remains limited to $2,600.

The FCC also developed the Fairness Doctrine on the premise that the public's right to be informed overrides the right of broadcasters to carry their "own particular views on any matter" (Supreme Court decision in *Red Lion Broadcasting Co. v. FCC*, 395 U.S. 367, 1969). In theory, this concept required stations to schedule time for controversial programming on issues and then to ensure the expression of opposing views. In practice, the FCC did not require stations to carry issue-oriented programming, so the rule focused on the right of reply to controversial points of view. Broadcasters argued that the right of reply had a "chilling effect" on free speech that led stations to avoid controversial programming, and that view finally prevailed as the Supreme Court struck down the right of reply.

Even with the "chilling effect" of the Fairness Doctrine removed, the mainstream media avoided giving platforms to political extremists for fear of offending their audiences. However, more politically charged speech emerged first on talk radio and then on some cable news channels like Fox News and MSNBC.

Political speech is highly protected even at the extremes, although it has limits that anyone who posts their opinions online should be aware of. It is permissible to criticize prominent politicians and their policies ("the president's policies are stupid") and attack their character and intelligence, as long as the insult is a matter of opinion rather than of fact ("the candidate is a coward" is permissible but "the candidate ran away at the Battle of Bull Run" is a fact that could be checked and proven to be true or false). However, the same is not true of the clerk at the local Department of Motor Vehicles or your professors who, though they may be government employees, enjoy the same protections you do as a private citizen. You can criticize government policies ("Stop the war!") and also the system of government ("Smash capitalism!"), and call for its overthrow, even by violent means ("Up the Islamic revolution!"). Hate speech and even bomb-making instructions published online are protected speech in the United States. But you may not directly incite people to imminent violence with your words ("Now take that bomb we showed you how to build and set it off at the shopping mall this Saturday").

Obscenity and Indecency. The First Amendment was originally framed to protect political speech and religious choice but has gradually been extended to speech that is regarded by some as morally wrong. For example, D. H. Lawrence's *Lady Chatterley's Lover* (1928) was censored in the United States for nearly 30 years but is far less "steamy" than the romance novels that can be found on the shelves of local supermarkets today. In 1957, in *Roth v. United States,* the U.S. Supreme Court defined **obscenity** in community-based terms: "whether, to the average person, applying contemporary community standards, the dominant theme of the material taken as a whole appeals to prurient interest [i.e., makes the average person sexually aroused]." In *Miller v. California* (1973), the Court added that states might prohibit works "which portray sexual conduct in a patently offensive way, and which, taken as a whole, do not have serious literary, artistic, political, or scientific value." That allows some communities to define books, magazines, and videos as pornographic and restrict their sales to adult bookstores or require their covers to be concealed when on public display.

Child pornography has no protection because of the harm done to the children who are its victims. In the United States (18 U.S.C. §2256), child pornography is defined as the visual depiction of persons under 18 engaging in actual or simulated explicit sexual acts or who display genitals or breasts. Advertisers who feature underage models in their sexy fashion layouts arguably violate this law. Teens who engage in "sexting" by sending naked pictures of themselves to their boyfriends or girlfriends are also technically child pornographers. Many states are crafting new laws to avoid treating teens as sex offenders. However, college-age social media users who post pictures of underage boyfriends or girlfriends could still be treated as felons for trafficking child pornography.

The 1934 Communications Act extended freedom of speech to broadcast media, but their use of the public airwaves makes them accessible to children and subjects them to limits on **indecent speech** as well as obscenity. The current standard for indecent speech was set when the FCC disciplined a radio station for broadcasting a comedy monologue that poked fun at the rules against saying "swear words" on the air. The FCC defined indecency as "language that describes, in terms patently offensive as measured by contemporary community standards . . . sexual or excretory activities or organs," and its action was upheld by the Supreme Court (Heins, 1993, p. 26). However, the prohibition applies only to radio and television broadcasts during hours when children are likely to be listening or watching. There is a "safe haven" for unfettered free speech from 10 p.m. to 6 a.m. Cable television, satellite radio, and streaming media are not covered because they require an extra fee and thus do not enter the home "unbidden" where they might be seen or heard by children.

1957

Roth v. United States defines obscenity

Obscenity refers to material where the dominant theme taken as a whole appeals to prurient, or sexually arousing, interest.

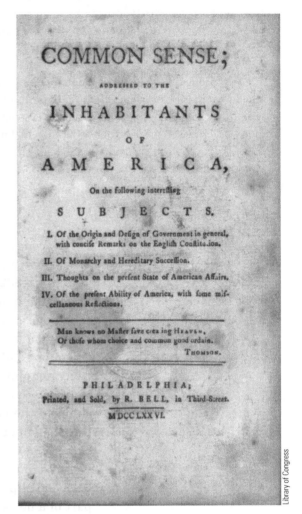

Library of Congress

COMMON SENSE AGAINST CENSORSHIP
Publications, such as Thomas Paine's *Common Sense,* challenged British censorship and promoted the American Revolution. U.S. citizens have the right to question their form of government just as Paine questioned the legitimacy of the British monarchy to rule its American colonies.

Indecent speech is graphic language that pertains to sexual or excretory functions.

GEORGE CARLIN AND THE "SEVEN DIRTY WORDS"

The *FCC v. Pacifica Foundation* case defined a number of key issues relevant to obscenity and indecency. The case centered on whether the Pacifica radio station could play a provocative 12-minute monologue about the "seven dirty words you can't say on radio" by the late comedian George Carlin that included multiple instances of each of the seven words.

The FCC argued that, judged by contemporary community standards, these words are offensive; that broadcasting is an intrusive medium; and that obscenity is separate from indecency. The FCC made a later clarification that media can use such words when children are in the audience when the words have legitimate artistic, political, or social value (e.g., a Shakespearean play).

The Supreme Court decided (in *FCC v. Pacifica Foundation*, 98 Supreme Court 326, 1978) that the FCC may sanction licensees who use indecent words because broadcasting is the least protected by the First Amendment and it enters the privacy of people's homes where children have easy access. The FCC can review programming after broadcast and can use that review when considering licensing. So, the seven dirty words can still not be uttered on radio or on broadcast television programs transmitted by TV stations that are licensed by the FCC. If you are not offended by "dirty words" (or are curious about what those are) you can find Carlin's dialog on YouTube. Strict indecency rules do not apply there, either, although YouTube does have an age verification requirement for pornographic videos.

Indecency rules continue to evolve. After Janet Jackson's "accidental" breast baring during the 2004 Super Bowl, Congress increased the fines 10-fold (to $325,000) for each station that the offending party owned (CBS Television had 10 owned and operated stations). However, an incident the year before in which Bono used the "f-word" to describe his feelings about winning a music award undermined the crackdown. A federal judge ruled that Bono's offense was a fleeting one and that since the FCC had previously not punished brief instances of indecency, they had no right to do so in the Bono case without providing notice of a change in their policy. The FCC changed the rule to cover fleeting obscenity, but the Supreme Court ruled they could not do that after the fact, although the commission can apply the rule going forward. Currently making its way toward the Supreme Court is a fine imposed by the FCC against WBJM of Roanoke, VA, which aired a 3-second clip in 2012 containing a tiny image from a pornographic film as part of a news story.

Industry self-regulation also plays a role. The parental advisories that precede broadcast network television programs (see next section) are an example, as are the film ratings supplied by the Motion Picture Association of America (MPAA), and the video game ratings provided by the Entertainment Software Rating Board (ESRB), an industry trade group. In the United States, all such limits are a matter of self-regulation. The First Amendment prohibits government **censorship** before the fact. The FCC and federal prosecutors can respond to consumer complaints only after the fact.

The Internet poses unique challenges. Congress tried to hold the Internet to the same indecency standards as broadcasting, but the Supreme Court ruled that this infringed unfairly on the rights of adults. The 1998 Child Online Protection Act narrowed the prohibitions to cover commercial sites only, targeted

Censorship is the formal restriction of media or speech content by government, political, or religious authorities.

only content harmful to children, and required age verification on adult sites in hopes of passing muster with the First Amendment, but the Supreme Court declined to uphold the law in a 2009 decision. For now, the only form of protection in effect is the Children's Internet Protection Act, which requires schools and libraries that receive government subsidies for their Internet connections to use filtering software.

Some social media have imposed their own self-regulation in an effort to make their networks friendly to all. YouTube screens submissions and removes pornography, although that happens after the material has been uploaded; thus obscene videos may live a fleeting life before they are removed. Facebook bans nudity, including pictures of breastfeeding, a prohibition that some mothers find excessive. Most social media sites have self-imposed minimum age requirements but compliance is voluntary.

Obscenity laws also apply to us as individuals. Though seldom enforced, it is unlawful to use the "f-word" in phone conversations, and some states have passed laws against using obscenity in texting. Possession of pornography is not a crime. Possession of child pornography is a crime, and its distribution is not protected by the First Amendment. Talking about sex on the Internet is also protected, but not if one of the parties is a minor. A growing number of states have laws against that and federal laws are pending.

Violence. Concerns about the effects of media on children (see Chapter 14) also underlie efforts to curb violence in the media. A provision in the 1996 Telecommunications Act required the V-chip, which permits parents to block out television programs rated as containing sex or violence. Industry leaders reluctantly created a rating system in 1997, modeled on the age-based rating of films (see Chapter 7). Critics had hoped for a system that would have a separate rating for levels of sex, violence, and indecent language in each program, but the industry chose not to comply with that request. And surveys of viewers with V-chip sets have shown that very few were using this option. Now the attention of lawmakers has turned to the marketing of violent content to children. At issue are releases of "director's cut" versions of films to home video that contain depictions of sex and violence that were cut to earn child-friendly ratings in theaters.

Commercial Speech. Commercial speech advertises a product or service for profit or for a business purpose. It is entitled to much less protection than noncommercial speech, since it is not seen as part of the political marketplace of ideas. Misleading commercial speech or commercial speech that proposes unlawful actions has no protection. Businesses have free speech rights as long as their products are legal (see Chapter 14). That is why we still see cigarette and liquor ads even though those products harm their consumers when used

INDECENT? Did M.I.A. commit an indecent act when she flashed her middle finger during the 2012 Super Bowl half-time show? Now that the Supreme Court is making the FCC reconsider its indecency rules, should this gesture qualify?

in excess. The Federal Trade Commission (FTC) intervenes if (1) the message is likely to mislead the consumer; (2) the consumer is found to be acting reasonably under the circumstances; and (3) the omission, falsehood, or representation is "material" or likely to affect actual purchase decisions. The FTC can issue a cease-and-desist order prohibiting further communication of the deception and mandate corrective advertising requiring public clarification and admission of the falsehood.

Protecting Privacy

Although many Americans assume that they have a right to **privacy**, this right is not clearly established. Some argue that the first 10 amendments to the U.S. Constitution focus on protecting people from invasions of their privacy by government. This broad view of privacy remains controversial. Private companies as well as the government now pose privacy threats.

Preventing Government Snooping. The clearest privacy protection against government snooping is found in the Fourth Amendment to the Constitution, which guarantees "the right of the people to be secure in their persons, houses, papers, and effects, against unreasonable searches and seizures." It also states that "no (search) warrants shall issue but upon **probable cause** ... particularly describing the place to be searched, and the persons or things to be seized." Government criminal investigators can intercept conversations via wiretap and open your mail but only with a court warrant, as specified in the Fourth Amendment. The Electronic Communications Privacy Act (ECPA) of 1986 extended wiretap protections to electronic mail, teleconferences, and other new media. However, the warrants can currently be served on the e-mail service provider without notifying the end user and legislation to require user notification is stalled in Congress.

1986

Electronic Communications Privacy Act extends wiretap protection to e-mail

Probable cause is a judge's decision that provisional evidence of criminal violation or national security danger justifies a wiretap.

The ECPA may not go far enough. Although e-mail from home computers and personal accounts is protected, e-mail from office or school computers or accounts may be monitored by employers or school officials. Reformers would like to see the privacy act revised to require warrants for all law enforcement searches of e-mail and phone records, including those that just reveal the time of the communication and the parties involved. Location-based information generated by cell phones, data captured by smart TVs, and information stored on *cloud computing* sites also demand further protections.

Passed in the wake of the September 11, 2001 terror attacks, the USA PATRIOT Act of 2001 loosened the rules in cases where the FBI or other officials convince special courts that U.S. national security is threatened. The standard of probable cause was reduced so that approval of intercepts was almost automatic in national security cases. However, several court decisions have restored somewhat stricter requirements for probable cause. In 2002, Congress passed the Homeland Security Bill that permits federal officials to track and locate Internet users who pose an imminent threat to national security interests or who may perpetrate attacks on protected computers belonging to government or key private interstate commerce or communications companies. It also encourages cooperation from Internet and computer companies by protecting them from being sued for releasing personal information to the government. Congress fully legalized the monitoring in 2008.

Still, it came as a shock to many in 2013 when a low-level government contractor by the name of Edward Snowden revealed that the National Security Agency (NSA) was engaged in massive global snooping. The NSA collects everything from logs of telephone calls placed inside the United States, to postings in social media, to the private cell phone conversations of German Chancellor Angela Merkel and other foreign leaders. In 2015, congress reauthorized most of the PATRIOT Act and renewed other provisions under the name USA Freedom Act. The Freedom Act put a stop to wholesale data collection by the NSA, although the data is still collected by phone companies and can be obtained by law enforcement through a court order.

Privacy and national security are often in conflict with each other, which became clear in two developments in 2016. A court decision in the European Union triggered by Snowden's revelations forced a renegotiation of the treaty governing the transfer of personal information across the Atlantic. The EU–U.S. Privacy Shield agreement gave EU residents new rights to contest misuse of their personal data by U.S. firms as well as by the government and established an ombudsman to look into their complaints. The FBI asked Apple to help it decrypt messages on an iPhone that was involved in a terrorist attack in San Bernardino, California. Apple refused and the FBI eventually paid a third party to crack into the phone. This episode revived calls to give law enforcement a "back door" into encrypted communications.

Preventing Commercial Snooping. Ironically, Apple may be a bigger threat to our privacy than the Federal government is. The private sector intrusion begins with credit rating bureaus that gather credit information about individuals to sell to banks, loan agencies, and mortgage companies. *Data brokers* compile and resell credit card transaction data to determine buying habits and preferences, and match that with information compiled from public records, such as drivers' licenses and property deeds, and with information Internet users leave behind as they navigate social media. Internet services merge that data with proprietary data they collect from us on their own websites. For example, according to the privacy policy on Apple's iTunes website, they reserve the right to "share" user data with any of their 'affiliates," for any purpose they deem appropriate, and to match it to any other "nonpersonal" data they can lay their hands on.

Privacy advocates, and the FTC, would like to see legislation that allow consumers to access their personal information, to correct errors, and to receive notification whenever it is "shared" for commercial purposes (see Chapter 14). However, attempts to enact a bill of rights for consumer privacy into law bogged down and industry self-regulation efforts have not caught on. For example, data disclosure labels for smartphone apps, modeled after nutrition labels on food, were created but only a few app developers have adopted them. Likewise, FTC guidelines for the use of information about online behavior to target ads are mostly ignored by e-commerce websites, as are the Do Not Track notifications activated through the latest Internet browsers. Perhaps if privacy is really as central to the Apple brand as the company claims, then they should require the privacy labels on all listings in their App Store and ask permission whenever their users' personal information is shared with their affiliates.

The accuracy and control of computer databases is becoming a critical issue. When you apply for a credit card or loan, you may be refused because someone with a similar name or Social Security number has not made payments.

Even if the data on file are accurate, that could be used unfairly, such as by charging you more for products you buy online than other customers or for denying insurance coverage. Control over the use, release, and sale of information (see Media & Culture: Consumer Privacy Tips and Rights) was addressed by the Data Quality Act, which permits more scrutiny of government data for accuracy. The Health Insurance Portability and Accountability Act (HIPAA) set a national standard for electronic transfers of health data, but privacy advocates contend that it prioritizes medical needs over privacy concerns. However, political campaigns benefit enormously from the ability to target interest groups that commercial databases give them, so politicians are reluctant to regulate them. Still, public pressure for relief from intrusive telemarketing led to the FTC's Do Not Call Registry, which permits people to register telephone numbers that telemarketers cannot call, or at least know they should not call.

Protection against hacker attacks on commercial websites became an issue after an attack on Target's retail customer database exposed millions of credit card numbers in 2013. The FTC has proposed that companies be required to issue prompt notification of security breaches and impose fines that would discourage lax security practices, but those initiatives have bogged down in Congress.

Some privacy advocates now see Facebook as the biggest privacy threat. Many social media fans seem blithely content to make this statement: "We have no privacy, get over it." However, a key principle of privacy law is one's expectation of privacy. So, in not expecting to have any privacy and going along with Facebook's privacy policies, social media fans are helping to assure that neither they will have privacy rights, nor will anyone else. The issue is particularly acute for children. COPPA prohibits websites from collecting private information from children under 13. On one hand, Facebook would like to see an end to the policy, arguing that millions of young children are already using the site. On the other hand, privacy advocates would like to see the protections applied to children through age 17 and bans on online tracking of children and the use of facial recognition and location information that might aid marketers, but also child molesters.

Disclosure of personal identities associated with online personae is another controversial privacy issue. Internet users who use the Web to gripe about products or people may become the targets of lawsuits when their information service providers expose their identities. Widely available Internet search tools can be used to track down everything you write in blogs or post on social networking sites, and it can archive your rash statements for years. Many a recent college graduate has learned to his or her dismay that employers now routinely look up the Facebook profiles of job applicants and demand that applicants show them content that is restricted to online friends, although some states now prohibit that. ISPs (including colleges and universities) are also required to provide information about Internet pirates under the Digital Millennium Copyright Act (DMCA) of 1998.

Protecting Intellectual Property

Intellectual property laws protect the original ideas of individuals and institutions through patents, copyrights, and trademarks. The goal of the laws

Intellectual property is a creative work of art, writing, film, or software that belongs to a legally protected owner.

Media & Culture

CONSUMER PRIVACY TIPS AND RIGHTS

- Periodically review your consumer credit files.
- If you dispute the information in your file, append your own explanation.
- If you want to have your name removed from telemarketing lists, contact the Do Not Call Registry of the FTC.
- Never give out your Social Security number except to your employer or government agencies.
- Do not write your telephone number on credit applications, on subscription forms, or even on the checks you cash.
- Assume that everything you say on a cordless phone can be overheard.
- Assume that all of your computers or e-mail accounts from school or work are monitored by those institutions.
- Activate the Do Not Track feature in your Web browser.
- Set your Web browser privacy settings to the highest level so that you can tolerate and delete cookies regularly.
- Remove private details from social networking sites, including your birth date.
- Set your Facebook account to "Pair my social actions with ads for NO ONE."
- Wipe your smartphone memory when you turn it in or sell it.

Consumer Privacy Rights

A right to privacy has been articulated in a series of decisions by the federal courts and has been extended to information privacy by several pieces of legislation over the past decades. All consumers should be aware of their rights under these laws.

- **The right to inspect.** Under the Fair Credit Reporting Act of 1970, consumers have the right to inspect the information contained in a credit agency's file. The Fair and Accurate Credit Transactions Act (FACTA) of 2003 established a right to obtain free credit reports once a year and required financial institutions to institute protections against identity theft.
- **The right to challenge.** Consumers have the right to challenge the accuracy of the information and to append their own explanations.
- **The right to updates.** Credit agencies must purge items that are more than 7 years old, including records of old arrests and lawsuits.
- **The right of control.** Inquiries for purposes other than hiring, insurance investigations, or credit checks can be made only with the permission of the subject or under a court order. The Privacy Act of 1974 constrains federal agencies—though not state and local governments or private companies—from transferring information without consent and from using information for purposes other than that for which it was originally collected. The Family Education Rights and Privacy Act (FERPA) gives students and their parents control over the release of academic information.
- **The right to refuse.** The Privacy Act of 1974 stipulates that citizens can refuse to disclose their Social Security number except where required by law. This limits the use of Social Security numbers to match data between sources.
- **The right to notification.** The Right to Financial Privacy Act of 1979 requires that federal law enforcement agencies notify individuals when their financial records are subpoenaed. The Privacy Act of 1974 prohibits secret files and requires government agencies to publish descriptions of the files they keep and the types of information they contain each year.
- **Freedom from intrusion.** The National Do Not Call Registry, instituted by the FTC in 2003, gives you the right to register your telephone number to avoid marketing calls at home from commercial sales groups or marketers with whom you are not already doing business. The Controlling the Assault of Non-Solicited Pornography and Marketing (CAN-SPAM) Act requires commercial spammers (while exempting religious and political institutions and companies with whom we have a prior relationship) to identify themselves accurately and to offer the ability to opt out of future mailings. Also, sexually explicit content must be clearly labeled as such.
- **The right to electronic privacy.** A 1967 Supreme Court decision held telephone wiretaps to be unconstitutional, although Congress later legalized wiretaps conducted under court order. The Electronic Communication Privacy Act of 1986 extended this protection to electronic mail messages. HIPAA governs the release of medical records and gives patients the right to inspect and correct them. The Children's Online Privacy Protection Act (COPPA) prohibits websites from collecting personal information from children under age 13 without parental permission.

is twofold: to encourage new ideas by allowing inventors and artists to profit from their innovations, while not unduly depriving society of the benefits of those ideas and making it possible to synthesize fresh ideas from old ones. The key to achieving that balance is to give creators exclusive rights to their works for a period of time, after which they enter the public domain and may be used freely by all.

Encouraging Creativity. **Patents** give inventors the exclusive rights to their inventions for 20 years, during which time they can demand royalties from others who use them. Smartphone manufacturers Apple and Samsung engaged in a global patent war for years over, for example, who has the right to the "pinch to zoom" patent, which Apple claims, and the courts have affirmed, is its invention.

The question of whether patents are restricted to tangible things, like Bell's telephone patent (see Chapter 11), is a controversial issue. Computer software was once considered unpatentable on the grounds that computers merely executed mathematical formulas that were the product of mental processes, rather than patentable devices. But that changed dramatically in the 1990s when patents were extended to business processes. For example, Amazon was awarded a patent on the "one-click" shopping method that lets return visitors to the site place orders without reentering their credit card information. In 2010, the Supreme Court ruled that business processes that were merely abstract ideas (e.g., an idea for a new form of online dating) were not patentable but left the door open for business method patents in the future. A thorny issue is whether patents should be issued for software applications that are "obvious," such as those that are merely computerized versions of well-established procedures, like holding money aside to pay future real estate tax bills.

Article 1, Section 8, of the U.S. Constitution authorized a national **copyright** system to "promote the Progress of Science and useful Arts, by securing for limited Times to Authors . . . the exclusive Right to their . . . Writings." The United States (in 1791) and most developed countries established laws to protect authors' works. With the movement of books across borders, a need for international agreement on copyright became apparent, resulting in the Berne Convention in 1886. The United States expanded the range of works covered by copyright in 1976 to include computer programs, adding to more traditional protection of literature, music, drama, pantomimes, choreography, pictures, graphics, sculptures, motion pictures, audiovisual works, and sound recordings.

Patents are superior to a mere copyright in that they protect against *reverse engineering*—for example, making an imitation of an invention that performs the same basic functions as the inventor's but uses different underlying computer instructions. That was the issue in the battles between Apple and Samsung over smartphone patents. Copyright offers protection only against duplication of the underlying computer instructions and of the screen display and command sequences—the general "look and feel" of software, such as a spreadsheet program.

Efforts to prove that someone else has copied your idea may meet with varying degrees of success. Apple was unable to convince courts that Microsoft Windows copied the "look and feel" of the Macintosh graphical user interface, which Apple in turn had copied from Xerox. Aspiring Hollywood writers

A **patent** gives an inventor the exclusive right to make, use, or sell an invention for 20 years.

1791

U.S. Copyright Law protects the rights of authors to profit from their works

Copyright is the legal right to control intellectual property. With it comes the legal privilege to use, sell, or license creative works.

1998

Copyright Term Extension Act increases copyright protection to 70-plus years who write scripts "on spec" have had a notoriously difficult time proving that the resulting films based on their ideas were plagiarized. Some infringement claims do succeed, though. Robin Thicke and Pharrell Williams were successfully sued by the family of Marvin Gaye for copying parts of a 1977 song in the 2013 Grammy winner, "Blurred Lines."

Many believe that the balance is tipping too much in favor of the copyright owners. In 1998, the U.S. Congress passed the Copyright Term Extension Act (CTEA). It extended the period of protection to the life of the author plus 70 years. A major impetus for the law was to extend the "life" of cartoon characters such as Donald Duck and Bugs Bunny, whose copyright protections were due to run out in the early 2000s. Mass media conglomerates, such as Disney (Donald Duck) and Warner (Bugs Bunny), have become very aggressive in closing down sites that use images from copyrighted works they control. The media conglomerates do not always win, though. Warner Music lost the copyright to "Happy Birthday" when a court found that it had been in circulation years before the date Warner had claimed and its copyright had expired. Now you can sing "Happy Birthday" again without incurring a royalty fee.

Another trap in intellectual property law is "work for hire," the principle that awards the property rights to the entity that pays the creator for his or her work. The heirs of Jack Kirby, originator of the X-Men comic book characters, were denied their inheritance when a court ruled that he had created them as work for hire. A word of caution to our readers: students who write computer code or design Web pages for pay also lose their intellectual property rights.

New digital technologies make it easy to duplicate copyrighted material without paying anything to the creators or to those who have bought the distribution rights. One solution has been to make unauthorized copying a crime. Another has been to legally regulate copying technologies to make illegal copying harder. A companion law to the CTEA, the DMCA, made Internet service providers liable if they knowingly carry sites that violate copyright rules and forces them to identify the names of users who make illegal copies. However, if websites quickly remove copyrighted materials when notified, they are protected from prosecution. YouTube successfully defended itself against a lawsuit seeking damages for unauthorized postings of SpongeBob clips because it promptly responded to notices by SpongeBob's owners at Viacom. The recording industry has stopped suing its customers but continues to pursue file-sharing services in court. The recording industry has successfully sued file-sharing services like Napster and Kazaa into submission, although Bit-Torrent sites remain a problem. The DMCA also outlawed circumvention of

COPY PROTECTION Copyright laws protect the owners of the rights to music including "Happy Birthday to You" whose owners had the right to claim royalties whenever the song was sung in public until their claim was overturned by a 2015 court ruling.

copy protection technologies. Using this provision, the industry successfully sued the creators of software (known as DeCSS) that broke the anticopying technology incorporated in DVDs.

Internet piracy continues to plague media industries that claim each and every illegally copied file as a financial loss, and a criminal act. In 2012, the media industries urged Congress to pass new restrictions that would make Internet service providers responsible for taking down illegal material, empower copyright owners to remove material themselves, and force search engines to block access to foreign websites that carried it. A mass protest by the Internet community focusing on the First Amendment implications of the proposed law resulted in the withdrawal of the proposal. The industry's response was implementation of the *Copyright Alert System*. It uses third parties to monitor BitTorrent for copyright violations that are then reported to the copyright owners, who in turn complain to Internet providers. Offenders receive a series of six warnings from the Center for Copyright Information, culminating in "mitigation" procedures that might include slowing or terminating the user's Internet access (CCI, 2014).

Piracy is also an international trade issue because software and entertainment products are among America's main exports. It is particularly difficult to ensure that no one copies these products in international markets without paying for their use. Illegal copying and nonpayment of royalties have been an ongoing issue between the United States and China. New international agreements extend copyright protection to digital formats and treat intellectual property as an export commodity like any other so that powerful trade sanctions can be imposed on countries that act unfairly.

Protecting Consumer Rights. The protection of copyright holders is only half the story. The other side is that users of creative works are entitled to reasonable access to them. This concept of **fair use** permits academic and other noncommercial users to make copies of parts of copyrighted works for personal use and also for purposes of analyzing them in classrooms, in academic publications, or in artistic works, so long as they do not diminish the market for the complete work. In 2016, Google finally won a long-running court battle in which it claimed that the snippets of the 20 million books it has posted online are covered by fair use, although a group representing authors is certain to appeal that decision to the Supreme Court. Guidelines are given for how much of a copyrighted work can be reprinted or redisplayed without incurring the need to pay a license fee, for example, no more than 10 percent of a textbook. Consumers also have some rights under the Audio Home Recording Act of 1991. That law establishes the right of consumers to make copies of their own records and tapes for noncommercial use. But the Home Recording Act protects only hardware devices (like tape recorders) that make copies, not software that makes copies, which makes software-based programs, like Internet file-sharing programs, open to challenge.

To shield yourself from media industry lawyers, it is a good idea to avoid "sharing" copyrighted material online. It's also best to avoid well-known images from popular culture when making your own Web pages, recordings, or online videos. If you are dedicated to the idea that culture should be free, practice what you preach by yielding some of your own intellectual property rights through the Creative Commons approach (see Chapter 10).

Fair use permits users limited copying of copyrighted works for academic, artistic, or personal use.

Competition Issues

Media Concentration. In Chapter 2, we described the dangers of having a **monopoly,** where a single company controls an industry, or **oligopolies,** where a few companies dominate and have a much greater influence than would a broader, more competitive group of owners. Dominant media firms may charge excessive amounts for their products, withhold innovations, or discourage new competitors. This kind of activity is an unlawful abuse of market power, according to the **Sherman Antitrust Act of 1890.**

U.S. courts, the U.S. Department of Commerce, and the FCC are charged with prohibiting any **restraint of trade** arising from excessive concentration of media ownership. The concentration of ownership may come about through **vertical integration,** when a company owns key assets in multiple aspects of a single industry. In approving Comcast's acquisition of NBCUniversal in 2011, the FCC required that the company give fair access to its newly acquired television and Internet content properties to other cable, satellite, and Internet network providers. Another form of concentration is **horizontal integration,** in which a company owns many outlets of the same kind of medium or dominates a market on its own. For example, in 2016 cable TV giant Charter Communications bought two other cable companies, Time Warner Cable and Bright House Networks. That gave Charter control over a large portion of both the broadband Internet and the cable television markets that might limit competition in the online video services market. In approving the acquisitions, regulators imposed conditions designed to protect online video distributors like Netflix and Hulu and to increase broadband competition. Anticompetitive collusion is also forbidden. Apple and major book publishers were found to have colluded over prices for e-books in a 2013 court decision.

The 1996 Telecommunications Act eliminated national ownership limits on the number of TV stations a company may own, raised the proportion of the nation that could be covered by a television network's own stations from 25 percent of homes to 35 percent (and raised it again to 39%), and set a cap (later struck down in court) of 30 percent on what proportion of U.S. households could be covered by a cable system owner. Even these expanded national limits are being challenged as interfering with free speech of media owners. In 2001, the FCC lifted its ban on one company owning more than one broadcast TV network. For radio, there are no national limits, and local ownership caps increase with market size (see Chapter 7).

Another ownership question has to do with **cross-ownership**: should a company be allowed to own various kinds of media? Traditionally, U.S. regulators did not allow a single company to own radio, television, and newspapers in the same area, in order to prevent one company from controlling too much content in one locality, thus limiting diversity of ideas. The 1996 Telecommunications Act largely deregulates vertical and horizontal integration and voids cross-ownership rules. In 2008, the FCC issued new rules that allowed limited TV–newspaper cross-ownership, but only when the TV station in question was not dominant in its market. That rule was struck down in court on the grounds that proper notice had not been given to the industry, but as of this writing the FCC is again reconsidering the issue. The commission has clamped down on

1890

Sherman Antitrust Act prohibits monopoly ownership

> **Oligopoly** is the domination of a market by a few firms.

> **Monopoly** is the domination of a market by a single company.

> **The Sherman Antitrust Act (1890)** prohibits monopolies and the restraint of free trade.

> **Restraints of trade** limit competition.

> **Vertical integration** occurs when a company with the same owner handles different aspects of a business within the same industry, such as film production and distribution.

> **Horizontal integration** is the concentration of ownership by acquiring companies that are all in the same business.

1996

Telecommunications Act updates regulation of telecommunications

> **Cross-ownership** occurs when one firm owns different media outlets in the same area.

local management agreements that allow television station owners to manage multiple stations in a market, a loophole that was being used to evade single market ownership limits.

Companies integrated very quickly after 1996, leading a few major firms, such as Disney and Fox, to dominate film and television production, film distribution, network and cable TV distribution, and syndication (see Chapters 8 and 9). Critics called for a reassessment of unbridled vertical integration (McChesney, 2000). Horizontal integration has also run rampant, particularly in the telecommunications industry, where Southwestern Bell has reconsolidated most of the old AT&T empire (see Chapter 11). Recently, there has been a consolidation wave in television group ownership in response to growing horizontal integration in the cable television industry (see Chapter 9).

In the past, there was no apparent need to regulate newspaper ownership because there was lively competition. The government tried to sustain the industry by allowing competing newspapers within a city, such as Detroit's *Free Press* and *News,* to merge their business operations under what is called a *joint-operating agreement.* The goal was to allow limited horizontal integration in exchange for preserving diversity of content in the form of separate newsrooms and editorial policies (see Chapter 4).

Network neutrality (see Chapter 10) presents a new type of ownership issue. That is the policy of requiring Internet service providers to treat all of the data that pass through their networks on an equal basis to prevent them from favoring their own content. The network neutrality rules enacted by the FCC in 2015 reclassified Internet providers as telecommunications services and thus subject to *common carrier* regulation that forces telephone companies to offer service to all on an equal basis at published prices. The rules cover both wireline and mobile carriers and specifically prohibit blocking or slowing of content or giving some content priority for pay. The commission will review interconnection agreements between content providers like Google and Netflix and Internet providers like Comcast and Verizon on a case-by-case basis but will stop short, for now, of setting prices. Legal challenges to the new rules, particularly the criteria used for those case-by-case determinations, are certain to follow.

Concentration of ownership is an issue in all industries, but diversity of content is an issue unique to the media. One of the major goals of the FCC since it was established by the Communications Act of 1934 has been to promote diversity of content among broadcasters. Limited frequencies and high initial costs pose *barriers to entry* so that relatively few people can actually participate in the "marketplace of ideas." The FCC decided that it needed to actively promote diversity of content under these conditions.

In an effort to preserve diversity, U.S. policy once gave preference to minorities, local owners, and female applicants for broadcast station licenses in the hope that they would increase diversity and better serve their communities. These preferences were gradually eliminated in the 1980s and 1990s, and minority and female ownership of broadcast stations remains very low (see Chapter 9). Furthermore, past industry consolidation into a few large ownership groups has resulted in many minority owners selling their stations to larger groups (Irving, 1998). The FCC has renewed policy initiatives on minority ownership, but not much has actually changed.

2015

FCC sets net neutrality rules

Network Neutrality is the principle that Internet providers should treat all forms of content equally regardless of the origin of the content.

1934

Communications Act establishes the FCC

Does diversity of ownership guarantee diversity of content? Even with fewer, less diverse owners, the number of channels of music and television has actually increased on FM radio and cable television. However, if one looks at diversity of ideas and artists within those channels, some critics still maintain that ownership concentration limits the number of people making decisions. The evidence is clear on one point: concentration of ownership has made for less local ownership, so decisions about what content to provide to local audiences are increasingly made by people farther away from listeners to radio and viewers of local TV news.

UNIVERSAL SERVICE? Photos like these of racially diverse, smiling tots using computers belie the fact that Internet access lags for children in minority homes.

UNIVERSAL SERVICE

The Graham Act of 1921 first established the concept of **universal service** in U.S. Law. For most of the twentieth century, universal service meant trying to get a wireline telephone into as many homes as possible. With the spread of mobile phones and more people using the Internet for their essential communication needs, attention has turned to making Internet service universal. As we saw in Chapter 9, the digital divide still exists, in that rural, low-income, and minority homes are less likely to have access to the Internet than urban, high-income, majority citizens and their access to broadband Internet also lags. But also, the United States lags behind many industrialized nations in broadband. How to close these gaps?

Following a mandate from the Telecommunications Act of 1996, the FCC created the E-Rate program to help fund Internet connections in schools and libraries using subsidies from telecommunication carriers. As part of the 2009 Recovery Act initiative, the federal government invested $7.2 billion in improving broadband Internet service in underserved areas where adoption lags. The FCC has set a goal of having broadband in 90 percent of all U.S. homes in 2020, so sustained support is needed. In 2011, the FCC redesigned the Universal Service Fund that is paid for by monthly fees of $1 to $2 that appear on consumer phone bills. The Connect America Fund aims to extend broadband Internet service to all rural areas that lack high-speed Internet service by the 2020 deadline. Future E-Rate support will also prioritize broadband Internet connections.

Yet, public infrastructure investments may not be enough by themselves if people cannot afford Internet connections. Home broadband connections may be in decline and their cost, especially when bundled together with cable TV service, is a problem in low-income homes. As conditions for approving merger deals, the FCC prodded Comcast, Charter, and AT&T make limited time offers of low-cost (between $5 and $10 per month) broadband Internet service to families with children living in targeted areas and participating in the school

1921

Graham Act codifies the universal access doctrine

Universal service is the principle that everyone should have basic access to telecommunication services.

lunch program. ConnectHome is a new federal program to offer low-cost home connections in public housing nationwide. In 2015, the FCC voted to remake the current subsidies for universal telephone service into universal Internet service and is considering rules for implementing that policy as of this writing. The Commission also acted to lift restrictions on community broadband providers, such as public power utilities, who might be able to offer broadband service at a lower cost than cable or telephone companies. Longer hours at computer labs in public libraries and better public transportation to reach them would also help, but those policies are beyond the reach of the FCC. However, if further adoption is to take place, the public needs to learn about effective uses of broadband Internet for personal and community development (LaRose et al., 2011).

Who Owns the Spectrum?

One of the main reasons for the regulation of communication has long been the need to allocate the scarce supply of radio and television channels. The Communications Act of 1934 established the FCC. It determined how close stations could be to each other geographically and still use the same channels. That put government regulators in the position of deciding who got to broadcast, so they made rules for awarding and renewing **licenses.** Historically, the main criterion was the public interest, but that term was left for the FCC to define, and it has never been given a precise definition. In practice, the FCC tried to promote **localism** by giving licenses to stations in cities of a variety of sizes. The FCC also reserved some licenses in FM and television specifically for noncommercial stations that emphasized education and culture.

After 1980, the FCC decided that there was no longer a scarcity of radio stations, given the proliferation of FM stations. They also saw television as inherently competitive because an increasing number of U.S. homes had multichannel cable TV (Fowler & Brenner, 1982). Therefore, the **scarcity argument** for regulation was diminished. Furthermore, pro-business FCC commissioners proposed a lottery to pick applicants at random—or an auction—to sell frequencies to the highest bidder. Auctions are increasingly used to award frequencies for new telecommunication services.

The FCC auctioned off television channels 52 to 69 as part of the transition to digital television in 2008. The scarcity of channel space for mobile communications has long been an issue in the United States, and the UHF television frequencies are "prime real estate" in the communications spectrum because those signals travel long distances and pass through walls with ease. With advances in wireless technology (see Chapter 11), this channel space could become the home for new entertainment services as well as mobile telephone and data services. The FCC is also reallocating spectrum space reserved for government users such as the Department of Defense and opening up the "white space" where television channel slots are unoccupied in local markets. In 2016, a plan to cluster TV stations in adjacent channels so that more spectrum could be auctioned off to wireless providers was implemented. Some stations plan to go off the air and others, including several PBS member stations, offered to share spectrum space with others to take advantage of nine-digit sales of spectrum territory that they never really owned to begin with. What a deal!

Licenses grant legal permission to operate a transmitter.

Localism is ownership and program decision making at the community level.

The **scarcity argument** states that because there are a small number of stations and the cost of entry to broadcasting is high, extra regulation is required.

The basic uses of radio spectrum frequencies are defined by the International Telecommunications Union (ITU). This body also allocates radio spectrum frequencies to countries, which their governments then allocate internally. Allocation issues are decided at the World Radiocommunication Conference (WRC), held every 3 years, and at regional conferences held in each of the three ITU regions (the Americas are in Region 2). It is the WRC that decides, for example, which frequencies will be available for mobile service in various countries, which frequencies will be reserved for satellite communication, and how far apart the satellites must be. The regional conferences then deal with communications issues that crop up between neighboring countries.

Technical Standards

Another regulatory function of governments is technical oversight for electronic media. The FCC works with private companies and with engineering-oriented standards organizations. Private companies often develop standards for their own equipment, and then compete to set the industry-wide standard, such as the race between the HD-DVD and Blu-ray formats for high-definition home video that ended when key industry players gave their support to Blu-ray.

Agreement on basic technological standards signals manufacturers when to mass-produce a new technology. But when a technology continues to improve and evolve, when do we say the moment is right to set standards? Cell phones offer a clear example. Lack of agreement on which system to use and the proliferation of different digital technologies in the United States resulted in a less advanced system with more incompatibilities and less complete coverage than in Europe, which agreed early on to a common digital cellular standard, GSM. A world standard has been adopted for fourth-generation (4G) cell phones (see Chapter 11).

1865

International Telecommunications Union forms to standardize telegraphy

Standards Bodies. In the United States, some standards are created by professional associations, such as the Institute for Electrical and Electronics Engineers (IEEE), and are subsequently ratified by the government. Some standards, like the Windows computer operating system of Microsoft, evolve from a single company. Sometimes the FCC forces industry to create a working group to resolve a conflict over standards. The Advanced Television Systems Committee that set the digital high-definition television (HDTV) standard is an example. In recent years, the government has tended not to set standards for new technologies, but rather has let industry work them out, sometimes leading to incompatible systems and consumer confusion, as in the case of cell phones.

International Standards. International bodies exist because of the need for connections among countries with

SETTING THE STANDARD Technical standards for telecommunication services are set at international conferences like this one organized by the International Telecommunications Union.

STOP &
REVIEW

1. What is the difference
   between a copyright and a
   patent?

2. What is the relationship
   between vertical and horizontal integration?

3. What is the Sherman Antitrust Act?

4. How have ownership rules
   changed since 1996?

5. What is universal service?
   Why is it important?

6. Why did the relative scarcity
   of radio spectrum frequencies require government
   regulation?

7. How are international standards set?

telephony, fax, and data. The ITU, first formed in 1865 to standardize and enable telegraph traffic between countries, is the oldest international body in the
world. The ITU standards process involves negotiation and ratification of
technical approaches to providing telecommunications services. Representatives from equipment manufacturers, telecommunications carriers, and
national regulatory bodies confer within committees to define the standards.
The spectrum allocation process described in the previous section is part of
the ITU's work. The organization also plays a role in fostering international
development. Sustainable broadband development topped the agenda for the
ITU's World Telecommunication Development Conference in 2014.

THE POLICY-MAKING PROCESS

The United States has three branches of government: legislative, judicial,
and executive. Government policy is made by representatives elected to Congress or state legislatures, judges appointed to various courts, and those
appointed to regulatory agencies in the executive branch of government. Also,
corporations make policy through their decisions, such as the types of services to offer and how much to charge, and work through professional lobbyists and industry trade associations to influence legislation. Researchers and
journalists may help set the agenda for regulation by bringing issues to the
attention of government or corporate policy makers: witness the decades of
research done on the effects of television and video game violence on children.

Federal Regulation and Policy Making

All three branches of the federal government play an active role in communications regulation (see Figure 16.2). Laws are proposed by the executive branch or
by Congress. Executive-branch regulatory agencies, such as the National Telecommunications and Information Administration (NTIA), propose legislation in
consultation with Congress. Members of Congress frequently initiate legislation
as well. Congress then considers, alters, and passes the legislation—first in specialized committees, such as the House Subcommittee on Telecommunication and
the Internet, and eventually by the full House of Representatives and Senate.
Legislation can be modified at all stages. Lobbyists for industries and various
public interests also try to affect legislation in favor of their clients at each step of
the process. Finally, bills of proposed legislation are either defeated or passed by
Congress and then sent to the president, who may either sign or veto them.

The executive branch implements the laws. Cabinet departments monitor
industry compliance. For example, the Antitrust Division of the Justice Department examines whether companies are violating the Sherman Antitrust
Act. If so, the department then brings a suit against the offender. It can also
reject deals that it finds will undermine competition, as it did in turning down
AT&T's acquisition of T-Mobile in 2011. The FCC can discourage other deals,
such as Comcast's proposed merger with Time Warner Cable, by signaling
their likely rejection or attaching conditions, as it did in approving the acquisition of Time Warner Cable by Charter Communications in 2016. Other
laws are implemented by executive-branch regulatory agencies, such as the
FCC and the FTC. Because actions of the FCC or FTC are taken to federal

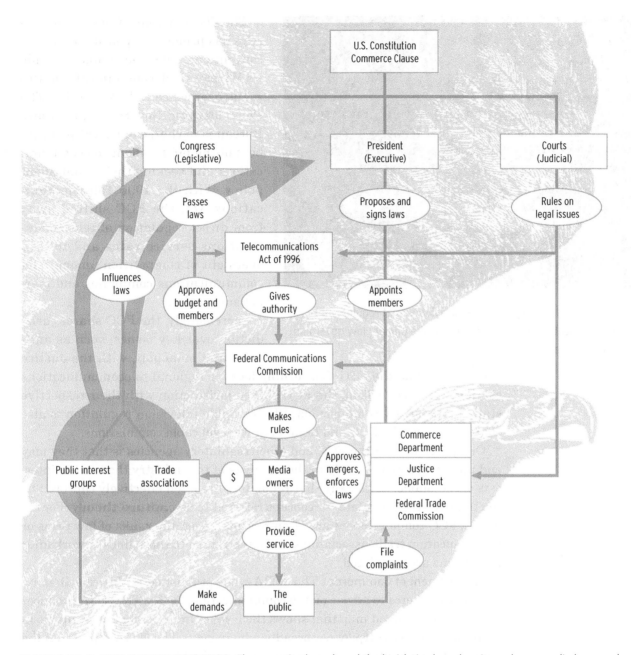

FIGURE 16.2 **THE POLICY PROCESS** The executive branch and the legislative branch write and pass media laws, such as the Telecommunications Act of 1996. If the laws are challenged, the courts then rule on their constitutionality.

district courts under the Telecommunications Act of 1996, these courts are often the key media-related element in the judicial branch. Ultimately, though, the Supreme Court hears cases that are appealed from lower courts, especially if there is a question as to whether the law that is being applied violates any principles of the U.S. Constitution, such as freedom of speech.

The Federal Communications Commission. The FCC regulates broadcasting, satellite/cable TV, and telecommunications. The FCC Media Bureau oversees licensing and operation of broadcast stations and interprets legislation by Congress by making and enforcing regulations, such as those on cable system ownership. The FCC takes the wording of legislation and goes through a rule-making process. It solicits suggestions from industry, academics, and others; then FCC staff draft rules, which are put up for comment, then implemented.

MAKING POLICY The U.S. Congress passes legislation that regulates the media. The Telecommunications Act of 1996 remains the primary law governing the media in the United States.

The FCC's Wireline Competition Bureau has primary responsibility for the conventional telephone industry, while its Wireless Telecommunications Bureaus oversee cell phone service. The Consumer and Governmental Affairs Bureau is in charge of educating members of the public about telecommunications and seeking their input about policy. With the 1996 Telecommunications Act, the FCC shifted away from direct regulation of telecommunications service rates and toward oversight of competition among telecommunications companies and market entry rules.

Increasingly, the FCC shares jurisdiction over key issues, such as antitrust and monopoly, with the Justice Department and the FTC. Concerning local or regional telecommunications carriers, such as Verizon, the FCC shares jurisdiction with their respective state public utility commissions (PUCs). Cable television regulation is also shared between the FCC and local- or state-level cable commissions.

One problem with the FCC and other regulatory agencies is that they may end up attuned more closely to the interests of the industry than to the interests of the public. Critics say that regulators are often effectively captured by the industry they regulate—a concept referred to as **capture theory**. For example, FCC commissioners are often recruited from the ranks of law firms or communication trade associations and often return to those lines of work after their terms are completed.

Capture theory explains that regulators are unduly influenced by the industry they regulate.

Department of Commerce. The NTIA was established within the Department of Commerce to advise on telecommunications policy. The NTIA produces a national broadband map that shows the level of Internet service available in local communities (http://www.broadbandmap.gov/). The NTIA represents the United States in international bodies, such as the ITU, that set international telecommunications trade policies and make satellite orbit and communication frequency allocations.

Along with the Office of the United States Trade Representative, NTIA has been active in **multilateral trade negotiations.** These include the North American Free Trade Agreement (NAFTA) and the World Trade Organization (WTO). NTIA also negotiates issues such as the settlements of revenues from international phone calls. In addition, it is working on current topics such as expanding digital literacy.

Multilateral trade negotiations occur among a number of countries at the same time.

The U.S. Patent and Trademark Office and the United States Copyright Office of the U.S. Library of Congress address international copyright issues in communications media with the World Intellectual Property Organization.

The Federal Trade Commission. The FTC is the regulatory agency charged with domestic trade policy. It monitors trade practices such as **deceptive advertising.** It also investigates companies' actions in restraint of trade. It

Deceptive advertising makes misleading or untruthful claims.

began an investigation of possible anticompetitive practices in computer operating systems that eventually led to an antitrust suit filed against Microsoft by the Justice Department. The FTC scrutinizes privacy policies and practices by companies online, as well as the advertising of violent media products to children.

The Justice Department. The Justice Department plays an important role in the enforcement of general laws that apply to communications as well. To enforce the Sherman Antitrust Act, the Justice Department initiated the suit that eventually broke up AT&T. In accordance with the 1996 Telecommunications Act, the Justice Department shares jurisdiction on monopoly issues with the FCC. It monitors competitiveness in important sectors of the information economy, such as monopoly practices in the computer industry, and competition in local TV and radio markets.

The Courts. The judiciary interprets challenges to laws written by Congress and rules made by the FCC and other federal agencies to see whether they are consistent with the U.S. Constitution. The Supreme Court is the ultimate court of appeals for decisions by lower courts, so it usually ends up reviewing decisions made in major cases such as penalties for indecency in broadcasting and local telephone competition. Courts can also interpret and enforce legal decisions. For example, the Third District Court of the District of Columbia supervised the breakup of the old Bell system in 1984, one of the most powerful government interventions in a communications industry.

Congress. It is the U.S. Congress that ultimately writes and rewrites the communications laws of the land. After years of debate, Congress updated the 1934 Communications Act in 1996 because so many crucial issues required substantial definition or redefinition in law, not just regulatory decree or judicial interpretation. In 1996, those issues included competition within and across media and telecommunications industries, ownership restrictions, and regulation of violent and sexual content on TV. Many congressional committees are involved in communications issues. For the 1996 Telecommunications Act, for example, much of the crucial debate and lobbying took place in the House Telecommunications Subcommittee, since renamed the Subcommittee on Telecommunications and the Internet, which shaped the basic provisions that went before the full House of Representatives.

State and Local Regulation

States and municipalities are increasingly involved in the regulation of telecommunications. They have been less involved in mass media, except in cable TV. For many years, state-level **public utility** commissions regulated local and regional telephone companies' rates. However, most states have drastically reduced their levels of regulatory oversight. They have deregulated

OPENING MARKETS The NTIA is involved in negotiating access to Chinese markets for American media companies and in encouraging the Chinese government to clamp down on copyright piracy. Media products are a major source of foreign trade revenues for the U.S. economy.

STOP & REVIEW

1. What were the media forms in pre-agricultural society?
2. Which media evolved in industrial societies?
3. What changes led to the development of the information society?
4. Which media have not become purely digital, end to end?

Public utilities are regulated monopolies.

telecommunications almost entirely by removing most of the restrictions on the nature and scope of activities that such companies engage in and the prices they charge. One area that states and localities are not involved in is regulation of the Internet. Congress has placed a moratorium on local regulation—and taxation—of the Internet in hopes of fostering the growth of the new medium. Yet, some states are beginning to impose their own regulations on privacy and consumer issues, as well as on financial issues like applying state sales taxes to Internet purchases.

Lobbies

Industry and public interest groups lobby to influence proposed legislation in the executive branch and in Congress. The term comes from the practice of confronting politicians in the lobbies of public buildings, although these days most of the activity takes place behind closed doors. Lobbies try to affect how laws and rules are interpreted and enforced once they are made. For example, since passage of the 1996 Act, broadcasters and cable companies have lobbied Congress and the president to get the FCC to permit more concentration of ownership and more cross-ownership among local media.

Verizon, AT&T, the National Cable & Telecommunications Association, and the National Association of Broadcasters (NAB) are among the top-spending lobbyists. Increasingly, telecommunications policy issues cut across industry boundaries, so the powerful lobbies of the publishing and motion picture industries end up getting involved. Technology companies, such as Apple, Google, and Facebook, are also active lobbyists. These groups not only lobby directly about the substance of legislation and enforcement of laws, but also reinforce their arguments with campaign contributions and form political action committees (PACs) to lobby and to run advertisements for candidates. Sometimes they give favorable publicity, travel junkets, or financial deals to politicians in exchange for preferential treatment. Other lobby groups serve the public interest. The American Association of Retired Persons (AARP) and the Benton Foundation lobbied for years to preserve universal, low-cost "lifeline" local telephone service for older and poverty-stricken Americans.

Industry lobbyists and public interest groups are frequently at odds, and the competing special interests and public interests make it difficult to pass legislation. For example, public interest groups succeeded in pressing for restrictions on television indecency, even though they were resisted strenuously by the NAB and the television networks. Content restrictions are ordinarily considered unconstitutional, but the public interest groups have persuaded the FCC to consider stricter standards. Although industry lobbyists and public interest groups can legally exert influence on the executive and legislative branches, the judicial branch is supposed to be beyond their reach. Still, Supreme Court justices are known to be frequent beneficiaries of free travel and accommodations supplied by parties who have business before the court.

The Fourth Estate

The mass media play an important role in the policy-making process by reporting stories about ongoing issues of interest to the general public, such as indecency and privacy. The media have a "watchdog" role (see Chapter 4) to alert society and policy makers to social trends that raise new issues that could require government action, such as the digital divide. However, some of the policy issues we have examined in this chapter, such as intellectual property, media ownership rules, and spectrum allocation, are not of much interest to the general public. Journalists working for trade publications, such as *Broadcasting and Cable* and *Telephony,* cover that territory, although often with a pro-industry slant. Increasingly, the "citizen journalists" who post their views on blogs (and social networking sites) play a role in public discussion, sometimes uncovering issues that the mainstream press may have overlooked and offering points of view not found in trade publications.

The mass media might act as lobbyists for their own interests, either directly in their own channels or through associations, such as the NAB and the MPAA. For example, few media reported on major telecommunications legislation in 1996 until it was drafted (Gustafsen, 2006), perhaps so that the media industry could present a unified message to the public. Media can have a much broader role as the forum in which much of the policy debate takes place.

The news media pursue the goal of reporting objectively, but they sometimes have a position or an agenda of their own. For example, do news media tend to have a generally liberal or generally conservative bias, and are they intentionally biased for or against specific groups, such as business or the military? Does FaceBook have a liberal bias in identifying trending items for its users? Observers disagree. For example, the group Fairness and Accuracy in Reporting (fair.org) tracks what it considers conservative bias in media coverage, whereas Accuracy in Media (www.aim.org) tracks perceived liberal bias.

STOP & REVIEW

1. How are media laws made and implemented?
2. What are the main institutions in the executive branch that participate in the media policy-making process?
3. What is the relationship of the FCC to other government agencies?
4. What is the role of the courts in media regulation?
5. What is a lobby group? What lobby groups are active in communications media issues?

WATCHING THE WATCHDOG PRESS The group Fairness and Accuracy in Reporting (fair .org) tracks what it considers conservative bias in media coverage. Accuracy in media keeps a similarly watchful eye out for liberal bias (www.aim.org).

SUMMARY & REVIEW

WHAT IS THE DISTINCTION BETWEEN POLICY AND LAW?

Policy is government and public consideration of how to structure and regulate media so that they contribute to the public good. Public policy involves a collective action of the whole society or its representatives. Laws are binding rules created by the legislature and enforced by the executive authority, like the FCC.

WHAT IS THE MARKETPLACE OF IDEAS?

The marketplace of ideas reflects the concept that, with free speech, the best ideas will win out in any competition with others. The concept of a free press is the extension of freedom of speech to media.

WHAT IS THE FIRST AMENDMENT?

The First Amendment to the U.S. Constitution says, "Congress shall make no law respecting an establishment of religion, or prohibiting the free exercise thereof, or abridging the freedom of speech, or of the press." Among the kinds of speech not protected by the First Amendment are libel, defamation, indecency, and inciting violence.

WHAT IS LIBEL?

Libel is harmful and untruthful written remarks that damage someone's reputation or good name. To be legally liable, the person or organization accused of libel must be shown to have known that the information was false, and its use must have been intended to damage the reputation of the person being libeled.

WHAT ARE THE RULES GOVERNING INDECENCY?

References to excretory or sexual organs or functions are indecent, and seven "dirty words" cannot be uttered on broadcast radio or television between the hours of 6 a.m. and 10 p.m. The FCC responds to public complaints about indecent content and may impose fines of $325,000 per occurrence.

HOW ARE MEDIA AND TELECOMMUNICATIONS STANDARDS SET?

Companies often develop standards for their own equipment and compete to set the industry-wide standard. Industry committees sometimes set collective standards, often when spurred or required by government bodies such as the FCC. Internationally, most standards are set or endorsed by the ITU.

WHAT IS THE PRIMARY LAW REGULATING ELECTRONIC MEDIA?

The Communications Act of 1934 established the FCC, regulated broadcasting by regulating scarce frequencies, and media ownership. The 1996 Telecommunications Act encouraged competition between industries, such as cable TV and telephony. It relaxed rules on how many stations a group could own and on cross-ownership of broadcasting, cable TV, telephone companies, and movie studios. It deregulated telephony ownership structures, areas of activity, and prices, but tried to maintain universal service. The act also proposed restrictions on Internet pornography, which were struck down by the Supreme Court.

HOW IS PRIVACY PROTECTED?

Many people are concerned about privacy or control of personal individual information held in consumer credit databases and gathered on the Internet. No overall laws have yet been written on privacy rights, although use of data by government and the interception of messages are controlled by law. A right to privacy has been judicially interpreted from the Fourth Amendment. Congress has written laws both extending and limiting information privacy rights, which have been interpreted and reviewed by the courts.

WHAT ARE THE RESTRICTIONS ON MEDIA OWNERSHIP?

The Telecommunications Act of 1996 reduced or eliminated many restrictions on media ownership. No one company may own TV stations that collectively reach more than 39 percent of TV households or any more than two TV stations in a given market. The number of radio stations owned is restricted on a market-by-market basis, depending on the total number of stations in each market. One company may own a newspaper and a television station in the same market but only if the television station is not a dominant one.

HOW ARE MEDIA OWNERSHIP AND MEDIA CONTENT LINKED?

Some owners may try to influence content to promote their own ideas and interests. If owners are too much alike, they may not produce diverse content, whereas a greater diversity of ownership may produce more diverse content.

HOW DOES THE "SCARCITY ARGUMENT" JUSTIFY GOVERNMENT REGULATION?

There are far fewer frequencies than people who want to use them, both for broadcasting and for two-way services, such as cellular telephony. Someone must allocate frequencies in such a way that radio spectrum users do not interfere with each other. Because the scarcity of frequencies requires that some people be given frequencies and others not, rules imposed by governments for allocating and renewing licenses were necessary.

WHAT ARE THE MAIN INSTITUTIONS IN THE MEDIA POLICY-MAKING PROCESS?

The main institutions in the executive branch are the FCC, which regulates most aspects of communication; the NTIA, which covers some aspects of policy research and international policy; and the FTC, which monitors trade and business practices. Congress passes laws about communication. The Justice Department and the court system, particularly the federal district courts, enforce and interpret the existing laws.

WHAT IS A LOBBY GROUP?

Lobbies are interest or business groups that try to influence lawmaking or enforcement. Some of the main business lobbies are Verizon, AT&T, the National Cable & Telecommunications Association, and the NAB.

THINKING CRITICALLY
ABOUT THE MEDIA

1. What should the government do to protect children from harmful media content?

2. Which is the greater threat to your privacy? The government or private industry? Defend your position.

3. What is the best use of the communications spectrum now occupied by broadcast radio and television?

4. What should the limits on media ownership be?

5. What does the FCC do, exactly?

KEY TERMS

capture theory (p. 464)

censorship (p. 448)

copyright (p. 454)

cross-ownership (p. 457)

deceptive advertising (p. 464)

fair use (p. 456)

First Amendment (p. 445)

freedom of speech (p. 445)

horizontal integration (p. 457)

indecent speech (p. 447)

intellectual property (p. 452)

laws (p. 442)

libel (p. 445)

license (p. 460)

localism (p. 460)

marketplace of ideas (p. 445)

monopoly (p. 457)

multilateral trade negotiations (p. 464)

network neutrality (p. 458)

obscenity (p. 447)

oligopoly (p. 457)

patent (p. 454)

policy (p. 442)

privacy (p. 450)

probable cause (p. 450)

public utilities (p. 465)

restraints of trade (p. 457)

scarcity argument (p. 460)

self-regulation (p. 443)

Sherman Antitrust Act of 1890 (p. 457)

standards (p. 443)

universal service (p. 459)

vertical integration (p. 457)

MEDIA ETHICS

LEARNING OBJECTIVES

After studying the topics in this chapter, you will be able to:

1 Distinguish morality from ethics.
2 Identify the guiding principle behind each of the following ethical philosophies: social contract theory, golden mean, golden rule, veil of ignorance, categorical imperative, principle of utility, and pragmatic ethics.
3 Given an ethical dilemma, apply Potter's Box to determine the best course of action.
4 Outline some ethical responsibilities of journalists.
5 Given an advertising campaign, critique its adherence to the advertising and marketing ethical guidelines.

ETHICAL THINKING

The First Amendment gives media professionals a great deal of freedom, but media professionals and others are always guided in their choices by community standards, professional ethics, and personal values and morals. In this chapter, we learn how media professionals make ethical choices.

Take a look at headlines today. Much of the crime news seems to be about people who don't have a moral compass (they can't tell the difference between right and wrong). Most people think they are ethical; yet, individuals have varying standards of what is right and wrong. In bygone days, all college students were required to take ethics classes. Now, students rarely have training in ethics; they receive their knowledge from their religion, family, and society. Do you know the definitions of morality and ethics?

- **Morality** is the ability to understand the difference between right and wrong.
- **Ethics** are standards of good conduct and moral rules in all situations whether or not they are governed by formal laws or policies.

YM YIK/EPA/Newscom

TRANSPARENCY TO THE PUBLIC IS AN IMPORTANT COMPONENT OF ETHICS. Apple invited journalists to see their restructured procedures for Chinese workers in iPhone factories, after years of charges of unsafe working conditions.

> **Morality** is the line between right and wrong behaviors and decisions.

> **Ethics** are standards of good conduct.

Indeed, we can hope for the day that the ethical conduct of all individuals would make laws unnecessary.

Media ethics codes try to set a standard or act as a guide for ethical decision making. Some ethics guidelines are codified by professional organizations, whereas others represent broad systems of ethics. Churches, private companies, industry trade groups, minority groups, and public-interest groups also monitor media performance. But individual media professionals themselves must always act as their own ethical watchdogs, guided by organizational codes and community standards. Increasingly, audiences face ethical dilemmas of their own as they may provide content for the Internet.

The ethics of journalists receive a lot of attention because their work is in front of millions of people, but professionals involved in all aspects of the media face moral dilemmas every day. Imagine what you would do in the following situations, and why:

- You work for a student news media organization on campus, and an Apple representative sends you the new iPhone! Wow! Do you keep it? What if an Apple public relations or advertising representative calls you and asks if you like the new iPhone, and then asks you to tweet or blog about it? Do you do it? If so, do you include in your post that Apple sent you an iPhone and that Apple asked you to endorse it? *Do you want your audience to believe you have integrity?*

- How do you think people would regard your (objective) story criticizing another company's smart phone if they knew you had been given an iPhone? *Does it appear as if you were biased or compensated for your story?*

- Does the iPhone gift affect your (objective) story about the international petition for Apple to end the exposure of 1.5 million of its Chinese workers to toxic chemicals that can cause leukemia and nerve damage when assembling iPhones? *How will audiences regard your opinions or news stories in the future?*

- You are a PR intern for Apple. Does the continued publicity about its apparent disregard for Chinese factory workers worry you? Do you want a full-time job with Apple after you graduate? *What do your choices say about your personal and professional ethics?*

- You work for the independent campus TV news show. You shot a video of the recent campus riot. The police want it to identify participants. Do you turn it over to them? *Will anyone else want to be a source for you in the future? And what about the First Amendment?*

- You work part time in advertising for a social media company. You sell banner ads. Does it matter that you have no clue how many people see the banner ads, but you assume it must be a lot because millions of people are online? *Are you selling false hopes to businesses? Will they continue to buy ads from you for other media outlets after they find out these numbers are not what you thought?*

- You work part time as a radio news reporter, and there is no time before the noon news show for you to interview a school authority about the latest school shooting. Is it okay to use a really great

MEDIA THEN··· MEDIA NOW

384–322 BCE
> Aristotle discusses the golden mean in Nicomachean Ethics

1787
> First Amendment to the U.S. Constitution

1790
> Kant introduces the categorical imperative in Critique of Practical Reason

1863
> John Stuart Mill publishes Utilitarianism

1947
> Hutchins Commission promotes social responsibility of the press

2000
> The Public Relations Society of America, formed in 1947, revised its latest code of conduct

2011
> The International Chamber of Commerce (ICC), a world business organization, revised its code for advertising and marketing practices

2014
> The Society of Professional Journalists, formed in 1909, revised its code of ethics

interview that you found online? *Do you attribute the source or do you want it to appear that the interview was with you?—And, in effect, lie to your audience?*

■ OMG! The tweet that you just received is perfect for your research paper on the effects of the economy on the media industry! Since it is just someone's opinion, do you need to reference it in your research paper? Would it make a difference if you found it in a blog? Does it matter if you don't know the person's real name? *After all, do you need to know whose ideas you are stealing? Does your audience need to know your source?*

Ethics guidelines can help us with these moral issues. We will look first at some general systems of ethics that are prevalent now and where they originated. Then, we will look specifically at some current ethical issues and how individual media professionals resolved them.

MindTap

Read, highlight, and take notes on the complete chapter text in a rich interactive online platform.

ETHICAL PRINCIPLES

Many ethical decisions are based on people's underlying religious, philosophical, and cultural ideals. Thousands of journalists and others who work in media make good, ethical decisions every day. Let us consider several ideals that have been useful in media ethics.

Socrates, Thomas Hobbes, and John Locke believed in a social contract theory—that people in society have an unwritten agreement with one another. For example, as long as news organizations uphold their social responsibility of reporting news with integrity, then society might not call for government regulation of news content.

384–322 BCE

Aristotle discusses the golden mean in *Nicomachean Ethics*

- Aristotle's golden mean holds that "moral virtue is an appropriate location between two extremes." Moderation and balance are the key points (Merrill, 1997). This means that stories should have balanced points of view or include various points of view to provide balance. For example, James Holmes went on a shooting spree in a movie theater in Aurora, Colorado, and was in the news repeatedly for his various trials and appeals. We saw his photo and read stories that questioned his sanity (imagine that!). Should news programs and bloggers spend time analyzing the accused, or should time be spent remembering the victims?

- The golden rule, "Do unto others as you would have them do unto you," comes from the Bible but can be found in many other cultural traditions as well. Translated into journalism, it means doing no harm to the subjects of your stories and treating them respectfully. In advertising, it means not lying to the public when promoting a service or product. In public relations, it means telling the truth to the public about a crisis caused by your client. It can also be applied to media technology companies. Facebook recently revised hundreds of thousands of users' news feeds without their knowledge. They changed positive and negative posts to see if they could control your emotions. Google's Street View cars (and now cameras on bicycles and in backpacks) photographed street views from all over the world while also collecting personal information from millions of nearby unsuspecting people on their computers. And Apple tracked and recorded detailed information from iPhones and iPads on customers' locations with a time stamp in an unprotected file. Any hacker could find out where you live and the places that you go. How would the developers like it if all of their keystrokes and personal information were recorded and sold? Or, if their newsfeeds were changed? Media developers should treat the public (you) as they would want to be treated.

- Using the "veil of ignorance" (Rawls, 1999) means treating all members of society equally, as if you didn't know who had a stake in an issue. Rawls would have admonished the industry for having a revolving door of FCC leaders and cable and wireless group lobbyists. When the FCC makes decisions that affect you and me and the nation, do we feel that those decisions are in everyone's best interests or the interests of a few large (stakeholder) media companies?

- Immanuel Kant's categorical imperative holds that you should "act on that maxim which you will [wish] to become a universal law." About 57,000 petitioners to *Teen Vogue* and 86,000 petitioners to *Seventeen* asked the magazines to stop using models who appear to have an eating disorder and to stop airbrushing and changing the faces and body sizes of the females in their photographs. What's wrong with being natural and liked for who you are? Fake images of ideal beauty lower young women's self-esteem and can lead to depression or ways of trying to "fix" themselves through anorexia or bulimia to be acceptable. Fake images also can affect boys' (and men's) expectations. Kant would say that fashion magazines should act in a way to be responsible to the society.

- John Stuart Mill's principle of utility holds that we should seek the greatest happiness for the greatest number. Mill was concerned about what would bring the greatest good for society, which he defined as benefiting the largest number of people (Christians, Rotzoll, & Fackler, 1991). Here, we consider potential benefits and harm, determine which action would benefit the most people (or harm the fewest), and choose that. For example, the video game industry is known for the harassment of women and general misogyny. Games usually center on males, and many female characters are "things," for male gratification. Male characters do the action, whereas women are acted upon. Males are clothed and women appear partially naked or naked. Winners are rewarded by "abusing or having sex with females." And, female breasts and bottoms are enlarged and spotlighted for the player. The list goes on (Sarkeesian, 2015). John Stuart Mill would say that this "entertainment" has negative repercussions for society, and promotes men's and women's unrealistic images of each other and themselves and how they should behave.

- Pragmatic ethics were postulated by John Dewey, an early twentieth-century American social philosopher and educator. He argued that actions had to be judged by their results, not by whether they adhered to a particular philosophy or guideline. This directs us to think ahead about the consequences of our actions. For example, critics are worried about violence on prime time television. Yet, televised (college) football games are highly violent, socially acceptable, and celebrated. Much evidence has recently emerged about youth concussions and serious brain injuries. Dewey would ask if our spectator and TV "entertainment" of watching combative sports is worth a player's decline in quality of life, such as dementia, that they may soon experience.

- Situation ethics consider moral principles to be relative to the situation at hand, not absolute. Individuals may trust their intuitive sense of what is right, and guidelines might have exceptions if the overall purpose is good (Day, 1991). Situation ethics is not an ethical code like the others here, but rather urges consideration of alternate frameworks depending on the situation. For instance, using hidden recording devices to document lawbreaking is against the categorical imperative of respecting the privacy of subjects but might be acceptable as an application of the principle of utility if revealing the story will serve the public interest.

1790

Kant introduces the categorical imperative in *Critique of Practical Reason*

1863

John Stuart Mill publishes *Utilitarianism*

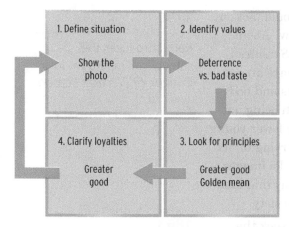

1. Define situation

Show the photo

2. Identify values

Deterrence vs. bad taste

4. Clarify loyalties

Greater good

3. Look for principles

Greater good
Golden mean

FIGURE 17.1 POTTER'S BOX Potter's Box gives a four-step model for thinking through ethical situations.

THINKING THROUGH ETHICAL PROBLEMS: POTTER'S BOX

Potter's Box is a process approach to deciding on ethical actions, developed by Harvard divinity professor Ralph Potter (see Figure 17.1). It is a four-stage model in which each stage helps clarify one aspect of the ethical problem at hand. Potter represented the stages as four quadrants of a box, hence the name.

Quadrant 1: We first identify the facts of the situation. For example, in designing a public campaign against drunk driving, the media planners want to address a serious public safety problem by making the consequences of drunk driving visible. They consider featuring a young woman who was disfigured in an accident caused by a drunk driver. She is willing to have her image used and signs a release form.

Quadrant 2: We identify our choices and the ethical options. Will the shock value of the images deter potential drunk drivers? Will the images be sensationalistic, violating community sensibilities, going beyond moderation? Despite being warned of possible outcomes, could the publicity harm the woman and affect her willingness to participate?

Quadrant 3: Next, we look for general principles that underlie our options. Based on Mill's utility principle or situation ethics, one could argue that the greater good of public safety outweighs the lesser evil of bad taste. Aristotle's golden mean might argue against using an extreme image, going beyond past practices. The golden rule might make us hesitate to put the young woman through an ordeal that we would not wish to suffer ourselves. This helps link concrete options to overarching principles, getting us to think about our own basic values.

Quadrant 4: We clarify our loyalties. Are we more concerned about being true to our own values or about the effectiveness of the campaign? Are we more excited about being connected to something edgy or new, or is it too close to sensationalism? Is the greater good more important than the golden mean?

Andrew Hetherington/Redux

USING POTTER'S BOX Phil Robertson of the A&E TV show *Duck Dynasty* made some remarks about gays, non-Christians, and African Americans, which resulted in controversy. Some groups were outraged about his comments and asked A&E to remove him from the show. Other groups criticized A&E for being intolerant of Robertson's right to free speech. A&E's golden mean was to distance itself from Robertson's opinions and suspend Robertson from the show for one week. The network also promised to initiate a national campaign promoting "unity, tolerance and acceptance among all people." How would you use Potter's Box to analyze this decision?

Potter's Box is not a solution—it is a process that helps us think about our options more clearly. It focuses on ethical or moral issues, not legal ones. Everyone will run into ethical dilemmas where laws, professional training, or organizational rules are not always clear. Potter's Box can help us think through what to do.

CODES OF ETHICS

To assist their members in ethical decision making, various professional groups and media organizations have adopted ethics guidelines or codes. The recommendations of the 1947 Hutchins Commission on social responsibility in journalism have been quite influential among journalists and other professionals in all media.

The guidelines were based on two fundamental ideas: One, whoever enjoys a special measure of freedom, like a professional journalist, has an obligation to society to use their freedoms and powers responsibly. Second, society's welfare is paramount, more important than individual careers or even individual rights. The Commission went further to list five guidelines for the press: (1) present meaningful news, accurate and separated from opinion; (2) serve as a forum for the exchange of comment and criticism, and expand access to diverse points of view; (3) project a representative picture of the constituent groups in society, by avoiding stereotypes and by including diverse voices; (4) clarify the goals and values of the society; implicit was an appeal to avoid pandering to the lowest common denominator, with sensationalism, for example; and (5) give broad coverage of what was known about society. This has been interpreted as prying open government secrets and presenting scientific discoveries.

These principles inspired the Society of Professional Journalists' Code of Ethics, revised in 2014. It tries to anticipate situations and offer guidance on how to deal with them (see Media & Culture: Society of Professional Journalists' Code of Ethics). If journalists follow the Society's guidelines, many ethical missteps could be avoided.

Corporate Ethics

Wow! Wouldn't it be great to be a wildly profitable company *and* have taxpayers subsidizing the million-dollar salaries of your CEOs? Comcast, Starbucks, and Chipotle are among the companies that pay their CEOs with stock options. Stock options for CEOs are deducted from the taxes of publicly traded companies. When companies get tax breaks, there are fewer dollars for government-funded work. So, improvements for school buildings, parks, and water pipes, for example, might not happen if there isn't enough money collected

1947

Hutchins Commission promotes social responsibility of the press

2014

The Society of Professional Journalists, formed in 1909, revised its code of ethics

---

Media & Culture

SOCIETY OF PROFESSIONAL JOURNALISTS' CODE OF ETHICS

Seek Truth and Report It

Source: http://www.spj.org/ethicscode.asp

Ethical journalism should be accurate and fair. Journalists should be honest and courageous in gathering, reporting, and interpreting information.

from taxes. (Or, can you guess who might pay more taxes next year so it does get done?) Think about that every time your car rattles over another pothole. Comcast CEO Stephen Burke received about $49 million in stock options on top of $30 million in other compensation. Starbucks paid about $236 million to its CEO and got $82 million deducted from its tax bill, while Chipotle gave $200 million and subtracted $69 million from its taxes.

Sometimes powerful or high-profile personalities lose sight of the fact that their actions should benefit society. Can you imagine being the public relations representative for these companies and having to respond to the media and the public about increasing the price of cable, coffee, and tacos while the same company pays exorbitant salaries and gets huge tax deductions? Even Warren Buffett abstained from his vote as a board member to show that he thought the compensation plan for Coca-Cola executives was excessive.

So far, our discussion in this chapter has emphasized individual ethical choices. However, most media professionals work within large corporations that present a fundamental moral conflict on a daily basis: my ethics or my job? Professional ethics codes provide guidance when corporate ethics have lapsed such that media workers know when it is time to "blow the whistle" on unethical corporate practices.

Large media firms share some basic ethical dilemmas with other large corporations. Many critics believe that an ethical crisis exists, and it is the result of a fundamental shift in the values of large corporations and their top managers. The temptation to improve their numbers by hiding losses, recording phony profits, or shortchanging public service obligations has proven irresistible to some ethically challenged executives. In addition, many of these executives are obsessed with their own comforts and exorbitant incomes.

Perhaps it is time to return to the corporate responsibility model that preceded the obsession with the bottom line. This imperative parallels the social responsibility model that guides individual journalists. Ethical corporations are expected to "give back" to the communities in which they do business by making charitable contributions and performing public service. Their executives have an obligation to serve with community organizations and, individually and collectively, make their communities a better place to live.

Furthermore, corporations do have a responsibility to foster ethical behavior among their own employees. By emphasizing fair play and a respect for law and other individuals, they aim to develop a corporate culture that rewards ethical behavior, not just the pursuit of the bottom line. Many corporations behave responsibly toward their communities, although their good works sometimes do not attract as much attention.

Making Ethics Work

In some professions, notably medicine and law, ethical codes are tied to licensing requirements. The penalty for ethical violations can be revocation of one's license to practice. There is no licensing in media professions, although serious ethical lapses can be career threatening. This brings us to the question of how codes of ethics have any impact if they do not have the force of law or carry threats to one's livelihood.

Perhaps the most important impact of professional codes is the idea that media professionals have a responsibility to society. Because relatively few people create professional media content, those who do need to consider the impact of their actions on society. In the United States, this sense of social responsibility is the prevailing ethic for media.

Although compliance with professional media codes is voluntary, there are nonetheless severe consequences for violating them. This is because media managers hold them up as norms for employee conduct. In several well-publicized cases, media professionals have been fired from their jobs and—because news travels fast on social media—they were unable to find work at any other media organization. Managers also lose their jobs if their oversight is too lax. But who oversees the boss's boss in a large media organization?

One approach to focus on ethics is to require employees in media organization to read and sign the ethics code. Another approach is for instructors to make ethics an important component of education, which is a required part of the curriculum in accredited journalism programs everywhere. So, if you plan a career in media, communication, or a related field, it is not too soon to start thinking about the choices you will face and the personal values you will bring to those decisions and the social good you can do.

ETHICAL ISSUES

Now that we understand some of the principles, challenges, and procedures involved in media ethics, we turn to consider some recurring ethical issues. These are organized around the various media professions.

Journalism Ethics

Whether they write stories for traditional media, tweet an update, or blog about an issue, journalists face ethical dilemmas that affect people at every turn—because people are included in their stories and people use the information that they read in stories.

Ethical Limits on Free Speech. The First Amendment was originally framed to ensure freedom of the press, but that is not an absolute freedom, and is still not enjoyed in many parts of the world today. In Chapter 16, we discussed legal limits on freedom of the press having to do with libel, public safety, indecency, and obscenity. But even perfectly legal stories are still subject to ethical restraints.

Accuracy. In conventional news media, prevailing journalistic ethical principles about the accuracy of information are quite strict. Journalists do not fabricate evidence, make up quotes, create stories or events, or manipulate misleading photographs, any of which might deceive the public. Celebrated NBC news anchor Brian Williams painted a vivid picture that he and a news crew were shot down in a helicopter in Iraq and detailed how they

1787

First Amendment to the U.S. Constitution

UNLIMITED What are the ethical limits of reporting government secrets? Where is the line between holding governments and powerful organizations accountable, and protecting citizens?

were saved. The pilot remembered it differently. After his apology, Williams was suspended without pay from his job at the No. 1 evening news show with 9.3 million regular viewers. "By his actions, Brian has jeopardized the trust millions of Americans place in NBC News," said Stephen P. Burke, the chief executive of NBCUniversal.

Few journalists make these types of mistakes. Accuracy is taken very seriously by news organizations because audiences depend on media credibility.

When students read news and information online, they should know that some Internet sites are not news organizations with ethics codes in place, and blogs and tweets are usually opinions without supporting evidence.

> **Fairness and balance** is making sure that varied points of view are known equally.

Fairness and Balance. Journalists and editors constantly make choices about what to cover. They can advance certain companies, people, and causes over others by the decisions they make on whom and what to cover, and whom to quote first and how much to quote. So it is important to be fair.

On the other hand, should reporters publicize someone they know, a cause they agree with, or a company they are employed by at the expense of others?

As conglomerates become owners of television stations, critics wonder if it is difficult for television newscasts not to run "news stories" that are thinly disguised promotions for entertainment shows on the same station. Vertical integration creates the potential for interference with negative news coverage affecting media owners. For example, to please its corporate parent, Disney Corporation, ABC News canceled a story about child molesters employed by Disneyland. Although the news editor protested, the story did not air. This creates a climate of self-censorship in which reporters know that it isn't a good idea to prepare critical stories about their corporate cousins. On the flip side, positive news about competitors could also be squelched—which contributes to a decline in trustworthy, objective reporting.

Confidentiality. News reporters protect the confidentiality of their sources so that they have the trust of citizens who may have inside information about important stories. For example, if a reporter is doing a story on the drug trade, she could talk to drug dealers. Because the knowledge the reporter gains from her sources could help convict them, law enforcement officials sometimes try to get reporters to reveal the identity of the sources. However, this is one ethical issue on which there is fairly widespread agreement: the reporter has promised either implicitly or explicitly to keep secret the source's identity and any of the details that could incriminate the source. After all, a journalist who breaks her promise of confidentiality to a source will get no more interviews or tips from others.

Furthermore, news organizations do not relish the idea of being considered an arm of the police or authorities. For example, Michigan State University students rioted (happily but dangerously) when the football team won the Big Ten Championship against Ohio State and was on its way to the Rose Bowl. MSU police and the city police asked reporters for videos and photos showing students involved with the riots. The student journalists' refusals were not challenged, most likely because they had won an earlier case, citing shield laws.

A related question is source attribution—how to cite sources. Rarely should journalists attribute something to an anonymous source, or someone whose identity is not revealed. A reporter reveals as much as possible about the competence and position of his source in order to support the credibility of the story. After all, the public wonders why unnamed "official sources" do not have to be held accountable for their statements.

Many sources will talk only if they cannot be identified from what is said about them in the story. Stories with nonattribution are a bad idea because the source is not held accountable. However, sometimes the gamble has overridden positive effects. The most famous example was the Watergate scandal of the 1970s that brought the downfall of President Nixon. *All The President's Men* movie showed that key inside information was supplied by a confidential source known only as "Deep Throat" to *Washington Post* reporters Robert Woodward and Carl Bernstein. It wasn't until 2005 that Deep Throat was revealed as W. Mark Felt, former assistant director of the FBI during the Nixon administration. You might be more familiar with the recent movie *Spotlight* that told how *Boston Globe* reporters interviewed many people, who did not want to be identified, about the Catholic Church clergy's sexual abuse of children and the decades-old cover-up. In both cases, the journalists stood by their promises to the victims and to the public.

JOURNALISM AT ITS BEST. The journalists at the Boston Globe investigated child sex abuse in the Roman Catholic Church, winning the 2003 Pulizer Prize for Public Service, and inspiring the acclaimed film *Spotlight.*

Sensationalism. Hearst and Pulitzer relied on sensational stories, titillating details, and graphics to compete for readers (see Chapter 4). Some consider sensationalism simply a matter of pandering to bad taste.

Sensationalism can sometimes be attributed to commercialism. A conflict can occur between news value and shareholder values. Many stations run sensationalized stories ("How clean are the kitchens in your favorite restaurants?") during "sweeps" rating weeks, even though there is not really anything new to report. Broadcast news focuses on stories that have a dramatic visual element that makes for good ratings. There is an inclination to lead newscasts with footage of car wrecks, wars, or airplane crashes because of the visual nature of the medium. There is also a temptation to ignore or downplay an important story because it doesn't have eye-catching footage to go with it. This ideology is changing with multimedia stories on the Internet. Now, news editors ask what the important story is and how it can best be told.

Sometimes media get carried away and forget to take the pulse of their audiences: are you really sitting on the edge, hungering for the latest news to find out why Justin Bieber just spent $250 on tacos at a fast food restaurant (no pun intended)?

Conflicts of Interest. Some freelancers and journalists may be tempted to let someone else pay for their travel to exotic locations, such as the Bahamas, or to high-profile events, like the North American International Auto Show. Sponsors hope that **junkets**—paid trips for journalists— will attract the

> **Conflict of interest** is when professionals, such as journalists, have an invested interest that might affect their decision making, making them less objective.

> A **junket** is an expense-paid trip intended to influence media coverage.

attention of reporters or influence how a subject is portrayed. For example, a resort operator might pay for travel writers to visit in hopes of getting a favorable story into a newspaper or magazine—free advertising—that might entice visitors. Or, a company might fund a trip that is only vaguely related to a particular topic but might make the writer feel more positive toward the sponsoring organization when a story in the future pops up. If you liked their luxury resort (and want to be invited back), you should also like their parent company's stock, right? Another form of conflict of interest is **freebies**—gifts from sources and news subjects. It is sometimes tempting for journalists to accept free gifts, such as dinners, T-shirts, books, and passes to sports events or to the theater. Even the smallest of gifts can leave a big impression, and you should say no.

The problem with junkets and freebies is that the journalists are not experiencing the event as regular customers who have to pay fees and haggle with managers. Another problem is that journalists who are feeling good from having been lavishly wined and dined are reflecting positively instead of objectively on the free experience.

Most publications have very strict rules against all freebies and junkets. When journalists are given gifts—before or after stories—the gifts are returned or given to charity, citing company policy. These journalists avoid even the appearance of a conflict of interest. Also, an accepted practice is to disclose the relationship that raises a conflict of interest so that the audience can be alerted to the potential bias. If there is too much of a conflict, then another journalist is assigned to the story.

Privacy. Journalists weigh the public's right to know with an individual's privacy. How far should reporters go in their coverage of the subject of a story? Where should they draw the line on details? And to what degree are they responsible for consequences to that person? When their privacy has been invaded, some subjects move away from the local area, change their names, and in rare cases, even commit suicide. Journalists determine what information is central to the objective of the story and remove extraneous details. Often, journalists can report the "who," "what," "where," and "when" for a story immediately, but wait on the "how" and "why" until facts can be verified.

Thousands of journalists show sensitivity and good judgment in the many decisions they make daily. However, a few get caught up in the moment. For example, Christin Cooper went too far in her interview with Bode Miller after he won an Olympic bronze medal. Instead of celebrating the moment, she chose to ask questions that included the recent death of his brother and other family issues. She continued to push and the camera continued to roll even as Miller bowed his head, cried, and was unable to answer. Former athletes, such as Cooper, often become sports announcers and some do not understand professional ethics because they are not trained journalists.

The international press exercises different standards concerning privacy. When a hotel maid accused the French former International Monetary Fund advisor of rape, French reporters named the alleged victim and her daughter, described her personality and looks (which has nothing to do with rape), but discouraged photos of the politician in handcuffs.

> **Freebies** are gifts of any value from sources and potential news subjects.

M.Flynn / Alamy Stock Photo

ETHICS CHALLENGES Corporations employ media professionals who must advise their clients and tell the truth to the public when disaster strikes. The Carnival Corporation has experienced passenger deaths, plumbing problems, refrigeration issues, overflowing toilets, power outages, and fires. It may be a challenge to promote the next cruise vacation to keep the company afloat.

Meanwhile, American journalists refrained from naming the housekeeper with whom former California governor Arnold Schwarzenegger had an affair, even though it was consensual, until after her name came out in blogs. They also held back the name of Schwarzenegger's and the housekeeper's boy and blurred his face in baby photos.

Ethical Entertainment

Why should we care how much violence or misogyny children or adults are exposed to in computer games? What about television's thousands of murders that elementary school children see and the hundreds of thousands of acts of media violence that teenagers are exposed to by the time they graduate from high school? (See Chapter 15.) Will they think that hurting others is no big deal as they confuse fantasy with real life? Should filmmakers think about the social impacts of their films?

Who's responsible for media effects? Should producers take responsibility for the social effects of their creations? Or is their role to create "art" and let the chips fall where they may? Most filmmakers, musicians, and television entertainment producers, for example, say that they are not responsible for the social impacts of their creations. If children get hurt imitating an action, then that is their problem, not the producers'. The same issue applies to depictions of rude behavior or vulgarity in popular movies, TV shows, computer games, and music. Yet, young viewers might be influenced

STOP & REVIEW

1. What are the main areas of concern in media ethics?

2. What are some of the classic ethical principles that people apply to issues that arise in media ethics?

3. What is Potter's Box?

4. What are the ethical responsibilities of journalists?

to think that the behavior they see so often on the screen or hear in songs is attractive or even socially acceptable. What happens when we have a whole society thinking that such dispositions on how to treat one another are commonplace?

Parents have protested Nickelodeon's *Teenage Mutant Ninja Turtles* movies because it is an extremely violent show targeted to a young audience. Young children often can't tell the difference between fantasy and reality. When the first Ninja Turtles movie appeared, schools in Indiana had to issue a warning to their young students that the Turtles were not real; unfortunately, too many children were falling down storm drains looking for them and imitating dangerous situations. The second movie was excessively violent and the third movie in the series begins with an antagonist's head being blown off (a murder). How has watching a violent murder become an acceptable form of entertainment? And, the fourth movie continues the sci-fi carnage fun.

As Chapter 15 discusses, researchers do not always agree on how deep or pervasive the effects of violence or sex in the media are, but they do agree that the amount of graphic violence in media has increased. Headlines constantly remind us that some people seem to imitate specific acts of violence or reckless behavior that they have seen on the screen or heard about in music. What if larger numbers of people don't directly imitate the televised actions but come to see it as more normal or acceptable?

Young people form their values through what they see. For example, many reality shows are detrimental to young woman's self-image and attitudes. The *Kardashians* spend inordinate amounts of time on physical appearance and are inconsiderate and disrespectful of others. The *Housewives* programs focus on appearance, bickering, and backbiting. Even the title "real housewives" is condescending and hints that women cannot achieve a certain lifestyle without being married. Many reality TV shows teach misplaced values, destructive behavior, and a false sense of reality and expectations.

These false expectations are compounded through magazine models who appear emaciated and airbrushed; female comics characters with inordinately large chests, tiny waists, and few clothes; and female video game characters that are generally nonessential (and offensive). Immanuel Kant would admonish these entertainment producers and players to respect women and men equally and in a way that should be universal common law. John Stuart Mill would reprove the producers and players to aspire toward doing the greatest good for society.

And, we can't move away from entertainment ethics without a word about TV football. Many football players have been arrested for domestic violence against their wives or girlfriends. Yet, they are cheered, celebrated, and paid millions of dollars to be violent in games. Many players experience multiple concussions that will damage their brains within a few, short years. Yet, they are urged to get back in the game and be more aggressive. While some researchers have studied the effects of violence on TV shows and video games (as noted in Chapter 15 in Media and Anti Social Behavior), others have found a connection between men's TV football viewing and family violence, especially if a favored team had an unexpected loss (Card & Dahl, 2011).

In the face of these issues, industry representatives usually make two counterarguments: (1) individuals are not as vulnerable as is commonly supposed and (2) individuals and families have a responsibility to make their own decisions about what to watch and what to make of it. For the mainstream of society, making responsible choices is probably the right answer. But how can people make informed choices? One current response within public schools is to teach media literacy so that children and adolescents understand the industry and what they are watching. A number of churches and other groups are also doing this to supplement what children do or don't learn at home about making such choices.

Indecency is a particularly sensitive issue since the courts ruled that moral standards vary among communities, which are permitted to develop local standards for treatment of sexuality. Media professionals think about the ethics of indecency in individual terms ("Do I really think this is a good idea?"), in institutional terms ("What do we as a company want to say to the public?"), and in terms of community standards and values ("Is this an appropriate thing to say to this community?").

> **Indecency** is when behavior or decisions are not appropriate and negatively deviate from social standards.

Many viewers were upset when Miley Cyrus "performed" at the Video Music Awards (VMAs) on MTV in 2013. Many complaints about various parts of her act were filed with the Federal Communications Commission (FCC). Unfortunately for them, the FCC couldn't do anything because it has no jurisdiction over cable channels. But even if something is legal to do, is it ethical? Usually, unethical decisions lead to bad publicity or to bad business.

Until recently, the prevailing trend in America was toward unrestricted artistic freedom divorced from social considerations. But religious critics and social philosophers have argued that the artist is not absolved from responsibility to contribute positively to society. These critics argue that artists should either raise people's consciousness about issues or, at the very least, refrain from contributing to social harm.

Social Media Ethics

Privacy. Social media are profoundly ethically challenged. The entire social media phenomenon is predicated on a massive ethical breach: selling private information to commercial interests under the false pretense of running a place where friends and family can meet, and then shielding themselves behind baffling privacy protection policies. Research on cyber security has shown that users should also be more responsible in reading the fine print of social media privacy guidelines and also using different passwords for each social media site and changing their passwords often.

Unfortunately for Facebook and Cornell researchers, angry users did not agree that the fine print of Facebook's "informed consent" policy covered the attempted manipulation of their moods. Hundreds of thousands of users' newsfeeds were changed to be either positive or negative to see if they altered users' moods. Facebook reviewed users' subsequent status updates and found they were affected by what they read. (Imagine that!) Four months later, Facebook changed its policy to say that user information might be used in research. (So read the fine print before you click "agree" on website "security" policies!) In a subsequent review, it was found that Cornell University's ethics board did not preapprove the study (Sullivan, 2014).

Trolling is being deliberately offensive online to others with the objective of upsetting them or getting a reaction or baiting them to do something.

Trolling. Facebook chooses to remain willfully ignorant of the many children under age 13 who use its website, making the youngsters vulnerable to stalkers, bullies, and unscrupulous marketers. These trollers try to bait users into doing what they want. In days gone by, bullies might catch you at recess or after school, but you were safe at home. With computers, bullying has changed. Mobile devices and social media are 24/7, and so is the opportunity to offend and be offended, sometimes with tragic consequences (MSU School of Journalism, 2012).

Social media follow the lead of the mass media when it comes to explaining away media effects, even including cases of suicide induced by cyberbullies: it is the parents' (or the schools' or law enforcement's) fault but never theirs.

Public Relations Ethics

In any job, choices of doing good or evil exist. Public relations can be used for the public good while advancing private advantage. Or it can be used to manipulate the public interest or hide selfish commercial objectives. Most practitioners are very ethical.

The Center for Media & Democracy's PR Watch is a modern-day critic that identifies and investigates PR spin by corporations and government agencies that affect the democratic process and people's lives. Its website (http://www .prwatch.org) criticizes assaults against the public interest. It helps expose those whose moral compass is broken.

There are many PR examples in which businesses give back to customers and are good citizens within the community. For instance, Flint, Michigan, experienced an extended crisis when drinking water was contaminated from nearby lakes and also from the old lead pipes that carried the water. People and animals became ill, which was one of many problems associated with the water. Governor Snyder asked President Obama for aid. Meanwhile, Walmart and Sam's Club published a full-page ad, declaring their help by sending 6.5 million bottles of water to the schools in the community. Their partners in this endeavor were Coca-Cola, Nestle, and PepsiCo. The PR on this goodwill gesture cultivated a positive relationship with the community (whose citizens might choose one of these soft drinks in a future shopping trip).

The key to ethical behavior for both individual practitioners and the institutions they serve is organizational performance. If a company, for example, acts in a manner that harms rather than helps the people it depends on for success, no amount of public relations can save the day, no matter how well the effort is designed or executed. The only real solution for the guilty party is for management to correct the problem. For example, Orogold cosmetics has been lambasted on several social media sites for its sales tactics—customers all over the world complain about sales staff pushing and holding women hostage with cream on their faces while giving an extended sales pitch, refusing to refund products, using trickery, and generally lying to sell their expensive products (e.g., ripoff.com, complaintsboard.com). When a positive review was posted amidst the overwhelming negative ones, customers responded with, "You are so fake," assuming the post was a PR tactic (Craig, 2011). The point is that if a company is known for being unethical, then no amount of PR will help.

2000

The Public Relations Society of America, formed in 1947, revised its latest code of conduct

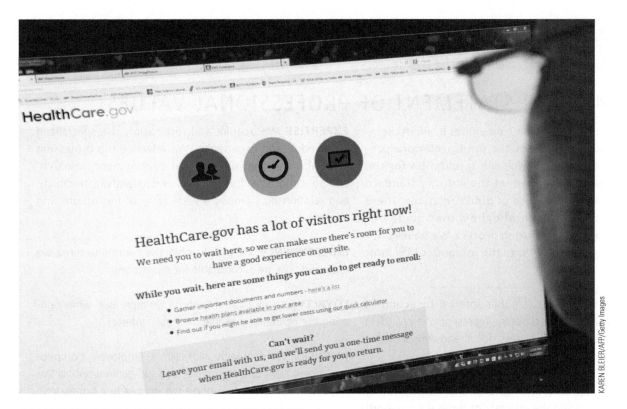

COMMUNICATING HONESTLY WITH THE PUBLIC The HealthCare.gov website was intended for people to learn about and apply for affordable health care. The launch of the site was less than stellar. Instead of ignoring complaints, government media representatives admitted the website needed improvements. In an effort to better understand the situation, they also provided a place for people to submit comments or questions: http://www.hhs.gov/digitalstrategy/blog/2013/10/making-healthcare-gov-better.html

Ethical and legal breaches of conduct, down through the years, led to the formation of the Public Relations Society of America (PRSA) in 1947 and its Code of Professional Standards in 1950 (see Media & Culture: PR Ethics). The code is framed as a self-directed teaching tool that expresses the "universal values that inspire ethical behavior and performance." Other public relations membership organizations, such as the International Public Relations Association (IPRA) and the International Association of Business Communicators (IABC), have codes of conduct with specific examples of what they consider unprofessional and/or unethical behaviors.

Advertising Ethics

In advertising, ethical decisions revolve around selecting one moral value over another when writing, designing, or placing advertisements.

Harmful Products. The promotion of harmful products creates obvious ethical dilemmas

VIOLATING YOUR PERSONAL RIGHTS? Google's Street-View cars collected personal information (e-mails, passwords, etc.) from open Wi-Fi networks for years as they also took pictures of streets. From the perspective of a media professional, is this ethical? Could the golden rule be applied here?

PRSA MEMBER STATEMENT OF PROFESSIONAL VALUES

This statement presents the core values of PRSA members and, more broadly, of the public relations profession. These values provide the foundation for the Member Code of Ethics and set the industry standard for the professional practice of public relations. These values are the fundamental beliefs that guide our behaviors and decision-making process. We believe our professional values are vital to the integrity of the profession as a whole.

ADVOCACY We serve the public interest by acting as responsible advocates for those we represent. We provide a voice in the marketplace of ideas, facts, and viewpoints to aid informed public debate.

HONESTY We adhere to the highest standards of accuracy and truth in advancing the interests of those we represent and in communicating with the public.

EXPERTISE We acquire and responsibly use specialized knowledge and experience. We advance the profession through continued professional development, research, and education. We build mutual understanding, credibility, and relationships among a wide array of institutions and audiences.

INDEPENDENCE We provide objective counsel to those we represent. We are accountable for our actions.

LOYALTY We are faithful to those we represent, while honoring our obligation to serve the public interest.

FAIRNESS We deal fairly with clients, employers, competitors, peers, vendors, the media, and the general public. We respect all opinions and support the right of free expression.

Source: PRSA Member Code of Ethics. https://www.prsa.org /aboutprsa/ethics/codeenglish/#.V4OwiFd1bnY

---

for advertising professionals. Emerson Foote resigned as chairman of McCann-Erickson, one of the world's largest and most prestigious ad agencies, in protest over its willingness to create cigarette advertising. He was making a choice between the value of free expression (tobacco companies produce legal products and have a right to advertise) and the value of health concerns (the link between nicotine and cancer).

Other advertising professionals have not been so scrupulous. Children are attracted to e-cigarettes wrapped in rainbow colors and filled with candy flavors—such as cupcake, chocolate candy bar, lemonade, and cotton candy—that mask the nicotine. Manufacturers are looking to cultivate new consumers, and apparently are successful. The Center for Disease Control (CDC) reported that e-cigarette use doubled from 2011 to 2012 for children in grades 6 to 12. And almost 2 million middle and high school students have tried e-cigarettes. As use has increased, so have the calls to poison centers—from one a month in 2010 to 250 a month in early 2014. The liquid nicotine produces poisons that can be inhaled, ingested, or absorbed through the eyes and skin (CDC, 2014). E-cigarettes by any other name—"e-hookahs" or "vape pens"—are still e-cigarettes (with addictive nicotine that arrests brain development and is linked to cancer).

E-cigarette manufacturer Lorillard is responsible for about 82 percent of the e-cig ads viewed by 12- to 17-year-olds (Healy, 2014). It's an advertiser's business to know the market. So, you can bet Lorillard's advertising professionals

WHAT'S THE GREATER GOOD? Nicotine can be addictive, arrest brain development, and cause cancer. Would e-cigarette manufacturers, advertisers, PR professionals, or media executives want their mothers, brothers, or daughters to experience these potentially deadly health problems as a result of advertising?

knew what they were doing when they created ads targeted to youth and decided where to place the ads. So why do it? Perhaps a sense of professional responsibility to the advertising client or the desire to continue their employment by cigarette companies outweighs the advertising professionals' ethical responsibility to the children of the United States and elsewhere. Although they can claim First Amendment rights to advertise to whomever they want, is it ethical to do so?

And what about the media that run these ads during programs watched by teens? Shouldn't they just say no? Congress removed cigarette advertising from TV because of the influence that TV advertising has on youth. Yet, from 2011 to 2013, exposure to e-cigarette ads increased 256 percent among children ages 12 to 17 (Healy, 2014).

Stereotyping. There are also questions about the ethics of using ethnic and sex-role stereotypes in advertising. Did you ever notice that almost all the women who appear in ads are unnaturally thin and beautiful, while the African-American males tend to be professional athletes? Are such portrayals harmless appeals to advertising target markets, or do they perpetuate harmful stereotypes that foster racism and sexism?

In addition to promoting a product that is harmful to one's health, e-cigarette advertisers are designing images that are harmful to the society it stereotypes, and even raunchy. On a *Sports Illustrated* cover with young women wearing only bikini bottoms, Lorillard Inc. placed a Blu e-cigs logo on a tiny bikini triangle. The online version offers a magnification option for readers to "zoom in." The accompanying text? "Slim. Charged. Ready to Go. Available Nationwide."

Lorillard's e-cigs are legal products, the ad agency's advertisements are legal, the targeting to children is legal (for now), and *Sports Illustrated* has a right to run the ads. But are any of these ethical decisions? E-cigs are linked to health issues, the ads stereotype women and the expectations of men, and many youth are socialized by what they see in magazines, such as *Sports Illustrated*. Critics protest ethical breaches and lax standards. If the government becomes involved, then laws might be passed that tighten free speech. Thus, professionals must weigh the potential consequences of their actions that might bring in revenue but also might lower customer approval or attract government enforcement.

Another issue is, why is it that all women must be thin? Many young girls strive to achieve the impossible and boys may think the unnatural is the standard. It's bad enough that many models look anorexic, and that if a real woman looked like Barbie, she'd topple over. A personal favorite of one of the authors is the Slumber Party Barbie that came with a book on "How to Lose Weight." It included this tip: "Don't Eat" (McDonough, 2009). Photographers add to girls' and women's insecurities by airbrushing and cutting those thin models in half: just liquefy, freeze, and wrap in Photoshop. The images also socialize boys and men to have unnatural expectations. Thus, the ethical dilemma for manufacturers, advertisers, PR practitioners, and publications that showcase images such as these is finding out whether or not consumers approve of the images by voting with their dollars at the cash register.

Images of groups portrayed in advertising may have negative effects even when they do not include blatant stereotypes. Numerous studies show that models appearing in ads do not reflect the racial and gender balance of the American population. Indeed, some groups, such as Native Americans, female business executives, and people with glasses, are nearly invisible in ads. Perhaps that sends the message that minorities, females, and those with physical impairments are invisible—and therefore, not important—in society. There are also valid concerns about targeting vulnerable groups with potentially harmful products, like selling high-alcohol malt liquor or cheap wine in low-income areas or potentially unhealthful diet aids to females. Some advertisers and publications go according to their client's wishes and others have ethical standards they won't compromise. The business decision is, on one hand, doing what is ethically right and hope consumers will approve, and on the other hand, experiencing a potential loss of income if an advertiser won't submit a different ad for publication or a client goes to another agency that will do what it wants.

Consumer Privacy. So, what's the first thing the clerk asks when you step up to the counter to purchase your party shoes at DSW or your tennis shoes at Dick's Sporting Goods? "Let me sign you up for our rewards program!" The coded language from some companies is "Our company wants all of your contact information, and we want to record your purchases." Yikes! The ability to compile massive individual files of consumer and media behavior data takes market segmentation to the extreme, making it possible to address consumers as individuals, which is the practice of relationship marketing. However, this type of research is also important in data mining, which allows advertisers to sift through huge databases to identify unique market segments, such as skin care products for young men.

These capabilities raise concerns about the misuse of personal information collected and stored through databases and websites. Many websites require the disclosure of your personal information including name, address, telephone number, and credit card numbers. They can also track your keystrokes while at their websites, collate that information with information obtained from your visits to other websites and from your own computer, merge it with consumer credit information from the offline world, and sell the information on you to third parties (see Chapter 12).

Industry self-regulation has thus far been the preferred method of dealing with privacy issues. The Federal Trade Commission issued "Rules of the Road" guidelines that require websites to disclose their privacy policies, and privacy certification authorities have been established to monitor compliance. However, websites with these disclosures may seem to give the appearance of trustworthiness, whereas in fact they only inform the website visitor *how* their privacy will be invaded (LaRose & Rifon, 2006). Thus, consumer privacy protection is still largely a matter of the ethical choices made by website proprietors who weigh user privacy against potential profits.

Intrusiveness. It's even at the gas pumps! The ubiquitous nature of advertising has raised another type of privacy question: are there places that should be protected from advertising? In recent years, advertising has spread to speaker boxes at gas stations, on eggs, on parking meters, and in public bathroom stalls. Proposals have been made to put commercial messages on postage stamps. Now marketers send attractive, young undercover marketing representatives to cyber cafés and bars to plant plugs for computers and liquor products in casual conversations and pay others to impersonate consumers in social media. Consumers are often annoyed when they are powerless to separate themselves from commercialism. Telemarketers interrupt family meals. Advertisers tie up fax machines and spam e-mails, and they use satellite channels, such as Channel One, for commercials shown in public schools, a domain that was previously commercial free.

As you walk into stores in the not-too-distant future, cameras will automatically scan your facial features to match with their database of your purchasing habits. Now they know almost everything about you!

With the exception of the Do Not Call lists for telemarketers, recent antispam legislation, restrictions on cigarette advertising, and the do-not-track initiative (see Chapter 12), there is little legal protection from the advertising barrage. Advertising on broadcast network television is limited by a voluntary agreement among broadcasters, and most media organizations have

IT'S EVERYWHERE! IT'S EVERYWHERE! Should we be confronted with advertising every moment of our lives?

standards that prohibit ads for certain products, such as condoms. Other than that, advertisers enjoy broad free-speech protections, so incessant advertising bombardment comes down to a choice between ethics and commerce for the advertiser.

Subliminal Messages in Media. You can receive messages without even knowing it. Subliminal ads are words and messages that are presented below the audience's level of awareness, and were banned by the FCC. One type of subliminal messaging is product insertions in movies that promote power of suggestion: you see actors drinking Coca-Cola in a movie and soon you want a Coke to drink. Some subliminal messages are in the form of faint writing on images that only your subconscious sees. And another type is the insertion of frames into a movie that flip by so quickly that you don't realize you are seeing something other than what is in the surrounding frames. Games have subliminal messages as well.

Deceptive Advertising. In order to preserve their good name, most advertisers go to great lengths to avoid deceptive advertising. However, blunders and differences of opinions can happen. For example, Weight Watchers sued Jenny Craig over "misleading and deceptive ads" in which Jenny Craig compared the two programs in a study that Weight Watchers said never happened and was not backed by scientific fact. The government does not usually regulate aggrandizing or bragging in advertising that can't be proved. This is called *puffery* (see Chapter 12). The problem is that many children and adults believe such claims. If these statements get out of hand, then it is possible that society may call for government regulation of advertising.

Research Ethics

Communications research is a vital component of many media professions. It is everywhere: from surveys appearing in your e-mail to phone calls at home to the questionnaires your professor asks you to fill out in class. Sometimes you try to make it stop, but that only triggers more mailings and phone calls (because you responded at all).

What gives the researchers the right to intrude? It is important to remember that both society and you can benefit from your cooperation in research studies. Ratings and other surveys provide the feedback that the media industry needs to serve you better. The studies that social scientists conduct help increase our knowledge of the role that communications media play in society (see Chapter 15), or they help to inform public policy debates. Your opinions truly do count in communications research studies, so you should provide them willingly and honestly when you can.

However, not all surveys are legitimate, and not all researchers adhere to accepted ethical guidelines. This is a special problem with phone surveys. Too many times, what starts out as a survey winds up being a sales pitch. Or, if you don't go along, the so-called interviewer may resort to abuse, begging, or intimidation to keep you on the line. The information you give, along with your name, address, and phone number, may be turned over to direct marketers who put you at the top of their "sucker lists."

The Do Not Call list offers a little protection (except with researchers, who are exempt). According to the ethical guidelines of the American Association for Public Opinion Research, professional researchers may not lie to you or coerce you in any way. All information that can be used to identify you through your responses must be kept confidential and your name may not be disclosed for nonresearch purposes (marketing, for instance).

Academic researchers must adhere to even stricter standards. The American Psychological Association (APA), for example, expects ethical researchers to stress that your participation is voluntary and that you may withdraw at any time. They must tell you of the nature of the study and the amount of time—or other commitment—that is expected of you and ask for your informed consent. And if you are participating in the study for extra credit in a class, an alternative activity should be available by which you could earn the same credit.

Experimental and ethnographic studies raise their own issues. Experimental manipulations (such as those that administer simulated electrical shocks) can have harmful psychological effects on participants. Ethnographic studies that observe people in Internet discussion groups may violate the privacy of participants if they think they are "speaking" to a closed group of associates. Only content analysis studies are generally free of human subjects' ethics concerns (except when analyzing posts in online forums where privacy may be expected).

Most colleges and universities have a human subjects committee and a set of guidelines mandated by the federal government to safeguard your rights as a research subject. Such committees review and approve research studies prior to their implementation, especially if an experimental design involving deception is used or if sensitive information (such as questions about sexually transmitted disease) is collected. Some human subjects committees also uphold the APA guidelines and have special provisions of their own. The Belmont Report from the Department of Health and Human Services outlines basic ethical principles on the use of human subjects in research and is found online at http://www.hhs.gov/ohrp /humansubjects/guidance/belmont.html.

Consumer Ethics

In the evolving world of innovative digital media, an important change is that the receiver, or audience, for the media is also the source of media content (see Chapter 1). That raises ethical issues for you, the audience.

Web Surfing. Sometimes it may seem that the Internet has no rules, but that is not true. Most Internet providers have a code of ethics on their home page under "Acceptable Uses" or "User Policy." These are guidelines, not laws, but the penalty for disobeying them can be the heavy Internet users' equivalent of "death": termination of your account. The following sections discuss some general rules to follow.

Harassment. Here the golden rule might apply. If you don't want to receive abusive e-mail, spam, or "mail bombs" of repetitive, unwanted messages, then it might be a good idea not to send them either. "Trolling"—making provocative statements in newsgroups to get people to visit your website or buy your client's project, for example—might also be avoided. If your account is at a university, school authorities will take an especially dim view of sexual or racial harassment, and it may have legal or disciplinary consequences far beyond cancellation of your e-mail privileges.

Misrepresentation. Americans are swindled out of millions of dollars each year because of fraud—sometimes as people posing as FBI agents or banks wanting your account numbers or "friends" needing you to send money. However, if "no misrepresentation" is your "categorical imperative," it also precludes using someone else's name to sign up for services or "borrowing" other people's passwords. Of course, if you are in a multiuser game or another Internet environment where everyone has a false identity and everyone knows and agrees on the rules, this "misrepresentation" is acceptable. That's an example of adapting your ethics to the situation. However, "stealing" someone's identity online is a serious issue that could create real damage to the person you are pretending to be.

Hacking. Some forms of hacking are unlawful, such as gaining unauthorized access to people's telephones, bank accounts, or computers and stealing credit card numbers. But sabotaging other people's websites and writing malicious programs to distribute on the Internet are unethical as well. You may think that "the greater good" is served by defacing a particular website, but the owners of the site and their visitors certainly won't agree.

Your own provider may have additional guidelines. Universities, for example, generally have a policy that prohibits the commercial use of the Internet. Using your Web page to promote your rock band or your favorite politician might get you into trouble, and using it to sell pirated recordings of Grateful Dead or Pharrell Williams concerts almost certainly will.

Providers also vary in how they check for violations. Some respond only to complaints, whereas others take it upon themselves to seek out abusers by monitoring chat rooms and discussion areas. Also, be advised that if your e-mail or website is an organizational account (and that does include student accounts), you have no right to privacy. Employers (and university administrators) have the legal right to inspect your e-mail for violations of their acceptable uses policies. The FBI is working with a trade group, the Information Technology Association of America, to promulgate ethical guidelines to young Internet users, their schools, and their parents. These are phrased as biblical commandments, examples of what Kant called "categorical imperatives":

"Thou shalt not vandalize Web pages.

Thou shalt not shut down Web sites."

Sharing or Stealing? Intellectual property rights are now on a collision course with the freewheeling culture of the Internet. Let there be no doubt, it is unlawful to share copyrighted music and video files over the Internet without permission from (and also payment to) the copyright owner (see Chapter 16). You may call it "sharing" or "downloading," but in fact it is stealing. The Recording Industry Association of America and the Motion Picture Association of America have abandoned the strategy of prosecuting individual downloaders, at least for now, so the ethics issue remains important. Like speeding and underage drinking, file sharing is illegal, but the odds of getting caught seem small. So what weak ethical justification can you produce? I won't get caught? Everyone else is doing it? The Big Media are ripping off all of us? I can't afford the DVD anyway? If so, you might want to check the social contract theory again.

Social Media User Ethics. As we saw earlier, proprietors of social media websites are ethically challenged, so you, the user, need to supply ethical standards. You might consider refusing requests from underage friends (i.e., under age 13) to discourage them from using social media that have a real potential of harming them. You should mind your own online behavior, refraining from making posts that are certain to provoke hostility or encourage lewdness and drunkenness. Don't disclose the private information of others: if they are careful not to reveal their home address, phone number, or current whereabouts, you should not disclose those, either. When you see inappropriate content, take your "friends" to task and report it to the system administrator. Be sure to observe the journalistic ethics discussed previously. Even if you do not aspire to be an online journalist, you must respect the rights of private citizens in your tweets and blog posts. You are not free to "dish the dirt" on everyone you know as they do in the tabloids. And private citizens and businesses can sue you if they feel you have besmirched their reputations.

Responsible Viewing. If you are concerned about violence, vulgarity, and stereotyping in the media, then are you part of the problem if you continue to view it? For example, the dangers of concussions from participation in sports like football and soccer have recently become a concern. By continuing to view football games on television, you support a systematic exploitation of human suffering for the profit of sports channels and team owners and for your own entertainment. Indirectly, you contribute to the injuries of young children (as seen on the Esquire Channel's *Friday Night Tykes* TV series) who imitate their sports heroes, including learning how to get away with violent behavior on the field (LaRose, 2014). How might you balance your love of sports with the health hazard that they pose and that you, the viewer, contribute to? Is entertainment a "greater good" that outweighs the mangling of young bodies?

Plagiarism. Another ethical dilemma for students is downloading material from the Internet into term papers, or downloading (or even buying) entire papers. Some sites offer term papers for sale (we won't tell you where), but many students use Google to find relevant snippets of documents and cut and paste them into their own papers. It's so easy! However, both are plagiarism.

Perhaps you would like some nice graphics to spice up your paper (and fill out the minimum page requirement). Don't be tempted! Copying just about anything from a website or from a print publication is probably a copyright violation unless you obtain permission from the author. Sometimes the site explicitly says that you are free to use the images there as long as you credit the source, but you have to be sure that the site from which you copied owns the rights to the work in the first place. Many websites are sources of free graphics, photos, or other images (e.g., www.freedigitalphotos.net). Be careful to read the fine print or terms of use. They might vary depending on the image itself or the reason you want the image. Some demand citation or permission, and others limit use to offline applications. However, even if citation is not required, copying someone else's diagram, photo, or artwork into your paper is as much an act of plagiarism as copying their words.

Most colleges and universities have honor codes that specifically prohibit plagiarism, with penalties ranging from flunking the assignment to failing the

2011

The International Chamber of Commerce (ICC), a world business organization, revised its code for advertising and marketing practices

STOP & REVIEW

1. Why should we care about entertainment ethics? What are some of the concerns?

2. What do the International Chamber of Commerce guidelines say about data protection and privacy information?

3. What are your rights as a research subject?

4. What is the problem with stereotyping in advertising and other media?

5. What are some forms of plagiarism in class assignments, and how can you avoid it?

course to expulsion from the program or university. Just to be clear, plagiarism is not only a copyright violation but also a breach of your school's honor code, even when you take the trouble to look up synonyms for a few words and rewrite the lead sentences. Don't use Wikipedia as a guide to organize your paper. Even copying the order in which the arguments are made in someone else's work is plagiarism. You need to quote and cite exactly what you copy and paraphrase and cite ideas that you borrow. And having a reference to the work containing the paragraph you are stealing somewhere else in your paper does not cover you; every quote you copy or paraphrase must be properly cited at the point it is found in the text.

Beware—professors can Google, too, and can find the original work you stole. Some colleges and universities buy site licenses for faculty tools to review your papers, such as http://www.turnitin.com, that can pick out passages that were edited to replace keywords. So how many words is it ethically acceptable to copy? None! You need to reinterpret everything, process it in your own words and thoughts, and cite the sources you have used for inspiration. Don't copy and paste information for your notes; reinterpret the information in your own words as you attribute.

Media & Culture

GUIDELINES FOR INTERNET ADVERTISING AND MARKETING

The International Chamber of Commerce developed guidelines to promote high standards of ethics on all forms (text, audio, visual) of advertising and marketing communications. The following is a subset of the original guidelines.

1 – Basic principles All marketing communications should be legal, decent, honest, and truthful.

All marketing communications should be prepared with a due sense of social and professional responsibility and should conform to the principles of fair competition, as generally accepted in business.

No communication should be such as to impair public confidence in marketing.

2 – Honesty Marketing communications should be framed so as not to abuse the trust of consumers or exploit their lack of experience or knowledge.

Relevant factors likely to affect consumers' decisions should be communicated in such a way and at such a time that consumers can take them into account.

3 – Decency Marketing communications should not contain statements or audio or visual treatments that offend standards of decency currently prevailing in the country and culture concerned.

4 – Social responsibility Marketing communications should respect human dignity and should not incite or condone any form of discrimination, including that based upon race, national origin, religion, gender, age, disability, or sexual orientation. Marketing communications should not without justifiable reason play on fear or exploit misfortune or suffering. Marketing communications should not appear to condone or incite violent, unlawful, or antisocial behavior. Marketing communications should not play on superstition.

5 – Truthfulness Marketing communications should be truthful and not misleading.

Marketing communications should not contain any statement, claim, or audio or visual treatment that, directly or by implication, omission, ambiguity, or exaggeration, is likely to mislead the consumer.

6 – Use of technical/scientific data and terminology Marketing communications should not misuse technical data, for example, research results or quotations from technical and scientific publications, present statistics in such a way as to exaggerate the validity of a product claim, or use scientific terminology or vocabulary in such a way as falsely to suggest that a product claim has scientific validity.

7 – Use of "free gift" or "free offer" and "guarantee" This means there is no obligation at all. If shipping is charged or bought in conjunction with another items, then the shipping and the accompanying items should not exceed the price of the "free" product.

8 – Substantiation Descriptions, claims, or illustrations relating to verifiable facts in marketing communications should be capable of substantiation. Such substantiation should be available so that evidence can be produced without delay and upon request to the self-regulatory organizations responsible for the implementation of the Code.

9 – Identification Marketing communications should be clearly distinguishable as such, whatever their form and whatever the medium used. When an advertisement appears in a medium containing news or editorial matter, it should be so presented that it is readily recognizable as an advertisement and the identity of the advertiser should be apparent.

Marketing communications should not misrepresent their true commercial purpose. Hence, a communication promoting the sale of a product should not be disguised as, for example, market research, consumer surveys, user-generated content, private blogs, or independent reviews.

10 – Identity The identity of the marketer should be apparent. Marketing communications should, where appropriate, include contact information to enable the consumer to get in touch with the marketer without difficulty.

11 – Comparisons Marketing communications containing comparisons should be so designed that the comparison is not likely to mislead, and should comply with the principles of fair competition. Points of comparison should be based on facts that can be substantiated and should not be unfairly selected.

12 – Denigration Marketing communications should not denigrate any person or group of persons, firm, organization, industrial or commercial activity, profession, or product, or seek to bring it or them into public contempt or ridicule.

13 – Testimonials These should be genuine and relevant and not out of date.

14 – Portrayal or imitation of persons and references to personal property Permission must be obtained from individuals and private property who are portrayed.

15 – Exploitation of goodwill Marketers must not take advantage of the goodwill of another organization without prior consent.

16 – Imitation Marketing communications should not imitate those of another marketer in any way likely to mislead or confuse the consumer, for example, through the general layout, text, slogan, visual treatment, music, or sound effects.

17 – Safety and health Marketing communications should not, without justification on educational or social grounds, contain any visual portrayal or any description of potentially dangerous practices, or situations that show a disregard for safety or health, as defined by local national standards. Instructions for use should include appropriate safety warnings and, where necessary, disclaimers.

Children should be shown to be under adult supervision whenever a product or an activity involves a safety risk.

18 – Children and young people Special care should be taken in marketing communications directed to or featuring children or young people. The following provisions apply to marketing communications addressed to children and young people as defined in national laws and regulations relevant to such communications.

- Such communications should not undermine positive social behavior, lifestyles, and attitudes;
- Products unsuitable for children or young people should not be advertised in media targeted to them, and advertisements directed to children or young people should not be inserted in media where the editorial matter is unsuitable for them.

19 – Data protection and privacy When collecting personal data from individuals, care should be taken to respect and protect their privacy by complying with relevant rules and regulations.

Collection of data and notice When personal information is collected from consumers, it is essential to ensure that the individuals concerned are aware of the purpose of the collection and of any intention to transfer the data to a third party for that third party's marketing purposes.

Security of processing Adequate security measures should be in place, having regard to the sensitivity of the information, in order to prevent unauthorized access to, or disclosure of, the personal data.

Children's personal information Permission should be obtained from parents or legal guardians before children 12 and younger give any information. As little information as needed should be obtained for the child to participate in the desired activity. The communication with children should not be a means to market communications to the parents or give information to a third party.

Privacy policy Anyone who collects data should have a privacy policy that is readily available to visitors. It should include a clear statement as to whether or not data is being collected.

Rights of the consumer Appropriate measures should be taken to ensure that consumers understand and exercise their rights to opt out of marketing lists (including the right to sign on to general preference (services), to require that their data are not made available to third parties for their marketing purposes, and to rectify incorrect data which are held about them.

20 – Transparency on cost of communication It is to be made clear at the time of a customer's action if a premium cost will be assessed for the purposes of communication.

21 – Unsolicited products and undisclosed costs Customers are not to be charged after-the-fact for unsolicited items. Communications are not to appear as if they require payment, if no payment is necessary.

22 – Environmental behavior Marketers are not to encourage actions that go against policies and standards of good environmental behaviors.

23 – Responsibility Media owners, publishers, marketers, advertising and PR agencies, and individuals are responsible for their decisions and actions.

24 – Effect of subsequent redress for contravention Although a correction might be made, it does not excuse the original action.

25 – Implementation Marketers should be familiar with this Code. Organizations and agencies should apply it where appropriate.

26 – Respect for self-regulatory decisions Marketers should respect the decisions made by self-regulatory bodies and not contradict decisions.

Source: International Chamber of Commerce, the World Business Organization. Available: http://www.iccwbo.org /advocacy-codes-and-rules/document-centre/2011/advertising-and-marketing-communication-practice-(consolidated-icc-code)/

SUMMARY & REVIEW

WHAT ARE MEDIA ETHICS?

Ethics guide communicators in how to behave in situations in which their activities may have a negative impact on others.

WHAT ARE THE MAIN AREAS OF CONCERN IN MEDIA ETHICS?

The main ethical issues that arise in communications media are accuracy or truthfulness, fairness and responsibility of treatment, privacy for media subjects and people in information services, and respect for the intellectual property or ideas of others.

WHAT ARE SOME OF THE BASIC ETHICAL PRINCIPLES?

Some are absolute standards. Kant's categorical imperative directs us to act according to rules that we would like to see universally applied. The "veil of ignorance" involves treating all members of society equally. Other principles make judgments more relative to situations. With situation ethics, for example, moral ideas and judgments must be made in the context of the situation at hand. According to Aristotle's golden mean, "moral virtue is an appropriate location between two extremes." Mill's principle of utility states that we should "seek the greatest happiness for the greatest number." Dewey's pragmatic ethics ask us to judge actions by their results.

WHAT ARE MAJOR CODES OF ETHICS FOR COMMUNICATORS?

The Society of Professional Journalists' Code of Ethics and the Public Relations Society of America's Code of Professional Standards are major codes of ethics for communicators.

WHAT IS POTTER'S BOX?

Developed by Harvard divinity professor Ralph Potter, Potter's Box is a process approach to deciding on ethical actions. In four stages, it defines the facts of the issue, identifies the different values for choices that can be made, looks for general principles that underlie the options identified, and clarifies the ethical priorities.

WHAT ARE THE BASIC ETHICAL PRINCIPLES FOR JOURNALISM?

Journalists are not to fabricate evidence, make up quotes, create hypothetical individuals to focus stories around, or create or manipulate misleading photographs, any of which might deceive the public. They avoid favoritism or partisanship in coverage; protect sources; and avoid corruption, bribery, or accepting favors. Sensationalism in news coverage can affect the process of legal trials. It can affect perceptions of violence, fear, and racial tensions. Pressure to improve ratings or sales can lead to overdramatizing sensational elements and compromising news values. Corporate strategies and vertical integration can lead to unfairly favoring in-house interests. Reporters are usually concerned about protecting their sources, but they also need to refer to them as explicitly as possible to increase the credibility of what they write. Confidentiality of sources is crucial to reporters, both to protect those sources and to gain and maintain access to them. Reporters must make decisions about when to disturb the privacy of individuals.

WHAT ARE THE ETHICAL ISSUES IN PUBLIC RELATIONS?

PR practitioners should deal fairly and responsibly with both clients and the public, not harming the public interest. If a practice is in the best interest of the community, then it probably is in the best interests of the organization. Most practitioners would prefer to be proactive in their public responsibilities, rather than deal with crisis communications—having to react to and clean up a disaster. Some practitioners have to decide between their own moral compass of what is right and the requests of corporate executives who want to make more money at all costs (and who might not have taken an ethics class).

WHAT ARE THE ETHICAL RESPONSIBILITIES OF ENTERTAINMENT PRODUCERS?

Should producers avoid content that can harm their audience? Those who hold the idea of social responsibility for media professionals would say yes, but most entertainment creators say no. Research shows that entertainment may have considerable impact, but industry groups minimize social effects and say that people should make more responsible choices about what they consume.

WHAT ARE THE ETHICS ISSUES FOR ADVERTISING?

In advertising, ethics is about the process of selecting and balancing moral values against profits when writing, designing, or placing advertisements; protecting privacy in direct marketing; and avoiding promotion of harmful products and deceptive advertising.

WHAT ETHICAL BEHAVIOR SHOULD INTERNET USERS CONSIDER?

Internet users should avoid harassment of other users, not misrepresent themselves or others, not violate others' privacy, not use Web sources for plagiarism, and should obtain permission for material they copy onto their websites.

WHAT ARE THE MAIN ETHICAL ISSUES FOR MEDIA CONSUMERS?

Consumers owe reasonable compensation to people who produce intellectual property—the things you read, watch, and listen to—so don't illegally download copyrighted music or videos.

THINKING CRITICALLY
ABOUT THE MEDIA

1. Use Potter's Box to analyze the examples on page 472.

2. Using the ethical principle of your choice, decide if a journalist could justify revealing a source, rather than spending months in jail for contempt.

3. Is it true that exposure to violent TV harms young children? Explain your answer.

4. How do you ethically justify "sharing" music on the Internet? How would you explain that position to Katy Perry or Justin Timberlake?

5. What is plagiarism, and how can you avoid it?

MindTap

Test your knowledge with online printable flashcards and online quizzing.

KEY TERMS

conflict of interest (p. 481)

ethics (p. 472)

fairness and balance (p. 480)

freebies (p. 482)

junket (p. 481)

indecency (p. 485)

morality (p. 472)

trolling (p. 486)

> **MindTap** Log on to the MindTap Communication for *Media Now* to access a variety of additional material, including this chapter's ebook, learning objectives, comprehension quizzes, videos, and more!

GLOBAL COMMUNICATIONS MEDIA

LEARNING OBJECTIVES

After studying the topics in this chapter, you will be able to:

1 Differentiate a "free flow of information" from a "free and balanced flow of information."
2 Define globalization, glocal, regionalization, and cultural proximity.
3 Given an example of entertainment media in a country, determine the most likely countries for exportation based on cultural proximity.
4 Explain why music and television are considered both globalized and localized industries.
5 Weigh the argument that American and European entertainment industries have operated as cultural imperialists throughout the less-developed world.
6 Discuss at least three international challenges that face all Internet users.
7 Consider how globalization will change the nature of some U.S. media.

ACTING GLOBALLY, REGIONALLY, AND NATIONALLY

The global aspect of media is very striking. Sometimes it looks like **cultural imperialism,** in which media products made in the United States dominate popular culture worldwide. *The Simpsons* was on television in over 200 countries in 2015, while *Star Wars: The Force Awakens* covered many movie and video screens worldwide, making far more money abroad than inside the United States. Young women in South Korea once outraged their elders by modeling their lives on *Sex and the City*, but now star in Korean dramas seen worldwide. Australian media magnate Rupert Murdoch's various companies reach about three-fourths of the globe with satellite TV signals and even more countries with movies and TV programs.

Hu Zhiqing/Newscom/ZUMA Press/Beijing/China

WHAT'S ON IN CHINA IS SOME-TIMES THE SAME as what's on where you live. A growing number of countries are not only taking in U.S. imports, but also creating their own media and exporting to other countries.

501

MindTap®

Start with a quick warm-up activity.

However, global media are far from a Hollywood monopoly. *The Simpsons* is made by animators in South Korea, for example. Some major U.S. media companies are or have recently been owned by Japanese (Sony) or Canadian (Warner Records) companies. Rupert Murdoch is a good example of a global media empire based first in Australia, then the United Kingdom, and now the United States but reaching far beyond all three. Mexican and Brazilian soap operas (telenovelas) reach as many countries as *Friends* and are extremely popular in some places, such as Eastern Europe and Central Asia. Facebook is one of the most popular websites in over 130 countries worldwide, but faces significant local competition in some parts of the world, from companies such as Renren in China. When AT&T invested in foreign telecommunications companies, it had to compete closely with British Telecom (Great Britain) and Telefónica (Spain) abroad and with T-Mobile (Germany) in the United States.

Although American-made films, TV programs, and music remain attractive to world audiences, other global, regional, national, and local media industries, audiences, and regulatory bodies are emerging, with a wide variety of ideas, genres, and agendas. More countries are competing to sell or transmit media to others (see Figure 18.1). Some, such as Mexico, Brazil, India, and South Korea, compete worldwide. Popular music from South Korea is gaining audiences across the globe, building on "Gangnam Style" by Psy, which topped Billboard charts in the United States and was the first music video to top 1 billion views globally. Turkey, Egypt, and Lebanon dominate a regional market in the Middle East characterized by shared geography, language and /or culture, similar to the regional market for Mexican television that includes U.S. Hispanics.

Globalization of media is probably most pervasive at the level of technology and media industry models—ways of organizing and creating media. The

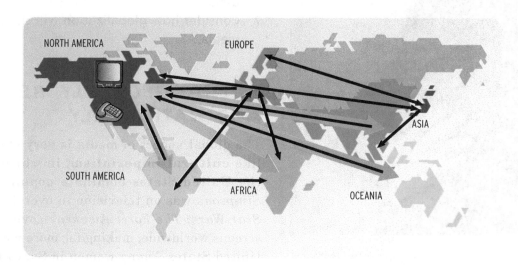

FIGURE 18.1 INTERNATIONAL MEDIA FLOWS Although the United States has initially dominated international flows in most media, other countries are beginning to sell more media and information to each other. (In the figure, wider arrows indicate heavier flows.)

world is becoming a more integrated market based in capitalist, or market-place, economics. This exerts pressures on nations to make media more commercial, supported by advertising, aimed at consumers, and to privatize or commercialize telecommunications or other media companies that were once government owned.

Most countries produce increasing amounts of their own television, music, Internet content, and magazines. But if they produce them by drawing on U.S., British, or Japanese models and genre ideas or formats licensed from media companies headquartered in those countries, those "national" media products are still at least somewhat globalized. And even if a national soap opera reflects largely local culture in its plot and characters, it still helps Colgate-Palmolive and other multinational firms sell soap in yet another part of the global market, as it did when Colgate-Palmolive sponsored the Chinese production of the Colombian (and U.S.) soap opera *Ugly Betty*. Roland Robertson (1995) called such combinations **glocal**—local productions done with global forms and ideas.

> **Glocal** is local people borrowing or adapting global ideas.

At the same time, truly globalized markets are emerging as many youth the world over are exposed to the Internet and shop online for the latest fashions and consumer products. Procter and Gamble finds that teenage girls everywhere seem to have the same questions about puberty, for example, so they can simply translate the material on their website into 40 different languages instead of developing a separate website in each country. Controversy rages about global campaigns, however, and other firms find it better to go local in their marketing strategies.

Global institutions and companies also have a major impact. Global regulatory bodies, such as the International Telecommunication Union (ITU), allocate satellite orbits, determine broadcast frequencies, and define the standards for telephones, mobile phones, faxes, and Internet connections. The ITU is the oldest part of the United Nations, dating back to 1865, because some international regulator was required to achieve compatibility of telegraph standards and rates between countries, to enable commerce and news flows between them. The ITU would like to allocate Internet domains and other resources, too. The United States had opposed that idea, but under considerable global pressure, is moving to make Internet governance more global (see Chapter 10). Global telecom companies, like Cable & Wireless of the United Kingdom or Telefónica of Spain, run much of the world's communications infrastructure of optical fiber cables, satellites, and high-speed lines. Global media companies, like Rupert Murdoch's News Corporation, not only reach people directly with media but also force domestic competitors to react to them. When Murdoch's Star TV started broadcasting in India, the state television broadcaster had to respond with more competitive entertainment or lose its audience. However, when Murdoch went into China, he had to bend to their rules to do business, which shows that global companies are not equally powerful everywhere. Nation-states can still be powerful if they are well organized and determined; witness the 2014 ruling in the European Union giving its citizens the "right to delete" links to misleading, defamatory content about themselves.

1865

ITU (International Telecommunication Union) begins as the International Telegraph Union

MEDIA THEN··· MEDIA NOW

1865
> ITU (International Telecommunication Union) begins as the International Telegraph Union

1914–1945
> World Wars I and II permit Hollywood to outplace competitors

1945
> UN founded, incorporating ITU, starting UNESCO

1976
> UNESCO hosts critical discussion for proposals for a New World Information Order

1990
> Satellite TV begins to compete with national control of television

2003
> ITU hosts World Summit on the Information Society to promote use of the Internet in poorer countries

2010
> Google violates European Union privacy protections by collecting street-level data

2016
> Facebook has 1.59 billion members worldwide

MindTap

Read, highlight, and take notes on the complete chapter text in a rich interactive online platform.

Regionalization links nations together based on geographic, cultural, linguistic, and historical commonalities.

The other major aspect of globalization is the increasingly worldwide penetration of media technology. All nations now have quite a few people using the Internet and satellite television. Those new media can greatly increase global reach and access for many. However, global new media reach coexists with a global digital divide. Twenty years ago, both the rich and the poor's experience with media relied on television. Now, this has changed. While over 90 percent of South Koreans have broadband Internet access, less than 2 percent of Mozambicans have any kind of Internet access.

Regionalization

Regionalization of media is growing as well. In several regions of the world (such as Europe, North and South America, and the Middle East), magazines, newspapers, and books have been transported easily across borders for centuries, serving regions of common language or culture. In South and East Asia, such communication by print and by movement of teachers has been going on for millennia. Radio, television, and satellite television signals also spilled directly from one country to its neighbor. Well over half of the Canadian population can directly receive U.S. radio and television signals, for example.

In the European Union (EU) and the North American Free Trade Agreement (NAFTA) regions (Canada, the United States, and Mexico), governments have negotiated agreements on how to handle such media border crossings. The EU went further in 1989 to try to have "television without frontiers" within the EU. However, the attempt to produce programming for a Europe-wide television market proved difficult, despite being promoted heavily by the EU. Europeans are still divided by language and culture, and many don't want to watch, read, or listen in another language (Schlesinger, 1991), although sports and music, which transcend cultural and linguistic barriers more easily, have helped pan-European television channels grow and find audiences. The French still prefer French television to German or British television. However, Europeans are more willing to listen to other nations' music. The Eurovision song contest is one of the most widely watched pan-European productions, even though many tune in to cheer on whoever is representing their country that year. So the music industry has regionalized somewhat farther in Europe than television, even as some countries, particularly France, still tend to protect their national film industries.

Cultural Proximity

Although geographical closeness or proximity helps media cross borders, language and culture seem more important than geography, as the example of Europe shows. It seems that people there and elsewhere tend to look for television programming, Internet sites, and music that are more culturally proximate, or relevant, to them.

Cultural proximity is the desire for cultural products as similar as possible to one's own language, culture, history, and values. Thus, even though people often like the cosmopolitan appeal of some European or American television, movies, and music, they tend to choose most of their media from their own or a similar culture because it is more familiar and interesting to them.

Language is a crucial divider of media markets. Historically, trade in television between countries has been shaped by language (Straubhaar, 2007), and language seems to be shaping Internet patterns as well, so far. Language provides a strong natural barrier to media imports. The United States is a prime example. Most of what little imported television and film Americans watch comes from Great Britain, Canada, New Zealand, or Australia, culturally similar English-speaking countries. Likewise, British pop music is widely accepted, whereas other musicians, such as the Icelandic group Sigur Rós, have to sing in English to break into the U.S. market. This also indicates a countertrend: many global youth are getting more used to listening to music in English, to the point where the band playing at a wedding in the global television hit *Game of Thrones,* in 2014, was Sigur Rós.

Besides language, other aspects of culture are important in defining audiences: jokes, slang, historical references, political references, the familiarity of landscapes and cityscapes, gossip about stars, and remarks about current people and events are often culture or nation specific. Such cues, where they are shared across borders, can help build cross-national markets. For instance,

> **Cultural proximity** is the preference of audiences for media in their own language and culture.

CRIME PAYS GLOBALLY Although most countries produce an increasing number of their own TV shows, highly produced U.S. shows that emphasize crime or action-adventure, such as *CSI: Crime Scene Investigation,* can still sell to many countries.

Latin American countries used to import American situation comedies in the 1950s and 1960s. Now they tend to import comedy shows from each other, because the cultural proximity of Spanish-speaking Latin American nations makes slang, jokes, and references to current events easier to understand. This is also true for U.S. Spanish-speaking audiences, who usually prefer Mexican shows to Hollywood, since Mexican, Colombian, or even Brazilian shows (in translation from Portuguese to Spanish) feel more familiar.

However, many producers have discovered that when they make too many references to current politics, use too much slang, or otherwise focus too narrowly on current local issues, their programs are less well received around the world. Hollywood has long experienced this dilemma. Sometimes a very popular sitcom, such as *Seinfeld,* is too specific to the United States for broad export in the global market, whereas a show such as *Sex and the City* or *The Simpsons* does better abroad.

Although cultural proximity is a strong factor, audiences in many countries still respond very well to some kinds of imported programs, particularly those whose emphasis is on action, sex, and violence, where dialogue or cultural nuances are minimized. So many of the most popular U.S. films now focus on action and are explicitly aimed at foreign markets, since they often bring in up to three times as much revenue as the North American market itself (MPAA, 2015).

Conversely, a rising trend calls for local versions of popular shows, such as the Brazilian version *of Big Brother,* in its 15th season in 2015. Those who prefer an imported program are also more likely to be well-off, better educated, and urban. Among the few foreign, non-English-speaking genres to be hits in the United States are stylish, violent action films from Hong Kong and China, love dramas from Korea, and sexy, violent cartoons from Japan. Sports are another genre with nearly universal appeal. And some elements of pop music are globalized, whereas others are **localized:** another example that complicates the logic of cultural proximity.

Smaller than global, but larger than national, **cultural–linguistic markets** build on transnational cultural proximity. These markets build on common languages and common cultures that span borders. Just as the United States grew beyond its own market to export globally, a number of companies have grown beyond their original national markets to serve these cultural–linguistic markets, such as Mexico for Latin America and much of the Hispanic United States.

> **Localization** refers to a global company adapting its programs to local markets to make them more attractive.

> **Cultural–linguistic markets** build on common languages and common cultures that span borders.

National Production

However, even as global and cultural linguistic markets for media are all increasingly important, the main point at which media are paid for through advertising or fees, created, regulated, and consumed remains the nation. The majority of media companies have been structured, at least at first, to serve national markets, even though transnational and global companies are on the rise. National governments have far more effective control over media through station licensing, economic controls, technology controls, and subsidies than regional or global institutions or treaties. And ratings and audience research over the years tend to show that, given a choice, people tend to prefer to see national content in media (de Sola Pool, 1983; Straubhaar, 2007; Tracey, 1988).

Nations vary considerably, however, in what they can or will do to create media. Companies based in larger, more prosperous nations can create more media content than those in small, poorer nations. Production companies in the United States, the United Kingdom, Japan, India, South Korea, and other mediamedia powers can afford lavish production values that may overwhelm the modest productions of local media. This has been especially notable in film, where U.S. exports dominate more than in television or websites. There can be a contradictory tug-of-war between cultural proximity and imported production values, or the cosmopolitan appeal of sophisticated imported programs.

National governments can help or hinder media growth. National goals for media, reflected in government policies, are often very different, and they significantly affect how media are structured and what they create. Some nations, like China, expect media to cooperate with government political and economic goals. Some, like Saudi Arabia or Pakistan, expect media to project a certain set of religious values.

The Global Media

Thirty years ago, people talked about Americanization of media in the world. Today, they talk more about globalization. Although American media still play a prominent role in the global scene, media industries from a number of other countries are also heavily involved across the world. There are also media whose goal is to cover a region, like Al Jazeera in the Middle East, or the globe, like the BBC World Service. And some media, like Facebook, now explicitly target the world even if they started in a very specific place, like Harvard University.

A handful of publicly traded firms dominate the most globalized part of the media system. Some of the largest are Disney (U.S.), Comcast (U.S.), Rupert Murdoch's News Corporation (Australian/U.S.), AT&T (U.S.), Bertelsmann (German), Viacom (U.S.), Warner-EMI (Canada), and Sony/Columbia/TriStar (Japanese). The other main global firms are Apple (U.S.), Microsoft (U.S.), Google (U.S.), Facebook (U.S.), Amazon (U.S.), and Vivendi (French). Of the top 12–13 global media firms, eight to nine are American, depending on how one defines groups like News Corp (Anglo-American). These types of companies are growing and globalizing quickly. Time Warner and Disney generated around 15 percent of their income outside of the United States in 2014. By 2014, countries outside

BONO, FROM GLOBAL SUPERSTAR TO GLOBAL DEVELOPMENT AID ACTIVIST A number of entertainment superstars, such as Bono, Shakira, and Angelina Jolie, are trying to convert the fame and symbolic capital they have acquired into a different kind of star power to try to draw people to the cause of increasing development aid for the world's poor, which all are promoting in different ways. This kind of activism goes back at least to George Harrison's Concert for Bangladesh in the early 1970s.

the United States represented 70 percent of the total box office for all films (MPAA, 2015). AT&T's recent acquisition of satellite TV giant DirecTV was motivated, in part, by a desire to expand into South American markets, where DirecTV had millions of subscribers.

Behind the top global firms is a second tier of 30 to 40 media firms that make between $1 and $10 billion yearly in media-related business. These firms have national or cultural–linguistic strongholds or specialize in specific global niches, as the BBC specializes in news and documentaries. Some are American (including Gannett and Cox). Most of the rest come from Europe (Hachette, Havas, EMI) or Canada (Rogers, Shaw). Some are based in East Asia (NHK, Chinese Central TV) and Latin America (TV Globo, Televisa). It is no stretch to add computer media, games, and telecommunications, so we should add Google, Apple, and Microsoft; game companies Nintendo and Electronic Arts; and telecoms like AT&T, Deutsche Telecom, TelMex /América Movil (Mexico), and Telefónica to the list. Social media giant Facebook could be a dominant force in global media if it achieves its plans to reach most of the world's mobile phones. So are messaging/social media programs, like WhatsApp, purchased by Facebook in 2014 to extend its reach both in the United States and globally.

Some media industries, such as advertising agency J. Walter Thompson, former radio giant RCA, and the Hollywood film and TV studios represented by the Motion Picture Association of America (MPAA), have been global since the 1920s. They control many of the companies in other countries that distribute and exhibit (in theaters) the films produced in the United States. However, the ownership of Hollywood itself became globalized, when Sony purchased Columbia and TriStar film groups. Critics scrutinized the results to see whether films produced by Sony reflected Japanese rather than American sensibilities. No real changes were found. However, both Bollywood (India) and Nollywood (Nigeria) are challenging Hollywood by turning out thousands of films at lower cost, and releasing them for much lower costs, too.

Record companies are similarly structured except that they have a more diverse set of origins and an even more international ownership. Parts of the music Big Three are based outside the United States, including Warner-EMI (Canada/Russia), Sony-BMG Music Group (Japan–Germany), and Vivendi-Universal (France). Russian company Access bought a 2 percent stake in Warner Music Group in 2011 before it acquired EMI (a British record label). These companies also have large foreign branches that produce and distribute records within other markets, as well as distribute American and European music.

However, as music production becomes much cheaper all over the world, more groups are recording at all levels: local, national, and regional. Those sell now in many forms—cassettes, CDs, MP3s, and streaming online. Piracy is also so prevalent inmost places that music groups earn a living mostly from live performances.

Still, there are some important distinctions in the ways that various media are organized around the world. In the following sections, we will consider those differences and analyze the flow of media between them.

News Agencies

News has flowed across borders for hundreds of years. Many early newspapers and newsletters installed correspondents in other countries so that they could publish foreign news for their readers.

After the 1840s, newswire services, based on the then-new technology of the telegraph, the U.S. Associated Press (AP), British Reuters, and Agence France Presse (AFP) were the first electronic news services, anticipating the increase in speed and volume of information of the Internet. By the 1970s, many critics asserted that the major newswire services had too much control over international news flow. They followed standard American and European definitions of what was news: disasters, sensational or unusual events, political upheaval, wars or conflicts, famous personalities, and current (versus long-term) events. Although this approach fits the Western ideal of the press as a critic and watchdog, it often produces negative coverage and images of other countries.

As radio and television became the dominant news media in many countries, the wire services developed material for them, and later, so did satellite news channels like CNN. News agencies now have to compete with the many news sources now available to everyone online. Al Jazeera (Doha), CCTV 9 (China), and Russia Today have also pushed television news operations into a number of countries, becoming alternative news sources, although often with a strong national point of view and questionable credibility. Now information and reporting by a variety of people on Twitter have become both direct news sources for many and sources that professional news reporters use in their own stories. This became particularly clear with microblogging in China and Twitter's role in the Arab Spring political and social revolutions of 2011, although many now argue that face-to-face communication, grassroots organizing, and mass media were all more important than Twitter in terms of lasting effects.

Radio Broadcasting

Because the print media's reach is limited in many countries by low literacy and purchasing power, broadcast media took on increased importance. In the poorest countries, radio is still the main mass medium for many people. However, in parts of Africa and South Asia, some people do not even have access to radio because the signal doesn't reach them, they can't afford a receiver, or they don't have electricity or the means to recharge batteries.

International radio. In some of the poorest countries, where domestic radio stations don't cover the whole country, people in remote areas may listen to international broadcasters. International radio, whether continent-spanning

STOP & REVIEW

1. What is globalization?

2. What is cultural proximity?

3. What are some of the bases that define cultural–linguistic markets for media?

4. What are the main reasons why companies buy or start up media in other countries?

5. Which companies are the main global owners of media?

6. How does news flow between countries?

commercial radio stations such as Africa One, or foreign government stations such as the Voice of America (VOA), Radio France, and the BBC, is usually on short-wave frequencies that can carry across thousands of miles (Straubhaar & Boyd, 2007). New services have begun in hotspot areas, like Radio Sawa by the United States in Arabic in the Middle East. Such international radio programs now try to use medium wave radio, which can be received by more people than short wave.

National radio. In most countries, national and local radio become much more important than international radio. Many countries have important national radio networks, which are widely listened to, but in many places radio is becoming more local. Radio can cater to the apparently widespread audience desire for local news, local weather and information, local talk shows, and local music. In radio, the urge for cultural proximity by audiences and market segmentation by advertisers often favors the very local, although people still want to hear national and global music and news. Local music can reflect local preferences in local languages, and local news and talk tend to cover the things that most concern people in daily life. In Wales, some radio stations try to attract people to listening in Welsh in order to help keep the language alive and sell ads to the locals. A growing global community radio movement, trying to get more community groups on the air, strengthens this trend, usually bringing together community groups, nonprofits, and, sometimes, international aid agencies.

Music

Music around the world seems to be both the most globalized and the most localized of media. Travelers to almost any country will hear a great deal of American and European music, but they will also hear an astonishing variety of local music—nearly all cultures have a musical tradition (and a market niche for it). Such traditional music usually adapts well to being recorded, played on the radio, streamed online, and sold on CDs.

The strength of national and local radio has a great deal to do with a revival in national and local music around the globe. Beyoncé, as well as transnational artists like Shakira, can be heard around the world on many stations that appeal to affluent and globalized young people, but other stations are playing music by local artists as well, which tend to appeal to more middle-class, working-class, and poor people (IFPI, 2015).

There is a truly global music industry, based primarily in the United States and Europe, which speaks to a globalized youth culture. But there are also thriving national and regional music industries, with a wide variety of genres and audiences, which also remain popular in most countries. Historically, audience tastes tend to be multilayered, with many people listening to global music, regional or national music, and local music to suit different needs and interests, including local advertisers (Colista & Leshner, 1998). Technology changes, like global flow of music files over the Internet, can increase access to U.S. music, but new

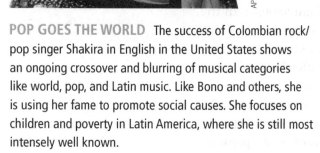

AP Images/Andrew Medichin

POP GOES THE WORLD The success of Colombian rock/pop singer Shakira in English in the United States shows an ongoing crossover and blurring of musical categories like world, pop, and Latin music. Like Bono and others, she is using her fame to promote social causes. She focuses on children and poverty in Latin America, where she is still most intensely well known.

technologies, like Internet radio, digital downloads or streaming, and videos on YouTube are all increasingly used for regional and national music.

Governments sometimes require that a certain proportion of nationally produced music be played on radio stations. For example, Canada requires satellite radio Sirius to include Canadian content. Some also subsidize national music industries to make sure that local music is produced. Most often, music development has been left to musicians' initiative, market forces, and audience demand. Audience members are often willing to pay for local and national music, although they also listen to and purchase global music. Music, too, is much cheaper to produce than film or television—so much so that it serves a wide variety of subcultures and market niches within and across nations, such as Turkish music among Turkish residents in Germany.

One threat to both global and local music industries is piracy. In many countries, like Russia, local and national musicians simply cannot make any money at all by selling recordings, since nearly all copies sold are pirated illegally. The only way such artists support themselves is by touring and giving concerts, which deters many from being professional musicians.

The major companies that dominate international music import and sell the dominant American and European pop music around the world. In many countries and regions, they also record and sell works by national or cultural–linguistic market artists. That gives them a stake in promoting those artists, both at home and abroad, when they perceive that there might be an export market. Multinational firms record Jamaican reggae and dance hall as well as Caribbean salsa and Mexican *norteño,* sell them at home, and also export them to the United States. Those international companies are willing to risk distributing national music recordings, because musical tastes are more diverse and the costs (and financial risks) of recording, distributing, and promoting music recordings are much lower than those of film or TV. So global firms end up selling both global and local music.

Film

Of all the international media examined here, film is perhaps the most globalized and the most difficult to produce on a sustained national basis. A map produced by UNESCO for 2013 shows how few countries produce large numbers of film (see Figure 18.2).

Historically, Hollywood film gained a decisive advantage when World War I and then World War II destroyed or weakened competing film industries in Germany, Italy, France, Japan, and Great Britain. After World War II, U.S. government pressure on both conquered nations and former allies pushed them to open their markets wider to U.S. films in order to receive postwar aid.

There are also several current reasons why film production, finance, and distribution remain concentrated in the United States and its coproduction partners. First, film is a relatively expensive medium to produce. Even cheap feature films, paying almost nothing to actors and technicians, cost hundreds of thousands of dollars, and an average Hollywood film costs over $85 million. Cheaper digital production equipment has started to change this, as seen with the proliferation of thousands of quickly shot, low-budget Nigerian "Nollywood" films on video. However, overall, global promotion costs continue to rise sharply. Second, the economic success of a film is never guaranteed, so it represents an expensive, risky

1914–1945

World Wars I and II permit Hollywood to outpace competitors

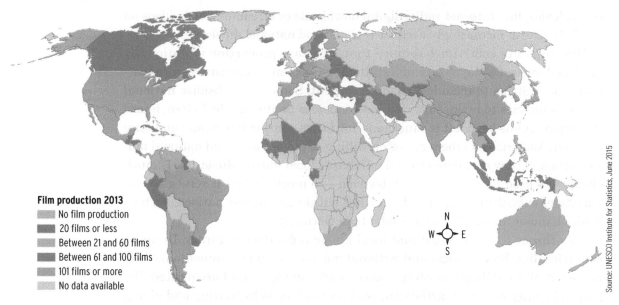

Film production 2013

- No film production
- 20 films or less
- Between 21 and 60 films
- Between 61 and 100 films
- 101 films or more
- No data available

Source: UNESCO Institute for Statistics, June 2015

FIGURE 18.2 **THE HIGH CONCENTRATION OF FILM MAKING IN THE WORLD:**
Very few counties in the world make over 100 films a year.

investment to the producer, investors, and other funding sources, which many countries are unable to sustain. Third, the distribution channels to enable a film to make money have been globalized to a greater degree than any other medium, except news services. Films from independent producers or from outside the English-speaking world have a hard time breaking into the international distribution system, which is largely controlled by companies associated with the Motion Picture Association of America (MPAA). However, as overseas markets like China grow larger than the U.S. market, the Chinese government can and does demand edits in Hollywood films released in China, to better fit Chinese sensibilities. And films that do strongly offend other nations, like "The Interview," which showed a comic assassination attempt against the leader of North Korea, led to a major 2014 computer hack of Sony and the release of many documents very embarrassing to it.

However, an increasing number of firms, like Fox and Sony, do actively look for international films to distribute in the United States and abroad, as well as for opportunities to coproduce films with foreign companies (see Figure 18.3). That can reverse, too, as Chinese and Indian producers have begun to invest in U.S. companies and initiate coproductions in the U.S. Figure 18.3. Even Disney has begun to look for international cartoons to distribute, like those of Japanese Hayao Miyazaki, such as *The Wind Rises* (2013). Some foreign films, like *The Past* (France/Iran, 2013), are internationally distributed and do well, but most films produced in other countries never get distributed outside their home countries. Even some of the more successful ones, such as the well-regarded original Swedish version of *Girl with the Dragon Tattoo* (2009), do less well with American audiences than U.S. remakes, like the 2011 U.S. version of *Girl with the Dragon Tattoo.*

Films of significant quality and interest have been produced in many countries, but few countries are currently producing many feature films. A number of poor nations, such as the Dominican Republic, have produced only a few feature-length films in their histories—and some have made none at all. Furthermore, film production has slowed down in many countries, such as most of Latin America and Africa, as many companies or government production institutes have fallen

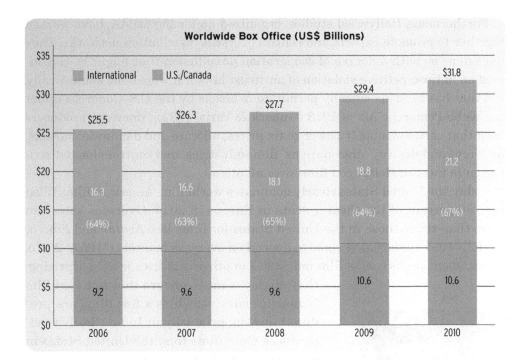

Worldwide Box Office (US$ Billions)

FIGURE 18.3 **RISING IMPORTANCE OF GLOBAL FILM EXPORTS TO HOLLYWOOD**
Although the U.S. and Canadian markets remain the most important to Hollywood, other markets, like Europe and the Asia Pacific, have grown greatly between 2006 and 2015.

into debt or suffered other economic crises. In a number of countries where film production had been heavily subsidized, governments have found themselves unable to continue support. Some countries, including France and Spain, still continue to subsidize their film industries, but this led to conflicts in trade talks (such as the World Trade Agreement) with the United States, which considers these subsidies an unfair form of protectionism (U.S. Department of Commerce, 2004). The big problem is that international films, even when produced at national expense, do not break through the largely Hollywood-based control of international distribution, and most national markets, with the exception of larger nations like Brazil, India, Nigeria, and China, are not big enough to make money with films that have little chance of international distribution.

There are several key reasons why American films have dominated in a variety of markets. One is the enormous size of the U.S. market for movies, which for many years permitted Hollywood to recover most of the costs of films in their domestic release, although now Hollywood depends increasingly on overseas sales for much of their profits. Even now, however, few other countries have such a large and affluent national film audience, although China has just overtaken the United States as the most lucrative market. Second is the heterogeneous nature of the U.S. audience, which includes diverse groups that demand simple, more entertainment oriented, and more universal films. Because of these elements, Hollywood has been the world's film production center, drawing money and talent from around the world and away from competing film industries abroad. Since the 1920s, Hollywood has drawn actors, directors, writers, and musicians from Europe, Latin America, and Asia (Guback & Varis, 1982). This continues with recent talent like Alejandro González Iñárritu, from Mexico, who just directed the Oscar best film winner in 2016, *The Revenant*.

Furthermore, Hollywood studios, organized under the MPAA, have worked together to promote exports and control overseas distribution networks. They have done so with a degree of cooperation or collusion that might be considered an anticompetitive violation of antitrust laws if it were done domestically, but that has been specifically permitted overseas by the U.S. Congress under the Webb-Pomerene Act of 1918 (Guback & Varis, 1982). American producers used that cartel monopoly power to fix prices, allocate and dominate markets, undercut and destroy other nations' film industries, and control global distribution in favor of Hollywood films over all others.

Today, the United States clearly dominates world film. American films filled over 80 percent of the theater seats in Europe in 2014. Overseas sales can more than triple those in the United States for films like *Avatar* and *Frozen,* so Hollywood studios have come to depend on overseas markets (MPAA, 2015). Government protection of film industries in other countries is not surprising: they simply want to ensure that national film industries survive. Quite a few films are produced in Asia, primarily in India ("Bollywood" produces more films than the United States in most years) and China. Egypt is the film center of the Arab world and Nigeria ("Nollywood") of West Africa. Brazil and Mexico produce far more films than other Latin American countries. These countries show that film industries can be maintained, even in some developing countries, if the domestic market is large or if the film companies produce for a multicountry audience and market. Some countries are also getting creative with financial incentives to promote national film production. Since Brazil, for example, began letting national and international companies deduct any losses on Brazilian film investment from their taxes, film investment and production has shot up to over 100 films a year, a small number compared to the United States, Nigeria, China, or India, but significant by international standards. While some countries, like Brazil or France, are primarily aiming to be more self-sufficient in film, others, like China, clearly have their eyes on producing more for global markets, whether alone; with regional partners, as is common in Europe; or with Hollywood. Similarly, to enter China's market, where foreign films are limited by government quota, many U.S. groups are now coproducing with Chinese groups to either avoid those quotas or simply make the films more attractive to Chinese audiences.

Many international producers have started working with Hollywood in financing,

Nigel Bowles/John Connor Press Associates LTD/Newscom

STAR OF YOUTUBE Swedish web-based comedian and video producer, Felix Arvid Ulf Kjellberg, known by the followers of his YouTube Channel as PewDiePie, has won awards, raised money for charities, and influenced video game sales through the international popularity of his YouTube channel.

distribution, or even broader coproduction. Some countries, like Canada, offer sizable production incentives, which have moved Hollywood companies to shoot there. It is becoming common to shoot exteriors in one country and sound stage scenes in another, edit sound in another, and add special effects in yet another. The *Narnia* and *Lord of the Rings* films all featured British stories; actors from the United Kingdom, the United States, Australia, and New Zealand; New Zealand locations and special effects; and U.S. financing and distribution. In many ways, Hollywood is becoming a very globalized force, with different parts of the labor of making films shifting to a variety of countries (special effects to the United Kingdom and New Zealand), low-cost shooting locales to many places, while finance and distribution remain centered in Hollywood itself.

Video

In many countries, films are now most commonly seen on video or on television, rather than in cinema houses. In the more affluent parts of most countries, increasing numbers of the middle class and economic elite have DVDs, satellite or cable TV, and Internet downloads or streaming to watch films or TV. U.S. productions largely dominate video rental stocks as well, since the same Hollywood firms that dominate theatrical distribution supply them. DVD sales or rentals are actually somewhat more diverse, since there are parallel circuits for distributing films and television programs from local producers in China, Korea, Turkey, Nigeria, and India to immigrant populations around the world who miss media from home. An increasing number of countries created cable channels that show nationally produced movies almost exclusively, which provides a notable distribution vehicle for national films that many viewers would not otherwise see.

Another new trend, streaming on-demand services, like Netflix, are complicating film and television distribution. Netflix has been pushing international growth hard, and now services over 130 countries in 20 languages. Its largely U.S. catalog is drawing many younger, usually more affluent, viewers. That seems to create a new wave of U.S. or Hollywood dominance; even Netflix is also pushing into coproduction in many countries, including Brazil, Colombia, and Norway.

Film finance is also drifting offshore. Mainland China is beginning to emerge as a financial power in film production. Both private investors and a government-backed media fund are backing coproductions with Hollywood studios. *Iron Man 3,* for example, was a Chinese-American coproduction.

Television

Television broadcasting in many countries is divided among public, governmental, and private ownership. Television had been very expensive, too expensive for private media to make it profitable in some very poor countries. Through their frequency licensing power, almost all governments get involved in planning who gets to own or operate radio or television stations, which also leads many of them to get involved in controlling content. However, as "television" becomes more broadly defined to include a variety of video production on channels like YouTube, a much bigger variety of actors are getting involved.

Satellite TV begins to compete with national control of television

In Africa, Asia, and Eastern Europe, governments often have owned-and-operated broadcasting systems in order to control radio and TV content. Their stated intention has usually been to use radio and television as powerful tools to develop their societies, but controlling politics is often the hidden agenda. India's state television, Doordarshan, initially tried to use television to teach better health and agricultural practices to villagers, but in the 1970s and 1980s, then-prime minister of India, Indira Gandhi, also discovered it to be a very powerful political tool (Kumar, 2006). In addition, urban and middle-class viewers of the single national channel rebelled, demanding more entertainment. After that, Doordarshan had to be content to insert subtle pro-development themes, such as child health care and family planning, into soap operas that people like to watch (Singhal & Rogers, 2001). Satellite and cable television after 1990 also brought in new forms of competition in much of the world, which forced broadcast television to change. This has been true in India, Europe, Turkey, several Arab nations, and several parts of Asia. So, now India's Doordarshan has to compete with hundreds of commercial television channels, all on satellite or cable TV, aimed not only nationally but also at over a dozen regional languages, not to mention an explosion of television on the Internet.

Access to television is still somewhat unequal around the globe. In some parts of the world, including much of Africa, most of the population still doesn't watch television, particularly outside the main cities. In Mozambique, one of the poorest countries, only around 35 to 40 percent of the population has a television, mostly the same 30 to 35 percent who speak Portuguese, the language used on television. In contrast, most people in Latin America and East and South Asia have television, even the poor. Most people in the world have worked very hard to gain access to television, perhaps more than any other medium, other than cell phones, which many now use to watch digital video or even more conventional television programs. One of the authors of this book has visited Brazilian, Peruvian, and South African homes where auto batteries powered the TV sets in homes with no other electricity.

In many countries, including most of Western Europe, either governments or not-for-profit public corporations originally operated television broadcasting. Since the 1990s, a number of these countries have also introduced commercial television, which became economically and culturally powerful. The goal of public broadcasters has been to use broadcasting to promote education and culture. An example is the BBC in Great Britain. To a large extent, the public broadcasters in Europe and Japan have outpaced the U.S. Public Broadcasting System (PBS) and National Public Radio in creating more educational, informational, and cultural programming. However, in some countries,

DRAWING POWER In many places, people see TV as so important that it comes before almost all other purchases. Even temporary shelters like this one may have a dish to receive satellite TV.

AP Images/Enric Marti

public broadcasters sometimes have let political parties control their news and information programs. A good example is Italy, where Silvio Berlusconi rose to political power by controlling the dominant three private networks, then maintained power, despite his conviction for tax evasion, by also controlling the three public television networks as prime minister.

State broadcasters are usually supported from government funds. Public radio and television networks are often supported by audience license fees. This is in order to maintain independence from both government budget control and commercial pressures by advertisers. In Britain and Japan, everyone who owns a radio or a television set pays an annual license fee. That fee goes directly to the public broadcasters (BBC in Britain and NHK in Japan), who use it to finance program production and development. Some audiences in Great Britain have complained that programming tends to be elitist and stiff. In 2007, the hallowed and venerable "beeb," as it is known, was told point blank by the British government to be more entertaining if it wanted its license renewed in the future. Faced with a growing unwillingness on the part of the government to support higher license fees, the "beeb" was forced to make deep cuts in its staff and cut back on original programming in 2014. It was also forced to make its overseas operations commercial to try to raise money to support its domestic production, which theoretically remains noncommercial, but obviously has to coordinate with the global commercial operations, like BBC America.

Broadcasting has mostly been privately owned in Canada, Central America, and South America, in part because of the strong influence of U.S. media corporations and advertisers, who promoted commercial approaches in the 1930s and 1940s (Schwoch, 1990). However, government controls over private broadcasters have varied among these countries. In contrast to the minimal controls in the United States, there are stricter controls in Canada, where the government has tried to restrict the importation of programs from the United States. Many Latin American and Eastern European governments have exerted strong control over private broadcasters to obtain political support, mostly through economic pressures, such as selectively awarding licenses or government advertising to supportive broadcasters. In most of the private broadcasting systems, entertainment programming has dominated to meet the demands of advertisers for large audiences.

Since 1990, European, Asian, and other countries have increased private commercial broadcasting and reduced government and public ownership. Publics often push for more broadcast choices (especially when more channels are already coming in via satellite and the Internet), and advertisers, both foreign and local, pushed to have commercial stations to put advertising on. Most countries have liberalized competition in broadcasting by permitting new private companies and individuals to enter the market. They often come from print publishing, such as Silvio Berlusconi, ex-prime minister of Italy, who still controls the three major private Italian television networks. Many countries also privatized some public or government broadcast stations and networks. Sometimes this was to reduce government political control over state stations, such as when France privatized some of the state television networks to reduce state political power. Sometimes, too, **privatizing** was done to take broadcasting out of the public budget and make it privately supported through

Privatizing government assets refers to selling them to private owners.

advertising. Many public broadcasters are feeling budget pressures, so many public and state channels now carry advertising.

Television flows. Television has a much more complicated flow between countries than film. American television programs are very common and visible globally, but many other producers sell programs to national and transnational cultural linguistic markets as well. At first, U.S. film studios and independent producers sold television programs worldwide with the same economic and cultural advantages that American film producers had enjoyed. In the 1960s and 1970s, American films, sitcoms, action-adventures, and cartoons flooded into many other countries. Since then, many countries have begun to create much of their own television and to buy more from other countries besides the United States.

A number of countries, from Great Britain to Taiwan, established quotas limiting the amount of imported television programming that could be shown. In 1989, the European Economic Community required member nations to carry at least 50 percent of television programming produced within Europe. Hollywood and U.S. government officials protested these rules at trade talks in the World Trade Organization (WTO) and in regional treaties like NAFTA. However, quotas or barriers to the import of film and television lose some of their force when young, tech-savvy viewers can download *Big Bang Theory* in Beijing even though that show has been banned from broadcast or local cable. Another major force in television flow is the existence of global companies that stream television contents between nations, either legally like Netflix, or illegally, like a number of websites, largely based outside the United States.

American television exports represent a steadily increasing share of television producers' profits. Because many shows made more money overseas than in the United States, as in film, a number of American producers began to shape their programs to anticipate and maximize overseas sales in the 1980s and 1990s (Waxman, 1998). However, now the high cost of U.S. TV programs also limits their distribution. The fees charged to foreign stations are set in relation to ratings, which sometimes makes U.S. shows more expensive than domestic ones. In other cases, lower local ratings often relegate foreign shows to late-night hours when few are watching.

American television programs face increased competition in a number of areas. More nations at virtually all levels of wealth are creating more of their own programming, particularly if we count new forms of television like videos on YouTube. Production technology costs are going down, groups of experienced technicians and artists have been trained in most countries, new stars /producers emerge on YouTube, and a number of low-cost program forms or genres have been developed, including talk, variety, live music, reality shows, live comedy, and game shows. Even more expensive shows, like soap operas, are increasingly produced nationally (see Worldview: Soap Operas Around the World).

Format sales give countries a sort of "program in a box" to produce locally. Foreign format shows are invading television in the United States and elsewhere in a big way. *American Idol* was a ratings hit based on a format developed in Great Britain, for example, with productions in over 20 countries and unlicensed copies in another half dozen. Licensing formats like *Wheel of Fortune* or *Survivor* are now a rapidly increasing global business. A great deal of "local" or "glocal" programming is now based on such international formats and models. Imported TV formats are often replacing imported TV programs, since they have some advantages of cultural proximity (local stars, jokes, etc.) while retaining the value of using formulas that are proven ratings successes elsewhere.

A significant exception to the localization of television in many places is TV news. Since the 1970s, television news flow began to increase steadily from wire services, such as the Associated Press and news film sources from Great Britain. They offered filmed (and later video) footage for various national television news operations to use in their newscasts. Television news flow increased dramatically as CNN, the BBC, Al Jazeera, Russia Today, CCTV-9 from China, and other satellite-based news operations began to offer entire newscasts and even all-day news coverage across borders, primarily to satellite television receivers and cable television operations. Now television news also flows on the Internet, so U.S. viewers can see Al Jazeera International, even if U.S. operators refuse to carry it. Al Jazeera also localized a version in English, aimed at the United States, but after several years of trying to gain an audience, it failed in 2015. China also has an official English language news channel, CCTV-9, now known as CCTV News. So television news flow is slowly becoming more diverse, although audiences for these channels in the United States have been low. In contrast, the BBC has developed a large U.S. audience base, in part due to its cultural proximity to the United States.

INTERNATIONAL BROADCASTS Shows that are popular in America often find audiences worldwide. The Showtime hit *Homeland* is also broadcast in Canada, Ireland, Australia, India and Pakistan.

Cable, Satellite, and Internet TV

Cable TV has been expanding in most countries of the world. **Direct broadcast satellite (DBS)** or direct-to-home (DTH) has also rapidly spread, often spanning the borders of neighboring countries.

A number of channels quickly became global in reach—CNN, MTV, HBO, ESPN, TNT, Nickelodeon, the Cartoon Network, Discovery, and Disney—to sell their existing channels in these countries or even to translate and adapt their U.S. channels to the languages and cultures of the new audiences. MTV is a prolific example, with over 200 different versions worldwide, but has succeeded by localizing what it does to each market, with local music and programs.

> **Direct broadcast satellite (DBS)** is a television or radio satellite service that transmits signals from satellites to compact home receivers.

World View

SOAP OPERAS AROUND THE WORLD

Although American soap operas are still popular in many other countries, now they have to compete with soaps from Mexico, South Korea and Turkey. In Latin America, telenovelas run in prime time and usually depict romance, family drama, and upward mobility. The archetypal telenovela for many was *Simplemente Maria,* about a Peruvian peasant girl who moves to the city, works as a maid, saves money, buys a sewing machine, and becomes a successful seamstress. All sewing machines in Lima sold out after that plot development. Mexico, India, and South Africa have all used soap operas to convey themes that development planners want to communicate, such as family planning in Mexico and India, and working against domestic violence in South Africa. On the commercial side, Brazilian telenovelas' product placement often represents close to 50 percent of the advertising money spent on the program. Telenovelas are also hot exports, still playing to large audiences in Romania, Russia, and even China. But Romania has largely replaced Mexican telenovelas with its own that build on the Mexican style.

Martial arts dramas from Hong Kong and China follow some soap opera themes—romance, love, family intrigues, and rivalries—but add martial arts action, dramatic battles, dynastic court intrigue, historical plots, and period costumes. These are popular throughout Asia. Japan makes its own versions, focused on the Samurai era and featuring a similar mix of rugged heroes, beautiful heroines, and battles. These programs are also becoming popular worldwide. Korea has exported contemporary family and romance melodrama throughout East Asia, which has now broken into global popularity, along with Korea pop music, as "the Korean Wave."

Indian soap operas can be epic, mythological, and even religious. One of the first popular soap operas retold the national Hindu religious epic the *Ramayana,* the story of the Hindu gods. It had a powerful effect, according to critics, who saw it as reinforcing nationalist Hindu political parties and standardizing throughout India a previously diverse set of versions of the *Ramayana.*

Many of these series are also popular in other markets, especially those that share languages and cultures. Telenovelas now sell to all of Latin America; Hong Kong soaps sell in southern China and feature on satellite Star TV; Turkish soaps are popular in the Mid-East, dubbed into Arabic; and Indian soaps are popular even in neighboring (and rival) Pakistan. Some of these exporters are also breaking into the global market. Mexican soap operas are popular now in Eastern Europe and the Mid-East, and Hong Kong martial arts serials can be seen in Los Angeles dubbed into Spanish. If the theme is interesting enough—like in the Colombian telenovela *Yo soy Betty la tea* (I Am Betty the Ugly Girl), about a spunky but plain girl dismissed by the fashionistas she works with—then people who don't even speak the language watch the program for its emotional impact. This was true of many English-language viewers when *Betty* played on Spanish-language television in the United States in 2001. (*Betty* touched such a nerve in the United States that from 2006 to 2010 ABC aired its own version, called *Ugly Betty,* and the series was nominated for a Golden Globe award.) That popularity led to more U.S. shows like "Jane the Virgin" that is loosely based on a Venezuelan telenovela, "Juana la Virgen."

What do people find most interesting about international soap operas, like telenovelas? Colombian professor Jesus Martin-Barbero thinks that melodrama speaks very deeply to key issues for almost everyone: the need to get ahead, the need to keep your family together while you do that, the ups and downs of romance, and the complex emotions that family life stirs up (Martin-Barbero, 1993).

A number of cable channels and DBS services started with a specific language or regional target. Some European channels focused on news, music, sports, films, children's shows, and other targeted programming. One satellite television service in Asia, Star TV, owned by Rupert Murdoch, originally targeted the whole of Asia with American (MTV, film), European (BBC, sports), and Chinese-language channels. That largely failed, since relatively few people wanted to watch in English. It had to target more specific markets, such as

India, Taiwan, China, South Asia, Indonesia, and Japan, with more localized programming.

Several nations (China, Hong Kong, Mexico, Egypt, Saudi Arabia) have developed their own satellite television channels aimed both at national audiences and at neighbors within the same cultural–linguistic markets. For example, the Qatar channel Al Jazeera has provided regional news to the Middle Eastern regional market of Arabic speakers for almost two decades, effectively creating a region-wide television news audience. By covering the 2003 U.S. war against Iraq in a way that gave considerable coverage to Iraqi civilian casualties as well as providing pro-Palestinian coverage of the Israeli–Palestinian conflict, Al Jazeera has won many viewers in the region and has come into major conflict with Western governments who found they had little leverage over it. Other countries use Al Jazeera footage as a news source. However, the unique power of Al Jazeera has diminished as more people watch news on Internet channels.

Internet-based television is also revolutionizing much of the world, at least the parts that have broadband access. Amateur and professional producers in many places are using YouTube, national equivalents to YouTube, and a variety of social networks, to reach audiences with everything from bloodthirsty ISIS recruiting videos to local folk music recorded at concerts on smartphones. These new forms of television are doing very recognizeable comedy, music video, short dramas, and other "television" genres, but are redefining genres like documentaries with an enormous amount of recorded video documenting everything from birthday parties to political demonstrations. As more and more mobile phones can record video and permit viewers without other forms of Internet access to watch, this new television will explode futher and continue to redefine what the medium means.

NEWS WITH AN ARAB SPIN? Since 1996, Al Jazeera, based in Qatar, has become "the CNN of the Arab World." By taking a very independent line on covering the Israeli-Palestinian conflict and on the wars in Afghanistan and Iraq, it has also become very controversial outside the Arabic-speaking world. It now has an international service in English, which many Americans use to get a local take on Afghanistan and Iraq.

Telecommunications Systems

The infrastructure for international media and information services has also become increasingly globalized. For transoceanic transmission, there are several worldwide satellite networks, both government and commercial. Quite a few national satellite systems also offer telephone and television transmission services to neighboring countries.

Satellite orbits, like radio frequencies and telephone/mobile phone standards, are regulated by the ITU, which was absorbed into the larger United Nations system, when it was started in 1945. Unlike the ITU, UNESCO (United Nations Educational, Scientific, and Cultural Organization) started in 1946 not with a regulatory focus, but with a mandate to increase exchanges of knowledge, education, and media between countries, hoping to reduce war and conflict in the long run.

As elements of the telecommunications infrastructure, satellites compete with an extensive set of world and regional fiber-optic networks owned by AT&T, Cable & Wireless of Great Britain, and others. Fiber-optic cables carry

1945

UN founded, incorporating ITU, starting UNESCO

STOP & REVIEW

1. What role has radio played in communication between countries?

2. Why is music more likely to be produced in a wider variety of countries than film or TV?

3. Why did American films come to dominate world film markets?

4. What competes with American media products, such as *The Simpsons,* around the world?

5. Why is television more often locally produced around the world than film?

6. How do changes like privatization affect TV production and flow?

the same kinds of signals carried by satellites across transoceanic distances, with greater speed and less distortion.

In another globalizing development, a number of national telecommunications companies are going international or regional. AT&T, France Telecom, Telefónica of Spain, and others bought telephone, cellular telephone, and data communications companies in Latin America, Africa, and Asia in the 1990s. However, after the global telecommunications capacity glut and bust in the early 2000s, as well as the decline in profitability of many telecommunications-operating companies, some of these firms, like AT&T, sold off some of their international interests. One pattern that emerged was of companies refocusing on markets where they traditionally had influence and knew best how to operate, like Telefónica in Latin America and Cable & Wireless in the Caribbean. Major companies also suffered setbacks speculating in licenses for emerging wireless technologies like third-generation (3G) wireless. However, as smartphones become a primary means of accessing the Internet, those networks are finally being built and becoming profitable—particularly in developing areas where fixed lines and cable never existed. Middle-income countries like Brazil are pushing to complete national 3G coverage while advanced markets move into 4G or LTE (see Chapter 11).

The United States, Japan, and a few other countries have more than 60 wired telephones and 90 to 110 mobile phones per 100 people and have an Internet built on the telephone and cable television infrastructures. But some African and South Asian nations have less than one wired telephone line per 100 people, and have moved to a largely cellular based phone and Internet system (see Figure 18.4). Mobiles have exploded globally so

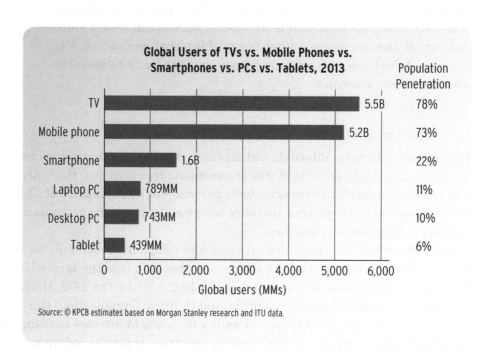

FIGURE 18.4 **TELEVISIONS, COMPUTERS, AND CELL PHONES AROUND THE WORLD** Most people in the world have a television, and almost as many now have cell phones. Smartphones, able to access the Internet, are now twice as common as computers. So much of the world now accesses the Internet over phones, not via computers.

that there is an average of 90 mobiles per 100 people in most of the world. Although the poorest areas lag behind, mobile phones are probably the fastest diffusing communications service since television. In most countries in Africa, Eastern Europe, Latin America, and South Asia, people mainly have cell service as their primary telephone, and increasingly as their major form of access to the Internet as well.

Text messaging and some Internet access, such as Facebook and WhatsApp, are widespread over cell phones, more so than over phone or cable wires. Also spreading fast is wireless (Wi-Fi) access to smartphones, laptops, and other computers in both rich and poor countries. An increasing numbers of global calls are made via computers on Internet networks like Skype or WhatsApp for very low cost or even for free.

CAN YOU HEAR ME NOW? In many countries, where telephone lines are limited, the first phone for most people is now a cell phone.

Computer and Tablet Access

The production of computers has been limited to a few countries in North America, Europe, Latin America, and East Asia. Although China, Korea, and Taiwan have developed successful computer hardware industries, the efforts of most other less industrialized countries, such as Brazil, to develop computer hardware industries have often been frustrating and expensive, although India and others have developed successful software industries. The relatively high cost of hardware and software and the unequal distribution of incomeallow fewer people in the developing world to afford computers.

Even though personal computers can cost less than $300 in the United States, they tend to be considerably more expensive in many other countries. Citizens of many countries have average monthly incomes well under $200, which makes acquiring even a $300 computer difficult for most of the world's population. Figure 18.5 shows how computers are quickly being overtaken by tablet sales at the global level. In many places, tablets often cost less than half of even low-cost laptops, so they are often becoming the device of choice, particularly for students or consumers who want to access the Internet.

The purchase and use of computers and tablets have been spreading worldwide, but unequally. In some countries, like Mozambique, relatively well-off

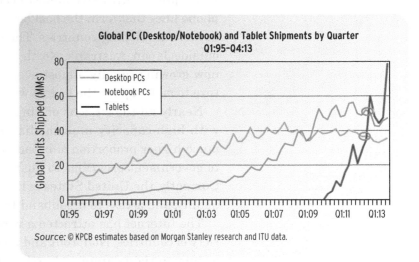

Source: © KPCB estimates based on Morgan Stanley research and ITU data.

FIGURE 18.5 COMPUTER AND TABLET ACCESS Most people in the world lack access to computers, which, before the smartphone and tablet revolutions, also cut them off from the Internet. Now, tablet sales have shot past computers, which will be another major way that people access the Internet from now on.

professionals and business owners can afford access to computers. In others, such as North Korea or Cuba, dictatorial regimes prevent their citizens from owning computers for fear their citizens will learn inconvenient truths about their living conditions. Many experts fear that relatively limited access to computers will keep businesses and professionals in the poorest developing countries from competing in a globalized market where others have a sophisticated computer infrastructure to work with, particularly those in Europe, North America, and East Asia (Castells, 2004). Others now hope that smartphones and tablets may make up some of the gap in receiving and creating information (ITU, 2014).

The Internet

Computers entered into business globally at a considerable rate, along with Internet use. The first significant global impact of information services and data communications worldwide was the interconnection of far-flung operations of multinational corporations via data networks. Today, it is most likely that the customer service representative we are talking to on the phone is based in India, where there is a large industry that trains people to talk to Americans or Australians.

In India, telecommunications networks and the Internet permit outsourcing of work from the United States, ranging from computer programming to telephone call centers. The arrival of the Internet standardized many of these technologies into a single network that was much cheaper to use, so small business and individual users outside of big business and government can now afford access to rapid, high-capacity international data, text, and graphics communications. However, lack of access to information communication technology still hampers many poorer countries (World Bank, 2015).

The Internet exploded out of the United States into the rest of the world. It has proved attractive almost everywhere. However, the computers and telephone lines that form the backbone of the Internet are in much shorter supply in most developing countries. The spread of the Internet was initially slower outside Japan, Australia, North America, and northern Europe, although it is now growing rapidly almost everywhere, often using the cellular infrastructure to make up for the lack of wireline phone or cable TV infrastructure.

Nearly all the citizens of Singapore and South Korea are on the Internet, with high-capacity multimedia broadband networks. In fact, Korea has a much higher proportion of broadband users than does the United States, due to government programs to push this infrastructure and make it affordable. Currently, the United States is barely in the top 20 globally in terms of speed, quality, and access to broadband Internet (OECD, 2013).

The Internet has attracted a wide variety of unexpected new users in a variety of countries. Nonprofit and nongovernmental organizations (NGOs), such as human rights groups, churches, labor unions, and political party networks, have found the Internet a useful communications tool. For example, mass protests against elections held in Iran in 2009, which many citizens perceived as rigged, were organized through the Internet (especially through e-mail and Twitter) and cell phones. Now social networking is used by political activists around the world, as was visible during the Arab Spring in the Middle East in the early 2010s. Unfortunately, it has also become a tool for dictators who use social media to identify dissidents whom they arrest.

The Internet raises a number of new prospects for communication across borders. The structure of the Internet permits anyone with access to a computer or smartphone to send or receive e-mail to or from anyone else on the planet who has an Internet connection. Use of the World Wide Web, social networks, or music and video downloading is much more problematic for many global users, because Internet connections in developing countries at first relied on unreliable telephone lines that permitted only the slowest connections, making the transmission of graphics, let alone music and video, impractical. However, both Google and Facebook are pressing into these countries, creating deals with local cell providers to carry special simplified versions of their services on feature phones (the level below smartphones). So for hundreds of millions of people with only a cell phone, Facebook will be the only Internet they know, for at least the near future. However, Facebook's plan to increase such services in India was blocked by government regulators out of concern that offering poor, rural people only a few services associated with Facebook's Free Basics plan over cell phones violated principles of net neutrality. In many other places, particularly in Southeast Asia, Latin America and Africa, such plans are moving rapidly forward, often arranged at local levels by cell phone providers who see that offering free or heavily discounted access to Facebook or WhatsApp is an excellent way to get new customers introduced to Internet service. Facebook is also exploring new technologies from wifi towers to drones or balloons to get basic Internet access out to its billions of prospective customers.

A student in Lebanon can read news about his country not only from official sources but also from foreign newspapers, international newswire services, political dissidents and Islamic movements such as Al Manar, and other sources not approved by his government. This makes the Internet a revolutionary force in global information flow, as we shall see in the next section. It also makes the Internet the main current challenge for many governments, such as China, Iran, and Singapore, that are concerned about controlling information flows into their country (see Technology Demystified: A Closed or an Open Internet— The Great Firewall of China). China, Iran, North Korea, and other nations that wish to control political, sexual, or religious content on the Internet are working hard to give people access to the information they need to participate in a global information economy—while also controlling access to politically threatening information and news from the rest of the world. Access to the Internet has grown rapidly, but the government continues to use various controls to limit access to critical political commentary, particularly from outside

Facebook has 1.59 billion members worldwide

THE MAIN SOURCE Most people in the world now have access to TV, which brings images from around the world.

China. This effort continues to cast considerable doubt on the idea that the Internet would tend to eliminate political control over information. However, dissidents can be creative. North Korean exiles float packets of flash drives containing South Korean television shows and news information across rivers into North Korea to reach computer users there whose Internet connections are limited or controlled.

Technology Demystified

A CLOSED OR AN OPEN INTERNET—THE GREAT FIREWALL OF CHINA

For a number of years, the PRC (People's Republic of China) has blocked thousands of foreign websites that carry objectionable material by preventing IP addresses from being routed through its servers. It does this using standard firewalls and proxy servers at Internet gateways. Public security uses keyword-filtering technology to identify sites and sends the current list of objectionable sites to the entry points periodically, while human spies paid by the government are planted in Internet cafés. Chinese news outlets are also required to hire in-house censors who block politically sensitive stories from being posted online or take them down when they appear. Social networking sites are also monitored and censored.

China monitors new perceived technological threats to its information control. "As more and more illegal and unhealthy information spreads through the blog and search engine, we will take effective measures to put the BBS, blog, and search engine under control," according to Cai Wu, director of the Information Office of China's Cabinet (French, 2006).

A 2004 crackdown, a "people's war" on pornography, showed earlier Chinese attempts at control. Government regulations require Internet service providers to implement registration systems forbidding the collection of service charges from pornographic websites. Those caught violating the rules will be blacklisted by supervisory officials. They have requested that Internet cafés install software to monitor their customers. Internet cafés are not allowed to permit people under 18 to use their services. The government has cracked down on domestic microblog services that people used to criticize government policies and organize protests. Such restrictions have increased under the most recent national government, which seems even more concerned with information control.

That has been reinforced by prosecution and severe punishment of those who use the Internet in forbidden ways. The government has also required search engines like Google or Yahoo! to censure search possibilities in their Chinese versions, in order to gain permission to operate legally and accept advertising in China. In 2009, a group of hackers with links to the Chinese government broke into files containing information about Google e-mail accounts held by Chinese citizens. This led Google to decide to stop cooperating with government censorship requests and withdraw direct search services from China. As of June 2010, it referred queries to its Hong Kong Chinese language site, in the hopes that more lenient rules would exist there, but the sites Chinese users on the mainland try to link to can still be blocked by government filters.

E-mail was initially less affected by blocking. Dissident organizations outside China collected thousands of e-mail addresses and send them to Chinese net users, although several people have been prosecuted over the years for providing such e-mail lists to outsiders. The Chinese government is also working on controlling access, particularly at public cybercafés, by making people register and making cybercafé owners responsible for what is accessed.

The government has also recently cracked down on the use of the Internet for entertainment. For years, young Chinese downloaded foreign television programs over the Internet and organized networks of translators who created subtitles for them. However, recent laws place strong limits on such activities, as it couples Internet restrictions with concerns about the effect of foreign television on Chinese culture.

Source: This builds on several sources, including newspaper coverage, and "Internet Censorship–China" in M/Cyclopedia of New Media.

INTERNATIONAL REGULATION

International media and telecommunications systems are regulated differently from national media systems. As with most aspects of **international law,** there is usually no direct enforcement power, and regulation requires a consensus among nations that the proposed regulations or changes serve their various interests. Failing that, nations have tended to assert their self-interest, and the larger, more powerful nations tend to get their way (Padovani, 2005).

One of the few international organizations to have achieved any real power and real changes is the ITU. Common or compatible technical standards are required so that users of telegraph, telephone, fax, and e-mail equipment in various countries can communicate with each other across borders. For instance, the ITU encouraged ICANN (Internet Corporation for Assigned Names and Numbers; see Chapter 10) to create URLs in all languages to enable truly global use of the Internet. One of the main ITU divisions, ITU-T (telecommunications), is primarily involved with technical standards for telecommunications.

The ITU controls some of the same crucial regulatory problems that individual nations solve within their borders. For example, radio spectrum frequencies have to be allocated to different uses in various nations to avoid interference among users. Even more important, the ITU allocates the space orbits for satellites, since those orbits lie above and across national boundaries. **Satellite footprint** areas almost automatically cover multiple countries, requiring international agreements on coverage and standards. Frequency and orbit allocations are routinely recorded by the ITU's B (broadcasting) division and are overseen by periodic World Administrative Radio Conferences that decide ultimately which country gets which orbits and frequencies. Poorer countries have complained since the 1970s that this process favors the larger, more industrialized countries. The ITU responded by creating a third major division, Development, to work with developing countries to accelerate their adoption of new telecommunications and broadcast-related technologies. That group organized the World Summit on the Information Society (WSIS), which from 2003 onon focused on the need to promote greater Internet access in developing countries. The summit also challenged U.S. control over Internet standards via ICANN, a private corporation in the United States created in 1998.

The Internet has posed interesting challenges to international regulation. It has required some new regulatory mechanisms for basic tasks like setting standards and assigning domain names, such as ICANN, ISOC, and IETF (see Chapter 10). Much of the discussion in the WSIS ended up focusing on the need to globalize the functions of ICANN in assigning domain names that use world languages, for example. Subsequent debates have pushed hard to shift power over ICANN from the United States to the ITU. That may have been hastened by recent revelations of the U.S. National Security Agency (NSA) spying on both Internet and telephone traffic. The president of Brazil, whose cell phone was one of the ones tapped by the NSA, created a new global conference with that agenda, NetMundial, in 2014. Led by global lobbying from outside the UUnited States, opposed by many in the United States, ICANN is

> **International law** includes treaties between countries, multi-country agreements, and rules established by international organizations.

2003

ITU hosts World Summit on the Information Society to promote use of the Internet in poorer countries

> A **satellite footprint** is the surface area covered by the satellite's signal.

planning on transferring some of its functions to the ITU, although that has been delayed in 2015.

The other major player in global regulation is now the European Union, which has begun to set de facto global standards on antitrust and privacy issues. Since global corporations have to meet EU rules to operate in that large part of the global economy, those rules may become their working global standards. For example, the 2014 EU ruling that people have a right to delete coverage of their pasts on the Internet will have an enormous impact on Google.

Privacy laws have already required intense negotiation between EU standards, which are very protective of privacy, and American standards, which have been much looser and less defined. In order for American firms to do Internet business in Europe, they have to negotiate an adjustment to those European rules. In fact, this is an area in which European standards may well push the United States toward stricter rules on privacy than would otherwise have been the case. In 2010, Google was forced to turn over private data it had collected while making street-level images of cities in Europe that violated EU privacy standards. The EU has also pushed against monopoly dominance by U.S. companies, threatening to take Apple to court for closing iTunes to competitors and fining Microsoft for restricting competition with its proprietary technologies like Internet Explorer or Windows Media Player, and investigating Google for similar restriction of competition by forcing companies who license the Google Android cellular operating system who feature Google applications on their home screens.

2010

Google violates European Union privacy protections by collecting street-level data

There are other tough regulatory issues on the near horizon for the global Internet, like setting and collecting taxes on Internet commerce. Even more than with American states, many European and other countries get much of their revenue from sales taxes that are evaded by Internet commerce. Countries around the world also have very different positions on things like pornography or hate speech. For example, Germany attempts to regulate cross-border anti-Semitic hate speech, which violates strict laws put in place after the Holocaust during World War II. The Internet is challenging not only global rules but also regional ones, like the privacy rules of the European Union. So far, the EU has successfully pushed large Internet companies like Google to change its policies on privacy and the right to be left alone, or the right to delete old information on the Internet. The EU is also proposing to unite regulation on such issues across the whole EU region.

MEDIA *LITERACY*

WHOSE WORLD IS IT?

Among the main issues in globalization of communications media are cultural imperialism, media and information flows, free flow of information, media trade, hacking and cyber-warfare between nations (and possibly large companies, as well), and the effects of media on national development.

POLITICAL ECONOMY OF THE INTERNET

Although computers can promote U.S. or other major nations' corporate centralization of global operations and dominance of various data flows (Schiller, 1981), such as being the center points of Google, Amazon, and Facebook, computer networks and data transfers also permit high-level jobs, such as computer programming, to be transferred to low-wage nations such as India, which has become an offshore outsourcing center for many corporations.

This situation represents an economic opportunity for millions of Indians but a loss of jobs for many Americans who had previously done the work. And high-level programming and systems analyst jobs are also being increasingly exported to countries such as India, reversing the pattern of dominance that Schiller alerted us to. In fact, an increasingly dense and complex connectivity and integration of companies' operations between the United States, India, and many other places via the Internet is now one of the most crucial defining characteristics of globalization for many people. This enables outsourcing of jobs in areas like telephone call centers, database entry, software development, and television and film production from the United States to India and other countries where labor costs are low (see Chapter 1). Workers there can be easily and relatively cheaply connected to companies in the United States, given that the cost of telecommunications between the two countries is lower than the cost of labor in the United States.

POLITICAL ECONOMY OF CULTURAL IMPERIALISM

Perhaps the biggest international issue in communications media has been what many nations call *cultural imperialism,* particularly the unequal flows of film, television, music, news, and information from the United States and Europe to other nations, as well as drawing developing countries into the global consumer economy. This unbalanced flow bothers many nations on several levels. First, it is seen as a cause of cultural erosion and change. So many media products and cultural influences flow into other countries from the United States that some people there fear American ideas, images, and values will replace their own. Some of the fears seem trivial to U.S. observers, as when French authorities fought to keep American words, such as "drugstore" and "weekend", from creeping into common use by French. However, some consequences of media flows can be deadly serious. Some poor countries in Africa saw epidemics of infant diarrhea and death when mothers gave up breastfeeding for bottle-feeding, which they had seen in European and American television programs and advertising. (Mixing infant formula with unsanitary water caused the problem.)

Other critics of cultural imperialism have been more concerned about the increasingly global economics underlying the structures of media. Underlying the fear of commercial media, in particular, is the idea that they tend to tie countries into a global economy based on advertising and consumption, which pushes poor people to want goods they cannot afford, to get people to think of themselves primarily as consumers.

The cultural imperialism argument lost much of its force as many countries increased the amount and kinds of media contents they produce.

Some governments, such as Japan and Taiwan, pressured national television broadcasters to produce more programming. Others, such as France, subsidize their national film industries to keep them strong. Another solution is to limit media imports, such as the amount of foreign television and film. For example, China allows in only 34 foreign feature films per year. However, such limits have been strongly opposed by the United States in the WTO, and China will have to renegotiate that quota in 2017. The MPAA has been negotiating for increased film imports into China. Many countries have discovered that national and regional television and music production tend to increase more or less naturally, because they are increasingly feasible economically and because audiences want them. However, for many critics, the global transformation of the economics of media into steadily more capitalist, commercial forms of operation in most countries reflects the continuation of many of the economic issues of cultural imperialism into the new framework of globalization.

CULTURAL IMPACT OF MEDIA AND INFORMATION FLOWS

Even though nations differ culturally and politically, they are seldom isolated. As we look at the globalization of media, we see that one of its most obvious aspects is an extensive flow of a variety of media contents between countries. Elements of media, such as books, songs, stories, and news, have always flowed across borders; cultures have never been truly isolated. Even before Gutenberg's printing press, the Christian Bible and the Islamic Koran had both moved powerfully across a number of countries and cultures, as handwritten copies motivated leaders who led millions into massive religious and cultural change.

However, many people worry that modern media move new ideas and values across borders in such quantities, and at such speed, that we have entered a new age of much more pervasive and rapid change in the world's cultures. Marshall McLuhan (1964) looked at the electronic media and anticipated a "global village." What kind of global village might the media construct? Much of what flows across borders originates in Hollywood, so some fear that the "village" will be as Americanized as a San Fernando Valley mall multiplex theater. However, as detailed earlier in this chapter, observers like Castells (1997) and Straubhaar (2007) pointed out that media flows from television to the Internet began to be more balanced, although film and news remainexceptions.

A major issue is the impact of Hollywood-style material on other cultures. Because Hollywood films, television, and Anglo-American pop music often include sex, violence, drugs, and gender roles and racial images that clash strongly with local values around the world, many people fear its influence, particularly on the young. After September 11, 2001, some in the Arab nations cited such clashing images as part of what made a number of religious Muslims fear U.S. cultural influence on their national values. Many worry that media like satellite television and the Internet simply amplify the availability of these messages. However, after the 2003 invasion of Iraq, satellite television in the Arab nations also became notable for carrying Al Jazeera's Arab version of the news, which competed very strongly with both commercial American news media, like CNN, and recent official U.S. media in the region, like Al Sawa and Al Hura.

An alternative vision of the global future is that new information technologies will decentralize the global village, so that information and culture will flow in many directions, from a variety of sources, with many different messages. This scenario sees a variety of companies and groups, such as environment or human rights groups, reaching broader audiences across borders. An example might be Doctors without Borders, which provides medical and other support to refugees in places like Darfur. However, some countries, such as Russia and Egypt, have moved to limit the impact of U.S. human rights groups and other activist groups, seeing them as threats to their national sovereignty.

FREE FLOW OF INFORMATION

One of the fears in many countries is that unbalanced media flows will diminish **national sovereignty,** reducing countries' cultural autonomy and governments' abilities to support and protect their cultures. In contrast, the idea of a **free flow of information** reflects the basic concept of freedom of speech, whereby all people ought to be as free as possible to both send and receive information across borders. So U.S. news media oppose any attempt to balance or regulate news flows. But according to the idea of national sovereignty, governments or other domestic forces are entitled to assert national control over natural resources, culture, politics, and so on. Both approaches are established as basic principles in the UNESCO charter and the 1948 UN Declaration on Human Rights. A 2005 convention on protection of endangered cultures in UNESCO raised these issues again.

Those who consider the current international flows of information and culture unequal tend to emphasize national sovereignty as a justification for a country's asserting control over media flows. The United States has opposed many such proposals. It does so in part because American commercial media interests are threatened by proposed restrictions on media sales and flows. But the United States has also opposed certain proposed restrictions on principle. The United States and a number of other nations believe it is important to keep as free a flow of information as possible to promote freedom of speech globally, independent of government censorship.

Debate raged in UNESCO over these issues from 1976 to 1983, until the United States decided to withdraw in protest of proposed policies that it thought violated the values of the free flow of information and journalistic freedom. UNESCO proposed that countries create national policies to balance the flow of information. The United States feared that these policies would give too much power to governments that would be likely to restrict free speech and the free flow of information. The compromise proposal by UNESCO (subsequently rejected by the United States after 1980) promoted a free and balanced flow by helping developing countries build up their own abilities to produce and export media and cultural products. When the U.S. proposal was defeated, it pulled out of UNESCO in 1983, returning only in 2002.

Although this idea received little financial support, a number of developing nations succeeded in producing more media anyway. Most countries now do much more of their own television, music, news, and websites. The most notable regional news agency launched in among developing countries has been

National sovereignty is the policy of keeping domestic forces in control of a nation's economy, politics, and culture.

Free flow of information occurs when information flows as freely as possible between countries.

1976

UNESCO hosts critical discussion for proposals for a New World Information Order

Al Jazeera. More recently, the Internet has permitted a much more diverse flow of news, although most major news media continue to use the same old commercial news agencies. As described earlier in this chapter, a number of national media ventures have begun to balance the flow of television, film, and music among nations. A new wrinkle in the free flow of information arises with the Internet, which enables vastly largely flows of information, music, film, television, and socialsocial media between countries. In theory, Internet advocates thought it would be impossible for nations to control, but China, Cuba, Iran, and others have succeeded in controlling key aspects of Internet flow. (See Technology Demystified: A Closed or an Open Internet—The Great Firewall of China, page 526.) Cuba has agreed in principle to open and expand Internet access, but many of those who remain powerful in its government are very concerned about maintaining control over information.

TRADE IN MEDIA

Media flow and trade issues have been raised in regional treaty organizations, such as the European Union (EU) and NAFTA, as well as in the WTO. The United States tends to see cultural industries as a trade policy issue, because such exports are a significant part of the American balance of trade, compensating for American purchases of Japanese, Korean, and Chinese DVD players, television sets, and other consumer electronics, for example. European. Chinese and Canadian governments, desiring to boost their own producers, see these matters partially as a trade issue, but they also see a cultural policy issue and believe the distinctness of national cultures ought to be preserved on television, music, and film.

The issue came up repeatedly in the General Agreement on Tariffs and Trade (GATT), which was dedicated to lower **tariffs** on trade, and its successor, the WTO. In the last round of GATT negotiations, in the early 1990s, the United States pushed hard to impose new international trade rules on audiovisual materials (television and film) that would keep countries from protecting their own national film and television industries or setting quotas to keep out imported films and programs. The EU rallied around the French, who opposed such a change (existing GATT rules permitted protection and subsidy of film industries), but audiovisual materials are subject to more liberal trade rules under the WTO. At the same time, the European Union has been opening up Europe for greater competition, trade, and non-European investment in telecommunications, since telecommunications is not seen as having the same cultural impact as film and television.

In the late 1990s, the WTO moved into another crucial area for new digital media: copyright and intellectual property protection. It created significantly stronger copyright protection in digital media, such as the Internet and digital recordings (CDs, DVDs, digital music, and film), in 1998. However, enforcement in places like China has been difficult. A specific organization, the World Intellectual Property Organization (WIPO), was created in 1974 to safeguard copyright and related interests. It has become an increasingly central part of world trade in information, media, and cultural products, as those products now assume a larger role in world trade. U.S. industry organizations like the MPAA also push hard for international enforcement of copyright protection.

Tariffs are taxes imposed by governments on goods imported from other countries.

HACKING AND CYBER-WARFARE

Another rising issue is various forms of cyber-warfare. In cyber-espionage, both countries and corporations try to steal economic, technological, military, and political secrets from each other. Most people tend to think of espionage as political and military, but increasingly, countries like China have blended various forms of espionage. The United States has denounced Chinese army units for stealing economic secrets as much as military ones. But the United States and other major powers do this, too, as do terrorist groups, who increasingly act separately from nations. Even companies, environmentalists, and others do this for profit or to make a political point, as did Edward Snowden in 2013 when he disclosed thousands of National Security Agency secrets to denounce the extensive degree of U.S. cyber-espionage. Nations also conduct other forms of cyber-warfare, as when the United States and Israel temporarily damaged Iranian nuclear capabilities with computer viruses and other cyber-attacks.

MEDIA AND NATIONAL/LOCAL DEVELOPMENT

Another main issue is whether media, information technologies, and telecommunications can be made to better serve national or local development. As noted earlier, part of the fear expressed in international debates is that media are primarily serving global commercial interests, not the needs of the populations of the various countries, whether rich or poor. Many government planners and social critics feel that most people in developing nations need media that offer more than slick American entertainment and advertising.

Many governments and international organizations, such as UNESCO, worked hard to create models using media to promote education, health, agriculture, local religious and cultural values, and so on. Some of these programs succeeded, particularly radio programs based in rural areas (McAnany, 2012). The latest development focus has been to try to address health issues in areas like Africa and to get laptops or other computers to students and others in developing countries (ITU, 2010), as well as to reach out with new services on cellphones.

The ITU and the World Bank encourage national governments and foreign investors to invest more funds in expanding of developing world telephone and Internet systems, such as building the telecommunications systems necessary for Internet coverage of more of their populations. World Bank and other research shows that such investment contributes to economic growth. This issue is currently discussed primarily in terms of poor countries' access to the Internet, including bringing the infrastructure to provide mobile broadband on phones. Debate at the 2003 World Summit on the Information Society showed countries feared falling behind in their abilities to compete in economic areas where widespread and fast Internet connection was crucial. Since many people in most countries do not have access to the Internet, one of the main immediate impacts is increased economic and social stratification between those who can e-mail and surf the Net and those who cannot.

STOP & REVIEW

1. Why would countries privatize telephone companies?

2. What are the barriers to increasing Internet access in many countries?

3. What kinds of new challenges does the Internet bring to international regulators? To nations?

4. What is cultural imperialism?

5. What are the counterarguments to cultural imperialism?

6. What are considered unequal flows of media?

7. What is the conflict or trade-off between national sovereignty and the free flow of information?

SUMMARY & REVIEW

WHY DO GOVERNMENTS OWN MORE BROADCASTING THAN PRINT MEDIA IN MANY COUNTRIES?

Broadcast media always require frequency regulations or standards by governments, which led many governments to take control of radio and television they regulated. In some poor countries, governments are the only institution with enough money to support television. Electronic media also have the potential to affect more people. Some governments see electronic media as valuable tools for either development or political control. In some of the poorest countries, governments may be among only a few bodies that have enough money to run broadcasting or telecommunications.

WHY DOES HOLLYWOOD DOMINATE WORLD FILM MARKETS?

American films were made to appeal to a large immigrant audience through a universal and entertainment-oriented style, which made it easy for diverse international audiences to accept its films. The United States also benefited from the destruction or blockage of foreign film industries during World War I and World War II. U.S. producers developed an efficient export cartel, the MPAA, which owned much of the world distribution and exhibition structure.

WHY DO MORE COUNTRIES PRODUCE TELEVISION THAN FILM?

U.S. television programs were also produced primarily by the MPAA film studio companies, which gave them the benefit of an existing international distribution structure. American television also used many of the popular techniques and formulas of Hollywood film producers, which gave its productions much of the same universal entertainment appeal. Many other countries found that showing American television programs was cheaper than the cost of local production and provided an easy solution to filling schedules, although U.S. programs are increasingly expensive, so they are sometimes not cheaper than local productions in some countries. However, because U.S. programs are frequently much less popular than local ones, most countries have increasingly produced more and more national television.

As technology costs for television production decline and experience in producing shows increases, people in many countries are finding it easier to make their own shows, particularly now with tools as cheap as smartphones, producing material for YouTube. Furthermore, once countries develop television genres that are popular at home and in nearby cultural linguistic markets, audiences tend to prefer the local programs, and companies now export formats to the United States, reversing the conventional flow of entertainment programs.

Soap operas, variety shows, and music and talk shows tend to be more prominent in programming abroad than in the United States. Some countries are too small to produce certain kinds of programming. Smaller countries tend to focus on these lower-cost genres. New genres are developing on YouTube and other sites that focus on even cheaper productions with phones and laptops that are still popular with millions of people.

WHY DO MORE COUNTRIES PRODUCE MUSIC THAN TELEVISION?

Recorded music is cheaper to produce than television shows. Musical preferences are often more localized to regions within countries and to subcultures defined by age, ethnicity, and religion. Thus, there is demand for a large, diverse set of artists and recording companies.

WHAT ARE THE MAIN GLOBAL IMPACTS OF THE INTERNET?

Since many people in most countries do not have access to the Internet, one of the immediate impacts is increased economic and social stratification between those who can e-mail and surf the Net and those who cannot. For those with access, the Internet helps globalize economic activity, making it easier to sell things and outsource jobs across borders. It also challenges attempts at news control and censorship. The Internet enables nontraditional groups, from EcoNet to Al Qaeda, to network and coordinate across the world. It also enables new forms of television, music, documentary, and propaganda.

WHICH COMPANIES ARE THE MAIN GLOBAL OWNERS OF MASS MEDIA?

The main companies are Time Warner (U.S.), Disney/ABC (U.S.), Rupert Murdoch's News Corporation (Australia), DirecTV (U.S.), and Comcast (U.S.). Others include Seagram-Universal (Canada), Bertelsmann (Germany), Vivendi (France), and General Electric/NBC (U.S.). Companies beyond traditional mass media, such as Apple, Google, Microsoft, and Telefónica (Spain), should be considered, too.

WHAT ORGANIZATIONS MOST REGULATE INTERNATIONAL MEDIA?

The main international regulatory organization is the ITU, which has telecommunication, broadcasting, and development divisions. It allocates frequencies and satellite orbits to countries and, together with the International Standards Organization, sets international standards for telecommunications. UNESCO debated the unbalanced flows of media and news between countries and whether countries have a right to protect their cultures from outside influence. The EC (European Commission) sets standards, establishes rules about media flow, and creates regional markets. The WTO has also become important in regulation of trade in media products and information services.

WHAT IS CULTURAL IMPERIALISM?

Cultural imperialism is an unbalanced relationship in culture and media between countries. The main issue is unequal flows of film, news, television programs, cable channels, and music from the United States to other countries. Other aspects include the globalization of media ownership, foreign investment in national media, and the use of foreign media models. International media flows seem to become more balanced as other countries produce and export more. This tendency toward balance is more notable in music and television than in film or news.

WHAT IS THE TRADE-OFF BETWEEN NATIONAL SOVEREIGNTY AND THE FREE FLOW OF INFORMATION?

The United States promotes the free flow of information as an international extension of its national values about freedom of expression. Other countries complain that the free flow of ideas permits the United States to dominate international flows of media. These countries wish to exercise their national sovereignty. However, giving such power to government raises the prospects of censorship and control of information.

THINKING CRITICALLY
ABOUT THE MEDIA

1. What type of conditions in the media relations between countries led people to call it media imperialism?

2. Why do people characterize the media relations between countries and cultures in the past 20 years as increasing globalization?

3. Why does Hollywood dominate global film production and distribution much more than it does television, music, and the Internet?

4. What is the difference between a free flow of media and a free and balanced flow?

5. What are the different impacts of media on developing countries?

KEY TERMS

cultural imperialism (p. 501)

cultural proximity (p. 505)

cultural–linguistic markets (p. 506)

direct broadcast satellite (DBS) (p. 519)

free flow of information (p. 531)

globalization (p. 502)

glocal (p. 503)

international law (p. 527)

localization (p. 506)

national sovereignty (p. 531)

privatizing (p. 517)

regionalization (p. 504)

satellite footprint (p. 527)

tariff (p. 532)

GLOSSARY

AAC is advanced audio coding.

Abolitionists wanted to abolish slavery.

Account executives are the liaisons between the agency and the client.

Acoustic is a sound that is not electronically amplified.

Advertising is communication that is paid for and is usually persuasive in nature.

Advertising media are the communication channels that carry messages to consumers.

The **advertising plan** is a written document outlining the objectives and strategies for a product's advertising.

An **affiliate** is a station that contracts with networks to distribute their programming.

Affiliate fees are monthly per-subscriber fees that cable programming services charge local cable operators.

Affordances are the technical features of communication channels that allow their users to perform useful functions.

Almanacs are book-length collections of useful facts, calendars, and advice.

AM, or **amplitude modulation**, carries information in the height, or amplitude, of the radio wave.

Analog communication uses continuously varying signals corresponding to the light or sounds originated by the source.

Anonymous sources are people who give reporters information but do not allow the publication of their names.

Apps (short for *applications*) are software applications for use on smartphones.

Artificial intelligence (AI) is the property of an interactive medium that convinces users that they are interacting with a real person.

Asynchronous media are not consumed simultaneously by all members of the audience.

Audience is the number of readers of a magazine.

Audiobooks can be heard on a CD, the radio, or downloaded onto a mobile device.

Augmented reality superimposes game objects on a real-world environment.

Auteurs are directors who also see themselves as artists. They want to control all aspects of their production, often writing, sometimes shooting or editing, their films.

Backlist books are older books that are not actively promoted but are still in print.

Backpack journalism is the term for reporters who carry a digital video camera (a mini DV; see Chapter 8), tape recorder, notebook, telephone, and computer, often in a backpack.

Barriers to entry are obstacles companies must overcome to enter a market.

Basic cable is the lowest level of cable service that includes local broadcast stations.

A **blog,** short for *Web log,* is commentary addressed to the Web audience. A blog is similar to an online opinion journal.

Bluegrass came from white music in the South and Appalachia, building on Irish and Scottish instruments and traditions.

Blues came from music by black slaves in the South, which was characterized by specific chord progressions and moods.

B movies are cheaply and quickly made genre films.

Book publishers offer an array of services, from editing to promoting to selling a book.

Book was defined traditionally and narrowly as a set of pages bound together between covers.

A **brand** consists of all the dimensions that identify and give unique value to a product or company.

Brand loyalty is the consumer's propensity to make repeat purchases of a specific brand of product.

Broadband refers to high-speed Internet connections.

The **bullet model,** or hypodermic model, posits powerful, direct effects of the mass media.

The news industry **business model** was totally dependent on advertising revenues. Thus, revenues fluctuate with the advertising whims and budgets of other businesses.

The **buying motive** explains the consumer's desire to purchase particular products.

Cable modems connect personal computers to cable TV systems.

Cable television transmits television programs via coaxial cable or fiber.

CAN-SPAM Act regulates commercial e-mail.

Capture theory explains that regulators are unduly influenced by the industry they regulate.

Casual games are informal games that can be completed in short periods of time.

Censorship is the formal restriction of media or speech content by government, political, or religious authorities.

Chain broadcasting is synonymous with a broadcasting network.

A **channel** is an electronic or mechanical system that links the source to the receiver.

Circulation is the number of copies distributed to the public, for a price or free.

Click-through rate is the percentage of readers who click on an ad to visit the advertiser's page.

Coaxial cable is the high-capacity wire used for cable television transmission.

Common carriers provide service to all on an equal basis.

Compositing is merging several layers of images that were shot separately.

Computer-to-plate technology transfers page images composed inside a computer directly to printing plates.

Communication is an exchange of meaning.

The **communications spectrum** includes the range of electromagnetic radiation frequencies that are used in wireless communication systems.

Community access means created by community residents without the involvement of the cable operator.

Concentration of ownership occurs when several kinds of media or many outlets of the same kind of media are owned by a single owner.

Conflict of interest is when professionals, such as journalists, have an invested interest that might affect their decision making, making them less objective.

Conglomerates are big businesses or corporations that own seemingly unrelated holdings. They are made up of diverse parts from across several media industries and are involved in multiple areas of business activity.

Consumer magazines are magazines that contain general-interest topics.

Content analysis is a quantitative description of the content of the media.

Convergence is the integration of mass media, computers, and telecommunications.

Cookies are small files that websites leave on their visitors' computers.

Copy testing evaluates the effectiveness of advertisements.

Copyright is the legal right to control intellectual property. With it comes the legal privilege to use, sell, or license creative works.

A copyright royalty fee is a payment for use of a creative work.

Corantos were news sheets that appeared around 1600.

Corporate communications refers to when a practitioner is employed by a single company to do its public relations work, rather than contract out the work to a PR agency.

Correlated means that there is a statistical measure of association between two variables.

Cost per thousand is how much a commercial costs in relation to the number of viewers who see it, in thousands.

Covers are artists' performances of others' songs.

Critical studies examine the overall impact of media.

Cross-ownership occurs when one firm owns different media outlets in the same area.

Cultivation theory argues that mass media exposure cultivates a view of the world that is consistent with mediated "reality."

Cultural imperialism occurs when some countries dominate others through the media.

Cultural proximity is the preference of audiences for media in their own language and culture.

Cultural studies is a branch of scholarship that argues that media and audiences work together to define culture.

Cultural–linguistic markets build on common languages and common cultures that span borders.

Culture is a group's pattern of thought and activity.

Database marketing is used when advertisers store information about consumers so that they can personalize messages.

Datelines appear at the beginning of a story and note the location where a story happens.

Deceptive advertising makes misleading or untruthful claims.

Demographic segmentation is based on social or personal characteristics, such as age, sex, education, or income.

Dependent variables are the consequences, or effects, of media exposure.

Desktop publishing is the process of editing, laying out, and inserting photos to design and display a page using a desktop computer.

Diffusion is the spread of innovations.

Digital means computer-readable information formatted in 1s and 0s.

Digital video is recorded, edited, and often transmitted in digital form as used by computers.

The **digital divide** is the gap in Internet usage between rich and poor, Anglos and minorities.

A **digital game** is a game in which a digital computer facilitates the game play.

Digital subscriber line (DSL) sends high-speed data over existing phone lines.

Dime novels were inexpensive paperback novels of the nineteenth century.

Direct broadcast satellite (DBS) is a television or radio satellite service that transmits signals from satellites to compact home receivers.

Direct marketing is a form of advertising that requests an immediate consumer response.

A **disc jockey (DJ)** is a radio station announcer who plays records and often emphasizes delivery and personality.

Diversity includes all points of view from people of different races, cultures, political leanings, gender, age, and life experiences, for example.

A **duopoly** exists when two companies dominate a market.

E-books are book content that appear in digital text format. They can be read on mobile devices, computer tablets, and e-readers.

E-commerce (electronic commerce) is the ability to buy and sell online.

Economics studies the forces that allocate resources to satisfy competing needs.

Economies of scale result when unit costs go down as production quantities increase.

Electromagnetic recording is a method of storing information as magnetized areas on a tape or disk.

Encryption is used when a message is written in a secret code.

E-readers are devices that are used to display digital content found in books, magazines, and newspapers.

In the **era of creativity**, advertisers emphasized entertainment as well as information.

Ethics are standards of good conduct.

Ethnography is a naturalistic research method in which the observer obtains detailed information from personal observation or interviews over extended periods of time.

Experimental research studies the effects of media in carefully controlled situations that manipulate media exposure and content.

Fabrication is information that is made up instead of emerging from facts.

Fairness and balance is making sure that varied points of view are known equally.

Fair use permits users limited copying of copyrighted works for academic, artistic, or personal use.

Feature films are story films, usually over one and a half hours.

The **Federal Communications Commission (FCC)** regulates communication in the United States.

Fiber-optic systems use light instead of electricity to transmit information.

Film noir comprised the "dark," moody American films of the 1940s, often focused on detectives or similar themes.

The **First Amendment** to the U.S. Constitution guarantees freedom of speech and of the press.

First-run distribution for film productions is made specifically for movie theaters.

First-run syndication is the rental or licensing for original productions made specifically for the syndication market.

FM, or **frequency modulation**, carries information in variations in the frequency of the radio wave.

Format clock is an hourly radio programming schedule.

Formats are radio label content aimed at a specific audience.

Freebies are gifts of any value from sources and potential news subjects.

Freedom of speech is the idea that speech and media content should be free from government restriction.

Free flow of information occurs when information flows as freely as possible between countries.

Frequency is the number of cycles that radio waves complete in a second.

Front projection lets actors be photographed in front of an image so that they appear as part of it.

Game engine refers to the software components that govern the physical properties of the game world, interact with the user, and render images for the player.

Gatekeepers decide what will appear in the media.

Generalizability is the degree to which research procedures and samples may be generalized to the real world.

Genres are distinctive styles of creative works. The term is also used to represent different types or formats of media content.

Globalization is reducing differences that existed between nations in time, space, and culture.

Glocal is local people borrowing or adapting global ideas.

Gospel music derives from white and black southern church hymns.

Gross is the total box office revenue before expenses are deducted.

Group owners own a number of broadcast stations.

Hard news is the immediate coverage of recent events, such as accidents and crime.

Hegemony is the use of media to create a consensus around certain ideas so that they come to be accepted as common sense.

Hertz (Hz) is a measure of the frequency of a radio wave in cycles per second.

High fidelity is accurate reproduction of natural sound.

High-definition television (HDTV) is digital television that provides a wider and clearer picture than standard television.

Horizontal integration is the concentration of ownership by acquiring companies that are all in the same business.

Horizontal integration is the concentration of ownership by acquiring companies that are all in the same business.

Hybridizing genres or music blends different traditions into a new form.

Hypertext markup language (HTML) is used to format pages on the Web.

Hypertext transfer protocol (http) is the Internet protocol used to transfer files over the Web.

Indecency is when behavior or decisions are not appropriate and negatively deviate from social standards.

Indecent speech is graphic language that pertains to sexual or excretory functions.

Independent (indie) films are films not made by the major studios.

Independent variables are the causes of media effects.

Infomercials are paid television programs that promote a product.

Information campaigns use the techniques of advertising in an attempt to convince people to adopt prosocial behaviors.

In an **information society**, the exchange of information is the predominant economic activity.

Information workers create, process, transform, or store information.

The **infrastructure** is the underlying physical structure of communication networks.

Integrated marketing communications (IMC) assures that the use of all commercial media and messages is clear, consistent, and influential.

Intellectual property is a creative work of art, writing, film, or software that belongs to a legally protected owner.

Interactive communication allows the user to modify and control a message as it is presented.

International law includes treaties between countries, multi-country agreements, and rules established by international organizations.

Internet service providers (ISPs) provide connections to the Internet.

Internet2 is a new, faster version of the Internet.

Joint operation agreements (JOAs) allow competing newspapers to share resources while maintaining editorial independence.

A **junket** is an expense-paid trip intended to influence media coverage.

The **law of supply and demand** describes the relationship among the supply of products, prices, and consumer demand.

Laws are binding rules passed by legislatures, enforced by the executive power, and applied or adjudicated by courts.

Libel is harmful and untruthful written criticism from the media that intends to damage someone.

Licenses grant legal permission to operate a radio transmitter.

The theory of **limited effects** holds that the effects of the mass media on individuals are slight.

Literacy is the ability to read and understand a variety of information.

Live stream is when the events are streamed on the Internet and watched as they are happening live.

Local area networks (LANs) link computers within a department, building, or campus.

Localism is ownership and program decision making at the community level.

Localization refers to a global company adapting its programs to local markets to make them more attractive.

Local market monopoly occurs when one company owns (controls) the media in that community.

Local origination means created within the community by the cable operator.

Location-based services use information about the location of mobile phone users to tailor content to specific locations.

Low-power stations have more limited transmission power and cover smaller areas than regular FM stations.

Major film studios like Fox or Disney integrate all aspects of production and distribution.

Marginal costs are the incremental costs of each additional copy or unit of a product.

Marketplace of ideas is the concept that the truth and the best ideas will win out in competition.

A **mash-up** combines several audio and/or video segments or tracks into a new creation.

Mass audience is a large, broad audience interested in a variety of general topics.

Mass communication is one-to-many, with limited audience feedback.

Massively multiplayer online role-playing games (MMORPGs) are online games that thousands play at the same time in a virtual world.

Mattes are background paintings or photographs that are combined with performers in the foreground.

M-commerce means electronic shopping transactions completed with a cell phone.

Media departments negotiate on behalf of the advertiser to buy space from media companies.

Media effects are changes in knowledge, attitudes, or behaviors resulting from media exposure.

Media literacy means learning to think critically about the role of media in society.

Media relations focus on establishing and maintaining good relations with the media.

Mediated refers to communication transmitted through an electronic or mechanical channel.

Metered pay models require readers to pay a price to read more than a few articles.

Microwave systems transmit information between relay towers on highly focused beams of radio waves.

Miscellanies were magazines with a wide variety of content.

Mobile devices are handheld computers or cell phones with display screens. They access and send information using cell phone or Wi-Fi connections to the Internet.

Mobile virtual network operators (MVNOs) offer mobile services by leasing capacity from network owners.

Modems (modulator-demodulators) convert digital data to analog signals and vice versa.

Mods are modifications to game play or game environments made by users and amateur game developers.

Monopoly is the domination of a market by a single company.

Morality is the line between right and wrong behaviors and decisions.

Motion Picture Code of 1930 (Hays Code) was a self-regulation of sex on screen by the motion picture industry.

MPAA (Motion Picture Association of America) is a trade organization that represents the major film studios.

MPAA ratings are part of a movie-rating system instituted in 1968.

MP3 is a sound digitization and compression standard, short for MPEG-2 Layer 3.

Muckraking is investigative journalism that "rakes off the muck"—dirt and filth— to expose corruption and scandal.

Multilateral trade negotiations occur among a number of countries at the same time.

The **multistep flow** model assumes that media effects are indirect and are mediated by opinion leaders.

Multiple system operators (MSOs) are cable companies that operate systems in two or more communities.

Must carry is the policy that requires cable companies to carry local broadcast signals.

Narrowcasting targets media to specific segments of the audience.

National sovereignty is the policy of keeping domestic forces in control of a nation's economy, politics, and culture.

Net neutrality means users are not discriminated against based on the amount or nature of the data they transfer on the Internet.

New journalism was the investigative reporting of the nineteenth century.

New media are digital, interactive, social, asynchronous, multimedia, and narrowcasted.

News aggregates take stories from the original news sources for display on their own sites, hoping to attract audiences. Most do not pay the originators, who should be paid and referenced.

News magazines are weekly periodicals with coverage (text and visual) on current news events.

A **nickelodeon** is a phonograph or player piano operated by inserting a coin, originally a nickel.

Nonlinear editing uses digital equipment to rearrange scenes to make the master copy.

Novels are extended fictional works, usually of book length.

An **O&Os** is a TV or radio station that is owned and operated by a network.

Objectivity fosters news stories free of biases and opinions.

Obscenity refers to material where the dominant theme taken as a whole appeals to prurient, or sexually arousing, interest.

Oligopoly is the domination of a market by a few firms.

On demand means that audiences can download podcasts whenever they want.

Orphaned books are older books, perhaps still under copyright, whose authors are unknown.

Packet switching breaks up digital information into individually addressed chunks, or packets.

Partisan press are newspapers sponsored by a person or groups that support particular ideas, causes, politics, or individuals.

Pass-along rate is the number of people who see a single copy of a magazine.

A **patent** gives an inventor the exclusive right to make, use, or sell an invention for 20 years.

Pay TV charges cable customers an extra monthly fee to receive a specific channel.

Payola occurs when record companies give bribes to DJs to get their records played.

Paywall model limits the number of free articles that a reader can access.

Penny Press included daily newspapers that sold for 1 cent and had content that interested the average person.

Persuasion is the use of convincing arguments to change people's beliefs, attitudes, or behaviors.

Phishing is an online scam in which criminals pretend to be someone you trust in an effort to obtain money or sensitive information.

Plagiarism is using someone else's ideas and work without citation.

Platform is a basic type or brand of game system.

Playlists are the songs picked for air play.

Podcasting is recorded messages or audio programs distributed through download to computers, iPods, or other portable digital music players.

Policy is a public framework for structuring and regulating media, so they contribute to the public good.

Political economy analyzes patterns of class domination and economic power.

Popular culture is made up of elements mass produced in a society for the mass population.

Portals are Web pages that users launch when they first log on to the Web.

Postproduction includes editing, sound effects, and visual effects that are added after shooting the original footage.

PR agencies have multiple clients they represent.

Priming theory states that media images stimulate related thoughts in the minds of audience members.

Print-on-demand technology prints books only when they are ordered by customers.

Privacy is the right to avoid unwanted intrusions or disclosure.

Privatizing government assets refers to selling them to private owners.

Probable cause is a judge's decision that provisional evidence of criminal violation or national security danger justifies a wiretap.

Profits are what is left after operating costs, taxes, and paybacks to investors.

Propaganda is the intentional influence of attitudes and opinions.

Prosocial behaviors are those that a society values and encourages.

Protocols are technical rules governing data communication.

Public broadcasters aim to serve public interests with information, culture, and news.

Public opinion is the aggregate view of the general population.

Public relations activities are intended to favorably influence the public.

Publics are the different audiences that PR practitioners communicate with as part of their daily work.

Public utilities are regulated monopolies.

Radio Act of 1912 first licensed radio transmitters.

Radio waves are composed of electromagnetic energy and rise and fall in regular cycles.

Ratings measure the proportion of television households that watch a specific show or how many people are listening to a radio station.

Rear projection effects have images projected behind performers who are in the foreground.

Regional Bell operating companies (RBOCs) are the local telephone operating companies that AT&T divested in 1984.

Regionalization links nations together based on geographic, cultural, linguistic, and historical commonalities.

Regulation is government restriction or supervision of privately owned activity.

With **relationship marketing,** consumers develop a strong preference for brand through one-to-one communication.

Reliability is the extent to which a result is stable and consistent.

Research organizations compile statistics about consumers and their media habits and evaluate advertising messages.

Restraints of trade limit competition.

Retransmission fees are monthly per-subscriber fees that local broadcasters charge cable companies for the right to carry their programs.

Sales promotions are specific features like coupons that directly spur sales.

Satellite systems send information back and forth to relays in orbit around the earth.

A **satellite footprint** is the surface area covered by the satellite's signal.

The **scarcity argument** states that because there are a small number of stations and the cost of entry to broadcasting is high, extra regulation is required.

To **scoop** a rival newspaper is to be the first one to get the story and publish it.

Seditious speech is aimed at overthrowing the government.

Segmented audiences are consumers that can be grouped together because of specific demographics or special interests such as hobbies or politics.

Self-regulation pertains to communication industry codes and practices of monitoring and controlling the media's performance.

The **Sherman Antitrust Act** (1890) prohibits monopolies and the restraint of free trade.

Shoppers are free to readers and are supported by advertisers. Content sometimes includes news stories, but advertising is the main objective.

Smartphones are mobile phones that can access the Internet.

Snowball effects happen when a small event or issue builds quickly.

Social learning theory explains media consumption in terms of its expected outcomes.

Social media are media whose content is created and distributed through social interaction.

Social responsibility model calls on journalists to monitor the ethics of their own newsgathering and reporting.

Soft news stories can be covered or published at almost anytime.

Softcover books are usually printed and distributed in a manner similar to that of hard cover books. They are larger, exhibit more intricate artwork on the cover, and are more expensive than mass-market paperbacks.

The **Source-Message-Channel-Receiver (SMCR)** model of mass communication describes the exchange of information as the message passes from the source to the channel to the receiver, with feedback to the source.

Spamming is unsolicited commercial e-mailing.

Spyware is malicious software that secretly sends information about your online activities.

Standards are agreements about technical characteristics of communication systems.

The **star system** was the film studios' use of stars' popularity to promote their movies.

Stereo is splitting recorded sound into two separate channels.

Stereotyping is the making of generalizations about groups of people on the basis of limited information.

Stop Online Piracy Act (SOPA) was an antipiracy initiative by the film and music industries, defeated in 2011 because it seemed to limit Internet rights.

Streaming video converts video to continuous streams of data for transmission over the Internet.

The **studio system** in Hollywood emphasized key stars as a way to promote studio films.

Subscription libraries lent books to the public for a fee.

Survey studies make generalizations about a population of people by addressing questions to a sample of that population.

Syndication is the rental or licensing of media products.

Tabloids are newspapers focused on popular, sensational events.

Talkies are motion pictures with synchronized sound for dialogue.

Tariffs are taxes imposed by governments on goods imported from other countries.

Technological determinism explains that the media cause changes in society and culture.

The Telecommunications Act of 1996 is federal legislation that deregulated radio ownership rules and the communications media. It opened the U.S. telecommunications industry to competition.

Teletext was an early way to transmit digital news by cable or broadcast signals for display on TVs.

Theatrical films are those released for distribution in movie theaters.

Theories are general principles that explain and predict behavior.

Third-generation (3G) cell phones have high-speed data transmission capacity for video and Internet.

Top 40 is a radio format that replays the top 40 songs heavily.

Trade magazines are magazines that are targeted toward a particular profession.

Transmission-control protocol/Internet protocol (TCP/IP) is the basic protocol used by the Internet.

Trolling is being deliberately offensive online to others with the objective of upsetting them or getting a reaction or baiting them to do something.

UHF stands for ultrahigh frequency, channels 14 to 69.

Uniform resource locators (URLs) are the addresses of Web pages.

Unique visitors per month is the measure of how many different people visit the site within a month. A visitor can make many visits to the site, but is counted once. (It is the computer origination that is counted and not the person.)

Universal service is the principle that everyone should have basic access to telecommunication services.

Uses and gratifications is the theory that media are actively selected to satisfy our needs.

Validity is the degree to which we are actually measuring what we intend to measure.

Vertical integration occurs when a company with the same owner handles different aspects of a business within the same industry, such as film production and distribution or phone manufacturing and phone service.

VHF is the very high-frequency television band, channels 2 to 13.

Victrola was the trade name for an early phonograph.

A **video game** uses a television or similar screen to display the game play.

Videotex was an early way to transmit digital news by phone lines for display on TVs or early desktop computers. A modem and special software were needed to transmit the analog signals to digital ones and vice versa.

Viral marketing spreads ideas about products through chat rooms, blogs, social networking sites, or other Internet-based avenues.

Virtual reality is a computer-generated environment that immerses the user in a make-believe world.

Web 2.0 are Internet applications in which users can provide content as well as consume it.

A **webcast** is a real-time event transmitted over the Internet.

Wide area networks (WANs) connect computers that are miles apart.

Wi-Fi is short for *wireless fidelity,* a standard for wireless data.

Windows are separate film release times for different channels or media.

Wire services supply news to multiple paying news organizations; they were named originally for their use of telegraph wires. Modern wire services are digital and are called "news services."

Woodcuts were used to make illustrations by carving a picture in a block of wood, inking it, and pressing it onto paper.

Yellow journalism was the sensationalistic reporting of the nineteenth century.

REFERENCES

Ackley, S. (2013, November 14). Despite increased competition, local radio maintains competitive position in local ad market. *Local Media Watch, BIA Kelsey.* Retrieved from http://blog.biakelsey.com/index .php/2013/11/14/despite-increased-competition-local -radio-maintains-competitive-position-in-local-ad-market/

Adorno, T., & Horkheimer, M. (2007). The culture industry: Enlightenment as mass deception. In *Stardom and Celebrity: A Reader* (pp. 34–43). London and Thousand Oaks, CA: Sage.

Ahlbom, A., Feychting, M., Green, A., Kheifets, L., Savitz, D. A., & Swerdlow, A. J. (2009). Epidemiologic evidence on mobile phones and tumor risk: A review. *Epidemiology, 20*(5), 639–652.

Allen, R. (1992). *Channels of discourse, reassembled.* Chapel Hill: University of North Carolina Press.

Alsop, R. (Ed.). (1997). *The Wall Street Journal almanac, 1998.* New York: Ballantine Books.

Alter, A. (2015, September 22). The plot twist: E-book sales slip, and print is far from dead. *The New York Times.* Retrieved from http://www.nytimes. com/2015/09/23/business/media/the-plot-twist-e-book-sales-slip-and-print-is-far-from-dead.html?_r=0

Altheide, D. (1974). *Creating reality.* Beverly Hills, CA: Sage.

Altschull, H. (1995). *Agents of power* (2nd ed.). New York: Longman.

American Library Association. (2008). *Frequently challenged books of the 21st century.* Retrieved July 16, 2012, from http://www.ala.org/ala/issuesadvocacy/ banned/frequentlychallenged/21stcenturychallenged/ index.cfm

——. ALA Press Release. (2011, April 11). *Jobs-seekers, entrepreneurs continue to turn to their local library for help: State of America's Libraries Report 2011.* Retrieved April 11, 2011, from http://www.ala.org/ news/pr?d=6865

——. (2014). *State of America's libraries 2014.* Retrieved July 16, 2014, from http://www.ala .org/ news/state-americas-libraries-report-2014/ executive-summary

American Psychatric Association. (2013). *Diagnostic and statistical manual of mental disorders DSM-V.* Arlington, VA: Author.

Anderson, B. (1983). *Imagined communities: Reflections on the origin and spread of nationalism.* New York: Verso.

——. (2015). Technology device ownership: 2015. *Pew Research Center.* Retrieved from http://www.pewinternet.org/2015/10/29/ technology-device-ownership-2015/

Anderson, C. A., Berkowitz, L., Donnerstein, E., Huesmann, R. L., Johnson, J. D., Linz, D., et al. (2003). The influence of media violence on youth. *Psychological Science, 4*(3), 81–110.

Anderson, C. A., Gentile, D. A., & Buckley, K. E. (2007). *Violent video game effects on children and adolescents: Theory, research, and public policy.* New York: Oxford University Press.

Anderson, C. A., & Wolff, M. (2010, September). The web is dead. Long live the Internet. *Wired Magazine.* Retrieved April 22, 2012, from http://www.wired.com/ magazine/2010/08/ff_webrip/all/l

Anderson, J., & Meyer, T. (1988). Mediated communication. Newbury Park, CA: Sage.

Aoyama, Y., & Castells, M. (2002). An empirical assessment of the informational society: Employment and occupational structures of G-7 countries, 1920–2000. *International Labour Review, 141*(1/2), 123–160.

Apperley, T. H. (2006). Genre and game studies: Toward a critical approach to video game genres. *Simulation Gaming, 37*(1), 6–23.

Apte, U., Karmarkar, U., & Nath, H. (2012). The US information economy: Value, employment, industry structure, and trade. *Technology, Information and Operations Management, 6*(1), 1–87.

Arsenault, D. (2009). Video game genre, evolution and innovation. *Eludamos Journal for Computer Game Culture, 3*(2), 149–176.

Auletta, K. (2010). *Three blind mice: How the TV networks lost their way.* New York: Random House LLC.

Auletta, K. (2014, February 3). Outside the box: Netflix and the future of television. *The New Yorker,* 54–61.

Bachmair, B. (2006). Medien padagogik. *Medienpaed.* Retrieved July 10, 2013, from www.medienpaed .com/06-l/bachmair2.pdf

Bandura, A. (1965). Influence of models' reinforcement contingencies on the acquisition of imitative responses. *Journal of Personality and Social Psychology, 1,* 589–595.

——. (1986). *Social foundations of thought and action.* Englewood Cliffs, NJ: Prentice Hall.

Barlett, C. P. (2009). Video game effects—Confirmed, suspected, and speculative: A review of the evidence. *Simulation Gaming, 40,* 377–403.

Barnes, B. (2016, March 19). An educated guess on how much 'Star Wars: The Force Awakens' will make for Disney. *New York Times,* p. B6.

Barnouw, E. (1966). A *history of broadcasting in the United States.* New York: Oxford University Press.

Baron, M., Broughton, D., Buttross, S., Corrigan, S., Gedissman, A., González de Rivas, M. R., et al. (2001). Media violence. *Pediatrics, 108*(5), 1222–1226.

Bartsch, A., & Oliver, M. B. (2011). Making sense of entertainment on the interplay of emotion and cognition in entertainment. *Experience Journal of Media Psychology, 23*(1), 12–17. doi:10.1027/1864-1105/a000026

Baudrillard, J. (1983). *Simulations.* New York: Semiotext(e), Inc.

Bell, D. (1973). *The coming of post-industrial society.* New York: Basic Books.

Bellis, M. (2000). *The walkie-talkie: Al Gross.* Retrieved July 26, 2006, from http://web.mit.edu/invent/iow/gross.html

Bennett, W. L., & Iyengar, S. (2008). A new era of minimal effects? The changing foundations of political communication. *Journal of Communication, 58,* 707–731.

———. (2010). The shifting foundations of political communication: Responding to a defense of the media effects paradigm. *Journal of Communication, 60*(1), 35–39.

Benoit, W., & Hansen, G. (2004). Presidential debate watching, issue knowledge, character evaluation, and vote choice. *Human Communication Research, 30*(1), 121–144.

Benson, K., & Whitaker, J. (1990). *Television and audio handbook.* New York: McGraw-Hill.

Berg, M. (2015, November 2). The world's highest-paid YouTube stars 2015. *Forbes.* Retrieved from http://www.forbes.com/sites/maddieberg/2015/10/14/the-worlds-highest-paid-youtube-stars-2015/

Berger, A. (1992). *Popular culture genres.* Newbury Park, CA: Sage.

———. (2013). *Media analysis techniques.* Thousand Oaks, CA: Sage Publications.

Berkowitz, L. (1984). Some effects of thought on anti- and pro-social influences of media effects. *Psychological Bulletin, 95,* 410–427.

Berlo, D. K. (1960). *The process of communication: An introduction to theory and practice.* New York: Holt, Rinehart and Winston.

Bernard, R. M., Abrami, P. C., Borokhovski, E., Wade, C. A., & Ta, R. M. (2009). A meta-analysis of three types of interaction treatments in distance education. *Review of Educational Research, 79*(3), 1243.

Bernays, E. (1961). *Crystallizing public opinion.* Norman: University of Oklahoma Press.

Bessiere, K., Kiesler, S., Kraut, R., & Boneva, B. (2008). Effects of Internet use and social resources on changes in depression. *Information, Communication and Society, 11,* 47–70.

Billboard. (2011, December 17). Retrieved January 10, 2012, from http://www.billboard.com/author/6262

Blau, R. (2014). Brooklyn public library researchers answered 3.5 million questions in 2013, records show. *Daily News.* Retrieved March 27, 2014, from http://www.nydailynews.com/new-york/brooklyn/brooklyn-public-library-researchers-answered-3-5-million-questions-2013-records-show-article-l.1734547

Bluestone, M. (2015). U.S. publishing industry's annual survey reveals $28 billion in revenue in 2014. *Association of American Publishers.* Retrieved from http://publishers.org/news/us-publishing-industry's-annual-survey-reveals-28-billion-revenue-2014

———. (2016). AAP statshot: Publishers net revenue from book sales declines 2.0% through third quarter of 2015. *Association of American Publishers.* Retrieved from http://newsroom.publishers.org/aap-statshot-publisher-net-revenue-from-book-sales-declines-20-through-third-quarter-of-2015/

Bogost, I. (2007). *Persuasive games: The expressive power of videogames.* Cambridge, MA: MIT Press.

Bourdieu, P. (1984). *Distinction: A social critique of the judgment of taste.* Cambridge, MA: Harvard University Press.

Bouwman, H., & Christofferson, M. (Eds.). (1992). *Relaunching Videotext.* Boston: Kluwer Academic Publishers.

———. (1998). *On television.* New York: New Press.

Bowker. (2013). *2013 U.S. book consumer demographics & buying behaviors annual review* [Preview PDF]. Retrieved January 10, 2014, from http://www.bookconsumer.com/store/product.php?id=51

Boyd, D. (2014). *It's complicated: The social lives of networked teens.* New Haven, CT: Yale University Press.

Boyland, E. J., Nolan, S., Kelly, B., Tudur-Smith, C., Jones, A., Halford, J. C., & Robinson, E. (2016). Advertising as a cue to consume: A systematic review and meta-analysis of the effects of acute exposure to unhealthy food and nonalcoholic beverage advertising on intake in children and adults. *The American Journal of Clinical Nutrition, 103,* 519–599. doi:10.3945/ajcn.115.120022

Braestrup, P. (1977). *Big story: How the American press and television reported and interpreted the crisis of Tet 1968 in Vietnam and Washington.* Boulder, CO: Westview Press.

Braudel, F. (1994). *A history of civilizations.* New York: Penguin.

Braunstein, Y. (2000). The FCC's financial qualification requirements: Economic evaluation of a barrier to entry for minority broadcasters. *Federal Communications Law Journal, 53*(1), 69–90.

Brinkley, J. (1997, July 21). Companies are on a quest for your ears. *New York Times.* Retrieved from http://www.nytimes.com/1997/07/21/business/companies-are-on-a-quest-for-your-ears.html

Brody, G. (1990). Effects of television viewing on family interactions: An observational study. *Family Relations, 29,* 216–220.

Broom, G. (2009). *Cutlip and center's effective public relations* (10th ed.). Englewood Cliffs, NJ: Prentice Hall.

Brown, J. D., & L'Engle, K. L. (2009). Sexual attitudes and behaviors associated with U.S. early adolescents' exposure to sexually explicit media. *Communication Research, 36*(1), 129–151.

Bryce, J., Rutter, J., & Sullivan, C. (2006). Digital games and gender. In J. Rutter & J. Bryce (Eds.), *Understanding digital games* (pp. 185–204). Thousand Oaks, CA: Sage.

Brynjolfsson, E., & McAfee, A. (2011). *Race against the machine: How the digital revolution is accelerating innovation, driving productivity, and irreversibly transforming employment and the economy.* Lexington, MA: Digital Frontier Press.

Buijzen, M., & Valkenburg, P. (2003). The unintended effects of television advertising: A parent-child survey. *Communication Research, 30*(5), 483–503.

———. (2013). The intended and unintended effects of advertising on children. In E. Scharrer (Ed.), *Media effects / media psychology: The international encyclopedia of media studies* (pp. 586–607). San Francisco, CA: Wiley-Blackwell.

Bureau of Labor Statistics (BLS). (2012). *Telecommunications.* Retrieved January 5, 2013, from http://www.bls.gov/oco/cg/cgs020.htm

———. (2014). *Occupational outlook handbooks.* Retrieved March 13, 2014, from http://www.bls.gov/oob/media-and-communication/editors.htm

———. (2015a). *NAICS 541800 – advertising, public relations, and related services.* Retrieved January 29, 2016 from http://www.bls.gov/oes/current/naics4_541800.htm

———. (2015b). *Occupational outlook handbook.* Retrieved January 27, 2016 from http://www.bls.gov/ooh/a-z-index.htm

———. (2016). Industries at a glance: Telecommunications: NAICS 517. Retrieved February 6, 2016 from http://www.bls.gov/iag/tgs/iag517.htm.

Burke, K. (2015, August 6). How financial aid is driving up college textbook prices. *Market Watch.* Retrieved from http://www.marketwatch.com/story/400-for-a-book-why-college-textbooks-are-going-the-way-of-the-dinosaur-2015-08-05?page=1

Burke, M., Marlow, C., & Lento, T. (2010, April 27). *Social network activity and social wellbeing.* Paper presented at the Computer Human Interaction Conference, Atlanta, Georgia.

Bushman, B. J., & Anderson, C. A. (2009). Comfortably numb: Desensitizing effects of violent media on helping others. *Psychological Science, 20*(3), 273–277.

Bushman, B. J., & Cantor, J. (2003). Media ratings for violence and sex: Implications for policymakers and parents. *The American Psychologist, 58*(2), 130–141.

Button, L. (2016, March 1). Wi11 education session reveals overall trends in book retailing. *American Booksellers Association.* Retrieved from http://www.bookweb.org/news/wi11-education-session-reveals-overall-trends-book-retailing

Campbell, J., & Carlson, M. (2002). Panopticon.com: Online surveillance and the commodification of privacy. *Journal of Broadcasting & Electronic Media, 46*(4), 586–606.

Capella, M. L., Webster, C., & Kinard, B. R. (2011). A review of the effect of cigarette advertising. *International Journal of Research in Marketing, 28*(3), 269–279.

Card, D., & Dahl, G. (2011). Family violence and football: The effect of unexpected emotional cues on violent behavior. *Quarterly Journal of Economics, 126*(1), 103–143. Retrieved from http://www.ncbi.nlm.nih.gov/pmc/articles/PMC3712874/

Carey, J. (1972). *Politics of the electronic revolution or 1989 commas culture?* Urbana: University of Illinois.

———. (1989). *Communication as culture: Essays on media and society.* Boston, MA: Unwin Hyman.

Carnagey, N., Anderson, C., & Bushman, B. (2007). The effect of video game violence on physiological desensitization to real-life violence. *Journal of Experimental and Social Psychology, 43*(3), 489.

Caroli, M., Argentieri, L., Cardone, M., & Masi, A. (2004). Role of television in childhood obesity prevention. *International Journal of Obesity, 28,* S104–S108.

Cassell, J., & Jenkins, H. (1998). *From Barbie to Mortal Kombat: Gender and computer games.* Cambridge, MA: MIT Press.

Castells, M. (1997). *The Power of Identity.* Malden, MA: Blackwell Publishers.

———. (2000). *Rise of the network society: The information age: Economy, society and culture* (2nd ed.). Cambridge, MA: Blackwell Publishers, Inc.

———. (2004). *The power of identity* (2nd ed.). Cambridge, MA: Blackwell Publishers, Inc.

Catalano, F. (2015, January 18). Paper is back: Why "real" books are on the rebound. *Geek Wire.* Retrieved form http://www.geekwire.com/2015/paper-back-real-books-rebound/

Center for Copyright Information (CCI). (2014). Retrieved July 16, 2014, from http://www.copyrightinformation.org/

Centers for Disease Control and Prevention. (2013). Notes from the field: Electronic cigarette use among middle and high school students—United States, 2011–2012. *Morbidity and Mortality Weekly Report, 62*(35), 729–730. Retrieved September 10, 2013, from http://www.cdc.gov/mmwr/preview/mmwrhtml/mm6235a6.htm?s_cid=mm6235a6_w

Centers for Disease Control and Prevention. (2014). *New CDC study finds dramatic increase in e-cigarette-related calls to poison centers.* Retrieved April 30, 2014, from http://www.cdc.gov/media/releases/2014/p0403-e-cigarette-poison.html

Chandra, A., Martino, S. C., Collins, R. L., Elliott, M. N., Berry, S. H., Kanouse, D. E., et al. (2008). Does watching sex on television predict teen pregnancy? Findings from a national longitudinal survey of youth. *Pediatrics, 122*(5), 1047–1054.

Chang, A., Aeschbach, D., Duffy, J., & Czeisler, C. (2015, January). Evening use of light-emitting ereaders negatively affects sleep, circadian timing, and next-morning alertness. *Proceedings of the National Academy of Sciences, 112*(4), 1232–1237. Retrieved from http://www.pnas.org/content/112/4/1232.full.pdf

Chess, S., & Shaw, A. (2015). A conspiracy of fishes, or, how we learned to stop worrying about #GamerGate and embrace hegemonic masculinity. *Journal of Broadcasting & Electronic Media, 59*(1), 208–220.

Chlapowski, F. (1991). The constitutional protection of informational privacy. *Boston University Law Review, 71,* 133.

Chmielewski, T. (n.d.). The average author's salary for one book. *Houston Chronicle.* Retrieved from http://work.chron.com/average-authors-salary-one-book-7181.html

Cho, J. (2011). The geography of political communication: Effects of regional variations in campaign advertising on citizen communication. *Human Communication Research, 37,* 434–462. doi:10.1111/j.1468-2958.2011.01406.x

Chomsky, N., & Herman, E. (1988). *Manufacturing consent: The political economy of the mass media*. New York: Pantheon Books.

Christians, C., Rotzoll, K., & Fackler, M. (1991). *Media ethics: Cases and moral reasoning* (3rd ed.). New York: Longman.

Christman, E. (2014, January 3). Digital music sales decrease for first time in 2013. Retrieved January 4, 2014, from http://www.billboard.com/biz/articles/news/digital-and-mobile/5855162/digital-music-sales-decrease-for-first-time-in -2013

Cisco. (2015). Cisco visual networking index: Forecast and methodology, 2014–2019. Retrieved January 15, 2016 from http://www.cisco.com/c/en/us/solutions/collateral/service-provider/ip-ngn-ip-next-generation-network/white_paper_c11-481360.pdf

Clark, C. (1972). Race, identification and television violence. In G. Comstock, E. Rubenstein, & J. Murray (Eds.), *Television and social behavior* (Vol. 5, pp. 120–184). Washington, DC: U.S. Government Printing Office.

Clark, D. B., Tanner-Smith, E. E., & Killingsworth, S. S. (2015). Digital games, design, and learning a systematic review and meta-analysis. *Review of educational research, 18,* 79–122. doi:10.3102/0034654315582065

CNET. (2014). *Sega Dreamcast: Gaming's most magnificent failure*. Retrieved February 12, 2014, from http://www.cnet.com/news/sega-dreamcast-gamings-most -magnificent-failure-video/

Colista, C., & Leshner, G. (1998). Traveling music: Following the path of music through the global market. *Critical Studies in Mass Communication, 15,* 181–194.

Common Sense Media. (2006). *New national poll: The Internet now seen as #1 media concern for parents*. Retrieved Februrary 1, 2007, from http://www.commonsensemedia.org/news/press-releases.php?id=23

Computing Research Association. (2011). *Taulbee survey report 2009–2010*. Retrieved January 30, 2012, from http://www.cra.org/resources/taulbee/

comScore. (2013a). *comScore announces availability of U.S. mobile commerce sales estimates by product category and leading individual retailer*. Retrieved August 29, 2013, from http://www.comscore.com/Insights/Press_Releases/2013/8/comScore_Announces_ Availability_of_US_Mobile_Commerce_Sales_ Estimates

——. (2013b). *comScore releases November 2013 U.S. online video rankings*. Retrieved December 22, 2013, from http://www.comscore.com/Insights/Press_Releases/2013/12/comScore_Releases_November_2013_US._Online_Video_Rankings

——. (2014). *comScore reports November 2013 U.S. smartphone subscriber market share*. Retrieved January 8, 2014, from http://www.comscore.com/Insights/Press_Releases/2014/1/comScore_ Reports_November_2013_US_Smartphone_ Subscriber_Market_Share

——. (2015). comScore releases October 2015 U.S. desktop online video rankings. Retrieved from http://www.comscore.com/Insights/Market-Rankings/comScore-Releases-October-2015-US-Desktop-Online-Video-Rankings

Connell, P. M., Brucks, M., & Nielsen, J. H. (2014). How childhood advertising exposure can create biased product evaluations that persist into adulthood. *Journal of Consumer Research, 41*(1), 119–134.

Cook, T., Appleton, H., Conner, R., Shaffer, A., Tamkin, G., & Weber, S. (1975). *Sesame Street revisited: A case study in evaluation research*. New York: Russell Sage Foundation.

Cox, K. (2011). *The Gamer's Gaze*. Retrieved March 3, 2012, from http://www.your-critic.com/2011/06/gamers-gaze-part-l.html

Craig, T. (2011, Novemeber 21). Orogold cosmetics: Fool's gold. Retrieved from http://www.snobessentials.com/2011/11/oro-gold-cosmetics-fools-gold.html

Crawford, G., & Rutter, J. (2006). Digital games and cultural studies. In J. Rutter & J. Bryce (Eds.), *Understanding digital games* (pp. 148–165). Thousand Oaks, CA: Sage.

Cringely, R. (1998). *Nerds 2.0.1*. Retrieved September 17, 2002, from http://www.pbs.Org/opb/nerds2.0.l/

Croteau, D., & Hoynes, W. (2002). Social inequality and media representation. *In Media society: Industries, images, and audiences* (pp. 185–216). Thousand Oaks, CA: Pine Forge Press.

Curtis, A. (2011). *The brief history of social media*. Retrieved April 22, 2012, from http://www.uncp.edu/home/acurtis/NewMedia/SocialMedia/ SocialMedia-History.html

Czitrom, D. (1982). *Media and the American mind*. Chapel Hill: University of North Carolina Press.

Dailey, D., Bryne, A., Powell, A., Karaganis, J., & Chung, J. (2010). *Broadband adoption in low-income communities*. A Social Science Research Council report. Retrieved April 20, 2012, from http://www.ssrc.org/publications/view/lEB76F62 -C720-DF11-9D32-001CC477EC70/

Dates, J., & Barlow, W. (1997). Does mass media realistically portray African American culture? No. In A. Alexander & J. Hanson (Eds.), *Taking sides: Clashing views on controversial issues in mass media and society*. Guilford, CT: Dushkin/Brown & Benchmark.

Davenport, L. (1987). A *co-orientation analysis of newspaper editors and readers' attitudes toward videotex, online news and databases: A study of perceptions and opinions*. Doctoral dissertation, Ohio University.

——. (1988, July). *Are update: 1976 and 1987 editors' predictions of audience reactions to videotex; and a comparison: 1987 audience reactions and 1976 and 1987 editors' predictions*. Paper presented to the Newspaper Division, Association for Education in Journalism and Mass Communication National Convention, Portland, Oregon.

Davenport, L., Fico, F., & DeFleur, M. (2002, Spring). Computer-assisted reporting in classrooms: A decade of diffusion. *Journalism Educator, 57*(1), 6–22.

Davenport, L., Randle, Q., & Bossen, H. (2007). Now you see it, now you don't: The problems with newspaper photo archives. *Visual Communication Quarterly, 14*(4), 218–230.

Davis, K. (1985). *Two-bit culture*. Boston, MA: Houghton-Mifflin.

Davis, K. C., Farrelly, M. C., Messeri, P., & Duke, J. (2009). The impact of national smoking prevention campaigns on tobacco-related beliefs, intentions to smoke and smoking initiation: Results from a longitudinal survey of youth in the United States. *International Journal of Environmental Research and Public Health, 6*(2), 722–740.

Day, L. (1991). *Ethics in media communications: Cases and controversies.* Belmont, CA: Wadsworth.

de Sola Pool, I. (1983). *Forecasting the telephone: A retrospective technology assessment of the telephone.* Norwood, NJ: Ablex.

De Zuniga, H. G., Jung, N., Valenzuela, S. (2012). Social media use for news and individuals' social capital, civic engagement and political participation. *Journal of Computer-Mediated Communication, 17*(3), 319–336.

Deacon, D., Mudrock, G., Pickering, M., Golding, P. (2007). *Researching communications: A practical guide to methods in media and cultural analysis.* New York: Bloomsbury.

Dibbel, J. (1993, December 21). A rape in cyberspace. *The Village Voice,* 36–42.

DiGrazia, J., McKelvey, K., Bollen, J., & Rojas, F. (2013). More tweets, more votes: Social media as a quantitative indicator of political behavior. *PLoS ONE, 8*(11), e79449. doi:10.1371/journal.pone.0079449

Dizard, W. (1997). *Old media, new media.* New York: Longman.

Douglas, S. (2004). *Listening in: Radio and the American imagination.* Minneapolis: University of Minnesota Press.

Downs, E., & Smith, S. L. (2010). Keeping abreast of hypersexuality: A video game character content analysis. *Sex Roles, 62,* 721–733. doi:10.1007/S11199-009-9637-1

Durkin, S. J., Biener, L., & Wakefield, M. A. (2009). Effects of different types of antismoking ads on reducing disparities in smoking cessation among socioeconomic subgroups. *American Journal of Public Health, 99*(12), 2217–2223.

Eagan, K., Stolzenberg, E. B., Bates, A. K., Aragon, M. C., Suchard, M. R., & Rios-Aguilar, C. (2015). *The American freshman: National norms fall 2015.* Los Angeles, CA: Higher Education Research Institute, UCLA. Retrieved April 17, 2016 from http://www.heri.ucla.edu/monographs/TheAmericanFreshman2015.pdf

Eagan, K., Stolzenberg, E. B., Ramirez, J. J., Aragon, M. C., Suchard, M. R., & Hurtado, S. (2014). *The American freshman: National norms fall 2014.* Los Angeles, CA: Higher Education Research Institute, UCLA. Retrieved January 27, 2016 from http://www.heri.ucla.edu/monographs/TheAmericanFreshman2014.pdf

Eastin, M. S. (Ed.). (2013). *Encyclopedia of media violence.* Thousand Oaks, CA: Sage.

Eastman, L. (1993). *Broadcast Icable programming.* Belmont, CA: Wadsworth.

Edmonds, R. (2015). Worldwide newspaper circulation revenues pass advertising for the first time. *WAN-IFRA* (World Association of Newspapers and Newspaper Publishers). Retrieved from http://www.poynter.org/2015/worldwide-newspaper-circulation-revenues-pass-advertising-for-the-first-time/347771/

Edwards, B. (2004). *Edward R. Murrow and the birth of broadcast journalism.* New York: Wiley.

——. (2009). *30 years of handheld game systems.* Retrieved from http://www.pcworld.com/article/183679/30_years_of_handheld_game_systems.html

Egan, K., Lozano, J. B., Hurtado, S. & Case, M. H. (2013). *The American freshman: National norms fall 2013.* Retrieved February 11, 2014, from http://www.heri.ucla.edu/monographs/TheAmericanFreshman2013.pdf

Egenfeldt-Nielsen, S., Smith, J. H., & Tosca, S. P. (2008). *Understanding the video games.* New York: Routledge.

Ellison, N., Steinfeld, C., & Lampe, C. (2007). The benefits of Facebook "friends": Social capital and college students' use of online social network sites. *Journal of Computer-Mediated Communication, 12*(4), article 1. Retrieved from http://jcmc.indiana.edu/vol12/issue4/ellison.html

Ellul, J. (1990). *The technological bluff.* Grand Rapids, MI: Eerdmans.

eMarketer. (2016). Digital Ad spending to surpass tv next year. Retrieved April 17, 2016 from http://www.emarketer.com/Article/Digital-Ad-Spending-Surpass-TV-Next-Year/1013671

ESA (Entertainment Software Association). (2011). Essential facts about the computer and video game industry. Retrieved March 3, 2012, from http:// www.theesa.com/facts/pdfs/ESA_EF_2011.pdf

——. (2015). Essential facts about the computer and video game industry. Retrieved February 8, 2016 from http://www.theesa.com/wp-content/uploads/2015/04/ESA-Essential-Facts-2015.pdf

Everett, G. (1993). The age of new journalism, 1883–1900. In W. Sloan, J. Stovall, & J. Startt (Eds.), *Media in America: A history* (2nd ed.). Scottsdale, AZ: Publishing Horizons.

Ewen, S. (1976). *Captains of consciousness.* New York: McGraw-Hill.

——. (2008). *Captains of consciousness: Advertising and the social roots of the consumer culture.* New York: Basic Books.

Fairchild, A. L., Bayer, R., & Colgrove, J. (2014). The re-normalization of smoking? E-cigarettes and the tobacco "endgame." *New England Journal of Medicine, 370,* 2354.

FCC. (2012a). *Local telephone competition as of December 31, 2012.* Retrieved from http://hraunfoss.fcc.gov/edocs_public/attachmatch/DOC-324413Al.pdf

——. (2012b). *Report on ownership of commercial broadcast stations.* Retrieved March 1, 2014, from http://www.fcc.gov/guides/ownership-report-commercial-broadcast-station-form-323

——. (2013). *16th mobile wireless competition report.* Retrieved March 1, 2014, from http://www.fcc.gov/document/16th-mobile-competition-report

——. (2014). Report on ownership of commercial broadcast stations. Retrieved January 11, 2016 from https://apps.fcc.gov/edocs_public/attachmatch/DA-14-924A1.pdf

——. (2015). 18th mobile wireless competition report. Retrieved February 5, 2016 from https://www.fcc.gov/document/18th-mobile-wireless-competition-report

Featherstone, M. (1990). Perspectives on consumer culture. *Sociology, 24,* 5–22.

Federman, J. (1998). *National television violence study, vol. 3, executive summary.* Santa Barbara: University of California, Santa Barbara, Center for Communication and Social Policy.

Ferguson, C. J. (2009). Media violence effects and violent crime: Good science or moral panic? In C. J. Ferguson (Ed.), *Violent crime: Clinical and social implications* (pp. 37–57). Thousand Oaks, CA: Sage.

Ferguson, C. J., Coulson, M., & Barnett, J. (2011). A meta-analysis of pathological gaming prevalence and comorbidity with mental health, academic and social problems. *Journal of Psychiatric Research, 45*(12), 1573–1576.

Ferguson, C. J., Coulson, M., & Griffiths, J. B. (2011). A meta-analysis of pathological gaming prevalence and comorbidity with mental health, academic and social problems. *Journal of Psychiatric Research, 45*(12), 1573–1578. Retrieved from http://www.tamiu.edu/~cferguson/Video%20Game%20Addiction.pdf

Ferguson, C. J., & Kilburn, J. (2010, March). Much ado about nothing: The misestimation and overinterpretation of violent video game effects in Eastern and Western nations: Comment on Anderson et al. (2010). *Psychological Bulletin, 136*(2), 174–178. doi:10.1037/a0018566

Feshbach, S., & Singer, R. (1971). *Television and aggression.* San Francisco, CA: Jossey-Bass.

Fisch, S., & Truglio, R. (Eds.). (2001). *"G" is for growing: Thirty years of research on children and Sesame Street.* Mahwah, NJ: Erlbaum.

Fischer, C. (1992). *America calling.* Berkeley: University of California Press.

Flew, T. (2012). *The creative industries culture and policy.* London: Sage.

Foasberg, N. (2014). Student reading practices in print and electronic media. *CUNY Academic Works.* Retrieved from http://academicworks.cuny.edu/qc_pubs/10

Folkerts, J., & Teeter, D. (1994). *Voices of a nation: A history of mass media in the United States.* New York: Macmillan.

Ford, T (1997). Effects of stereotypical television portrayals of African-Americans on person perception. *Social Psychology Quarterly, 60*(3), 266–275.

Fowler, M., & Brenner, D. (1982). A marketplace approach to broadcast regulation. *Texas Law Review, 60,* 207–257.

Fox, J., Bailenson, J. N., & Tricase, L. (2013). The embodiment of sexualized virtual selves: The Proteus effect and experiences of self-objectification via avatars. *Computers in Human Behavior, 29*(3), 930–938.

Fox, S. (1984). *The mirror makers: A history of American advertising.* London: Heinemann.

Franz, M. M., Freedman, P., Goldstein, K., & Ridout, T. N. (2008). Understanding the effect of political advertising on voter turnout: A response to Krasno and Green. *The Journal of Politics, 70,* 262–268.

Fratrik, M., Boland, M., & Ducey, R. (2015). BIA/Kelsey's U.S. local advertising forecast for 2016. Retrieved from http://www.biakelsey.com/webinars/BIAKelsey-U-S-Local-Advertising-Forecast-for-2016-Key-Findings.pdf

Freemuse. (2007). *Freedom of musical expression.* Retrieved October 12, 2007, from http://www .freemuse.org/

FreePress. (2011). *Who owns the media?* Retrieved July 14, 2012, from http://www.savetheinternet.com/ownership/chart

French, H. W. (2006, June 30). China vows broad new censorship measures. *New York Times.* Retrieved June 30, 2006, from http://www.nytimes .com/2006/06/30/world/asia/30iht-china.2093703 .html?_r=1

Freud, S. (1949). *An outline of psychoanalysis.* (J. Strachey, Trans.). New York: W. W. Norton.

Fridkin, K. L., Kenney, P. J., Gershon, S. A., & Woodall, G S. (2008). Spinning debates: The impact of the news media's coverage of the final 2004 presidential debate. *The International Journal of Press / Politics, 13*(1), 29–51.

Frost, R. (1996, November 21). The electronic Gutenberg fails to win mass appeal. *Wall Street Journal,* p. B6.

Fuchs, C. (2009). Information and communication technologies and society: A contribution to the critique of the political economy of the Internet. *European Journal of Communication, 24*(1), 69–87.

Galtung, J., & Ruge, M. H. (1965). The structure of foreign news. *Journal of Peace Research, 2*(1), 64–91.

Gandy, O. (1982). *Beyond agenda setting: Information subsidies and public policy.* Norwood, NJ: Ablex.

Garth, J. (2003). *Tolkien and the Great War: The threshold of Middle-Earth.* New York: Houghton-Mifflin.

Gee, J. P. (2003). *What video games have to teach us about learning and literacy.* New York: Macmillan.

Gentile, D. A., Lynch, P., Linder, J., & Walsh, D. (2004). The effects of violent video game habits on adolescent hostility, aggressive behaviors, and school performance. *Journal of Adolescence, 27,* 5–22.

Gentile, D. A., Maier, J. A., Hasson, M. R., & de Bonetti, B. L. (2011). Parents' evaluation of media ratings a decade after the television ratings were introduced. *Pediatrics, 128,* 36–44. doi:10.1542/peds.2010–3026

Gerbner, G., Gross, L., Morgan, M., & Signorelli, N. (1994). Growing up with television: The cultivation perspective. In J. Bryant & D. Zillmann (Eds.), *Media effects: Advances in theory and research* (pp. 17–41). Hillsdale, NJ: Lawrence Erlbaum.

Gilder, G. (2000). *Telecosm: How infinite bandwidth will revolutionize our world.* New York: Free Press.

Gitlin, T. (1983). *Inside prime time.* New York: Pantheon Books.

GLAAD. (2013). Where we are on TV: 2012–2013 season. Retrieved from https://www.glaad.org/publications/whereweareontvl2

Glascock, J. (2001). Gender roles on prime-time network television: Demographics and behaviors. *Journal of Broadcasting & Electronic Media, 45*(4), 656–669.

——. (2003). Gender, race, and aggression in newer TV networks' primetime programming. *Comunication Quarterly, 51,* 90–100.

Gomery, D. (1991). *Movie history: A survey.* Belmont, CA: Wadsworth.

Gramsci, A. (1971). *Selections from the prison notebooks.* New York: International Publishers.

——. (1994). *Letters from prison.* New York: Columbia University Press.

Gray, H. (1995). *Watching race: Television and the struggle for "Blackness."* Minneapolis: University of Minnesota Press.

Green, R. (2015). The game changer: Social media and the 2016 presidential election. *The Huff Post Politics.* Retrieved from http://www.huffingtonpost.com/r-kay-green/the-game-changer-social-m_b_8568432.html

Greitemeyer, T., & Mügge, D. O. (2014). Video games do affect social outcomes: A meta-analytic review of the effects of violent and prosocial video game play. *Personality and Social Psychology Bulletin, 40*(5), 578–589. doi: 10.1177/0146167213520459

Grossman, D., & DeGaetano, G. (2009). *Stop teaching our kids to kill: A call to action against TV, movie and video game violence.* New York: Crown Publishing. Retrieved from http://www.enotalone.com/personal-growth/45 73.html

Guback, T., & Varis, T. (1982). *Transnational communication and cultural industries* (Reports and Papers on Mass Communication no. 92). Paris: UNESCO.

Guernsey, L. (2001, September 20). An unimaginable emergency put communications to the test. *New York Times.* Retrieved September 20, 2001, from http://www.nytimes.com/2001/09/20/technology/circuits/201NFR.html

Gustafsen, K. (2006). *Deregulation and the market in public discourse: The AT&T divestiture, the 1996 Telecommunications Act, and the development of a commercial Internet.* PhD dissertation, University of Texas Libraries, Austin, TX.

Hall, S. (1980). Encoding/Decoding. In S. Hall, D. Hobson, A. Lowe, & P. Willis (Eds.), *Culture, media, language.* London: Hutchinson.

Hammermeister, J., Brock, B., Winterstein, D., & Page, R. (2005). Life without TV? Cultivation theory and psychosocial health characteristics of television-free individuals and their television-viewing counterparts. *Health Communication, 17*(3), 253–264.

Hargittai, E., & Hinnant, A. (2008). Differences in young adults' use of the Internet. *Communication Research, 35*(5), 602–621.

Harris, R. J., & Barlett, C. P. (2008). Effects of sex in the media. In J. Bryant & M. B. Oliver (Eds.), *Media effects advances in theory and research* (3rd ed., p. 324). New York: Erlbaum.

Heine, C., & Swant, M. (2015, December 23). Why the beatles needed digital streaming to maintain their brand. *AdWeek.* Retrieved from http://www.adweek.com/news/technology/why-beatles-needed-digital-streaming-maintain-their-brand-168742

Heins, M. (1993). *Sex, sin and blasphemy.* New York: New Press.

Hilbert, M., & López, P. (2011, April 1). The World's Technological Capacity to Store, Communicate, and Compute Information. *Science, 332*(6025), 60–65. Published online 10 February 2011. doi:10.1126/science.1200970

Hesmondhalgh, D. J. (2008). Cultural and creative industries. In T. Bennett & J. Frow (Eds.), *The SAGE handbook of cultural analysis* (pp. 553–569). London: Sage.

——. (2013). *The cultural industries* (3rd ed.). London: Sage.

HHS. (2010). *Childhood obesity.* Retrieved May 10, 2010, from http://aspe.hhs.gov/health/reports/child_obesity/

Hilmes, M. (1997). *Radio voices: American broadcasting, 1922–1952.* Minneapolis: University of Minnesota Press.

Hilmes, M., Newcomb, H., & Meehan, E. (2012). Legacies from the past: Histories of television. *Journal of Communication Inquiry, 36*(4), 276–287.

Holbert, R. L., Weeks, B. E., & Esralew, S. (2013). Approaching the 2012 U.S. presidential election from a diversity of explanatory principles understanding, consistency, and hedonism. *American Behavioral Scientist, 57*(12), 1663–1687.

Holzmann, G., & Pherson, B. (1994). *The early history of data networks.* Retrieved from http://www.it.kth.se/docs/early_net/toc.html

Horkheimer, M., & Adorno, T. W. (1972). *Dialectic of enlightenment* (J. Cumming, Trans.). New York: Herder and Herder.

Hovland, C., Lumsdane, A., & Sheffield, F. (1949). *Experiments on mass communications.* Princeton, NJ: Princeton University Press.

Huber, G., & Arceneaux, K. (2007). Identifying the persuasive effects of presidential advertising. *American Journal of Political Science, 51*(4), 957.

Huesmann, L. R., Dubow, E. F., Boxer, P., Souweidane, V., & Ginges, J. (2012). Foreign wars and domestic prejudice: How media exposure to the Israeli-Palestinian conflict predicts ethnic stereotyping by Jewish and Arab American adolescents. *Journal of Research on Adolescence, 22*(3), 556–570.

Huesmann, L. R., & Eron, L. D. (1986). The development of aggression in American children as a consequence of television violence viewing. In L. Huesmann, & L. Eron (Eds.), *Television and the aggressive child* (pp. 45–80). Hillsdale, NJ: Lawrence Erlbaum.

——. (2013). The development of aggression in children of different cultures: Psychological processes and exposure to violence. In *Television and the aggressive child: A cross-national Comparison* (pp. 1–27). London: Routledge.

Huesmann, L. R., Moise-Titus, J., Podolski, C., & Eron, L. (2003). Longitudinal relations between children's exposure to TV violence and their aggressive and violent behavior in young adulthood: 1977–1992. *Developmental Psychology, 39*(2), 201–221.

Huntzicker, W. (1993). The frontier press 1800–1900. In W. Sloan, J. Stovall, & J. Startt (Eds.), *Media in America: A history* (2nd ed.). Scottsdale, AZ: Publishing Horizons.

Hust, S. J., & Brown, J. D. (2008). Gender, media use, and effects. In S. L. Calvert & B. J. Wilson (Eds.), *The handbook of children, media, and development* (98–120). Malden, MA: Wiley-Blackwell.

Hwang, Y., & Jeong, S. (2009). Revisiting the knowledge gap hypothesis: A meta-analysis of thirty-five years of research. *Journalism & Mass Communication Quarterly, 86*(3), 513–532. doi:10.1177/107769900908600304

IDC. (2015). Smartphone vendor market share 2015 Q2. Retrieved February 6, 2016 from http://www.idc.com/prodserv/smartphone-market-share.jsp

IGN Entertainment. (2010). IGN's top 100 games. Retrieved January 11, 2011, from http://top100.ign.com/2005/001-010.html

Ingram, M. (2015, December 22). Print books sales are up, but don't start celebrating just yet. *Fortune.* Retrieved from http://fortune.com/2015/12/22/print-book-sales/

International Federation of the Phonographic Industry (IFPI). (2014). *IFPA digital music report 2014.* London: Author.

——. (2015). *Digital music report.* London: Author. Retrieved from http://www.ifpi.org/downloads/Digital-Music-Report-2015.pdf

——. (2016). IFPI digital music report 2015 [Press release]. Retrieved from http://www.ifpi.org/downloads/Digital-Music-Report-2015.pdf

Internet Advertising Bureau. (2015). IAB internet advertising revenue report 2014 full year results. Retrieved February 3, 2016 from http://www.iab.com/wp-content/uploads/2015/05/IAB_Internet_Advertising_Revenue_FY_2014.pdf

Irving, L. (1998, September 18). *Minority commercial broadcast ownership report.* Washington, DC: National Telecommunications and Information Administration.

Issenberg, S. (2012). The victory lab: The secret science of winning campaigns. New York: Crown Publishers.

Ito, M., Horst, H., Bittanti, M., Boyd, D., Herr-Stephenson, B., Lange, P. G., et al. (2009). *Living and learning with new media: Summary of findings from the digial youth project.* Retrieved March 7, 2012, from http://digitalyouth.ischool.berkeley.edu/report

ITU. (2010). *World telecommunication / CT development report 2010.* Geneva: Author.

——. (2014). *Measuring the information society.* Geneva: Author. Retrieved February 10, 2014, from http://www.itu.int/en/ITU-D/Statistics/Pages/publications/mis2013.aspx

Jarrad, S. (2016, February 16). Retail Sales at Bookstores Up in December. *American Booksellers Association.* Retrieved from http://www.bookweb.org/news/retail-sales-bookstores-december-0

Jenkins, H. (1999, July). Professor Jenkins goes to Washington. *Harper's Magazine,* 19–23.

Jensen, M., Danziger, J., & Venkatesh, A. (2007, January/February). Civil society and cyber society: The role of the Internet in community associations and democratic politics. *Information Society, 23*(1), 39.

Jenson, J., & De Castell, S. (2010). Gender, simulation, and gaming: Research review and redirections. *Simulation & Gaming, 41*(1), 51–71.

Jhally, S. (2000). Advertising at the edge of the apocalypse. In R. Andersen & L. Strate (Eds.), *Critical Studies in Media Commercialism* (pp. 27–39). New York: Oxford University Press.

Johnson, J. G., Cohen, P., Smailes, E. M., Kasen, S., & Brook, J. S. (2002, March 29). Television viewing and aggressive behavior during adolescence and adulthood. *Science,* 295(5564), 2468–2471.

Jones, S. (1992). *Rock formation: Music, technology, and mass communication.* Newbury Park, CA: Sage.

Jung, C. G. (1970). *Analytical psychology: Its theory and practice; the Travistock lectures* (Foreword by E. A. Bennet). New York: Vintage Books.

Kafai, Y. B., Heeter, C., Denner, J., & Sun, J. Y. (2008). *Beyond Barbie and Mortal Kombat: New perspectives on gender and gaming.* Cambridge, MA: MIT Press.

Kahin, B., & Varian, H. (Eds.). (2000). *Internet publishing and beyond: The economics of digital information and intellectual property.* Cambridge, MA: MIT Press.

Katz, E., & Lazarsfeld, P. (1955). *Personal influence.* New York: Free Press.

Kearney, M. S., & Levine, P. B. (2014). *Media influences on social outcomes: The impact of MTV's 16 and pregnant on teen childbearing* (No. wl9795). Cambridge, MA: National Bureau of Economic Research.

Keller, P., & Lehmann, D. (2008). Designing effective health communications: A meta-analysis. *Journal of Public Policy & Marketing, 27*(2), 117–130. doi:10.1509/jppm.27.2.117

Kenski, K., Hardy, B. W., & Jamieson, K. H. (2010). *The Obama victory: How media, money and message shaped the 2008 election.* New York: Oxford.

Kent, S. L. (2001). *The ultimate history of video games.* Rocklin, CA: Prima Publications.

Kerr, A. (2006). The economics of digital games. In J. Rutter & J. Bryce (Eds.), *Understanding digital games* (pp. 58–74). Thousand Oaks, CA: Sage.

Kilborn, P. (1993, March 15). New jobs lack the old security in time of "disposable workers." *New York Times,* p. A1.

Kim, H. K. (2009). Analyzing the gender division of labor: The cases of the United States and South Korea. *Asian Perspective, 33*(2), 181–229.

Kiriakidis, S., & Kavoura, A. (2010). Cyberbullying: A review of the literature on harassment through the Internet and other electronic means. *Family & Community Health, 33,* 82–93.

Kirriemuir, J. (2006). A history of digital games. In J. Rutter & J. Bryce (Eds.), *Understanding digital games* (pp. 21–36). London and Thousand Oaks, CA: Sage.

Kitchen, P. J., & Burgmann, I. (2004). *Integrated marketing communication.* John Wiley & Sons, Ltd.

Klapper, J. (1960). *The effects of mass communication.* New York: Free Press.

Knight, A. (1979). *The liveliest art.* New York: New American Library.

Koponen, J. M. (2010). *The future of personal digital information—Scarce resource, valuable commodity or an efficient utility?* University of Art & Design Helsinki. Retrieved January 4, 2010, from http:// www.jarnokoponen.net/file_download/9/OPEN _TheFutureOfDigitalInformation_JM Koponen _021109_final.pdf

Koster, R. (2002). *Online world timeline.* Retrieved February 17, 2010, from http://www.raphkoster.com/gaming/mudtimeline.shtml

Kowalski, R. M., & Limber, S. P. (2013). Psychological, physical, and academic correlates of cyberbullying and traditional bullying. *Journal of Adolescent Health, 53*(1), S13–S20.

Kraut, R., Kiesler, S., Boneva, B., Cummings, J., Helgeson, V., & Crawford, A. (2002). The Internet paradox revisited. *Journal of Social Issues, 58,* 49–74.

Kraut, R., Patterson, M., Lundmark, V., Kiesler, S., Mukophadhyay, T., & Scherlig, W. (1998). Internet paradox: A social technology that reduces social involvement and psychological well-being? *American Psychologist, 53*(9), 1017–1031.

Kumar, S. (2006). *Gandhi meets primetime.* Urbana, IL: University of Illinois Press.

Kunkel, D. (1998). Policy battles over defining children's educational television. (Children and Television). *The Annals of the American Academy of Political and Social Science, 57*(15), 37.

Kunkel, D., Maynard Farinola, W. J., Farrar, K., Donnerstein, E., Biely, E., & Zwarun, L. (2002). Deciphering the V-chip: An examination of the television industry's program rating judgments. *Journal of Communication, 52*(1), 112–138.

Kutner, L., & Olson, C. K. (2008). *Grand theft childhood: The surprising truth about violent video games and what parents can do.* New York: Simon & Schuster.

Labor, U. S. D. O. (2016). *Occupational outlook handbook.* Retrieved February 26, 2016, from http://www.bls.gov/ooh/occupation-finder.htm

Lachlan, K., Smith, S., & Tamborini, R. (2005, December). Models for aggressive behavior: The attributes of violent characters in popular video games. *Communication Studies, 56*(4), 313–330.

LaRose, R. (2014). The psychology of interactive media habits. In S. Sundar (Ed.), *The psychology of communication technology.* New York: Wiley Blackwell.

LaRose, R., & Atkin, D. (1992). Audiotext and the re-invention of the telephone as a mass medium. *Journalism Quarterly, 69*(2), 413–421.

LaRose, R., Connolly, R., Lee, H. G., Li, K., & Hales, K. (2014). Connection overload? A cross cultural study of the consequences of social media connection demands. *Information Systems Management, 31*(1), 59–73.

LaRose, R., DeMaagd, K., Chew, H. E., Tsai, H.-Y S., Steinfield, C., Wildman, S. S., et al. (2012). Measuring sustainable broadband adoption: An innovative approach to understanding broadband adoption and use. *International Journal of Communication, 6,* 2576–2600.

LaRose, R., & Eastin, M. (2004). A social cognitive theory of Internet uses and gratifications: Toward a new model of media attendance. *Journal of Broadcasting and Electronic Media, 48*(3), 358–377.

LaRose, R., Kim, J. H., & Peng, W. (2010). Social networking: Addictive, compulsive, problematic, or just another media habit? In Z. Pappacharissi (Ed.), *A networked self: Identity, community, and culture on social network sites* (pp. 59–81). New York: Routledge.

LaRose, R., & Rifon, N. (2006). Your privacy is assured—of being invaded. *New Media and Society, 8*(4), 1009–1030.

LaRose, R., Strover, S., Gregg, J., & Straubhaar, J. (2011). The impact of rural broadband development: Lessons from a natural field experiment. *Government Information Quarterly, 28,* 91–100.

Latham, A. J., Patston, L. L., & Tippett, L. J. (2013). The virtual brain: 30 years of video-game play and cognitive abilities. *Frontiers in Psychology, 4,* 629.

Lau, R. R., Sigelman, L., & Rovner, I. B. (2007). The effects of negative political campaigns: A meta-analytic reassessment. *Journal of Politics, 69*(4), 1176–1209.

Lauzen, M., Dozier, D., & Reyes, B. (2007). From adultescents to zoomers: An examination of age and gender in prime-time television. *Communication Quarterly, 55*(3), 343.

Lazarsfeld, P. (1941). Remarks on administrative and critical communication research. *Studies in Philosophy and Social Science, 9,* 2–16.

Lee, K. (2004). Presence, explicated. *Communication Theory, 14*(1), 27–50.

Leiner, B. M., Cerf, V. G., Clark, D. D., Kahn, R. E., Kleinrock, L., Lynch, D. C., et al. (2009). Abrief history of the Internet. *ACM SIGCOMM Computer Communication Review, 39*(5), 22–31.

Leipzig, A. (2015). Sundance infographic 2015: Dollars and distribution. *Cultural Weekly.* Retrieved from http://www.culturalweekly.com/sundance-infographic-2015-dollars-and-distribution/

Lemmens, J. S., Valkenburg, P. M., & Peter, J. (2009). Development and validation of a game addiction scale for adolescents. *Media Psychology, 12,* 77–95.

Lessig, L. (2004). *Free culture: How big media uses technology and the law to lock down culture and control creativity.* New York: Penguin.

Levy, P. (2001). *Cyberculture* (R. Bononno, Trans.). Minneapolis: University of Minnesota Press.

Liebert, R., & Sprafkin, J. (1988). *The early window.* New York: Pergamon Press.

Lievrouw, L. A. (2006). New media design and development: Diffusion of innovations v social shaping of technology. *Handbook of new media,* (pp. 246–263). Thousand Oaks, CA: Sage.

Lim, S., Sauter, S., & Schnorr, T. (1998). Occupational health aspects of work with video display terminals. In W. Rom (Ed.), *Environmental and occupational medicine* (3rd ed., pp. 1333–1344). Philadelphia, PA: Lippincott-Raven.

Liming, D., & Vilorio, D. (2011). Work for play: Careers in video game development. Retrieved February 11, 2016, from http://www.bls.gov/careeroutlook/2011/fall/art01.pdf

Limmer, J. (Ed.). (1981). *The Rolling Stone illustrated history of rock and roll.* New York: Random House.

Lin, C. (2003). An interactive communication technology adoption model. *Communication Theory, 13*(4), 345–365.

Lin, J. (2007). *College students perceptions of credibility of blogs and traditional media as a function of the blog usage.* Master's thesis, Michigan State University.

Lindlof, T. R., & Taylor, B. C. (2010). *Qualitative communication research methods.* Thousand Oaks, CA: Sage.

Ling, R. (2004). *The mobile connection: The cell phone's impact on society.* San Francisco, CA: Morgan Kaufmann.

Lippmann, W. (1922). *Public opinion.* New York: Macmillan.

Littlefield, M. B. (2008). The media as a system of racialization: Exploring images of African American women and the new racism. *American Behavioral Scientist, 51*(5), 675–685.

Livingstone, S. (1998). *Making sense of television: The psychology of audience interpretation* (2nd ed.). New York: Routledge.

Livingstone, S., & Helsper, E. J. (2008). Parental mediation of children's Internet use. *Journal of Broadcasting & Electronic Media, 52*(4), 581–599.

Lotz, A. (2015). Assembling a toolkit. *Media Industries, 1*(3).

Lotz, A. D. (2001). Postfeminist television criticism: Rehabilitating critical terms and identifying post-feminist attributes. *Feminist Media Studies, 1*(1), 105–121.

Lu, A. S., Kharrazi, H., Gharghabi, F., & Thompson, D. (2013). A systematic review of health video games on childhood obesity prevention and intervention. *Games for Health: Research, Development, and Clinical Applications, 2*(3), 131–141.

Lynam, D. R., Milich, R., Zimmerman, R., Novak, S. P., Logan, T. K., Martin, C., et al. (1999). Project DARE: No effects at 10-year follow-up. *Journal of Consulting and Clinical Psychology, 67*(4), 590–593.

Lyotard, J. (1984). *The postmodern condition.* Manchester, UK: Manchester University Press.

Maes, K., De Haes, S., & Van Grembergen, W. (2011). *How IT enabled investments bring value to the business: A literature review.* This paper appears in: System Sciences 44th International Conference on System Sciences, Kauai, Hawaii, January, 1–10.

Magazine Publishers of America (MPA). (2011). Retrieved January 9, 2012, from http://www.magazine.org /consumer_marketing/circ_trends/1318.aspx

Magazine Publishers Association. (2014). *MPA Factbook 2013/2014.* Alberta: Author

Martin-Barbero, J. (1993). *Communication, culture, and hegemony: From the media to the mediations.* Thousand Oaks, CA: Sage.

Mast, G., & Kawin, B. (1996). *The movies: A short history.* Needham Heights, MA: Simon & Schuster.

Mastro, D. (2008). Effects of racial and ethnic stereotyping. In J. Bryant & M. B. Oliver (Eds.), *Media effects advances in theory and research* (3rd ed., pp. 325–341). Mahwah, NJ: Erlbaum.

McAnany, E. (1980). *Communication in the rural third world: The role of information in development.* New York: Praeger.

McAvoy, K. (2011). TV's top 30 group owners. *TV news check.* Retrieved April 29, 2011, from http://www.tvnewscheck.com/article/2011/03/30/50206 /tv-group-ranking-could-see-shakeup-in-11

McChesney, R. (2000). *Rich media, poor democracy: Communication politics in dubious times.* Urbana: University of Illinois Press.

——. (2013). *Digital disconnect.* New York: New Press

——. (2015). *Rich media, poor democracy: Communication politics in dubious times.* New York: The New Press.

McCombs, M. E., Shaw, D. L., & Weaver, D. H. (2014). New directions in agenda-setting theory and research. *Mass Communication & Society, 17*(6),781–802.

McDonough, P. (2009). *TV viewing among kids at an eight-year high.* Retrieved February 14, 2011, from http://blog. nielsen.com/nielsenwire/media_entertainment/ tv-viewing-among-kids-at-an-eight-year-high/

McGuinness, M. (2015). The three biggest ways musicians get ripped off (and how to avoid them). Retrieved from http://lateralaction.com/articles/music-business/

McKearns, J. (1993). The emergence of modern media, 1900–1945. In W. Sloan, J. Stovall, & J. Startt (Eds.), *Media in America: A history* (2nd ed.). Scottsdale, AZ: Publishing Horizons.

McLuhan, M. (1962). *The Gutenberg galaxy: The making of a typographic man.* Toronto, ON: University of Toronto Press.

——. (1964). *Understanding media: The extensions of man.* New York: McGraw-Hill.

Means, B., Toyama, Y., Murphy, R., Bakia, M., & Jones, K. (2009). *Evaluation of evidence-based practices in online learning: A meta-analysis and review of online learning studies.* Washington, DC: U.S. Department of Education, Office of Planning, Evaluation and Policy Development, Project Report, Centre for Learning Technology, Retrieved January 15, 2010, from http:// repository.alt.ac.uk/629/

Merrill, J. (1997). *Journalism ethics: Philosophical foundations for news media.* New York: St. Martin's Press.

Michigan State University, School of Journalism. (2012). *The new bullying: How social media, social exclusion, laws and suicide changed bullying.* Canton, MI: Read the Spirit Books.

Milavsky, J., Kessler, R., Stipp, H., & Rubens, W. (1982). Television and aggression: Results of a panel study. In D. Perarl, L. Bouthliet, & J. Lazar (Eds.), *Television and behavior: Ten years of scientific progress and implications for the eighties* (Vol. 2, pp. 138–157). Washington, DC: National Institute for Mental Health.

Miller, T. N., Govil, J., Mcmurria, R., Maxwell, T., & Wang. (2005). *Global Hollywood 2.* Berkeley: University of California Press.

Milliot, J. (2014). Book sales rose 1% in 2013. *Publishers Weekly.* Retrieved April 5, 2014, from http://www. publishersweekly.com/pw/by-topic/industry-news/financial-reporting/article/61667-book-sales-rose-l-in-2013.html

Mitchell, K. J., Finkelhor, D., Jones, L. M., & Wolak, J. (2012). Prevalence and characteristics of youth sexting: A national study. *Pediatrics, 129*(1), 13–20. doi:10.1542/peds. 2011–1730

Mitchell, K. J., Finkelhor, D., & Wolak, J. (2003). The exposure of youth to unwanted sexual material on the Internet: A national survey of risk, impact, and prevention. *Youth and Society, 34*(3), 330–359.

MobieTV. (2016). MobiTV Board of Directors. Retrieved June 20, 2016 from http://www.mobitv.com/about/ corporate-overview/management-team/

Mody, B., Bauer, J., & Straubhaar, J. (1995). *Telecommunications politics: Ownership and control of the information highway in developing countries.* Hillsdale, NJ: Lawrence Earlbaum.

Moore, G. (1996). *Nanometers and gigabucks—Moore on Moore's Law.* University Video Corporation Distinguished Lecture. Retrieved January 29, 1997, from http://www.uvc.com/

Morgan, M., & Shanahan, J. (1997). Two decades of cultivation research. In B. R. Burelson (Ed.),

Communication Yearbook 20 (pp. 1–47). Thousand Oaks, CA: Sage.

Morley, D. (1992). Television, audiences and cultural studies. New York: Routledge.

Morozov, E. (2011). The net delusion: The dark side of Internet freedom. New York: Public Affairs.

Morrissey, B. (2007, November 5). Social network ads: Too close, too personal? Retrieved March 1, 2008, from http://news.yahoo.eom/s/adweek/20071106/ad_bpiaw/socialnetworkadstooclosetoopersonal

Motion Picture Association of America. (2011). 2010 U.S. theatrical market statistics report. Retrieved March 15, 2011, from http://www.stop-runaway-production.com/wp-content/uploads/2009/07/2010-MPAA-market-stats.pdf

——. (2014). Theatrical market statistics report 2013. Retrieved April 1, 2014, from http://www.mpaa.org/wp-content/uploads/2014/03/MPAA-Theatrical-Market-Statistics-2013_032514-v2.pdf

MPAA. (2015). Theatrical Market Statistics Report. Motion Picture Association of America, Los Angeles, CA.

Mulligan, J. (2000). History of online games. Retrieved March 13, 2010, from http://tharsis-gate.org/articles/imaginary/HISTOR-l.HTM

Mutz, D. C., & Young, L. (2011). Communication and public opinion: Plus Ça change? Public Opinion Quarterly, 75(5), 1018–1044. doi:10.1093/poq/nfr052

NAA (Newspaper Association of America). (2013). Newspaper media revenue 2013: Dollars grow in several categories. Retrieved from http://www.naa.org/Trends-and-Numbers/Newspaper-Revenue.aspx

——. (2015a). 20 tweetable truths about the newspaper industry. Retrieved from http://www.naa.org/Topics-and-Tools/Digital-Media/Social-Media/2015/Tweetable-Truths.aspx

——. (2015b). Improving digital subscription adoption: A look at two newspaper approaches. Retrieved from http://www.naa.org/Topics-and-Tools/Digital-Media/Paid-Content/2015/Improving-Digital-Subscription.aspx

——. (2015c). Newspper digital audience springs forward to 176 million, boosted by mobile users. Retrieved from http://www.naa.org/Topics-and-Tools/Digital-Media/Mobile/2015/march-digital-audience

——. (2015d). Young adults feel most informed with traditional media. Retrieved from http://www.naa.org/Topics-and-Tools/Audience-and-Circulation/Research/2015/millennials-research.aspx

Nacos, B. L., & Torres-Reyna, O. (2007). Fueling our fears: Stereotyping, media coverage, and public opinion of Muslim Americans. Lanham, MD: Rowman & Littlefield.

Napoli, P. (2002). Audience valuation and minority media: An analysis of the determinants of the value of radio audiences. Journal of Broadcasting & Electronic Media, 46(2), 169–184.

Nathanson, A. (2004). Factual and evaluative approaches to modifying children's responses to violent television. Journal of Communication, 54(2), 321–336.

Nathanson, A. I., Wilson, B. J., McGee, J., & Sebastian, M. (2002). Counteracting the effects of female

stereotypes on television via active mediation. Journal of Communication, 52(4), 922–937.

National Center for Educational Statistics. (2004). A nation online: Entering the broadband age. Retrieved April 16, 2005, from http://www.ntia.doc.gov/reports/anol/index.html

——. (2005). National assessment of adult literacy results. Commissioner Mark Schneider speech on 2003 data. Retrieved from http://nces.ed.gov/whatsnew/commissioner/remarks2005/12_15_2005.asp

National Science Foundation. (2015). Women, minorities and persons with disabilities in science and engineering. Retrieved from http://www.nsf.gov/statistics/2015/nsf15311/digest/theme2.cfm#engineering

National Telecommunication & Information Administration. (2002). A nation online: How Americans are expanding their use of the Internet. Retrieved March 10, 2003, from http://ntia.doc/gov/ntiahome/dn/index.html

Newspaper Association of America. (2013, March). Retrieved from www.naa.org

New York Times. (1901). Tweed ring—its beginnings and its methods [sic.]. Retrieved May 10, 2014, from http://querynytimes.com/mem/archive-free/pdf?res=F3071EF73C5415738DDDA10994D1405B818CF1D3

Nielsen. (2012). State of the media: U.S. digital consumer report Q3-Q4 2011. Retrieved February 25, 2011, from http://www.nielsen.com/content/dam/corporate/us/en/reports-downloads/2012%20Reports/Digital-Consumer-Report-Q4-2012.pdf

——. (2013). The cross platform report: A look across media. Retrieved January 9, 2014, from http://www.nielsen.com/us/en/reports/2013/a-look-across-media-the-cross-platform-report-q3-2013.html

——. (2014). State of the media: Audio today—A focus on African American and Hispanic audiences. Retrieved March 10, 2014, from http://www.nielsen.com/us/en/reports/2014/state-of-the-media-audio-today-a-focus-on-african-american-and-hispanic-audiences.html

——. (2015). The total audience report Q3 2015. Retrieved from http://www.nielsen.com/us/en/insights/reports/2015/the-total-audience-report-q3-2015.html

——. (2016). 2015 U. S. music year-end report. Retrieved from http://www.nielsen.com/us/en/insights/reports/2016/2015-music-us-year-end-report.html

Nielsen Media Research. (2010). Television audience 2009. New York: The Nielsen Company.

——. (2015). Total audience report Q3 2015. Retrieved February 1, 2016 from http://www.nielsen.com/us/en/insights/reports/2015/the-total-audience-report-q3-2015.html

Noam, E. (1983). Telecommunications regulation today and tomorrow. New York: Law and Business.

Noelle-Neumann, E. (1984). The spiral of silence: Public opinion—Our social skin. Chicago: University of Chicago Press.

Noonan, M. C., & Glass, J. L. (2012). Hard truth about telecommuting. Monthly Labor Review, 135, 38.

NPD Group. (2014). Research shows $15.39 billion spent on video game content in the U.S. in 2013, a 1 percent *increase over 2012*. Retrieved February 11, 2014, from https://www.npd.com/wps/portal/npd/us/home/

NSF (2013). *Women, minorities, and persons with disabilities in science and engineering: 2013*. Retrieved March 21, 2014, from http://www.nsf.gov/statistics/wmpd/2013/pdf/nsf13304_full.pdf

NTIA. (1995). Falling through the net. Retrieved January 14, 2016 from https://www.ntia.doc.gov/ntiahome/fallingthru.html

——. (2013). *Exploring the digital nation: America's emerging online experience*. Retrieved January 11, 2014, from http://www.ntia.doc.gov/files/ntia /publications/exploring_the_digital_nation_-_ americas_emerging_online_experience.pdf

——. (2015). *Digital nation data explorer*. Washington, DC: National Telecommunications and Information Administration. Retrieved January 16, 2016 from https://www.ntia.doc.gov/other-publication/2015/digital-nation-data-explorer

Odlyzko, A. (2001). *Content is not king*. Retrieved April 9, 2002, from http://firstmonday.org/issues/issue6_2/odlyzko/index.html

OECD. (2013). *Time for the U.S. to reskill? What the survey of adult skills says*. OECD Skills Studies, OECD Publishing. Retrieved March 20, 2014, from http://dx.doi.org/10.1787/9789264204904-en

——. (2014, June 2013). *Fixed and wireless broadband subscriptions per 100 inhabitants*. Retrieved March 20, 2014, from http://www.oecd.org/sti/broadband/oecdbroadbandportal.htm

Okorafor, N., & Davenport, L. (2001, August). *Virtual women: Replacing the real*. Commission on the Status of Women, Association for Education in Journalism and Mass Communication National Convention, Washington, DC.

O'Neill, M. (2010). *How much money do the top grossing YouTube partners make?* Retrieved from http://socialtimes.com/money-youtube-partners_b21335

OpenSignal. (2015). The state of LTE. Retrieved February 4, 2016 from http://opensignal.com/reports/2015/09/state-of-lte-q3-2015/

Oppliger, P. A. (2007). Effects of gender stereotyping on socialization. In R. W. Preiss, B. M. Gayle, N. Burrell, M. Allen, & J. Bryant (Eds.), *Mass media effects research: Advances through meta-analysis* (pp. 199–214). Florence, KY: Routledge.

Ouellette, J. A., & Wood, W. (1998). Habit and intention in everyday life: The multiple processes by which past behavior predicts future behavior. *Psychological Bulletin, 124*, 54–74.

Outing, S. (2011). *The 11 layers of citizen journalism*. Retrieved January 12, 2012, from http://www.poynter .org/uncategorized/69328/the-ll-layers-of-citizen -journalism/

Packard, V. (1957). *The hidden persuaders*. New York: Simon & Schuster.

Padovani, C. (2005). Debating communication imbalances from the MacBride report to the world summit on the information society: An analysis of a changing discourse. *Global Media and Communication, 1*(3), 316–338.

Paek, H. J., Nelson, M. R., & Vilela, A. M. (2011). Examination of gender-role portrayals in television advertising across seven countries. *Sex Roles, 64*(3–4), 192–207.

Paik, H., & Comstock, G. (1994). The effects of television violence on social behavior: A meta-analysis. *Communication Research, 21*, 516–545.

Palmer, K. (2015, June). *M-commerce and beyond*. Paper presented at PATA Global Insights Conference, Auckland, New Zealand. Retrieved February 2, 2016 from http://www.comscore.com/Insights/Presentations-and-Whitepapers/2015/m-Commerce-and-Beyond

Palmgreen, P., & Rayburn, J. (1985). An expectancy-value approach to media gratifications. In K. Rosengren, L. Wenner, & P. Palmgreen (Eds.), *Media gratifications research: Current perspectives* (pp. 61–72). Beverly Hills, CA: Sage.

Papacharissi, Z., & Rubin, A. M. (2000). Predictors of Internet usage. *Journal of Broadcasting and Electronic Media, 44*, 175–196.

Pappas, C. (2000, July 10). Ad nauseam. *Advertising Age*, 16–18.

Pariser, E. (2011). *The filter bubble: What the Internet is hiding from you*. New York: Penguin Press.

Parlett, D. S. (1999). *The Oxford history of board games*. New York: Oxford University Press.

Parton, J. (1874, July). Falsehood in the Daily Press. *Harper's New Monthly Magazine, 49*, 274. Retrieved March 1, 2010, from http://harpers.org/archive /1874/07/0044438

Payne, D. (1993). The age of mass magazines, 1900–present. In W. Sloan, J. Stovall, & J. Startt (Eds.), *Media in America: A history* (2nd ed.). Scottsdale, AZ: Publishing Horizons.

Perrin, A. (2015). Social media usage: 2005-2015. *Pew Research Center*. Retrieved from http://www.pewinternet.org/2015/10/08/social-networking-usage-2005-2015/

Petry, N. M. (2011). Commentary on Van Rooij et al. (2011): "Gaming addiction"—a psychiatric disorder or not? *Addiction, 106*, 213–214. doi:10.1111/j.1360-0443.2010.03132.x

Pew Research Center. (2010). *The state of the news media: Americans spending more time following the news*. Retrieved May 5, 2011, from www.people-press.org/2010/09/12/ americans-spending-more-time-following-the-news/

——. (2013a). *The 2013 state of the news media*. Retrieved from thestateofthenewsmedia.org/2013

——. (2013b). *Section 4: News sources, election night and views of press coverage*. Retrieved from http://www.people-press.org/2012/ll/15/section-4-news-sources-election-night-and-views-of-press-coverage/

——. (2015). Newspapers: Fact sheet. Retrieved from http://www.journalism.org/2015/04/29/newspapers-fact-sheet/

Pew Research Center for Excellence in Journalism (2011). *Overview by Tom Rosenstiel and Amy Mitchell on the annual report of American journalism 2011*.

Retrieved May 5, 2012, from http://stateofthemedia.org/2011/overview-2/

Picard, R. G. (2002). *The economics and financing of media companies.* New York: Fordham University Press.

——. (2011). *The economics and financing of media companies* (2nd ed.). New York: Fordham University Press.

Pieterse, J. N. (2004). *Globalization and culture: Global melange.* Lanham, MD: Rowman & Littlefield.

Postman, N. (1986). *Amusing ourselves to death: Public discourse in the age of show business.* New York: Penguin Books.

——. (1992). *Technopoly.* New York: Knopf.

Powell, K., & Abels, L. (2002). Sex-role stereotypes in television programs aimed at the preschool audience: An analysis of Teletubbies and Barney & Friends. *Women and Language, 25*(1), 14–22.

Purcell, K., Rainie, L., Mitchell, A., Rosenstiel, T., & Olmstead, K. (2010). *Understanding the participatory news consumer.* Pew Research Center's Internet & American Life Project.

Putnam, R. (2000). *Bowling alone: The collapse and revival of American community.* New York: Simon & Schuster.

Radway, J. A. (1984). *Reading the romance: Women, patriarchy, and popular literature.* Durham: University of North Carolina Press.

Rafaeli, S. (1988). Interactivity: From new media to communication. In R. P. Hawkins, J. M. Weimann, & S. Pingree (Eds.), *Sage annual review of communication research: Advancing communication sciences* (Vol. 16, pp. 10–134). Beverly Hills, CA: Sage.

Rafaeli, S., & LaRose, R. (1993). Electronic bulletin boards and "public goods" explanations of collaborative mass media. *Communication Research, 28*(2), 277–297.

Rakow, L. (1992). *Gender on the line.* Urbana: University of Illinois Press.

Rainie L., & Perrin, A. (2015). Slightly fewer Americans are reading print books. *Pew Research Center.* Retrieved from http://www.pewresearch.org/fact-tank/2015/10/19/slightly-fewer-americans-are-reading-print-books-new-survey-finds/

Rawls. (1999). *A theory of justice: A revised edition.* Boston, MA: Belknap Press.

Razlogova, E. (2011). *The listener's voice: Early radio and the American public.* Philadelphia: University of Pennsylvania Press.

Real, M. (1989). *Super media: A cultural studies approach.* Thousand Oaks, CA: Sage.

Reed, B. (2010). A brief history of smartphones. *Network World.* Retrieved from http://www.networkworld.com/slideshows/2010/061510-smartphone-history.html

Reeves, B., & Nass, C. (1996). *The media equation.* New York: Cambridge University Press.

Rice, R., & Atkin, C. (2000). *Public communication campaigns* (3rd ed.). Thousand Oaks, CA: Sage.

Riddler, I., & Denison, S. (1998, February). When there is no end to a good game. *British Archaeology.* United Kingdom: Council for British Archaeology, 31. ISSN 1357–4442.

Rideout, V. (2007). *Parents, children & media. Kaiser family foundation.* Retrieved April 8, 2008, from http://www.kff.org/entmedia/upload/7638.pdf

Riley, S. (1993). American magazines, 1740–1900. In W. Sloan, J. Stovall, & J. Startt (Eds.), *Media in America: A history* (2nd ed.). Scottsdale, AZ: Publishing Horizons.

Roberts, M., Wanta, W., & Dzwo, T. (2002). Agenda setting and issue salience online. *Communication Research, 29*(4), 452–65.

Robertson, L. A., McAnally, H. M., & Hancox, R. J. (2013). Childhood and adolescent television viewing and antisocial behavior in early adulthood. *Pediatrics, 131*(3), 439–446.

Robinson, T N., & Borzekowski, D. L. G. (2006). Effects of the SMART classroom curriculum to reduce child and family screen time. *Journal of Communication, 56*(1), 1–26.

Rogers, E. (1986). *Communication technology—The new media in society.* New York: Free Press.

——. (1995). *Diffusion of innovations* (4th ed.). New York: Free Press.

Romanowski, P., & George-Warren, H. (1995). *The new Rolling Stone encyclopedia of rock & roll.* New York: Fireside.

Rosser, J. C., Jr., Lynch, P. J., Cuddihy, L., Gentile, D. A., Klonsky, J., & Merrell, R. (2007). The impact of video games on training surgeons in the 21st century. *Archives of Surgery, 142*(2), 181–186.

Rubin, A. (1983). Television uses and gratifications. *Journal of Broadcasting, 27,* 37–51.

Sadowski, C. (2011, July). *Newspaper websites post consecutive quarterly traffic increase.* Retrieved March 11, 2012, from http://www.naa.org/News-and-Media/Press-Center/Archives/2011/Newspaper-Websites-Post-Consecutive-Quarterly-Traffic-Increase.aspx

Sandage, C. H., Fryburger, V. R., & Rotzoll, K. B. (1989). *Advertising theory and practice.* White Plains, NY: Longman.

Sarkeesian, A. (2015). How videogames reward misogyny and abuse. *Takepart.com.* Retrieved from http://www.takepart.com/video/2015/09/02/women-video-games

Sayre, B., Bode, L., Shah, D., Wilcox, D., & Shah, C. (2010). Agenda setting in a digital age: Tracking attention to California proposition 8 in social media, online news and conventional news. *Policy & Internet, 2*(2), 7–32. doi:10.2202/1944–2866.1040

Schement, J., & Curtis, T. (1997). *Tendencies and tensions of the information age.* New Brunswick, NJ: Transaction books.

Scheufele, D., Shanahan, J., & Kim, S. (2002). Who cares about local politics? Media influences on local political involvement, issue awareness, and attitude strength. *Journalism and Mass Communication Quarterly, 79*(2), 427–44.

Schiller, D. (1996). *Theorizing communication: A history.* New York: Oxford University Press.

Schlesinger, P. (1991). *Media, state and nation.* Newbury Park, CA: Sage.

Schmidt, M., & Park, M. (2013). *Trends in consumer book buying [Infographic].* Retrieved January 17, 2014, from http://randomnotes.randomhouse.com/trends-in-consumer-book-buying-infographic/. (Original source: Bowker Market Research, 2013 U.S. Book Consumer Demographics & Buying Behaviors Annual Review.)

Schramm, W. (Ed.). (1954). *The process and effects of communication.* Urbana, IL: The University of Illinois Press.

——. (1982). *Men, women, messages and media.* New York: Harper & Row.

Schramm, W., Lyle, J., & Parker, E. (1961). *Television in the lives of our children.* Palo Alto, CA: Stanford University Press.

Schudson, M. (1984). *Advertising, the uneasy persuasion.* New York: Basic Books.

Schwoch, J. (1990). *The American radio industry and its Latin American activities, 1900–1939.* Champaign: University of Illinois Press.

Sears, D. O., & Freedman, J. L. (1972). Selective exposure to information: A critical review. In W. Schramm & D. Roberts (Eds.), *The process and effects of mass communication* (pp. 209–234). Urbana, IL: University of Illinois Press.

Seiter, E. (1992). Semiotics, structuralism, and television. In R. Allen (Ed.), *Channels of discourse, reassembled* (2nd ed., pp. 31–66). Chapel Hill: University of North Carolina Press.

Sethuraman, R., Tellis, G. J., & Briesch, R. A. (2011). How well does advertising work? Generalizations from meta-analysis of brand advertising elasticities. *Journal of Marketing Research, 48*(3), 457–471.

Shaheen, J. G. (2003). Reel bad Arabs: How Hollywood vilifies a people. *The Annals of the American Academy of Political and Social Science, 588*(1), 171–193.

——. (2012). *Reel bad Arabs: How Hollywood vilifies a people.* Northampton, MA: Interlink Publishing.

Shannon, C. E., & Weaver, W. (1949). *The mathematical theory of communication.* Urbana, IL: University of Illinois Press.

Sharma, R. (2013). Community clip show: Examining the recursive collaboration between producers and viewers of a postmodern sitcom. *The Journal of Fandom Studies, 1*(2), 183–199.

Shefrin, D. (1993). Rediscovering an old technology: Facsimile newspaper lessons of invention and failure. In J. Pavlik & E. Dennis (Eds.), *Demystifying media technology.* Mountain View, CA: Mayfield Publishing.

Sherry, J. (2004). Flow and media enjoyment. *Communication Theory, 14,* 328–347.

——. (2007). Violent video games and aggression: Why can't we find links? In R. Preiss, B. Gayle, N. Burrell, M. Allen, & J. Bryant (Eds.), *Mass media effects research: Advances through meta-analysis* (pp. 231–248). Mahwah, NJ: Routledge.

Siwek, S. E. (2014). Video games in the 21st century. Retrieved February 11, 2016 from http://www.theesa. com/wp-content/uploads/2014/11/VideoGames21st-Century_2014.pdf

Shoemaker, P. J. (1991). *Gatekeeping.* Newbury Park, CA: Sage.

Shoemaker, P. J., & Vos, T. P. (2009). *Gatekeeping theory.* New York: Taylor & Francis.

Shonfeld & Associates. (2012). *2011 advertising to sales ratios by industry sector.* Retrieved March 7, 2012, from http://www.saibooks.com/adv-ind-sector-ratios .html

Signorielli, N. (1989). Television and conceptions about sex roles: Maintaining conventionality and the status quo. *Sex Roles, 21*(5–6), 341–360.

——. (2003). Prime-time violence 1993–2001: Has the picture really changed? *Journal of Broadcasting & Electronic Media, 47*(1), 36–58.

——. (2009). Race and sex in prime time: A look at occupations and occupational prestige. *Mass Communication and Society, 12*(3), 332–352.

Signorielli, N., & Bacue, A. (1999). Recognition and respect: A content analysis of prime-time television characters across three decades. *Sex Roles, 40,* 527–544.

Singhal, A., & Rogers, E. M. (2001). *India's communication revolution: From bullock carts to cyber marts.* New Delhi: Sage/India.

Sisario, B. (2016). Adele album resists the streaming trend in music sales. *New York Times.* Retrieved from http://www.nytimes.com/2016/01/06/business/ media/adele-album-resists-the-trends-in-music-sales. html?_r=0

Sivulka, J. (2012). *Soap, sex, and cigarettes: A cultural history of American advertising.* Belmont, CA: Cengage Learning.

Sloan, D. (Ed.). (2005). *The media in America: A history* (6th ed.). Northport, AL: Vision Press.

Sloan, W., Stovall, J., & Startt, J. (Eds.). (1993). *Media in America: A history* (2nd ed.). Scottsdale, AZ: Publishing Horizons.

Smith, A. (2013). *Smartphone ownership 2013.* Retrieved from http://pewinternet.org/Reports/2013/Smartphone-Ownership-2013/Findings.aspx

——. (2015). Cell phones, social media and campaign 2014. *Pew Research Center.* Retrieved from http://www.pewinternet.org/2014/11/03/ cell-phones-social-media-and-campaign-2014/

Smith, L. A., & Foxcroft, D. R. (2009). The effect of alcohol advertising, marketing and portrayal on drinking behaviour in young people: Systematic review of prospective cohort studies. *BMC Public Health, 9,* 51–62.

Spence, L. (2005). *Watching daytime soap operas: The power of pleasure.* Middletown, CT: Wesleyan University Press.

Sporkin, A. (2013). *U.S. publishers see ongoing sales growth in print.* Association of American Publishers website. Retrieved March 3, 2014, from http:// publishers.org/press/111/

Standage, T. (1998). *The Victorian Internet.* New York: Berkley Books.

Statista. (2016). Leading social media websites in the United States in October 2015, based on share of visits. Retrieved January 18, 2016 from http://www. statista.com/statistics/265773/market-share-of-the-most-popular-social-media-websites-in-the-us/

Stepanikova, L., Nie, N. H., & Xiaobin, H. (2010, May). Time on the Internet at home, loneliness, and life satisfaction: Evidence from panel time-diary data. *Computers in Human Behavior, 26*(3), 329–338. ISSN 0747-5632, doi:10.1016/j.chb.2009.11.002

Sterling, C., & Kittross, J. (2002). *Stay tuned—A concise history of American broadcasting* (2nd ed.). Belmont, CA: Wadsworth.

Stewart, D. W., & Pavlou, P. A. (2008). The effects of media on marketing communication. In J. Bryant & M. B. Oliver (Eds.), *Media effects advances in theory and research* (3rd ed.). New York: Erlbaum.

Stowe, H. B. (1852). *Uncle Tom's cabin; or, life among the lowly.* Boston, MA: John P. Jewett & Co.

Straubhaar, J. D. (2007). *World television: From global to local.* Thousand Oaks, CA: Sage Publications.

Straubhaar, J. D., & Boyd, D. (2007). International broadcasting. In Y. R. Kamalipour (Ed.), *Global communication* (2nd ed.). Belmont, CA: Wadsworth.

Straubhaar, J. D., Spence, J., Tufekci, Z., & Lentz, R. G. (Eds.). (2012). *Inequity in the Technopolis: Race, class, gender and the digital divide in Austin.* Austin: University of Texas Press.

Strayer, D. L., Cooper, J. M., Turrill, J., Coleman, J., Medeiros-Ward, N., & Biondi, F. (2013). *Measuring cognitive distraction in the automobile.* Washington, DC: AAA Foundation for Traffic Safety. Retrieved February 25, 2014, from https://www.aaafoundation.org/sites/ default/files/MeasuringCognitiveDistractions.pdf

Stone, A. (n.d.). 10 twenty-first century bestsellers people tried to ban (and Why). *Mental Floss.* Retrieved from http://mentalfloss.com/article/59059/10-twenty-first-century-bestsellers-people-tried-ban-and-why

Streeter, T. (1996). *Selling the air: A critique of the policy of commercial broadcasting in the United States.* Chicago: University of Chicago Press.

Strover, S. (2003). Remapping the digital divide. *The Information Society, 19*(4), 275–277.

Sullivan, G. (2014, July 1). Cornell ethics board did not pre-approve Facebook mood manipulation study. *The Washington Post.* Retrieved from https://www.washingtonpost.com/news/morning-mix/wp/2014/07/01/facebooks-emotional-manipulation-study-was-even-worse-than-you-thought/

Sundar, S. S., & Limperos, A. M. (2013). Uses and grats 2.0: New gratifications for new media. *Journal of Broadcasting & Electronic Media, 57*(4), 504–525.

Sundar, S. S., Jia, H., Waddell, T. F., & Huang, Y. (2015). Toward a theory of interactive media effects (TIME). *The handbook of the psychology of communication technology,* 47–86. New York: Wiley Blackwell.

Swanson, C. (2015). The Bestselling Books of 2014. *Publishers Weekly.* Retrieved from http://www.publishersweekly.com/pw/by-topic/industry-news/bookselling/article/65171-the-fault-in-our-stars-tops-print-and-digital.html

Swing, E. L., Gentile, D. A., Anderson, C. A., & Walsh, D. A. (2010). Television and video game exposure and the development of attention problems. *Pediatrics, 126*(2), 214–221.

Synovate. (2007, August 30). *New study shows Americans' blogging behaviour.* Retrieved January 23, 2008, from http://www.synovate.com/news/article/2007/08/new-study-shows-americans-blogging-behaviour.html

Tan, T. (2014, July 8). College students still prefer print textbooks. *Publishers Weekly.* Retrieved from http://www.publishersweekly.com/pw/by-topic/digital/content-and-e-books/article/63225-college-students-prefer-a-mix-of-print-and-digital-textbooks.html

Tebbel, J. (1969). *The American magazine: A compact history.* New York: Hawthorne Books.

Tiggemann, M. (2014). The status of media effects on body image research: Commentary on articles in the themed issue on body image and media. *Media Psychology,* (ahead-of-print), 1–7.

Tracey, M. (1988). Popular culture and the economics of global television. *Intermedia, 16*(2), 9–25.

Turing, A. M. (1950). Computing machinery and intelligence. *Mind, 59*(236), 433.

Turkle, S. (1995). *Life on the screen: Identity in the age of the Internet.* New York: Simon & Schuster.

——. (2011). *Alone together: Why we expect more from technology and less from each other.* New York: Basic Books.

——. (2012). *Alone together: Why we expect more from technology and less from each other.* New York: Basic Books.

TV-Free America, (n.d.). *Television statistics.* Retrieved from http://www.csun.edu/science/health/docs/tv&health.html

UNESCO. (2003). *Convention for the safeguarding of the intangible cultural heritage.* Paris: Author.

U.S. Department of Commerce. (2004). *A nation online: Entering the broadband age.* Washington, DC: National Telecommunications and Information Administration.

U.S. Department of Health and Human Services (U.S.D.H.H.S.). (2001). *Youth violence: A report of the Surgeon General.* Rockville, MD: Author.

USA Today. (2004, December 11). Wal-Mart sued over Evanescence lyrics. Retrieved July 14, 2012, from http:// www.usatoday.com/life/music/2004-12-ll-walmart -music_x.htm

Vakratsas, D., & Ambler, T. (1999). How advertising works: What do we really know? *Journal of Marketing, 63*(1), 26–43.

Valentino, N., Hutchings, V., & Williams, D. (2004). The impact of political advertising on knowledge, Internet information seeking, and candidate preference. *Journal of Communication, 54*(2), 337–354.

Van Erva, J. (1990). *Television and child development.* Hillsdale, NJ: Lawrence Erlbaum.

Van Rooij, A. J., Schoenmakers, T. M., Vermulst, A. A., Van Den Eijnden, R. J. J. M., & Van De Mheen, D. (2011). Online video game addiction: identification of addicted adolescent gamers. *Addiction, 106*(1), 205–212.

Vandercruysse, S., Vandewaetere, M., & Clarebout, G. (2012). Game-based learning: A review on the effectiveness of educational games. In M. Cruz-Cunha (Ed.), *Handbook of research on serious games as educational, business and research tools* (pp. 628–647). Hershey, PA: Information Science Reference.

Vandewater, E. A., Shim, M. S., & Caplovitz, A. G. (2004). Linking obesity and activity level with children's television and video game use. *Journal of Adolescence, 27*(1), 71–85.

Varnelis, K. (2012). *Networked publics.* Cambridge, MA: The MIT Press.

Vinjamuri, D. (2013). Is publishing still broken? The surprising year in books. *Forbes.* Retrieved March 9, 2014, from http://www.forbes.com/sites/davidvinjamuri/2013/10/04/is-publishing-still -broken-the-surprising-year-in-books/

Virnoche, M. (1998). The seamless web and communications equity: The shaping of a community network. *Science, Technology & Human Values, 23*(2), 199–218.

Vlad, T., Becker, L. B., Simpson, H., & Kalpen, K. (2013). *2012 annual survey of journalism and mass communication enrollments.* Athens, Georgia, Grady College of Journalism & Mass Communication, University of Georgia. Retrieved from www.grady.uga.edu /annualsurveys/

Vogt, N. (2015). State of the news media 2015, Audio: Fact Sheet. Retrieved from http://www.journalism.org/2015/04/29/audio-fact-sheet/

Volkow, N. D., Tomasi, D., Wang, G. J., Vaska, P., Fowler, J. S., Telang, F., et al. (2011). Effects of cell phone radio frequency signal exposure on brain glucose metabolism. *Journal of American Medical Association, 305*(8), 808–813.

Wakefield, M. A., Loken, B., & Hornik, R. C. (2010, October 9–15). Use of mass media campaigns to change health behaviour. *The Lancet, 376*(9748), 1261–1271. ISSN 0140-6736, doi:10.1016/S0140-6736(10)60809-4. Retrieved from http://www.sciencedirect.com/science/article/pii/ S0140673610608094

Wakefield, M., Terry-McElrath, Y., Emery, S., Saffer, H., Chaloupka, F. J., Szczypka, G., et al. (2006, December). Effect of televised, tobacco company-funded smoking prevention advertising on youth smoking-related beliefs, intentions, and behavior. *American Journal of Public Health, 96*(12), 2154–2161.

Waldman, S. (2011). *The information needs of communities.* Washington, DC: Federal Communications Commission. Retrieved February 5, 2012, from http://www.fcc.gov/info-needs-communities

Walther, J. (1996). Computer mediated communication: Impersonal, interpersonal and hypersonal. *Communication Research, 23*(1), 3–41.

Wanta, W. (1997). *The public and the national agenda.* Mahawh, NJ: Lawrence Erlbaum.

Waverman, L., & Dasgupta, K. (2009). *Connectivity scorecard 2009.* Retrieved January 25, 2010, from http://www.connectivityscorecard.org/images/uploads/media/TheConnectivityReport2009.pdf

Waxman, S. (1998, November 29). As Hollywood looks afar, minorities often lose out. *Washington Post News Service in Austin American-Statesman,* G-l.

The Week. (2011). Occupy Wall Street: A protest timeline. Retrieved January 18, 2012, from http://theweek.com/article/index/220100/occupy-wall-street-a-protest-timeline

Wells, W., Burnett, J., & Moriarty, S. (1995). *Advertising principles and practice.* Engelwood Cliffs, NJ: Prentice Hall.

White, D. (1949). The gate-keeper: A case study in the selection of news. *Journalism Quarterly, 27* (4), 383–390.

Williams, B., & Delli Carpini, M. (2004). Monica and Bill all the time and everywhere: The collapse of gatekeeping and agenda setting in the new media environment. *American Behavioral Scientist, 47*(9), 1208–1230.

Williams, D. (2006). Virtual cultivation: Online worlds, offline perceptions. *Journal of Communication, 56,* 69–87.

Williamson, P. (2007). *Ratings and their reasons: An investigation of the efficiency, application and unintended consequences of the Motion Picture Association of America's film rating system.* Dissertation, Michigan State University, MI.

Wilson, B., Martins, N., & Marske, A. (2005). Children's and parents' fright reactions to kidnapping stories in the news. *Communication Monographs, 72*(1), 46.

Wilson, B., Smith, S. L., Potter, W. J., Kunkel, D., Linz, D., Colvin, C. M., et al. (2002). Violence in children's television programming: Assessing the risks. *Journal of Communications, 52*(1), 5–35.

Wimmer, R. D., & Dominick, J. R. (2011). *Mass media research* (9th ed.). Boston, MA: Cengage.

Winseck, D. (2011). Introductory essay: The political economics of media and the transformation of the global media industries. In D. Winseck & D. Y. Jin (Eds.), *The political economies of media: The transformation of the Global Media Industries* (pp. 3–48). London: Bloomsbury Academic.

Winter, D. (2006). *Noughts and Crosses—the oldest graphical computer game.* Retrieved from http://www.pong-story.com/1952.htm

Wolff, E. N. (2006). The growth of information workers in the US economy, 1950–2000: The role of technological change, computerization, and structural change. *Economic Systems Research, 18*(3), 221–255.

World Bank. (2009). *World development report 2010: Development and climate change.* Washington, DC: World Bank Group.

——. (2015). *World development report.* Washington, DC: World Bank.

Wright, C. (1974). Functional analysis and mass communications revisited. In J. Blumler & E. Katz (Eds.), *The uses of mass communications* (p. 86). Beverly Hills, CA: Sage.

Wright, P. J. (2013). U.S. males and pornography, 1973–2010: Consumption, predictors, correlates. *Journal of Sex Research 50*(1), 60–71. doi:10.1080/0 0224499.2011.628132

Ybarra, M. L., Mitchell, K. J., Hamburger, M., Diener-West, M., & Leaf, P. J. (2012). X-rated material and perpetration of sexually aggressive behavior among children and adolescents: Is there a link? *Aggressive Behavior, 37,* 1098–2337. Retrieved from http://dx.doi.org/10.1002/ab.20367

Yioutas, J., & Segvic, I. (2003). Revisiting the Clinton/Lewinsky scandal: The convergence of agenda setting and framing. *Journalism and Mass Communication Quarterly, 80*(3), 567.

Zickuhr, K. (2010). *Generations 2010.* Retrieved March 12, 2011,from http://www.pewinternet.org/Reports/2010/Generations-2010.aspx

Zillmann, D., & Bryant, J. (1985). Affect mood and emotion as determinants of selective exposure. In D. Zillmann & J. Bryant (Eds.), *Selective exposure to communication* (pp. 157–189). New York: Routledge.

Zuboff, S. (1984). *In the age of the smart machine.* New York: Basic Books.

INDEX

DVD (digital video disc) players, 13
  effect on film industry, 195
  renting, 204–205
  technology of, 230
Dylan, Bob, 136

E

eBay, 253
e-books. *See also* e-publishing
  defined, 60
  e-reader, 62
  mobile devices, 62
  sales of, 67
e-cigarette, 488–490
ecological validity, 403
e-commerce, 275–276
  advertising, 373–374
  defined, 62
economic development, stages of, 11
economics, 25–37
  of book publishing, 63–65
  CBS Television, 27
  classical view of, 26
  of competition, 27–28
  defined, 26
  magazine industry, 122–125
  new media, 35–37
  political view of, 37–39
  of production and distribution, 26–27
  profit motives, 31–33
economies of scale, 27, 28
The Economist (magazine), 127
ECPA. *See* Electronic Communication Privacy Act (ECPA)
Edison, Thomas A., 133, 185, 341
editors, 107–108, 120
education
  distance, 425
  entertainment, 425
  formal, 425–426
  informal, 425
Edwards, Bob, 172
electromagnetic recording, 142, 143
electromagnetism, 168–169
Electronic Arts, 315, 325
Electronic Communication Privacy Act (ECPA), 309, 450
electronic news gathering (ENG) systems, 231
electronic numerical integrator and calculator
      (ENIAC), 251
electronic publishing, 270–271
Eliot, T. S., 59
Ellul, Jacques, 50
Elrick, M. L., 87
e-mail, 45, 347, 412
Eminem, 135
Emmis, 171
encoder, 14
encryption, 257
ENG systems, 231
ENIAC. *See* electronic numerical integrator and calculator
      (ENIAC)
Entercom, 171
entertainment, 46, 232–233
  Internet, 271–272
entertainment education, 425
Entertainment Software Rating Board (ESRB), 332, 448
entrepreneurs, and public relations, 340–341
e-publishing, 61–62. *See also* e-books

Equifax, 373
era of creativity, 367
E-Rate program, 459
e-reader, defined, 62
ESPN, 221, 234, 242
ESRB. *See* Entertainment Software Rating Board (ESRB)
Ethernet, 252
ethics
  advertising. *See* advertising ethics
  codes of, 477–479
  confidentiality, 480–481
  conflicts of interest, 481–483
  consumer, 493–496
  consumer privacy, 490–491
  corporate, 477–478
  deceptive advertising, 492
  defined, 471
  entertainment, 483–485
  guidelines, 473
  hacking, 494
  harassment, 493
  harmful products, 487–489
  Internet advertising and marketing, 496–498
  intrusiveness, 491–492
  in journalism, 105–106, 472, 479–483
  media, 472
  misrepresentation, 494
  piracy, 144
  plagiarism, 495–496
  Potter's Box, 476
  pragmatic, 475
  principles, 474–475
  public relations, 486–487
  and public relations, 356–357
  research, 492–493
  sharing/stealing, 494
  situation, 475
  social media, 485–486
  stereotyping, 489–490
  subliminal messages, 492
  Web surfing, 493
  working of, 478–479
ethnicity
  advertising and, 40–41
  media studies of, 40–41
ethnographers, 400, 406
ethnographic research, 405–406
European Economic Community, 518
European Union (EU), 282, 505, 532
"EverQuest" (video game), 316
experimental research, 402–403
experimental treatments, 402, 403
eXtensible hypertext markup language (XHTML),
      261–262

F

fabrication, 105
Facebook, 7, 255, 256, 257, 279, 304, 407, 428, 452, 502
  informed consent policy, 485
  and public relations, 348
  social media, 273, 274–275
Fairbanks, Douglas, 188
Fairness and Accuracy in Reporting, 245
Fairness Doctrine, 245, 446
FairPlay (software), 144
fair use concept, 456
Fanning, Shawn, 138

interpretive communities, 417
knowledge gap hypothesis, 429–430
learning behavior, 409–411
limited effects theory, 414
longitudinal survey studies, 405
making money in, 33–34
multistep flow model, 413
narrowcasted, 20
and national/local development, 533
national production, 507
new, 19
observational learning, 414
online, 256
prejudice, 419–421
priming theory, 415
privacy protection, 450–452
prosocial behaviors, 400, 423
and public opinion, 46–47
qualitative method, 401
quantitative method, 401
and racial depictions, 40–41
reliability, 403
risk factors, 398
selective processes, 413–414
self-efficacy, 410–411
serious games, 426
and sexual behavior, 421–422
social inequality, 429–438
social learning theory, 414
social presence, 411
societal impacts, 429
spectrum allocation, 460–461
survey studies, 405
technical standards, 461–462
theories of, 25
theories of impacts, 412–423
theories of usage, 408–412
on third screen, 294–295
trade in, 532
uses and gratifications theory,
    408–409
validity, 403
video games. *See* video games
violence in. *See* violence in media
well-being, 428–429
media bashing, 397
media center, 346
media consumption, 43
media department, 378
media effects, defined, 400
media kits, 346
media literacy, 37, 69
media relations, 350
Media Research Center, 245
media scholar, 29
mediated communication, 17
MegaUpload, 140
"MegaWars I" (video game), 316
Merkel, Angela, 451
message, defined, 14
Metcalfe, Bob, 252, 258
Metcalfe's Law, 258
    computer technology trends, 264–265
    description, 258
    Internet trends, 258–262
    network technology trends, 263–264
metered pay model, 95
metropolitan dailies, 98

Mexican-American War, 81
MGM, 192
Michigan State University (MSU), 480
Microsoft Corporation, 252, 266
    Kinect system, 321–322
    monopolies and, 29
    XBox, 265, 316, 319
    Xbox One, 323
microwave system, 298
middleware, 325
Mill, John Stuart, 475
Miller, Bode, 482
Miller, Glenn, 133
Miller, Mac, 167
Miller v. California, 447
Milton, John, 78
Minow, Newton, 218
60 Minutes (TV show), 46
miscellanies, defined, 113
misrepresentation, ethics, 494
Miyamoto, Shigeru, 315, 316
mobile advertising, 372–373
mobile device, defined, 62
mobile networks, 297–301
mobile radios, 291
mobile virtual network operators (MVNOs), 302
MobiTV, 303
modems (modulator-demodulators), 251, 252, 295
Modern Family (TV show), 241
Modified Final Judgment (MFJ), 291
mods, defined, 327
Monday Night Football (TV show), 234, 243
Monogram Studio, 191
monopolies
    in communications media, 30–31
    defined, 28, 457
    formation of, 28–31
Moore's Law, 138
    computer technology trends, 264–265
    description, 258
    Internet trends, 258–262
    network technology trends, 263–264
morality, 471
Morley, David, 215
Morning Edition (radio show), 177
Morse, Samuel F. B., 81, 289
Morse code, 158
Morse's telegraph, 295
"Mortal Kombat" (video game), 317, 332
Mother Jones, 117
Motion Picture Association of America (MPAA), 194, 208–209,
    211, 448, 508, 512
Motion Picture Code, 188
Motion Picture Export Association of America
    (MPEAA), 190
Motion Picture Producers and Distributors of America, 188
motivational research, 382
Motown, 136, 165
Movietone (newsreel), 191
MP3 (Motion Picture Expert Group-2 audio layer III),
    143, 144
MPEG-2, 228
MSNBC, 233, 244, 433
MTV, 148
muckraking, 85, 108, 115, 116–117, 128
multicasting, 227
multilateral trade negotiations, 464
multimedia communication, 20–21